P9-CDL-514

VICTORY AT SEA

VICTORY
AT SEA

WORLD WAR II
IN THE PACIFIC

James F. Dunnigan
and
Albert A. Nofi

William Morrow and Company, Inc.
New York

To John Lindemann, Corporal, USMC, 1942–1945
E Company, 2nd Battalion, 25th Marines,
4th Marine Division
Roi, Saipan, Tinian, Iwo Jima

Library of Congress Cataloging-in-Publication Data

Dunnigan, James F.
    Victory at sea : World War II in the Pacific / James F. Dunnigan and Albert A. Nofi.
        p.   cm.
    Includes bibliographical references (p.) and index.
    ISBN 0-688-05290-8
    1. World War, 1939–1945—Campaigns—Pacific Area.
    2. World War, 1939–1945—Naval operations.   I. Nofi, Albert A.   II. Title.
    D767.D78 1995
    940.54'26—dc20   94-41232
                                                               CIP

Printed in the United States of America

3   4   5   6   7   8   9   10

P R O L O G U E

T his book was first written in an electronic edition (called a GameBook), for inclusion in a computer wargame of the same name (published by 360-Pacific in 1994), researched and designed by the same authors. We wrote that book and designed the game mainly because of the opportunity to integrate a history book into a history game. This led to the idea of doing an edition of the GameBook as a more traditional book, on paper. The GameBook had the advantage of hypertext and the resulting easier access to information. It was something of a challenge to take the GameBook "manuscript," custom written for electronic presentation, and turn it into its current format. Basically, we went over the entire GameBook manuscript and rewrote about a third of it (and fixed up bits and pieces in the rest). About 20 percent of the material in this book did not appear in the GameBook. We reorganized everything and added new illustrations. While an electronic book is more efficient, not every reader has a computer, and it will be a few years before a one-pound electronic book reader is widely available at an affordable price. Thus, we had the challenge (and interesting opportunity) to take the same subject and present it in two rather different venues (paper and electronic).

This book may be read in several ways. Or perhaps "used" is a better way of putting it. You could start at page one and go right on through to the end, the "normal" way to read a book. You will find doing so quite satisfactory. However, you might also consider just flipping it open to any section and reading whatever you find there. This method will prove just as satisfactory, and possibly a lot more entertaining. Of course, you could also consider *Victory at Sea* a reference book, which is probably the least satisfactory way of using it. The choice is yours.

ACKNOWLEDGMENTS

D ennis Casey, Richard L. Di Nardo, the editors and the staff of *Strategy & Tactics* magazine, the members of the New York Military Affairs Symposium, Fun H. Fong, Jr., Brian Sullivan, Patrick Abbazia, Wayne McKinney, Kathleen Williams, Steve Laroe, Susan Leon, Bob Shuman, John Boardman, David E. Schwartz, Roger Covington, Steven J. Zaloga, Norman Friedman, Tom Holsinger, Mike Peterson, Tom Trinko, and Mary Spencer Nofi, who has to put up with one of us.

C O N T E N T S

CONTENTS

T E R M S   A N D

C O N V E N T I O N S

TIME: In most cases we use the military form of telling time. Thus, 7:05 A.M. would be 0705 hours, and 9:30 P.M. would be 2130 hours.

ABBREVIATIONS

AA	antiaircraft	CVE	escort aircraft carrier
A/C	aircraft	CVL	light aircraft carrier
Art	artillery	DD	destroyer
A/T	antitank	DE	destroyer escort
BB	battleship, including battlecruisers	Div	division
		ETO	European Theater of Operations
Br	British/Britain		
CA	heavy cruiser	Fr	French/France
CAP	Combat Air Patrol (aircraft maintained over a carrier, for defensive purposes)	Ger	German/Germany
		g.r.t.	gross register tons; describes size of nonwarships
CBI	China-Burma-India Theater of Operations	HIJMS	"His Imperial Japanese Majesty's Ship"
CINCPAC	commander in chief, Pacific (U.S. Navy)	HMAS	"His Majesty's Australian Ship"
CL	light cruiser	HMS	"His [Britannic] Majesty's Ship"
CLAA	antiaircraft light cruiser	HNMS	"Her Netherlands Majesty's Ship"
CV	aircraft carrier		

TERMS AND CONVENTIONS

IJN	Imperial Japanese Navy
Inf	infantry
It	Italian/Italy
Jap	Japanese/Japan
knot	nautical mile, equal to 1.15 land miles or 1.85km
MG	machine gun
Mtr	mortar
Neth	Netherlands
PBY	multi-engine floatplane used for reconnaissance
RAF	Britain's Royal Air Force
RCT	regimental combat team (a U.S. task group consisting of an infantry regiment, an artillery battalion, and sundry support forces, about a third of a division)
RN	Britain's Royal Navy
SNLF	Special Naval Landing Force, Japanese "Marines"
SS	submarine
TF	task force, group of warships traveling together
TG	task group, portion of a task force
U.S.	the United States
USAAF	the United States Army Air Forces
USMC	the U.S. Marine Corps
USN	the U.S. Navy
USS	"United States Ship"

VICTORY AT SEA

O N E

THE CAMPAIGNS

The campaigns and battles of the Pacific war were unlike any others before or since. For example, the first carrier battles occurred during the Pacific war, and there haven't been any more since 1944. Similarly, prior to the Second World War, amphibious operations were relatively rare in warfare; yet they were a commonplace of the Pacific war, and rather frequent even in the European portion of World War II. Since World War II, however, there has only been one amphibious assault against a defended beach. That was at Inchon in 1950. There hasn't been another island-hopping campaign since the Pacific war. Given the world situation today, it may be some time, if ever, before we see anything like the battles and campaigns that were fought in the Pacific from 1941 to 1945.

THE COURSE OF THE WAR

The Pacific war did not simply start at Pearl Harbor and move west until Japan was reached. The battles took place on over a third of the earth's surface and often simultaneously, thousands of miles apart. Understanding how this came to be requires that we take a look at the reasons why Japan decided to start the war.

Many of Japan's top military leaders realized that they could not win a long war against the United States. But that was not enough to keep Japan from entering World War II. Since the 1920s, the government had been increasingly dominated by Army officers. This is what had gotten Japan involved in its aggressive war in China and what, in response, had led to the oil embargo by the Western nations. This last action put the Japanese generals on the spot. They could not afford to abandon their operations in China, as that was their principal justification for running the government. But they could not ignore the oil embargo either, as the Western countries controlled the world's oil supply and without oil the Japanese armed forces would be largely crippled within a year.

For the military, it was a case of use it or lose it. The Japanese generals convinced themselves that some chance of military victory in the Pacific was preferable to guaranteed impotence from a lack of oil. The generals saw the embargo as an offensive move, and their military response as a defensive reaction. Even in the 1990s, many Japanese still see it that way.

While the Imperial Navy's admirals did not exercise nearly as much control over the government, they went along with the generals. Japan was a maritime nation; it depended on control of the seas. The generals recognized this and the Navy budget remained relatively large throughout the twenty years preceding Pearl Harbor. But the generals were in firm control of the government and the admirals followed the generals' lead.

The basic plan for the Pacific war was to destroy the Allied forces in the region, seize all the Allied colonies and possessions, and then sue for peace on favorable terms. It was felt (though not all Japanese leaders believed it) that the Allies would prefer some kind of settlement rather than fight a long war in the Pacific. It was a desperate gamble that at first appeared to be working.

The Japanese had a high opinion of their own military prowess. This attitude certainly helped, because the numbers didn't look quite so favorable. Most of the Japanese Army was tied down in China. Only about a quarter of a million ground troops could be scraped together for the Pacific offensive. Japan's target list was impressive; the Philippines, sundry Central Pacific islands, the Netherlands East Indies (modern Indonesia), New Guinea and nearby island groups, Indochina (Vietnam and environs), Malaya (Malaysia and Singapore), Thailand, Burma, and parts of India. In these territories there were over half a million Allied troops. But it was more than numbers that counted. Many of the Allied troops were poorly trained, inexperienced, or both, and many were local recruits who were not necessarily completely happy with the rule of the "mother country."

The French Vichy troops in Indochina were neutral (and, technically, allies of Japan, because of Vichy France's relationship with Japan's ally Nazi Germany). Thailand (Siam) was pro-Japanese, primarily out of fear rather than enthusiasm for the Japanese cause.

But the biggest asset the Japanese Army had was the Japanese Navy. The Pacific war began with the Allies and Japan having a rough parity in naval forces (except for carrier superiority), as well as larger and more capable air forces.

Most of the Japanese target areas were not heavily garrisoned. The British had large forces in Singapore, as did the United States in the Philippines. But the nearby Japanese forces were better trained and led and had superior air support. Many areas were held by token forces and all the Japanese had to do was walk in and take over.

The initial Japanese attacks in December 1941 and January 1942 soon overwhelmed all resistance. The Japanese used their naval superiority to isolate Allied forces. This not only cut the Allied forces off from resupply and reinforcement, it also allowed the Japanese to take care of Allied strongholds one at a time. For example, Japanese troops conquered Malaya before going on to the Netherlands East Indies and Burma.

What stopped the Japanese eventually, and slowed them down in the meantime, was a lack of merchant shipping to move the troops

NAVAL FORCES IN THE PACIFIC, DECEMBER 1941

	TOTAL JAPAN	U.S.	OTHER ALLIES	TOTAL ALLIED
A/C: Carrier	545	280	—	280
A/C: Other	2,140	1,180	600	1,780
Carriers	10	3	—	3
Battleships	11	9	2	11
Heavy Cruiser	18	13	1	14
Light Cruisers	17	11	10	21
Destroyers	104	80	20	100
Submarines	67	73	13	86

NOTES: "A/C" is aircraft, with "Other" including nonnaval land-based craft. U.S. A/C figures include aircraft in California, Washington, and Oregon. Figures for carriers exclude ships working up (i.e., not yet fully operational) and escort carriers. Including these would raise the Japanese totals to 13 carriers with about 650 aircraft; U.S. ships in these categories were all in the Atlantic.

"Other Allies" were the British Commonwealth (Britain, Australia, New Zealand, Canada, and India) and the Netherlands. Obviously the United States also had its Atlantic Fleet, from which it quickly withdrew three carriers to improve the carrier ratio in the Pacific, as well as a number of battleships and other vessels, but these were not available on December 7, 1941.

and supplies forward. But in the first six months of the war, Japan had seized all the Central Pacific islands, all of what is now called Indonesia, all of Southeast Asia except for western Burma, and most of New Guinea and adjacent islands. In less than half a year, Japan's carriers attacked targets from the Hawaiian Islands to southern India, literally going halfway around the world in the process. Japan's fleet, and particularly its carriers, was what protected the relatively small Japanese ground forces from retribution by Allied land, air, and naval forces.

But in May, with more U.S. carriers in the Pacific, Japan began to lose carriers. First, a light carrier was lost in the Battle of the Coral Sea and a heavy carrier damaged. A month later, four heavy carriers were lost at Midway. That essentially evened up the carrier situation in the Pacific, despite the United States' loss of two carriers (one each at the Coral Sea and Midway). Equally important was the United States' pouring land-based aircraft into the theater. This restricted where Japan's carriers, and its ships in general, could operate with relative safety.

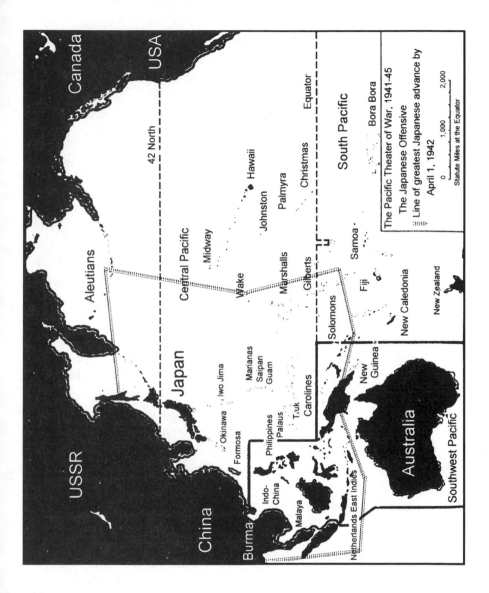

The Pacific Theater of War, 1941-45
The Japanese Offensive
Line of greatest Japanese advance by April 1, 1942

0   1,000   2,000
Statute Miles at the Equator

Canada

USA

42 North

Hawaii

Johnston

Palmyra

Christmas

Equator

Bora Bora

South Pacific

Aleutians

Central Pacific

Midway

Wake

Marshalls

Gilberts

Samoa

Fiji

Solomons

New Caledonia

New Zealand

USSR

Japan

Okinawa   Iwo Jima

Marianas
Saipan
Guam

Truk

Carolines

New Guinea

Formosa

Philippines
Palaus

China

Burma

Indo-China

Malaya

Netherlands East Indies

Australia

Southwest Pacific

Had it not lost five carriers in the first seven months of the war, Japan planned to keep pushing its defensive perimeter outward. These planned conquests (as far south as the Fiji Islands and, eventually, Hawaii to the east and India and the Persian Gulf in the west) would be garrisoned slowly (because of the lack of cargo ships) by troops withdrawn from China and new units raised in Japan. The Japanese Army had misgivings about these expansion plans, even though it agreed with the Navy about the need to grab as much territory as possible as a prelude to the eventual peace negotiations with the Allies. The Army did draw the line at an attempt to land in Australia. That nation was simply too large for the Japanese Army's scant resources to handle, particularly in light of the hostile population there.

But in the spring of 1942, there was much optimism and little clear thought in Japanese military headquarters.

The early victories had been more spectacular than even the most enthusiastic Japanese militarists envisioned. For a few months, anything seemed possible. But after Midway, reality set in. However, the worst news was not the loss of the carriers at Midway, but the refusal of the Allies to negotiate. Pearl Harbor had wakened the sleeping tiger (as many Japanese officers who had studied in America had warned) and America now wanted vengeance.

Japanese who knew a bit about world economics and U.S. history knew that the Americans would not rest until Japan was a smoldering ruin, and that the Americans were quite capable of Japan's destruction. No one in Tokyo would ever admit this publicly until near the end. But it became clear that the Americans were coming, with murder in their hearts.

In August 1942, the United States landed a Marine division on Guadalcanal and seized an unfinished Japanese airfield. Meanwhile, to the northwest, the Japanese were continuing to fight over possession of New Guinea. The Guadalcanal battle lasted six months and resulted in a Japanese defeat. This was but one of a series of battles in this area that took Allied troops right up the Solomon chain of islands, past Rabaul, across New Guinea, and on toward the Philippines by April 1944. Meanwhile, the fighting on New Guinea continued into 1945.

During late 1942 there was a series of carrier battles that demonstrated U.S. capabilities in carrier warfare, and killed many of

Japan's hard-to-replace carrier pilots. In the summer of 1944, the rebuilt Japanese carrier force was destroyed once and for all in the Battle of the Philippine Sea (the "Great Marianas Turkey Shoot").

Meanwhile, two other fronts gave the Japanese even more trouble. In Burma, the Japanese offensive stalled by mid-1942. Noting that the Allies were building railroad, truck, and air routes into China, the Japanese eventually tried in 1943–1944 to push the British back into India and away from any access to China. But the opposing forces were more evenly matched now and the Japanese offensives failed. By early 1945, the Allies were on the offensive and eventually pushed the Japanese out of most of Burma.

While Burma was a stalemate the Japanese could afford, the third prong of the Allied counteroffensive led right to Tokyo. In late 1943, the United States began the series of amphibious operations in the Central Pacific that would, eight months later, seize islands close enough to Japan for B-29 bombers to reach Tokyo and other home-island cities. In late 1944, the Philippines were retaken. In early 1945, islands even closer to Japan were taken and the bombing campaign against Japanese industry and population intensified.

By the summer of 1945, Japan was isolated and broken.

PEARL HARBOR

Japan opened the war with three major attacks and several minor ones. The first strike (by a number of hours) was at Pearl Harbor. The objective was to cripple the only force in the Pacific (the U.S. Pacific Fleet, and particularly its battleships) that could interfere with the other two Japanese attacks (on the Philippines and Malaya). Surprise was essential in the Pearl Harbor attack. This was so not just because surprise put the defender at a disadvantage, but also because attacking a major naval base with carrier aircraft in broad daylight had never been done before and no one was sure how successful it would be. On paper it appeared it would work, and the British had been rather successful in a nighttime air raid on the Italian fleet in Taranto Harbor on November 11–12, 1940. The experienced and history-savvy officers of the Japanese fleet knew that

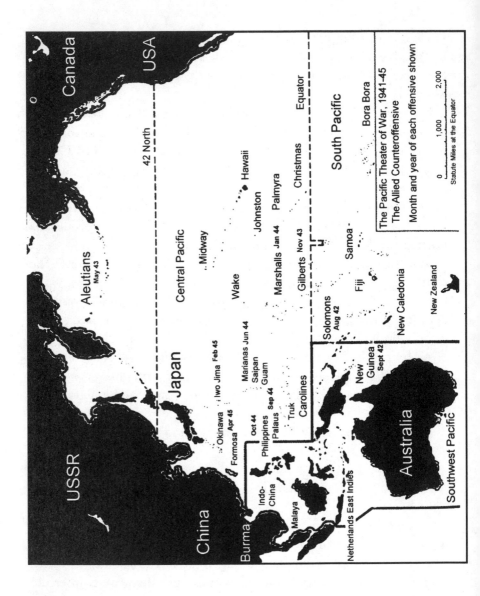

USSR

Canada

Japan

China

Burma

Indo-China

Malaya

Netherlands East Indies

Australia

New Guinea Sept 42

New Caledonia

New Zealand

Solomons Aug 42

Fiji

Samoa

Bora Bora

Southwest Pacific

South Pacific

Aleutians May 43

Central Pacific

Midway

Wake

Hawaii

Johnston

Palmyra

Christmas

Equator

Marshalls Jan 44

Gilberts Nov 43

42 North

USA

Okinawa

Iwo Jima Feb 45

Formosa Apr 45

Marianas Jun 44

Saipan

Guam

Oct 44

Philippines

Palaus Sep 44

Truk

Carolines

The Pacific Theater of War, 1941-45
The Allied Counteroffensive
Month and year of each offensive shown

0   1,000   2,000

Statute Miles at the Equator

the first time anything is tried, particularly something risky, the unexpected can be expected.

The Pearl Harbor operation was the brainchild of Japanese Admiral Isoroku Yamamoto, who ordered planning for the undertaking to begin in the spring of 1941. The basic concept was to injure American military power in the Pacific to such an extent that Japan would be able to overrun a vast territory; then the United States would ultimately decide on a negotiated peace rather than a protracted war. Japan could not grab a lot of territory in the Pacific if a large enemy fleet was in the same waters. America had the only other large fleet, and most of it was based at Pearl Harbor in the Hawaiian Islands. Cripple that fleet, and Japan could do whatever it could get away with in the Pacific.

The Pearl Harbor Strike Force (six carriers, two fast battleships, two heavy cruisers, a light cruiser, nine destroyers, and three submarines, supported by eight tankers and supply ships) was concentrated in great secrecy at a secure anchorage in the Kurile Islands north of Japan. As part of the undertaking, another group of submarines was assigned to ferry two-man midget subs tasked with penetrating Pearl Harbor from the sea at the same time the airmen attacked.

On November 26, 1941, the strike force sailed, under the command of Vice Admiral Chuichi Nagumo. Maintaining total radio silence, the strike force took a route through the North Pacific, which had proven wholly devoid of shipping under normal circumstances. The progress of the strike force across the Pacific was relatively fast, despite the necessity of having to refuel by the inefficient tow method.

Although American and Allied intelligence services were aware that war was increasingly imminent, the much less secretive concentration of Japanese forces for an offensive southward into the "Southern Resources Area" (Malaya, the East Indies, the Philippines, and so on) attracted their attention. War warnings to Pacific Theater commanders only confirmed their expectations that something would soon happen in that quarter.

In December 1941 the naval and air base at Pearl Harbor and other installations on Oahu, in the central Hawaiian Islands, represented the greatest concentration of American military power in the world. In normal circumstances the island was the home of nine or ten battleships, three carriers (with over 250 aircraft), a score or more cruisers, and literally dozens of destroyers, submarines, mine warfare vessels, and support ships, plus about 500 land-based aircraft and two understrength infantry divisions.

In addition to combat forces, Oahu had elaborate maintenance and repair facilities, extensive warehouses, and a large fuel dump. Command of these forces was divided between Admiral Husband Kimmel and Lieutenant General Walter C. Short. In a typical example of the haphazard command structure that prevailed in the U.S. armed forces before (and to some extent during) World War II, neither officer was in overall command. Short was responsible for the defense of Hawaii from attack, including air attack, and the protection of the fleet when in port. Kimmel was responsible for all naval forces and for the direction of naval operations. Although the two had a smooth working relationship, neither effectively consulted with the other on potential threats to the security of the command.

As early as February 1941, Short had dismissed the possibility of a carrier air raid on the place, despite the fact that the Navy had several times practiced such a strike against the Panama Canal, San Diego, and Pearl Harbor itself. These practice raids had demonstrated that such operations were not all that difficult. Despite that, Short's principal concern seems to have been the threat of sabotage by members of Hawaii's large resident Japanese and Japanese-American population.

The Japanese strike force arrived at a point some 275 miles north of Pearl Harbor late on December 6. At 6:00 the next morning, Admiral Nagumo launched his first strike, of forty-nine high-level bombers, forty torpedo bombers, and fifty-one dive bombers, escorted by fifty-one fighters. As these flew southward, they split up into different sections, each with its particular objective.

Although U.S. Army enlisted personnel manning an experimental radar system spotted the incoming aircraft, the duty officer at air defense headquarters dismissed the bogey, suggesting that it was a flight of B-17s due in from California.

At about the same time, a destroyer exercising outside the harbor entrance spotted a submarine periscope, made a vigorous attack, and confirmed a kill (getting one of the five midget subs that were trying to enter the harbor), but no one took the destroyer skipper's frantic messages seriously. As a result, the strike achieved complete surprise, the first bombs falling at 7:55. Air bases were hit first, to ensure no interference from American aircraft. Then the bombers went after the fleet, anchored neatly in the shallow and narrow waters of Pearl Harbor.

Although it was a Sunday morning, and many of the ships' companies were understrength, having sent men ashore on weekend passes, fleet antiaircraft guns came into action quite quickly. The first strike worked the ships over heavily. The principal objectives were the battleships, of which seven were tied up along "Battleship Row" and an eighth was in dry dock. These took an enormous pounding, notably the ships moored outboard of Ford Island. Within a half hour, all eight battleships were damaged or sunk, as were ten other warships. The strike ended at 8:25.

Within minutes a second strike almost as strong as the first (fifty high-level bombers, eighty dive bombers, and forty fighters) came over, Nagumo having launched it at 6:45. Hampered by dense smoke from the damage inflicted by the first strike, and by increasingly voluminous antiaircraft fire, the second strike inflicted relatively little damage.

Even as the second strike flew back to the carriers, a critical argument was going on aboard the Japanese flagship. Impressed by the success of their first strike, air-minded officers were trying to convince Nagumo to undertake a third strike, this time against the harbor installations, warehouses, and fuel dumps. Nagumo demurred, concerned over the location of the American carriers, which had not yet been located. As a result, as soon as the second strike had been recovered, the strike force turned back for Japan. No Japanese naval task force would ever again penetrate so far eastward.

Pearl Harbor was a devastating defeat for the United States. A total of eighteen warships were sunk or heavily damaged, including two battleships that were total losses, *Arizona* and *Oklahoma*. In addition, nearly 200 aircraft were destroyed, virtually all on the ground, and over 2,400 soldiers, sailors, and Marines were killed.

Japanese losses were five midget submarines and about twenty-eight aircraft, for a total of less than fifty men. Arguably, the defeat could have been worse. The three Pacific Fleet carriers escaped the debacle (*Saratoga* was undergoing a refit at San Diego, while *Lexington* and *Enterprise* were at sea, returning from delivering additional aircraft to Wake and other island garrisons). And a case can be made that Nagumo's decision not to undertake a third strike was in error, for it would have destroyed the fuel dumps, thereby crippling the remnants of the fleet, and so seriously damaged the harbor facilities that minor repairs would not be practical, thereby in effect forcing the United States back to the west coast. While such a possibility existed, it is important to note that Nagumo's second strike had been relatively ineffective (in fact, most of the Japanese aircraft losses occurred during the second strike). Moreover, since his own pilots had just demonstrated the devastating effectiveness of carrier aviation, his concern over the location of the U.S. carriers was by no means unreasonable.

WAKE ISLAND

Wake Island, some 2,000 miles west of Pearl Harbor, is a small atoll in the Central Pacific. In late 1941 it was a way station on the Pan Am Clipper route to the Far East, with a small U.S. seaplane base and a modest garrison of sailors and Marines.

The Japanese occupation of Wake Island was a subsidiary aspect of the Pearl Harbor operation. The island first came under attack by Japanese surface ships and aircraft operating out of the Mandates on December 8. These severely punished the garrison, destroying many of the handful of fighter planes available. Three days later a detachment of the Special Naval Landing Force (the "Imperial Marines") essayed a landing, only to be beaten off with considerable loss, the defenders sinking a destroyer in the process.

The carriers *Soryu* and *Hiryu*, returning from the Pearl Harbor operation, were detached from the Pearl Harbor Strike Force and called in to work over the island's defenses by air attacks. These carriers lingered in the vicinity of Wake for most of three days, December 21–23, on the last of which the Japanese attempted another landing, which was successful. Historically, that was the end of the struggle for Wake. But there might have been more.

As the U.S. Navy began picking up the pieces from the Pearl Harbor disaster, Admiral Kimmel, still commanding the Pacific Fleet, decided to strike back at the Japanese, and ordered the three carriers in the Pacific to the support of Wake. One, *Saratoga*, under Rear Admiral Frank Jack Fletcher, was in position to intercept the

Japanese carriers before the island fell. At dawn on December 23, *Saratoga* was about 425 miles northeast of the island, and about the same distance due east of the Japanese carriers. Moreover, at that moment *Lexington* and her escorts were less than 750 miles southeast of Wake, and the *Enterprise* group a little more than 1,000 miles east of the island. In the event, the attempted relief of Wake was called off by Vice Admiral W. S. Pye, who had just replaced Kimmel in an acting capacity pending the arrival of Chester W. Nimitz. Had Pye not called off the operation, it is perfectly possible that the first carrier battle of the war would have taken place off Wake. And the outcome of that engagement would certainly have dramatically altered the entire course of the Pacific war.

Had the U.S. carriers succeeded in sinking both of Japan's carriers at Wake, the sudden loss of a third of its first-line carriers might have seriously injured Japanese morale, provoking a major offensive against Hawaii early in 1942, rather than the Midway operation in June of that year. But it is also possible that the Japanese could have won the battle. One U.S. carrier air group was still equipped with Brewster Buffaloes, older aircraft even more outclassed by the Zeros than were the Wildcats on the other two flattops. A Japanese victory at Wake, with the attendant loss of one or maybe two carriers, would have seriously crippled the U.S. war effort in the Pacific. And such a victory might also have brought on a much earlier Japanese offensive against the Hawaiian Islands than was actually the case, at a time when American resources would have been much slenderer than they were at Midway.

THE JAPANESE INVASION OF HAWAII

Despite the Japanese attack, Pearl Harbor was still the most important American base in the Pacific, sustaining the offensives that ultimately brought Japan to its knees. The Japanese actually planned a Hawaiian invasion and alerted two infantry divisions for that purpose early in 1942. The loss of four aircraft carriers at Midway, however, killed the Hawaii invasion plans. The two divisions were sent to other battles in the Pacific.

A successful Japanese occupation of the Hawaiian Islands would have seriously hampered America's ability to carry on the war. Almost certainly the "Europe first" doctrine would have been tossed out, and a major reshuffling of American resources to the Pacific, even greater than that engendered by Pearl Harbor, would have begun. The principal U.S. effort in the Pacific would have been focused on recovering Hawaii, which would have given the Japanese something of a free hand in the South and Southwest Pacific, with dire consequences for Australia and New Zealand.

However, the possibility of a successful Japanese seizure of the Hawaiian Islands was low.

Even on December 7, 1941, the United States already had two infantry divisions on Oahu, the 24th and 25th, both at about 75 percent of full strength, plus the Hawaiian National Guard, various auxiliary and Army Air Force personnel troops, and numerous sailors and Marines, not to mention some rather elaborate coast defense installations, with the troops to man them.

Shortly after the Japanese attack, additional forces began to arrive in considerable numbers, including several battalions of light tanks and antiaircraft artillery, and the entire 27th Infantry Division, an oversized prewar National Guard formation (it still had four infantry regiments).

By March 1942 there were nearly 75,000 Army and Marine combat troops on Oahu, plus all those support troops and sailors, most of whom had some infantry training. And then there were all those new aircraft that were rapidly funneled into the islands.

In order to seize Oahu, the Japanese would first have had to attain control of the surrounding seas and skies. They could have done this in most of the Pacific, what with their "First Air Fleet" of six carriers, but would have had trouble going up against the considerably enhanced American resources in airplanes and antiaircraft defenses in Hawaii in early 1942. Since it's unlikely that they would have been able to duplicate their December 7 feat of destroying American air power on the ground, they would have been at a distinct disadvantage, particularly since there would have been some U.S. carriers lurking in the neighborhood as well. Of course they could have attempted to grab one or two of the less well defended islands first, in order to establish air bases from which to overwhelm the defenses of Oahu, but that would have tied up a lot of the troops needed for the main assault. Such a move would also have delayed the attack on Oahu, putting a severe strain on their already overstretched logistical resources, possibly forcing them to curtail offensive operations in other areas, and subjecting them to the attentions of U.S. submarines, a marginal but very real threat.

Finally, the Japanese were not too successful when landing against opposition, and were several times beaten off beaches during 1942, in operations in which the defenders were not particularly well prepared, such as at Milne Bay. So it seems likely that the Japanese would have suffered a severe reverse.

The major obstacle the Japanese faced in attacking Hawaii was logistical. There were not enough cargo ships available to sustain a major operation as far away as Hawaii. The offensives the Japanese did undertake required so much shipping that industry on the home islands was deprived of essential transport. An invasion of Hawaii would have required more sea transport than any previous Japanese operation. Moreover, to keep a garrison supplied in far-off Hawaii would have continued this drain on Japanese shipping.

However, even an unsuccessful Japanese attempt to take Oahu might have had interesting, and negative, effects on the course of the Pacific war. Such a victory would certainly have drawn U.S. resources rather decisively into the Central Pacific, with the possibility of offensive movements against the Mandates in mid-1942, particularly if the Philippines was still holding out. This would have been a dangerous proposition, given that carrier and amphibious warfare doctrines were both still in the formative stages. At the same time, the lessened attention given over to the South and Southwest Pacific might have permitted the Japanese to secure control of New Guinea and the Solomons (Guadalcanal), making the defense of Australia and New Zealand more difficult. In the end, of course, the United States would still have won, but just possibly at greater cost.

THE FALL OF THE PHILIPPINES: WHERE DUGOUT DOUG GOT HIS NAME

While General Douglas MacArthur is generally considered one of the most capable military leaders America ever produced, he had his failures. One of the most devastating was the manner in which he conducted the defense of the Philippines. In late 1941, the Philippines was defended by 25,000 U.S. and Philippine regular troops and over 100,000 poorly trained Philippine reservists and conscripts. Using air bases in Taiwan (then called Formosa), the Japanese first established air superiority over the Philippines; then their Navy established maritime supremacy around the islands. The Japanese Army then invaded with 50,000 troops and, after five months of hard fighting, conquered the islands.

Despite ample warning of a Japanese attack, nearly a half day after Pearl Harbor MacArthur allowed his air force to be largely destroyed on the ground. Although the Japanese air bases were 500 miles away, MacArthur did not order his aircraft dispersed nor did he take pains to resist the Japanese air attacks effectively. Similar errors were made with the ground forces. Although MacArthur had been in the Philippines for several years, he failed to take into account the low training levels of his Philippine troops when reacting to the actual Japanese invasion. Most of the Philippine Army's troops had less than a month's training on December 7, 1941 (December 8 in the Philippines, Japan, and other places west of the International Date Line).

When the Japanese invaded, MacArthur, rather than implement the long-standing operational plan, which called for an immediate withdrawal to the rugged Bataan peninsula, decided to try to halt the Japanese in mobile operations on the North Luzon Plain. The results were disastrous. The American and Philippine troops fought bravely, if not skillfully, and actually managed to slow the Japanese advance. But in the process many of MacArthur's handful of experienced men and much of the best equipment were lost.

Meanwhile, troop and supply movements were bungled before and during the land battles with the Japanese invasion force. When the surviving U.S. and Philippine troops finally did retreat to the Bataan peninsula, they did so short of ammunition, food, and spare parts, all of which were available but had not been ordered moved in time. Overall, MacArthur performed in a decidedly lackluster manner, especially compared to his later accomplishments.

What prevented "MacArthur's Disaster" from becoming "The End of MacArthur's Career" was largely MacArthur's reputation, his skill at public relations, and the need for a presentable hero in the dark days of early 1942. MacArthur was one of the most famous American officers of the post–World War I period. A genuine hero of World War I, he had been the head of the U.S. Army during the 1930s and had accepted the job of leading the infant Philippine Army (which brought with it the title field marshal) partially because the Japanese threat was recognized and everyone felt safer with someone of his caliber in charge out there. Although many military leaders back in the United States could see that MacArthur was screwing up big time in December 1941, the political leaders looked at the bright side. While British and Dutch forces were collapsing in weeks all over the Pacific, MacArthur's forces continued to hold out through the spring of 1942. Although the American situation in the Philippines was hopeless, MacArthur was declared a hero and was evacuated just before his army had to surrender and march off to three years of Japanese captivity. This gave MacArthur a chance for a rematch, with better results later. But the veterans of this campaign always remembered that "Dugout Doug" spent most of his time in a bunker (a "dugout") and then fled.

STUBBORN DEFIANCE IN THE JAVA SEA

One of the few ship-to-ship naval battles between Allied and Japanese forces during the initial Japanese expansion occurred in the Java Sea. On February 27, 1942, five cruisers and nine destroyers (the ABDA, or American-British-Dutch-Australian, Force), commanded by a Dutch admiral, sallied forth to prevent further Japanese landings in what was then the Netherlands East Indies (Indonesia). Over the next three days, most of this force was sunk by Japanese ships and aircraft. Slight damage was done to the Japanese. But it was only some bad luck that prevented this Allied force from doing significant harm to the Japanese invasion force. The Japanese were fairly reckless in pushing their troop-laden transports forward. Several times the Allied warships came dangerously close to sinking these vulnerable transports. As it was, the presence of Allied warships in the area threw the tight Japanese schedule into a state of confusion.

The reason the Japanese were moving so quickly was that they had to seize the oil fields and refineries on Sumatra before they could be destroyed beyond recovery. The Japanese oil situation was desperate and was the primary reason Japan had gone to war in the first place. As it turned out, the Japanese were luckier than the Allies. The oilfield defenders were surprised by Japanese paratroopers, who were soon reinforced by forces landed from the sea. Had the ABDA Force gotten a few of those Japanese transports, the Sumatra oil fields would have remained in Allied hands long enough to be devastated beyond repair (at least with the resources Japan had available). That done, Japan would have been out of fuel by 1944, and would have suffered severe oil shortages for over a year before that. Japanese resistance to the Allied advance would have been weaker. In short, a little bit of Allied luck in the Java Sea during February 1942 would have changed the course of the war.

SHOWING THE FLAG AND LEARNING THE ROPES: THE 1942 CARRIER RAIDS

Immediately after Pearl Harbor, there wasn't much the United States could do in the Pacific. The Japanese quickly seized most of the major Allied bases in the region and the shock of this rapid conquest left the Allies in need of some morale building. This needed morale boost came in the form of a series of raids by the U.S. carriers, including the two ships that had escaped destruction at Pearl Harbor.

The Japanese cooperated by committing their dozen carriers to supporting ground operations and a largely unnecessary sortie into the Indian Ocean. They made no effort to follow up on their success at Pearl Harbor by tracking down and destroying the numerically fewer U.S. Pacific carriers.

After Pearl Harbor, the United States quickly added two carriers from the Atlantic (*Hornet* and *Yorktown*) to the three already in the Pacific (*Enterprise*, *Lexington*, and *Saratoga*). However, on January

11, 1942, *Saratoga* was torpedoed by a Japanese sub 500 miles south of Hawaii, forcing her back to a west coast shipyard for several months of repairs and modernization. Since *Saratoga*'s pilots and aircraft were distributed to the other carriers and training centers, this gave the United States four fully staffed carriers for use against the Japanese.

Despite the risk of losing more carriers, a policy of raiding was adopted. The first two attempts involved Wake Island. In mid-December 1941, an attempt was made to aid the hard-pressed U.S. garrison there, which if successful might have resulted in the first carrier-to-carrier battle ever. Then, in January 1942, an attempt was made to hit the newly installed Japanese garrison on the island. Both attempts failed through a combination of inexperience, excessive caution, and bad luck.

In early February, however, the Marshall Islands were hit in the first successful raid. In late February, a raid on Rabaul (in the Bismarcks) was called off when the U.S. carrier was spotted by Japanese recon aircraft. Early March saw a successful raid on Marcus Island, only 1,000 miles from the Japanese home islands.

In mid-March, two carriers hit Japanese forces landing on the north coast of New Guinea, in a daring raid over the Owen Stanleys, some of the highest mountains in the Pacific area. Then came the most spectacular raid of all, in mid-April, when sixteen Army B-25 bombers launched from *Hornet* bombed Tokyo.

At this point the Japanese decided to try to make a decisive attempt to crush the USN, resulting in the Battles of the Coral Sea (May 7–8) and Midway (June 3–5). The two battles evened up the carrier situation in the Pacific when the Japanese lost five carriers (*Shoho* at the Coral Sea, and *Akagi*, *Kaga*, *Soryu*, and *Hiryu* in about five minutes at Midway) at a cost of two American ones (*Lexington* and *Yorktown*). This ended the period of desperate carrier raids by the United States.

By allowing these raids, the Japanese enabled the American carriers to gain valuable experience. As with all their ships and sailors, the Japanese carriers and air groups had begun the war better trained than their Allied counterparts. Without these raids, and their opportunity for relatively risk-free practice, the Battle of Midway might easily have gone the other way.

NEW GUINEA: A LITTLE
CORNER OF HELL ON EARTH

While Guadalcanal is generally regarded as the pivotal land battle in the first year of the Pacific war, it was actually only an extension of operations in New Guinea, which was the main campaign in the South Pacific.

New Guinea, a large tropical island north of Australia, was, before the war, controlled by Holland (the western half) and Australia (the rest). Smaller groups of islands extended to the northeast (the Bismarcks) and southeast (the Solomons, at virtually the tail end of which was Guadalcanal). All three island groups were considered vital parts of the Japanese defensive system.

New Guinea was the scene of some of the longest and toughest ground combat of the Pacific war. The Japanese landed on the north coast of New Guinea in early March 1942. The Australians (and later Americans) were on the south coast. Fighting first raged in the Owen Stanley Mountains, which formed the rugged spine of New Guinea. This fighting combined the worst aspects of jungle and mountain combat. The Japanese had managed to struggle over the mountains against Australian rearguard resistance, but had been halted almost literally a few dozen miles north of Port Moresby, the principal Allied base in New Guinea. Then they fell back, in an agonizing retreat that cost the lives of many men.

By late 1942, the fighting was concentrated on Japanese positions on the north coast. This fighting continued into 1944 as the Japanese continued to reinforce their battered forces, while American and Australian forces leapfrogged their way up the coast, isolating Japanese strongpoints. Japanese stragglers were still being hunted down into 1945.

New Guinea was something of a forgotten battle. Partially this was because of the way the media worked. New Guinea was almost wholly an Army affair. There were few Marines and relatively little action by the Navy. In addition, more even than Guadalcanal, New Guinea was a dreary, grinding jungle campaign, characterized by mud, heat, and disease. New Guinea was a tropical meat grinder of constant combat through steaming jungles and steep mountains. All the aircraft operated from primitive, often mud-soaked airfields. While Guadalcanal was over in six months, New Guinea went on for years. In the eyes of the American public, New Guinea got old real quick. That attitude carried on in the public's memory after the war.

Although the New Guinea fighting did more to cripple the Japanese armed forces, Guadalcanal got a higher place in the pantheon of Pacific battles.

THE BATTLE OF THE CORAL SEA

The Battle of the Coral Sea was the first battle between aircraft carriers. As such, it was the first naval battle in which neither side could see the other. All the fighting involved aircraft attacking ships or other aircraft. The engagement, fought on May 7–8, 1942, set the pattern for all the other 1942 carrier actions. The Coral Sea operation was the result of Japan's desire to occupy New Guinea and the Solomon Islands.

In March, U.S. carrier aircraft had carried out a daring attack on an earlier group of Japanese ships landing troops on the north coast of New Guinea. Flying over the supposedly too-high Owen Stanley Mountains by taking advantage of favorable thermals to catch the Japanese completely off guard, the U.S. aircraft had struck when the Japanese were not expecting it. The raid was only moderately successful, as the ships had already discharged their troops and cargoes. Had the U.S. carriers arrived a little earlier and caught the Japanese ships still loaded, the Japanese landing might well have been stopped entirely. As a result of this raid, the Japanese decided to occupy the balance of New Guinea, to push their defensive frontier farther southward.

Japanese forces, concentrated at Rabaul, were to sortie by ship into the Coral Sea and secure Port Moresby on the south coast of New Guinea and Tulagi in the eastern Solomons. As with most Japanese plans, there were a plethora of task forces involved. The principal striking element was a task force built around the carriers *Shokaku* and *Zuikaku*, plus two heavy cruisers and six destroyers. Earmarked for the occupation of Port Moresby were three light cruisers, five destroyers, a seaplane tender, a flotilla of smaller warships, and eleven troop-carrying transports, plus various supply ships, all covered by a light carrier, four heavy cruisers, and a destroyer. Finally there was the Tulagi occupation force: two destroyers, a troop transport, and various small warships. The plan was for the carrier task force, under Vice Admiral Takeo Takagi, to enter the Coral Sea from the east, and engage and destroy any Allied warships encountered, thereby enabling the landing forces to go about their business.

This did not seem an overly difficult assignment, as the Allies were believed to have only slender resources. This was true. Allied forces comprised Rear Admiral Frank Jack Fletcher's Task Force 17: the carriers *Yorktown* and *Lexington*, with eight American and Australian cruisers and eleven destroyers, supported by a fueling group of two oilers and two destroyers. Both sides, of course, committed some submarines and long-range reconnaissance aircraft to the operation, and some land-based fighters and bombers were within range.

The battle ranged over the Solomon Sea and the northern portions of the Coral Sea. On May 3 the Japanese occupied Tulagi unopposed, and a raid from *Yorktown* the next day did little damage. This gave away Fletcher's position, but the Japanese were unable to take advantage of the situation since their carriers had been ordered to drop off some fighters at Rabaul. Over the next two days each fleet maneuvered cautiously, trying to locate its opponent without revealing its own location. Reconnaissance was poor, and despite the fact that the two task forces passed within about 70 miles of each other at one point, neither side spotted the other. Not until the seventh was first blood drawn.

Early on May 7, the dawn patrol from *Shokaku* and *Zuikaku* located the American oiler *Neosho* and destroyer *Sims*. Acting on an erroneous report that the two ships were a carrier and cruiser, Admiral Takagi ordered an air strike, which quickly sent the two vessels to the bottom, at the cost of six aircraft lost. Meanwhile, U.S. carrier planes were also acting on a false lead, a *Yorktown* scout having reported "two carriers and four heavy cruisers" some 175 miles northwest of TF 17. Not until both American carriers had launched full deckloads of aircraft was it discovered that the scout had intended to say "two heavy cruisers and two destroyers" but miscoded his message. So the air strike was aborted. Then Lady Luck, the true goddess of war, took a hand. Just as the American aircraft were preparing to return to their ships, they came upon the Port Moresby support group, steaming southeastward in the Solomon Sea. They promptly jumped the carrier *Soho*, taking only ten minutes before the cry "Scratch one flattop" went out over the radio waves for the first time by an American pilot. This so upset Vice Admiral Shige-yoshi Inouye, overall Japanese commander in the area, that he effectively aborted the Port Moresby operation.

Meanwhile, Fletcher, realizing that he had located the Port Moresby invasion force, ordered a cruiser squadron under British Rear Admiral J. G. Grace to go after it, thereby weakening his defensive screen. Grace's mission turned into a wild-goose chase, but he did successfully beat off an attack by thirty-one land-based Japanese aircraft and then had to endure another by USAAF (U.S. Army Air Forces) B-17s, which tried a high-altitude bomb run on him, with no loss either time. The Japanese airmen reported two battleships and a heavy cruiser sunk; the American flyboys were almost as optimistic (even though they had attacked friendly ships).

Toward evening, Takagi sent out an offensive scouting mission, with orders to sink Fletcher's carriers. Intercepted by Fletcher's CAP (Combat Air Patrol), the Japanese planes were roughly handled, losing nine. Attempting to return to their ships after dark, six tried to land on *Yorktown* and were duly shot down, while eleven others splashed while trying to make night landings on their own carriers.

So as of the end of May 7, both sides had little to brag about, the United States having accounted for a light carrier and about twenty enemy aircraft and the Japanese for an oiler and a destroyer. Then came the eighth.

Each side sent out predawn reconnaissance patrols on May 8, and each managed to locate the other's carriers. Each side immediately launched massive strikes, the Japanese of 121 aircraft and the Americans of 122. Although the air strikes were of virtually identical size, and indeed the two task forces were quite closely matched as well (United States: two carriers, five cruisers, seven destroyers; the Japanese: two carriers, four cruisers, six destroyers), meteorological conditions favored the Japanese. The Japanese were operating from the

Solomon Sea, just then overcast and subject to occasional rain squalls, while the Americans were in the bright and sunny Coral Sea, one of the calmest expanses of water in the world.

The American air strikes went in first. At about 10:57 A.M., *Yorktown*'s bombers, having failed to locate *Zuikaku*, took on *Shokaku*, scoring only two hits, but damaging her flight deck sufficiently to prevent further operations. Half of *Lexington*'s bombers missed the Japanese entirely, while the other half put another bomb into *Shokaku* at about 12:40; Takagi immediately ordered her to retire to Truk. By this time Japanese air strikes were working over Task Force 17. Between 11:18 and 11:40, *Yorktown* took a bomb hit, but *Lexington* took a real pounding, two torpedoes and two bombs, which left her listing and on fire. As both sides recovered aircraft, Takagi decided to leave the area, conceding a strategic victory to Fletcher, despite his heavier loss in ships (the fleet carrier *Lexington*, which went down despite heroic damage-control efforts, oiler *Neosho*, and destroyer *Sims*, against only the light carrier *Shoho*). In addition to having their strategic intention frustrated in this action, the Japanese lost the services of two carriers, for *Shokaku*'s damage required about two months to repair, while *Zuikaku*'s plane and pilot losses required a month to make up. As a result, neither carrier was present for Midway.

The Coral Sea also revealed the bad habits, and inexperience at this new form of warfare, of both navies. Japanese communications were sloppy, with admirals being in the habit of not passing on vital information. This was a trait the Japanese were never able to overcome throughout the war. Japanese admirals tended to fight as if each commanded the only Japanese force engaged, and constantly missed opportunities to coordinate with other Japanese forces—a real problem, given their propensity to scatter offensive elements hither and yon, apparently in order to deceive the U.S. forces as to where the main blow was to fall. The Japanese also lacked the rapid repair techniques of the Americans. While the heavily damaged *Yorktown* was repaired in time for the Battle of Midway, the less heavily damaged *Shokaku* was not ready until a week after Midway was over. The major U.S. errors were largely due to inexperience. The Japanese had more experience in carrier operations and were able to attack American carriers more efficiently, expertly maneuvering their aircraft groups to search out and attack enemy ships. American officers closed this experience gap by the end of 1942.

THE BATTLE OF MIDWAY

The Japanese began planning for a June 1942 decisive battle in the vicinity of Midway shortly after the Doolittle Raid on Tokyo in April. Indeed, the Coral Sea operation was actually an integral part of the overall strategic plan that was to bring about this battle. The intention was to smash the remnants of American naval power in the Pacific, and advance Japan's outer defensive perimeter more than 1,000 miles farther by seizing the western Aleutians, Midway Island, and ultimately Fiji, Samoa, and New Caledonia, simultaneously severing the Allied lifeline between the U.S. west coast and Australia. Like the Pearl Harbor operation, the Midway operation was the brainchild of Isoroku Yamamoto. But it was neither as well planned nor as well executed.

Yamamoto's plan for the Midway operation was complex. The principal striking force would be Chuichi Nagumo's First Air Fleet (the Pearl Harbor Strike Force), down to four fleet carriers due to losses at the Coral Sea, plus two fast battleships, two heavy cruisers, a light cruiser, and a dozen destroyers. This would be supported by the Advanced Force of sixteen submarines. The actual capture of the objective would be the responsibility of the Midway Occupation Force of 5,000 troops in a dozen transports, supported by two battleships, a light carrier, two seaplane carriers, eight heavy cruisers, two light cruisers, and twenty destroyers, plus a dozen smaller warships organized into seven task groups. Giving deep support was the Main Body: three battleships, a light carrier, two seaplane carriers, a light cruiser, and seventeen destroyers. Then there was the Northern Area Force, comprising a support group of four battleships and two light cruisers, plus two light carriers, three heavy cruisers, three light cruisers, a dozen destroyers, three submarines, and about a dozen miscellaneous small warships, organized in no fewer than six task groups, including two of troop transports. All of these task groups, of course, had supply ships and oilers assigned. The plan was for the Northern Area Force to make a demonstration against the Aleutians, grabbing a couple of uninhabited islands in an effort to divert American attention from the principal objective. While the U.S. Navy raced northward to cope with the threat to the Aleutians, perhaps suffering losses to the Advanced Force, meanwhile the Midway Occupation Force would take its objective under the protection of the First Air Fleet. Presumably, the Americans would then race south to relieve Midway, once more running the gantlet of the Advanced Force, and right into an aerial ambush by the First Air Fleet. Should the Americans try for a surface action, the Main Body would be ready to come up from its supporting position, several hundred miles behind the First Air Fleet.

This plan may have looked fine on paper, but it was seriously flawed. Not only was the Japanese organization very complex, scattering task forces across half of the western Pacific, but the Aleutians operation consumed too many resources for a proper diversion (90 carrier aircraft, a quarter of the approximately 350 available). Moreover, by early May, American Pacific commander Chester W. Nimitz had a pretty good notion as to the identity of the principal Japanese objective, partially as a result of good guessing and partially as a result of fortuitous code breaking. Nimitz intended to counter Yamamoto's offensive by a careful concentration of everything he had, which admittedly was not much. He had three carriers (with 233 aircraft, only about a dozen fewer than those on Nagumo's four carriers), including *Yorktown*, mostly repaired from her Coral Sea damage, as well as seven heavy cruisers, one light cruiser, and seventeen destroyers. These were organized into two task forces under Rear Admiral Fletcher and supported by nineteen submarines, plus as much shore-based air power as could be jammed onto Midway's tiny surface (sixty Navy combat aircraft and twenty-three Army B-26s and B-17s, plus about thirty-two Catalina patrol bombers). There were also three destroyers, some PT boats, and some miscellaneous smaller warships assigned to patrol portions of the long chain of islets and atolls linking Midway with Hawaii (where the Japanese had once established a temporary flying-boat base using submarines, and planned to do so again).

Aware of the "threat" to the Aleutians, Nimitz grudgingly assigned five cruisers, thirteen destroyers, six submarines, and some seaplane tenders, patrol boats, and minesweepers. He also ordered the carrier *Saratoga*, completing repairs from a torpedo hit, up from

San Diego with her escorts, and the battle fleet, composed of the more lightly damaged Pearl Harbor survivors plus reinforcements from the Atlantic, with an escort carrier, to sortie from San Francisco Bay, where it was temporarily housed.

With Nimitz's approval, Fletcher deployed his carriers northeast of Midway, reasoning that the Japanese would most likely come from the northwest, the west, or the southwest. This conceded the initiative to the Japanese. Normally, giving away the initiative is a bad idea in war. But in this case it was perfectly reasonable, since in order to hit the Japanese one had to find them. Locating the enemy could be done by patrol planes reaching out from Midway or, failing that, by letting them hit something first. In this case, the something was Midway. And that is precisely what took place.

The Japanese hit the Aleutians on June 3, 1942, and by the seventh had occupied Attu and Kiska, there being no one there to oppose them. But Frank Fletcher had not, in the interim "raced north." On June 3 a PBY Catalina patrol bomber had spotted the Midway Occupation Force. Early the next morning another PBY spotted the Japanese carriers. So Fletcher knew where the enemy were, while they were still in ignorance of his location. At 0630 Fletcher ordered Raymond Spruance, commander of TF 16, to prepare to launch a strike against the Japanese carriers from *Enterprise* and *Hornet*, holding back his own *Yorktown* for a follow-up strike. Even as this strike was getting into the air, Nagumo hit Midway with 108 aircraft. Spotted by radar, the Japanese air strike met resistance from Midway-based fighters.

Now came the critical moment of the battle. When dispatching his strike against Midway, Nagumo had ordered a second strike readied in the event American carriers had to be attacked. Meanwhile the leader of the Midway strike returned, ahead of his colleagues, and urged that a second strike be made against Midway, in order to destroy the island as a useful base. As Nagumo mulled over this suggestion, Midway-based bombers hit the fleet. Although the air strike was a failure, inflicting no loss on the Japanese carriers and suffering heavily itself, it seems to have helped convince Nagumo to have another go at Midway (he may also have recalled that his failure to authorize a third strike at Pearl Harbor had had unfortunate results). Confident that the American carriers were nowhere in the vicinity, Nagumo ordered the ninety-three fueled and armed aircraft to be rearmed for another go at Midway. Fifteen minutes into this operation, a reconnaissance plane reported spotting American ships to the northwest. Nagumo dithered for another fifteen minutes, then ordered the rearmament reversed so that the ninety-three aircraft could be dispatched to attack these American vessels. Soon the hangar decks of the Japanese carriers were littered with ammunition, as general-purpose bombs were being removed from the aircraft while torpedoes and armor-piercing bombs were being loaded. And on their flight decks the four carriers were recovering the aircraft returning from the Midway strike.

Meanwhile, Spruance's TF 16 air strikes had lifted off at about 0700: 116 fighters, dive bombers, and torpedo bombers. About two hours later, Fletcher put 35 of his own *Yorktown* planes into the air as well. Spruance had calculated the odds closely. Aware of the Japanese air raid on Midway, he had estimated the time it would take for the attackers to return to their carriers, and launched his strike with the intention of catching the Japanese aircraft as they were rearming on deck. But he had a run of bad luck. Nagumo ordered a course change at 0905, just as the last of the Midway strike planes were returning. This caused the *Hornet*'s fighters and dive bombers to miss the Japanese task force entirely. As a result, Torpedo Squadron 8, 15 TBD Devastators, went in unsupported, with the loss of all the airplanes and all but one of the forty-five crewmen to Zeros or antiaircraft fire. A similar fate awaited the *Enterprise* and *Yorktown* TBDs. Of 41 TBDs involved in attacks on the Japanese carriers only eight survived, and none scored a hit. By the time the *Yorktown* TBD strike had been beaten off, 1024, the Japanese thought they had won the battle.

But then, within about ninety seconds the whole outcome of the battle was reversed. Lieutenant Commander C. Wade McClusky arrived over Nagumo's carriers with thirty-seven *Enterprise* dive bombers just as the last TBD was downed. With Nagumo's CAP "on the deck" (at low altitude) from having annihilated the TBDs, McClusky's SBD Dauntless attacks were largely unopposed and thus accurate. The SBD attacks proved deadly. Within seconds *Kaga* and *Akagi* took bombs to their hangar decks that touched off ammunition and fueled aircraft, starting uncontrollable fires. Then, within seconds, *Yorktown*'s seventeen Dauntlesses showed up and put three 1,000-pound bombs neatly into the center of fueled and armed aircraft on *Soryu's* deck, turning her into an inferno as well. By 1030 Nagumo had lost three carriers, all burning uncontrollably. He ordered his last carrier, *Hiryu*, to launch a strike on *Yorktown*, while bringing up all available escorts to cover the ship.

Hiryu's strike, fifty fighters and bombers, followed the American aircraft home, arriving over *Yorktown* at about 1440 hours. A furious action ensued, as *Yorktown's* CAP and escorts accounted for most of the Japanese attackers. But some got through, and the carrier took three bombs and two torpedoes. Not completely recovered from the damage she had taken at the Coral Sea, *Yorktown* began to list dramatically, and soon had to be abandoned. Admiral Fletcher shifted his flag to a cruiser and basically turned direction of the battle over to Spruance.

Having spotted *Hiryu*, at 1530 *Enterprise* launched fourteen of her own SBDs and ten of *Yorktown's*, which jumped *Hiryu* at 1700. Nagumo's last carrier went down quickly after taking four hits. Apprised of the outcome of Midway within minutes of the loss of his carriers, Yamamoto reacted by ordering the Main Body and the light carriers in the Aleutians to the support of the now-carrierless First Air Fleet, a classic instance of too little, too late. The Battle of Midway was over, the Imperial Navy having lost four of its finest carriers and any chance to annihilate the U.S. Navy in the Pacific.

Midway, the second carrier battle of 1942, was the most decisive of the war. But not for the reasons the Japanese had thought it would be, even if they had captured the place. In fact, the Battle of Midway would have turned into "the Siege of Midway" if the Americans had not known what the Japanese were up to or did not have forces available to ambush the Japanese.

The Japanese plan was to seize Midway quickly and then advance down the chain of islands the 1,000 or so miles to Hawaii, sinking any U.S. naval forces rushing out to the defense of Midway. But that was the Japanese way of thinking.

The U.S. Navy had other ideas. If the Japanese had seized Midway, the United States would have put it under siege with long-range aircraft and submarines. Midway was over 2,000 miles from the Japanese home islands and quite isolated. It would have to be supplied by sea, and the Japanese never fully grasped the problems of logistics in the Pacific war. A Japanese-held Midway would have turned into another of many Japanese logistics disasters. While the

Japanese played down logistics, they played up the importance of "military honor." They felt the Americans would come out to defend Midway no matter what. The Americans felt otherwise.

Without the advantage of reading the coded Japanese messages, the United States would not have risked its three carriers against the Japanese. Midway would have fallen to the Japanese, but the effect of this success on the course of the war might actually have been relatively minimal.

GUADALCANAL: A 3-D FIRST

Guadalcanal was neither the biggest nor the longest battle of the Pacific war. Its main claim to fame was not as "the turning point" in the Pacific war, but rather as history's first three-dimensional campaign. For the first time in history, air, land, and sea forces were combined as never before.

It all began in May 1942, when the Japanese landed construction troops on Guadalcanal Island in order to build an airstrip. The field would enable them to interdict Allied supply convoys going to Australia and provide a springboard for further advances to the south. Recognizing the danger from this strategy, the United States decided to make Guadalcanal the site of the first Allied counteroffensive. In August, the U.S. 1st Marine Division made a virtually unopposed landing on Guadalcanal and a landing on nearby Tulagi (where there was some heavy fighting), cleared the Japanese troops away from the incomplete airfield, and quickly completed it.

For the next six months, Japanese ground, naval, and air forces fought desperately to take the airfield back. Two carrier battles, half a dozen major (and some thirty smaller) naval surface battles, over a dozen land battles, and over hundreds of air raids were conducted in that six-month period. The Japanese effort failed. By early 1943, the Japanese had abandoned attempts to retake the airfield and left Guadalcanal.

This was the first of many three-dimensional battles in the Pacific war. Crucial, and often desperate, combat was seen on land, sea, and air. Guadalcanal was also the only campaign in which the Japanese had virtual parity in resources with the Allies, which is why it was such a close-run thing.

The Solomons Campaign

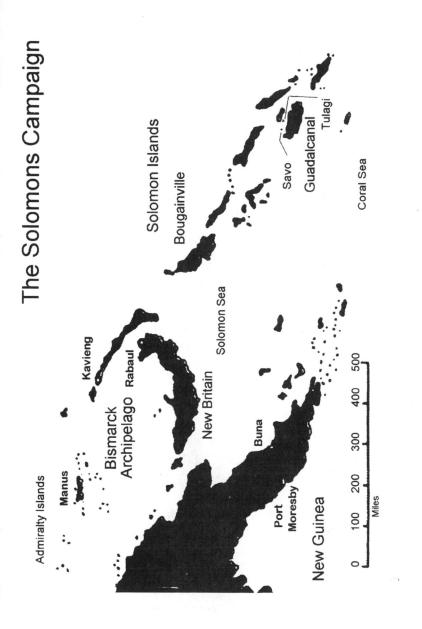

Admiralty Islands

Manus

Bismarck
Archipelago

Kavieng

Rabaul

New Britain

Buna

Solomon Sea

Port
Moresby

New Guinea

Bougainville

Solomon Islands

Savo

Guadalcanal

Tulagi

Coral Sea

0   100   200   300   400   500

Miles

The Guadalcanal campaign consisted of four rather distinct series of battles:

1. Air combats in defense of Guadalcanal
2. Ground fighting on the island
3. Carrier battles in the vicinity
4. Surface naval clashes in waters near the island

The series of nearly forty surface engagements in the waters between Guadalcanal and Florida islands in the Solomons ("Ironbottom Sound") in 1942 set a number of records for the U.S. Navy. To begin with, Guadalcanal was the Navy's first major amphibious operation since 1898. And—barring the Java Sea battles, which were under Allied command—the Battle of Savo Island on August 9 was the U.S. Navy's first fleet action since 1898 (and only about the fifth in its entire history), its first ever night fleet engagement, its first ever defeat in a fleet action, and its worst ever defeat (after Pearl Harbor). At Savo Island, four heavy cruisers (one of them Australian) and a destroyer were sunk, 1,270 men killed, and 709 wounded in an action lasting little more than a half hour, with virtually no loss to the enemy. This was the worst Allied defeat in the Solomons campaign.

The Battle of Cape Esperance (October 11–12, 1942) provided three firsts: the Navy's first victory in a fleet action since 1898, its first victory in a night fleet action, and its first surface victory against a Japanese squadron.

A month later a less fortunate "first" occurred: the first death of an American admiral in a fleet action, when Rear Admiral Norman Scott was killed on the bridge of his flagship in the opening moments of the First Naval Battle of Guadalcanal (November 12–13), followed within minutes by the death of Rear Admiral Dan Callaghan, the task force commander. The two men immediately became the first and second admirals ever to receive a posthumous Medal of Honor for a fleet action (one MOH had been awarded to an admiral posthumously for Pearl Harbor, a very different kind of battle).

The Second Naval Battle of Guadalcanal (November 14–15, 1942) saw four American battleship firsts. Very early on November 15 there occurred the first encounter between battleships in the Pacific war, when USS *South Dakota* and *Washington* took on HIJMS *Kirishima*, which was also the first time American battleships had ever encountered an enemy battleship at sea (and only the second encounter between U.S. and enemy battleships ever). The action was also the first (and last) time a U.S. battleship was hit by fire from an enemy battleship, when *South Dakota* took one 14-inch round from *Kirishima*, plus possibly a 5-incher. And a few minutes later occurred the first (and last) time a U.S. battlewagon "sank" an enemy battleship, when *Washington* turned *Kirishima* into a burning wreck, her broadsides scoring with nine 16-inch hits, followed up by about forty 5-inch shells.

Most of these surface actions took place at night between August and November 1942. There were also two carrier battles (Eastern Solomons, August 23–25, and Santa Cruz, October 26), many minor surface actions, and many encounters between land-based aircraft and ships. Never before, or since, had the U.S. Navy engaged in such a furious round of surface combat. As hard fought as the ground fighting on Guadalcanal was, four times as many sailors lost their lives in the naval battles fought in support of the ground and air forces on the island as did Marines and soldiers.

There was another unique dimension to the American experience at Guadalcanal. It was the first genuine joint-services operation in American history. That is, there was virtually no distinction among the services in staffs or operations, and no interservice squabbling. In some of the desperate ground actions, GIs and Marines literally fought shoulder-to-shoulder against fierce Japanese attacks.

Even in the air, there was no distinction as to service, or even nationality. A Japanese air strike might be met rather indiscriminately by aircraft being flown by Army, or Navy, or Marine pilots, or even New Zealanders or Australians, and occasionally all at once, sometimes even flying very different aircraft. Guadalcanal was also just about the only such battle during World War II, and there have been few others since. But then, never has the need been so desperate.

THE *SECOND* OFFENSIVE, AND WHY IT WAS IMPORTANT

The U.S. capture of Guadalcanal on August 7, 1942, is rightly considered the first Allied offensive operation of the Pacific war. But ten days later, on August 17, 221 U.S. Marine "Raiders" landed on the Japanese-held island of Makin. The Marines, including Major Elliot Roosevelt, the president's son, came ashore from two submarines. Within hours they had destroyed a new seaplane reconnaissance base and killed the 90-man Japanese garrison. The Marines lost 30 dead and 14 wounded.

The island was quickly evacuated before Japanese reinforcements could arrive. The departure was in such haste that a few Marines were inadvertently left behind, and the Japanese murdered them.

The raid was mainly for propaganda purposes, although it did serve some military function. But the raid had an enormous impact on the subsequent fighting in the Pacific. The Japanese were alarmed at the vulnerability of dozens of similar island bases throughout the Pacific. The decision was made to increase the garrisons of these islands and to build the fortifications with which the Marines became so intimately acquainted during the rest of the war.

This was not the only case in which the Japanese reacted strongly to a minor American operation. The Doolittle Raid (on April 18, 1942, when sixteen B-25 bombers flew from a carrier to bomb Japan) caused the Japanese to keep hundreds of combat aircraft in the home islands to prevent another attack, thereby greatly easing the plight of Allied forces elsewhere in the Pacific.

THE BATTLE OF THE EASTERN SOLOMONS

The late-August 1942 Battle of the Eastern Solomons was a consequence of the American landing on Guadalcanal on August 7, 1942. On the night of August 9, a Japanese cruiser-destroyer squadron inflicted a serious defeat on American and Australian cruisers off Savo Island, in an effort to gain control of the waters around Guadalcanal, so as to enable the Japanese to land reinforcements on the island and at the same time strangle the Marines' tentative hold on the place. Meanwhile, from his headquarters on Truk, Admiral Isoroku Yamamoto began concentrating a major force for a decisive blow against the U.S. fleet in the South Pacific, an operation that would at the same time cover the landing of additional reinforcements on Guadalcanal.

In late August, Yamamoto concentrated two battleships, three carriers, a seaplane carrier, eight heavy cruisers, three light cruisers, twenty-three destroyers, two dozen submarines, and a number of smaller warships and auxiliary vessels at Truk, while three heavy cruisers, a light cruiser, eight destroyers, and three submarines concentrated at Rabaul to escort the reinforcements to Guadalcanal.

As usual with Japanese plans, forces were divided into numerous subordinate groups scattered rather widely over the ocean. The Truk-based task force comprised five groups organized into two task forces, all under Vice Admiral Nobutake Kondo, while the Rabaul force, under Rear Admiral Raizo Tanaka ("Tenacious Tanaka") comprised no less than four task groups. The plan called for the submarines to spread out ahead of the fleet in order to ambush American warships. Then the light carrier *Ryujo*, a heavy cruiser, and two destroyers, serving as bait, were to steam well ahead of Vice Admiral Chuichi Nagumo's two fleet carriers to provoke an American reaction both by her presence and by air strikes on the Marines at Henderson Field on Guadalcanal. When the American carriers took the bait, they would in turn be jumped by massive air strikes from *Shokaku* and *Zuikaku* and annihilated.

When the Japanese began to move, reconnaissance aircraft and Australian coast watchers (men who stayed behind when the Japanese occupied the islands, hiding in the jungle to radio information as available) quickly apprised U.S. Vice Admiral Robert Lee Ghormley of the fact. As a result, he ordered Vice Admiral Frank Fletcher into action.

Fletcher had three carrier task forces, each built around a single carrier, supported by two or three cruisers (and in one case a fast battleship) and five to seven destroyers. By dawn on August 23, Fletcher was about 150 miles northeast of Henderson Field, actually on the Pacific side of the Solomons. Misinformed by fleet intelligence that the Japanese carriers had not yet passed Truk, Fletcher decided that he had a few days' grace, and promptly dispatched Task Force 18, *Wasp* and her escorts, southward to refuel, thereby reducing his effectives by a third.

The next morning a PBY spotted *Ryujo*, Kondo's "bait," about 280 miles northwest of Fletcher's position. Fletcher took the bait. At 1345 (1:45 P.M.) on August 24, he launched thirty-eight bombers plus escorts. As these aircraft were on their way, one of Fletcher's scouts came across *Zuikaku* and *Shokaku*, just 60 miles beyond *Ryujo*. Although Fletcher tried to switch the air strike to the more valuable targets, communications problems interfered. *Ryujo* was hit hard, and went down at about 2000. By then Nagumo had already launched two strikes, one at 1507 and the other at 1600.

Aware that the Japanese air strike was coming, Fletcher deployed his two carriers about 10 miles apart, each closely surrounded by its escorts. He also put up fifty-one Wildcats as CAP and flew off bombers that could not be defueled and demunitioned in time to be struck below. CAP intercepted the first Japanese strike at 1629. Although the U.S. Navy fighters accounted for a good many of the attackers, twenty-four Japanese dive bombers got through, concentrating on the carrier *Enterprise* and battleship *North Carolina*, the former taking three bombs that caused considerable damage, including a steering problem that plagued her for several hours. By 1647 the survivors of the first Japanese air strike were winging their way home. The second Japanese air strike went totally astray and returned to its carriers.

During the Japanese attack, the carrier *Saratoga* had received only minimal attention. As a result, she was able to organize an air strike of her own, albeit a modest one (seven bombers with no escorts). At 1745 *Saratoga*'s planes hit Kondo's main body, severely damaging a seaplane carrier. By the time these planes returned to *Saratoga*, Fletcher had decided to break off the action, and the fleet was soon steaming southward. Although Kondo attempted to pursue with his battleships and heavy cruisers, he soon gave up the effort.

The Eastern Solomons was a battle in which both sides made serious errors. Yamamoto could have committed heavier forces, and Fletcher sent a third of his force off to refuel. Strategically and tactically it was an American victory, for with a loss of just seventeen aircraft Fletcher had killed a light carrier, a destroyer, and several dozen aircraft, while the Japanese had not even come close to annihilating American sea power in the South Pacific.

THE BATTLE OF THE SANTA CRUZ ISLANDS

The late-October 1942 Battle of the Santa Cruz Islands was the result of a Japanese effort to undertake a major ground offensive on Guadalcanal supported by carrier aircraft. Unable to secure command of the sea through a naval engagement, the Japanese now decided to do so by means of a land attack, capturing Henderson Field, through a combination of ground attack and naval air assault.

As Yamamoto was willing to commit four battleships, five carriers (with 267 aircraft), eight heavy cruisers, three light cruisers, plus thirty-eight destroyers, a dozen submarines, and a number of auxiliary vessels, as well as considerable land-based air power, this might have worked if the Japanese Army had not taken too long to "soften up" the Marines. The fleet was supposed to intervene in the ground action on October 22, but the Army stretched out the softening-up process until the twenty-sixth. This gave newly appointed Allied theater commander Vice Admiral William F. Halsey time to strengthen his forces, calling up the *Enterprise* task force, which was at Nouméa on the twenty-second (thus giving him two carriers with 169 aircraft, plus one battleship, six cruisers, and fourteen destroyers), while sending all available troops and aircraft to bolster Guadalcanal.

So while Halsey grew stronger during the protracted ground fighting for Henderson Field, Yamamoto grew weaker, as his ships kept to sea for days on end, consuming precious fuel, developing engine trouble (which forced one carrier back to Truk), and exhausting their crews. The Japanese Army, of course, lost the battle for Henderson, which for a time was so desperate that U.S. Army infantrymen were fed into the front-line Marine units. Had Yamamoto known that, there would never have been a Battle of the Santa Cruz

Islands. But at 0126 on October 25, an Imperial Navy liaison officer with the troops on Guadalcanal signaled that the airfield was now in Japanese hands. So Yamamoto ordered the fleet south.

American PBYs spotted Vice Admiral Nagumo's carriers, *Shokaku* and *Zuikaku*, at about noon on October 25. Rear Admiral Thomas Kinkaid, commanding the *Enterprise* task force, attempted a strike that afternoon, which failed to locate the enemy. Although each side groped for the other, neither was successful. During the night of October 25–26, Kinkaid maintained a steady course northwestward, toward the probable location of the Japanese. Before dawn he launched several scouts, and these soon apprised him of the location of the enemy carriers. Passing the word back to Halsey in Nouméa, he received the order "ATTACK—REPEAT—ATTACK!" Kinkaid was ahead of him, having already dispatched a scouting group, and at 0740 several dive bombers inflicted severe damage on the light carrier *Zuiho*, knocking her out of the battle. However, Japanese fleet commander Nobutake Kondo's scouts had by this time spotted *Hornet* and ordered a major strike. Shortly afterward, *Hornet* and *Enterprise* both dispatched major strikes (by some accounts the two hostile air groups actually passed each other en route to their respective targets; it is unclear as to whether this actually occurred).

Kinkaid adopted what was the then standard defensive formation, with his carriers each surrounded by a ring of escorts (later in the war it was found better to concentrate all carriers within a single ring of escorts), with a healthy CAP overhead. *Enterprise* was about 10 miles from *Hornet* when the Japanese struck, at just about 0900. A fortuitous rain squall sprang up, shielding *"The Big E"* from the enemy, who promptly concentrated on *Hornet*. The latter took several bombs, two suicidal crash dives, and two torpedoes, knocking her completely out of action, before the Japanese broke off the attack on her to work over *Enterprise* as she emerged from the squall. Superb ship handling, and voluminous fire from the battleship *South Dakota* and antiaircraft cruiser *San Juan*, kept *Enterprise* from serious harm. At just about the time *Hornet* was being battered, the American air strikes hit Nagumo's carriers, quickly inflicting damage on *Shokaku*, knocking her out of action, and heavily damaging a cruiser as well. But the Japanese had more carriers than the Americans. Kondo ordered strikes from his two undamaged carriers, *Zuikaku* and *Junyo*.

Kondo's strike hit at 1101. Although *Enterprise's* escorts took some damage, she escaped unscathed. Not so the already severely battered *Hornet*, which took three more hits. She would later have to be abandoned after an unsuccessful attempt to sink her; Japanese destroyers sank her with torpedoes the next day. As Kondo's strike winged its way home, Kinkaid decided to break off the action and began steaming southward. Surprisingly, Kondo did not pursue. He might have essayed another air strike, still having two intact carriers and lots of pilots. Apparently unaware of the extent of the damage he had inflicted on the U.S. Navy, Kondo believed that the action would be renewed the next day. It was not to be.

Santa Cruz was a tactical victory for the Japanese, and, indeed, it left them with the only undamaged carriers in the Pacific. But they had suffered about 100 pilots lost, and pilot replacement was becoming an increasingly serious problem. Strategically the battle was an American success, the Japanese once again failing to crush the numerically inferior U.S. Navy.

THE CARTWHEEL
THAT ROLLED OVER THE JAPANESE

Cartwheel was the campaign to isolate, but not capture, Rabaul, one of the largest Japanese bases in the Pacific. As such, it was the most far-ranging encirclement battle of the war, with the two Allied pincers advancing over 1,000 miles. It all began when, in the spring of 1942, the Japanese occupied the Bismarck island group (northeast of New Guinea) and began turning it into their principal bastion in the Southwest Pacific. The spacious natural harbor of Rabaul was the center of this complex. The Japanese put into it over 100,000 troops and hundreds of aircraft. The port generally held the second largest concentration of Japanese warships in the Pacific (after Truk, the main base). Rabaul's cruisers and destroyers escorted transports feeding troops and supplies to sustain protracted battles in New Guinea and the Solomons.

General MacArthur, the Allied commander for the Southwest Pacific, decided that it would be easier to encircle Rabaul with Allied-held islands than it would be to assault so heavily fortified a place directly. This encircling operation was called Cartwheel. The offensive took place between September 1943 and early 1944. The key attack was a series of carrier air raids on Rabaul, which destroyed local Japanese air power. These raids also destroyed the viability of Rabaul as a base for warships, thus leaving over 100,000 Japanese troops isolated and starving by mid-1944.

The last link in the fence thrown around Rabaul was put into place when two island groups north of Rabaul were taken in early 1944 (the Admiralty Islands in February and the St. Matthias Islands in March). Once Rabaul was surrounded by Allied-held islands, few reinforcements or supplies could reach these Japanese, thus making them relatively harmless.

THE BIG BACKWATER, THE CBI

One of the more obscure theaters of World War II was the CBI (China-Burma-India). This was an area that was ignored for good reason, as there was little chance of anything happening there that would likely change the outcome of the war. Most of the crucial military action in the CBI was in Burma, which the Japanese invaded in early 1942. Throughout the war, fighting continued in this area, mainly because it was "the gateway to India." The British were concerned about Japan's instigating further unrest in an already unstable India, especially if Japanese forces battled their way across the Indian border.

Burma also provided land access to China over the "Burma Road." In 1942, the Japanese were stopped just short of the Indian border, cutting the Burma Road. For the next three years, British, African, Indian, U.S., and Chinese troops prosecuted a series of campaigns against dogged Japanese resistance. The CBI consumed Allied resources, but also tied up some first-line Japanese divisions.

The war in Burma began in January 1942, with a Japanese invasion of this British colony. The Japanese had two large, quite capable divisions to face two lower-quality British divisions (containing a mix of British, Indian, and Burmese troops). The fighting proceeded slowly, the opposing forces being infantry units operating in jungle and rice paddy terrain. By April, the Japanese held the southern part of the country. The Chinese were alarmed at this development, as much Allied military aid to China came in over the Burma Road. This route went from Burmese ports via a long twisting road, over the mountains into southern China.

The Nationalist Chinese sent two "armies" (each the size of a U.S. corps) south along the Burma Road. About half of these troops were veterans, the rest less reliable, untrained soldiers. The Japanese responded by sending two more divisions into Burma and diverting troops from the retreating British toward the oncoming Chinese. This stopped the Chinese cold and sent them reeling back into China (most of the 95,000 troops were lost to desertion and sickness). The British were forced back into India, with the Japanese in possession of all of Burma.

The battles in Burma, like those in the rest of the Pacific Theater, were defined by the inhospitable terrain. Most of the subsequent fighting in the country took place in the northern part, and that area was largely mountains and jungle. Disease and logistical difficulties were constantly present for both sides.

For the rest of 1942, both sides rebuilt their forces and prepared to go on the offensive. The British got going first and began advancing down the Burmese coast, in a region called the Arakan, during December. The Japanese fell back. By March 1943, the British attack had faltered, after advancing some 100 miles down the Burmese coast. The Japanese, now reinforced, began their own attack. By May, the Japanese had recovered half of the lost coastline. Then came the monsoon rains, and combat had to slow down because of the nasty weather.

While the Japanese were pushing the British back up the Arakan coast, one of the more striking operations of the Burma war took place. Orde Wingate, a British artillery officer, convinced his superiors that he could train British soldiers to operate in the jungle. Thus prepared, he would send groups of several hundred men each behind Japanese lines in order to attack rear-area installations (particularly railroads). Wingate's troops were called Chindits after a mispronunciation of the Burmese word for "lion" (chinthe) and introduced a new form of warfare. Wingate wasn't just unleashing light infantry to terrorize the enemy rear area (an ancient tactic), he was using modern technology (radios to coordinate the raids and aircraft to supply them) to do the job in a more effective manner. While the Chindits caused the Japanese a lot of trouble, this was not of much assistance to the main British operations on the coast. There, the Japanese regained the initiative while the Chindits were rampaging through their rear area. But in the long run, the Chindits had a noticeable effect. The Japanese logistical arrangements were threadbare to begin with, and the Chindits (and, later, the American "Merrill's Marauders") caused the Japanese supply situation to fail during later operations. This was a big help to the major British offensives. Also, there was the propaganda value of Allied troops' going into the Japanese rear area.

Overall, 1943 did not go very well for the Allies. The Japanese were poised to invade India and prospects of substantial reinforcements were meager. Throughout the year, however, the Chinese had been encouraged to renew operations in northern Burma. There, from the town of Ledo, a new road was being built into China, over which to carry military matériel. The Chinese had a vested interest in seeing the "Ledo Road" completed; thus they were enthusiastic about providing the troops to protect it from possible Japanese interference.

In 1944, the Burmese fighting developed into three different campaigns. In the north were the Chinese, fighting against Japanese efforts to disrupt work on the Ledo Road. On the coast, preparations went ahead for an Allied advance south, assisted by amphibious operations (if enough ships could be pried away from other theaters). In the center, the Japanese were getting ready to move into India, firmly believing that this would cause the Indian people to rise up in rebellion against the British. This was not entirely out of the question, but the British had been aware of the danger for several years and had made political moves (promising India independence after the war) to keep the peace.

The battle in north Burma developed well for the Chinese throughout 1944. But in November they were forced to withdraw two divisions to deal with a major Japanese offensive in central China. Thus the Chinese were not able to inflict any decisive damage on the Japanese, although the Ledo Road remained secure.

Farther south, the Japanese began an offensive in March that led to the sieges of Imphal and Kohima, just across the border in India. The Japanese logistical situation was bad to begin with and they were depending on the British retreating and leaving Allied supplies behind. This didn't happen; the British stayed and fought even when surrounded. Increased Allied air power gave the Allies air superiority by mid-1944 and enabled isolated forces to be resupplied regularly by air. This was something the Japanese had not expected either. By the end of summer, the Japanese offensive collapsed. The lack of supplies led to enormous Japanese losses due to disease and starvation. Less than half their 65,000 dead were from combat causes.

Down along the coast, the fighting was desultory, with little progress being made by the Allies.

In early 1945, the Japanese paid for the desperate offensives they had launched in 1944. The Allies—mostly Indians—advanced on all fronts and by May were driving across all of Burma. Rangoon fell and the fighting became more a hunt for the many Japanese units that were still in the bush and unwilling to surrender.

Looming behind all the action in Burma, whose main purpose was to keep the Japanese out of India, was the war in China.

THE WAR (A BIG ONE) IN CHINA

Most Americans don't think of the war in China as part of the Pacific war. In fact, the fighting in China was much more intense and bloody than what Americans faced in the Pacific. Casualties in China were in the millions, both before and after Pearl Harbor. It was Japan's invasion of China (which began in 1931 or 1935 or 1937, depending on how one wishes to count various "incidents") that eventually got the United States into World War II in the first place. And it was in China, not Poland, that the earliest battles of World War II were fought.

Japan had been making steady inroads in China and Korea since the 1880s. Initially, the Japanese saw themselves as competing on equal terms with European powers (particularly Britain and Russia) that struggled for colonial trading privileges in China. But the Japanese soon realized that they could attempt to conquer China. Not right away, but a piece at a time. The Japanese tended to take the long view.

Their war with China in 1894–1895 got the Japanese a free hand in Korea and control of some of Manchuria and all of Formosa. A war with Russia in 1904–1905 got them control of all of Korea and

43

more of Manchuria. Note that the Russians had already grabbed much of Manchuria before the 1904–1905 war (partly to keep the Japanese out), and this was used as Japan's justification for expanding its control in the area.

After World War I, the Japanese were given more leeway in China because they had sided with the Allies against the Germans during the war. As a result of that cooperation, the Japanese received the German colonies in the Pacific, including many well-placed islands in the Central Pacific, and wanted the German concessions on the large Shantung Peninsula southeast of Peking (now called Beijing).

While the European colonial powers were by then largely gone from China, the Chinese themselves had begun to get their act together. A revolution had deposed the monarchy just before World War I and the rebels were attempting to weld the various warloads into a cohesive government. But during the 1920s there came a Communist revolution. This actually helped the Japanese, who played one Chinese faction against another through the 1920s. Meanwhile, the Japanese increased their military strength in Korea and parts of Manchuria. More important to the Japanese, they increased their economic presence. This meant getting access to raw materials and markets, as well as favorable trading terms. The Japanese built railroads and other facilities and staffed them with Japanese colonists.

The Japanese generals running the show in China became more and more independent of the government back in Tokyo. Using subversion and threats, Japanese military leaders gained control over larger portions of Manchuria. In 1931, the Japanese Army staged an "incident" with local Chinese troops that gave them an excuse to conquer all of Manchuria. This took about a year, after which they promptly declared Manchuria an independent nation. While the Japanese government was not happy with this freelancing by the Army commanders in China, political leaders were not about to risk a military coup by attempting to assert civilian control over the Army. Through the 1930s, over a million Japanese settlers moved into Manchuria.

Although the Japanese government never made any serious attempts to rein in its ambitious generals in China, this did not satisfy the increasingly bold Japanese Army officer corps. In 1936 there was an attempted coup in Tokyo by junior army officers. Several senior civilian officials were assassinated before the coup was suppressed. These junior officers wanted even more support for the Chinese war, and although the coup failed, they had made their point.

In 1937, Japan began large-scale warfare against China. Attacking from enclaves in Manchuria and along the coast, the Japanese advanced into central China. Japan had 300,000 troops in China at the time, plus 150,000 Manchurians and Mongolians under Japanese officers. The Chinese had over 2 million troops under arms, but these were much less well equipped, trained, and led than the Japanese invaders. For two years the Japanese advanced deeper into China. But progress was slow and casualties mounted.

Gradually, the Japanese came to control much of northern China and nearly all the coastal areas. In 1939, they decided to return to their earlier subversion and attrition tactics. With control of all Chinese ports, the Japanese felt that Chinese military resistance would soon wither. But there were still two supply routes open to the Chinese: One was the railroad from French Indochina (Vietnam) and the other the Burma Road. America and other Western nations were still willing to support China, and these two routes kept the Chinese armed forces going. The Japanese, naturally, sought to shut down these two routes, and they would do so once they were at war with the United States and Britain (which controlled Burma).

Many Western nations were not happy with Japanese attempts to conquer China. Diplomatic protests had no effect. In the summer of 1941, the Western nations raised the ante by freezing Japanese assets and then invoking a trade embargo. Because the Japanese were dependent on Western-controlled raw materials (particularly oil) to keep their economy going, the embargo gave them a choice of getting out of China or seeing their economy (and military power) collapse. Their only other choice was war with America, Britain, and Holland (which controlled most of the local oil supplies).

At the start of the Pacific war, most of the Japanese Army was in China. In Manchuria, keeping an eye on Russia, were thirteen divisions. In China were another twenty-three divisions, not to mention a goodly number of independent brigades. There were also about twenty divisions of Japanese-controlled Chinese troops representing the government of the "independent Manchuria" the Japanese had set up.

The Japanese only had about ten divisions to spare for the conquest of the Pacific (including Malaya and Burma). It was very much a shoestring operation in the Pacific because of the massive number of troops needed to keep an eye on China. While China got the bulk of the troops, the Japanese effort in the Pacific got most of everything else. As a result, the Japanese Army in China spent the rest of the war fighting a poor man's war. The most common offensive operations were short, local advances for the purpose of stealing the rice crops at harvest time. This helped feed the Japanese troops and made the Chinese weaker.

After their supply lines from Indochina and Burma were cut in late 1941, the Chinese received only a trickle of supply flown in over the Himalayan Mountains by U.S. aircraft. Thus neither side had the ammunition or other supplies to sustain any major operations. For most of the war, the Chinese front was a stalemate. Moreover, the Nationalist Chinese (who received all the support from the Allies) devoted over a third of their troops to watching the Communist armies. Despite the threat of Japanese conquest, the Chinese civil war went on.

In 1944, the Japanese took advantage of this situation by establishing a truce with the Chinese Communists. This allowed the Communists to strengthen their hold over the northwestern Chinese territory they controlled, and enabled the Japanese to send troops south for their 1944 offensive against American airfields.

From May through November of 1944, the Japanese again advanced, overrunning U.S. airfields in central China. Much of the supply being flown in by American transports went to support U.S. combat aircraft. As small as this air force was, it bothered the Japanese a great deal, and they scraped together what resources they had to knock out the American airfields.

As with the 1937 campaign, the 1944 operation was hampered by logistical problems and constant resistance from the Chinese population. Moreover, the Chinese Nationalist Army had been receiving more military aid and training from the United States since 1941 and had become a more competent force.

However, the American commanders in China were convinced that air power could stop the Japanese if there was a major offensive. Thus the Chinese ground troops were not as well equipped as they could have been if a lot of the airlifted supply had gone to building up the Chinese Army instead of the bombing campaign.

Despite the obstacles, the Japanese managed to capture the airfields and link up with their forces in Indochina. This cut Nationalist Chinese–controlled territory in half, thus making the Nationalist situation much worse.

The 1944 offensive went on for almost a year and exhausted Japanese forces in China, making them ripe for rapid defeat by the Russians in the summer 1945. In April 1945, the Russians made their intentions clear by abrogating the nonaggression treaty with Japan. Realizing that their Manchurian army had been bled dry to support the Pacific and Chinese operations, Japanese commanders were ordered to send troops from China to Manchuria. This evened up the situation sufficiently for the Chinese to recover a lot of the territory the Japanese had taken earlier.

When the Russians attacked in August 1945, the Japanese, even reinforced, were not able to stop them. When Japan surrendered on August 15, the Communists and Nationalists were quick to grab the surrendered weapons and continue their civil war (which the Communists won by 1949).

Throughout the Pacific war, most of the Japanese Army was in China. While the Chinese troops were not active much of the time, many of Japan's best troops were thus occupied, rather than being sent against Allied troops in the Pacific or in Burma. So China's role, though generally neglected, was critical to the Allied victory.

THE BATTLE OF THE PHILIPPINE SEA

The greatest (and last) carrier battle of the war, at least in terms of the number of carriers and aircraft involved, the Philippine Sea resulted from an effort by the Japanese Navy to reverse the fortunes of war in the Pacific. The Japanese plan was rather simpler than previous ones, a tribute to the direction and clear thinking of Vice Admiral Jisaburo Ozawa.

Ozawa had assumed command of the First Mobile Fleet, comprising most of Japan's surface warships, in late 1943. Ordered by the chief of naval operations, Admiral Soemu Toyoda, to annihilate the American Fifth Fleet, Ozawa concentrated five battleships, nine carriers (with 430 aircraft), eleven heavy cruisers, two light cruisers, thirty-four destroyers, and several auxiliaries at Tawitawi, a small island group at the southeastern end of the Philippines, with a fine, albeit rather open, anchorage in close proximity to the Borneo oil fields, which produced a crude so light it could be burned by ships' engines without refining.

While this fleet was concentrating, hundreds of aircraft were being ferried into the Marianas and Carolines, as also were twenty-five submarines, all intended as part of a trap that Ozawa would spring on Raymond Spruance's Fifth Fleet.

Ozawa's plan was simple. When word came that the Americans were hitting the Marianas, their next logical target for an amphibious landing, he would sortie from Tawitawi and head directly to intercept the attackers, deployed in such a fashion that three of his light carriers would act as bait about 100 miles in advance of the main body (which was deployed in two task forces). Considering the circumstances, Ozawa's plan was probably the best he could do, and a lot better than most previous Japanese carrier battle plans.

Raymond Spruance, commanding the Fifth Fleet, had an enormous amount of resources at hand for the Marianas operation. In addition to the fast carriers (Task Force 58: fifteen carriers with over 890 carrier aircraft embarked, plus seven battleships, eight heavy cruisers, thirteen light cruisers, and sixty-nine destroyers), assigned to defend the landings from interference by the Imperial Navy, he had available nearly a dozen escort carriers and numerous older battleships, cruisers, and destroyers assigned to actually support the landings. So Spruance was overwhelmingly superior to Ozawa.

On June 15, learning that the Americans had landed on Saipan, Admiral Toyoda ordered Ozawa to implement the attack plan, "Operation A-Go." For three days Ozawa steamed slowly northeastward.

Spruance, apprised of Ozawa's coming by submarine reconnaissance, calmly laid his plans. One task group was dispatched on a scheduled raid to the Bonin Islands, where it took out numerous aircraft assigned to assist Ozawa in the destruction of the Fifth Fleet. Meanwhile, Spruance borrowed a few additional ships from the invasion force to bolster his defensive screen further, and ordered the fleet to rendezvous about 140 miles west of Tinian at 1800 hours on June 18.

Marc Mitscher, the actual Task Force 58 commander, formed his task groups into a T. Three task groups formed the crossbar, supported by another task group forward and to their left, with the upright base of the T formed by his fast battleship task group, pointing toward the enemy. Despite his great superiority, Spruance moved with caution, as Japanese reconnaissance aircraft were longer-legged than American ones. This was wise, as Ozawa knew where Spruance was, while Spruance did not know where Ozawa was.

On the morning of June 19, Task Force 58 made some air strikes at Japanese air bases on Guam, usefully destroying aircraft intended to support Ozawa. Meanwhile, at about 0800, Ozawa launched sixty-nine aircraft from his three "bait" light carriers against the American carriers. Spotted on radar at 0959, the strike was quickly intercepted and only about sixteen of the attackers got through the swarm of Hellcats that met them, inflicting insignificant damage on the U.S. fleet. Only twenty-four of the sixty-nine Japanese aircraft made it back to their carriers.

Ozawa's second strike, 130 aircraft dispatched from the main body at about 0900, did even worse than the first, 98 falling after having inflicted only minor damage. Worse, even as this strike was getting off, a U.S. submarine put a torpedo into Ozawa's newest and largest carrier, *Taiho*, which shortly succumbed to a series of massive internal explosions.

Ozawa launched a third strike at 1000 hours, consisting of forty-seven aircraft, all but seven of which returned safely because they completely failed to intercept the American ships, the others falling to roving patrols of Hellcats.

At 1100 hours Ozawa launched eighty-two aircraft from *Zuikaku*, *Ryuho*, and *Junyo*. Although these too followed a false contact, the strike commander led them farther and they managed to attack Task Force 58, but they inflicted no damage and only twenty-eight made it back to the carriers, most badly shot up. Meanwhile Ozawa lost yet another carrier, *Shokaku*, to an American submarine. By now night was falling.

So far the battle had been one of Japanese air strikes on American ships, since Mitscher had difficulties locating the enemy carriers.

During the night of June 19–20, Mitscher kept feeling for the enemy, while Ozawa maneuvered to keep within range yet undetected. Not until 1540 on June 20 was Mitscher able to get a fix on the enemy, when Ozawa was about 275 miles southwest of Task Force 58. At 1620 Mitscher launched 216 planes from ten carriers. These reached Ozawa at about 1840. With darkness closing in, the aircraft attacked, sinking the carrier *Hiyo*, damaging *Zuikaku* and some other ships, and disabling two fleet oilers. In this action Ozawa lost 65 more aircraft, while the United States lost only 20.

With night falling, the American aircraft hastened back to their carriers, and several were damaged or lost making night landings, despite the fact that Mitscher gallantly ordered the carriers to light up their flight decks (thus making it easy for any nearby Japanese subs to find targets).

The final count of Japanese losses on June 19–20 was three carriers sunk plus damage to another, and two oilers so badly damaged they had to be scuttled. The Japanese lost about 410 aircraft, and nearly 200 land-based planes, not to mention hundreds of men. All of this was done at the cost of 130 U.S. aircraft lost, plus some slight damage to a few ships. Only seventy-six Americans had been killed.

During the night of June 20–21, Ozawa tried to put as much distance as possible between himself and Spruance. The latter undertook a pursuit, but then broke it off to rescue downed aircrewmen (fifty-nine of whom were fished out of the sea). The massacre of Japanese carrier aviation was promptly dubbed the Great Marianas Turkey Shoot.

It seems clear that Spruance should have pursued Ozawa more vigorously in the aftermath of the battle, so that he might have inflicted a decisive defeat on the twenty-first. But Spruance had two missions, one to defeat the Imperial Navy and the other to support the landings on Saipan.

THE FLYING SAMURAI RUN OUT OF GAS (ETC.)

All was not as it appeared during the Great Marianas Turkey Shoot.

It is commonly accepted that the cause of this lopsided battle was the relative quality of the pilots. There is some truth to this. A look at trends in pilot training during the war reveals that the quality of Japanese pilots, among the best in the world (if not *the* best) at the onset of the war, declined steadily during it. However, it turns out that, although important, this was not the principal reason for Japan's poor pilot performance against the Americans in 1944. It was a host of other factors that, combined, resulted in a disaster for Japanese carrier aviation. These reasons were:

- FUEL (or the lack of it). Japan had been short of oil since the beginning of the war and its inability to boost production at captured oil fields, or to produce enough tankers to carry the oil, made it impossible for ships to stay at sea long, or for pilots to fly much. The lack of sea and air time led to less capable sailors and pilots. Practice makes perfect and since 1942 the Americans had had a lot more practice.
- SUBMARINES (too many American ones). U.S. submarines not only made steady inroads on the available Japanese tankers and merchant ships, but also limited the amount of time carriers could spend at sea. One, *Shinano*, was ten hours into her maiden voyage when she was sent to the bottom by a prowling U.S. sub. Carriers could not be risked when too many U.S. subs were in the area, and the Japanese never had enough land-based aircraft and destroyers to keep large areas free of U.S. subs. In the Philippine Sea, the Japanese lost their newest, and arguably best, carrier, *Taiho*, to a U.S. sub even before the battle was well joined.
- BETTER COORDINATION (by the Americans). The U.S. Navy had developed the CIC (Combat Information Center) concept. Because of the wide use of radios in aircraft and powerful shipboard radars, the admiral in the CIC (on his flagship) could thus control hundreds of aircraft at once and coordinate them against large Japanese attacks. The Japanese had nothing quite as effective as the CIC, and suffered much from the efficient American CICs.
- BETTER ANTIAIRCRAFT CAPABILITY (on U.S. ships). American heavy (5-inch) antiaircraft shells were equipped with proximity fuzes (which had a small radar set in them, causing the shell to detonate when it was close to a target), and there were literally thousands of efficient smaller-caliber (20mm and 40mm) automatic antiaircraft guns in the American fleet as

well. The CIC, using the reports from radar, would activate the long-range fire of relatively large caliber shipboard AA guns (mostly 5-inch) against those Japanese aircraft that got past the CIC-controlled U.S. fighters. The proximity fuzes would cause the shells to explode whenever they came close to an aircraft, unless they made a direct hit. The CIC directed thousands of shells into the path of approaching Japanese aircraft, forming a wall of radar-equipped shells that the planes would have to fly through. Those Japanese aircraft that survived the wall then had to face the thousands of 20mm and 40mm automatic cannon on the defending ships. As a result, in one case an attack of over 300 Japanese aircraft was practically annihilated. The hundreds of Japanese aircraft were able to secure only one hit. It was on a battleship, with a bomb that caused minimal damage.

THE BATTLE OF LEYTE GULF

The greatest naval battle in history, Leyte Gulf was the Imperial Navy's last attempt to engage in a decisive battle with the U.S. Navy. It was actually a series of interrelated engagements fought over tens of thousands of square miles of ocean in October 1944.

Aware that the next major American move in the Pacific was almost certainly a landing in the Philippines, the Imperial Navy developed a series of possible defensive plans, the precise one to be used depending upon the actual site of the American landings. The plan recognized several serious obstacles to the success of the Japanese, the most significant being the virtual incompetence of their naval aviators by this point in the war. So the plan envisioned the use of Japan's remaining carriers (with minimal air groups) as bait to lure the main American strength northward, away from the invasion beaches, which would then be hit by surface forces that had quietly made their way through the numerous small seas and straits in the Philippine archipelago.

The version of Operation Sho ("Victory") that was put into effect was predicated upon an American landing on Leyte, in the central part of the eastern Philippines. This envisioned four main task forces, all under Vice Admiral Jisaburo Ozawa. Ozawa's Main Body of the Mobile Force, concentrated in the Inland Sea and comprising four carriers and two hybrid battleship/carriers, would steam southward from Japan into the western Philippine Sea, constituting the baiting of the trap. The actual offensive elements were A Force, C Force, and the Second Striking Force.

A Force, five battleships, including the behemoths *Yamato* and *Musashi*, with nine heavy cruisers and accompanying destroyers, would concentrate at Brunei Bay (where it was easy to get fuel). It would then thread its way through the Sibuyan Sea in the central Philippines, debouch from San Bernardino Strait, and speed south to shoot up American transports off Leyte.

The Second Striking Force, two heavy cruisers, a light cruiser, and four destroyers in the Inland Sea, would sail south through the China Sea and into the Sulu Sea, where it would unite with C Force.

C Force, with two battleships, a heavy cruiser, and four destroyers, was to start from Brunei Bay.

Once the Second Striking Force and C Force united in the Sulu Sea, the two squadrons would thread their way through the many islands, and debouch from Surigao Strait right into Leyte Gulf, to devastate American shipping off the beaches.

Operation Sho was put into effect on October 20, as various elements began to steam for their objectives. Meanwhile, the U.S. Navy had brought over 200 warships (including 2 Australian ones) into action off the Philippines, supporting over 400 transports and hundreds of other smaller vessels that were actually effecting the landings on Leyte Island.

The fleet was widely dispersed. The Fast Carrier Task Force, still under Marc Mitscher, was deployed about 100 miles east of Leyte, with the individual task groups rotating into and out of action in order to refuel and remunition. With Mitscher was Third Fleet commander William F. Halsey, over fifteen carriers, seven fast battleships, and dozens of cruisers and destroyers. Between Mitscher and Leyte were three escort carrier task groups, assigned to support the beachhead. And in Leyte Gulf itself was the Seventh Fleet: six old battleships (five of them Pearl Harbor veterans), eight cruisers, nearly twenty destroyers, and numerous PT boats, protecting the transports and lending fire support to the combat troops on Leyte itself.

Not until October 23 did Halsey learn that the Japanese fleet was on the move. At 0630 that day, two U.S. submarines sank two and disabled one of the heavy cruisers accompanying Vice Admiral Takeo Kurita's A Force. Although he had to cope with attacks from Japanese land-based aircraft, which sank the light carrier *Princeton*, Mitscher launched a major strike with 259 aircraft against Kurita's squadron. These intercepted Kurita in the Sibuyan Sea and heavily worked him over. The superbattleship *Musashi* went down, after taking enormous punishment, and the other ships turned back. So one of the Japanese attack forces had been defeated by the evening of October 24.

Meanwhile, before noon on October 24 carrier reconnaissance aircraft had spotted the combined C Force and the Second Striking Force. Vice Admiral Kinkaid, commanding the Seventh Fleet, correctly concluded that these ships were headed for Surigao Strait and ordered the old battleships off Leyte to intercept.

Rear Admiral Jesse Oldendorf, commanding the fire support vessels, deployed his old battleships, cruisers, destroyers, and torpedo boats in a massive ambush at the northern end of Surigao Strait, not 50 miles south of the invasion beaches. Oldendorf's torpedo boats began harassing Vice Admiral Shoji Nishimura's ships shortly before midnight. Around 0200 Oldendorf's destroyers began getting their licks in, and at 0300 the battleship *Fuso*, struck by several torpedoes, began to burn and then blew up, while *Yamashiro* took one, and then a second torpedo.

But the two Japanese squadrons kept coming, firing on whatever targets they could locate. The American battleships opened fire at 0353. It did not take long. By 0411 only a wounded cruiser and the destroyer *Shigure* had escaped, fleeing south past the second Japanese squadron, C Force, which shortly retired, having already taken some damage. So the Japanese had now lost two rounds.

Meanwhile, shortly after 1500 on October 24, reconnaissance aircraft from Task Force 38 had spotted the Japanese carriers coming south. Now that Halsey knew where the enemy was, he went after him. By midnight on October 24, Admiral Halsey was steaming north with the fast carriers and battleships, intent upon intercepting Ozawa's carriers. This was precisely what the Japanese wanted, as their carriers were worthless anyway. By his action, Halsey exposed the landings to terrible danger.

During that same night, Kurita's A Force, having turned eastward seemingly in abandonment of its mission, now reversed course once more to steam for San Bernardino Strait. Early on October 25, Kurita's squadron debouched into the broad waters of the Philippine Sea and began racing southward, wholly undetected by American air reconnaissance. Actually, a recon plane had spotted them shortly before midnight, but Halsey dismissed the contact. False contacts were a common problem during World War II.

At 0646, Kurita's four battleships, six heavy cruisers, and dozen or so destroyers blundered into Taffy 3, a group of six escort carriers, three destroyers, and four destroyer escorts. A wild melee ensued, as Kurita's heavy ships strove to overwhelm the American vessels. Since Kurita thought the American vessels were fleet carriers and cruisers, he moved somewhat cautiously, which worked against him.

Straining hopelessly to pile on speed, the jeep carriers and their escorts fought back with air attacks (some made without ammunition), gunfire, and torpedo attacks. American losses were heavy: two escort carriers, a destroyer, and two destroyer escorts. Kurita might have done worse damage, but other escort carrier groups in the area began lending Taffy 3 a hand, and then he received word that the Second Striking Force had been annihilated at Surigao Strait. He lost his nerve, and at 1236 began steaming northward.

During Taffy 3's ordeal off Samar, the bulk of Task Force 38 was steaming northward in the hope of intercepting and destroying Ozawa's carriers. The first air strikes were launched at dawn, and by 0800 Ozawa's carriers were being heavily worked over. This continued throughout the day, so that by early afternoon Ozawa had lost four carriers and a destroyer, some finished off by gunfire from Halsey's heavy cruisers; the latter, by that time, had been apprised of his error in leaving San Bernardino Strait unguarded and had dispatched his fast battleships southward, to arrive off Samar just in time to sink a damaged Japanese destroyer, the battleships having gotten clean away.

Thus ended the Battle of Leyte Gulf, the greatest naval battle in history. It was an overwhelming American victory, and virtually marked the death of the Imperial Navy.

TWO BATTLES FOR THE PHILIPPINES

The Philippines had the grim distinction of suffering two major invasions during World War II. The Japanese put a lot more into defending the Philippines in late 1944 than the United States had in 1941. America had had about 130,000 mostly untrained troops defending the islands in 1941. Japan had 350,000 troops as a garrison in 1944. The Japanese troops were also better trained, motivated, and equipped. Japan also had a larger air force and fleet to defend the islands. In turn, the United States went after the Philippines with far larger forces than Japan had used in 1941. During their invasion, the Japanese had actually had fewer troops than the defending Americans. In 1941, the Japanese had gone straight for the main island of Luzon (containing the capital, Manila), while in 1944 the United States first landed on Leyte, in the east central part of the Philippines. In both cases, the area first invaded was dictated by the presence of friendly air bases.

The 1941 Japanese invasion had been staged out of Taiwan, which was a few hundred miles north of Luzon. In 1944, the Allies came from the south because they had just established air bases on recently captured islands northwest of New Guinea. In 1944 the Japanese were under far more pressure than the Americans had been in 1941. For Japan, the Philippines was the Allied staging area for an invasion of the Japanese home islands. This brought out the Japanese air and naval forces in large numbers, which the United States proceeded to destroy. After that, a series of amphibious landing extending into early 1945 led to the capture of all the Philippine Islands. By early March, 1945, Manila was again in U.S. hands. Although fighting continued in remote areas until Japan surrendered, the Philippines was effectively liberated. MacArthur had kept his promise to the Philippine people and "returned."

THE FIVE-FRONT WAR

An ancient bit of military wisdom is that it is unwise to fight a two-front war. Japan went into World War II struggling to deal with five fronts.

Two of these are familiar to Americans, with General MacArthur's offensive in the Southwest Pacific, from the Solomons and New Guinea northwestward toward the Philippines, and Admiral Nimitz's series of island assaults across the Central Pacific.

A third campaign is rather less familiar to Americans: Burma and the Indian frontier, where sizable Japanese armies struggled with British and Indian soldiers for three years.

There was a fourth front where most of the Japanese Army (which ultimately comprised 10 percent of Japan's adult population) was occupied with a war in China. Here, millions died during the war, mostly Chinese.

In addition, throughout the war, Japan had to maintain large forces in Manchuria to guard against an attack by the Soviet Union, an attack that did not come until literally the last week of the war.

Because Japan is an island nation, all these battlefronts had to be supplied by ship. Japan began the war with a shipping shortage and this only got worse. Japan's prospects of success on any of these fronts were dim. Indeed, even if Japan had had but one front, her shipping problems would have been enormously difficult.

America opened two widely separated fronts in the Pacific because U.S. industry was able to produce enough ships and aircraft to support two separate assaults on Japan.

The war in China had been dragging on since the early 1930s, with slim prospects for eventual Japanese success. The occupation of Burma and subsequent invasion of India were largely based on the assumption that if the Japanese got into India proper, the Indians would rise up and drive the British out. The British took the precaution of promising the Indians independence when the war was over; the Indians believed the British, and hence most of the "British" fighting the Japanese were actually Indian.

To add to Japanese problems there was that potential fifth front, as tensions had existed between the Soviet Union and Japan for a long time. In 1939 the Japanese initiated several battles with Soviet forces on the Manchurian border. The Japanese lost, and decided to defer their plans to run the Soviets out of eastern Siberia.

Japan had long seen Russia, and later the Soviet Union, as its major enemy in Asia. The war with America and her allies was something Japan wanted to avoid, and believed she could avoid. But the Soviet Union bordered the Japanese colony of Manchuria. Until 1941, there were over forty Soviet divisions in what the Russians called the Far East (Siberia was to the north and west). Japan had only a dozen divisions in Manchuria, but the Japanese believed they could eventually increase this force and successfully attack the Russians.

In 1939, relations between the Japanese and Soviets had deteriorated, largely because of the usual rambunctiousness of the independent-minded and aggressive Japanese generals in China. From 1938 on, there were incidents on the Manchurian border, and several small battles took place. In May 1939, the Japanese decided to teach the Soviets a lesson in an area bordering Soviet-controlled Mongolia. Here, there was an ongoing dispute as to where the border really was, and the Japanese intended to put their troops where they felt the border should be.

Moving forward an infantry division near the Khalkhin-Gol River, the Japanese were handily repulsed by the Soviets. This came as something of a shock to the Japanese, because they had long thought themselves militarily superior to the Russians. After all, they had defeated them in the 1904–1905 war. Undeterred, the Japanese brought up reinforcements (70 tanks in two tank regiments and an infantry regiment) and went at it again in July. The Russians responded with a force that included 300 tanks and crushed the Japanese offensive again. The Japanese then brought forward heavy artillery and found that the Soviets outclassed them in that area also. In August, the Russians decided to make their own attack, and brought up four divisions that proceeded to push the two Japanese divisions back to where the Russians considered the Manchurian border should be.

This series of battles was relatively large for 1939, but puny by later World War II standards. The Japanese used 40,000 troops and suffered 18,000 casualties. The Soviets committed 70,000 troops and took 14,000 casualties. The Japanese fought hard, but the Soviets fought smarter and with more weapons and equipment. Japanese air power was not decisive, but Soviet armor was. The Japanese kept the peace on their border with the Soviet Union from then on and assumed that all would be forgotten, especially when the Japanese did not take advantage of Soviet weakness after most Russian divisions were sent west against the Germans in late 1941. In 1942, the Japanese made plans to rebuild their Manchurian forces and send the Russians back west. But defeats in the Pacific soon undercut these aspirations.

The Soviets did not forget, and in August 1945, the Soviets opened Japan's fifth front with a massive invasion of Japanese-controlled Manchuria. Japan surrendered to the Allies on August 15, 1945.

THE WAR AGAINST JAPANESE SHIPPING

While the Germans got most of the bad publicity for their spectacular U-boat defeat in the Atlantic, less is said about America's successful campaign against Japanese shipping in the Pacific. U.S. submarines accounted for over half of Japanese merchant shipping and were able to prowl to every corner of Japan's maritime empire. Complementing this effort were the increasing reach and dominance of American carrier- and land-based aviation at the front lines. Japanese ships had to run an obstacle course from the time they left port (and promptly encountered waiting American subs) until they reached front-line bases and were pummeled by U.S. bombers.

In 1945, U.S. subs and B-29s began planting thousands of mines in Japanese coastal waters. In addition to the shipping sunk, these mines virtually shut down Japanese ports. The mines worked day and night and in any weather. Japanese ships had neither bad weather nor darkness as protection from the mines, as they did from enemy subs and aircraft.

The Allied antishipping campaign not only wiped out Japan's merchant marine by the end of the war, it crippled it by the end of 1943. Thus Japan had less ability to meet the multiple American amphibious offensives during 1944. Japan began the war with about

JAPANESE SHIPPING SUNK (IN THOUSANDS OF TONS)

SUNK BY	TOTAL	1942	1943	1944	1945	% OF TOTAL
Submarines	5,880	69%	83%	69%	23%	62%
Carrier A/C	1,740	11%	2%	23%	28%	18%
Land A/C	825	9%	11%	6%	12%	9%
Mines	600	0%	0%	0%	28%	6%
Misc.	450	11%	3%	2%	8%	5%
Total	9,495	875	2,175	4,330	2,115	
% per Year		9%	23%	46%	22%	

NOTES: "Carrier A/C" is primarily carrier-based aircraft but also includes land-based Navy planes. "Misc." includes accidents at sea (storms, breakdowns, and so on) as well as losses to enemy surface warships. Due to rounding, not all columns add up to 100%.

6.5 million tons of shipping. That amount steadily declined throughout the war.

The Japanese fought a poor man's fight for the entire war, using much less ammunition and fewer weapons per combatant. This lowered their combat capability and increased their casualties. They had little choice in the matter, as they were simply unable to move much over the water because they never had enough shipping.

Japan's shipping crisis was made worse by the policies of its Army and Navy. At the beginning of the war, each service appropriated large amounts of shipping (1.8 million tons for the Navy, 2.1 million for the Army) to support its offensive operations. This left the civilian economy about a million tons short of its minimum needs. Since the arms factories depended on imports for most of their raw materials, production took a beating from the beginning. To make matters worse, the Army and Navy would not cooperate with each other or industry in the use of shipping. The Army would send a supply ship to Java and, instead of coming back with raw materials, it would come back empty because moving raw materials was not an Army responsibility. This situation was not rectified until 1944, and then it was too late.

It got worse. Japan never developed an effective convoy system or antisubmarine techniques. But underlying all of this was the fact that Japan was still a minor industrial power. It was during the 1930s

JAPANESE MERCHANT SHIPPING AVAILABLE (IN MILLIONS OF TONS)		
SHIPPING	IN SERVICE	SUNK TO DATE
Dec. 1941	6.4	0
Jan. 1943	5.9	0.9
Jan. 1944	4.8	3.1
Jan. 1945	2.4	7.4
Aug. 1945	1.5	9.3

that Japan had begun to industrialize in a serious way. Even so, by 1940 Japan was only producing half a million tons of shipping a year. This was less than a tenth of what the United States was capable of. Even with a massive effort, Japan was never able to produce more than 1.7 million tons of shipping a year. That was in 1944, the year that American subs and aircraft sank 2.7 million tons.

The Japanese did have one item in their favor. For the first eighteen months of the war American submarines were equipped with defective torpedoes. It wasn't until September 1943 that this problem was completely resolved, although by the end of 1942 many submarine crews had developed ways to get some use out of their torpedoes. Nevertheless, this gave the Japanese merchant marine something of a free ride through the middle of 1943. After that, Japanese shipping disappeared beneath the waves with great rapidity.

Oddly enough, Japanese submarines were never a menace to Allied shipping. The Japanese felt that the only proper targets for their submarines were enemy warships. It was considered a waste of good torpedoes to shoot at merchant ships. However, the Japanese subs did have some success against Allied warships. Two carriers were sunk (one an escort carrier), as were two cruisers. Several other major warships—carriers and battleships—were put out of action for months by Japanese submarine torpedoes.

The Americans also went after Japanese warships when there was no merchant shipping handy. Arguably, the U.S. submarines were better at it than their Japanese counterparts.

American subs spent 31,671 days on patrol, or about three weeks per patrol. Many patrols were cut short by mechanical problems and

U.S. SUBMARINE ACTIVITY IN THE PACIFIC

	1941–1942	1943	1944	1945	TOTAL
Warships Sunk	2	22	104	60	188
Merchantmen Sunk	180	325	603	186	1,294
Patrols	350	350	520	330	1,550
U.S. Subs Lost	7	15	19	8	49

NOTES: "Patrols" consist of one sub going out looking for the enemy for up to two months, or until it is damaged or runs out torpedoes.

Not counted among sinkings are enemy warships and merchantmen damaged by submarine attacks. These amounted to a smaller number than those sunk, mainly because warships attacked tended to be small escort types and Japanese ships were, on average, rather smaller than Western ones. These smaller ships were much less likely to survive a torpedo hit.

Not all sinkings resulted from torpedo hits. When the opportunity presented itself (no enemy warships were around), a sub would surface and use its 76mm deck gun to sink smaller ships. This saved torpedoes, desirable because only about twenty-four to thirty were carried by an American sub.

some were in support of fleet operations. These fleet patrols were much shorter than others.

To attack 4,112 Japanese merchant ships, 14,748 torpedoes were used. This was 3.6 torpedoes per attack and indicates that the typical attack involved firing a "spread" of torpedoes to maximize the chances of hitting something. Even at that, only about a third of these attacks succeeded in sinking anything. Because of defective torpedoes, the odds of sinking a ship were under 20 percent from 1941 to late 1943, and rose to over 50 percent thereafter. For the entire war, some 350 tons of enemy shipping were sunk for every torpedo fired.

The submarine war in the Pacific cost the United States some 50 submarines. The Japanese lost 130 subs during the war, most of them to aircraft attacks. The British also lost 3 subs, and the Dutch 5, in the Pacific. Allied subs operating in the Pacific accounted for about 2 percent of the Japanese shipping sunk.

At the beginning of the war, Japan was the premier submarine user in the Pacific, with 67 boats. The United States had 56 in the Pacific, more in the Atlantic, and the ability to outproduce Japan in this area. This is precisely what America did, building over 200 new subs. Japan was able to build only 120.

But what principally defanged Japanese subs was American air power and warships using effective antisubmarine weapons and tactics. Thousands of American patrol aircraft constantly crisscrossed the Pacific, making life decidedly uncomfortable for Japanese subs. America also produced over 600 destroyers and destroyer escorts. While over half of these initially went to the Atlantic (to confront German U-boats), plenty were left for the Pacific. Japan produced fewer than 100 destroyers and smaller antisubmarine ships during the war and used them much less efficiently.

Another serious shortcoming of Japan's was its many long and exposed sea routes. Many of these were outside the range of friendly aircraft, and the Japanese had far fewer long-range patrol aircraft anyway. Round trips for merchantmen from Japan to outlying bases took from thirty to ninety days. This was particularly true of bases in the Central Pacific. By the end of the war, many of these bases could no longer be reached anyway because American forces had seized nearby islands and installed air bases. Japanese troops on these bypassed islands often starved before the war ended, but not before resorting to cannibalism. Even some shot-down American pilots ended up in the stewpot.

As successful as they were, American sub crews still took high losses, with 22 percent of the U.S. submariners being killed during the course of the war. This was the highest percentage loss of any arm of the service.

THE CENTRAL PACIFIC CAMPAIGN

Tarawa, Saipan, Iwo Jima, Tinian, Okinawa. The image most people have of the war in the Pacific is of amphibious assaults on these islands in the Central Pacific. While the island assaults took place, they were not in fact the centerpiece of the Pacific war. The Central Pacific campaign didn't really get under way until late 1943. Until, and after, that time most of the fighting took place in the Solomons, New Guinea, and northwestward on the road to the Philippines. Several of the epic island assaults weren't actually part of the Central Pacific offensive, but rather, further stops on the road that went from New Guinea to the Philippines.

The campaign that began in New Guinea during early 1942 could have been the sole offensive that eventually would fight its way north to the islands just south of Japan. From bases there, the B-29s could (and ultimately did) fly north to trash Japan's cities.

But the American warship-building program begun in 1940 started to fill the fleet with new ships in 1943. By 1944 the fleet would be much larger than anything the Japanese could muster. The naval battles in 1942, particularly at Midway and in defense of Guadalcanal, had crippled Japanese carrier power and made the enemy vulnerable to an American naval offensive. So it was decided that, rather than risk all these new U.S. carriers in the New Guinea area (where the Japanese had a substantial number of land-based aircraft), a second offensive would be launched across the vast Central Pacific.

To a certain extent, this second offensive was suggested by the admirals so that the Navy could play a major, and singular, role in the Pacific fighting. In New Guinea, General MacArthur was capable of advancing north with minimal Navy support. The Army's amphibious divisions did indeed make more amphibious landings than the Navy's Marines during the war. The Army also has ample land-based aircraft (and effective tactics for attacking enemy ships) as well as a lot of shipping under its control.

MacArthur suggested that all resources be devoted to his drive north to the Philippines and Japan itself. He felt that a Navy offensive through the Central Pacific would delay the taking of Formosa and the isolation of Japan from its vital oil supplies to the south. MacArthur also made the point, later proven to be true, that the amphibious assaults in the Central Pacific would be far bloodier than the ones he was undertaking in the larger, and less widely scattered, island groups between Australia and the Philippines.

The Navy won the argument. MacArthur eventually did make it to the Philippines and Japan lost access to its oil not because Formosa was taken (it wasn't) but because USN subs sank most of Japan's oil tankers by 1944.

The Central Pacific campaign did ensure that the remaining Japanese fleet, which included a lot of battleships and smaller warships, as well as thousands of aircraft, were tied up in the Central Pacific and not sent south to oppose MacArthur. The USN offensive also stretched Japanese resources so thin that they were weaker everywhere, and thus speeded up the destruction of Japanese military power. We'll never know if MacArthur's strategy would have been more effective, but the dual offensive approach did annihilate Japanese military power in the Pacific.

All of the Central Pacific invasions were undertaken over unprecedented distances. The troops embarked thousands of miles away in places like Hawaii, the west coast of the United States, and the Solomons. The invasion fleets stayed at sea for months at a time, supplied by hundreds of tankers and freighters. While the fighting was usually over in less than a month, the casualties were high and the divisions involved were sent back to their bases for rest, retraining, and replacements. Then these divisions went out for yet another invasion. These divisions, with their usual specialist units for amphibious operations, numbered 15,000 to 20,000 men.

In eleven months, the U.S. Navy advanced 4,200 (statute) miles, from Hawaii to Peleliu. This was unheard of in military history. The advance averaged nearly 400 miles a month. The first jump, from Hawaii to the Gilberts, took U.S. forces 1,600 miles from Hawaii. The next advance, to the Marshalls, increased the distance to 2,400 miles. The third operation, to the Marianas, reached 3,700 miles from Hawaii. The final leg, to the Palaus, completed the drive, some 4,200 miles from where it had begun eleven months earlier. By way of comparison, the distance from New Guinea to the Philippines was only some 2,000 miles. And while it was only 4,000 miles from Hawaii to Tokyo, there were no islands along that northern Pacific route. The islands were the key, as they provided unsinkable aircraft carriers and land bases to support the fleet.

The Central Pacific offensive got started in November 1943 when the 2nd Marine Division and the Army's 27th Infantry Division stormed Tarawa and Makin islands in the Gilberts. These atolls (little island groups created by the coral) were the closest to Allied-held territory and would provide air and naval bases for further advances. Tarawa was controlled by the Japanese Navy and garrisoned by naval infantry (SNLF) troops. Tarawa itself contained only two battalions of combat troops; the rest of the personnel belonged to various support units. This was typical of the Japanese island garrisons, although the many support troops could be just as lethal as trained infantrymen when armed with a rifle and secure in a bunker. All Japanese troops would fight to the death no matter what their military specialty.

Tarawa set the tone for future operations. The Japanese would not surrender, so all but 146 of the 4,836-man garrison died. The United States suffered 3,300 casualties (including 900 dead). Tarawa was the first of the classic "island assaults" of the Pacific war. Much went wrong and it was a bloody lesson for the Marines, who changed tactics and techniques before undertaking their next invasion.

The next phase of the Central Pacific drive came two months later. In January 1944, Kwajalein and two smaller atolls in the Marshall Islands, several hundred miles north of the Gilberts, were attacked by the 4th Marine Division and the Army's 7th Infantry Division. The Japanese garrison of some 10,000 men was wiped out, with the Americans suffering 1,700 casualties. The Japanese had learned some lessons from the loss of Tarawa, but this next assault came so quickly that there was not sufficient time to radically change the existing defenses in the Marshalls. Not only were the Americans faster in making this next attack, but they were able to incorporate lessons from Tarawa. These landings in the Marshalls went much more smoothly.

So successful were the Marshall Islands operations that it was decided to go straight for the Mariana Islands. MacArthur still urged that all available resources be directed toward the liberation of the Philippines. But continuing U.S. carrier raids on the main Japanese fleet base on Truk (in the Carolines) had been so devastating to enemy air and naval forces in the area that it appeared Truk could be bypassed. Moreover, the Army's new B-29 bomber was entering mass production and bases in the Marianas were needed for the bombing of Japan to begin.

In June and July 1944, the Mariana Islands (Guam, Saipan, and Tinian) and their 50,000-man garrison, several hundred miles northeast of Truk, were invaded by the 2nd, 3rd, and 4th Marine Divisions, a Marine brigade, and the Army's 27th and 77th Infantry Divisions.

This was the largest transoceanic invasion ever launched. The 105,000 assault troops were supported by 29 carriers of various kinds (carrying 891 aircraft), 14 battleships, 25 cruisers, and 152 destroyers, plus hundreds of freighters, tankers, and amphibious ships. The Marianas were truly in the middle of nowhere and the U.S. armada gathered from as far away as the west coast of North America and Australia.

As usual, nearly all the Japanese fought to the death, and the struggle went on into August. Nearly 23,000 Americans became casualties. The Japanese Army was in charge of defending the Marianas, and it deployed four infantry divisions to the defense of Guam, Saipan, and Tinian. More troops were on the way, but U.S. submarines were intercepting many of these reinforcement convoys.

Meanwhile the Japanese could not ignore MacArthur's steady progress from Allied bases in eastern New Guinea. The Allied capture of western New Guinea would endanger Japan's oil supplies. Thus, just before the American invasion fleet appeared in the Marianas, Japan had sent off aircraft and ships to deal with MacArthur, unaware that the U.S. fleet was fast approaching the Marianas. As a result, the Japanese got beaten by both MacArthur in the south and the U.S. fleet in the Marianas. The defeat in the Marianas was made more catastrophic by the Japanese decision to offer battle with their rebuilt carrier fleet. This resulted in the Great Marianas Turkey Shoot (the Battle of the Philippine Sea), as more experienced and better-trained U.S. pilots chopped their Japanese counterparts to pieces. The Japanese not only lost the Marianas, they also saw their fleet reduced to near impotence.

During the summer of 1944, MacArthur gained control of western New Guinea and began moving north to take island bases within aircraft range of the Philippines. With the Marianas now in American hands, MacArthur urged an immediate drive on the Philippines.

Earlier in the year it had been agreed that the Palau Islands would be taken in the fall to provide further air bases and to complete the encirclement of the Japanese base at Truk. Some Navy commanders urged that Palau be bypassed and all resources put into the Philippine assault. But prudence took precedence and a slightly scaled-back Palau operation went forward while the Philippine invasion was moved up to October 1944.

In September, Peleliu Island (in the Palaus, 1,000 miles west of Truk) was taken by the 1st Marine Division and the Army's 81st Infantry Division. The 10,500 Japanese were well fortified and turned the battle into something nearly as bloody as Tarawa, with 10,000 Americans becoming casualties. In hindsight, the Peleliu attack could have been dropped. The Japanese threat in the area was not nearly as powerful as was thought at the time. But that's hindsight. At the time, Peleliu seemed necessary and so the assault went forward.

These operations in the Gilberts, Marshalls, Marianas, and Palaus completed the encirclement, and neutralization, of the main Japanese naval base at Truk. Now surrounded by U.S.-held islands (crammed with bombers and fighters) the Japanese were forced to withdraw their fleet from Truk. This, in turn, made it easier for MacArthur's forces coming up from the south to invade the Philippines during November 1944.

Peleliu was also, in effect, the end of the Central Pacific offensive. For shortly after Peleliu, MacArthur invaded the Philippines and the two separate offensives merged. The next island assaults to the north were, for all practical purposes, the combined American offensive toward Japan.

By early 1945, the Philippines was pretty much under Allied control, although thousands of Japanese fought on in jungles and mountains, while several hundred thousand more Japanese troops were isolated in places like Rabaul and the Caroline Islands (especially Truk). Meanwhile B-29 bombers were operating from the Marianas and systematically burning down Japan's urban areas.

The remaining island assaults were for the purpose of providing forward bases for land-based aircraft and the late 1945 invasion of Japan itself.

In February 1945, the 3rd, 4th, and 5th Marine Divisions attacked Iwo Jima. This small volcanic island just south of the Japanese home islands was an important part of the Japanese defense system against B-29 raids. In American hands, it would provide an emergency airfield for damaged or crippled aircraft returning from raids (the B-29 had a lot of engine trouble). Some 20,000 Japanese were dug in to resist an invasion. A third of the invading American force (23,000 troops) were killed or wounded in five weeks of fighting to secure the island.

In April 1945, the 1st and 2nd Marine Divisions and the Army's 27th, 7th, 77th, and 96th Infantry Divisions attacked Okinawa and some smaller outlying islands. Okinawa, considered by the Japanese as a part of Japan, was garrisoned by 110,000 troops, including many recently conscripted Okinawans. The fighting was the toughest yet seen in the Pacific. The island was not conquered until the end of June. Nearly 110,000 Japanese troops were killed on Okinawa, plus possibly as many civilians. It was somewhat encouraging to note that 7,000 Japanese surrendered, but many of these were recently conscripted civilians.

Thousands of civilians on Okinawa committed suicide rather than be "conquered." America suffered a record number of combat deaths (12,281, including 4,907 Navy personnel). Over 50,000 Americans were wounded. There were also over 14,000 combat fatigue casualties and nearly 30,000 noncombat casualties. It was a rough campaign.

During the protracted ground fighting on Okinawa, the Japanese made heavy use of Kamikaze suicide aircraft, losing over 1,900 of them (plus 2,300 other aircraft) in attacks against the fleet. There were 36 Allied ships sunk (26 by Kamikazes) and 368 damaged (164 by Kamikazes).

The stubborn and bloody resistance at Okinawa gave rise to very real fears that it would be repeated if the Allies had to proceed with their invasion of the Japanese home islands. However, the atomic bombs, and the Soviet invasion of Manchuria in August, caused the Japanese to surrender before the planned amphibious invasion came off.

The invasion of Japan itself, scheduled for November 1, never happened, leaving Okinawa as the last major amphibious operation of the war. The Central Pacific offensive lasted only eleven months (from Tarawa in November 1943 to Peleliu in September 1944). Most of the amphibious operations in the Pacific were launched by MacArthur's American, Australian, and New Zealand army troops rather than Marines. But the boldest and bloodiest island assaults were carried off by the Marines during the eleven-month Central Pacific offensive. The audacity and ferocity of these amphibious operations made far more of an impression on the American memory of the Pacific war than the less glamorous island hopping and years of jungle fighting MacArthur's army troops endured.

THE INVASION OF JAPAN

The United States began making plans for the eventual invasion of Japan surprisingly early in the war. By early 1943, it was felt that the first phase of this assault would take place in late 1945. The target date shifted back and forth somewhat over the next two years until, at the time of the Japanese surrender on August 15, 1945, the date was set for November 1.

Because Japan was a collection of major islands, the invasion would take place in phases. The overall operation was called Downfall.

First, there would be some preliminary operations involving the seizure of various small islands off the Japanese home islands, to provide bases for air, naval, and logistical support.

Then would come Operation Olympic, wherein the southernmost of the principal Japanese islands, Kyushu, would be hit with ten infantry divisions, three Marine divisions, and one parachute division. There would also be 2,458 oceangoing ships (including 63 carriers, 22 battleships, 50 cruisers, 458 destroyers, and small boys), plus 8,000 aircraft adding their firepower to the attack. But the bulk of the casualties would be taken by the 250,000 ground combat troops going ashore. Resistance was expected to be so heavy that one Marine division was not even mentioned in the tentative plans for operations following the securing of the beachheads, as it was assumed that this division would be so depleted by losses it would no longer be fit for action. Over 800,000 Allied troops would be involved in the Olympic campaign. This would be, in many respects, a larger amphibious operation than the D-Day assault against Normandy.

Until the day they surrendered, the Japanese went ahead with their preparations for resisting the expected Allied invasion. By the end of 1945, the Japanese planned to have 2.5 million troops under arms in the home islands. These would be organized into fifty divisions and numerous smaller units.

Japan's aircraft factories were still operating, although just barely, and planes were being held back for the final defense of the home islands. Thus Japan would have had about 9,000 aircraft to resist the invasion with. About half of these would be used in Kamikaze suicide attacks. Unlike the earliest Kamikazes, not all the pilots were volunteers and few had much flying experience. The veteran, or at least trained, pilots were now reserved for interceptor and bomber aircraft.

The Japanese were confident that they could do serious damage with their Kamikazes, and they were probably right. Through the end of the war, for each 15 Kamikaze aircraft lost, one Allied ship was damaged, and for every 100 Kamikazes shot down, one Allied ship was sunk. American defenses against the Kamikazes were getting better as the war went on, but these attacks would still be effective. During the first Kamikaze attacks in late 1944, 1 in 6 aircraft hit something. By the time of the Okinawa campaign in early 1945, only 1 Kamikaze in 9 was doing any damage. Both sides calculated that only 1 in 12 to 20 Kamikazes would connect during the Downfall operation. But the Japanese also decided to change their Kamikaze tactics, going for troopships and landing craft rather than carriers and battleships. This was expected to destroy the equivalent of two divisions (over 30,000 soldiers and sailors) before they got ashore.

To defend Kyushu, the Japanese expected to have some 600,000 troops available by November. This may have been overly optimistic, as by August 1945, Allied naval and air power had effectively sealed off each of the Japanese home islands. But even a lack of reinforcements from the main island of Honshu would have still left some 400,000 Japanese troops on Kyushu.

For the Allies, the battle was expected to depend on air power to destroy Japanese mobility on Kyushu. The Allies expected the battle to resemble the fighting in the Philippines (the very large islands) more than the smaller islands in the Pacific. Moreover, most of the newly raised Japanese divisions were spending most of their time building coastal fortifications, not training. These "static divisions" were expected to stay in their entrenchments and keep shooting until killed. Not much training was required for this, and the Japanese had regularly shown a preference for fighting to the death. American troops had developed better tactics for destroying troops holding out in fortifications, but these new methods did not eliminate all risk to the attackers. It would still be a bloody battle.

In the Philippines, the Japanese had withdrawn when there was an opportunity, and scattered Japanese units were still holding out when the war ended. There would be some of this on Kyushu and these Japanese troops would have to be hunted down. In the Philippines, this "hunting" was greatly aided by local Filipino guerrillas. But in the Philippines, the local population was pro-American. On Kyushu, the locals were not only going to be hostile, but were organized to resist.

Nearly a quarter of the Japanese population, including many

women, was conscripted (or volunteered) for local defense forces. While these irregulars were not well armed, they were nearly as determined as the uniformed troops. So there would be no friendly locals giving information about where the Japanese troops were or what shape they were in. No, the locals could be expected to attack you when your back was turned, or perhaps when it wasn't. Allied planners foresaw widespread resistance and great slaughter. So did the Japanese. But these were the people who coined the phrase "Death is lighter than a feather."

The second phase of Downfall was Coronet. This was to be the invasion of the main island, Honshu, in March 1946. The Allies were transferring troops from Europe for this and the assault force would consist of nineteen infantry divisions, three Marine divisions, one airborne division, and, in a first for the Pacific war, two armored divisions.

Since this invasion would involve the taking of Tokyo, and the surrounding Kanto Plain, it was expected to be the final battle. And a bloodier battle than was fought for Kyushu (where fighting would probably still be going on when Coronet kicked off).

Despite their unbroken string of victories, Allied troops did not look forward to an invasion of Japan with any enthusiasm. They were pretty sure about what would happen, mainly because two Japanese-populated islands (Saipan and Okinawa) had already been invaded and the reactions of Japanese civilians were now known. The Japanese civilians on these islands had actively assisted the Japanese troops. Moreover, many of the civilians had committed suicide when it was clear that the battle was lost. On Saipan, two thirds of the civilian population had died and, as usual, nearly all the troops fought to the death. On Saipan, 30,000 Japanese troops had caused 14,000 American casualties. On Okinawa, 107,000 Japanese troops (and at least 75,000 civilians) had died, but there had been over 60,000 U.S. combat casualties and over 40,000 noncombat injuries.

But the Kyushu invasion (Operation Olympic) would be more like the Philippines fighting, which had cost the United States 60,000 casualties including 13,000 dead. Based on this experience, and taking into account the differences between the two campaigns, U.S. Army planners estimated that the Kyushu fighting would incur 125,000 American casualties (including 31,000 dead). The Honshu invasion (Operation Coronet) in early 1946, since it involved about twice as many troops, was expected to incur about twice as many casualties. Thus, if Japan was to be conquered by invasion, the American casualties, based on recent experience, would be about 370,000 (including about 80,000 dead).

In the face of this, U.S. commanders contemplated the use of chemical weapons and (for the senior officers who knew about it) atomic bombs. It was decided not to use chemical weapons because the Japanese could respond in kind. With atomic bombs, there were doubts about how many would be available by the November 1 invasion date. There was also uncertainty as to how this new weapon should actually be used. The effects of radiation were known, and this complicated any plans to use atomic bombs anywhere near friendly troops. In the end, more practical new techniques, like flamethrower tanks and point-blank fire from 155mm and 8-inch guns, were seen as better ways of digging diehard Japanese troops out of their fortifications.

What was certain was that the Japanese would resist fiercely. This they had done consistently throughout the war. While the Okinawa battle had, for the first time, featured Japanese civilians organized to resist U.S. troops, there had also been an increase in the number of Japanese who surrendered. But this increase in prisoners was not all that encouraging, as it amounted to only a few percent of the enemy soldiers in the area. The rest had fought to the death. In the defense of their own homeland, Japanese resistance could be expected to be more determined, not less so. Nor was such a suicidal policy by an entire nation unknown. In the 1860s, Paraguay had attacked three of its neighbors, with the result that most of Paraguay's population had died in a protracted and hopeless defensive struggle.

The oft-quoted figure of "one million American dead if Japan was invaded" appeared after the war in the memoirs of politicians who were depending on fragile memories, or trying too hard to make their case for the use of the atomic bomb. This mythical million deaths began as an exaggeration of the 370,000 casualties figure (sometimes given by staff officers as "250,000 to 500,000"). Half a million soon became a million and casualties became deaths. The actual staff estimates have been sitting in unclassified archives, and the memories of those staff officers who calculated them, since

1945. But the media picked up on the "million American dead" figure because it made more compelling reading. While the "million American dead" is a myth, the estimates of 80,000 dead and 290,000 wounded were very realistic, based as they were on recent experience. An invasion of Japan would have increased the American deaths in World War II by 27 percent. Avoiding this invasion by any means possible was no trivial matter.

Fortunately, other factors were working to bring the Japanese to terms before the nation dragged itself to an epic of suicidal resistance. Since the spring of 1945, the naval blockade of Japan had been growing tighter. Food was tightly rationed, with the average citizen getting about 75 percent of the minimum caloric intake. The winter of 1945–1946 would have been one of starvation and general weakening of the entire population. Keep in mind, however, that Japan was minimally self-sufficient in food production. While many would starve, most could survive indefinitely. The food shortage hurt the Japanese, but would not necessarily lead to social disintegration. Starvation would not guarantee a Japanese surrender, and the Allies could not, for political reasons (the voters wanted the war over, now), keep over a million soldiers and sailors under arms for a year or more blockading Japan.

The problem that faced the Allies was how to get Japan to surrender as soon as possible. The Japanese were already, in mid-1945, offering to surrender as the Germans had in World War I. In this case, the German Army was allowed to remain as an institution, and this was what the Japanese Army (still in control of the Japanese government) wanted. This was refused. After all, leaving the German Army intact after World War I had played a part in its reemergence in World War II.

Going into August, the negotiations came down to whether or not the Japanese emperor would be able to remain on the throne. The Allies were willing to give way on this point. The reasoning was that the emperor, and his authority, would be needed to keep the population under control after the war. Unfortunately, the Japanese made the mistake of sending their surrender messages through their ambassador in Moscow. The Russians weren't ready to accept Japanese surrender just yet. Diplomats and politicians in Washington were still debating exactly how to understand and approach the Japanese government. This, as we have seen in subsequent decades, is a difficult task that, fifty years later, has still not been mastered.

On August 8, 1945, the Soviets invaded Manchuria and swept away the half-million-man Japanese garrison. Millions of Japanese colonists were also at risk, as were the Japanese armies to the south in China proper and Indochina. It was to maintain their position in China that Japan had gone to war with America in the first place. Now China was lost. American bombers had already burned out most of Japan's cities. Then, on August 6 and 9, came the atomic bombs. There seemed no end to the calamities that were to befall Japan. Although many Japanese preferred to fight to the death anyway, the emperor issued the order for surrender on August 15 and Olympic and Coronet joined the long list of historical "what if's?"

Many historians have since questioned the need for the atomic bombs. But that is hindsight. At the time, nothing seemed likely to dissuade the Japanese from making a suicidal last stand on their home islands. The Japanese had already demonstrated their do-or-die stubbornness in dozens of battles. Saipan and Okinawa merely confirmed that Japanese civilians were every much as determined as their soldiers. Japan had never surrendered; the nation had never been defeated.

A naval and air blockade was the only other alternative to an invasion and no one was sure how long this would take to bring the Japanese to terms. Most estimates had a blockade bringing a surrender at the end of 1945 or sometime in 1946. But it was also pointed out that the Japanese could drag the process out for several years. In America, this was politically unacceptable. The United States had now been at war for over three years. Germany had been defeated. The American people wanted peace. While some troops had been demobilized, many others had not, and there were already signs of unrest in the ranks. Mutinous behavior was becoming increasingly common through the summer of 1945 as troops were transferred from Europe to the Pacific. The government could not deal too harshly with these reluctant soldiers—the voters would not stand for it. The troops had done their job; the people wanted peace. Japan must be defeated as soon as possible, by whatever means available.

The atomic bomb, which was not successfully tested until July

1945, was seen as one more weapon to induce surrender. In strictly military terms, the atomic bomb was not a decisive weapon. There were only two of these bombs available after the first one was tested. While only one B-29 was required to deliver an atomic bomb, the damage caused would be less than that already inflicted by raids using 600 B-29s carrying explosive and incendiary bombs. What the atomic bomb did have going for it was shock—one bomb doing the work of hundreds of bombers. The Japanese didn't know how many atomic bombs America had, and the United States left to their imaginations how many it might have and how quickly it would use them. Against a people who seemed to disdain death, there was doubt that even the atomic bomb would bring the Japanese to surrender.

Japan required an unprecedented series of calamities before surrender became possible. Destruction of her fleet, isolation of nearly 400,000 troops in Pacific island garrisons, most of her cities being burned down, blockade of her ports, and, finally, atomic bombs and destruction of the last of her intact armies (in Manchuria) were what it finally took. No one knew, until it was all over, how much it would take. Fortunately, the invasion was not needed. On August 15, the emperor of Japan did one of those things Japanese emperors rarely did. He overrode all opposing counsel and broadcast the order to surrender. With no assurances that the Allies would respect the imperial institutions of Japan, the emperor threw himself, and his people, upon the uncertain mercies of the same peoples Japan had savagely fought for the past four years.

OCCUPIED JAPAN

By one estimate, the American occupation forces in Japan during the late 1940s expended an average of $200 million a year on prostitutes, providing a considerable stimulus to the local economy. The U.S. armed forces aided the recovery of Japan in other, more direct ways, as well. During the Korean War a lot of defense procurement contracts were let in Japan, and U.S. warships were routinely refitted and repaired in dockyards built for the Imperial Navy, which had been idle since 1945. The postwar fortunes of several major Japanese corporations were more or less derived from this war work.

The Korean War also marked the rebirth, albeit unofficially, of the Japanese Navy. Although officially completely disarmed after her surrender, Japan actually still maintained a small naval capability. There was a pressing need for this, as the United States had laid an extraordinary number of mines in Japanese waters late in the war in order to strangle shipping. The Japanese had engaged in extensive mining as well, in anticipation of an American invasion. So even as the Imperial Army and Navy were being disbanded from 1945 onward, some former naval officers, in one case even a former battleship skipper, and ratings were hired, officially as civilians, to man a large number of minesweepers. When the Korean War came, a lot of these vessels were pressed into service, crews and all, to support the U.S. amphibious landing at Inchon and the evacuation of Wonsan. Soon afterward the Japanese Maritime Self Defense Agency was created.

THE "OTHER" NAVAL WAR

Although Americans are wont to think that the naval war against Japan was where the seagoing action was during the Second World War, in fact the hottest maritime war was that against Germany and Italy, not only in terms of the loss of shipping, but also in terms

MAJOR WARSHIP LOSSES BY THEATER

THEATER AND AREA	NUMBER	%
European Theater	856	58.9
Atlantic Ocean	399	27.4
Baltic/Black Seas	126	8.7
Mediterranean Sea	331	22.8
Pacific Theater	598	41.1
Indian Ocean	25	1.7
Pacific Ocean	573	39.4
Total	1,454	100.0

of the loss of major warships, destroyers, cruisers, carriers, and bat-tlewagons.

Note also that the Axis actually inflicted and suffered losses in the Indian Ocean, where German and Italian submarines and surface raiders operated with some success against Allied shipping. The Axis accounted for a couple of warships in the Indian Ocean. For example, the German armed merchant raider *Kormoran* sank HMAS *Sydney* off Western Australia on Armistice Day 1941, being sunk in turn by her opponent. The Allies suffered no warship or merchant ship losses in the ETO (European Theater of Operations) at the hands of the Japanese.

TWO

THE SHIPS

The war in the Pacific was the largest naval war in history. Literally tens of thousands of ships went into harm's way. Moreover, it was the first naval war that saw the widespread use of aircraft carriers, aircraft, and a host of new electronic devices. The ships that served in the Pacific war established patterns of design and employment that remained a standard for the rest of the twentieth century. Modern sailors still study how ships were handled in the Pacific war because, in many respects, the experiences of the World War II sailors are still relevant. Moreover, there was a great deal of experimentation with ship design during the Pacific war. The multitude of ship designs used in the war demonstrated a lot about what worked and what didn't.

THE AIRCRAFT CARRIERS: FLEET, ESCORT, AND IN BETWEEN

The aircraft carrier was the newest and ultimately the most decisive category of warship in World War II. Essentially a fast-moving, floating airstrip, the carrier had been invented during World War I. The very earliest carriers were converted from vessels of various types: colliers, ferries, and the like. By the 1920s, several nations had carriers, most converted from partially completed battleships or battlecruisers. Since they lacked the big guns and, usually, the heavy armor protection of the battlewagons, the newer carriers were often about as fast as cruisers or destroyers.

Carriers also began to be built from scratch, and the principal navies (British, American, and Japanese) began to incorporate improvements based on their experience with the converted vessels. As a result, conversions aside, most prewar carriers were larger than heavy cruisers, but smaller than battleships, running between 14,000 and 24,000 tons' displacement, although there were a few that were smaller, notably several Japanese ones. Actually, the size of the carrier was not as important as its speed, higher-speed vessels being better able to get into and out of harm's way quickly, and its capacity to carry and operate aircraft, two rather different functions, affected by but not totally dependent upon size.

Several of the converted carriers, being essentially experimental vessels, had poor aircraft capacities. The United States was lucky in this regard, as its two converted carriers, *Lexington* and *Saratoga*, were roomy vessels, as were all subsequent American purpose-built carriers. In contrast, the Japanese adopted some unusual design elements, with the result that even the carriers they built from the keel up could not operate all the aircraft that they could carry, due to poorly laid-out hangar decks and stowage facilities. In addition, the Japanese adopted a policy of not storing aircraft on deck, whereas the U.S. Navy embraced deck storage with enthusiasm upon the outbreak of the war. As a result, U.S. carriers of comparable size usually could operate as many as 65 percent more aircraft (90 to 100 as against 55 to 65). British carriers tended to have a smaller aircraft capacity (55 to 65), but this was due to a decision to provide relatively heavy armor, the excess weight of which had to be paid for by a smaller air group. In compensation, British carriers were much more survivable ships.

Another critical factor that was more important than carrier size was the ship's capacity to carry aviation fuel (avgas) and carrier fuel, which determined operational endurance. While this was, of course, partially connected to the size of the vessel, once again policy decisions and design were factors. In consequence, U.S. carriers tended to have greater fuel capacity than either Japanese or British ones, which meant American carriers could generate more missions between trips to the barn.

The pressures of the war led to several variations on the aircraft carrier. The larger ships (CVs) soon became the primary weapons of sea power, and were in extremely short supply during the first eighteen months of the war. This shortage had been anticipated even before the Pacific war broke out, as prescient observers of naval affairs noted the value of aircraft in antisubmarine warfare. As a result, in 1941, under prodding from President Franklin D. Roosevelt, the U.S. Navy authorized the experimental conversion of a merchant ship into an escort carrier (CVE), a type that the Royal Navy was finding of some value. CVEs were smallish vessels, often less than half the size of CVs, rather slow (12 to 18 knots), and able to carry only a handful of aircraft (fifteen to thirty-six). Despite their limitations, they proved so useful—not only as convoy escorts, but as supports for the fleet in offensive operations—that the United States eventually built scores from scratch. They were also cheap and could be made available quickly. Through the war the United States commissioned some seventy-seven escort carriers, the British Commonwealth forty-three (some operated by Canada), and Japan five, although the Japanese used theirs primarily to transport naval aircraft from place to place, but one of many roles that the Allies found for these useful vessels.

In addition, the shortage of carriers early in the war led the United States and the Japanese to convert unfinished vessels of other types into light aircraft carriers (CVLs). These were rather larger than escort carriers. CVLs were generally capable of operating only about thirty aircraft, the same as CVEs, but had much better engines, enabling them to keep up with the CVs and other fast elements of the fleet, and making them an important element in the fast carrier task forces.

THERE ARE CARRIERS AND THERE ARE CARRIERS

The aircraft carrier was the premier naval weapon of World War II. But it wasn't perfect. Carriers were also among the most vulnerable of ships. While they could inflict enormous damage, they could take much less than any other ships their size because of their relative lack of armor and all the aviation gas and aircraft munitions they carried. Plus, that big flight deck made a wonderful target for attacking aircraft.

Aircraft carriers can be considered as weapons that "expend" aircraft for ammunition. As a result, the single most significant datum about carriers is the number of aircraft they can operate, not how big they are or how many of them you have or how survivable they may be, which are important too, but less so. To operate aircraft you have to carry them, yet some aircraft "carriers" were extraordinarily inefficient at this task. Consider the relationship between the size of carriers and their aircraft complements in the table on pages 83–84.

It is interesting to note that the worst-case U.S. ships in regard to TpA/C, the *Independence* Class light carriers, were better than most of the Japanese or other carriers on the list. This class was converted from light cruiser hulls, and a relatively high TpA/C was quite common for conversions, as can be seen in the case of several other ships, such as *Akagi* and *Kaga*, the worst examples being *Shinano* and *Eagle*.

British carriers had a high TpA/C because they tended to be more heavily armored, including an armored flight deck. While there were obviously some advantages in terms of stability and survivability to a relatively high TpA/C, it was not very cost-effective; you had a huge vessel (and an enormous crew) with low firepower. Generally, the lower the TpA/C, the better the carrier was, operationally.

CARRIER DISPLACEMENT PER AIRPLANE CARRIED

SHIP, NATIONALITY, YEAR IN SERVICE	A/C	DISPLACEMENT (IN THOUSANDS OF TONS)	TpA/C OF CV
CV Ranger—U.S. (1934)	76	17.6	0.23
CV Wasp—U.S. (1940)	76	18.5	0.24
CV Yorktown—U.S. (1937)	96	25.5	0.27
CV Unryu—Jap (1944)	65	20.0	0.31
CV Soryu—Jap (1937)	63	19.8	0.31
CV Hiryu—Jap (1939)	64	21.9	0.34
CVL Ryujo—Jap (1933)	37	13.7	0.37
CVL Saipan—U.S. (1946)	48	17.8	0.37
CV Essex—U.S. (1942)	91	34.9	0.38
CVE Casablanca—U.S. (1943)	27	10.9	0.40
CV Aquila—It (1943*)	66	27.8	0.42
CV Midway—U.S. (1945)	137	59.9	0.44
CV Shokaku—Jap (1941)	72	32.1	0.45
CVL Hosho—Jap (1922)	22	10.0	0.45
CV Lexington—U.S. (1927)	96	43.1	0.45
CV Ark Royal—Br (1938)	60	27.7	0.46
CV Courageous—Br (1928)	48	22.7	0.47
CVL Zuiho—Jap (1940)	30	14.3	0.48
CVL Majestic—Br (1945*)	37	17.8	0.48
CVL Colossus—Br (1944)	37	18.0	0.49
CVL Independence—U.S. (1943)	30	14.8	0.49
CV Chitose—Jap (1944)	30	15.3	0.51
CV Junyo—Jap (1942)	53	28.3	0.53
CV Implacable—Br (1944)	60	32.1	0.54
CVL Ryuho—Jap (1942)	31	16.7	0.54
CV Kaga—Jap (1928)	81	43.7	0.54
CVL Ibuki—Jap (1945*)	27	14.6	0.54

SHIP, NATIONALITY, YEAR IN SERVICE	A/C	DISPLACEMENT (IN THOUSANDS OF TONS)	TpA/C OF CV
CVL *Centaur*—Br (1946)	42	24.0	0.57
CV *Joffre*—Fr (1942*)	40	23.0	0.58
CVL *Unicorn*—Br (1943)	35	20.3	0.58
CV *Eagle II*—Br (1945*)	78	46.0	0.59
CV *Akagi*—Jap (1927)	72	42.8	0.59
CVE *Shinyo*—Jap (1943)	33	20.6	0.62
CV *Furious*—Br (1925)	36	22.5	0.63
CVL *Hermes*—Br (1923)	20	13.0	0.65
CV *Indomitable*—Br (1941)	45	29.7	0.66
CVE *Kaiyo*—Jap (1943)	24	16.5	0.69
CV *Malta*—Br (1946*)	81	56.8	0.70
CV *Bearn*—Fr (1927)	40	28.4	0.71
CV *Taiho*—Jap (1944)	53	37.7	0.71
CVE *Taiyo*—Jap (1941)	27	19.7	0.73
CV *Illustrious*—Br (1940)	33	28.6	0.87
CV *Argus*—Br (1918)	18	15.7	0.87
CV *Graf Zeppelin*—Ger (1942*)	42	37.0	0.88
CV *Shinano*—Jap (1944)	70	71.9	1.03
CV *Eagle*—Br (1923)	20	26.2	1.31

NOTES: This table lists each fleet carrier (CV) and light carrier (CVL)—a distinction often without a difference—in service or under construction during the war, plus a sample of escort carriers (CVEs) by way of comparison. Year is that of completion (completion as a carrier in the case of other types converted to carrier). Asterisk (*) indicates probable year of completion of ships that never entered service.

"A/C" is the carrier's maximum capacity, but note that Japanese carriers often had twelve to fifteen of their aircraft partially disassembled, since they could not operate all aircraft for which they were rated. "Displacement" is at full load (in thousands of tons), with all fuel and stores necessary for wartime operations. "TpA/C" stands for "tons (of ship) per aircraft," the displacement tonnage divided by the number of aircraft—in other words, how efficient the ship was in carrying the maximum number of aircraft. This is the figure with which the carriers have been arranged, from the smallest to the largest.

There were some disadvantages: *Ranger*, which proved to be the only U.S. fleet carrier that did not operate in the Pacific, was rather overcrowded, and *Wasp* not much better. By and large, the carriers with a TpA/C under 0.45 were the most successful in the war, and certainly among the busiest, including *Yorktown*, *Hornet*, *Enterprise*, *Shokaku*, *Zuikaku*, *Essex* and her sisters, and HMS *Ark Royal*, more or less the prototypical World War II carrier, which had the lowest TpA/C of all British carriers.

Of course, in addition to carrying the aircraft you had to keep them flying. This required avgas, a very volatile commodity that aircraft consumed in enormous amounts—some 300 gallons, roughly a ton, per sortie on average. As the war progressed, larger and thirstier aircraft were introduced. The newer planes had a longer range, largely because they carried a lot more fuel.

If we arrange the carriers on the basis of thousands of gallons of avgas (which was actually just high-grade gasoline) per aircraft, we get a somewhat different perspective, as in the table on pages 86–87.

Carriers were almost always short of fuel due to the constant aircraft operations, most of which were noncombatant in nature (patrolling, training, administrative movements, and so forth). Prudence dictated that carriers always have sufficient avgas on hand for combat operations (two to three sorties per aircraft); thus they were always slowing down to take on additional avgas from fleet tankers. Carrier captains were always keeping a close eye on onboard avgas available and much time and effort went into getting back to a port for refueling, or meeting up with a tanker for underway replenishment.

Note that combat operations, particularly early in the war, usually resulted in the loss of most of a carrier's aircraft. It was also normal to lose more aircraft from noncombat accidents than from enemy fire. Thus carriers also had to replenish their supply of aircraft constantly. Pilots tended to be more durable than the aircraft, but these highly trained men had to be replaced also as their numbers dwindled. Thus the carriers with larger capacity for aircraft and avgas were much better prepared for combat than larger carriers that had smaller capacities.

CARRIER AVGAS STOCK PER AIRPLANE

SHIP, NATIONALITY, YEAR IN SERVICE	A/C	GALLONS (IN THOUSANDS)	GpA/C	SORTIES PER A/C
CV Hosho—Jap (1922)	22	98.0	4.5	15.0
CVL Independence—U.S. (1943)	30	120.0	4.0	13.3
CVE Casablanca—U.S. (1943)	27	100.0	3.7	12.9
CV Taiho—Jap (1944)	53	176.0	3.3	11.0
CV Akagi—Jap (1927)	72	225.0	3.1	10.3
CVL Saipan—U.S. (1946)	48	140.0	2.9	9.7
CV Kaga—Jap (1928)	81	225.0	2.8	9.3
CV Essex—U.S. (1942)	91	240.0	2.6	8.7
CV Shokaku—Jap (1941)	72	187.0	2.6	8.7
CV Midway—U.S. (1945)	137	350.0	2.6	8.7
CV Shinano—Jap (1944)	70	171.0	2.4	8.0
CV Hiryu—Jap (1939)	64	150.0	2.3	7.7
CVL Colossus—Br (1944)	37	80.0	2.2	7.3
CV Wasp—U.S. (1940)	76	162.0	2.1	7.0
CVL Majestic—Br (1945*)	37	75.0	2.0	6.7
CV Malta—Br (1946*)	81	160.0	2.0	6.7
CV Yorktown—U.S. (1937)	96	178.0	1.9	6.3
CV Ranger—U.S. (1934)	76	135.0	1.8	6.0
CVL Centaur—Br (1945*)	42	75.0	1.8	6.0
CV Indomitable—Br (1941)	45	75.1	1.7	5.7
CV Ark Royal—Br (1938)	60	100.0	1.7	5.7
CV Implacable—Br (1944)	60	94.7	1.6	5.3
CV Graf Zeppelin—Ger (1942*)	42	65.0	1.5	5.0
CV Illustrious—Br (1940)	33	51.0	1.5	5.0
CV Soryu—Jap (1937)	63	96.0	1.5	5.0
CV Lexington—U.S. (1927)	96	137.5	1.4	4.7
CV Eagle—Br (1945*)	78	103.3	1.3	4.3

SHIP, NATIONALITY, YEAR IN SERVICE	A/C	GALLONS (IN THOUSANDS)	GpA/C	SORTIES PER A/C
CVL *Ryujo*—Jap (1933)	37	47.0	1.3	4.3
CV *Aquila*—It (1943*)	66	72.0	1.1	3.7
CVL *Unicorn*—Br (1943)	35	36.0	1.0	3.3
CV *Courageous*—Br (1928)	48	34.5	0.7	2.3
CV *Bearn*—Fr (1927)	40	26.0	0.7	2.3
CV *Furious*—Br (1925)	36	20.8	0.6	2.0

NOTES: This list is somewhat shorter than the previous one, due primarily to the extreme difficulty of securing information on the avgas capacity of some carriers, even a half century after the war. "Gallons" refers to thousands of gallons of avgas. "GpA/C" is thousands of gallons of avgas per aircraft. "Sorties per A/C" indicates the number of missions each airplane could undertake on the basis of the ship's GpA/C, at a notional average of about 300 gallons per mission. Obviously, the higher the sortie figure, the better the carrier. All other things being equal, like being able to carry a useful number of aircraft, it is interesting to note that most American and Japanese carriers had a GpA/C figure of about 2.0 or better, allowing a relatively high sortie rate, while British ones were much worse off, a further consequence of Britain's preference for armoring its carriers.

"... AND PASS THE AMMUNITION!"

Since the whole idea was to inflict damage upon the enemy, carriers had to carry ammunition as well as airplanes and fuel. Surprisingly, although they expended it in enormous amounts (in late 1942 a full U.S. Navy carrier air group of thirty-six fighters, thirty-six dive bombers, and eighteen torpedo bombers could deliver about 50 tons of ammunition in a single sortie), it was rare that a carrier exhausted its ordnance stocks, which were quite ample for extended combat operations.

The total weight of the pile of explosive devices on the carrier *Essex* came to something like 325 tons, more or less. There were enough torpedoes for two sorties by each of the ship's eighteen torpedo bombers and enough heavy bombs (500-pounders and above) for seventeen or eighteen sorties by each of her thirty-six dive bombers, not to mention the smaller stuff, suitable for use by fighters. Note that from time to time the proportions of ammunition were altered to reflect the changing military environment, and the potential mission of the ships in question.

AMMUNITION ALLOCATION: USS ESSEX, DECEMBER 31, 1942	
ITEM	NUMBER
Bombs, 100 lb, High Explosive	500
Bombs, 100 lb, Incendiary	300
Bombs, 500 lb, High Explosive	300
Bombs, 1,000 lb, General Purpose	400
Bombs, 1,600 lb, Armor Piercing	20
Bombs, 2,000 lb, General Purpose	20
Torpedoes, Aerial	36
Depth Charges	300

BATTLESHIPS

Until well into the twentieth century battleships (BBs) were the principal arbiters of sea power. They were large vessels, 20,000 tons or more, heavily armored (for example, 12-inch belts of specially hardened steels along their sides, if not more), and armed with eight to a dozen of the heaviest-caliber cannon possible, from 11-inch (firing 750-pound shells) on up to 18.1-inch (3,200-pound shells). Their job was to fight their own kind in large, decisive battles.

Battleships were the lineal descendants of the old wooden ships-of-the-line of Nelson's day, changed by an evolving technology. The threat of surface attack by light forces—torpedo boats and destroyers—led to the introduction of rapid-fire secondary armament, and the introduction of the submarine led to changes in tactics and great increases in the role of the destroyer, but on the eve of World War I the battleship was the undisputed capital ship.

The battleship emerged from the First World War with its reputation intact. Of the approximately seventy modern "battlewagons" that saw service in the war, only two were sunk, one by a mine (planted by a submarine) and the other by an internal explosion, probably caused by deterioration of ammunition. The record of the two dozen or so battlecruisers, which toted battleship artillery but sacrificed armor protection for superior speed, was less impressive, four being lost in action, all to enemy gunfire.

Although this confirmed the relative invulnerability of the battle-wagons, it was also rather surprising. After all, the admirals of the age were perfectly aware that their ships could be sunk, by gunfire, mines, or torpedoes, whether launched by surface vessels or submarines. Of course, by the end of World War I aviation enthusiasts like Brigadier General William "Billy" Mitchell were claiming that the battleship was vulnerable to the airplane. Although much has been made of their alleged foresight, these people were overstating the case a great deal, considering the capabilities of aircraft at the time. Even the famous sinking of the German prize *Ostfriesland* by U.S. Army bombers on July 21, 1921, was not a particularly valid test, given that the trial had been rigged in favor of the airmen. It was a clear, calm day and the ship was firmly anchored in Chesapeake Bay. The air enthusiasts cheated in the bargain, as they attacked at such low speed and altitude that had the ship been maneuvering they would certainly not have hit it, and had it been firing back the aircrewmen would all have been killed.

More objective tests against other vessels, including far newer, albeit incomplete, battleships whose completion had been canceled by the disarmament treaties of the 1920s, provided some valuable clues as to the vulnerability of battleships. The sailors asserted that a battleship under way and fully manned could avoid or shoot down attacking aircraft. And if, per chance, a battleship was hit, the armor would protect it. Finally, the large crews of the battlewagons could surely bring any damage under control. In all this the sailors were correct, but not correct enough.

During the 1920s and 1930s, most navies still considered the battleship the principal arm of sea power. But the bigger ones—the Royal Navy, the Imperial Japanese Navy, and the U.S. Navy—also invested their money in aircraft carriers. This was partially out of concern that the new weapon had potential and partially because various naval disarmament treaties restricted the number of battleships, which made having some aircraft carriers around to provide billets for senior officers rather attractive. These navies began to debate the ways in which the future of naval warfare would develop.

Ultimately, they all came to assume that the battleship and the carrier were complementary to each other. In fleet actions, carrier aircraft would scout ahead of the battleline, feeling for the enemy, and, having found him, soften him up with air attacks. Then the battleships would go in to slug it out. Afterward the carrier aircraft would follow up victory by harrying the enemy, or cover defeat by serving as the rear guard.

The most important technological development in the battleship following World War I was in its machinery. Earlier battleships had been slow, at best able to make two-thirds the 30 knots or so that destroyers and light cruisers could make, this a penalty for their enormous weight of armament and armor. But by the 1930s it was possible to provide machinery for battleships that eliminated most of the speed differential between them and small vessels.

In contrast, advances in gunnery had been relatively modest. Meanwhile, of course, bigger and better battleships were being built. Simply defined, a battleship is a very large (over 20,000 displacement tons), heavily armored warship toting eight to a dozen very large guns (11-inch caliber or greater). By the mid-1930s, when large-scale battleship construction was resumed, the ships and guns were growing very large: 35,000 tons and 14-inch guns were minimal. They were also growing faster.

Earlier generations of battlewagons had been quite slow, a problem that had fostered the development of the battlecruiser, with its lighter armor protection traded for higher speed. The battlecruiser had not worked out very well in combat, and by the late 1930s the surviving battlecruisers were even more obsolete than the older battleships, although they often found themselves in the company of the newer battlewagons, still being able to keep up. Then came World War II and the aircraft carrier took a while to establish itself as the primary warship.

The primacy of the airplane—and the carrier—did not occur with great suddenness. Neither the British air raid on Taranto (November 11, 1940) nor the Japanese one at Pearl Harbor (December 7, 1941) was a particularly good test of the survivability of the battleship against air power, inasmuch as in both instances the ships were surprised while at anchor in port, and only partially manned.

The sinking of HMS *Prince of Wales* and HMS *Repulse* by Japanese aircraft on the high seas off Malaya on December 10, 1941, was a much clearer demonstration that battleships were vulnerable to air power. However, even this was not necessarily a decisive demonstration, given the limited antiaircraft ability of both vessels.

Later in the war battleships, or at least American and British ones, which became almost literally floating antiaircraft fortresses, would survive even more intensive attacks. In fact, battleships proved immensely valuable in helping to defend carriers—which were even more vulnerable than battleships—from air attack, while protecting themselves. On one occasion, USS *South Dakota* shot down nearly three dozen attacking aircraft in about five minutes. And battleships' heavy guns were extremely useful in covering amphibious assaults all over the world, not a few landings being largely decided by the support of battleship gunfire. During the protracted ground struggle for Okinawa, for example, U.S. battleships and large cruisers (sort of glorified heavy cruisers carrying light battleship armament) expended 23,157 rounds of 16-inch, 14-inch, and 12-inch ammunition, a weight of metal of over 12,000 tons.

CRUISERS

To some extent descendants of the frigates of sailing navies, cruisers were nevertheless very much a twentieth-century type of warship. Much smaller than battleships but two or more times larger than destroyers, cruisers did not have as sharply defined a role as either of those two types.

As originally conceived, in the late nineteenth century, cruisers were in fact the descendants of the frigate, their duties being to "show the flag" in remote areas in order to keep the locals from stirring up trouble and, in wartime, to provide scouts with some firepower for the fleet. They were large enough for these tasks, but not so large and expensive as battleships. Many cruisers were in effect large destroyers, equipped with torpedoes and capable of doing most jobs destroyers were designed for. Indeed, in the Japanese Navy light cruisers were normally used as leaders of destroyer squadrons. But cruisers usually had larger, and longer-ranged, guns than destroyers. Cruisers also had some armor. So cruisers could usually defeat destroyers, unless the DDs got in a spread of torpedoes first. Cruisers were relatively valuable, and merited protection by destroyers, but were sometimes sent out on missions unescorted. The vague role of cruisers led to experimentation in their design.

Light cruisers (CLs) were between 2,500 and 12,000 tons in displacement, usually carrying six to a dozen 5-inch or 6-inch guns, but occasionally more, plus one or two banks of torpedoes, and some antiaircraft armament. Lightly armored, they were usually fast and relatively cheap, and could outshoot most things they couldn't outrun. Heavy cruisers (CAs) were from 8,000 to 18,000 tons in displacement, toting six to ten guns of 8-inch caliber plus antiaircraft weapons. Although the U.S. Navy dispensed with torpedoes on its heavy cruisers, the Japanese continued to include torpedoes on theirs, which proved a considerable asset. Generally much better armored than light cruisers, heavy cruisers were usually slower.

During the late 1930s, with aircraft looming larger as an antiship threat, a new variety of light cruiser was developed. This was the antiaircraft light cruiser (CLAA). The first few were created by the simple expedient of reequipping older light cruisers with a copious battery of 4-inch or 5-inch antiaircraft or dual-purpose guns and some radar, sometimes with a healthy allocation of torpedoes as well. Later, purpose-built antiaircraft cruisers appeared in several navies. Although very light, these vessels proved immensely valuable in combat, and not only in an antiaircraft role.

Ideally, the light cruisers were supposed to do the show-the-flag jobs in peacetime, and in war serve as antidestroyer protection for fleets, provide firepower to help defend convoys from surface attack, and, in some navies, serve as flagships for destroyer squadrons. Antiaircraft cruisers were supposed to protect the fleet from air attack. And heavy cruisers were supposed to serve as muscular scouts, able to locate enemy fleets, fight off enemy scouts, and, in battle, add their firepower to that of the battlewagons.

Unfortunately, by World War II a lot had changed and the role of the cruiser had become somewhat uncertain—particularly that of the heavy cruiser, since its scouting function had been usurped by aircraft and radar. Moreover, since one had to fight with what one had on hand, it was not uncommon in the numerous battles among the islands of the South and Southwest Pacific for heavy cruisers, light cruisers, and even antiaircraft cruisers to find themselves slugging it out in surface-action melees against enemy vessels of like type or even battleships.

Late in the war, the United States introduced something called a large cruiser (CB), which was sort of a super heavy cruiser; these ships were sometimes called battlecruisers due to their considerable size (over 34,000 tons at full load, as much as a fleet carrier) and heavier armament (nine 12-inch guns). They had the least well defined role of any type of cruiser, or any other category of warship, for that matter.

DESTROYERS

Destroyers (DDs) were the real workhorses of the fleet—anyone's fleet. They did everything.

Destroyers were created before the turn of the century to defend heavier ships against attacks by torpedo boats, from which role they derived their name, "torpedo-boat destroyers." Originally rather small vessels (250 to 300 tons), destroyers gradually grew in size and capability, and by World War II displaced from about 1,000 to about 2,500 tons, with some exceptional designs even reaching the vicinity of 3,000 tons. Meanwhile their missions expanded.

Through World War I destroyers continued to protect larger ships against torpedoes, although increasingly the torpedoes came from submarines. Between the wars, as destroyers continued to be general-purpose bodyguards for larger ships, they came to be equipped to defend against aircraft as well. Destroyers were usually also armed with torpedoes, which they could use against enemy surface ships.

Destroyers were fast, so they could keep up with any other type of ship and also maneuver around a formation of ships as they sought to head off any enemy threats, or deliver torpedo attacks. They were also small, cramped, and rather uncomfortable, particularly in heavy weather. Because of their high fuel consumption, destroyers had to be refueled frequently. At full steam, the typical U.S. DD ran out of fuel in about four days.

Operationally, although enemy attacks were generally against larger ships, destroyers took their "screening" role seriously and as a result took a disproportionate number of losses.

One consequence of World War II was the creation of a variety of destroyer types. The destroyer escort (DE) was a sort of pocket-variety destroyer, with lighter surface armament and lower speed on a smaller hull, specialized for antisubmarine duties. There were also destroyers that, through the fitting of additional radars and antiaircraft armament, became specialized in the antiaircraft defense of fleets. Later in the war such vessels were often posted at some distance from the main body of a fleet as "radar picket ships," to give early warning of the approach of enemy aircraft.

Destroyers, particularly older models, were also frequently converted for service as high-speed transports (AVPs), being able to carry modest but sometimes critical quantities of men and supplies to isolated garrisons on remote islands. Even before the war, the United States and Japan began converting older destroyers to a variety of odd jobs, such as minesweeping (DMSs) and mine laying (DMLs), or serving as general-purpose patrol boats and escorts.

THE LITTLE GUYS

In addition to the major warship types, there were numerous classes of "small boys." These included:

- GUNBOATS (PGs), a catch-all designation which included vessels that ranged in size from 30 to 2,000 tons
- FRIGATES (PFs), essentially cut-rate destroyer escorts of about 500 tons, in some navies called sloops
- TORPEDO BOATS (TBs), speedy vessels much smaller than destroyers (600 to 800 tons) designed primarily to deliver torpedo attacks against surface vessels
- MOTOR TORPEDO BOATS (MTBs), very small (50 to 60 tons), high-speed motor boats (35 to 40 knots) armed with a small number of torpedoes
- MINE WARFARE VESSELS (AMs), small ships specializing in the planting and clearing of mines
- CORVETTES and SUBMARINE CHASERS (PCs), very small (250 to 300 tons), very uncomfortable vessels that could be produced cheaply in great numbers

Mine warfare vessels aside, most of the small boys were of only marginal value, at best expedients. Gunboats were highly specialized vessels, designed to impress the various "natives" in peacetime. Although some navies continued to build torpedo boats, by World

War II they had long been supplanted by destroyers. Gunboats, frigates, sloops, torpedo boats, and the like were all pressed into service as antisubmarine escort vessels when the war came, to be quickly joined by submarine chasers and corvettes, and anything else that could be adapted to the role. Motor torpedo boats had some value for coastal operations, but on balance they were probably not worth the money, resources, and manpower invested in them.

Several navies, including those of Japan and the United States, converted obsolescent warships for use as minor combatants, such as old destroyers to minelayers (DMLs) and sweepers (DMSs), patrol boats, and the like. This was an economical use of available resources in a wartime emergency.

THE JAPANESE ARMY'S AIRCRAFT CARRIERS

In order to ferry airplanes to distant theaters, the Imperial Army converted seven merchant ships to serve as aircraft transports. These vessels looked like escort carriers, but their appearance was deceiving. These vessels carried eight to thirty-five aircraft, depending upon type. Although their principal function was to move airplanes from one place to another, these ships are occasionally listed as escort carriers in some works on the Pacific war, and have given rise to the legend that the Imperial Army built its own aircraft carriers to spite the Imperial Navy.

The real story is quite amusing. The Navy refused to provide the aircraft transportation services the Army required, so the Army procured its own transports, which looked like carriers. Since it was cheaper and more efficient to move aircraft fully assembled than crated, the Army "carriers" had what looked like a flight deck upon which the aircraft were parked. American experience demonstrated that disassembled fighter aircraft required up to 250 man-hours to put back together, and it required trained technicians to do the job right. The Army "carriers" had a limited capability to operate aircraft, to the extent that lightly loaded airplanes could fly off to nearby land bases. This was essential, since many air bases were on islands that lacked port facilities to unload the aircraft the traditional way. The Allies used true escort carriers for the same purpose, allowing Army pilots to make one carrier takeoff in order to reach their island air base.

SHIP CLASSES OF THE PACIFIC WAR

The Pacific war was primarily a naval war, despite the masses of aircraft in use. The largest fleets of warships ever were brought to bear in the Pacific campaigns.

Although occasionally single ships are built to unique designs, it is more usual for warships to be built in groups, called classes, with each vessel in the class being more or less identical with all the others. This saves money on design, and makes it easier to create homogeneous squadrons. Some classes contain more than 100 vessels; others comprise 2 or 3 ships.

The tables on pages 98–99, 106–107, 115, 118, 123, 128, 130, 137, and 140 detail the principal characteristics of the major classes of warships that served in the Pacific during World War II. They are accompanied by a series of short anecdotal comments about each class. The tables and comments are arranged alphabetically by type.

BATTLESHIPS AND BATTLECRUISERS

Alaska. Despite being a very fine design, combining high speed with considerable firepower, excellent protection, great endurance, and fine sea-keeping qualities, the *Alaska*s were white elephants. Frequently termed battlecruisers, they were not really similar to those World War I–era vessels, which were supposed to serve as scouts for the battle fleet. The ships in this class, *Alaska* and *Guam* (a third ship, *Hawaii*, was scrapped incomplete, while three others were never laid down), were really supercruisers, evolving out of concern that heavy cruisers were inadequate to meet the demands of modern warfare, and the suspicion that Japan was building something similar. Despite their rather odd origins, and their lack of a role, the *Alaska*s proved excellent ships, helping to escort carrier task forces and providing amphibious fire support in the last months of the war. They were enormously expensive, as the Navy spent a lot of money designing their main armament, experimenting with new-pattern 10-inch, 11-inch, and 12-inch guns in double and triple turrets before settling upon the final design. The needs of the service would have been better served by building another pair of *Essex* Class carriers, which would have been available much sooner, would have done a lot more work, and would have cost a lot less.

Arkansas. The oldest American battleship (laid down when Teddy Roosevelt was president), indeed the oldest American major combatant in the war, *Arkansas* saw some service in the Pacific, providing fire support for amphibious landings during the last year of the war, after turning in a virtuoso performance during amphibious assaults all over the European Theater. After the war she was expended during the Bikini atomic bomb tests, being virtually at ground zero.

California. Like all the older U.S. battleships, the *"Prune Barge"* and her sisters were rather slow, but were powerful, well-protected vessels. Extensively damaged at Pearl Harbor, they were reconstructed and emerged with greatly enhanced antiaircraft armament and protection. They served through the war, mostly providing fire support to amphibious landings, but played a major role in the night battleship action off Surigao Strait in October 25, 1944, when, with *West Virginia*, they collectively fired 225 fourteen-inch and sixteen-inch rounds at the Japanese fleet. *California*, launched in 1919, is the largest American warship ever built on the west coast, and is one of only two major American warships ever built out there (the other being the famous old battlewagon *Oregon*, way back in 1896), escort carriers of the *Casablanca* and *Commencement Bay* classes aside.

Fuso. The *Fusos* were good battleships, reasonably well protected and relatively fast for such old vessels. However, like all Japanese battleships they saw little action during World War II, before being blasted to pieces by U.S. battleships, cruisers, destroyers, and torpedo boats during the night action in Surigao Strait on October 25, 1944.

Iowa. The ultimate manifestation of U.S. battleship design, the *Iowas* were quite possibly the most powerful battleships ever built, their 16-inch guns being of a new model that gave them a range only a few hundred yards less than that of the Japanese 18.1-inch gun, with virtually the same penetrability and a considerably higher

Navy	Class	Combat Surf	AAA	Displacement Std	Full	Length	Beam	Draft	HP	Spd	Armor Belt	Turret	Deck	Tower	A/C	Guns Main	Sec	DP	AAA	HMG	TT	DC	Crew	Tot	Year
US	Alaska	24	27	29.8	34.3	241.3	27.8	9.7	150.0	33.0	9.0	12.8	5.2	10.6	2	9x12	None	12x5	None	90	0	0	1571	6	1944
US	Arkansas	26	8	26.1	30.1	168.9	32.3	9.1	28.0	21.0	11.0	12.0	4.3	11.5	2	12x12	16x5	None	8x3	24	0	0	1242	2	1912
US	California	36	9	34.9	40.3	182.9	34.8	10.1	29.5	20.5	13.5	18.0	5.5	16.0	2	12x14	14x5	None	8x5	24	0	0	2375	2	1921
Jp	Fuso	34	4	34.7	38.5	210.0	30.6	9.7	75.0	24.8	12.0	12.0	7.0	12.0	3	12x14	14x6	8x5	None	20	0	0	1396	2	1915
US	Iowa	50	38	48.1	57.5	262.1	33.0	11.0	212.0	32.5	13.0	19.7	8.1	17.5	3	9x16	None	20x5	None	120	0	0	1921	6	1943
Jp	Ise (A)	34	4	35.8	39.5	213.4	31.7	9.2	80.0	25.3	12.0	12.0	8.0	12.0	3	12x14	16x5.5	8x5	None	20	0	0	1376	2	1917
Jp	Ise (B)	22	9	35.4	38.1	219.6	31.7	9.0	80.0	25.3	12.0	12.0	8.0	12.0	22	8x14	16x5.5	16x5	None	57	0	0	1463	2	1943
Br	King George V	30	14	36.7	42.1	213.4	31.4	8.8	110.0	28.0	15.0	12.0	3.0	4.5	2	10x14	None	16x5.25	None	32	0	0	1422	5	1940
Jp	Kongo	23	3	27.5	32.2	214.5	28.0	8.4	136.0	30.5	8.0	10.0	2.3	10.0	3	8x14	14x6	8x5	None	12	0	0	1220	4	1913
Br	Lion	38	18	40.6	46.3	225.6	31.7	9.1	130.0	30.0	15.0	15.0	4.0	4.5	2	9x16	None	16x5.25	None	48	0	0	1680	4	MHB
US	Maryland	40	15	34.9	40.3	182.9	34.8	10.1	30.0	21.0	13.5	18.0	5.5	16.0	3	8x16	14x5	None	8x5	24	0	0	2375	3	1923
US	Montana	62	38	60.5	70.5	271.3	36.9	11.2	172.0	28.0	24.3	22.5	9.0	18.0	3	12x16	None	20x5	None	120	0	0	2150	5	MHB
Jp	Nagato	36	4	39.1	42.8	221.1	33.0	9.5	82.0	25.0	11.8	14.0	7.7	14.6	3	8x16	18x5.5	8x5	None	20	0	0	1368	2	1920
Br	Nelson	38	14	33.3	44.3	201.2	32.3	8.6	45.0	23.0	14.0	16.0	3.0	14.0	2	9x16	12x6	6x4.7	None	48	2	0	1314	2	1927
US	Nevada	30	9	29.1	31.7	175.3	32.9	9.0	25.0	20.5	13.5	18.0	5.0	16.0	2	10x14	12x5	None	8x5	24	0	0	1374	2	1916
US	New Mexico	34	9	33.4	36.2	182.9	32.4	9.4	40.0	22.0	13.5	18.0	5.5	16.0	2	12x14	12x5	None	8x5	24	0	0	1443	3	1918
US	New York	30	8	27.0	31.9	172.2	32.3	9.2	28.1	21.0	12.0	14.0	6.3	16.0	2	10x14	16x5	None	8x3	24	0	0	1290	2	1914
US	North Carolina	48	15	37.5	44.4	217.8	33.0	9.2	121.0	28.0	12.8	16.0	7.6	14.7	3	9x16	None	20x5	8x5	28	0	0	1880	2	1941
US	Pennsylvania	34	14	33.4	35.9	182.9	32.4	9.2	33.4	21.0	13.5	18.0	4.8	16.0	2	12x14	12x5	None	8x5	24	0	0	1052	2	1916
Br	Queen Elizabeth	21	14	32.0	37.0	181.8	31.5	9.3	80.0	24.0	13.0	11.0	3.0	14.0	2	8x15	12x6	20x4.5	8x5	32	0	0	1150	5	1915
Br	Renown	21	12	30.8	37.0	227.3	31.1	8.1	120.0	29.0	9.0	2.0	11.0	10.0	2	6x15	12x4	8x4.5	6x4	32	2	0	1200	2	1916
Fr	Richelieu	28	28	35.5	43.3	242.0	33.0	9.6	150.0	30.0	13.5	17.5	8.8	15.0	3	8x15	None	9x6	12x3.9	104	0	0	1670	4	1940
Br	Royal Sovereign	28	8	29.2	33.5	175.8	31.1	8.6	40.0	21.0	13.0	13.0	1.5	11.0	2	8x15	12x6	None	8x4	24	2	0	1100	5	1916
US	South Dakota	48	21	38.0	44.5	203.0	33.0	10.7	130.0	27.5	13.1	18.0	7.9	16.0	3	9x16	None	16x5	None	60	0	0	1793	4	1942
Br	Vanguard	28	24	44.5	51.4	231.6	32.9	9.4	130.0	30.0	14.0	13.0	4.0	3.0	2	8x15	None	16x5.25	None	70	0	0	1893	1	1946
Jp	Yamato	45	5	62.3	70.0	244.0	36.9	10.4	150.0	27.0	16.1	25.6	9.1	19.7	7	9x18.1	12x6.1	12x5	None	29	0	0	2500	4	1941

NOTES TO ALL SHIP TABLES: "Navy" is nation the ship belonged to; "Au" is Australia; "Br" is Britain; "Cn" is Canada; "Fr" is France; "Nth" is Netherlands; "NZ" is New Zealand; "Jp" is Japan; "US" is the United States.

"Class" is the name of the lead ship in the class. Some classes are not mentioned in the text.

"Combat" is a calculation of the relative combat value in the following areas: "Surf" is value in surface engagements; "AAA" is value against attacking aircraft.

"Displacement" is the amount of water the ship displaces (i.e., the weight of the water that would occupy the space occupied by the ship), expressed in thousands of tons. There are two values for this: "Std" is standard, or weight with basic crew, fuel, munitions and other supplies; "Full" is fighting weight, loaded with all the items needed to go to war.

Dimensions are expressed in meters. There are three of them: "Length"; "Beam," or width; and "Draft," or how deep into the water the bottom of the ship is at full load.

"HP" is maximum horsepower generated by the ship's engines.

"Spd" is top speed in knots (nautical miles per hour).

"Armor" is the protection many ships had against enemy fire, given in inches for the following positions on the ship: "Belt" is an area along the waterline to protect engines and ammo magazines; "Turret" is where the main guns are; "Deck" is for protection from shells or bombs; "Tower" is a tower in which the fire control crew operate. "A/C" is aircraft carried.

Guns: "Main" is the largest guns, on battleships from 11 to 18 inches in bore diameter; "Sec" is secondary guns for use against surface targets; "DP" is dual purpose, for use against surface and air targets; "AAA" is antiaircraft artillery, guns whose only purpose is to attack aircraft; "HMG" is heavy machine guns, caliber varying from 12.7mm to 40mm.

"TT" is torpedo tubes carried.

"DC" is depth charges carried (for use against submarines).

"Crew" is number normally carried.

"Tot" is total number of ships in this class, including units never completed.

"Year" is when the first ship in the class entered service. "MHB" is might have been, a class that was not, but could have been, in action.

rate of fire, which, coupled with radar fire control and their much higher speed (33 knots to 27, a difference of about 20 percent) and greater maneuverability, would have made them more than a match for an equal number of *Yamatos*. They spent the war providing antiaircraft cover for carrier task forces and bombarding enemy installations ashore. Since the war they've spent a lot of time in mothballs, being occasionally hauled out for various wars (Korea, Vietnam, the Persian Gulf). Since the introduction of ironclads, no other battleship class has seen such long and active combat service. With the retirement of the last of this class in 1992, the era of the cannon-armed ship-of-the-line came to an end, after a run of nearly four centuries. Maybe.

Ise. Somewhat improved versions of the *Fuso* Class battleship, the *Ises* saw little action in World War II. After Midway they were taken in hand for conversion to battleship/aircraft carriers (the "A" and "B" on the table on page 98 give the particulars of the original and the converted designs). The conversion tied up precious shipyard space and consumed valuable materials for nearly two years. The after pair of turrets was removed and replaced by a hangar deck and short flight deck with catapults, which permitted the *Ises* to operate about twenty-two aircraft. Actually, they were really glorified seaplane tenders, as they could only launch aircraft, which then had to land on the sea, from which they were recovered by cranes. In fact, no aircraft ever seem to have been allocated to either ship, and their only operational mission was as bait in the Northern Force during the Battle of Leyte Gulf. Both were later sunk in port by U.S. naval aircraft. A remarkable waste of resources.

King George V. The "KGVs" were good battleships, but undergunned because they were designed in the early 1930s, when Britain was attempting to secure a newer, and more restrictive naval limitation treaty. Their peculiar gun arrangement (two quadruple turrets and one double) was dictated by the need to scale back from a planned twelve-gun main battery. The quadruple turrets proved rather successful in service. Although they saw extensive service, they were never tested to their limits, but seem to have been reasonably resilient ships. *Prince of Wales* was lost off Malaya on December 10, 1942, after she had taken four aerial torpedo hits and numerous bombs, while *Duke of York* performed credibly in a night shoot-out with the German *Scharnhorst* on Boxing Day (December

26), 1943. Like all British ships, they had an inadequate antiaircraft fire control system, but nevertheless those serving in the Pacific in 1945 proved able to beat off repeated Japanese air attacks.

Kongo. HIJMS *Kongo* was built in a British shipyard, to a British design. Her sisters were built in Japanese yards, to the same design. Originally built as battlecruisers, during the 1930s they were extensively reconstructed. Given newer, more powerful engines, they were able to carry additional armor, which permitted them to be reclassified as "fast battleships." Although the 1930s upgrades did permit the *Kongo*s to accompany carrier task forces, the armor improvements were of only marginal value. *Hiei* was turned into a burning wreck by about fifty shells of 5-inch to 8-inch caliber off Guadalcanal on November 12–13, 1942; *Kirishima* had to be scuttled after taking just nine 16-inch and about forty to fifty 5-inch shells off Guadalcanal two nights later; and *Kongo* was sunk by a single torpedo on November 21, 1944.

Maryland. Virtually identical to the *California*s, save for their main armament (eight 16-inch guns rather than twelve 14-inchers), the *Maryland*s were the most powerful of the prewar American battleships. *West Virginia* was extensively damaged at Pearl Harbor, where *Maryland* suffered relatively lightly. As a result, *Maryland* and *Colorado*, not at Pearl due to a refit, were not as extensively rebuilt as *West Virginia*, which emerged as a virtual sister of *California*. The reconstruction was so extensive that neither *West Virginia* nor the *California*s could thereafter pass through the Panama Canal, their beams having been increased to 114 feet, while the locks were only 110 feet wide. Nevertheless, all three rendered excellent service as fire support ships, while at Surigao Strait, *West Virginia* fired numerous salvos and *Maryland* got off forty-eight 16-inch rounds, six full broadsides, perhaps the most sustained series of broadsides ever fired by an American battlewagon.

Montana. The *Montana*s were designed to succeed the *Iowa* Class battleships, being much larger and much more heavily armed, albeit at some sacrifice in speed. However, even before they were laid down it was becoming clear that the days of the battleship were numbered, and they were soon canceled.

Nagato. Among the best older battleships in the world, the *Nagato*s were quite fast, well protected, and well armed. Like all Japanese battleships in the war, they saw little action. *Mutsu* sank in

Hong Kong Harbor after an internal explosion, the nature of which has never been ascertained. *Nagato* survived the war relatively unscathed and was expended as a target during the 1946 Bikini nuclear weapons trials.

Nelson. Britain's *Nelson* Class had an odd battleship design, to say the least. With three triple turrets forward of the superstructure (C turret was lower than B and could not fire ahead), intended to save weight, and actually rather successful, the *Nelsons* were the only battleships built during the "naval holiday" introduced by the disarmament treaties. They were armored on the "Nevada" ("all or nothing") plan, which stressed enormous protection for vital areas, and nothing at all elsewhere. They were good ships, but very slow by World War II standards. They saw considerable service in the Indian Ocean.

Nevada. Old battleships, but well designed. Both were at Pearl Harbor, where *Oklahoma* proved a total loss, but *Nevada* was extensively rebuilt and emerged as a very successful ship, mostly in amphibious-assault fire support. She was expended during the Bikini A-bomb tests.

New Mexico. The *New Mexico* Class battleships were substantially similar to the *Pennsylvanias* in design, although much different in appearance. In the Atlantic in December 1941, they were spared the trauma of Pearl Harbor, and also the extensive rebuilding that the veterans of that disaster underwent, so that aside from numerous additions to their antiaircraft armament, they remained substantially unmodernized. They served primarily as fire support vessels for amphibious landings, though *Mississippi* did get in a few rounds against Japanese battleships at Surigao Strait.

New York. So old that they were not considered worth modernizing, the battleships *New York* and *Texas* had been a disappointment in service even when new. They spent most of the war in the European Theater, providing gunfire support for landings from North Africa to Normandy, before going out to the Pacific, where they rendered good service supporting amphibious landings. After the war, *New York* was expended in the Bikini A-bomb tests, while *Texas* is preserved as a war memorial, anchored near the San Jacinto battlefield in Texas.

North Carolina. Arguably superior to the succeeding *South Dakota* Class, the *North Carolinas* were among the best battlewagons of the

THE SHIPS

war—good sea boats, handy, relatively fast, and with a tremendous main battery. Both saw considerable service in the war, and *Washington* put nine 16-inch rounds (of seventy-five fired) into the Japanese *Kirishima* off Guadalcanal on the night of November 14–15, 1942, turning her into a burning wreck. Both ships later supported the fast carrier task forces with antiaircraft fire, covered numerous amphibious landings, and bombarded targets in Japan.

Pennsylvania. A good design, the *Pennsylvanias* were among the strongest battleships of the prewar era. *Arizona* was lost at Pearl Harbor, where *Pennsylvania* was less seriously damaged. Less extensively refitted than the other ships damaged on December 7, 1941, *Pennsylvania* served through the war, mostly providing fire support to amphibious landings. While present at Surigao Strait, she did not fire. She ended her days in the Bikini A-bomb test.

Queen Elizabeth. The *QEs* were the finest battleships of their generation, the most powerful and speediest of World War I, and the decade after as well. They were the first capital ships to burn oil fuel exclusively. Well protected, heavily armed, and relatively speedy (25 knots), they had excellent sea-keeping qualities. Though old by World War II, they were still of considerable value, not for shore bombardment alone, as proven in several surface actions with German and Italian warships. Several saw service with the British Far Eastern Fleet.

Renown. As ships, Britain's *Renown* Class battlecruisers were speedy, maneuverable, and good sea boats. As warships they suffered from all the handicaps common to battlecruisers, being virtually unprotected and rather lightly armed. Her maneuverability helped *Repulse* survive for about an hour under Japanese air attack on December 10, 1942, but she could not escape and succumbed to five torpedoes. *Renown* saw extensive service in the Indian Ocean and as a convoy escort. When she went to the scrap yard after the war, she was the last genuine battlecruiser in the world.

Richelieu. Large vessels of unusual design, the *Richelieus* were very well protected. Like all World War II battleships except American and British ones, she had large-caliber secondary armament (nine 6-inch guns) which were of no use for antiaircraft purposes. *Richelieu* served with the Royal Navy in the Indian Ocean from 1943 onward. *Jean Bart,* incomplete at the time of the fall of France to the Nazis, managed to escape to Casablanca, where from dockside in November 1942 she traded shots with the USS *Massachusetts*, much to her loss. She finally entered service in the early 1950s, being thereby the last battleship to be completed.

Royal Sovereign. Apparently having expended all their ideas on the QEs, the Royal Navy's designers produced a very inferior battleship in the succeeding *Royal Sovereign* Class. They were poorly conceived and poorly designed, and, in a moment of panic over oil supplies, were designed to burn coal. Although converted to oil during construction, they never matched the older class either in performance or sea keeping. Unlike the older QEs, they were not extensively reconstructed between the wars. Their principal role in World War II was convoy escort. Many were sent to the Indian Ocean in early 1942, there being nothing else to spare. It is unlikely that they would have withstood the Imperial Japanese Navy had it taken a more aggressive role in the Indian Ocean in early 1942.

South Dakota. Although displacing slightly more than the *North Carolina* Class battleships, the *South Dakota*s were shorter by about 50 feet and narrower by about 2 feet. They were also built with several innovative ideas in mind, none of which had been adequately tested, and all of which proved unsatisfactory. As a result, these ships were not only rather cramped and uncomfortable, but were also slightly slower, less stable, and less maneuverable than were their predecessors. Although *South Dakota* was rather seriously engaged in the South Pacific, being heavily damaged by Japanese shell fire on the night of November 14–15, 1942, most of their careers were spent escorting carrier task forces and providing gunfire support to amphibious landings. Note that *South Dakota* was fitted as a fleet flagship, and in consequence had four fewer 5"/38 dual-purpose guns than the twenty carried by her sisters (in order to provide accommodations for the fleet staff).

Vanguard. The last battleship completed for Britain, *Vanguard* was not ready for sea until after the war. Although she was equal in size and protection to contemporary foreign battlewagons, *Vanguard*'s main battery dated from World War I, her turrets and guns being those removed from the "large light cruisers" *Glorious* and *Courageous* when they were converted into aircraft carriers during World War I.

Yamato. The largest battleships ever built, and the largest warships ever until the commissioning of the nuclear-powered USS *En-*

terprise in 1960, *Yamato* and *Musashi* were enormous yet graceful-looking behemoths mounting the heaviest guns afloat and impressively protected: *Musashi* sank only after absorbing a dozen or more torpedoes and seventeen bombs in the Sibuyan Sea on October 24, 1944, and *Yamato* went down while on a suicide mission north of Okinawa on April 7, 1945, having taken about a dozen torpedoes and at least six bombs. Nevertheless, they were probably a bad investment. Neither ship saw much service in the war. They were quite slow by World War II standards, lacked maneuverability, and were probably no better than an even match for U.S. battleships of the *Iowa* Class. They were also expensive, and their construction limited the expansion of the Japanese Navy in terms of other, more vital types of ships, such as aircraft carriers or destroyers. Construction of this class entailed building a special 13,000-ton g.r.t. ship to transport their guns to the shipyards and several enormous floating cranes to help mount the things. For the same investment in money, steel, and manpower, two or three *Shokaku* Class carriers (including aircraft) could have been built for each *Yamato* completed, and the carriers would have been available in considerably less time. The Japanese appear to have recognized this, for the third ship in the class was converted into a carrier while still on the ways and the fourth was canceled.

FLEET CARRIERS

Akagi. Designed as a battlecruiser, *Akagi* was converted into a carrier under the terms of the Naval Disarmament Treaty of 1922. She was fast and rather well protected for a carrier, but could only operate about two thirds of the aircraft that she was capable of storing. Flagship of the First Air Fleet at the beginning of the war, she served from Pearl Harbor to Midway, where she had to be scuttled after U.S. dive bombers turned her into a burning wreck.

Chitose. Converted from prewar seaplane carriers that had been designed with such a purpose in mind, *Chitose* and *Chikuma* were surprisingly good light carriers, with excellent aircraft operational capacity for their displacement. They saw little active service, due to Japan's increasing shortage of good pilots. Both were sunk by U.S. naval aircraft off Cape Engaño in October 1944.

AIRCRAFT CARRIERS (CV and CL)

Navy	Class	Combat		Displacement		Length	Beam	Draft	HP	Spd	Armor			Tower	A/C	Guns				HMG	TT	DC	Crew	Tot	Year
		Surf	AAA	Std	Full						Belt	Turret	Deck			Main	Sec	DP	AAA						
Jp	Akagi	9	5	36.5	42.8	235.0	29.0	8.1	133.0	31.0	10.0	0.0	1.0	1.0	72	6x8	None	None	12x4.7	28	0	0	2000	1	1927
Br	Centaur	2	11	18.3	24.0	198.1	27.4	7.5	76.0	29.5	0.0	0.0	0.0	0.0	42	None	None	8x4.5	None	34	0	0	1390	8	MHB
Jp	Chitose	2	4	11.2	15.3	174.0	20.8	7.5	44.0	28.9	0.0	0.0	0.0	0.0	30	None	None	8x5	None	30	0	0	800	2	1943
Br	Colossus	1	6	13.2	18.0	190.0	24.4	7.1	40.0	25.0	0.0	0.0	0.0	0.0	37	None	None	None	None	24	0	0	1300	10	1944
Br	Eagle II	2	11	36.8	46.0	245.0	34.4	9.5	152.0	23.0	4.5	0.0	4.0	0.0	78	None	None	16x4.5	None	64	0	0	2740	2	1945
US	Essex	4	24	27.2	34.9	249.9	28.3	8.4	150.0	32.7	4.0	0.0	4.0	4.0	91	None	None	12x5	None	78	0	0	2686	26	1942
Br	Furious	2	1	19.1	22.5	224.0	27.5	8.6	90.0	30.0	3.0	0.0	1.0	0.0	36	10x5.5	None	2x4	None	4	0	0	1218	1	1925
Br	Hermes	2	3	11.0	13.0	166.1	27.3	5.7	40.0	25.0	3.0	0.0	1.0	0.0	20	6x5.5	None	None	4x4	10	0	0	664	1	1923
Jp	Hiryu	3	6	17.3	21.9	210.0	22.3	7.8	153.0	34.3	5.9	0.0	2.2	0.0	64	6x5.5	None	12x5	None	31	0	0	1100	1	1939
Jp	Hosho	0	1	7.5	10.0	155.5	18.0	6.2	30.0	25.0	0.0	0.0	0.0	0.0	22	4x5.5	None	None	None	10	0	0	550	1	1922
Jp	Ibuki	1	6	12.5	14.6	187.8	21.2	6.3	72.0	29.0	0.0	0.0	0.0	0.0	27	None	None	None	4x3	50	0	30	1015	1	1945
Br	Illustrious	4	17	23.0	28.6	205.1	29.2	8.7	111.0	30.5	4.5	0.0	3.0	0.0	33	None	None	16x4.5	None	48	0	0	1229	3	1940
Br	Implacable	4	16	23.5	32.1	205.1	29.2	8.8	148.0	32.0	4.5	0.0	3.0	0.0	60	None	None	16x4.5	None	44	0	0	1585	2	1944
US	Independence	1	9	10.7	14.8	182.9	21.8	7.4	100.0	31.6	5.6	0.0	2.0	0.0	30	None	None	None	None	36	0	0	1569	9	1943
Br	Indomitable	4	17	23.0	29.7	205.1	29.2	8.8	111.0	30.5	4.5	0.0	3.0	0.0	45	None	None	16x4.5	None	48	0	0	1392	1	1941
Jp	Junyo	3	5	24.1	28.3	206.0	26.7	8.2	56.3	23.0	0.0	0.0	0.0	0.0	53	None	None	12x5	None	24	0	0	1200	2	1942
Jp	Kaga	10	5	38.2	43.7	240.3	32.5	9.5	127.4	28.3	11.0	0.0	1.0	1.0	81	10x8	None	16x5	None	30	0	0	2016	1	1928
US	Lexington	17	17	37.7	43.1	259.1	32.1	10.2	180.0	33.3	7.0	2.5	2.0	2.0	63	8x8	None	None	12x5	48	0	0	2330	2	1926
Br	Magnificent	1	6	14.0	17.8	192.0	24.4	7.0	40.0	25.0	0.0	0.0	0.0	0.0	37	None	None	None	None	24	0	0	1300	6	MHB
Br	Malta	4	19	46.9	56.8	249.9	35.4	10.5	200.0	32.5	4.5	0.0	4.0	4.0	81	None	None	16x4.5	None	55	0	0	2780	4	MHB
US	Midway	6	45	47.4	59.9	274.3	34.4	10.5	212.0	33.0	7.0	0.0	7.5	4.0	137	None	None	18x5	None	152	0	0	4104	3	1945
US	Ranger	3	3	14.6	17.6	222.5	24.4	6.8	53.5	29.3	2.0	0.0	1.0	2.0	76	None	None	None	8x5	None	0	0	1788	1	1934
Jp	Ryuho	2	5	13.4	16.7	197.3	19.6	6.7	52.0	26.5	0.0	0.0	0.0	0.0	31	None	None	8x5	None	38	0	0	990	1	1942
Jp	Ryujo	2	2	10.6	13.7	167.0	20.8	7.1	65.0	29.0	0.0	0.0	0.0	0.0	37	None	None	8x5	None	4	0	0	924	1	1933

AIRCRAFT CARRIERS (CV and CL), Continued

US	Saipan	1	9	14.5	17.8	202.4	23.4	8.2	120.0	33.0	4.6	0.0	2.5	0.0	48	None	None	None	None		0			
Jp	Shinano	5	18	62.0	71.9	244.0	36.3	10.3	150.0	27.0	8.1	0.0	10.6	8.0	70	None	None	16x5	None	150	0	2400	1	1944
Jp	Shokaku	4	8	25.7	32.1	236.1	26.0	8.9	160.0	34.2	6.5	0.0	5.1	1.0	72	None	None	16x5	None	43	0	1660	2	1941
Jp	Soryu	3	5	15.9	19.8	210.0	21.3	7.6	152.0	34.5	1.8	0.0	2.2	0.0	63	None	None	12x5	None	28	0	1100	1	1937
Jp	Taiho	2	8	29.3	37.7	238.0	27.7	9.6	160.0	33.0	5.9	0.0	8.0	0.0	53	None	None	None	12x3.9	51	0	1751	1	1944
Br	Unicorn	2	6	14.8	20.3	171.9	27.4	7.3	40.0	24.0	0.0	0.0	0.0	0.0	35	None	None	8x4	None	16	0	1200	1	1943
Jp	Unryu	3	8	17.2	20.0	207.0	22.0	7.8	152.0	34.0	5.9	0.0	3.2	0.0	65	None	None	12x5	None	51	0	1550	6	1944
US	Wasp	3	13	14.7	18.5	210.3	24.9	7.1	70.0	29.5	0.6	0.0	1.3	2.0	76	None	None	8x5	None	40	0	2167	1	1940
US	Yorktown	3	13	19.9	25.5	234.7	25.3	7.9	120.0	32.5	4.8	0.0	1.5	4.0	96	None	None	8x5	None	40	0	220	3	1937
Jp	Zuiho	1	2	11.3	14.3	185.0	18.2	6.6	523.0	28.0	0.0	0.0	0.0	0.0	30	None	None	8x5	None	8	0	785	2	1940

NOTE: See page 99 for an explanation of the items on this table. Some classes are not mentioned in the text.

Colossus. Classified as light fleet carriers by the Royal Navy, *Colossus* and her sisters (all but one of which were completed after the war) actually carried slightly more aircraft than did the much larger *Illustrious* Class fleet carriers, and had a superior avgas (aircraft fuel) capacity as well (about 2,600 gallons per plane against about 1,500). This was due to their almost complete lack of armor and their inferior machinery, which made them about 5 knots slower.

Essex. The largest and most successful class of carriers in the war. Of thirty-two ordered, sixteen were completed in time to serve in the war (and ten more soon afterward). The *Essex* Class carriers were designed on the basis of all previous U.S. experience with carriers. They were large, fast, roomy ships, well protected and with an enormous capacity to operate aircraft. From the time they began to enter service at the end of 1942, they increasingly came to dominate the shape of the war. Though they were intensively involved in combat, not one was sunk despite often horrendous damage. Off Okinawa, *Franklin* took an apparently accidental crash hit from a bomber (not a Kamikaze) that penetrated to the hangar deck before exploding, leading to extensive internal explosions among parked aircraft. This caused the deaths of over 700 men and injury to more than 200 others (nearly 40 percent of her crew), yet she managed to survive and, after some preliminary repairs, make it all the way to New York under her own power, despite a pronounced list, for permanent repairs. With periodic modifications and reconstruction, elements of the class formed part of the Navy's first-line forces until the 1980s.

Furious. One of the very first carriers ever, *Furious* began life as an extremely light battlecruiser in 1916 (very fast, wholly unprotected, with two 18-inch guns!). Gradually she was converted to a seaplane carrier/semi-battlecruiser (one 18-inch gun), and then to a full seaplane carrier, and finally to an aircraft carrier, by the early 1920s. She was not a successful carrier, having too few aircraft and too limited an avgas storage capacity (about 575 gallons per airplane) for her size. Nevertheless, she performed well in a variety of roles, operating against Japanese land targets and coastal shipping in the Indian Ocean in 1942 and 1943, until effectively removed from front-line service as newer carriers became available.

Hermes. Britain's first purpose-built aircraft carrier, *Hermes* was relatively fast and an excellent sea boat, but her aircraft complement (twelve) was much too small to permit her to serve as a fleet carrier. Operating in the Indian Ocean alone but for a light escort, she was overwhelmed by Japanese carrier-based dive bombers on April 9, 1942.

Hiryu. A slightly enlarged version of *Soryu, Hiryu* had greater range but only marginally more aircraft operating capacity. Paired with *Soryu*, she served from Pearl Harbor to Midway, where she took four bombs from U.S. dive bombers that caused extensive fires and forced her to be scuttled. She was the last of the four Japanese carriers to be sunk during the battle.

Hosho. The first aircraft carrier ever specifically designed and built as such from the keel up, *Hosho* served as an important test bed in the development of Japanese naval aviation. But by World War II she was useless as a first-line vessel, and served in a variety of escort roles, particularly in support of the battle fleet and as a training carrier. She survived the war.

Ibuki. Ordered by the Imperial Navy as a heavy cruiser of new design, *Ibuki* was laid down in April 1942 and launched the following May. As the Japanese carrier situation was desperate, in November 1943 the incomplete cruiser was taken in hand for conversion into a carrier. Construction lagged, however, due to wartime shortages, and work was halted in March 1945, when the ship was about 80 percent complete. She would have been an adequate light carrier.

Illustrious. A very well protected class, *Illustrious* and her sisters were Britain's best carriers in the war, and the first carriers to have a fully armored hangar deck. Of course, this limited aircraft capacity to that of an escort or light fleet carrier. Nevertheless, they were successful ships, handy and good in heavy seas as a result of their innovative "hurricane" bows, which brought the hull right up to the forward edge of the flight deck, and very tough. *Formidable* and *Victorious* each took two Kamikazes off Japan with little effect on operations. *Victorious* remained in service into the 1960s.

Implacable. A further refinement of the *Illustrious* design, incorporating lessons learned from *Indomitable, Implacable* was less successful than either of those classes, her hangar deck not being suitable for some of the taller late-war aircraft, and her fuel capacity being too low for the eighty-one aircraft that she was found capable of operating when using deck storage. Like her predecessors, however, she was sturdy, taking a Kamikaze with a 550-pound bomb on the flight deck at the base of her island with no significant effect.

Independence. By mid-1942 it was clear that the aircraft carrier was the new weapon of decision in naval warfare. It was also clear that there were not enough of them. As a result, President Roosevelt, who had been advocating such a step for nearly a year, ordered nine partially completed *Cleveland* Class light cruisers to be converted into light aircraft carriers. The work was done quickly and the first ships began to enter service in January 1943, with the last ready by the end of that year. The *Independence* Class ships were very successful improvisations, despite being cramped and uncomfortable. About a third the size of a fleet carrier, they operated about a third as many aircraft. They saw extensive service, and one was sunk, *Princeton*, which took a bomb that penetrated into her torpedo storage, setting off a series of explosions that caused the ship to be abandoned on October 24, 1944, during the Battle of Leyte Gulf.

Indomitable. A variant of Britain's *Illustrious* aircraft carrier design, *Indomitable* was less well protected, but this permitted her to carry nearly twice as many aircraft. She proved a generally successful aircraft carrier.

Junyo. Converted from the hulls of ocean liners that were still under construction, the *Junyo*s were not successful ships, being slow, crowded, virtually unprotected, poorly subdivided, and, apparently, mechanically unreliable (*Hiyo* missed the Battle of the Santa Cruz Islands due to an engine breakdown). They saw some active service. *Junyo* survived the war, to be scrapped, while *Hiyo* was sunk by a single submarine torpedo during the Battle of the Philippine Sea in June 1944.

Kaga. *Kaga* was originally designed as a battleship, and was scheduled to be scrapped on the ways under the Washington Naval Disarmament Treaty. She was reprieved and converted to a carrier when *Akagi*'s sister ship was wrecked abuilding by the Great Tokyo Earthquake of 1923. More or less a half-sister of *Akagi*, she was rather slower. She ranged the Pacific from Pearl Harbor to Midway, where U.S. dive bombers put four bombs into her, starting fires that caused her to blow up and sink.

Lexington. The *Lexington*s were laid down as battlecruisers, and converted to carriers under the terms of the naval disarmament treaties. The largest, most impressive-looking carriers in the U.S. Navy during the war, they had the most powerful engines in the fleet until the advent of the *Iowa* Class battleships, using a successful but very expensive electric turbine drive. The two ships were central to the development of American naval air power doctrine, serving as test beds for numerous experiments in strategy, tactics, and even logistics. Though they initially operated only about 65 aircraft, it was eventually realized that they could comfortably function with over 100. Even in her death *Lexington*, one of the most beloved ships ever to wear the American flag, provided lessons for the future of carrier aviation. At the Coral Sea (May 8, 1942) she was damaged by two torpedoes and two bombs, which caused a list and some fires. Her damage control parties appeared to have had everything under control when two severe internal explosions wracked the ship, caused by the accumulation of fumes from avgas. The ship had to be abandoned and sunk by "friendly" torpedoes. Adjustments were made to all other carriers to limit future incidents of this sort. *Saratoga*'s life was as long and uneventful as *Lexington*'s was short and glorious. She survived the war, despite being torpedoed several times and even taking a Kamikaze, to be expended as a target at Bikini.

Midway. The culmination of U.S. wartime carrier development, *Midway* and her two sisters were huge ships, yet fast, far better protected than any previous U.S. carriers, and possessing an enormous aircraft capacity (over 130 planes). Although built with considerable speed (twenty-two to twenty-three months each), they began to enter service only about the time that Japan surrendered. They were rebuilt from time to time, the last one not being withdrawn from service until the end of the Cold War.

Ranger. An unsuccessful ship, *Ranger* was America's first carrier designed as such from the keel up. However, this occurred before much experience had been gained in operating the *Lexingtons*. As a result, far too much was attempted on a limited hull. Her wartime career was confined to the Atlantic, where she rendered valuable service in support of the North African landings and in air strikes on German installations in Norway. She was eventually relegated to service as a training carrier.

Ryuho. Converted from a submarine tender that the Japanese had built with that notion in mind, *Ryuho* was not as successful a vessel as the *Zuihos*, being slow and poorly constructed. She served mostly as a training carrier, and was scrapped after the war.

Ryujo. A poorly designed vessel, lightly constructed, unstable, and top heavy, *Ryujo* took part in a number of critical operations as an aircraft carrier, before being sunk in the eastern Solomons.

Saipan. Inspired by the success of the USS *Independence* Class, the *Saipans* were intended as light carriers based on the *Baltimore* Class heavy cruiser design, but to be built from the keel up as carriers. They were not completed until after the war.

Shinano. Arguably the most poorly designed carrier built during the war, *Shinano* was laid down as a battleship of the *Yamato* Class, and ordered converted when about 50 percent complete. She retained much of her battleship armor. Intended to serve as an aircraft carrier support vessel, providing repair and replenishment facilities for other carriers, *Shinano* could store about 50 percent more aircraft than she could operate. She was sunk while under tow to a fitting-out yard when a U.S. submarine put four torpedoes into her on November 29, 1944, just ten days after she had been completed. She required seven hours to sink, testimony to her excellent protection. *Shinano* was the largest aircraft carrier built until 1960.

Shokaku. Japan's best prewar carriers, *Shokaku* and *Zuikaku*, entered service only a few months before Pearl Harbor. Much larger versions of *Hiryu*, they were better protected and had a greater avgas capacity, but could operate only about the same number of aircraft. They were at Pearl Harbor and the Coral Sea, where damage to *Shokaku* and losses among their air groups resulted in their missing Midway. *Shokaku* survived six bombs in the Battle of the Santa Cruz Islands, but succumbed to three submarine torpedoes during the Battle of the Philippine Sea in June 1944, while *Zuikaku* took seven torpedoes and six bombs from U.S. naval aircraft before sinking off Cape Engaño in October 1944.

Soryu. *Soryu* was a well-designed ship, lightly built and fast, with an aircraft operational capacity equal to that of *Akagi* or *Kaga*, both of which were about twice her displacement. She accompanied them from Pearl Harbor to Midway, where she took three bombs, burst into flames, and blew up.

Taiho. Arguably the culmination of Japanese carrier design, *Taiho* was a large, fast, well-protected ship, but, like all Japanese carriers, suffered from a limited aircraft-operating capacity: Displacing about 10 percent more than the American *Essex*, *Taiho* was rated at only about 85 aircraft, as against 100 on *Essex*, and in fact could actually operate only about 60 percent of those. Supposed to be the lead ship of a batch of seven carriers more or less on the same design, she was the only one ever laid down. *Taiho* was sunk on June 19, 1944, during the Battle of the Philippine Sea, when a U.S. submarine put a single torpedo into her, causing an avgas leak with which inept damage control failed to cope, leading to the accumulation of volatile fumes in confined spaces, resulting in a fatal explosion.

Unicorn. The British soon found that *Unicorn*, originally built as an aircraft maintenance ship, was eminently suitable as a light carrier, if slow. Lacking the extensive protection preferred by British carrier designers, she had aircraft capacity equal to that of the *Illustrious* Class fleet carriers. She served with the Royal Navy in Japanese waters in mid-1945.

Unryu. Essentially modified *Hiryus*, Japan's *Unryu* Class carriers were built quickly (twenty-two to twenty-four months from keel to completion). Good ships, despite their limited aircraft capacity, they saw little action, Japan being unable to provide adequate air groups. *Unryu* was sunk by two torpedoes from a U.S. submarine in the South China Sea on December 19, 1944, and *Amagi* capsized in Kure Harbor on July 24, 1945, after being pounded by U.S. naval aircraft. *Katsuragi* survived the war, to be scrapped, as were three incomplete units.

Wasp. Designed to squeeze the last few thousand tons out of the U.S. Navy's carrier allocation under the terms of the naval disarmament treaties, *Wasp* was a greatly improved *Ranger*, with better protection and stability. Although not wholly suited to the demands of war in the Pacific, she gave a good account of herself until sunk by three torpedoes from a Japanese submarine on September 15, 1942, off the Solomons.

Yorktown. One of the most successful classes of warship ever built, the *Yorktowns* were the model for all later U.S. carrier designs. Relatively large, fast, very seaworthy vessels with excellent protection and large aircraft complements, they played an enormous part in the Pacific war, garnering great distinction in the process. *Yorktown*, only partially repaired from bomb damage at the Coral Sea, took several bombs and two torpedoes at Midway (June 4, 1942) and was temporarily abandoned, to be taken in tow the next day. On June 6 a Japanese submarine put two more torpedoes into her and she finally went down. During the Battle of the Santa Cruz Islands (October 24, 1942) *Hornet*, built several years later to the same design, took four Japanese bombs and three aerial torpedoes plus two suicide crashes by damaged Japanese aircraft, which caused considerable damage and engine failure. Since her hull remained sound, she was taken under tow, only to absorb three more Japanese bombs the following morning. As Japanese surface units were known to be closing in, it was decided to scuttle the ship, but despite about 300 rounds of 5-inch shells and nine torpedoes from U.S. destroyers (not all of which went off), she refused to sink. Abandoned, she was found later by Japanese surface forces, which finished her off with four 24-inch Long Lance torpedoes. The third member of the class, *Enterprise*, "The Big E," saw the most extensive service of any U.S. ship in the war, and emerged from it as the most highly decorated vessel in American naval history.

Zuiho. The *Zuiho*s were converted from Japanese submarine tenders that had been designed with such a contingency in mind. Rather successful ships, fast and with a reasonable aircraft operating capacity, they were surprisingly tough: *Shoho* took eleven bombs and about seven torpedoes before sinking at the Coral Sea in May 1942, while *Zuiho* went down after a nearly equal pounding off Cape Engaño in October 1944.

ESCORT CARRIERS

Bogue. Escort carriers converted from reciprocating-steam-engined C3 merchant hulls under construction at the time the United States entered the war, the twenty-one *Bogues* (of which ten were built for Britain), although displacing less than *Long Island* (about 14,000 tons full load as against about 15,000) and no faster, were more responsive to their helms, had a much greater aircraft complement (initially sixteen fighters and twelve torpedo bombers), and possessed an island superstructure. Like *Long Island*, they were very cramped internally. They saw extensive antisubmarine service in the Atlantic, and several were employed in a variety of roles in the Pacific.

ESCORT AIRCRAFT CARRIERS

Navy	Class	Combat Surf	AAA	Displacement Std	Full	Length	Beam	Draft	HP	Spd	Armor Belt	Turret	Deck	Tower	A/C	Guns Main	Sec	DP	AAA	HMG	TT	DC	Crew	Tot	Year
US	Bogue	1	4	9.4	13.9	151.1	34.0	7.1	8.5	16.5	0.0	0.0	0.0	0.0	28	None	None	2x5	None	14	0	0	890	11	1942
US	Casablanca	1	5	8.2	10.9	149.4	19.9	6.3	9.0	19.0	0.0	0.0	0.0	0.0	27	None	None	1x5	None	20	0	0	860	50	1943
US	Commencement B	2	15	18.9	21.4	169.9	32.1	8.5	16.0	19.0	0.0	0.0	0.0	0.0	33	None	None	2x5	None	56	0	0	1066	22	1944
Jp	Kaiyo	2	4	13.6	16.5	155.0	21.9	8.0	52.0	23.0	0.0	0.0	0.0	0.0	24	None	None	8x5	None	24	8	0	829	1	1943
US	Long Island	1	2	11.5	15.0	141.7	21.2	7.7	8.5	16.5	0.0	0.0	0.0	0.0	16	None	None	1x4, 2x3	None	4	0	0	856	1	1942
US	Sangamon	6	5	10.5	23.9	160.0	22.9	9.3	13.5	18.0	0.0	0.0	0.0	0.0	31	None	None	1x5	None	20	0	0	1080	4	1942
Jp	Shinyo	2	4	17.5	20.6	185.0	25.6	8.2	26.0	22.0	0.0	0.0	0.0	0.0	33	None	None	8x5	None	30	0	0	942	1	1943
Jp	Taiyo	2	3	17.8	19.7	168.0	22.5	7.7	25.5	21.0	0.0	0.0	0.0	0.0	27	None	None	None	6x4.7	8	0	0	850	3	1941

NOTE: See page 99 for an explanation of the items on this table.

Casablanca. Based on experience gained from *Long Island* and other escort carriers converted from merchant hulls, the forty-nine ships of the *Casablanca* Class were ordered as purpose-built escort carriers in early 1942, laid down between March 1942 and March 1943, and took only three to four months each to complete due to innovative mass-production construction methods introduced by Kaiser Industries. They saw extensive service in the Pacific, where four were lost, two by battleship gunfire off Samar on October 25, 1944, and two by Kamikaze attack.

Commencement Bay. A large class (twenty-three units, of which four were canceled and only about eight completed in time to take part in the war) ordered in 1943, *Commencement Bay* and her sisters were based on the very successful *Sangamon* Class escort carriers, being slightly smaller (about 21,400 tons to 23,800) and somewhat faster (19 knots to 18) than their predecessors, and able to operate slightly more (thirty-three to thirty-one) aircraft. They were also more reliable, better sea boats, and much better armed (fifty-eight antiaircraft barrels as against thirty on *Sangamon*). *Commencement Bay* and her sisters were built in improvised Pacific Coast shipyards using mass-production techniques that proved enormously successful.

Kaiyo. Converted from a passenger liner, *Kaiyo* served as an aircraft transport and training ship rather than an escort carrier. Although severely damaged, she survived the war to be scrapped. Conversion of a sister ship was planned, but the vessel was sunk before the work could be undertaken.

Long Island. The first American escort carrier, *Long Island* was a pet project of President Roosevelt's, partially inspired by British efforts to build such vessels. Converted from an incomplete standard diesel-powered C3 cargo ship, M/S (Motor Ship) *Mormacmail*, in about a year. Although slow (16.5 knots), somewhat unresponsive to her helm, and with limited aircraft capacity (her first air group was ten observation planes and six scout bombers), *Long Island* proved very satisfactory. Shortly after Pearl Harbor she was transferred to the Pacific, where she supported the battleline (composed of Pearl Harbor survivors and other old battleships transferred from the Atlantic) during the Midway campaign. She was later used as a training ship and aircraft transport. Unlike later U.S. escort carriers, she had no island superstructure. Her near-sister USS *Charger* (CVE 30) was converted later, to a somewhat different plan.

Sangamon. Converted from incomplete tanker versions of the standard Maritime Commission C3 hull, the *Sangamons* were much superior to the *Long Island* or *Bogue* design, being larger (23,800 tons full load) and somewhat faster (18 knots), with slightly more aircraft (thirty-one), better defensive armament, and more internal space, making servicing the aircraft much easier. As an added bonus, they retained an enormous fuel capacity (over 12,000 tons), being, in effect, self-escorting tankers. They were among the best escort carriers, seeing extensive service, and inspiring the *Commencement Bay* design.

Shinyo. Converted into an escort carrier from a German passenger liner that found itself in Japan at the outbreak of the war, *Shinyo* had an uneventful career until July 17, 1944, when she was torpedoed by a U.S. submarine.

Taiyo. Converted from ocean liners under construction at the start of the war, the *Taiyos* were much larger than comparable Allied escort carriers. Their primary mission was not in an escort role, but rather as aircraft transports and training ships. All were sunk by U.S. submarines.

HEAVY CRUISERS

Aoba. Essentially improved *Furutaka* Class heavy cruisers, mounting their 8-inch guns in twin turrets from the start, the *Aobas* saw extensive service, notably in the Solomons. A very durable ship, at one point in her career *Aoba* was reduced to a total wreck above the main deck, yet was still able to make speed and ultimately returned to service. Both were sunk by U.S. carrier aircraft. With the *Furutaka* Class they were the smallest heavy cruisers ever built.

Australia. The *Australia* Class heavy cruisers shared with their sister ships of the British *Kent* Class a general lack of handiness at sea, having a very wide turning circle. As in all British-designed heavy cruisers, they had minimal protection in the form of an armored box. They were well built and resilient: *Canberra* sank after taking about twenty hits of 4.7-inch to 8-inch shells, plus possibly two torpedoes, in three minutes at Savo Island (August 9, 1942), while *Australia* survived six Kamikaze strikes off Okinawa in 1945.

Baltimore. These were the best American heavy cruisers of the

HEAVY CRUISERS

Navy	Class	Combat		Displacement		Length	Beam	Draft	HP	Spd	Armor				A/C	Guns		DP	AAA	HMG	TT	DC	Crew		Year
		Surf	AAA	Std	Full						Belt	Turret	Deck	Tower		Main	Sec						Crew	Tot	
Jp	Aoba	12	2	9.0	10.7	177.5	17.6	5.7	102.0	33.0	3.0	1.0	1.4	3.0	2	6x8	None	None	4x4.7	12	12	0	625	2	1927
Au	Australia	14	3	10.9	14.5	179.8	20.8	6.3	80.0	31.5	4.5	1.0	1.0	0.0	3	8x8	None	8x4	None	4	0	0	698	2	1942
US	Baltimore	16	23	14.5	17.0	202.4	21.6	7.3	120.0	33.0	6.0	8.0	2.5	6.0	4	9x8	None	12x5	None	72	0	0	2039	24	1943
US	Des Moines	16	23	17.2	20.9	213.4	23.0	7.9	120.0	33.0	6.0	8.0	3.5	6.5	4	9x8	None	12x5	None	72	0	0	1799	4	MHB
Br	Exeter	11	6	8.4	10.5	164.6	17.7	6.2	80.0	32.0	3.0	1.0	1.0	3.0	2	6x8	None	8x4	4x4.7	16	6	0	630	1	1930
Jp	Furutaka	12	2	8.7	10.3	176.8	16.9	5.6	102.0	33.0	3.0	1.0	1.4	3.0	2	6x8	None	None	None	12	8	0	625	2	1926
Br	Kent	14	4	10.9	14.5	179.8	20.8	6.3	80.0	31.5	4.5	1.0	1.0	3.0	3	8x8	None	8x4	None	8	8	0	698	5	1928
Br	London	14	4	10.8	14.4	181.4	20.1	6.3	80.0	32.3	3.5	1.0	1.0	3.0	3	8x8	None	8x4	None	16	8	0	700	4	1929
Jp	Mogami (B)	14	6	12.4	15.5	198.0	20.2	5.9	152.0	34.9	4.9	1.0	2.4	3.0	3	8x8	None	8x5	None	12	12	0	850	4	1940
Jp	Mogami (C)	7	3	12.2	15.5	198.0	20.2	5.9	152.0	35.0	4.9	1.0	2.4	3.0	11	4x8	None	8x5	None	30	12	0	850	1	1943
Jp	Nachi	16	5	13.0	16.5	201.7	20.7	6.3	130.0	33.0	3.9	1.0	1.4	3.0	3	10x8	None	8x5	None	10	16	0	773	4	1928
US	New Orleans	15	5	10.1	12.5	176.2	18.8	6.9	107.0	32.7	5.8	6.0	2.5	6.0	4	9x8	None	None	8x5	8	0	0	868	7	1934
Br	Norfolk	14	6	10.0	13.4	181.4	20.1	6.4	80.0	32.3	1.0	1.0	1.0	3.0	1	8x8	None	8x4	None	16	8	0	710	6	1930
US	Northampton	15	5	9.0	11.4	177.4	20.1	5.9	107.0	32.5	3.8	2.5	2.0	2.5	4	9x8	None	None	8x5	8	0	0	740	6	1930
US	Pensacola	16	5	9.1	11.5	173.7	19.9	5.9	107.0	32.5	4.0	2.5	1.8	2.5	4	10x8	None	None	8x5	8	0	0	631	2	1933
US	Portland	15	5	10.3	12.8	180.4	20.1	6.4	107.0	32.5	3.0	2.5	2.5	2.5	3	9x8	None	None	8x5	8	0	0	807	2	1933
Jp	Takao	16	5	13.4	16.5	201.7	20.7	6.3	130.0	34.2	4.9	1.0	1.4	3.0	3	10x8	None	8x5	None	12	16	0	773	4	1932
Jp	Tone	14	3	11.2	15.2	189.1	18.5	6.5	152.0	35.0	4.9	1.0	2.4	3.0	6	8x8	None	8x5	None	12	12	0	850	2	1938
US	Wichita	15	5	10.6	13.0	182.9	18.8	7.2	100.0	33.0	6.0	8.0	2.5	6.0	4	9x8	None	8x5	None	8	0	0	929	1	1939

NOTE: See page 99 for an explanation of the items on this table. Some classes are not mentioned in the text.

war, and the largest class of heavy cruisers ever built, twelve of an order of twenty-four being completed in two somewhat different designs (*Baltimore* and *Oregon City*), some after the war. Free of the restrictions of the naval disarmament treaties, the *Baltimores* displaced over 40 percent more than the older American heavy cruisers. Although not particularly better armored than the experimental *Wichita*, they were better constructed, had superior antiaircraft defenses, were much more stable, and were far more comfortable. They proved excellent escorts for carrier task forces, but were never tested in surface actions against their Japanese counterparts.

Des Moines. The culmination of U.S. heavy cruiser design, and the largest heavy cruisers ever built, the three *Des Moines* Class ships were superior to any previous heavy cruisers, having a fully automatic 8-inch gun, enormous displacement, extensive protection, and much better sea-keeping qualities. Begun late in the war, all were completed after it. They would have been deadly opponents in a surface action.

Exeter. *Exeter* was a British attempt to design a "lite" heavy cruiser, the larger eight-gunned vessels having proven unsatisfactory for Britain's peacetime naval requirements. A successful ship, though undergunned by the standards of the Pacific war, she was extremely sturdy. In the action with the German pocket battleship *Graf Spee* in December 1939, she survived seven 11-inch hits (over 5,000 pounds of explosive shells), although they put her out of action, and at the Sunda Strait (March 1, 1942) she succumbed only after having taken scores of hits from Japanese heavy cruisers.

Furutaka. Japan's first "treaty cruisers," the *Furutaka*s were quite small for heavy cruisers. As completed, they mounted their six 8-inch guns in single turrets, converting to double turrets only after an extensive refit in the late 1930s, when their protection, quite light, was somewhat improved, with a concomitant reduction in speed. Both saw extensive service, particularly in the Solomon Islands, where *Kako* was torpedoed on August 10, 1942, and *Furutaka* sunk in a night action off Guadalcanal on October 11, 1942.

London. Although apparently even less handy than the *Kent* Class heavy cruisers, which they greatly resembled, the *Londons* were otherwise satisfactory ships. One ship, *Shropshire*, was later transferred to the Royal Australian Navy and gave good service in the Southwest Pacific and the Philippines.

Mogami. Originally designed as light cruisers (A in the light cruiser table), mounting fifteen 6-inch guns, the *Mogami*s appear to have been poorly constructed. Refitted several times, in 1939–1941 they were converted to heavy cruisers mounting ten 8-inch guns (B in the heavy cruiser table). Despite their shortcomings, they were tough ships: *Mogami* was literally left a burning wreck after Midway, yet remained afloat, managed to restore power, and returned to Japan for an extensive refit, during which she was converted to something like the *Tone* Class, with six 8-inch guns in three turrets forward and a flight deck aft, to operate a large number of floatplanes (C in the heavy cruiser table). All members of the class became war losses.

Nachi. Good ships, designed with the experience of the *Furutaka*s and *Aoba*s in mind, the *Nachi*s were much better protected, more stable, and somewhat faster vessels, being much larger (in violation of the 10,000-ton limit imposed by the naval limitation treaties). Like all Japanese cruisers, they saw considerable service, spending much of the war in the East Indies and the Indian Ocean. All became war losses. Tough ships: *Haguro* sank after taking eight torpedoes from British destroyers on May 16, 1945, in the last surface action of the war, and *Ashigara* five from a British submarine on June 8, 1945.

New Orleans. Representing a significant break with the earlier series of U.S. heavy cruisers, the *New Orleans* Class was much better protected. Despite this, three of the ships in the class became war losses in less than five minutes in the Battle of Savo Island on the night of August 9–10, 1942, no design being able to ensure against overconfidence, inexperience, bad luck, and a daring foe.

Norfolk. The principal difference between *Norfolk* and earlier British heavy cruisers lay in improved turret design and ammunition handling arrangements. They were tough ships, *Dorsetshire* taking ten Japanese 250- to 500-pound bombs in about eight minutes on March 5, 1942, before sinking, while *Norfolk* once survived two 11-inch rounds from the German battleship *Scharnhorst*.

Northampton. Less heavily armed than the *Pensacola*s, the *Northampton*s were somewhat better protected. Prewar modifications removed their torpedo tubes, but enhanced their antiaircraft protection. All saw hard service, and three became war losses. Despite their rather light protection, they were tough ships: *Houston,* already damaged some days earlier, took at least four torpedoes and scores of 8-inch and 5-inch rounds before going down in the Sunda Strait on March 1, 1942.

Pensacola. The first American "treaty cruisers," the *Pensacolas* were provided with a powerful offensive armament but were lightly protected, a design policy that was not continued in later classes. Like all U.S. heavy cruisers, they had their torpedo tubes removed before the war, a loss that would be felt during the numerous surface actions of the Pacific war. They saw extensive service.

Portland. Essentially somewhat modified *Northampton* Class heavy cruisers, the *Portlands* were slightly better protected. They saw extensive service in the war. *Indianapolis* was lost to a Japanese submarine on July 29, 1945, the last major American vessel sunk in the war.

Takao. An improvement on the *Nachi* Class heavy cruisers, the *Takaos* were bigger and better protected. All had extensive war service, *Atago* as a flagship. All became war losses, taking considerable punishment before succumbing: *Atago* and *Maya* were sunk by four torpedoes each from a U.S. submarine on October 23, 1944.

Tone. Designed as light cruisers with a dozen 6-inch guns, in four turrets all forward, but converted to four 8-inch guns while still building, the *Tones* were the best Japanese heavy cruisers, combining high speed, heavy armament, extensive protections, good seakeeping qualities, excellent maneuverability, and a very large seaplane complement, to enhance their role as fleet scouts. Although rated at six aircraft, they apparently never carried more than five. Both were sunk by U.S. carrier aircraft.

Wichita. An experiment, *Wichita* was essentially a heavy cruiser version of the *Brooklyn* Class light cruisers. As those were by no means wholly successful, neither was she, being a bit top-heavy. She was, however, much better protected than earlier American heavy cruisers and had an improved 8-inch turret. Experience gained from *Wichita* proved enormously valuable in the design of the *Baltimore* Class.

LIGHT CRUISERS

Adelaide. A World War I–era cruiser, *Adelaide* was obsolete long before the Pacific war began, and was quickly relegated to escort duties.

Agano. Like all Japanese light cruisers, the *Agano* Class ships were designed to serve as flotilla leaders. As a result, they were much more lightly armed than contemporary foreign light cruisers, even considering their relatively small displacement. They were, however, good sea boats, fast and handy. Three were sunk by U.S. naval aircraft and one was expended as a target in the Bikini nuclear tests.

Ajax. The British *Ajax* Class light cruisers were sisters to New Zealand's *Leander* Class ships. They were good ships, but of only limited value in the Pacific, being rather undergunned and "short-legged" (i.e., of relatively short endurance). They were, however, well built: *Neptune* went down slowly after striking three mines in quick succession, demonstrating their resilience.

Brooklyn. Designed to counter the fifteen-gunned original version of the Japanese *Mogami* Class, America's *Brooklyns*—which differed somewhat among themselves—were only partially satisfactory. However, experience gained from them proved valuable in the design of subsequent American cruisers, both heavy and light. One ship became a war loss: *Helena*, which was sunk by three torpedoes at the Battle of Kula Gulf on July 6, 1943. Another, having been sold to Argentina, became the first warship sunk by a nuclear submarine, during the Falklands War with Britain in 1982.

Cleveland. The best American light cruisers of the war, and the most numerous class of light cruisers ever built, twenty-nine being commissioned out of an order of fifty-two (not including nine other hulls completed as light aircraft carriers), the *Clevelands* were superior to the *Brooklyns*, despite having three fewer 6-inch guns. The class was, however, rather top-heavy and cramped. Despite this they rendered excellent service in the war, none becoming casualties despite often being in the thick of surface actions in the Southwest Pacific.

DeRuyter. Well designed for her primary role, showing the Dutch flag in the Far East, *DeRuyter* was outclassed by contemporary Japanese and American light cruisers. Flagship of the ABDA squadron in the early months of the war, she went down fighting in the Java

LIGHT CRUISERS

Navy	Class	Combat Surf	AAA	Displacement Std	Full	Length	Beam	Draft	HP	Spd	Armor Belt	Turret	Deck	Tower	A/C	Guns Main	Sec	DP	AAA	HMG	TT	DC	Crew	Tot	Year
NZ	Achilles	4	3	7.1	9.2	159.1	17.0	5.8	72.0	32.5	4.0	1.0	1.3	1.0	1	8x6	None	4x4	None	8	8	0	570	2	1933
Au	Adelaide	6	1	5.1	6.1	140.2	15.1	5.4	25.0	25.5	3.0	0.0	2.0	0.0	0	8x6	None	4x4	None	None	0	0	470	1	1922
Jp	Agano	4	4	6.7	8.5	162.0	15.2	5.6	100.0	35.0	2.2	1.0	0.7	3.0	2	6x6	None	None	4x3	32	8	16	730	4	1942
Br	Arethusa	4	4	5.3	6.7	146.3	15.5	5.0	64.0	32.3	2.3	1.0	1.0	3.0	1	6x6	None	8x4	None	8	6	0	500	4	1935
US	Brooklyn	14	9	9.8	12.2	182.9	18.8	6.9	100.0	32.5	5.0	6.5	2.0	5.0	4	15x6	None	8x5	None	24	0	0	686	9	1938
US	Cleveland	6	14	11.7	14.1	182.9	20.2	7.5	100.0	32.5	5.0	6.5	2.0	5.0	4	12x6	None	12x5	None	38	0	0	1285	29	1942
Nth	De Ruyter	4	2	6.0	7.5	168.3	15.7	5.1	76.0	33.5	2.0	1.2	1.2	1.2	1	7x5.9	None	None	None	18	0	0	435	1	1935
Fr	Duguay Trouin	4	2	7.2	9.4	175.3	17.2	5.2	100.0	33.0	0.8	1.0	0.8	1.0	2	8x6.1	None	None	4x3	4	12	0	578	3	1926
Br	Edinburgh	6	6	10.6	13.2	176.5	19.3	6.5	80.0	32.5	4.5	4.0	2.0	3.0	3	12x6	None	12x4	None	16	6	0	850	2	1939
Br	Enterprise	4	3	7.6	9.2	162.1	16.5	5.0	80.0	32.0	3.0	1.0	1.0	3.0	1	7x6	None	None	5x4	6	16	0	572	2	1926
Br	Fiji	5	4	8.5	10.5	164.0	18.9	6.0	72.5	31.5	3.5	2.0	2.0	0.0	2	12x6	None	8x4	None	8	6	0	920	8	1940
Br	Gloucester	5	4	9.4	11.7	170.1	19.0	6.3	82.5	32.3	4.5	2.0	2.0	0.0	3	12x6	None	8x4	None	8	6	0	800	3	1939
Nth	Java	3	3	6.7	7.2	155.3	16.0	5.5	72.0	31.0	3.0	4.0	2.0	5.0	0	10x5.9	None	None	None	10	0	0	525	3	1925
Jp	Katori	2	1	5.9	6.2	123.5	16.0	5.8	8.0	18.0	0.0	0.0	2.0	0.0	1	4x5.5	None	2x5	None	4	4	0	400	4	1940
Jp	Kuma	2	1	5.6	7.0	162.1	14.2	4.8	90.0	33.6	2.5	1.0	1.3	0.0	0	7x5.5	None	None	2x3.1	2	8	0	450	5	1920
Fr	La Galissonniere	4	7	7.6	9.1	172.0	17.5	5.4	84.0	31.0	4.0	4.0	1.5	3.8	4	9x6	None	None	8x3.5	20	4	0	764	6	1935
NZ	Leander	4	3	7.1	9.2	159.1	17.0	5.8	72.0	32.5	4.0	1.0	1.3	1.0	1	8x6	None	4x4	None	8	8	0	570	3	1933
Jp	Mogami (A)	14	3	11.2	15.0	198.1	19.2	5.9	152.0	35.0	4.9	1.0	2.4	3.0	3	15x6	None	8x5	None	12	12	0	850	4	1935
Jp	Nagara	4	1	5.6	6.5	162.1	14.2	4.8	90.0	34.5	2.5	1.0	1.3	0.0	1	7x5.5	None	None	2x3.1	2	8	0	450	6	1921
US	Omaha	12	3	7.1	9.5	169.4	16.9	4.1	90.0	34.0	3.0	0.0	1.5	0.0	2	12x6	None	None	2x3	12	10	0	458	10	1922
Jp	Oyodo	4	2	8.2	11.4	180.0	16.6	6.0	110.0	35.0	2.0	1.0	1.4	0.0	6	6x6	None	None	8x3.9	12	0	0	750	1	1943
Au	Perth	4	2	7.1	9.1	159.1	17.3	6.0	90.0	32.5	4.0	1.0	1.1	0.0	1	8x6	None	8x4	None	None	8	0	570	3	1936
Jp	Sendai	4	1	5.2	7.1	152.4	14.2	4.9	90.0	35.2	2.5	1.0	1.0	0.0	1	7x5.5	None	None	2x3	2	8	0	450	3	1924
Br	Southampton	6	4	9.1	11.4	170.1	18.8	6.2	75.0	32.0	4.5	1.0	2.0	3.0	3	12x6	None	8x4	None	8	6	0	748	5	1937
Br	Swiftsure	5	6	8.8	11.1	164.0	19.2	6.4	72.5	31.5	3.5	2.0	2.0	3.0	0	9x6	None	10x4	None	16	6	0	960	2	1944
Jp	Tenryu	2	1	3.9	4.4	142.9	12.3	4.0	51.0	33.0	2.0	1.0	1.0	0.0	0	4x5.5	None	None	3x3.1	2	6	0	327	2	1919
Nth	Tromp	4	1	3.8	4.8	125.0	12.4	4.2	56.0	33.5	0.6	0.6	1.0	0.5	0	6x5.9	None	None	None	12	6	0	309	1	1940
Br	Uganda	6	5	8.5	10.5	164.0	18.9	6.0	72.5	31.5	3.5	2.0	1.0	0.0	2	9x6	None	8x4	None	12	6	0	920	3	1943
Jp	Yubari	3	0	3.4	4.4	132.6	12.0	3.6	57.5	33.0	2.3	1.0	1.0	0.0	0	6x5.5	None	None	1x3	2	4	0	328	1	1923

NOTE: See page 99 for an explanation of the items on this table. Some classes are not mentioned in the text.

Sea on February 28, 1942, having absorbed several torpedoes and numerous shells.

Duguay-Trouin. Fast, but virtually unarmored cruisers, *Duguay-Trouin* and her sisters were designed by the French Navy for Mediterranean conditions, and were not successful ships. One, *Lamotte-Picquet,* was stationed in Indochina and gave a fair account of herself against some Thai gunboats armed with 8-inch guns during the brief Vichy-Thailand War in early 1941. She was otherwise inactive during the war and was sunk by U.S. carrier aircraft in 1945. Note that since these ships mounted 6.1-inch guns, they were technically heavy cruisers under the terms of the various naval disarmament treaties of the 1920s.

Edinburgh. The best British light cruisers of the war, incorporating the experience of the *Southampton* and *Gloucester* classes, the *Edinburghs* were also the largest British cruisers in the war. *Edinburgh* was lost in action, while her sister, HMS *Belfast,* is a war memorial in the Thames.

Fiji. In the "Colony" or *Fiji* Class light cruisers, the British attempted to do too much on a relatively small displacement. As a result, although the ships rendered good service, they were somewhat top-heavy and vulnerable: *Fiji* succumbed to one bomb and some near misses, while several others were nearly sunk by single torpedo hits.

Java. Although completed in the mid-1920s, the Netherlands' *Java* Class light cruisers had been laid down during World War I, and despite some modernization were very outdated by the Second World War. *Java* went down fighting in the Battle of the Java Sea on February 27, 1942. *Sumatra* had been undergoing a leisurely refit at Soerabaja when the war began. Unfit for duty, she managed to escape but saw no service in the war, being scuttled to form part of the Normandy beach breakwaters in 1944.

Katori. A peculiar class, Japan's *Katoris* were designed as training cruisers, escorts, and flotilla leaders for submarines. Very underarmed and underengined, they were not particularly useful vessels and their construction demonstrates some of the muddle that prevailed in Japanese military circles prior to the war. One was sunk by U.S. naval aircraft and a second by naval aircraft and gunfire, while the third survived the war.

Kent. Britain's first "treaty cruisers," the *Kents* were sisters to the *Australias.* Although not the handiest ships, and relatively lightly protected, they were well designed and rather resilient: *Cornwall* took nine hits and six near misses by Japanese 250- to 500-pound bombs in twelve minutes before sinking on March 5, 1942.

Kuma. Small ships, essentially obsolete by World War II standards, like most Japanese light cruisers the *Kumas* served mostly as flotilla leaders. Shortly before the war began, two units of the class were converted into torpedo cruisers, mounting a record forty tubes, but they were never tested in a surface action. All members of the class were extensively modified during the war. All but one became war losses.

La Gallissonier. The best French light cruisers of World War II, these vessels were too small, too undergunned, and too lightly protected to be of much use in the Pacific, though some of them served in the Indian Ocean with the Royal Navy.

Leander. Good light cruisers in a European context, New Zealand's *Leanders* (sisters to Britain's *Ajax*) were of only limited value in the Pacific, having relatively short range and being rather lightly armed. Nevertheless, they were tough ships: *Leander* herself survived a Japanese 24-inch torpedo at Kolombangara, while *Achilles* and her British sister *Ajax* survived numerous 5.9-inch and 11-inch hits during their encounter with the German *Graf Spee* in December 1939.

Nagara. Like all older Japanese cruisers, the *Nagaras* were small, lightly built, fast, and very obsolete by World War II standards. They spent most of the war as flotilla leaders, though one was converted into an antiaircraft cruiser. All became war losses, three by submarine and three as a result of air attack.

Omaha. Although quite old, and no longer a match for contemporary light cruisers, the *Omahas* were excellent ships, well designed, reliable, fast, maneuverable, and very seaworthy, even by World War II standards, albeit rather crowded. They gave excellent service in all theaters, none becoming a war loss.

Oyodo. An enlarged version of *Agano*, *Oyodo* was intended to serve as a flagship for submarine flotillas, for which she was supposed to have a sizable complement of floatplanes on a design similar to that of the *Tone* Class heavy cruisers. During construction, plans were changed, and she emerged with enhanced antiaircraft defenses that were constantly improved during the war, so that by its end she was effectively an antiaircraft cruiser. This did not help her, as she was sunk in harbor by U.S. naval aircraft.

Perth. Australia's *Perth* Class cruisers were typical of British-designed light cruisers. Although lightly protected, they were rather resilient. HMAS *Sydney* was lost after she took at least one torpedo and numerous 5.9-inch rounds from the German raider *Kormoran* on November 19, 1941, having meanwhile accounted for her opponent, while *Perth* succumbed to three Japanese torpedoes and several 8-inch rounds in the Sunda Strait on March 1, 1942.

Sendai. The *Sendai*s served as flotilla leaders during the war, in which capacity two were sunk during surface actions, and the third by air attack. The best of the older Japanese cruisers, they took considerable punishment for such lightly built vessels.

Southampton. A very successful design, the *Southampton*s were the first British light cruisers comparable to contemporary U.S. or Japanese designs. They were good sea boats, had efficient ammunition handling arrangements, and had excellent firepower. They were also very sturdy. On January 11, 1941, *Southampton* took two or three German 550-pound bombs, which caused a series of fires that led to the abandonment of the ship, although she did not sink until five torpedoes were put into her.

Tenryu. Japan's oldest light cruisers, they were very small ships, and spent the war as flotilla leaders. Both were sunk by U.S. submarines.

Uganda. The *Uganda*s, sometimes referred to as the "Second Group" of the "Colony Class," were a rather successful attempt by the Royal Navy to improve the stability of the *Fiji* Class light cruisers by reducing the number of 6-inch guns from twelve to nine to save weight, and thereby improve stability. Several ships of this class accompanied the Royal Navy's carrier task force in the Pacific during 1945.

Yubari. An experimental light cruiser, *Yubari* was perhaps the most graceful-looking vessel in the Japanese Navy, but was otherwise a failure, as she was quite overloaded and unstable. On a hull designed to displace about 2,900 tons, she mounted virtually the same armament as the 5,900-ton *Sendai*. She was lost to U.S. naval aircraft.

ANTIAIRCRAFT CRUISERS

Atlanta. A highly successful design, the *Atlanta* Class antiaircraft light cruisers proved so valuable that even before the first batch of four had been completed, a second batch had been ordered to a slightly different design, and later a third batch, of three ships, was laid down, not to be completed until after the war. Although designed primarily to shoot down airplanes, the *Atlantas* did some of their hardest fighting in surface actions in the Solomon Islands, where their numerous rapid-fire 5-inch guns proved remarkably valuable. Two became war losses: *Atlanta* went down under the pounding of Japanese battleships and destroyers in a night action off Guadalcanal on November 12–13, 1943, during which *Juneau* was torpedoed, sinking quickly (and taking with her the five Sullivan brothers). Later versions of the design mounted their 5"/38 guns differently from earlier ones, and carried fewer pieces as well, which led to improved stability.

Bellona. The last and best variant of Britain's *Dido* group of antiaircraft light cruisers, the *Bellonas* had fewer 5.25-inch dual-purpose guns, but more light antiaircraft, making them much more stable ships. Like all British ships, however, they were handicapped by having a poor antiaircraft fire control system.

Charybdis. These were later versions of Britain's *Dido* Class antiaircraft light cruisers, with fewer 5.25-inch guns, the original design having attempted too much on so small a displacement.

Cleopatra. One of several variants of Britain's *Dido* Class antiaircraft cruisers, they were not significantly different from the preceding *Charybdis* group. Aside from some design changes, one reason for the numerous variations on the basic *Dido* design was Britain's great shortage of resources, which made it difficult to mass-produce ships to a single design.

Dido. A good antiaircraft cruiser design, modified through several subsequent versions as the Royal Navy gained experience with this type of vessel. The *Didos* had fine sea-keeping qualities. Although they were well designed for the antiaircraft role, they lacked an efficient fire control system and were not suited to a surface slugfest, as were their American counterparts, which were designed later. They were, in addition, rather fragile. Of eleven vessels in this and the slightly differing *Charybdis*, *Scylla*, and *Cleopatra* classes, two

ANTIAIRCRAFT CRUISERS

Navy	Class	Combat		Displacement		Length	Beam	Draft	HP	Spd	Armor				A/C	Guns			AAA	HMG	TT	DC	Crew	Tot	Year
		Surf	AAA	Std	Full						Belt	Turret	Deck	Tower		Main	Sec	DP							
US	Atlanta	8	12	6.7	8.3	161.6	16.2	6.3	75.0	32.5	3.8	1.3	0.3	3.8	0	None	None	16x5	None	24	8	0	623	11	1942
Br	Bellona	2	6	6.0	7.8	147.8	15.4	5.4	62.0	32.0	3.0	1.0	1.0	3.0	0	None	None	8x5.25	None	12	6	0	530	5	1943
Br	Charybdis	2	4	5.6	7.3	147.8	15.4	5.1	62.0	32.2	3.0	0.5	1.0	3.0	0	None	None	8x4.5	None	8	6	0	500	1	1941
Br	Cleopatra	3	6	5.6	7.3	147.8	15.4	5.1	62.0	32.2	3.0	0.5	1.0	3.0	0	None	None	10x5.25	None	8	6	0	530	6	1940
Br	Dido	2	5	5.6	7.3	147.8	15.4	5.1	62.0	32.2	3.0	0.5	1.0	3.0	0	None	None	8x5.25	None	8	6	0	500	3	1940
Nth	J van Heemskerck	4	4	3.8	4.8	125.0	12.4	4.2	56.0	33.5	0.6	0.0	1.0	0.5	0	None	None	10x4	None	10	6	0	309	1	1942
Br	Scylla	2	4	5.6	7.3	147.8	15.4	5.1	62.0	32.2	3.0	0.5	1.0	3.0	0	None	None	8x4.5	None	8	6	0	500	1	1942
US	Worcester	14	19	14.7	18.0	202.4	21.5	7.5	120.0	33.0	5.0	6.5	3.5	5.0	4	None	None	12x6	24x3	36	0	0	1401	2	1948

NOTE: See page 99 for an explanation of the items on this table.

succumbed to a single torpedo each, two went down after taking two torpedoes, and one was rendered a constructive total loss by a single mine, albeit that several others survived equivalent damage.

Jacob van Heemskerck. Designed by the Royal Netherlands Navy as a sister ship to *Tromp*, *van Heemskerck* was intended to be a very small, very fast light cruiser (really an enlarged flotilla leader) for service in the East Indies. Fitting out in the Netherlands when the Nazis invaded, both ships were towed to England and completed there. *Tromp*, much further along in construction, was completed to the original design, and saw extensive service in the Atlantic. *Van Heemskerck*, having only recently been launched when the Germans arrived, was completed as an antiaircraft cruiser. She saw considerable service with the British Far Eastern Fleet in the Indian Ocean, although her abilities as an antiaircraft cruiser were never tested.

Scylla. One of the numerous variations of Britain's *Dido* Class antiaircraft cruisers, differing mostly in armament and some technical details.

Worcester. Extremely large light cruisers laid down in early 1945, the *Worcesters* had a new double turret that permitted their 6-inch guns to be used in both antiship and antiaircraft roles, making them the most powerful antiaircraft cruisers ever built.

DESTROYERS

Akatsuki. Completed in the late 1920s, the four destroyers of the Japanese *Akatsuki* Class were modified versions of *Fubuki*, slightly smaller but with virtually the same capabilities. Refitted in the mid-1930s, they gained displacement but lost some speed. They saw considerable service, particularly in the Solomons, where *Akatsuki* was sunk during the night action off Guadalcanal on November 12–13, 1942. Only one unit survived the war.

Akitsuki. Japan ordered the sixteen destroyers of the *Akitsuki* Class in 1939–1941, but only thirteen were actually laid down and twelve completed, while thirty-seven others ordered in 1942 were never begun. Large vessels, designed as escorts for carrier task forces, the *Akitsuki* Class destroyers had an unusual main armament oriented primarily toward antiaircraft protection: eight 3.9"/65 dual-purpose (antiship and antiaircraft) guns, rather than the usual six

DESTROYERS

Navy	Class	Combat Surf	AAA	Displacement Std	Full	Length	Beam	Draft	HP	Spd	Armor Belt	Turret	Deck	Tower	A/C	Guns Main	Sec	DP	AAA	HMG	TT	DC	Crew	Tot	Ye
Br	Acasta	3	3	1.4	1.8	95.1	9.8	3.7	34.0	35.3	0.0	0.0	0.0	0.0	0	None	None	4x4.7	1x3	6	4	30	138	1	192
Jp	Akatsuki	2	2	1.7	2.0	106.7	10.4	3.3	50.0	34.0	0.0	0.0	0.0	0.0	0	None	None	4x5	None	14	9	36	200	4	193
Jp	Akitsuki	2	8	2.7	3.7	126.0	11.6	4.2	52.0	33.0	0.0	0.0	0.0	0.0	0	None	None	8x3.9	None	4	10	72	300	13	194
US	Allen M. Sumner	2	2	2.6	3.2	112.5	12.5	4.3	60.0	36.5	0.0	0.0	0.0	0.0	0	None	None	6x5	None	23	4	6	336	58	194
Au	Arunta	2	2	2.0	2.5	108.4	11.1	4.0	44.0	36.4	0.0	0.0	0.0	0.0	0	None	None	8x4.7	None	4	8	30	220	3	194
Jp	Asashio	2	3	2.0	2.3	111.0	10.4	3.7	50.0	35.0	0.0	0.0	0.0	0.0	0	None	None	6x5	None	4	8	16	200	10	193
US	Bagley	2	3	1.8	2.3	103.9	11.0	3.9	50.0	35.0	0.0	0.0	0.0	0.0	0	None	None	5x5	None	4	16	10	192	8	193
US	Benham	4	2	1.7	2.3	103.9	10.8	3.9	50.0	38.5	0.0	0.0	0.0	0.0	0	None	None	4x5	None	6	16	10	184	10	193
US	Benson/Gleaves	1	2	1.8	2.4	106.2	11.0	4.0	50.0	35.0	0.0	0.0	0.0	0.0	0	None	None	5x5	None	7	10	10	208	96	193
US	Clemson/Wickes	1	3	1.1	1.3	95.8	9.4	3.0	27.0	35.0	0.0	0.0	0.0	0.0	0	None	None	None	None	8	12	10	114	67	193
US	Farragut	2	4	1.8	2.3	103.9	11.0	3.9	50.0	35.0	0.0	0.0	0.0	0.0	0	4x4	None	5x5	1x3	6	8	8	192	8	193
US	Fletcher	2	5	2.3	2.9	112.5	12.1	4.2	60.0	34.0	0.0	0.0	0.0	0.0	0	None	None	5x5	None	8	10	18	273	175	194
Jp	Fubuki	2	2	1.8	2.1	111.9	10.4	3.2	50.0	36.8	0.0	0.0	0.0	0.0	0	None	None	6x5	None	6	9	24	197	19	192
US	Gearing	2	5	2.6	3.5	119.0	12.5	4.4	60.0	38.5	0.0	0.0	0.0	0.0	0	None	None	4x5	None	23	10	16	336	105	194
US	Gridley	2	2	1.6	2.2	103.9	10.7	3.9	50.0	33.0	0.0	0.0	0.0	0.0	0	None	None	5x5	None	6	16	9	158	4	193
Jp	Hatsuharu	2	2	1.7	2.1	103.5	10.0	3.9	42.0	35.0	0.0	0.0	0.0	0.0	0	None	None	6x5	None	6	9	16	200	6	193
Jp	Kagero	2	2	2.0	2.5	111.0	10.8	3.8	52.0	34.0	0.0	0.0	0.0	0.0	0	None	None	3x4.7	None	6	8	0	240	18	192
Jp	Kamikaze	2	1	1.5	1.7	102.6	9.1	2.9	38.5	33.0	0.0	0.0	0.0	0.0	0	None	None	None	None	3	6	16	148	9	192
Fr	L'Adroit	2	1	1.4	1.7	107.2	9.8	4.3	34.0	35.0	0.0	0.0	0.0	0.0	0	4x5.1	None	None	None	6	8	10	142	14	193
US	Mahan	2	3	1.8	2.3	103.9	11.0	3.9	50.0	34.0	0.0	0.0	0.0	0.0	0	None	None	5x5	None	6	8	10	192	18	193
Jp	Minekaze	2	1	2.1	2.9	111.9	10.4	3.2	50.0	34.0	0.0	0.0	0.0	0.0	0	None	None	3x4.7	None	6	6	18	148	13	191
Jp	Mutsuki	2	1	1.6	1.9	97.5	9.2	3.0	38.5	34.0	0.0	0.0	0.0	0.0	0	None	None	4x4.7	None	4	6	36	150	12	192
US	Porter	2	3	1.8	2.3	103.9	11.0	3.9	50.0	35.0	0.0	0.0	0.0	0.0	0	None	None	5x5	1x3	6	8	10	192	8	193
Cn	Saguenay	1	2	1.4	1.8	95.1	9.8	3.7	34.0	35.3	0.0	0.0	0.0	0.0	0	None	None	4x4.7	1x3	4	4	30	138	1	194
Br	Saumarez	2	2	1.8	2.5	103.5	10.9	4.3	40.0	36.8	0.0	0.0	0.0	0.0	0	None	None	4x4.7	None	6	8	18	200	16	194
Jp	Shimakaze	2	2	2.6	3.0	120.5	11.2	4.1	75.0	39.0	0.0	0.0	0.0	0.0	0	None	None	6x5	None	6	15	8	250	1	194
Jp	Shiratsuyu	2	2	1.7	2.0	103.5	9.9	3.5	42.0	34.0	0.0	0.0	0.0	0.0	0	None	None	5x5	None	6	8	10	200	10	193
US	Sims	2	3	1.8	2.3	103.9	11.0	3.9	50.0	35.0	0.0	0.0	0.0	0.0	0	None	None	5x5	None	4	8	10	192	12	193
US	Somers	2	6	2.0	2.8	116.1	11.3	3.8	52.0	37.0	0.0	0.0	0.0	0.0	0	None	None	8x5	1x4	10	12	10	294	5	193
Br	Tribal	2	2	2.0	2.5	108.4	11.1	4.0	44.0	36.4	0.0	0.0	0.0	0.0	0	4x4.9	None	7x4.7	2x3*	4	4	46	220	16	193
Nth	Van Ghent	2	2	1.3	1.6	93.6	9.5	2.9	31.0	36.0	0.0	0.0	0.0	0.0	0	None	None	None	None	4	6	4	129	4	192
Jp	Yugumo	2	2	2.1	2.9	111.6	10.8	3.8	52.0	35.0	0.0	0.0	0.0	0.0	0	None	None	6x5	None	4	8	16	228	20	194

NOTE: See page 99 for an explanation of the items on this table. Some classes are not mentioned in the text.

5"/50 dual-purpose guns of most recent Japanese destroyers. They proved very successful ships, but came along much too late to affect the course of the war. Six became war losses.

Allen M. Sumner. A U.S. wartime development, the forty-seven destroyers of this class completed during the war (of an order of fifty-eight, of which five were canceled) proved somewhat disappointing in service. On virtually the same physical dimensions as the very successful *Fletcher* Class, the *Sumner*s mounted three double 5"/38 dual-purpose turrets, rather than five single mounts. As a result, the *Sumner*s were overweight, slow, and top-heavy. A top-heavy ship has a high center of gravity, causing her to roll badly and presenting an increased danger of capsizing if broadsided by heavy seas. Despite their limitations, the *Sumner*s saw considerable service. None became war losses.

Asashio. Completed 1937–1938, the ten Japanese *Asashio* Class destroyers were good ships, specialized for surface actions. As with all vessels, during the war their armament was steadily upgraded. All were war losses, three during the Battle of Surigao Strait.

Bagley. Like the *Gridley*s, the U.S. *Bagley* Class destroyers were designed in response to questions raised about the capabilities of the *Mahan* Class. However, they were built by the Navy in its own yards, with no corners cut. As a result, although superficially not much different from the *Gridley*s, they were much better ships. Like the *Gridley*s, they had only four 5"/38 dual-purpose guns, plus sixteen torpedo tubes. But they were also much more stable, and during the war proved capable of mounting greatly enhanced antiaircraft batteries with no difficulties. The eight *Bagley*s saw considerable service in the Pacific, during which three were sunk.

Benham. Although they were a derivative of the *Bagley* Class destroyers, the ten ships of this class incorporated numerous lessons learned from the Navy's experience with the *Farragut* Class, which had proven somewhat unsatisfactory in service. As a result, they were larger, but had a smaller main battery and more torpedo tubes, with more powerful engines and a somewhat higher speed. Several *Benham*s were assigned to Neutrality Patrol in 1940, and were modified to enhance their antisubmarine capability, losing half their torpedo tubes in the process, while gaining a Y-gun (depth charge thrower) and more antiaircraft guns, alterations that proved so successful that they were soon effected on the Pacific Fleet units as well. All units later had further improvements made to their air defense capacity. They saw considerable service, and two were lost in action.

Benson/Gleaves. The U.S. *Benson* and *Gleaves* classes were the last prewar-designed destroyers to enter service. Essentially somewhat smaller versions of the *Sims* Class, they had four smaller boilers rather than three large ones, plus ten torpedo tubes in two banks of five, rather than eight in two banks of four. There were numerous versions of the basic design, and, in fact, on paper about forty of the ninety-six units belonged to the *Gleaves* Class, which was officially a few tons heavier and had some minor differences in appearance. To a great extent these were differences of no consequence. More important was the fact that the later units of the group—regardless of official class—were built to a modified wartime version, which had one fewer 5-inch gun and far more antiaircraft guns, changes that were effected to previously completed vessels as time and the exigencies of war permitted. Seventeen became war losses.

Clemson/Wickes. Completed soon after World War I, the *Clemson* and *Wickes* classes were famous as the "four-stack" destroyers, which constituted about a third of the U.S. Navy's assets in that type of warship at the start of the war. Although obsolete almost as soon as they were completed, they saw significant service during World War II, many taking part in the early battles of the Asiatic Fleet and others serving as high-speed transports and mine warfare vessels.

Farragut. The first genuine post–World War I destroyer design in the U.S. Navy, the *Farraguts*, of which eight were built in the early and mid-1930s, more or less set the model for American destroyers in the early part of World War II. They had a high forecastle to improve sea-keeping capacity, and they introduced the 5"/38 dual-purpose gun as their main armament. But they lacked adequate protection for the 5-inch guns, and were rather cramped, due to the necessity of adhering to the limitations of the naval disarmament treaties. They saw heavy service during the war, with frequent modifications to their armament. Three were lost in the Pacific: Two, *Hull* and *Monaghan*, veterans of some of the toughest surface fighting of the Solomons campaign, were lost to the great typhoon of December 18, 1944, and one to the Japanese.

Fletcher. Save for the 1936 *Somers* Class, the *Fletchers* were the first U.S. destroyers to displace more than 1,800 standard tons, being over 25 percent larger than their predecessors. The U.S. Navy's mobilization destroyers, they were the largest class of destroyer ever built, totaling 175 ships completed during the war, with a number of differences among various units. Excellent ships, they were versatile and tough, and actually superior in several ways to the succeeding *Allen M. Sumner* Class. They saw extensive service, and many became war losses.

Fubuki. The nineteen units of the *Fubuki* Class (one of the original twenty having been lost in a prewar accident) were in many ways the typical Japanese destroyers of the war. When completed in the late 1920s, they were the most heavily armed destroyers in the world, superior in many ways to those in American or British service. Reconstructed in the late 1930s, they emerged somewhat larger, with somewhat less speed than before, but with improved seaworthiness. They saw extensive service in the war, during which all but one were lost.

Gearing. The culmination of U.S. destroyer development in World War II, most of the 116 *Gearings* ordered were not completed until after the surrender of Japan; only about forty entered service during the war. They were very successful ships, much better designed than the *Sumners*, which they closely resembled save for being longer, and thus more stable. A number of units were modified as "radar picket" ships, designed to provide early warning for carrier task forces, with additional radar and antiaircraft armament. The *Gearings* continued in service after the war, some even surviving into the 1980s in reserve status in the U.S. Navy, and on active duty in other navies.

Gridley. Designed by Bethlehem Shipbuilding as a result of some controversy over the *Mahan* Class, the four *Gridleys* (whose construction was almost simultaneous with that of the *Mahans*) were not very successful destroyers, having apparently been built with a lot of short cuts designed to reduce costs. They proved a disappointment in the service, particularly as they could not be fitted with an adequate antiaircraft allotment without extensive reduction in their torpedo armament, and they were eventually relegated to the Atlantic Fleet, as soon as enough *Fletchers* became available in the Pacific.

Hatsuharu/Shiratsugu. Smaller than the *Fubuki* and *Akatsuki* Class destroyers that preceded them, the *Hatsuharus* as built carried virtually the same armament. This made them top-heavy, and after the torpedo boat *Tomozuru* capsized in 1933, the completed *Hatsu-harus* were extensively modified, and those still building finished to the new design. This increased displacement to about that of the *Fubuki* Class, while speed fell considerably. They saw a lot of service and were several times rearmed; all became war losses.

Kagero. Completed between 1939 and mid-1941, the *Kageros* were regarded in the Imperial Japanese Navy as ideal fleet destroyers: fast, heavily armed, and maneuverable. They saw extensive service in the war, during which they were modified to enhance antiaircraft capability at the cost of surface firepower. All but one of the eighteen units in the class became war losses, five in surface actions.

Kamikaze. A Japanese World War I design, the nine *Kamikaze* Class destroyers (all named after various winds, such as the "Divine Wind," Kamikaze) were obsolescent by 1941. Despite this, they saw extensive service, being several times rearmed and refitted during the war, in which seven were lost—one, *Hayate*, having the dubious distinction of being one of the few major warships ever sunk in action by shore batteries, at Wake Island on December 11, 1941.

L'Adroit. An older class, *L'Adroit* and her sisters were the last French destroyers of ordinary proportions for a decade (after them came the "monster" classes, the French developing a predilection for destroyers that approached the size of small light cruisers). Several saw service in the Indian Ocean and one was actually in the South Pacific during the Guadalcanal campaign.

Mahan. The largest U.S. interwar class of destroyers (eighteen ships), the *Mahans* were ordered partially to stimulate the economy during the Great Depression (a useful "economy of force" measure employed by President Roosevelt to get some rearmament money out of a penny-pinching and isolationist nation). They embodied many innovative ideas, including extremely high pressure boilers and a greatly enhanced torpedo complement, while reverting to the 5"/38 dual-purpose main battery of the *Farragut* Class. They were very good ships (indeed, three more were built for Brazil), and very stable, taking the weight of numerous wartime upgrades to their antiaircraft capability with little difficulty. Six were lost in action.

Minekaze. A Japanese World War I design, the *Minekazes* were comparable to the U.S. "four-stack" destroyers of the *Clemson* Class. They were obsolete even before the war; two of the fifteen vessels in the class had been converted into high-speed transports, with reduced armament and speed but able to carry 250 fully armed troops with landing craft, while a third had been fitted to serve as the command ship for a radio-controlled target vessel. They saw considerable service in the war, ten being lost in action.

Mutsuki. The first Japanese destroyers designed after World War I, the *Mutsukis* were refitted as fast transports early in the war, but retained considerable antisubmarine and surface combat capability. All became war losses, most in the Solomons.

Porter. Designed to serve as flotilla leaders (i.e., flagships) to squadrons of "four-stacker" destroyers, the eight U.S. *Porters*, completed in the mid-1930s, were large, benefiting from modifications to the naval disarmament treaties in this regard. However, they were badly armed, having only surface-capable main guns, rather than the dual-purpose ones of the preceding *Farragut* Class, albeit eight to the latter's five. They were rather cramped but seaworthy, and saw considerable service in the war, during which they were several times modified, and in which only *Porter* was lost in action. After the war several of the surviving units were retained for various experiments.

Saguenay. Canada's *Saguenays* were sisters to the British *Acasta* Class destroyers, and saw considerable service in the Northeast Pacific.

Saumarez. A further evolution of Britian's *Tribal* Class, the *Saumarez* Class destroyers began coming off the ways in 1942, and eventually about eighty ships more or less on this model were in service. Good ships.

Shimakaze. Begun in August 1941 and launched eleven months later, but not completed until May 1943, *Shimakaze* was intended as the prototype of a radically new Japanese destroyer design, being very large, very fast (over 40 knots on trials), and very well armed. The only one completed of seventeen ships planned to this design, *Shimakaze* was several times rearmed during the war, before succumbing to U.S. naval aircraft in the Philippines in late 1944.

Sims. The dozen destroyers of the American *Sims* Class were intended to be a major evolutionary development over preceding designs, which had been restricted to 1,500 tons by the various disarmament treaties. As completed they turned out unsuccessfully, displacing much more than expected, and they had to be extensively redesigned and refitted even before entering service. In this new

guise they proved rather successful, despite the loss of some armament, and they became the prototypes for the succeeding two classes. They saw considerable service, and five were lost in action.

Somers. Designed as flotilla leaders, the five destroyers of the *Somers* Class were about 10 percent larger and mounted 50 percent more
torpedo tubes than the *Porters*, completed two or three years earlier.
As their hull dimensions were virtually the same as that of the *Porters*, the *Somers* destroyers were rather top-heavy. They were a disappointment in service: In order to increase their antiaircraft
capability they had to lose four torpedo tubes and two 5-inch guns
to retain their stability. One became a war loss.

Tribal. The *Tribal* Class (named after the great warrior tribes of
the British Empire) marked a significant increase in British destroyer
size, being about 30 percent larger than the previous classes, and
set the model for subsequent British destroyer construction. Altogether, about twenty-four prewar and seventy-five wartime ships
were more or less on this pattern, including a wartime repeat run
of the original 1936 design.

Van Ghent. The Royal Netherlands Navy had eight destroyers in
the East Indies, of different but quite similar classes. They gave
good account of themselves, but all became casualties in February
and March 1942.

Yugumo. Japan ordered thirty-six *Yugumo* Class destroyers between 1939 and 1942, of which only twenty were completed, the
last not until May 1941. Closely resembling the *Kagero* Class, they
were better designed and their main armament had a superior ele-
vation, on virtually the same displacement and with the same speed.
Extensively modified during they war, they saw considerable service.
All were lost in action.

DESTROYER ESCORT–TYPE SHIPS

Buckley. The *Buckleys*, which totaled 102 ships, were the second
generation of U.S. destroyer escorts, built 1942–1944 on the basis
of experience with the earlier *Evarts* Class. They saw considerable
service and proved quite satisfactory, most being retained in reserve
by the Navy into the 1960s. They were sometimes referred to as the

Navy	Class	Combat		Displacement		Length	Beam	Draft	HP	Spd	Armor				A/C	Guns				HMG	TT	DC	Crew	Tot	Year
		Surf	AAA	Std	Full						Belt	Turret	Deck	Tower		Main	Sec	DP	AAA						
US	Buckley	1	4	1.4	1.8	91.4	11.3	3.4	12.0	23.0	0.0	0.0	0.0	0.0	0	None	None	3x3	None	12	2	8	186	102	1943
US	Cannon	1	3	1.3	1.6	93.3	11.2	3.2	6.0	21.0	0.0	0.0	0.0	0.0	0	None	None	3x3	None	8	3	8	186	157	1943
US	Evarts	1	4	1.2	1.4	88.2	10.7	3.1	6.0	19.5	0.0	0.0	0.0	0.0	0	None	None	3x3	None	13	0	8	156	68	1942
Jp	Matsu	1	1	1.3	1.9	92.2	9.4	3.3	19.0	27.8	0.0	0.0	0.0	0.0	0	None	None	3x5	None	4	4	36	200	18	1944
Jp	Otori	1	1	0.8	1.0	88.5	8.2	2.8	19.0	30.5	0.0	0.0	0.0	0.0	0	None	None	3x4.7	None	1	3	0	113	8	1935
US	Rudderow	1	4	1.4	1.8	93.3	11.3	3.4	12.0	23.0	0.0	0.0	0.0	0.0	0	None	None	2x5	None	14	3	8	156	109	1943
Jp	Tachibana	1	3	1.3	1.6	100.0	9.4	3.4	19.0	27.8	0.0	0.0	0.0	0.0	0	None	None	3x5	None	24	4	60	?	18	1944
Jp	Tomozuru	1	1	0.6	0.8	77.5	7.4	2.5	11.0	28.0	0.0	0.0	0.0	0.0	0	None	None	3x4.7	None	1	2	0	120	4	1935

NOTE: See page 99 for an explanation of the items on this table.

"TE" Class, because of their electric turbine engines. They were good ships, and lucky, very few becoming war losses.

Cannon. Ordered at the same time as the *Buckleys*, the sixty-six vessels of the *Cannon* Class (types "DET" and "FMR" destroyer escorts) were essentially enlarged versions of the *Evarts* Class, with about 200 tons' more displacement at full load, on a longer and wider hull, with slightly more powerful engines and a touch more speed. They had virtually the same main armament, but added three torpedo tubes. Like all ships, they saw their antiaircraft armament enhanced during the war. "DET" referred to DEs with diesel electric power plants, "FMR" to geared turbine diesels.

Evarts. The first production-model U.S. destroyer escorts, the sixty-eight completed units of the *Evarts* Class (five more were canceled) were all completed 1943–1944. They were small, cramped, slow, and underarmed, and came into service only after the U-boat menace had been beaten, but they performed a variety of useful duties. All were disposed of immediately after the war. Officially they were the "GMT" Class, referring to their diesel-electric tandem drive.

Matsu. An increasing shortage of escorts caused the Imperial Japanese Navy to order the *Matsu* Class destroyer escorts in 1942. Somewhat more heavily armed than U.S. DEs, they took a long time to build, the first unit not being completed until April 1944 and the last of the eighteen in January 1945, a further eleven having been canceled. They saw extensive service, and seven were lost in action.

Otori. Completed in the mid-1930s, Japan's *Otori* Class fleet torpedo boats were much enlarged and improved versions of the unsuccessful *Tomozura* Class. The eight ships were somewhat modified for wartime escort duties, at which, like the *Tomozura*s, they were quite effective, and seven were lost in action.

Rudderow. Derived from the *Buckley* Class destroyer escorts, the *Rudderow*s (the "TEV" Class) were about the same size and dimensions (roughly comparable to the old *Farragut* Class destroyers), but mounted two 5"/38 dual-purpose guns rather than three 3"/50 dual-purpose, with heavier antiaircraft and torpedo allotments as well (three tubes rather than two). This made the twenty-two *Rudderow*s, as well as the twenty-four virtually identical *John C. Butler*s ("WGT"), the most successful American destroyer escorts in the war. "TEV" refers to turboelectric drive DEs with 5-inch guns (hence the "V"), "WGT" to geared turbine engines using small gears.

Tachibana. A follow-on to Japan's *Matsu* Class destroyer escorts, the *Tachibana*s were somewhat larger, and somewhat better armed, but easier to build. Only twenty-three of nearly forty ordered were actually laid down, of which only fourteen were completed, three of which became war losses.

Tomozura. Like several nations, Japan continued to build so-called oceangoing or fleet torpedo boats, basically very small destroyers specialized for torpedo attack. They were poorly designed, being unstable (*Tomozura* once capsized in a storm, later to be salvaged and returned to service) and unsuited to their original purpose, coordinated high-speed torpedo attacks in fleet actions. They were pressed into service as convoy escorts after extensive modifications to their armament, a role in which they proved surprisingly effective, as they could carry forty-eight depth charges each, far more than most fleet destroyers. Three were lost in action.

SUBMARINES

Gato. Only a handful of *Gato* Class submarines were available at the outbreak of the war, but nearly 200 were completed by its end in three somewhat different versions. Most saw extensive service against Japanese shipping. They were the most successful U.S. submarine design of the war.

I-1. The four-boat *I-1* (or *J-1*) Class was similar to fifty-eight of Japan's prewar and nine of her wartime submarines. They were good fleet boats, but poorly employed.

I-46. Arguably Japan's best submarine design of the war, the three boats of the *I-46* Class were among thirty-four similar boats built during the war. They were large, fast boats.

K-XIV. The Netherlands relied upon its approximately two dozen submarines, of 515 to 998 tons surfaced, as its primary arm of maritime defense in the East Indies. The *K-XIV* Class, which numbered five boats, was typical. When war came, the Dutch submarines proved fairly ineffective.

Perch. About 40 of America's 100 prewar submarines were more

SUBMARINES

Navy	Class	Combat Surf	AAA	Displacement Std	Full	Length	Beam	Draft	HP	Spd	Armor Belt	Turret	Deck	Tower	A/C	Guns Main	Sec	DP	AAA	HMG	TT	DC	Crew	Tot	Year
US	Gato	0	1	1.5	1.8	95.0	8.3	4.7	5.4	20.3	0.0	0.0	0.0	0.0	0	None	None	1x3	None	4	10	0	80	73	1942
Jp	I-1	0	0	2.0	2.4	94.0	9.2	5.0	6.0	18.0	0.0	0.0	0.0	0.0	0	None	None	2x5	None	None	6	0	92	4	1925
Jp	I-46	0	0	2.2	2.6	103.8	9.1	5.4	11.0	23.5	0.0	0.0	0.0	0.0	0	None	None	1x5.5	None	2	8	0	101	3	1943
Nth	K-XIV	4	0	0.8	0.9	74.0	7.6	3.9	3.2	17.0	0.0	0.0	0.0	0.0	0	None	None	None	1x3.5	None	8	0	38	5	1932
US	Perch	0	1	1.3	1.6	89.2	7.7	4.6	4.3	19.3	0.0	0.0	0.0	0.0	0	None	None	1x3	None	4	6	0	54	6	1936
Jp	Ro-33	0	0	0.7	0.8	71.5	6.7	4.0	2.9	19.0	0.0	0.0	0.0	0.0	0	None	None	None	1x3	1	4	0	42	2	1935
Br	T-Class	0	0	1.1	1.3	83.3	8.1	4.5	1.5	15.3	0.0	0.0	0.0	0.0	0	None	None	1x4	None	None	11	0	61	16	1941
Br	Thames	0	0	1.9	2.2	105.2	8.6	4.9	2.5	22.0	0.0	0.0	0.0	0.0	0	None	None	1x4	None	None	6	0	61	3	1933
Br	Undine	0	0	0.5	0.7	58.2	4.9	4.6	0.8	11.3	0.0	0.0	0.0	0.0	0	None	None	1x3	None	None	6	0	27	3	1938

NOTE: See page 99 for an explanation of the items on this table.

or less similar to *Perch*, which actually entered service after the war began. These boats were designed as fleet scouts, to reconnoiter and harass the enemy, but proved good commerce raiders, once leadership, training, and equipment deficiencies were remedied.

Ro-33. The *Ro-33* Class, of two boats, was essentially similar to about a dozen of Japan's prewar and fifty-two of her wartime submarines. They were adequate oceangoing vessels, poorly employed.

T-Class. Britain built only thirty-eight boats of the *T-Class*, a "war emergency" submarine design, in two batches. A number saw service in the Indian Ocean and the waters around the Netherlands East Indies.

Thames. The *Thames* Class was fairly typical of the larger of Britain's prewar submarine designs. Although these submarines' range made them more suitable to operations in the Atlantic and Mediterranean, a number of them saw service in the Pacific Theater. About twenty-eight boats dating from 1926 to 1938 were more or less on this model.

Undine. Britain had about 15 boats of this type, a standard small-submarine design, at the onset of the war, and went on to build about 120 more boats with roughly the same characteristics.

KILLER FISH

World War II was the golden age of torpedo warfare. This was the only conflict in which torpedoes were used extensively by submarines, aircraft, and surface ships. The Japanese had a significant advantage in torpedo warfare for the first two years of the war. This was because their principal surface-ship torpedo was larger and more capable than anyone else's and because the principal U.S. submarine torpedo was defective. The Japanese aerial torpedo was also superior during this period, giving the Japanese an advantage in every torpedo category. This was a particularly decided edge for the Japanese during the first year of the war.

Japanese surface ships used their so-called Long Lance torpedoes to destroy far more Allied ships than their opponents could using the same technique. U.S. carrier aircraft caused less damage with their less capable torpedoes and U.S. submarines were practically

TORPEDO TYPES

OFFICIAL NAME	HEAD DIAMETER (IN INCHES)	USER	WEIGHT (IN POUNDS)	WARHEAD (IN POUNDS)	RANGE/SPEED (IN KILOMETERS/ KNOTS)		NOTE
Type 8	24	Jap—S	5,207	761	10/38	15/32	A
Type 89	21	Jap—U	3,677	661	5.5/45	10/35	B
Type 90	21	Jap—S	5,743	827	7/46	15/35	C
Type 95	21	Jap—U	3,671	893	9/50	12/46	D
Type 93	24	Jap—S	5,952	1,080	20/49	40/36	E
Type 97	17.7	Jap—U	2,094	772	5.5/45		F
Type 91-1	17.7	Jap—A	1,728	331	2/42		G
Type 91-2	17.7	Jap—A	1,841	452	2/42		H
Type 91-3	17.7	Jap—A	1,872	529	2/42		I
Type 04	17.7	Jap—A	2,169	670	1.5/42		J
Kaiten	39.4	Jap—U	18,300	3,420	23/30	78/12	K
Mark 10	21	U.S.—U	2,215	497	3.2/36		L
Mark 15	21	U.S.—S	3,841	825	5.5/45	13.7/26	M
Mark 14	21	U.S.—U	3,280	643	4.1/46	8.2/31	N
Mark 13	17.7	U.S.—A	2,216	600	6.7/33		O
Mark 18	21	U.S.—U	3,154	575	3.6/29		P
Mark 24	19	U.S.—A	680	92	3.6/12		Q
Mark 27	19	U.S.—U	720	95	4.5/12		R

NOTES: "User" is the nation using the torpedo. In that column, "S" is surface ships; "U" is submarines; "A" is aircraft. "Range/Speed" gives the two extreme settings for the torpedo, with range in kilometers and speed in knots (1 knot = 1 nautical mile or 1.9 kilometers per hour).

A. The Type 8 was a 1920s design that was still being used by older destroyers and light cruisers early in the war. An effective torpedo similar to the U.S. Mark 15.

B. The Type 89 was a 1920s design for submarines and was widely used during the first year of the war. During that period, it was much more effective than the newer U.S. Mark 14.

C. The Type 90 was a 1930s design for cruisers. Used extensively early in the war.

D. The Type 95 was a smaller, submarine version of the Type 93 Long Lance. Quite effective. There was also a Type 92 electric torpedo, which was produced from 1942 on in small quantities (650) to supplement the more widely used Type 95.

E. The Type 93 was the famous Long Lance torpedo. The Japanese were way ahead of everyone else with this 24-inch surface ship torpedo. Very reliable, fast, and deadly. Widely used throughout the war, especially in the first year. As good as the Type 93 was, it had the same "wander" problem that all torpedoes have. Wander is the maximum distance a torpedo will wander off course at different ranges. The wander of the Type 93 was typical of all torpedoes. At 15 kilometers, a Type 93 would wander off a straight-line course as much as

500 meters right or left. At 25 kilometers wander was 700 meters, and at 30 kilometers it was 1,000 meters. Even at ranges of a few kilometers, wander could be as much as 100 meters. For this reason, you usually launched a spread of torpedoes. Torpedo bombers, because of wander and the fact that they carried only one weapon per aircraft, carried torpedoes with very short ranges.

F. The Type 97 was an even smaller version of the Long Lance, for use in midget submarines. Only 100 Type 97s were built and they were used only by the midget subs at Pearl Harbor. The Type 97 was not very reliable in any event.

G. The Type 91-1 was the standard aircraft torpedo in the first year of the war. This was an early 1930s design and was being replaced by the Type 91-2 in 1941. All Type 91s could be launched at over 200 knots early in the war (twice the launch speed of early U.S. airborne torpedoes) and 350 knots by 1944. Launch altitude was, for tactical reasons, rarely more than a few hundred feet.

H. The Type 91-2 replaced the 91-1 in 1942.

I. The Type 91-3 replaced the 91-2 in 1943.

J. The Type 04 was a further development of the Type 91 that could be launched at speeds over 400 knots. In service by late 1944.

K. The Kaiten was a manned suicide torpedo. Although 330 were put into service, only one U.S. ship was ever hit (a fleet oil tanker at Ulithi atoll in the Caroline Islands, in November 1944).

L. The Mark 10 was a World War I torpedo still in use on "S" Class U.S. submarines early in World War II.

M. The Mark 15 was the standard destroyer torpedo throughout the war. Compared to the Japanese Type 93 Long Lance, the Mark 15 was decidedly inferior. But the Type 93 was arguably the most effective torpedo used by any navy during the entire war. The Mark 15 was reliable and effective, even though it was slower and had a 20 percent smaller warhead than the Type 93.

N. The Mark 14 was the 1930s replacement for the Mark 10 and got off to a rocky start. It was designed to explode under its target using a magnetic-field-detecting detonator. In this way it would do maximum damage ("breaking the ship's back," or generally breaking up the internal structure of the ship). It worked during tests in the Atlantic Ocean. But the water conditions in the Pacific turned out to be different enough to make the Mark 14 almost useless. It took nearly a year for submarine captains to convince the Navy's torpedo establishment that there was a problem. A new detonator of more conventional design was then put on the Mark 14, but this one also turned out to be unreliable, the "firing pins" being made of relatively cheap metal that bent at the critical moment. It wasn't until the middle of 1943 that the Mark 14 finally became a reliable torpedo. With more modifications, Mark 14s continued in use until the late 1970s.

O. The Mark 13 was the standard U.S. airborne torpedo for most of the war. While not a bad design, it suffered from the need for low altitude and slow launching speed (50 feet and 110 knots). This caused many lost aircraft, as at that altitude and speed the torpedo bombers were perfect targets for enemy fighters or antiaircraft guns. At Midway, an entire squadron of torpedo bombers carrying Mark 13s were shot down while approaching their targets. In early 1944, some simple modifications were made to the Mark 13 that allowed it to be dropped at 1,000 feet and speeds of over 200 knots. By the end of the war, the configuration of the Mark 13 had been tweaked to the point where it could be dropped at 2,400 feet while traveling at over 400 knots. Aside from the height and speed problems, the Mark 13 turned out to be an effective weapon, with 40 percent of those launched actually hitting a target. The Mark 13 was also used successfully on PT boats.

P. The Mark 18 was an unsuccessful copy of the more effective German G7e submarine torpedo. This model did not leave a track and was a lot cheaper to build than the Mark 14. But while the design could be copied, the reliability of the German original could not. Many Mark 18s were fired late in the war, but submarine captains tended to prefer the older Mark 14.

Q. The Mark 24 was the first effective homing torpedo. Four sensors steered it toward the noise of a diving or schnorkling (running on diesel engines by means of periscope-type air vent) submarine. The Mark 24 was quite effective, with 346 used and 101 obtaining hits (two thirds resulting in destroyed subs, the others badly damaged). Only about ten percent of subs attacked with air-dropped depth charges would be sunk or damaged. The Mark 24 was first used in the summer of 1943 against German subs in the Atlantic.

R. The Mark 27 was a submarine version of the Mark 24. Rails were added so that it would fit into the submarine's 21-inch torpedo tubes. The Mark 27 was used only against Japanese escorts. It was quite effective, with 106 fired to obtain 33 hits (73 percent of which were fatal to the surface ship, usually something smaller than a destroyer). First used in mid-1944.

disarmed because of their defective torpedoes. The table on page 142 shows the torpedo situation in detail. It's not a pretty picture.

One reason that the flaws in several U.S. torpedo designs were not detected earlier was that they were not fully tested before the war under wartime conditions. This was a way to cut costs, as it saved $8,000 to $10,000 for each torpedo not expended, but it would have been money well spent.

THE OTHER REVOLUTIONARY NEW SHIP

Historically, the submarine is a rather recent development. Submarines first became practical in the late nineteenth century. They were the first "Stealth" weapons, being essentially torpedo boats that had the capacity to operate underwater for limited periods, albeit with a considerable loss of speed and endurance.

Submarines proved of considerable value during World War I, when Germany almost succeeded in severing Britain's maritime lifeline through an aggressive submarine campaign. This campaign ultimately failed, but attracted considerable attention. As a result, between the wars many navies invested rather heavily in submarines. By World War II there were essentially two types of submarines.

The "coastal submarine," built in considerable numbers by many navies, was of modest dimensions, less than 800 tons in surface displacement. It generally had a relatively low surface speed, 18 knots being at the high end. Coastal submarines usually carried four to six torpedo tubes, plus a deck gun and one or two antiaircraft machine guns. They were designed to roam the oceans and snipe at enemy shipping, or linger along the coast and ambush enemy warships.

Then there was the "fleet submarine," to use its American name. The fleet submarine was large, 1,000 tons or more, and usually had a relatively high surface speed of 20 knots, from which came the term *fleet submarine*, since it was able to keep up with the battle fleet. Being larger, the fleet submarine was better armed, usually with six to ten torpedo tubes, plus the usual deck armament. Fleet submarines also had more endurance than coastal submarines, since they could carry more diesel fuel and more batteries. When they were submerged, there was little difference in speed between the two types, 8 knots being more or less the norm. The only other important technical difference was that the fleet submarine was relatively more habitable, though not by much.

Most navies had a mix of coastal and fleet submarines, the idea being that the coastal types would raid enemy commerce, while the fleet types served as supports for the battle fleet, scouting for the enemy, harassing him before battle, mopping up fleeing enemy vessels after a victory, or covering the retreat of friendly vessels after a reverse. For various reasons, however, the United States built only fleet submarines, since it intended to meet any enemy—specifically the Japanese—in a decisive surface clash as soon as possible. This proved of considerable benefit once the war began, because the main use of U.S. subs was attacking Japanese merchant ships at great distances from American bases.

THE ULTIMATE BATTLESHIP BATTLE

The Imperial Navy's *Yamato* and *Musashi* were the largest battlewagons ever built, displacing almost 70,000 tons at full load. They also toted the heaviest guns ever to put to sea, nine pieces of 460mm caliber (a bore diameter of 18.11 inches), capable of throwing a 3,219-pound shell a maximum distance of slightly over 45,000 yards.

The largest American battleships, *Iowa* and her sisters *New Jersey*, *Wisconsin*, and *Missouri*, displaced only about 55,000 tons at full load, and mounted nine 16-inch (406mm) guns, which fired a 2,700-pound shell only to about 42,000 yards.

There was one moment in the war when the *Yamato* and *Iowa* Class ships might have clashed, during the Battle of Leyte Gulf in the Philippines, on October 25, 1944. With a squadron consisting of *Yamato*, three older battleships, some cruisers, and several destroyers, Japanese Admiral Takeo Kurita had managed to elude U.S. aerial reconnaissance and, slipping through San Bernardino Strait, had emerged off Samar to fall on a clutch of escort carriers. The running fight that ensued turned into a moral victory for the Americans, when, despite losing two carriers and three destroyers or destroyer escorts to Japanese gunfire, they managed to put up such a fight that the Japanese decided to withdraw. As the faster enemy ships began steaming off, one U.S. bluejacket is supposed to have cried out, "They're getting away!"

U.S. planning for the invasion of the Philippines had envisioned the possibility that the Japanese might threaten the landings with surface forces. Admiral William F. Halsey had seven fast battleships helping to escort the carriers of his Third Fleet. In an emergency he was supposed to form these into Task Force 34 under Admiral Willis "Ching Chong China" Lee, the Navy's best battleship man, and leave them to guard the large concentration of shipping in Leyte Gulf. However, when Halsey took his fleet north to pursue the Japanese carriers, he took the battlewagons with him. Had he not done so, or had he heeded the initial warnings to dispatch them southward, a slug-out between the Japanese *Yamato, Nagato, Haruna,* and *Kongo* and the American *Iowa, New Jersey, Massachusetts, South Dakota, Washington,* and *Alabama* might easily have resulted. As Samuel Eliot Morison would later write, "What a brawl that would have been . . . !"

But aside from *Yamato,* the Japanese ships were all old and slow in comparison with the American ones. A true test would have pitted a squadron of *Iowa*s against a squadron of *Yamato*s.

The two classes are compared in the table on page 147.

The differences between the two classes of battleships are interesting. Since speed in a ship is partially a factor of hull length and fineness, her more powerful engines made *Iowa* about 20 percent faster than *Yamato.* In addition, *Iowa*'s deeper draft made for greater stability, making her a better "gun platform" than her rival. Both of these factors would have been important in an engagement at sea. Moreover, *Iowa* was a much handier ship, responding to the helm more rapidly, with a smaller tactical diameter (the minimum diameter necessary to make a full circle), which made her more maneuverable.

On paper, of course, *Yamato*'s thicker armor suggests a much better protected ship, but this is rather deceptive. Thickness of plate must make an allowance for quality. In the years before World War II, the U.S. Navy had made considerable strides in armor technology. As a result, the protection offered by its new armor plate was equivalent to about 25 percent more thickness in terms of the older type of armor carried by *Yamato.* Barbettes, by the way, are the rounded

	YAMATO	IOWA
Displacement (in tons)		
Standard	64,000	48,110
Full Load	69,988	57,540
Dimensions		
Length: Waterline	839'11"	860'
Overall	862'9"	887'3"
Beam (wide)	121'1"	108'2"
Draft	34'1"	36'2.25"
Machinery		
Boilers	12	8
Turbines	4	4
Shaft Horsepower	150,000	212,000
Speed, Maximum	27 knots	32.5 knots
	(31.2 mph)	(37.6 mph)
Armor, Maximums		
Belt	16.1"	12.9"
Deck	9"	8.1"
Barbettes (turret bases)	21.5"	17.3"
Turret Faces	25.6"	19.7"
Conning Tower	19.7"	17.5"
Armament		
Main Battery	9 × 18.11"/45	9 × 16"/50
Secondary Battery	12 × 6.1"/60	
Dual Purpose	12 × 5"/40	20 × 5"/38
Light AA	omitted	
Crew	2,500	1,921

MAIN BATTERY GUN PERFORMANCE COMPARISON

	JAPANESE 18.11"/45	AMERICAN 16"/50
Muzzle Velocity	2,559 fps	2,600 fps
Penetration at:		
0 Yards	34"	32.62"
20,000 Yards	about 20.4"	20.04"
30,000 Yards	about 14.7"	14.97"
Rounds per Minute	1	2

bases on which the turrets rest; the conning tower is an armored citadel from which the skipper and steersman can fight the ship in comparative safety.

An additional important factor was that *Iowa* appears to have been much better constructed than *Yamato*. On December 25, 1943, for example, *Yamato* took a torpedo that demonstrated that the jointing between the hull and her armor belt was faulty. As a full repair would have entailed the addition of over 5,000 tons to the ship's displacement, the Imperial Navy merely patched up the damaged section and pretended there was no problem.

Of course the big difference was in the main batteries, *Yamato's* 18.11-inch rifles (as battleship guns were traditionally called) making *Iowa's* 16-inchers seem puny by comparison, what with the Japanese armor-piercing shell weighing nearly 20 percent more and having almost 7 percent more range. But this is a superficial comparison.

A deeper look proves more interesting.

Gun caliber is given in inches and barrel length, so if a piece is described as 18.11"/45 the bore is 18.11 inches in diameter and the barrel is 45 times that in length, or slightly less than 70 feet. The 16"/50 was about 66.6 feet long. Longer barrel length lends stability to the shell in flight, which increases range, which is one reason why, although the Japanese gun had a bore diameter 13 percent greater than the American piece, its maximum range was only 7 percent greater.

Other factors of importance were the propellant used (the "gun-

148

powder") and shell aerodynamics. On this score the U.S. piece was better, with a slightly higher muzzle velocity (the speed with which the shell leaves the barrel, measured in feet per second, or fps).

Incidentally, the marginally greater maximum range of the Japanese gun would have been of no consequence. The greatest range at which a land-based heavy artillery piece ever hit a target deliberately aimed at appears to have been about 17.4 nautical miles (roughly 35,200 yards, 20 land miles), a feat accomplished by a U.S. Army model 16"/45 coast defense gun at Fort Weaver, Hawaii, in August 1938, under absolutely wonderful conditions of weather and sea. The longest-range deliberate hit at sea in naval combat occurred on July 9, 1940, off Calabria, Italy, in the Mediterranean, when the British battleship *Warspite* put a single 15-inch round into the Italian battleship *Giulio Cesare* at 26,000 yards, about 12.8 nautical miles.

It may seem odd to measure the penetrability of a gun at zero range (i.e., at the instant the projectile leaves the barrel), but it actually is of some value for comparison purposes.

The number of rounds per minute that the pieces were capable of firing is a rather optimistic figure, since it was dangerous and exhausting to attempt to sustain maximum rates of fire for more than a few minutes. Of course, this still gave the U.S. gun a higher rate of fire.

In effect, on technical grounds, the U.S. 16"/50 battleship rifle was by no means inferior in performance to the Japanese 18.11"/45. And in action, that performance would have been enhanced by fire control radar, a development with which the Japanese had very little success.

So in the ultimate battleship brawl of all time, a squadron of four *Iowas* would probably have defeated a squadron of four *Yamatos*.

By the way, there were two battleship-to-battleship engagements during the Pacific war:

- THE SECOND NAVAL BATTLE OF GUADALCANAL (NOVEMBER 14–15, 1942). In a wild action that commenced shortly before midnight, a Japanese squadron including *Kirishima* engaged the new *Washington* and *South Dakota*, the latter taking considerable damage, while the former pounded the modernized Japanese battlecruiser so badly (nine 16-inch hits in the first couple of minutes) that she had to be scuttled the next morning.

- THE BATTLE OF THE SURIGAO STRAIT (OCTOBER 24–25, 1944). A U.S. squadron including the refurbished old battleships *Mississippi, Maryland, West Virginia, Tennessee, California,* and *Pennsylvania* (all but the first veterans of Pearl Harbor), supported by numerous smaller warships, ambushed a Japanese force including the old battleships *Fuso* and *Yamashiro,* which were annihilated in an action so one-sided that *Pennsylvania* never got to fire. This was the last time battleships ever fired on each other.

Considering that both the Imperial Navy and the U.S. Navy had put so much emphasis on battleships in their prewar plans, it is worth noting that of only two of the nine battleship slug-outs during World War II occurred in the Pacific. Briefly, the others were:

- NORTH SEA (APRIL 9, 1940). The undergunned German battleships *Gneisenau* and *Scharnhorst* engaged the old British battlecruiser *Renown* in an indecisive action off Norway.
- MERS EL-KÉBIR (JULY 3, 1940). The old British battleships *Resolution* and *Valiant,* with the battlecruiser *Hood* and some other ships, attacked the French fleet near Oran in Algeria, destroying the old battleship *Bretagne,* severely damaging her sister *Provence,* and less seriously damaging the new *Dunkerque,* while the latter's sister *Strasbourg* managed to escape unscathed.
- CALABRIA (JULY 9, 1940). An Italian squadron including the reconstructed old battleships *Giulio Cesare* and *Conte di Cavour* was intercepted off Calabria by a British squadron including the older battleships *Warspite, Royal Sovereign,* and *Malaya,* resulting in an indecisive but often intense action of about fifty minutes.
- DENMARK STRAIT (MAY 24, 1941). In a brief morning encounter in the Denmark Strait (between Iceland and Greenland), the new German battleship *Bismarck,* with an escorting heavy cruiser, took several hits while sinking the British battlecruiser *Hood* and damaging the very new British battleship *Prince of Wales.* Later that afternoon *Bismarck* and *Prince of Wales* briefly clashed again, without ill effects to either.
- NORTH ATLANTIC (MAY 27, 1941). After a wide-ranging chase

across the Atlantic, *Bismarck*, slowed by several fortuitous aerial-torpedo hits, was pounded to pieces by the new British battle-ship *King George* V and the older *Rodney*, reducing the German battleship to a burning wreck that was finished off by several torpedoes.

- CASABLANCA (NOVEMBER 8, 1942). The new USS *Massachusetts* exchanged several hundred rounds of heavy-caliber shells with the partially completed French *Jean Bart*, tied up at a dock at Casablanca, with the latter (which had only half of her guns mounted and was not yet fully operational for sea) coming off poorly.
- NORTH CAPE (DECEMBER 26, 1943). Off the northernmost point of Europe, a British squadron including the new battle-ship *Duke of York* encountered the German *Scharnhorst*, resulting in the latter's sinking after a protracted slugfest.

So there was a lot more battleship action in the European Theater than in the Pacific. Of course, the Pacific was most eminently a carrier theater, although the battleship actions off Guadalcanal and in the Surigao Strait were both considerably more decisive actions than most of those in the European war.

HOW THE WAR
WAS FOUGHT AT SEA

The Pacific war was fought largely at sea and in ways that had never been seen before. It was aircraft that changed the rules for all the players, as well as the enormous distances involved. In addition, there were also some of the ancient toe-to-toe slugging matches by surface ships. But most of the action revolved around using, and avoiding, aircraft, as well as trying to keep all those thousands of ships supplied.

STRATEGIC PLANNING BY WISHFUL THINKING

Military planners tend to be an optimistic lot. After all, there are so many things that can go wrong in war that one has to have a pretty positive outlook in order to have any faith in success whatsoever. But optimism can be taken to extremes. And perhaps never in military history has wishful thinking come to substitute for solid planning as much as in the Imperial Japanese Navy during World War II.

For example, during staff wargames (simulated operations on paper, using elaborate rules), it was not uncommon for umpires to allow "operations" to proceed despite an absence of supplies. They often permitted units to "refuel" from tankers the fleet did not possess, without any loss of time, so that the planned operations could proceed as scheduled.

But there were worse cases of cheating at wargames than the refueling gambit. The Japanese naval general staff held a major wargame as part of the planning for the Midway operation. Early in the game, the American player managed to "sink" several of the attacking carriers, an event that so upset the umpires that they restored the carriers to play. Even the subsequent disaster at Midway did not prove a salutary lesson.

Aware of the shortcomings of these earlier wargames, the Japanese decided on a new approach. Shortly after Midway, there was another wargame with even more interesting results, and interesting players—namely, Japanese diplomats just returned from the United States. During the early part of the war, all the belligerents, including the United States and Japan, had arranged to repatriate diplomatic personnel (including military attachés) who had found themselves trapped in enemy countries by the outbreak of hostilities. This was a time-consuming affair, as elaborate arrangements had to be made to ensure the safety of the ship carrying the diplomats and their families, the Swedish liner *Gripsholm*. As a result, a number of senior and middle-ranking Japanese naval personnel actually spent much of the first eight or nine months of the Pacific war living in relatively comfortable circumstances in the United States.

When the last batch of these officers returned to Japan, shortly after Midway, they were deliberately not briefed on the status of the war as understood by the Imperial Navy, and were then organized into a team to play the American side in a simulation game that was to cover the next two years of the war. The idea was sound, as these officers, one of whom was a rear admiral, had had full access to the American press while awaiting repatriation, and might be expected to have a useful perspective on American notions of how the war should be fought.

The game was conducted around the time the Marines landed on Guadalcanal. Despite rules that were generally favorable to the Japanese (such as reduced U.S. industrial productivity), by October 1, 1944, the "Americans" were landing in the Philippines, a matter that was extremely upsetting to the naval staff. This despite the fact that the game could easily have been used to help develop more realistic industrial production and strategic plans. The results of these games so shocked the Japanese High Command that no official notice of the game was circulated, all documentation was destroyed, and the officers who had taken the part of the Americans were scattered to various obscure posts and told, "Keep your mouth shut."

The actual initial U.S. landings in the Philippines occurred approximately three weeks later than those in the wargame.

IT WAS HARDER THAN IT LOOKED

Before the war, air power enthusiasts claimed that they could disable warships with heavy bombers from considerable altitudes. In practice, this proved wholly impossible. Indeed, so few underway ships were hit by high-level bombers that the probability of hitting them was actually less than chance.

The problem was one of the relative size of the target when viewed from high altitude, and the fact that the target was usually moving in an unpredictable fashion. The farther up one went, the smaller the target got, and the more significant became even minor changes in position.

PERCEIVED SIZE OF *MIDWAY*	
ALTITUDE (IN FEET)	% OF ACTUAL SIZE
500	59.52
1,000	14.42
5,000	0.61
10,000	0.14
15,000	0.08

Consider the aircraft carrier *Midway*. Although she was actually commissioned too late to see action in the war, *Midway* had the largest target area of any ship of the day, her length of 968 feet and beam of 136 feet giving a total deck area of roughly 14,700 square yards (in fact, the area was a good deal less, as these figures are for overall length and maximum beam).

To make a homier comparison, think about a dollar bill. A paper dollar is 6 inches by about 2.5 inches, with a surface area of about 15 square inches. This is about 1 square inch for each of 1,000 square yards of the carrier's flight deck. Now consider the relative size of the dollar at various distances from one's eye as compared with the size of *Midway* from various altitudes, in the table on page 156.

To put it another way, place a dollar bill at your feet. Stand up and look down at it. That's what *Midway* would look like from about 10,000 feet. So the principal reason that high-level bombers found it "difficult" to hit surface ships was that they were very, very small targets. Add to that the fact that the ships were usually somewhat camouflaged, were almost always moving, were often making evasive maneuvers, and were probably shooting like mad, and that the attacking aircraft were also moving and might even be the object of the attentions of unfriendly fighter aircraft, not to mention that there might be smoke or clouds obscuring the view, and it's no surprise that the number of ships actually hit by high-level bombers was negligible. Indeed, considering the lack of success that strategic bombers had in hitting factories and such, it's remarkable that in postwar literature the bomber enthusiasts repeatedly argued that wartime experience vindicated their prewar claims to be able to hit

THE *MIDWAY*/DOLLAR RELATIVE SIZE COMPARISON	
MIDWAY AT THIS HEIGHT (IN FEET)	. . . IS LIKE A DOLLAR AT THIS HEIGHT (IN INCHES/FEET)
500	3.2/0.27
1,000	6.3/0.53
5,000	31.6/2.63
10,000	63.6/5.3
15,000	94.8/7.9
20,000	126.0/10.5

ships under way at sea from altitude. In fact, on the only occasion on which this appears to have occurred, the Japanese victims were dumbfounded: When a B-17 actually hit a Japanese destroyer in the South Pacific, the ship's crew at first thought that anything but a bomber had been the cause of their injury, and at an official inquiry the ship's skipper ascribed the incident to ill fortune, allegedly commenting, "Even the B-17s can get a lucky hit once in a while."

UNEXPECTED ENCOUNTERS: SURFACE BATTLES IN THE PACIFIC

Before the Pacific war actually began, on December 7, 1941, surface combat was still expected to be the decisive form of naval action in the long-anticipated Japanese-American war. Certainly nothing that had occurred in the European war, which by then had been raging for more than two years, suggested otherwise.

However, Pearl Harbor and the air-sea battles of the Coral Sea and Midway in mid-1942 seemed to demonstrate that aircraft carriers, rather than battleships and cruisers, now ruled the waves. But the Coral Sea and Midway were followed by the Eastern Solomons and the Santa Cruz Islands, which, together with some unfortunate torpedoings, effectively depleted everyone's carrier forces.

As a result, most of the naval actions from late 1942 until well into 1943 were surface engagements, occasionally influenced by the presence of aircraft. In fact, there were over a dozen major and several score minor engagements between battleships, cruisers, and destroyers during the Pacific war.

Aside from a number of surface actions in the Netherlands East Indies in early 1942 and in the Philippines in 1944, virtually all of the remaining surface engagements took place in the Solomon Islands, notably in the vicinity of Guadalcanal, where in the six months from August 1942 through February 1943 there occurred five major and about thirty smaller surface engagements.

Before the war, the Japanese and the Americans had developed differing notions about surface combat. The Japanese, mindful of their probable numerical inferiority in a war with the United States, trained for night actions and stressed the use of torpedoes by both destroyers and cruisers. They preferred putting their heavier ships in the van, and were willing to use multiple columns, permitting the tactical independence of different squadrons operating together. All of these techniques were intended to make it easier for a smaller Japanese force to defeat a larger Allied one. And they worked.

The U.S. Navy, in contrast, was fairly rigidly tied to the single-line-ahead formation, with destroyers at the van and rear and the heavier ships in the middle, all to operate under a single command. For all practical purposes, the U.S. Navy saw no need to innovate or question what it was doing or what it was likely to face when surface naval combat occurred. Little attention was paid to Japanese preparations for the coming war, even though little effort would have been required to discover what the Japanese were doing to get ready. In fact, some military attachés in Tokyo did discern that the Japanese Navy was rather more effective than conventional wisdom in the West had it. These reports were generally ignored until it was too late.

When the two navies began to clash in surface actions, it quickly became apparent that the Japanese were superior. The battles did not conform to the USN's expectations. Because of the presence of land-based aircraft, whoever controlled the air in daylight had a tremendous combat advantage and so surface battles were almost always at night. In night surface combat, the Japanese initially had an advantage. During peacetime they had trained hard for this type of combat. They had evolved more realistic tactics for night combat and drilled their ships' crews relentlessly in all types of weather, regardless of casualties. In addition, they had developed superior optical equipment for range finding.

American sailors had received a more leisurely diet of daytime training exercises, marred by a contestlike atmosphere that resulted in training being conducted in the calmest possible weather, so that no ship would have an unfair advantage.

Moreover, unlike their U.S. counterparts, all Japanese cruisers carried torpedoes and many of them were provided with torpedo reloads. The cruiser crews were well trained in the use of torpedoes, something rare with torpedo-equipped cruisers. The Japanese torpedoes were superior to all others in the world, being both larger, more reliable, and longer-ranged. The U.S. admirals had generally neglected the use of the torpedo in surface combat, omitting it entirely from most cruisers, for example, and not getting enough practice in coordinating torpedo-armed destroyers with heavier ships during maneuvers.

So from the Java Sea battles (February 27–March 1, 1942) through the summer and fall battles around Guadalcanal, the Japanese were generally triumphant at night. American sailors had to undergo the same grueling training process as the Japanese before U.S. surface ships could meet the Japanese on equal terms. A lot of material changes in late 1942 helped, but it was the training that made the difference.

Meanwhile, the USN gradually acquired superior ships, improved damage control techniques, and developed better communications methods. And it began to learn to use its torpedoes.

The torpedo was actually the most effective weapon used in the night battles, accounting for most of the ships lost. As it turned out, American destroyermen already knew how to make effective torpedo attacks, but had usually been kept on a tight leash by task force commanders lacking destroyer experience. Given a chance to operate on their own, they proved particularly effective in torpedo attacks, as at Balikpapan (January 23–24, 1942) and Cape Esperance (October 11–12, 1942). Despite this, it was not until mid-1943 that U.S. destroyers were routinely allowed to operate in conjunction with, rather than in line with, heavier ships.

Meanwhile, radar came along. Surprisingly, it may have actually handicapped U.S. night fighting abilities initially. The first radars were inefficient, temperamental, and not at all understood by most senior officers. At times the presence of Japanese warships was first detected by lookouts, if it had not already been announced by the arrival of their shells, before they were detected by radar, at which point it was usually too late to do anything but die bravely. As radar improved and commanders who understood its capabilities and limitations (like Willis "Ching Chong China" Lee) came along, things began to get better, and American ships began to feel more comfortable in night actions.

However, even as the U.S. Navy improved, the Japanese remained formidable opponents. At Kula Gulf (July 4–5, 1943) and Kolombangara (July 12–13, 1943), they gave better than they received, despite all the American advantages. But gradually their edge was lost, and in the last important surface actions of the war on anything like even terms, Vella Lavella (August 6–7, 1943) and Empress Augusta Bay (November 2, 1943), they came off second best. It had been a tough school, but the U.S. Navy had learned, albeit the hard way. Learning how to fight while in combat is the hard way; learning during tough, realistic peacetime training is the easy way.

ANATOMY OF A CARRIER
U.S. TASK FORCE

Except for submarines, warships rarely operate alone. They travel and fight in groups for greater safety and effectiveness. In the twentieth century, these groups came to be called task forces. Aircraft-carrier task force composition and the formations used were a crucial, although often unrecognized, aspect of the naval war.

Even before the war broke out, the Japanese Navy had figured out that carriers operating in groups were many times more effective than carriers operating singly. Right at the start of the war the Japanese created the world's first operational fast carrier task force, grouping six carriers together with some fast battleships, cruisers, and destroyers, and sending them against Pearl Harbor with devastating effect. This task force operated for about five months, roaming the western Pacific in support of Japanese operations, and even raiding into the Indian Ocean. This "First Air Fleet" carried all before it and appeared invincible. At the time, it was. But then it was broken up. The Imperial Navy was never again able to put together so many carriers, and its carriers were never again to be nearly so effective.

In contrast, the United States began the Pacific war with a poverty of carriers and a plethora of missions. There were only three carriers in the Pacific at the time of Pearl Harbor and only as many more were to trickle in from the Atlantic over the first year of the war, mostly to replace losses. So carriers had to operate singly, with small escorts, in order to accomplish everything that had to be done. Gradually, as more and more carriers became available, task forces grew larger, with consequent improvements in effectiveness.

Despite this, through mid-1943, several American admirals still believed that single-carrier, or two-carrier, task forces were best. The most air-minded, however, took the tack that "more is better," holding out for the largest possible task forces, to concentrate the striking power of several carriers, and, incidentally, to concentrate the defensive firepower of so many vessels. And gradually their view prevailed, so that by mid-1943 task forces of three and four carriers were considered best, and some men were advocating even larger groupings.

In each of the 1942 cases the carriers were really operating in small task groups, each having its own dedicated escorts, but were usually operating under a single higher command. At the Eastern Solomons and Santa Cruz, the carriers were deployed about 10 miles apart, each at the center of a ring composed of battleships, cruisers, and destroyers about 1,800 to 2,500 yards distant. This did not permit mutual support among the three task forces, and made it impossible to provide adequate CAP (Combat Air Patrol, fighters protecting their ships). In contrast, at the Philippine Sea, the fleet deployed in five task groups (TGs), one composed primarily of battleships. Each carrier TG formed a circle about 4 miles across, with the carriers in the middle, closely accompanied by two or three destroyers and surrounded by cruisers and still more destroyers; intervals between escorts and carriers were often as little as a half mile. The battleship TG formed a larger circle, about 6 miles across, with all of the ships save the flagship deployed on the perimeter. The relative disposition of the TGs was:

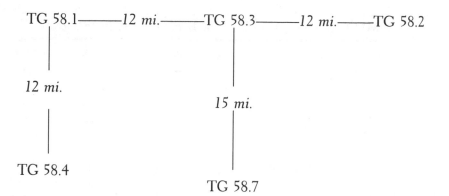

A picket of destroyers was deployed in a wide circle around the fleet. This formation was adopted to maximize antiaircraft firepower. Normally the battleships composing TG 58.7 were dispersed among the carrier task groups. However, Vice Admiral Raymond Spruance formed TG 58.7 and deployed it between his carriers and the Japanese, figuring that the battlewagons would likely prove irresistible to attacking enemy aircraft, while being both more able to defend themselves and more survivable than the carriers.

This sort of formation remained the norm through to the end of the war, by which time most TGs were composed of four heavy carriers plus one light carrier, for a total of about 430 aircraft. Some carrier admirals were by then thinking in terms of even larger task groups, with up to eight carriers, a development that would almost certainly have occurred had the war lasted into 1946.

In grouping their carriers for the Pearl Harbor operation, the Japanese had inadvertently hit upon the ideal size for a carrier task force. However, they failed to maintain it. One result of this was that they frittered away their superiority through dispersal, leading to their disaster at Midway, at which they committed only four of their nine available carriers, even granting that several of those sent off on unnecessary missions were relatively light. After Midway, their ability to build large carrier task forces was not as great as that of the United States, and steadily declined.

Although the First Air Fleet had given the Japanese a decided advantage in the early part of the war, the loss of the four carriers at Midway effectively reduced them to task forces of two or three carriers for the rest of 1942. At that, the Japanese approach was still

COMPOSITION OF U.S. CARRIER TASK FORCES

YEAR AND OPERATION	CV/CVL PER TASK FORCE	BB/CA/CL	DD	NOTE
1941				
Raids	1	3–4	5–9	A
1942				
Raids	1–2	4–6	5–10	B
Coral Sea	2	7	12	C
Midway: TF 16	2	6	11	D
TF 17	1	2	6	D
Eastern Solomons	1	2–3	5–7	E
Santa Cruz	1	3–4	6–8	F
1944				
Philippine Sea	3–4	3–5	9–12	G

NOTES:

A. These were the task forces that attempted to relieve Wake Island and then raided Jaluit in the Mandates.

B. Raids on the Mandates in early 1942 were by one-carrier task forces, but that which hit the Japanese in New Guinea had two carriers.

C. Actually there were two separate task forces operating cooperatively.

D. TF 16 and TF 17 operated in cooperation.

E. There were three task forces, operating under a single command, totaling three carriers, eight battleships and cruisers, and eighteen destroyers.

F. The two carrier task forces were supported by a surface combat group, for a total of two carriers, twelve battleships and cruisers, and eighteen destroyers.

G. The four carrier task forces (one of them with three carriers, the others with four) operated in conjunction with a battleship task force, for a total of fifteen carriers, seven battleships, twenty-one cruisers, and sixty-nine destroyers. This was basically the pattern to which the Third/Fifth Fleet adhered through the end of the war, a model that was also adopted by the Royal Navy task force that served in the Pacific in 1945.

superior to U.S. Navy practice, which remained uncertain as to the optimal size of a carrier task force until mid-1943.

Japanese tactical formations in the early period were based on single-ship defense. At Coral Sea, each carrier was covered by four to five cruisers and destroyers standing about 1,600 yards away. At Midway the Japanese grouped the carriers together and surrounded them with a screen of battleships, cruisers, and destroyers at less than a nautical mile's distance. For the defense of *Hiryu*, their last carrier at Midway, they grouped two battleships, one heavy cruiser,

COMPOSITION OF JAPANESE CARRIER TASK FORCES

YEAR AND OPERATION	CV/CVL PER TASK FORCE	BB/CA/CL	DD	NOTE
1941				
Pearl Harbor	6	5	9	
Wake	2	2	2	A
Rabaul	4	4	7	B
1942				
Indian Ocean	6	7	11	C
Coral Sea	2	4	6	D
Midway	4	5	12	E
Aleutians	2	2	4	
Eastern Solomons	2	6	17	F
Santa Cruz	3	7	15	G
1944 Philippine Sea				
Heavy TG	3	3	9–20	H
Light TG	1	3–4	3	H

NOTES:
  A. Actually, this task force comprised one division of the Pearl Harbor Strike Force (the First Air Fleet). Note, by the way, the extremely thin escort with which these carriers operated.
  B. Two divisions of the Pearl Harbor Strike Force.
  C. The reunited First Air Fleet.
  D. Excludes invasion force with one light carrier.
  E. Excludes invasion force and battle fleet, with one light carrier.
  F. Excludes a light carrier and supporting vessels serving as a bombardment group and bait.
  G. Excludes forces earmarked for surface action. The total Japanese force available comprised two fleet and two light carriers, five battleships, fifteen cruisers, and forty-four destroyers.
  H. There were two heavy task groups and three light ones, totaling five fleet and four light carriers, plus five battleships, nine cruisers, and twenty-eight destroyers.

and five destroyers within about a nautical mile. In neither case was this enough, and this certainly contributed to the demise of the First Air Fleet. Even this early in the war, U.S. escorts were routinely getting to within a half mile of the carriers.

After Santa Cruz, the Japanese carrier fleet was withdrawn from action for over a year, due largely to the enormous loss of trained pilots. This ought to have given the Japanese enough time to (1) train more pilots and (2) study U.S. carrier operations, since U.S.

carriers continued to operate in support of landings and in attacks on Japanese bases. They failed to do either very well.

For the Philippine Sea, Vice Admiral Jisaburo Ozawa formed two carrier task forces, one composed of three CVLs and one of five CVs and a CVL. He then proceeded to separate them by about 100 miles, sending the light carriers ahead of the main body, disposed in three task groups, each of one CVL plus escorts, deployed on a front of about 12 miles, while the main body formed two task groups. The fleet deployed roughly thus:

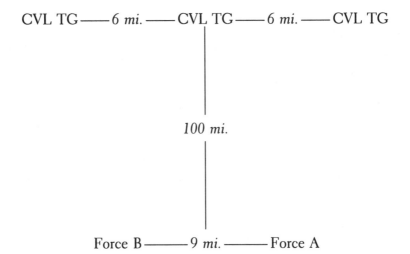

Ozawa appears to have intended to use the light carriers as bait, luring Spruance into a strike against them, so that he could in turn locate the U.S. carriers and hit them using his longer-range aircraft. Although the bait was rather far ahead of the main body, this might have worked, had his pilots been adequately trained. However, despite the longer range of his aircraft, he probably put too much distance between his striking force and his bait. And in any case, his resources were not adequate to the needs of the moment.

IT WAS IMPRESSIVE AS LONG AS IT LASTED

We think of the Pacific war as the "war of the carriers" and the "beginning of the carrier age." Well, that's technically true. But keep in mind that only *five* carrier-to-carrier battles were fought during the entire war. Moreover, there hasn't been another carrier-versus-carrier battle since the Battle of the Philippine Sea in June 1944. That's over fifty years, folks, and another one doesn't look too likely anytime soon.

The "carrier-versus-carrier era" lasted only twenty-five months (from the Coral Sea in May 1942 to the Philippine Sea in June 1944). And actually, the last carrier-to-carrier combat that was anything like an even fight was in October 1942 (Battle of Santa Cruz Islands). This was the last time an American carrier was sunk in a carrier battle. In effect, the "Golden Age of Carrier Battles" lasted from May to October 1942. Five months. Four battles. To be sure, there was a fifth carrier battle, which the Japanese lost, in mid-1944. But that one was called the Great Marianas Turkey Shoot, which gives you an idea of how lopsided it was.

Carriers proved to be more useful against everything but other carriers. Attacks on enemy bases and shipping and in support of amphibious landings composed the bulk of carrier activity throughout the war. Although land-based aircraft were two to three times as effective as carrier planes, the carriers could be swiftly moved across the vast expanse of the Pacific. It was this mobility that made carriers less effective. They could not lug around as much avgas or munitions as a land base could stockpile. Operating at sea caused more damage to the aircraft, and the shortage of space on a carrier made aircraft maintenance more difficult. But despite these limitations, the aircraft carrier reigned supreme across the Pacific. As long as the carriers stayed away from more numerous land-based aircraft (something the Japanese weren't able to muster by 1944), the carriers could slug it out with anything they came up against.

Note that the last American carrier lost in combat was a victim of land-based aircraft. And the second most dangerous foe of carriers was the submarine. Thus, since late 1942, the carrier situation hasn't changed. The U.S. carrier fleet is supreme and its only foes are large numbers of land-based aircraft and submarines.

NAVAL AIR DEFENSE

On balance, ships were usually not very safe in the presence of airplanes, particularly early in the war when air defenses were relatively weak.

There are several factors at work in determining just how survivable a ship is when under air attack. The first is the number of friendly fighters that one can put over the ships, since these can begin the process of defending them at some distance away. Lacking friendly fighters, or if the enemy gets past them, a ship must defend itself. So we start with individual ship antiaircraft armament.

Prewar estimates of the antiaircraft requirements of warships were uniformly inadequate. In practice, throughout the war, all navies continuously increased the antiaircraft capacity of all their ships, not only adding guns but developing new and more effective ones.

Consider the AA firepower of the U.S. battleship *South Dakota*:

DATE	5"/38	40mm	1.1"	20mm	.50 MG
Mar. 1942	16	—	28	6	8
Sept. 1942	16	16	20	36+	—
Feb. 1943	16	68	—	35	—
Dec. 1944	16	68	—	72	—
Mar. 1945	16	68	—	77	—

South Dakota was designed in the mid-1930s, laid down in 1939, launched in 1941, and commissioned in March 1942. When designed she had one of the heaviest allotments of antiaircraft guns of any ship, and her three sisters, who had four additional 5-inch guns, were even more heavily armed. This was an enormous antiaircraft capacity, but it was continuously upgraded throughout the war. The additional firepower added in September 1942 enabled her to survive the Battle of the Santa Cruz Islands (October 26, 1942), during which she was attacked by at least sixty-five Japanese dive bombers and torpedo bombers, downing twenty-six, the world's record for a single warship in a single engagement. Some of the attackers got through, hitting with three bombs plus a near miss, resulting in one death and fifty wounded, plus damage to one 16-inch gun turret.

The success of *South Dakota* at Santa Cruz was not only due to the volume of AA fire, but to:

1. Effective radar fire direction
2. The resiliency and maneuverability of the ship
3. The introduction of proximity-fuzed ammunition for her 5-inch guns

Given the sturdiness of her construction and the efficiency of American damage control techniques, *South Dakota* was probably a lot more survivable than any other ship in the fleet at the time. But she was also able to put up an enormous amount of AA fire. Nevertheless, that volume was still considered inadequate, and her antiaircraft defenses were repeatedly enhanced. Nor was this a unique experience. Apparently, virtually every ship in every navy that reported for repairs or an overhaul ended up with more antiaircraft firepower.

Consider some other examples in the table on page 168.

The Japanese actually added more antiaircraft weapons to their ships than did the Americans. However, U.S. and Allied ships usually started out with more, and better-quality, AA guns than did Japanese ships, and also tended to acquire air defense radar, radar fire direction, and the proximity fuze, which proved immensely important. Lacking these, as the war went on Japanese ships became relatively much more vulnerable to U.S. air attacks than U.S. ships were to Japanese air attacks, particularly as the quality of Japanese pilots declined.

The formation in which a ship found itself also affected air defense capability. Ships were safer traveling in relatively tight groups than in looser formations or singly. This is a simple matter of geometry: A group of ships has a smaller defensive perimeter than the sum of the defensive perimeters of the individual vessels. In groups they could share defensive responsibility, particularly if they had the doctrine, communications facilities, and training to do so.

The larger the formation, the more secure the ships at its center, although really enormous formations made captains and admirals nervous, which is probably why they never tried really huge task

U.S. SHIPS	5"	40mm	1.1"	20mm	.50 MG
CV *Enterprise*					
Dec. 1941	8	—	16	—	24
Jan. 1945	8	60	—	32	—
CL *Brooklyn*					
Dec. 1941	8	—	—	—	8
Jan. 1945	8	28	—	20	—
DD *Benson*					
Dec. 1940	5	—	—	—	6
Dec. 1941	4	4	—	7	—
Dec. 1945	4	12	—	4	—

JAPANESE SHIPS	5"	25mm	13.2mm
BB *Yamato*			
Dec. 1941	12	24	4
June 1943	24	36	—
Apr. 1944	24	98	—
July 1944	24	113	—
Jan. 1945	24	150	—
CV *Shokaku*			
Dec. 1941	16	42	—
June 1943	16	70	—
July 1944	16	96	—
DD *Kisumi*			
Dec. 1941	6	—	4
Dec. 1943	4	12	—
June 1944	4	28	4

forces. The most typical task force had three to five carriers plus escorts, despite the fact that some airmen were thinking in terms of task forces of eight carriers.

Aside from the Pearl Harbor Strike Force, the Japanese were never able to come close to emulating the virtually impregnable U.S. fast carrier task forces of 1944–1945. As their air defense capacity proved inadequate, we are unable to assess what their true capacity might have been.

However, despite the enormous volume of AA firepower generated by U.S. warships, a matter in which they were more or less emulated by the British and even the Japanese, the primary reasons U.S. surface forces were relatively immune from air attack by mid-1944 were:

1. The precipitous decline in the quality of Japanese pilots
2. The development of radar-controlled centralized air defense direction
3. The proximity fuze

Officially designated the VT, or variable telemetry, fuze (but more commonly called the "funny fuze"), the proximity fuze contained a miniature radar set. Thus equipped, a shell would explode when the returning radar signal indicated that there was an airplane within lethal range. This turned near misses into hits, and made antiaircraft fire by large (5-inch) guns much more effective. By mid-1943, although only about 25 percent of AA ammo issued to the fleet had proximity fuzes, these accounted for about 50 percent of Japanese aircraft shot down, making them about 300 percent more effective than the old timed or impact fuzes. By 1945 this had risen to nearly 600 percent, and this despite the fact that perhaps 30 percent of proximity-fuzed rounds were duds!

However, proximity-fuzed ammunition was in relatively short supply, so that even in 1945 the mix of AA ammo aboard ships was roughly 1:1 between proximity-fuzed and old-fashioned timed projectiles.

THE CARRIER AIR GROUP

The contingent of aircraft assigned to a carrier is called its air group. An air group in the Pacific war usually consisted of several squadrons, each of one type of aircraft. There was a mix of fighters, torpedo bombers, and dive bombers. The authorized number of aircraft in an air group varied a great deal during the war, as experience dictated various changes, as newer types of aircraft became available, and as newer carriers came into service. And of course, actual numbers of aircraft carried at any given moment would be affected by combat or administrative loss.

A number of unusual air groups were formed during the war. Three carriers were eventually equipped primarily for night operations. In June 1944, CVL *Independence* was converted to this role, followed in January 1945 by CV *Enterprise* and in the following June by CV *Bon Homme Richard*. These carriers had aircraft of all types fitted with special equipment for night flying and fighting, although they also regularly performed daytime missions.

From time to time it was proposed to equip one or two carriers entirely with fighters, so that they could assume the task of Combat Air Patrol over the fleet, freeing up the fighters of the regular carriers to escort their bombers. This was actually tried out experimentally in the spring of 1943, where there were only two Allied carriers operating in the Pacific, USS *Saratoga* and HMS *Victorious* (on loan from the Royal Navy). The two carriers shared their air groups, both of which were equipped with American aircraft, so that *Saratoga* ended up with seventy-two Avenger and Dauntless bombers and only twelve Wildcat fighters, while *Victorious* had thirty-six Wildcats and only twelve Avengers. The experiment was not judged a success and was never repeated. On the other hand, it was by no means unusual for escort carriers to be equipped entirely with fighters or bombers, especially when operating in support of amphibious landings.

Escort carriers were also often used as aircraft transports, in which role they were capable of carrying as many as seventy-four airplanes, if they were folding-wing Navy types. They could not, of course, operate these aircraft, which had to be loaded and offloaded by cranes.

Japanese carrier air groups tended to be much less uniform than American ones, partially because Japanese carriers tended to be much less uniform in their basic characteristics than American ones. In addition, the Japanese Navy tended to "marry" air groups to particular carriers, so that when the carrier was out of action, so too

CHANGING COMPOSITION OF U.S. CARRIER AIR GROUPS

MONTH	TYPE	FTRS	DBMRS	TBMRS	TOTAL	NOTE
Dec. 1941	CV	18	36	18	72	A
June 1942	CV	24	36	18	78	B
Aug. 1942	CVE	12	9	9	30	
Sept. 1942	CV	36	36	18	90	
Dec. 1942	CVL	21	9	0	30	
June 1943	CVE	12	8	0	20	C
Sept. 1943	CV	38	28	18	84	D
Jan. 1944	CVL	24	—9—		33	
	CVE	16	—12—		28	E
	CVE	15	—15—		30	F
June 1944	CV	54	24	18	96	
Dec. 1944	CV	71	15	15	101	G

NOTES: "Month" is that in which a new formula for air group composition was instituted. "CV" is fleet carrier; "CVE" is escort carrier; "CVL" is light carrier; "FTRS" is fighters; "DBMRS" is dive bombers; "TBMRS" is torpedo bombers.

Several trends are noticeable in these figures. Not only did the number of aircraft on carriers generally rise, but the proportion of fighters increased markedly, from 25 percent of the air group at the start of the war to 70 percent by its end. In addition, note that by early 1944 the advent of the Grumman Avenger, officially a dive bomber, had tended to blur the differences between torpedo bombers and dive bombers. A very good airplane, the Avenger could be employed in either role, or as a level bomber or even, with some modifications, as a light cargo and passenger transport. Totals exclude the two to three so-called utility aircraft on all carriers, usually light cargo/passenger planes.

A. At the time of Pearl Harbor, *Lexington* actually had only 63 aircraft embarked and *Enterprise* only 68, both ships having left some of their own planes behind in order to take on aircraft that they had just delivered to Wake and Midway respectively.

B. Actual totals at Midway were *Enterprise*, 79 aircraft (27 fighters, 37 dive bombers, 15 torpedo bombers); *Hornet*, 69 (17 fighters, 38 dive bombers, 14 torpedo bombers); and *Yorktown*, 75 (25 fighters, 37 dive bombers, 13 torpedo bombers), plus a couple of utility aircraft each.

C. *Bogue* Class CVEs, converted from merchant ships.

D. This was the authorized number, but many ships managed to have two to three additional combat aircraft.

E. *Bogue* and *Casablanca* Class escort carriers, displacing under 14,000 tons at full load.

F. *Sangamon* and *Commencement Bay* Class CVEs, displacing more than 20,000 tons at full load.

G. Actually, the official figure for fighters read something like "to capacity," so that most carriers had many more than is indicated here: *Saratoga*, for example, apparently carried 96 fighters. This was possible due to deck stowage, a practice not favored in the economy-minded prewar Navy, since the aircraft deteriorated rapidly with extended exposure to the elements. But deck storage was eminently practical once aircraft production had reached flood proportions, and heavy combat and operational losses would prevent any planes getting old enough to develop saltwater damage anyway. In addition, later U.S. naval aircraft had wings that folded tightly alongside the fuselage, which permitted some aircraft to be stored overhead, leaving the floor of the hangar deck available for additional airplanes; some older aircraft had often possessed only folding wing tips. Four fighters on each carrier were equipped for nighttime Combat Air Patrol, supported by a specially equipped Avenger that served as a night air control aircraft.

COMPOSITION OF JAPANESE CARRIER AIR GROUPS

MONTH	TYPE	FTRS	DBMRS	TBMRS	TOTAL	NOTE
Dec. 1941	CV	18	18	18–27	54–63	A
	CVL	16–24	21–0	0–21	37–45	B
	CVE	9–12	0	6–12	15–24	C
June 1942	CV	21	21	21	63	D
Aug. 1942	CV	27	27	18	72	E
	CVL	16	21	0	37	
Oct. 1942	CV	18–27	20–27	10–23	55–72	F
	CVL	18	0	6	24	G
May 1944	CV	26–27	26–25	17	69	
	CVL	20–21	0	9–10	29–30	

NOTES: "Month" is that in which a new formula for air group composition was instituted. "CV" is fleet carrier; "CVE" is escort carrier; "CVL" is light carrier; "FTRS" is fighters; "DBMRS" is dive bombers; "TBMRS" is torpedo bombers.

A. This despite the rated complements of the carriers: *Akagi* and *Kaga*, about 90; *Soryu* and *Hiryu*, about 70; *Shokaku* and *Zuikaku*, about 85. However, at Midway, *Kaga* does seem to have had 83 aircraft (30 fighters, 23 dive bombers, 30 torpedo bombers), although whether she managed to operate all of them is unclear.

B. *Zuiho*, *Shoho*, and *Ryujo*.

C. *Ryuho* and *Hosho*. Strictly speaking, these were not escort carriers, merely very small carriers. The Imperial Navy built a few escort carriers, which saw limited service. The Imperial Army built some aircraft transports, which looked like escort carriers and are sometimes so classified, but they had very limited aircraft operating capabilities, and in some cases none whatsover.

D. *Kaga*, however, had an additional 9 torpedo bombers.

E. However, at Eastern Solomons, *Shokaku* had only 14 dive bombers.

F. *Junyo*, 55; *Shokaku*, 61; *Zuikaku*, 72.

G. *Zuiho*.

was its air group. In contrast, the U.S. Navy viewed air groups and carriers as separate entities that could be mixed and matched as needed. When *Saratoga* was torpedoed in early 1942, her pilots and aircraft were immediately transferred to other carriers, whereas when *Shokaku* was put out of action at the Coral Sea, her air group was grounded until she was restored to service. As with American air groups, the Imperial Navy's also underwent evolution.

It is interesting to note that while there was a general increase in air group size, overall it was relatively minor. Similarly, although the tendency was to increase the proportion of fighters in air groups, this was not as marked as in the case of the U.S. air groups. One reason for this is that the Japanese did not adopt deck stowage of aircraft. Moreover, their poorly conceived folding wing designs (basically, the wings formed a triangle over the fuselage) consumed overhead space that prevented overhead stowage. In addition, due to technical problems concerning hangar deck stowage space and service area design, Japanese carriers were generally incapable of operating their full rated complements of aircraft, usually carrying some in a dismantled state. Most of the Japanese carriers appear to have been able to operate only about 85 percent of their rated aircraft capacity. The worst case seems to have been *Taiho*, able to operate only 65 percent.

Note that Japanese information is unavailable for 1943, during which the Japanese were desperately trying to rebuild their carrier fleet and air groups and undertook no combat operations. Although the Japanese did commit carriers in the Battle of Leyte Gulf in October 1944, the composition of their air groups is unclear. The four carriers (*Zuikaku*, *Zuiho*, *Chiyoda*, and *Chitose*) could operate about 170 aircraft, but actually had a total of 116 among them (80 fighters, 36 torpedo bombers). However, even before the battle was joined, most of these aircraft were flown off to land bases, leaving only 29 with the fleet, none of which did anything during the ensuing fighting. There were also two hybrid "battleship/carriers," which had no aircraft.

British carrier air groups lacked uniformity throughout the war. There were many reasons for this. The Royal Air Force was responsible for procuring aircraft and pilots for carriers, while the Royal Navy was responsible for operating them, reserving their command to Navy surface warfare officers. The result was airplanes that were either obsolete or wholly unsuited to carrier operations, pilots lacking adequate understanding of naval operations, and skippers much preferring to command battleships.

Given such handicaps it's a wonder that the Fleet Air Arm managed to garner a good deal of glory, its most notable success being the air strike against Taranto Harbor by twenty-one very obsolete Swordfish biplanes on the night of November 11–12, 1940, which put an important part of the Italian battle fleet out of action for several months. In the Indian Ocean and the Pacific, the Royal Navy's carriers did less well, until reequipped with American aircraft.

COMPOSITION OF BRITISH CARRIER AIR GROUPS

MONTH	TYPE	FTRS	DBMRS	TBMRS	TOTAL	NOTE
Feb. 1942	CV	21	—	24	45	A
	CV	12	—	21	33	B
	CVL	—	—	12	12	C
May 1942	CV	21–29	—	20–18	41–47	D
Nov. 1942	CV	24	—	18	42	E
May 1943	CV	36	12	—	48	F
May 1944	CV	28–42	18–0	21–15	57	G
Mar. 1945	CV	29	18	—	47	H
	CV	36–37	16–14	—	52–51	I
	CV	49	20	—	69	J
July 1945	CV	42	12	—	54	K
	CV	60	18	—	78	L

NOTES: "Month" is that in which a new formula for air group composition was instituted. "CV" is fleet carrier; "CVE" is escort carrier; "CVL" is light carrier; "FTRS" is fighters; "DBMRS" is dive bombers; "TBMRS" is torpedo bombers.

A. *Indomitable*, with 12 Fulmar and 9 Sea Hurricane fighters, and 24 Albacore torpedo bombers.

B. *Formidable*, with 12 "Martlet" fighters (Wildcats) and 21 Albacores. A very small air group, even for a British carrier. Note her aircraft complement for July 1945, in Note K, below.

C. *Hermes*, with a dozen Swordfish torpedo bombers.

D. *Illustrious*. The fighters were Wildcats, plus 1 to 6 Fulmars equipped for night patrol; the bombers were Swordfish.

E. *Victorious* as equipped for the North Africa landings. She had 12 Wildcat and 6 Seafire fighters, plus 6 Fulmar night fighters and 18 Albacore bombers.

F. *Victorious* while operating in company with *Saratoga* in the Pacific, equipped with 36 Wildcats and a dozen Avengers.

G. *Illustrious*, with Corsair fighters, Avenger dive bombers, and Barracuda torpedo bombers, as available, a very unstable air group.

H. *Indomitable*, with Hellcats and Avengers.

I. *Illustrious* was equipped with Corsairs and Avengers; *Victorious*, with Hellcats and Avengers. Numbers are for either configuration.

J. *Indefatigable*, with 40 Seafire and 9 Firefly fighters, plus 20 Avengers.

K. *Formidable*, sister ship to *Illustrious* and *Victorious*, with 36 Corsairs and 6 Hellcats, plus a dozen Avengers.

L. *Implacable*, with 48 Seafires and a dozen Fireflies, plus 18 Avengers.

British carrier air groups in the Pacific and Indian oceans are described in the table on page 174.

British carriers operated mostly in the Indian Ocean, but there were none there from about May 1942 until about May 1944. When *Victorious* operated in the South Pacific from May through August 1943, she did so only after several months of reequipping and retraining in Hawaii with U.S. aircraft. In early 1945, a British carrier task force began operating with the Third/Fifth Fleet, continuing until the surrender of Japan.

GAS-GUZZLING WARSHIPS

Warships are notorious fuel hogs. A "typical" 1944–1945 U.S. carrier task force of three fleet carriers, a light carrier, a couple of heavy cruisers, several light cruisers, and a dozen destroyers would consume nearly 50 tons of fuel oil an hour at 15 knots, or 1,200 tons a day. Even at this very economical speed, the task force would require a tanker loaded with fuel about every eight days. And at full speed, around 30 knots, consumption would more than triple.

Some figures based on U.S. and Japanese ships, in the table on page 176, are of interest.

Aside from the battleships *Nagato, Tennessee,* and *Yamato* and the escort carrier *Casablanca,* all of the ships on this table could do 30 knots or better at full speed, at the cost of skyrocketing fuel consumption. At full steam an American destroyer's fuel consumption roughly quadrupled. This was the main reason destroyers always seemed to be refueling, as at 30 knots they would run out of fuel in about four days.

Being short of fuel not only put you at a disadvantage operationally, but also created problems for the safety of the ship, particularly in a smaller vessel, since it affected stability. At full load (about 2,900 tons), fuel constituted about 17 percent of the displacement of a *Fletcher* Class destroyer. The three destroyers lost in the typhoon of December 17, 1944, all appear to have been rather low on fuel.

The most fuel-efficient ship on this list is the battleship *Iowa,* burning only 6.5 tons of fuel an hour to move some 57,000 tons of warship, or about 1 ton of fuel for each 8,800 displacement tons,

TYPE AND CLASS	LAUNCHED	FUEL CAPACITY (IN TONS)	HOURLY FUEL USAGE (IN TONS)	FUEL EFFICIENCY
Over 20,000 Tons				
BB *Nagato*	1919	5,600	8.4	5.8
BB *Tennessee*	1919	4,700	5.8	7.0
BB *Yamato*	1940	6,300	9.5	7.3
BB *Iowa*	1942	6,250	6.5	8.8
CV *Lexington*	1925	3,600	4.9	8.7
CV *Shokaku*	1939	4,100	6.2	5.2
CV *Essex*	1942	6,330	6.2	5.6
CV *Taiho*	1943	5,700	8.6	4.4
CB *Alaska*	1943	4,619	4.5	7.6
10,000–20,000 Tons				
CV *Ranger*	1933	2,350	3.1	5.7
CV *Soryu*	1935	3,670	5.5	3.6
CVL *Independence*	1942	2,600	3.0	4.9
CVE *Casablanca*	1943	2,200	3.2	3.4
CA *Mogami*	1934	2,163	3.2	3.4
CA *Baltimore*	1942	2,000	3.0	5.7
CL *Brooklyn*	1936	1,800	2.7	4.5
5,000–10,000 Tons				
CA *Aoba*	1926	1,800	3.0	3.0
CLAA *Atlanta*	1941	1,360	2.4	3.5
CL *Agano*	1941	1,400	2.1	4.1
Under 5,000 Tons				
DD *Fubuki*	1927	500	0.8	2.6
DD *Somers*	1937	400	0.8	3.5
DD *Akitsuki*	1941	1,097	1.6	2.3
DD *Fletcher*	1942	492	1.1	2.7

NOTES: Ships are grouped according to full-load displacement to make comparison between vessels of similar size easier. Within displacement groups, ships are listed according to their year of launching, which puts ships of comparable age (and level of engine technology) together. "BB" is battleship; "CV" is carrier; "CB" is large cruiser; "CVL" is light carrier; "CVE" is escort carrier; "CA" is cruiser; "CL" is light cruiser; "CLAA" is antiaircraft light cruiser; "DD" is destroyer. "Hourly Fuel Usage" is given at 15 knots because this was a common speed for long voyages, even by ships capable of much better. "Fuel Efficiency" is in terms of the number of tons (in thousands) of ship each ton of fuel could move at 15 knots, so the higher the figure, the more efficient the ship.

followed by the carrier *Lexington*, burning only 4.9 tons of oil an hour to move some 43,000 tons of warship, or little more than 1 ton of fuel per hour for each 8,700 tons of displacement. These were extraordinarily economical vessels.

In general, larger ships were more fuel-efficient than smaller ones, and newer ones more efficient than older ones; the exception, *Lexington* (commissioned in 1927), had unusually powerful engines (180,000 shp) and an experimental electric drive.

Other factors affecting fuel consumption were type of engines, time between engine overhauls, condition of the hull (clean or foul), weather, and crew training, not to mention basic design. Note also that U.S. ships were consistently more fuel-efficient than Japanese ones, a matter of superior technology.

TO SINK A SHIP

This is not as easy as it may seem. Among the factors that come into play are the nature of the basic structure of the ship (compartmentalization, armor, machinery spacing, and so on); size of the vessel; location of hits; time of day; casualties; damage control techniques, equipment, training, and experience; weather; type of ammunition used; and plain dumb luck.

As an example, three of the four U.S. carriers lost in 1942—*Lexington*, *Yorktown*, and *Hornet*—were considerably less damaged at the time they were abandoned than were a number of carriers that were saved despite severe damage in 1944–1945, such as *Bunker Hill* or *Franklin*. The difference lay in experience and in improved damage control techniques and equipment. Of the carriers lost in 1942, only *Wasp*, which succumbed to a spread of three torpedoes, would still have been lost even if late-war damage control techniques had been available.

The Japanese never caught on to some of the tricks that saved U.S. carriers later in the war. For example, while they carefully drained avgas lines during air attacks, they didn't hit upon the idea of filling these pipes and hoses with carbon dioxide. This removed volatile fumes from these elaborate plumbing systems, further reducing the danger of explosion.

HITS NECESSARY TO SINK A WARSHIP
(per thousand tons of displacement for battleships and cruisers)

| | NATURE OF AMMUNITION | | | | | | |
| | SHELLS | | | OTHER | | | |
SHIP TYPE	HEAVY	MEDIUM	LIGHT	BOMBS	TORPEDOES	KAMIKAZES	NOTE
BB	1–2	5–8	50+	1+	1+	1–3?	A
CV/CVL	8–10	15–25	50+	1–10	1–2	1–3?	B
CVE	1–6	3–10	15–40	1–2	1–2	1	B
CA	1–2	2–3	5–8	1–2	1–2	1–2	A
CL	1	1–2	3–5	1–2	1–2	1?	A
DD/DE	1–3	1–10	5–20	1–2	1–2	1	B
Merchant	1–2	2–3	5–10	1–3	1–2	1	B

NOTES: "Heavy" refers to shells of 11-inch caliber or greater, "medium" to those of 6- to 8-inch, and "light" to those of 4- to 5.5-inch. These are averages. For any ship, and especially the smaller ones, a single hit in a vital area (such as the ammunition magazine) can blow the vessel apart immediately. "Bombs" are taken to be of at least 500 pounds. Question marks in the "Kamikaze" column refer to the fact that no ship of the indicated type was ever sunk by this method.
   A. Numbers of shells and bombs given for battleships and cruisers, are per 1,000 tons of displacement, while torpedo and Kamikaze figures are totals. Thus a 40,000-ton battleship (BB) required forty to eighty heavy shell hits to sink it.
   B. Figures for carriers, destroyers, and merchantmen are totals.

The figures above, derived primarily from the experience of the Pacific war, should be taken as rough guidelines only.

These figures are actually rather conjectural, and are intended to give only an approximation of the sort of damage needed to do in a warship. The important thing is not so much the amount of damage that is inflicted on the ship as the rate at which it is inflicted: A lot of damage incurred over several hours may not be as deadly as a relatively small amount inflicted all at once, since the latter short-circuits the ship's damage control systems. Basically, if a ship doesn't sink at once, and is not a blazing inferno, the chances of saving her are pretty good, especially if her power plant is relatively unscathed. Some examples of the different degrees of damage that ships survived or did not survive can illustrate this.

• The carrier *Franklin* was almost lost when a Japanese bomber (not a Kamikaze) crashed—possibly accidentally—through her flight deck off Okinawa in 1945, setting off fueled and ammunitioned aircraft on the hangar deck. The resulting series of explosions killed over 700 and wounded more than 200 of her crew within minutes, while causing a nearly fatal list and extensive fires. Despite this, within hours she was able, with some assistance, to overcome the fires, restart her engines, and get out of the battle area. She then made a 12,000-mile voyage to the Brooklyn Navy Yard under her own power, stopping only once to take on stores and spare parts.

- The Italian battleship *Roma* was lost in September 1943 when a single unmanned German Felix guided missile (a radio-controlled glide bomb, actually) penetrated a magazine. This is the closest thing to a Kamikaze kill of a capital ship in the war.

- The light carrier *Princeton* was lost to a single bomb that penetrated several decks to detonate in a magazine, off Leyte in 1944.

- The Australian heavy cruiser *Australia* managed to survive a half-dozen Kamikaze hits suffered over several days off Okinawa in early 1945.

- The Japanese heavy cruiser *Mogami* was virtually a total wreck after the Battle of Midway (June 6–7, 1942), having been repeatedly bombed by U.S. aircraft, not to mention being crashed into by one of the attacking planes that she had just shot down (an incident that the Japanese attributed to the determination of the pilot, but that was probably an accident), yet managed to keep under way, get her engines back in order, and make it home safely, to be repaired and returned to service.

- The Japanese battleship *Hiei* was lost because, during the night action off Guadalcanal on November 12–13, 1942, she took about fifty hits from 5- and 8-inch shells, which started uncontrollable fires, leaving her dead in the water and an easy prey to U.S. aircraft the next morning.

- The upperworks of the Japanese heavy cruiser *Aoba* were turned into a total wreck by U.S. cruiser and destroyer gunfire during the Battle of Cape Esperance (October 11–12, 1942), yet within a couple of hours the ship was able to make 25 knots, getting away and living to fight another day.

- The heavy cruiser *San Francisco* survived a dozen hits by 14-inch high-explosive (not armor-piercing) shells, plus thirty-three more of 5-inch to 6-inch shells, off Guadalcanal on the night of November 12–13, 1942.

- The battleship *South Dakota* took one 5-inch, six 6-inch (including one AP, or armor piercer), eighteen 8-inch (of which five were AP), one 14-inch, and one unknown-sized shell, for a total of twenty-seven, during the night action off Guadalcanal on November 14–15, 1942. Two hits, both 8-inch AP, affected flotation, resulting in a list of about 0.75 percent, virtually imperceptible without instruments. Eighteen of the hits were in soft parts of the ship, one of which knocked out her search radar, and some of which caused a temporary loss of electrical power. This last might have been fatal were it not for the presence of USS *Washington*, which shot up the Japanese sufficiently to discourage them from continuing the fight. Total casualties were thirty-eight killed and sixty wounded.

- During her raid into the Atlantic in 1941, the German battleship *Bismarck* took an extraordinary beating. The blow-by-blow scorecard looked like this:

  24 MAY: Three 14-inch shell hits, which caused some flooding and reduced speed from 30 to 28 knots. That evening she took one aerial torpedo, which caused additional damage, reducing speed to 20 knots.

  26 MAY: Two or three aerial torpedoes struck the ship, one of which jammed the rudder, making her very slow and very difficult to steer.

  27 MAY: In her last fight, *Bismarck* absorbed perhaps some 300 to 400 hits from battleship and cruiser guns, including scores—if not hundreds—of 14-inch and 16-inch rounds, plus at least one torpedo. The last of these were taken at ranges as short as 2,200 yards. Although *Bismarck* was turned into a burning wreck, wracked by internal explosions, and unable to maneuver or return fire, she remained afloat, requiring three more torpedo hits before sinking. They don't build them like that anymore.

- The Japanese carrier *Taiho* was lost to a single submarine torpedo on the eve of the Battle of the Philippine Sea (1944). The hit, a relatively minor one, caused aviation fuel to leak into the ship's bilges. There it vaporized and eventually detonated, causing the ship to blow up.

- The Japanese battleships *Musashi* and *Yamato*, the largest warships in the world until the 1960s, both absorbed an extraordinary amount of damage before going down, the former taking perhaps nineteen torpedoes and seventeen bombs during the Battle of Leyte Gulf on October 24, 1944, and the latter about a dozen torpedoes and six bombs north of Okinawa on April 7, 1945.
- The U.S. light cruiser *Houston* (the second of that name in the war) was hit by two Japanese aerial torpedoes on October 16, 1944. These caused her to take on 6,500 tons of water, over 45 percent of her normal full-load displacement, yet she survived. No other vessel in history ever shipped that much water without sinking.

It's worth noting that, relatively speaking, battleships took more damage before sinking than any other type of vessel.

PLAYING THE TUBA

Sailors and strong drink have been an inseparable combination since time immemorial. Unfortunately for Uncle Sam's bluejackets, potable alcohol has been prohibited on U.S. Navy ships since teetotaling Secretary of the Navy Josephus Daniels banned it in 1914. The last night of legal booze found the fleet lying off Vera Cruz, with parties of officers rowing from ship to ship heroically trying to drink up every last drop before the midnight deadline.

So the hardest stuff officially available on American ships was coffee, of which endless gallons were consumed. Indeed, British officers often complained of caffeine overdoses after staff conferences on American warships. This was one reason why staff conferences tended to be on the foreign ships when U.S. vessels were operating in conjunction with British or other Allied ones. The Allies avoided caffeine jags and the Americans could be treated to some alcohol (in exchange, since the British were on tight rations for the entire war, the Americans always brought a few hams or some other items to donate to the officers' mess).

Tell an American that he can't have something, of course, and he'll figure out a way to get it. Improvisations were commonplace in the Navy throughout the war. Given some rice and raisins, the seamen would brew up a rather powerful homemade whiskey called "tuba" (after an Asian plant used to make alcoholic drinks). This was potent stuff, usually concocted by shipfitters, cooks, or other belowdecks types with access to the tools and supplies needed for putting a still together and operating it, and having a place to hide it.

Proof varied, but was usually high and unpredictable; "smoothness" varied from harsh on up. Other improvisations were common. For example, the advent of alcohol-fueled torpedoes was shortly followed by the discovery that "torpedo juice" was drinkable.

Some captains were more fanatical about eliminating tuba (and other such improvisations) than others. A few captains and even senior officers (like William Halsey) winked at minor violations of the ban. Some officers even went out of their way to circumvent it, procuring hard liquor for "medicinal" purposes and issuing it to their men on special occasions. There was also quite a lot of beer shipped to the fleet, which was periodically issued for consumption "off the ship." The sailors would literally take one of the ship's boats a few hundred yards from their vessel, consume their two cans of brew, and then come back so the next batch of men could do the same.

However, on the whole, let's just say that a sailor was in a lot more trouble if he left his ship drunk than if he returned to it in that state.

COULDN'T WAIT

It is estimated that several hundred boys under the age of seventeen managed to enlist during World War II using false documents. The youngest combatant in the United States armed forces during World War II (and probably the youngest since the Spanish-American War, if not the Civil War) was Calvin Graham (1930–1992) of Fort Worth, Texas. Early in 1942, twelve-year-old Graham forged his mother's name on enlistment papers and joined the Navy. He served in the battleship *South Dakota* during the Guadalcanal campaign, in which he was wounded. His correct age having meanwhile been established to the satisfaction of the ship's skipper, when *South Dakota* returned to the United States for repairs, Graham was given a one-way pass to his original recruiting station, which didn't know what to do with him. Meanwhile, since he did not return to his ship, he was classed as a deserter, arrested, and jailed. Released after he finally managed to convince the Navy that he was only thirteen, Graham was promptly given a dishonorable discharge and denied medical benefits because he had enlisted under false premises. Graham, who later reenlisted for a time after attaining the proper age, was eventually the beneficiary of special legislation to restore pay and benefits lost upon his original discharge. By a curious twist of fate, Graham's division officer while aboard *South Dakota* was Sargent Shriver, who was later President John F. Kennedy's brother-in-law, while another of his shipmates was a future teacher of one of the authors of this work, serving as one of the ship's steersmen.

The actual number of underage American boys who served in the war will never be known, as many of them were never detected. Nor can the number killed in action be determined.

(ALMOST) NEVER SURRENDER

Since the War of 1812, only one U.S. warship has ever struck its colors, the gunboat USS *Wake*, which surrendered without firing a shot at Shanghai on December 8, 1942, being then in a hopeless situation, tied up at a dock and surrounded by Japanese troops. *Wake* saw service with the Imperial Japanese Army and was eventually turned over to the Chinese. Note that in December 1968, the U.S. Navy electronic-intelligence-gathering ship *Pueblo* surrendered to North Korean warships off the coast of North Korea. *Pueblo* was not a warship, possessed minimal armament, and was not trained or intended to fight. However, some consider this a "warship surrender."

The Imperial Japanese Navy also acquired a U.S. destroyer, albeit not by surrender. USS *Stewart* (DD224), an old *Clemson* Class fourstacker, had been damaged during the fighting in the Netherlands East Indies early in 1942. She was put into a dry dock at Soerabaja, in Java, but was still undergoing repairs when the Japanese overran the island. Although demolition charges were set, these only slightly damaged the ship, and she was captured by Japanese troops on

March 2, 1942. Repaired, *Stewart* was commissioned as an escort in the Imperial Navy, and occasionally caused the radio waves to heat when spotted by American or Allied long-range reconnaissance aircraft. After a relatively uneventful career in the emperor's service, *Stewart* was returned to American control in 1945, and expended as a target during the nuclear weapons trials at Bikini in 1946.

FUELING THE FIGHT

After fuel oil, the most precious fluid in the Navy was coffee. The fleet lived on coffee, consuming it in endless gallons. There was usually a pot brewing almost anywhere one could be installed. Taste, of course, varied, but strong and black was not unusual, and the guys in the engine room ("the black gang") often put a little salt in theirs, to help them retain body salt in the extreme heat of their work areas. A cup of hot coffee was particularly appreciated by bluejackets standing watch on cold nights in northern latitudes, like the Atlantic convoy routes or the Aleutians, and special heavy mugs, without handles, were even issued, so that the men could grip them with mittens.

In normal circumstances a battleship used about 250 pounds of the stuff a day, nearly two tons a week. But the demand for coffee rose precipitously when a ship went into action, and it was not unusual for daily consumption to double. For example, during the protracted struggle with the Kamikazes off Okinawa, coffee was often the only sustenance many of the men on the picket ships bothered with for days on end.

As Samuel Eliot Morison said, "The U.S. Navy could probably win a war without coffee, but would prefer not to try." Of course, the men didn't live on coffee alone; there was other stuff, such as lemon pie. Lemon pie was very popular in the Navy, and on many ships was available virtually every night. And then there was ice cream.

Most of the bigger ships in the fleet had their own ice cream and soda fountains, affectionately known as the "gedunk bar." British tars often joked about their American cousins' addiction to ice cream, claiming that their grog ration was a superior privilege, but the Brits always seemed to head straight for the gedunk bar whenever they were guests on an American vessel.

There was an unwritten law in the fleet that on specific occasions (such as after duty on Sundays) a sailor had the right to eat as much ice cream as he wanted, in any combination. These indulgent concoctions were obtained from the ship's gedunk bar, and the "gedunk line" was a busy place, as men awaited their turn to whip up some fanciful concoction. One such line of anxious sailors was once the scene of a legendary encounter, when Admiral William F. Halsey dressed down two ensigns for trying to jump to the head of the line, considering that he himself was patiently waiting his turn.

By the way, the Navy also supplied proper food for its men. In contrast to the Army, in which the troops often had to subsist for weeks and months out of cans, the Navy provided a quite varied and balanced diet for its men. A large ship, such as a battlewagon or flattop, with, say, a crew of about two thousand officers and men, was usually provided with over 20 tons of food a week. A typical week's fare might consist of the following:

Beef, Frozen	10,000 lb
Veal, Frozen	2,000 lb
Ham, Smoked	750 lb
Fish, Frozen	500 lb
Luncheon Meat (Spam)	250 lb
Potatoes, White	9,000 lb
Potatoes, Sweet	900 lb
Carrots	1,500 lb
Lettuce, Iceberg	1,200 lb
Tomatoes	900 lb
Asparagus	900 lb
Cucumbers	850 lb
Celery	600 lb
Rhubarb	500 lb
Oranges	1,900 lb
Lemons	1,200 lb
Eggs	1,500 dozen

There were also several tons of flour and baking supplies, milk (fresh, condensed, and powdered), and hundreds of pounds of seasonings and condiments, plus about a ton of ice cream and one or two of coffee.

BREEZY CORNER

During the last ten months of the war, and particularly during the protracted struggle for Okinawa, many destroyers were placed on "picket duty," posted at some distance from the fleet in order to try to keep Japanese suicide aircraft from the carriers and transports. This was no easy task, for many of the "Emperor's Eagles" were very anxious to demonstrate their belief that "duty is a heavy burden, but death is lighter than a feather." In consequence, they would frequently attack the pickets rather than pass them by to try for the larger warships and transports farther on. As a result, destroyer-type vessels (DDs, DEs, and DMSs) bore the brunt of the Kamikaze onslaught; 16 were sunk by Kamikaze attack (19.3 percent of the 83 vessels sunk by Kamikazes) and 139 were damaged (39.7 percent of the 285 damaged vessels). What is surprising about this carnage is the battering that some ships survived. Take the case of the destroyer USS *Laffey*.

On the morning of April 16, 1945, *Laffey* (DD-724), an *Allen M. Sumner* Class destroyer commissioned in early 1944, was on radar picket patrol off Okinawa. From about 8:27 A.M. to 9:47 A.M., she was subjected to the attentions of about fifty Japanese aircraft. Although many of the attackers were downed by friendly fighters flying Combat Air Patrol, at least twenty-two of the enemy managed to get through to make attacks on the ship herself. Altogether, *Laffey* was hit by seven Kamikazes, six of which blew up spectacularly, while the seventh bounced off to explode in the sea hard by her port quarter. In addition, she was struck by four bombs and strafed several times by other Japanese aircraft.

Aside from the Kamikazes that actually struck her, *Laffey* managed to shoot down eight of her attackers. When the ordeal was over, *Laffey* had suffered thirty-one crewmen killed and seventy-two wounded, about 30 percent of her complement. She was down at the stern and unable to steer due to a jammed rudder. Her fire control director was gone and her only working guns were four 20mm antiaircraft pieces (out of six 5-inch, twelve 40mm, and eleven 20mm guns). Despite her damage, *Laffey* was repaired. After many years on active duty, *Laffey* was retired in 1977. She is today preserved as a war memorial in Charleston, South Carolina, along with the carrier *Yorktown*, second of that name in the war.

As can be seen, the destroyerman's lot off Okinawa was not a pleasant one. Thus it is understandable that one day during the long watch, the crew of one of the "tin cans" grew frustrated at the many Japanese pilots who persisted in attacking them rather than continuing on to try for bigger stuff. Knowing that the Japanese were supposed to be looking to sink carriers, the destroyermen erected a large sign proclaiming CARRIERS THIS WAY. It's doubtful that any of the attacking Japanese ever saw the sign, or if they did, that they could even read it, and hardly likely that had they done so they would have paid it much heed, but it may have made the destroyermen feel better.

SENIORITY

On March 27, 1993, the last of the prewar ships that fought in World War II and served continuously with the U.S. Navy was decommissioned. USS *Prairie* was a destroyer tender, providing maintenance and support for destroyers while far from base. Built in Camden, New Jersey, and entering service in late 1939, *Prairie* was for a time the flagship for the Atlantic Fleet support forces. During the war, the ship was assigned to the Pacific, and stayed there afterward. Over 10,000 sailors served on *Prairie*, including, since 1982, many women. Traditionally, the oldest serving ship flies the "Don't Tread on Me" pennant. Upon *Prairie*'s retirement, this was transferred to USS *Orion*, another tender, which had entered service during the war in 1944.

Many other prewar U.S. Navy ships continue in service, but not in the U.S. Navy. From 1945 until well into the 1970s, the huge U.S. World War II fleet provided the bulk of the secondhand warships for thrifty fleets around the world. There will still be some of these ships in service at the turn of the century.

The most senior major warship in the U.S. Navy during World

War II was the battleship *Arkansas* (BB-31). Commissioned in 1912, *Arkansas* served more or less continuously for over thirty-three years. Although no longer fit to accompany the fleet, even the battleline, she rendered yeoman service during the war in laying down support fire for amphibious landings on beaches as widely separated as Normandy and Okinawa. Decommissioned at the war's end, she was expended as a target in the nuclear weapons tests at Bikini atoll in 1946.

WEAPONS THAT WAIT

Naval mines were first introduced during the mid-nineteenth century. The "torpedoes" that Admiral David Glasgow Farragut "damned" at Mobile Bay were actually mines. But for a long time the threat from mines was largely theoretical. Then came the Russo-Japanese War (1904–1905), during which mines played a significant role. One battle was decided when the Russian flagship hit a mine and went down within minutes, taking with her the best Russian admiral of the day, and the Japanese lost a third of their battleships to mines (their own mines) in one disastrous afternoon. Through and after World War I, mine technology developed steadily, so that during World War II a variety of mines were available. There were the original contact mines, which go off when something hits them. New in World War II were magnetic mines, which detonate when large masses of steel pass by, and pressure mines, which go off if there is a change in water pressure, caused by a ship passing overhead. All of these could be delivered by surface ship, submarine, or increasingly, by airplane.

Mines have generally been considered the weapon of the inferior naval power. And certainly no one has ever thought of them as a "warrior's weapon." In fact, many of the most perceptive naval commanders have tended to regard them with disdain. Despite this, the U.S. Navy overcame its aversion to mines and used them extensively. Mines delivered by submarine and aircraft so effectively sealed off Japanese waters in 1945 as to completely shut down Japanese shipping, dealing the Japanese economy a deadly blow.

One reason that mines were so effective was that much of Japan's shipping was actually carried out by very small vessels, a response to Japan's long coastline and paucity of roads and railroads. Many of Japan's foodstuffs were moved in small craft of 80 tons or less, which could easily run along coasts at night and hide in bays, rivers, and others inlets by day, where they could be camouflaged against American aircraft. Mines made this a problematic proposition. As a result, Japan began running short of food. Had Japan not surrendered in August 1945, many Japanese would have starved or frozen to death by the end of the next winter.

The Japanese also used mines to good effect. Many U.S. subs that never returned probably ran afoul of minefields planted off Japanese ports. The Japanese used mines extensively to defend their island bastions. These mines had to be cleared before the troops could hit the beach. This was dangerous work, with the minesweepers often operating under fire from Japanese shore batteries.

Some of the mines used against landing craft were planted like land mines. The 107-pound, Type 96 Japanese mine could be submerged under a few feet of water. Small landing craft and amphibious vehicles were the typical victims of this weapon. The only antidotes were the UDT (Underwater Demolition Team) scuba divers the U.S. Navy organized. UDT swimmers would go in at night before an invasion to disable mines and demolish other obstacles with explosives. This was, as one can imagine, very dangerous work. Sometimes the Japanese guarding the beach were particularly alert and UDT casualties were very high. The UDT swimmers were an elite group and the only commando-type troops to be completely successful in the Pacific. The current U.S. Navy SEAL teams are direct descendents of the World War II–era UDTs.

TRADITION

Tradition is one of the mainstays of a military service. Some customs practiced during the Second World War go back centuries, literally into the dimmest past in many cases. For example, as late as World War II it was common for old chiefs (chief petty officers, the most senior enlisted men) to say that when they retired they were going to put an anchor over one shoulder and begin walking inland until someone said, "Where'd you get the funny fishhook?," whereupon they'd retire to raise chickens, as far from blue water as physically possible. This is a seaman's joke so old that it is virtually identical to one Homer told in the *Odyssey* nearly 3,000 years ago.

Several other old customs were (and are) still common in the Navy. For example, by early 1945 an astute observer aboard a U.S. Navy ship might have gotten a good sense of how soon the war was going to end by noticing that many of the sailors were working on "homecoming pennants." These are long, multicolored streamers that are flown from the mainmast as a ship returns victorious from a war. It's an ancient tradition, maintained by the old salts since time immemorial. By early 1945, with the fleet operating off Japan, sailors on many many ships began sewing homecoming pennants. Most ships had one by the time Japan surrendered in August 1945, and they can be seen streaming astern from the mainmasts in pictures of ships returning home after the war. By tradition, a homecoming pennant is one foot long for each day the ship was away from home. The longest belonged to *The Big E,* the carrier *Enterprise,* which, upon her return to the United States in late 1945, had been continuously away from the forty-eight states for well over 500 days. Her streamer was so long, in fact, that helium balloons were needed to keep it aloft.

The submarine service preserved another very old maritime tradition. Boats returning from successful war patrols customarily wore a broom at the top of the mainmast. This custom dates back to the seventeenth century, when the Dutch seadog Michel de Ruyter tied a broom to his mainmast to let everyone know that he had "swept" the seas of enemy ships.

There was one other hoary naval homecoming tradition not practiced in the U.S. Navy, the awarding of prize money upon the successful conclusion of a war. Originally a way to organize the division of loot, prize payments had passed out of fashion in the U.S. Navy shortly after the Spanish-American War. Highly successful Union Admiral David Dixon Porter, who greatly profited from prize, coined the immortal phrase "Armies loot, navies take prize." It was, however, still awarded in the Royal Navy, and shortly after the end of the war His Majesty's tars and jollies (sailors and marines) received a rather nice little bonus, amounting to several hundred dollars each for the common seamen, and proportionately more as one went up the ranks.

THE RIGHT BOMB FOR THE RIGHT TARGET

At the beginning of the war, there was not much to choose from in aircraft ordnance. There were bombs available in different weights, from a few pounds to more than a ton. There were several different types in each weight class, distinguished by armor-piercing ability, percentage of weight devoted to explosives, and type of fuze. The armor-piercing bombs were often converted naval gun shells, with as little as 5 percent of their weight comprising explosives. These bombs would have delayed-action fuzes so that the bomb could penetrate deep inside a ship before exploding.

In May 1942 the United States introduced an armor-piercing bomb that was specifically designed for the purpose (the AP Mk 1). It weighed 1,600 pounds, of which 209 pounds was explosive. This bomb could penetrate 5 inches of deck armor. Because so few enemy ships with armored decks (battleships) were encountered, most carriers had perhaps twenty of these bombs on hand. As the war went on, most of the bombs dropped were non–armor piercing (or "light case") types. These bombs (500 and 1,000 pounds being the most common) had 30 to 50 percent of their weight devoted to explosive.

From 1943 on, U.S. Forces began to use more air-to-surface rockets. The 3.5-inch (55-pound) rocket was developed for use against submarines. German U-boats would often be submerged by the time an approaching aircraft got close enough to drop a bomb, but the rocket solved that problem. A larger version, the 5-inch (90-pound) rocket, was developed for use in the Pacific against surface (and land) targets. Both types were in wide use by 1944.

Two other unconventional bombs deserve mention. The atomic bomb is well known, but only two were dropped. But there was another type of bomb that did more damage to Japanese cities, and killed more people. This was the Mk 69 incendiary bomb. Weighing only 6 pounds, millions were dropped and it was this bomb that destroyed Japans industrial power and most of the cities the factories were in. Tokyo, a city approximately the size of New York, was about 60 percent destroyed, mostly by incendiaries.

CARRIER LOSS RECORDS

The first aircraft carrier to be sunk in action in the war was HMS *Courageous*, a converted World War I "lite" battlecruiser, which took two torpedoes from the German submarine *U-29* on September 17, 1939, going down in fifteen minutes. Curiously, her sister ship HMS *Glorious* was the second carrier to be lost in action when she had the misfortune to encounter the German battleships *Scharnhorst* and *Gneisenau* off Norway on June 8, 1940. Despite a heroic but ultimately futile defense by the destroyer HMS *Glowworm*, the unlucky carrier was pounded with 11-inch shells for over an hour before she went down.

The first carrier killed in the Pacific war was also British, HMS *Hermes*, which was sunk by Japanese carrier aircraft near Ceylon on March 9, 1942; *Hermes* was the only British carrier lost in the Pacific. While the first U.S. carrier lost, *Langley*, was sunk by Japanese aircraft in the Java Sea in February 1942, she was officially no longer an aircraft "carrier," having been demoted to the status of an aircraft "tender" some years before the war. In this role the very slow *Langley*, which had a very short flight deck, was used to deliver aircraft, which was what she was doing when sunk.

The first Japanese carrier sunk in the war was HIJMS *Shoho*, done in by U.S. carrier aircraft at the Coral Sea on May 8, 1942, shortly before the first American carrier was lost: USS *Lexington*. The last American fleet carrier lost in action was *Hornet*, during the Battle of the Santa Cruz Islands on October 24, 1942; however, the light carrier *Princeton* was lost during the Battle of Leyte Gulf on October 24, 1944, and the escort carrier *Bismarck Sea* on February 21, 1945, off Iwo Jima, all to Japanese air attack.

The last of the twenty aircraft carriers lost by the Imperial Japanese Navy was *Amagi*, pounded to death by U.S. carrier aircraft in Kure Harbor on July 24, 1945.

"FOR THOSE IN PERIL ON THE SEA"

As if the normal hazards of war were not enough, war at sea adds to them a few extras. One enemy encountered often during the Pacific war was the typhoons ("cyclonic storms," or hurricanes) that regularly sweet across the ocean. On December 17, 1944, Task Force 38 was blindsided by a typhoon off the Philippines. Over 800 sailors were killed, three destroyers sunk, and twenty other ships severely damaged, while many aircraft were damaged or destroyed. This was not the only time a task force ran afoul of a storm, simply the worst. One reason for the seriousness of this incident may be due to the fact that Admiral Halsey flew his flag from a battleship, which was much more stable in foul weather than a destroyer, particularly one that was low on fuel. The "typhoon nursery" (for those north of the equator in the Pacific) is between 155 and 165 degrees east longitude, and from the equator to about 20 degrees north, at least for most of the year. From January through March, it's between 145 and 155 degrees. Further complicating matters, some ferocious storms form west of Japan in the Sea of Japan, and a few even farther north, over land in northeast Siberia, and then gain typhoon strength as they move out over the water. Most of these "northern typhoons" don't get beyond storm (over 34 knots' wind) strength, but some do. For every typhoon, there are several storms of somewhat lesser ferocity, which could be almost as bad as a typhoon because carrier operations were impossible during most storms, and this made it easier for enemy submarines to get close to the carriers. All of this storm activity happened smack in the middle of the Central Pacific Theater of Operations.

Making life even more difficult was the fact that since the Japanese held so many of the Central Pacific islands, there was often insufficient meteorological information on the formation of new storms or the paths of existing ones. For this reason, the U.S. Navy regularly used submarines to report on the weather, and maintained weather stations in China, including several in the Gobi in Inner Mongolia, probably about as far from blue water—perhaps from any open water—as the Navy has ever operated. The Japanese were not the only enemy ready to hit you while you weren't looking.

KAMIKAZE!

Most of what happened during the Pacific war was anticipated by American admirals and generals during the 1930s. One item was not foreseen, and this was the Japanese use of suicide aircraft. Even the Japanese did not expect to take such an extreme measure. But after the disastrous Battle of the Philippine Sea in June 1944, it was obvious that American carrier aircraft ruled the seas. Moreover, American ships now had formidable arrays of 20mm and 40mm antiaircraft guns, as well as radar fuzes for their 5-inch guns. Between these guns and the formidable Hellcat fighters, it was nearly impossible for Japanese bombers to make normal attacks on ships. Since aircraft were the best (and often only) way to attack enemy ships, the Japanese came up with the concept of one-way suicide attacks by their bombers.

The new attack method was called Kamikaze, a Japanese term meaning "Divine" or "Heavenly Wind." The term had a prominent place in Japanese history, as timely storms had twice saved Japan from amphibious invasion by Mongol fleets during the medieval period. Moreover, Japanese pilots were already accustomed to making suicide attacks when all else failed. This was part of Japan's military tradition, something Americans had witnessed time after time as Japanese ground troops fought to the death and refused to surrender in the most hopeless situations.

The first Kamikaze units were organized in the Philippines in the fall of 1944. There was no problem in getting pilots to volunteer for such duty. From the beginning, the Japanese sought to make as much as they could of their Kamikazes. These attacks would allow them to use even obsolete aircraft. Pilot training could be minimal, and often was, with many pilots receiving only a week's training. Precious aviation fuel would be saved, as aircraft need be given only enough for going out and (if no enemy ships were found) coming back. The third of a plane's fuel usually reserved for maneuvering and a margin of safety could be dispensed with.

The first Kamikaze attacks took place on October 25, 1944, off Samar Island in the southern Philippines. Shortly after American destroyers and escort carriers had fought off a Japanese battleship force, the Kamikazes struck. The results were encouraging, with two escort carriers damaged and one sunk. Between October and December, Kamikazes made more successful attacks on supply convoys steaming north to support further operations in the Philippines. Thus encouraged, the Japanese continued to expand their Kamikaze force and prepared to use it against the expected U.S. invasion of the main Philippine island, Luzon. In December, small groups of Kamikazes made successful attacks on American ships moving in for preliminary invasions of outlying islands. The major attacks, however, would come once the American invasion fleet was sitting off the coast in support of the amphibious assault.

In early January, the Kamikazes were unleashed on the first warships to arrive at Lingayen Gulf to shell the beaches before the amphibious ships arrived. Hundreds of Kamikazes flew out to meet the Americans, and inflicted losses the USN had not experienced since late 1942. While carrier fighters and numerous antiaircraft guns took their toll, many ships were hit. Since nearly all these were warships, the sinkings were few, but the American casualties were high. Because many of the injuries were from the aircraft's gasoline, the experience came as quite a shock to those sailors who survived. Previous Japanese air attacks had tried to put only bombs on their targets. Kamikazes put the entire aircraft on the target, and the exploding aircraft gas tanks added to the normal mayhem of an exploding bomb.

Fortunately, the Japanese had a limited number of aircraft. From the first Kamikaze attack on October 24, 1944, to the departure of the last Japanese aircraft from Luzon at the end of January, 378 Kamikazes were sent out. All were lost, as well as 102 escorting fighters. For this effort, 16 U.S. vessels were sunk (2 CVEs, 3 DDs, 1 DMS, plus 10 smaller vessels) and another 87 were damaged (including 7 CVs, 2 CVLs, 13 CVEs, 5 BBs, 3 CAs, 7 CLs, 23 DDs, 5 DEs, and 1 DMS). On the American ships there were thousands of casualties. Fortunately, this was as effective as the Kamikazes were ever going to get. The element of surprise was now lost; the American defenders were now thoroughly alerted to how the Kamikazes operated and began to change their defensive procedures to limit the damage from suicide aircraft.

The following month, the Kamikazes were again encountered during the Iwo Jima assault. Because the attacking aircraft had to fly in over open water, the attacks were not as devastating as those in the Philippines. Several ships were hit, but the only significant damage was to one CV and to a CVE that was sunk. However, worse was yet to come.

In April, Okinawa was invaded. In addition to the usual fanatical resistance on the ground, the Japanese launched over 1,500 Kamikazes and nearly as many regular aircraft at the American ships. Ship losses were heavy, with 21 sunk and 43 damaged so severely that repairs were not complete when the war ended; another 23 were damaged and required at least thirty days to repair. A further 151 ships received lesser damage. Worst of all, the crews sustained 9,700 casualties, 4,300 of which were fatal. For the Navy, this campaign was the most costly of the war. Seven percent of all the Navy's crew casualties for the Pacific war were incurred during the battles with the Kamikazes off Okinawa. And this was despite the many measures the American fleet had taken to counter Kamikazes. In addition to better control of fighters and antiaircraft guns, there was more crew training in damage control techniques. There was also the use of radar-equipped destroyers serving as a "picket line" to give early warning of the attacks and absorb some of the punishment. The destroyers contained air control parties that would direct fighters to the incoming Kamikazes as quickly as possible. But it was all never enough.

The problem with Okinawa was that the island and nearby ones were large enough to support many airfields. Kamikazes could also fly in from Taiwan and Japan itself (Kyushu.) This amounted to over 200 enemy airfields, too many for even the vast air power of America to shut down. Moreover, the airfields in distant Taiwan and Kyushu proved no problem for the Kamikazes. Since they did not have to return, they could nearly double their range.

The Japanese still allowed for a certain number of Kamikazes to turn back due to mechanical problems or due to a lack of targets. There were also fighter escorts for the Kamikazes, to prevent the inexperienced suicide pilots from being shot down before getting to their targets. The more experienced fighter pilots also served as navigators for the Kamikazes, who barely knew how to fly and were rarely up to the difficult task of navigating over open water.

The invasion fleet also had to worry about attacks by Japanese submarines, surface ships, and smaller suicide boats. Patrol aircraft and destroyers kept Japanese subs at bay, as well as the suicide boats. But the Kamikazes came in by the hundreds. During the Okinawa campaign, 1,900 Kamikaze aircraft attacked 587 Allied (U.S. and British) ships, of which 320 were warships. Each attack averaged 150 aircraft. One had 350 planes. Despite all the interceptors and anti-aircraft fire, 7 percent of the Kamikazes hit something.

After Okinawa, the next assault would be on Japan itself. For this eventuality the Japanese had over 5,000 Kamikazes ready. This was more than twice as many as were used during the Okinawa battle. Moreover, these would be coming over the hills of Kyushu, not over open water. Radar pickets and fighters would be less effective. The U.S. Navy could expect to take more than 10,000 casualties and see more than 300 ships hit during this battle. It was not something any sailor was looking forward to.

The atomic bombs on Hiroshima and Nagasaki ended the war without an invasion. This came as a relief to some of the Kamikaze pilots, for after the initial use of these suicide aircraft, fewer Japanese volunteered. Toward the end, Army and Navy pilots were simply ordered to join Kamikaze units. Japanese morale was weakening toward the end of the war, although it didn't seem that way in June 1945, as American sailors watched yet another swarm of suicide bombers headed right for them.

RECONNAISSANCE AT SEA

The very first, and perhaps most important, role that aircraft had in warfare was that of reconnaissance. Aircraft especially designed for reconnaissance were introduced in the decade before World War II. By the outbreak of the war there were essentially two types of reconnaissance aircraft, long range and short range.

Navies were particularly interested in long-range reconnaissance aircraft because of the need to patrol vast expanses of ocean and to escort convoys. Multi-engine aircraft were the norm, and flying boats were very popular, since they could operate with a minimum of basing facilities.

The ideal long-range reconnaissance airplane was not particularly fast, but had a very high endurance, giving it a long "loiter time," and was capable of attaining considerable altitude, to keep it safe from enemy fighters. Such aircraft usually had one or two machine guns for self-defense, and were often equipped to carry some small bombs or depth charges, to enable them to attack targets of opportunity. Bombers, particularly obsolete types, were often pressed into the role of maritime patrol, a duty for which they were generally satisfactory.

Short-range reconnaissance aircraft were designed to engage in tactical reconnaissance. Both armies and navies needed information on the enemy's local resources, information that could be obtained by relatively fast, small aircraft. During World War I navies began experimenting with catapult-launched seaplanes on major warships, and by World War II virtually all cruisers and battleships were equipped with such. Their duties were to help the ships' gunners find their targets. They proved valuable in this role, but by the end of the war were increasingly being dispensed with. There were two reasons for this. The increasing availability of carrier aircraft to support shore bombardment was an important factor, but perhaps even more significant was the extreme danger posed by the presence of the aircraft and their highly volatile fuel on the ships. Not a few battleships and cruisers suffered serious damage when their recon planes, or the fuel for them, caught fire, occasionally due to the blast effects of their own guns.

The U.S. Navy developed a third type of reconnaissance aircraft, the blimp. The blimp was a "nonrigid" airship, essentially a collection of helium gas bags loosely held together by an aluminum frame. Blimps were very slow, 80 to 90 knots being their maximum speed. But they had enormous range, and wonderful ability to loiter in an area for hours on end. Armed with depth charges, they proved immensely useful in convoy defense in the Atlantic, but saw little service in the Pacific.

While ships have always conducted searches for other ships and landward obstacles, aircraft were the premier search methods in World War II. Nevertheless, aircraft could not do it all. At night and in bad weather, ships still had to rely on their own onboard resources.

Search by ships was, and still is, performed by sailors "on watch." While most sailors on watch are doing vital jobs like manning the engines, steering the ship, and monitoring the radio, others are lookouts. The Japanese, in particular, carefully trained their lookouts and equipped them with excellent optical devices (binoculars and telescopes). Drilled at night and in bad weather, Japanese lookouts often outperformed the crude radar that U.S. ships had (and Japanese ships lacked) early in the war.

American radar soon got better, and by the end of 1942, the Japanese had lost their lookout advantage. Radar was first used on ships in the late 1930s and saw rapid development during the first few years of World War II.

By 1943, it was increasingly common for large aircraft to carry radar. This was particularly important for naval reconnaissance. Ships at sea could be spotted by airborne radar. You couldn't spot army units on land with radar because of the "clutter" created by hills, forests, and buildings. But at sea, ships stood out on radar screens. The bigger the ship, the farther away it could be spotted. Since most warships traveled in groups, you merely had to spot the largest ship in order to find the entire group.

Submarines were another matter, as they are the smallest of ships that operate on the high seas. But subs could still be spotted by airborne radar, and it was this vulnerability that eventually doomed the German U-boat threat in the Atlantic and made Japanese submarines much less lethal in the Pacific.

The Allies had the edge in radar development and the number of long-range aircraft built during World War II, and this provided them with a considerable advantage.

Effective radar and abundant search aircraft did not give the Allies perfect knowledge of what was afloat on the vast Pacific. There were never enough aircraft to cover all the ocean areas at all times. It was never possible to equip all recon aircraft with radar, and darkness and bad weather often made recon flights futile. What was possible was to increase the probability of spotting enemy ships depending on how many aircraft you had at a particular base, or on task force carriers. Moreover, spotting was also more likely the closer you got to the base or carriers that the aircraft were flying from. As the aircraft flew out from their base, the area to be covered increased. Recon aircraft customarily flew a course that resembled a slice of pie. Often they would fly back and forth across an area in much the same way a lawn mower covers an area of grass to be cut. Thus the range of the aircraft was critical not so much for the distance it traveled from its base as for the amount of sea area it could cover before it had to land. The farther you get from the aircraft base, the less likely you are to spot what is out there.

SEARCHING AND SPOTTING

The sharp-eyed lookout is an old naval tradition. There are many dangers at sea that can be seen before you run into them (including enemy ships) and there are always alert lookouts standing watch on ships. The twentieth century brought with it a new vantage point for naval lookouts: the floatplane, an airplane with pontoons instead of wheels, to enable it to operate from water.

About the same time aircraft carriers came into use, battleships and cruisers began to carry floatplanes for reconnaissance purposes. They were popular with all nations possessing cruisers (which carried one or two aircraft each) or battleships (which carried two or more).

The Japanese were quite fond of floatplanes and relied heavily on them for reconnaissance instead of their carrier aircraft. After 1942, the Japanese had little choice because most of their carriers were sunk. But in addition to floatplanes on warships, Japan formed floatplane units that operated from the coves and bays of Pacific islands.

The Japanese built special supply ships that could repair and maintain these floatplanes wherever their island base might be. Some of these support ships looked like carriers and could launch amphibious planes (with wheels and floats) from their decks. The Allies, on the other hand, had sufficient engineering units to build landing strips on islands quickly. Moreover, the Allies also had thousands of larger (two- or four-engined) floatplanes that had longer range than the normally single-engine Japanese floatplane.

RANGES OF SEARCH METHODS		
METHOD	RANGE (IN KM)	
	LOW	HIGH
Lookout	12	22
Aircraft	30	40

The low range in the preceding table is for smaller ships (with fewer lookouts) and smaller aircraft (with fewer crew members to keep a sharp lookout). These are clear-weather ranges and don't show the lesser probability of spotting something that is farther away. Weather is also a factor, mist and fog severely limiting range. Range at night is highly dependent on moonlight available, and even under the best of conditions is less than half the range of daylight.

Radar gave a spotting range just a bit greater than lookouts, but with greater probability of spotting something and considerable immunity from atmospheric and night effects. Radar early in the war was erratic, and it wasn't until late 1943 that Allied ship radar became routinely reliable. The Japanese were still struggling with radar technology when the war ended. A persistent problem with radar was the difficulty in using it close to land. It was very difficult to separate distant ships from the islands and other land forms.

THE NOT SO HIGH SEAS

As vast as the Pacific was, most large groups of ships endeavored to move in such a way that they were always within a few hundred miles of land, preferably land with an air base full of friendly fighters and bombers. This was an ancient custom, and the world's record for distance from the site of a sea battle to shore is still the British victory known as the "Glorious First of June" (June 1, 1794), fought some 400 miles from the nearest land, decidedly in the age of sail.

But having the protection of friendly air power, or avoiding enemy land-based aircraft, was seen as crucial during World War II. Moreover, aircraft could spot and attack lurking submarines or approaching enemy task forces. Friendly aircraft patrols provided weather reports, which were often protection against a more formidable foe than enemy torpedoes and bombs. Nearby land bases also provided anchorages and repair facilities for ships that broke down or were damaged in combat. Such nearby succor often made the difference between saving and losing a valuable ship.

THE AIRCRAFT

The Pacific war was the first naval war in which aircraft played a decisive role. Since manned flight was only thirty-eight years old when Pearl Harbor was attacked, there was not a lot of experience in the use of aircraft at war. Aircraft technology had been changing at a breakneck pace through the 1930s; the Japanese attack on Pearl Harbor was, in fact, the first massed use of carrier aircraft in combat. Six months later, there was the first carrier-versus-carrier battle. But it was land-based aircraft that truly ruled the skies over the Pacific. Carriers were normally too few in number to cope with land-based air power. Carriers were used to seize islands that could serve as airfields for the more numerous and capable land-based aircraft. All of this was new to warfare and the air generals and admirals had to write the book as they went along. Aircraft designs were also modified, and created, as the war went on. The development of aircraft design is very much a history of the Pacific war.

THE AIRCRAFT OF THE PACIFIC WAR

More than in any other theater of operations during the Second World War, the airplane played a vital role in the Pacific—not just carrier aircraft, but land-based ones as well. In fact, land-based aircraft were more numerous than carrier-based ones. Many different kinds of aircraft were in the Pacific, and, indeed, the table on pages 204-207 manages to omit many of the less numerous types.

A-20 HAVOC /BOSTON. The A-20 Havoc (or Boston, as it was known to the British) was originally built mainly for export, although the U.S. Army began to receive some in 1941. Several were present during the Pearl Harbor attack and A-20s saw action in New Guinea during the dark days of 1942. It was an odd duck. Although it looked like a twin-engine medium bomber, it performed like a single-engine light bomber and was actually quite small compared side by side to the B-25 or B-26 twin-engine bomber. The crew was usually just two (the pilot and a machine gunner, who faced the rear), although some aircraft were modified to add a bombardier. The A-20 was so narrow that there was no room for the crew to move from their seats. It was nimble and fast, but sacrificed range for payload, which could be up to 4,000 pounds of bombs. As the war went on, more .50-caliber machine guns were added. This made the A-20 a potent strafing aircraft. The short range, compared to the two-engine B-25 and B-26, made the A-20 less desirable in the Pacific; as a result, most served in Europe. Russia eagerly received 3,000 and the British 1,800 of the nearly 7,000 produced, and even the Dutch got a few. The United States used 2,000, including some converted to night fighters in late 1942 (the P-70) and some for photo reconnaissance. A few Dutch ones were captured intact by the Japanese in 1942 in Java.

A-26 INVADER. The U.S. A-26 Invader was a much improved A-20, so much so that, although it looked a lot like the A-20, it was

AIRCRAFT

Nation	Type	Designation/Name	Builder	AA	AS	Speed	Reach	Range	FPR	Armament	Load	Crew	Built	Year
US	BmrM	A-20 Havoc/Boston	Douglas	3	9	282	405	890	10	5x12.7mm	4,000	2	6,800	1940
US	BmrM	A-26 Invader	Douglas	6	16	324	550	1,210	24	12x12.7mm	4,000	2	2,500	1944
US	BmrM	A-28 Hudson	Lockheed	2	5	246	955	2,100	7	7x7.62mm	1,400	6	2,800	1939
US	BmrD	A-35 Vengeance	Vultee	2	2	279	236	520	8	4x12.7mm	1,000	2	1,528	1942
Jap	Ftr	A5M Claude	Mitsubishi	3	0	237	295	650	2	2x7.7mm	60	1	1,000	1936
Jap	Ftr	A6M Zero/Zeke	Mitsubishi	6	1	307	386	850	8	2x20mm + 2x7.7mm	550	1	10,937	1941
Jap	Ftr	A6M2-N Rufe	Mitsubishi	6	1	307	364	800	8	2x20mm + 2x7.7mm	550	1	327	1942
US	BmrT/D	AD Skyraider	Douglas	3	16	318	500	1,100	12	4x20mm	8,000	1	3,200	1946
US	BmrL	AM-1 Mauler	Martin	3	7	319	500	1,100	12	4x20mm	7,000	1	750	1946
Br	BmrT	Albacore	Fairey	1	4	140	364	800	3	3x7.62mm	2,000	2	803	1940
US	Bmr	B-10	Martin	1	2	260	909	2,000	3	3x7.62mm	2,260	4	300	1934
US	BmrH	B-17 Flying Fortress	Boeing	7	8	249	773	1,700	26	13x12.7mm	8,000	10	12,731	1939
US	BmrM	B-18 Bolo	Douglas	3	9	197	393	865	12	6x12.7mm	2,500	7	375	1937
US	BmrH	B-24 Liberator	Consolidated	5	8	261	818	1,800	20	10x12.7mm	8,000	9	18,800	1941
US	BmrM	B-25 Mitchell	North American	5	13	239	500	1,100	20	3x7.62mm & 4+12.7mm	3,200	5	9,800	1940
US	BmrM	B-26 Marauder	Martin	1	8	249	477	1,050	5	5x7.62mm	5,800	5	5,150	1941
US	BmrH	B-29 Superfortress	Boeing	6	20	355	1,614	3,550	22	11x12.7mm	20,000	13	3,100	1944
US	BmrH	B-36	Convair	5	84	450	4,545	10,000	20	16x20mm	84,000	15	382	1947
Jap	BmrT	B5N Kate	Nakajima	1	3	205	241	530	3	3-4x 7.7mm	1,750	2	1,150	1937
Jap	BmrT	B6N Jill	Nakajima	1	3	259	409	900	2	2-3x7.7mm	1,750	2	1,270	1944
Jap	BmrT	B7A Grace	Aichi	2	5	305	455	1,000	6	2x20mm+	2,200	2	100	1944
Br	BmrT	Barracuda	Fairey	1	3	198	250	550	2	2x7.7mm	1,500	3	2,500	1941
Br	BmrL	Battle	Fairey	1	2	209	409	900	2	2x7.7mm	1,000	3	2,400	1935
Br	FtrN	Beaufighter	Bristol	7	2	287	591	1,300	12	4x20mm	2,100	2	5,560	1940
Br	BmrT	Beaufort	Bristol	1	4	230	405	890	5	5x7.7mm	1,500	2	2,100	1939
Br	BmrL	Blenheim	Bristol	1	2	266	1,045	2,300	2	5x7.7mm	1,300	3	5,400	1936
Jap	DBmr	D3A Val	Aichi	1	2	231	382	840	3	3x7.7mm	816	2	816	1938
Jap	DBmr	D4Y Judy	Yokosuka	1	3	313	518	1,140	3	2x7.7mm + 1x7.9mm	1,300	2	2,319	1942
Br	Ftr	DH 100 Vampire	de Haviland	8	2	469	477	1,050	12	4x20mm	2,000	1	1,100	1946
Br	Ftr	DH 103 Hornet	de Haviland	8	2	472	1,182	2,600	12	4x20mm	2,000	1	420	1945
Br	BmrL	DH 98 Mosquito	de Haviland	0	2	369	1,364	3,000	0	nil	2,000	2	7,781	1940

Nation	Type	Model	Manufacturer								Armament		Production	Year
Jap	Boat	E13A Jake	Aichi	0	1	203	500	1,100	816	1	1x7.7mm	3	1,400	1939
Jap	Float	E16A Paul	Aichi	0	1	250	341	750	1,000	1	1x7.7mm	2	252	1944
Jap	Float	E7K	Kawanishi	0	1	149	455	1,000	500	1	1x7.7mm	3	530	1934
Jap	Float	F1M2 Pete	Mitsubishi	1	0	200	409	900	120	3	3x7.7mm	2	1,114	1940
US	Ftr	F2A Buffalo	Brewster	4	0	297	391	860	200	8	4x12.7mm	1	500	1940
US	Ftr	F4F Wildcat	Grumman	6	1	276	305	670	500	12	6x12.7mm	1	7,900	1939
US	Ftr	F4U Corsair	Chance-Vought	7	3	408	441	970	3,000	12	4x20mm	1	11,100	1943
US	Ftr	F6F Hellcat	Grumman	6	2	322	373	820	2,000	12	6x12.7mm	1	12,275	1942
US	Ftr	F6U Pirate	Chance-Vought	12	2	521	545	1,200	2,000	6	4x12.7mm	1	30	1948
US	Ftr	F7F Tigercat	Grumman	7	4	371	432	950	4,000	9	4x20mm or 12.7mm	2	210	1945
US	Ftr	F8F Bearcat	Grumman	10	2	366	436	960	2,000	8	4x12.7mm	1	730	1945
US	Ftr	FH-1 Phantom	McDonnell	11	2	439	273	600	2,000	8	4x12.7mm	1	61	1946
US	Ftr	FJ-1 Fury	Hawker	7-	2	391	273	600	2,000	8	4x20mm	1	31	1946
US	Ftr	FR-1 Fireball	Ryan	10	1	369	545	1,200	1,000	8	4x.50	2	66	1946
Br	Ftr	Firefly	Fairey	7	1	335	500	1,100	500	4	2x20mm	2	600	1943
Br	Ftr	Fulmar	Fairey	4	1	243	316	695	500	6	6x7.7mm	2	600	1940
Jap	BmM	G3M Nell	Mitsubishi	2	6	200	636	1,400	1,700	8	1x20mm + 4x7.7mm	4	1,050	1936
Jap	BmM	G4M Betty	Mitsubishi	3	9	237	1,682	3,700	2,200	13	4x20mm + 1x7.7mm	4	2,400	1941
Jap	Boat	H6K Mavis	Kawanishi	1	2	183	1,000	2,200	2,200	4	4x7.62mm	5	217	1937
Jap	Boat	H8K Emily	Kawanishi	3	4	252	1,761	3,875	4,400	10	2x20mm + 4x7.7mm	10	131	1942
Br	Ftr	Hurricane	Hawker	5	1	290	182	400	1,000	6	6x7.7mm	1	12,800	1937
Jap	Ftr	J2M Jack	Mitsubishi	5	1	370	257	565	550	8	2x20mm +2x7.7mm	1	450	1943
Jap	Ftr	J8M Shusui	Mitsubishi	8	0	521	23	50	0	6	2x20mm	1	1	1947
Jap	Ftr	Ki-100	Kawasaki	7	1	341	491	1,080	550	6	2x12.7 &2x7.7mm	1	396	1945
Jap	Ftr	Ki-102 Randy	Kawasaki	6	1	313	491	1,080	1,100	11	1x57mm, 2x20mm, 1x12.5mm	2	238	1944
Jap	Ftr	Ki-108	Kawasaki	6	1	324	545	1,200	550	10	1x57mm, 2x20mm, 1x12.5mm	1	4	1945
Jap	Ftr	Ki-109	Mitsubishi	6	1	291	932	2,050	550	14	1x75mm, 4x12.7mm	2	22	1945
Jap	BmrM	Ki-21 Sally	Mitsubishi	2	5	262	534	1,175	2,200	6	6x7.7mm	5	2,064	1938
Jap	Ftr	Ki-27 Nate	Nakajima	3	0	248	132	290	440	2	2x7.7	1	3,400	1937
Jap	BmrL	Ki-30 Ann	Mitsubishi	1	1	233	364	800	660	2	2x7.7	2	704	1938
Jap	Ftr	Ki-43 Oscar	Nakajima	5	1	287	409	900	550	4	2x12.7mm	1	5,900	1941
Jap	Ftr	Ki-44 Tojo	Nakajima	6	1	330	318	700	550	8	4x12.7mm	1	1,200	1942
Jap	Ftr	Ki-45 Nick	Kawasaki	6	1	295	364	800	550	5	1x20mm + 2x7.7mm	2	1,701	1942

Nation	Type	Name	Manufacturer						Armament					
Jap	Ftr	Ki-46 Dinah	Mitsubishi	1	1	370	800	1790	1x7.7mm	1	0	5	1700	1941
Jap	BmrL	Ki-48 Lily	Kawasaki	1	2	273	589	1,295	3x7.7mm	3	1,750	2	1,977	1940
Jap	BmrM	Ki-49 Helen	Nakajima	2	2	265	589	1,295	1x20mm + 6x7.7/12.7mm	9	2,200	8	800	1942
Jap	BmrL	Ki-51 Sonia	Mitsubishi	1	0	228	260	572	2x7.7	2	440	2	2,385	1940
Jap	Ftr	Ki-61 Tony	Kawasaki	7	1	320	289	635	2x12.7 & 2x7.7mm	6	550	1	2,791	1942
Jap	BmrM	Ki-67 Peggy	Mitsubishi	2	6	291	932	2,050	1x20mm + 4x12.7mm	7	2,600	7	700	1944
Jap	Ftr	Ki-84 Frank	Nakajima	7	1	337	416	915	4x20mm	12	550	1	3,480	1944
Jap	Ftr	MXY-7 Baka	Yokosuka	6	3	465	23	50	nil	0	nil	1	800	1945
Br	Ftr	Meteor	Gloster	9	2	514	273	600	4x20mm	12	2,000	1	3,550	1944
Jap	Ftr	N1K1 George	Kawanishi	6	2	321	409	900	2x20mm + 2x7.7mm	8	2,200	1	1,417	1944
US	Ftr	P-26 Peashooter	Boeing	3	0	203	142	313	2x 7.62mm/12.7mm	3	240	1	147	1934
US	Ftr	P-35	Seversky	3	0	245	455	1,000	1x7.62mm & 1x12.7mm	2	100	1	76	1941
Br	Ftr	P-36 Hawk	Curtis	4	0	261	326	718	2x7.62mm	2	250	1	350	1936
US	Ftr	P-38 Lightning	Lockheed	6	2	360	177	390	1x20mm, 4x12.7mm	11	1,600	2	8,600	1942
US	Ftr	P-39 Airacobra	Bell	5	1	334	268	590	1x37mm+	8	500	1	7,500	1941
US	Ftr	P-40 Tomahawk	Curtis	5	1	328	95	208	6x12.7mm	12	500	1	13,200	1939
US	Ftr	P-47 Thunderbolt	Republic	7	3	372	233	512	8x12.7mm	16	3,000	1	15,660	1942
US	Ftr	P-51 Mustang	North American	8	2	380	491	1,080	4x20mm	12	2,000	1	15,586	1942
US	Ftr	P-59 Aircomet	Bell	10	1	359	273	600	1x37mm+	8	1,500	1	190	1945
US	Ftr	P-61 Black Widow	Northrop	6	1	326	395	868	4x20mm + 4x12.7mm	20	1,000	3	691	1943
US	Ftr	P-63 Kingcobra	Bell	7	2	354	177	390	1x37mm+	8	1,500	1	3,303	1943
Jap	BmrM	P1Y1 Frances	Yokosuka	1	2	307	491	1,080	2x20mm	3	2,000	7	1,082	1943
US	Boat	PB2Y Coronado	Consolidated	4	1	298	409	900	8x12.7mm	16	1,200	11	210	1942
US	Boat	PBM Mariner	Martin	2	4	195	1,000	2,200	8x mg	7	4,000	9	1,600	1941
US	Boat	PBY Catalina	Consolidated	1	4	152	909	2,000	5x mg	5	4,000	7	3,300	1936
US	BmrM	PV-1 Ventura	Lockheed	1	5	271	636	1,400	2x12.7mm	4	3,000	6	2,145	1942
US	DBmr	SB2A Buccaneer	Brewster	1	2	200	409	900	2x7.62mm	2	1,000	1	750	1941
US	DBmr	SB2C Helldiver	Curtis	3	2	255	759	1,670	5x12.7mm	10	1,000	2	5,000	1943
US	DBmr	SBD Dauntless	Douglas	1	2	221	440	968	4x .30/12.7mm	5	1,000	2	5,936	1940
US	Float	SC Seahawk	Curtis	1	1	272	247	543	2x12.7mm	4	1,000	2	9	1944
US	FLoat	SO3C Seamew	Curtis	1	0	275	455	1,000	2x.30	2	0	2	800	1942
US	FLoat	SOC Seagull	Curtis	1	0	250	455	1,000	2x.30	2	200	2	258	1935

Nation	Type	Designation/Name	Builder	AA	AS	Speed	Reach	Range	FPR	Arm	Load	Crew	Built	Year
Br	Ftr	Seafire	Supermarine	6	1	339	273	600	8	8x7.7mm	500	1	2,000	1942
Br	Ftr	Spitfire	Supermarine	6	1	330	273	600	8	8x7.7mm	500	1	20,500	1935
Br	BmrT	Swordfish	Fairey	1	3	139	455	1,000	2	2x7.62mm	1,500	2	2,391	1935
US	BmrT	TBD-1 Devastator	Douglas	2	2	179	282	620	2	2x7.62mm	1,000	2	1,000	1937
US	BmrT	TBF Avenger	Grumman	2	6	240	399	877	7	1x.30 & 3x.50mg	2,000	3	9,830	1942
Br	FBmr	Tempest	Hawker	6	6	384	332	730	8	4x20mm	2,000	1	920	1944
Br	FBmr	Typhoon	Hawker	6	6	358	200	440	8	4x20mm	2,000	1	3,330	1941
Br	BmrT	Vildebeeste	Vickers	1	3	156	284	625	2	2x7.62mm	1,500	2	202	1937
Au	BmrL	Wirraway	Commonwealth	1	1	200	282	620	2	2x7.62mm	200	2	755	1937

NOTES: "Nation" is country of origin.

"Type" is type of aircraft—e.g., "Ftr" is fighter; "BmrD" is dive bomber (one engine, dives down on target); "BmrH" is heavy bomber (usually four engines); "BmrL" is light bomber (one engine); "BmrM" is medium bomber (two engines); "BmrT" is torpedo bomber; "FBmr" is fighter-bomber; "FtrN" is night fighter.

"Designation/Name" is the official designation and name; Allied nickname for Japanese aircraft. "Builder" is the manufacturer. "AA" is air combat capability. "AS" is antiship capability. "Speed" is maximum, in miles per hour. "Reach" is maximum one-way trip possible, in miles. "Range" is maximum operational round-trip range, in miles. "FPR" is firepower rating, a mathematical calculation of the aircraft's firepower. "Arm" is number and caliber of machine guns or cannon carried. "Load" is bomb/torpedo load possible, in pounds. "Built" is number manufactured. "Year" is year first in service.

considered a new aircraft. For all practical purposes, it was. It was faster (in fact, the fastest U.S. bomber of the war) and more heavily armed (up to twenty-two .50-caliber machine guns, although twelve were standard), and also had more armor than the A-20. With all those machine guns, and a 4,000-pound load, low-flying A-26s were the terror of German troops in late 1944. In the Pacific, the A-26 was murder on Japanese shipping. The concentrated fire of a dozen or more .50-caliber machine guns quickly shredded merchant ships and even destroyers. The plane also used rockets, and these caused problems, as the fast-moving A-26 was often right over the target seconds after the rockets hit, so that debris from the explosions was sometimes hurled into the underside of the aircraft. Some 2,500 A-26s were built.

A-28 HUDSON. The A-28 Hudson was a unique warplane. It was originally designed as a civilian airliner (the Lockheed 14) in 1937. The British were seeking combat aircraft in the United States during 1938 and Lockheed quickly modified its airliner to produce the Hudson, a light bomber, in 1939. Some 2,800 were eventually built, with about 80 percent of them being used by the British. The U.S. Army called its version the A-28 or A-29, depending upon details of design. The U.S. Navy got a few for recon work, calling them the PBO. It was not large for a two-engine aircraft: 10 tons. The Hudson's top speed was 246 mph, and it could fly over 2,000 miles. Because of its range, it was often used as an armed patrol aircraft. Armament consisted of seven .30-caliber machine guns and 750 pounds of bombs. During the early years of the war, the Hudson was a vital weapon in the Allied air arsenal, and many were present in the Pacific during 1942.

A-35 VENGEANCE. The A-35 Vengeance was a U.S. dive bomber built to British specifications by the American Vultee company. It entered service in 1942, when several hundred were used in the Burma area. Production ended in late 1944, after 1,500 had been manufactured. The A-35 (American name) Vengeance (British name) was a reasonably efficient bomber in 1942. It had a top speed of 279 mph and carried half a ton of bombs.

A5M CLAUDE. The first modern Japanese carrier fighter, the A5M Claude was introduced in 1936. Like the equally hapless U.S.

Buffalo, the A5M was too slow, underarmed, and, particularly for a carrier aircraft, short-ranged. However, in 1936, the A5M was quite an able interceptor. The superb Japanese prewar pilots were able to rack up a good combat record with the A5M in China. Fortunately for the Japanese, the new Zero had replaced the Claude on most Japanese carriers by late 1941. Aircraft technology moved quickly in the late 1930s: The U.S. F4F Wildcat, entering service only two years after the A5M, was already obsolete. By 1941 about 1,000 A5Ms had been manufactured, although production was resumed once more toward the end of the war, for Kamikaze service, since the Claude was cheaper to produce than the Zero.

A6M ZERO/ZEKE. The A6M Zero/Zeke was the most numerous Japanese fighter of the war (over 10,000 built) and, for the first year, one of the most lethal in the Pacific. The A6M was very fast and had exceptional range because of its light construction and correspondingly small engine. But this performance was not achieved without cost. While the A6M was fast and nimble, it was not as sturdy as American fighters. The large fuel supply was not protected by self-sealing fuel tanks, turning what for an American fighter would be a nonfatal hit into a fiery inferno for an A6M. American pilots soon learned how to avoid the A6M's advantages. After the first year of the war, more maneuverable U.S. fighters appeared, and by 1943 the A6M was no longer a fearsome opponent. The Zero did undergo upgrades throughout the war, and the 1944 model was about 20 percent more capable than the 1941 version. "Zeke" was the initial American code name for the airplane. The designation "Zero" has nothing to do with American contempt for things Japanese, as has been suggested, but rather was the name the Japanese themselves gave the airplane from its year of introduction, 1940, which was 2600 in their traditional calendar.

A6M2-N RUFE. The A6M2-N Rufe was a floatplane version of the Japanese A6M Zero carrier fighter. Because of the floats suspended underneath the aircraft, the Rufe had about 20 percent less combat capability than the original Zero. The idea behind this aircraft (of which only 327 were built) was to base it in forward areas where airfields had not yet been built. Operating from coves and bays, the Rufe could attack enemy reconnaissance aircraft and give protection to Japanese recon planes. The Rufe had some success operating in this fashion, but was still generally outfought by most Allied fighters.

AD SKYRAIDER. The U.S. AD Skyraider was the ultimate World War II carrier bomber. But because design work wasn't begun until 1944, and the first flight took place only in early 1945, the Skyraider didn't see action in the Pacific war. Proof of its effectiveness can be seen in its combat record during the Korean and Vietnam wars. The Skyraider remained in production until 1957, with nearly 3,200 being built. The most remarkable aspect of the aircraft was its armament (four 20mm cannon, 8,000 pounds of bombs) and endurance (over four hours). The Skyraider could loiter over a battlefield until it was needed, just the kind of service the troops most wanted. With a top speed of only 318 mph, the Skyraider was slow enough to find its target and hit it accurately. Also quite robust, the aircraft could take a lot of damage. Although originally designed as a dive and torpedo bomber, it spent all of its career hitting land targets. Had the Pacific war gone into 1946, the Japanese would have suffered much from the Skyraider.

AM-1 MAULER. The AM-1 Mauler, a carrier bomber, began development during the war, but did not reach the U.S. fleet until 1946. It's an example of what the Navy might have had if the war had started later or lasted longer, or if the United States had begun developing new aircraft more quickly. The first flight was in the summer of 1944. The AM-1 was faster than the Avenger, had a longer range, and carried over three times as much weight in bombs (7,000 pounds). Its firepower was also considerable: four 20mm cannon.

ALBACORE. The Albacore was one of the several obsolete 1930s aircraft the British used in the Indian Ocean early in the war. This one was a biplane torpedo bomber. The Albacore had a decent range and carrying capacity, but was woefully slow (140 mph). Nevertheless, it served into 1943.

B-10. Billed as the "first genuine strategic bomber," the B-10 was an early 1930s American design. The Army received 103 in 1935 and 1936. The aircraft was also exported, with 120 going to Dutch forces in the East Indies (Indonesia). It was these B-10s that played a minor role in the first few months of fighting in the Pacific war. By

1930s standards, the B-10 wasn't too shabby a bomber. It had a top speed of 260 mph and a range of 2,000 miles. However, it only had three .30-caliber machine guns for defense and carried but a ton of bombs. The B-10s were easy targets for Japanese fighters.

B-17 FLYING FORTRESS. The U.S. B-17 Flying Fortress was the first modern four-engine heavy bomber, entering combat in 1941. It promised more than it delivered, but what it did accomplish in combat was significant in the Pacific war. The B-17 entered service in 1939 and it was seen as a means of finding and destroying warships far out at sea. The initial experience with B-17s in the Pacific war was not encouraging. Many B-17s were destroyed on the ground by the Japanese at Pearl Harbor and in the Philippines. B-17 attacks on ships at sea were rarely successful (although the Air Corps made certain the newspapers printed otherwise). But the B-17 soon began to prove useful as a long-range reconnaissance aircraft that could fight its way past enemy interceptors. Japanese fighters were not as lethal to B-17s as were German ones. Although the vast majority of the 12,000 B-17s served in Europe, over 1,000 were in the Pacific during the war, serving as armed reconnaissance aircraft and bombers.

B-18 BOLO. The B-18 Bolo was a DC-3 transport redesigned as a U.S. bomber. It was a pretty respectable warbird. However, the B-18 came into use in 1936 and bomber technology advanced rapidly in the next few years. Most of the 375 B-18s built were converted to maritime reconnaissance use, and in this guise served in the early months of the Pacific war. The aircraft was slow (about 200 mph top speed), poorly armed, and able to carry, at most, a ton of bombs, but it did manage to kill a few German submarines off the east coast.

B-24 LIBERATOR. The B-24 Liberator was America's second-generation heavy bomber. Often unfavorably compared to the B-17, the B-24 was actually a superior aircraft and was produced in greater numbers than the B-17 (19,000 versus 12,000). The B-24 beat the B-17 by about 10 percent in range, speed, and payload. The longer range of the B-24 made it better suited for Pacific use. The Navy used a modified B-24 (PB4Y-2) with even longer range as patrol aircraft. The B-24 was a terrific antisubmarine aircraft, able to carry as many as twenty-four depth charges at ranges up to 1,000 miles. Over 1,000 B-24s constantly scoured the vast Pacific for enemy ships. Because of this patrol coverage, the Japanese were unable to stage many surprise attacks. There were also several hundred B-24s converted to transports, as the C-109 tanker (carrying nearly 9 tons of fuel) or C-87 freighter (hauling over 8 tons of freight or passengers).

B-25 MITCHELL. The U.S. B-25 Mitchell was produced in larger numbers (nearly 10,000) than any other twin-engine bomber of the war. Many considered it the most effective. The B-25 was particularly lethal in the Pacific, where many carried a 75mm gun and eight .50-caliber machine guns facing forward, plus six .50-calibers pointed in other directions. This "ship buster" version could also carry a torpedo or 3,200 pounds of bombs. A thousand of this antishipping version were built, with a quarter of them flying under Navy or Marine colors. These aircraft, with heavier armament than a tank, were the scourge of Japanese merchantmen and their escorts. The B-25 was flown off the carrier *Hornet* for the Doolittle Raid in 1942 and continued to fly in combat until the end of the war. As it had entered service in 1940, the B-25 was a major component of American air power from the very beginning. Thousands were given to the Allies, particularly Russia and Britain. Designed for use against land targets, the B-25 proved that bombers could take on warships, but only if they came down to sea level.

B-26 MARAUDER. The B-26 Marauder entered U.S. service a year after the B-25, and the two twin-engine bombers were often confused with each other, despite the fact that the B-25 had a twin tail and the B-26 the more common single tail rudder. Because the B-25 got there first, and did its job well, few B-26s were sent to the Pacific. Both aircraft were about equal in performance, with the more modern B-26 having a slight edge. Both weighed 15 to 16 tons fully loaded for a typical mission. Although the B-26 had a reputation for being difficult to land, it had the lowest accidental loss rate of any American combat aircraft. There were two groups of B-26s in the Pacific, and these generally performed the conventional bombing missions while the B-25 got down low and did all the glamorous stuff. Only about 5,000 B-26s were produced and their service lasted into the late 1940s.

B-29 SUPERFORTRESS. The U.S. B-29 Superfortress was the world's first truly strategic bomber. Weighing over 60 tons fully loaded, it could fly over 3,000 miles carrying 5 tons of bombs. It was fast, with a top speed of 355 mph and a cruising speed of 290 mph. It normally flew over 5 miles high, and the crew spaces were pressurized and heated. This was a big plus for the crew, who often suffered frostbite and oxygen starvation in B-17s and B-24s flying at those altitudes. What got the development of the B-29 going was the fall of France in 1940. Fearing that England would be next and needing a way for U.S.-based bombers to attack Nazi targets in Europe, the United States conceived the B-29 as a bomber with sufficient reach to hit European targets from North America or Iceland. This proved unnecessary, as Britain held and the Germans turned their attention to Russia in 1941. But by early 1942, the United States was faced with a war against Japan. And in early 1942, the Japanese were winning. An aircraft like the B-29 was now needed to bomb Japan across the even vaster Pacific Ocean. The first B-29 flew in late 1942. Production began in early 1943. After crews were trained and units sent overseas, the first B-29s saw combat in June 1944. Over 3,000 B-29s were eventually produced and the entire B-29 program cost more than the Manhattan Project (to build the atomic bomb). By early 1945, up to 600 B-29s at a time were flying against Japanese cities from bases in the Mariana Islands. The last B-29 was produced in 1946, but it continued to serve in the Korean War and in foreign air forces until the late 1950s.

B-36. The U.S. B-36, design work for which began in 1942, was the most ambitious World War II heavy bomber project. It was designed to bomb Germany from bases in North America. The first prototype flew a year after the Japanese surrendered, and production models didn't appear until 1948. This could have been speeded up, had the war in the Pacific lasted longer. With a longer reach (over 6,000 miles) than the B-29 and a bigger bomb load (38 tons, maximum), it could have pounded the Japanese home islands from halfway across the Pacific. Only 382 were built, and production ended in 1951 (as the B-47 and B-52 were approaching production). Later

("D") versions had four jet engines added to the six standard piston engines, which worked double "pusher" propellers (i.e., the props were on the rear edge of the wing). The B-36 was, indeed, the last World War II bomber.

B5N KATE. The B5N Kate was Japan's carrier torpedo bomber early in World War II. This was the aircraft that carried the torpedoes at Pearl Harbor. Although considered obsolete by 1941, it was superior to the U.S. Devastator, but not nearly as good as the Avenger. It entered service in 1937, with production continuing until 1942. Some 1,100 were manufactured, and some were still in service in 1944.

B6N JILL. The B6N Jill carrier torpedo bomber was the replacement for the B5N and didn't enter service until early 1943. The B6N was slightly superior to the two-year-older Avenger, its American counterpart. However, the B6N arrived at a bad time for Japanese carrier aviation. During 1944, most of Japan's carriers had been destroyed. The B6N ended its career in 1945 operating from land bases and making Kamikaze attacks.

B7A GRACE. The B7A Grace was the last-generation Japanese torpedo bomber. Problems with its engine delayed delivery from 1943 to 1944. Although only 114 were produced, it was probably the best torpedo bomber of the war. As fast as many fighters (over 300 mph) and quite maneuverable, it arrived too late to operate from carriers and flew from land bases until the end of the war.

BARRACUDA. The Barracuda was the successor to the Royal Navy's Albacore torpedo bomber. It was faster but had a shorter range. Coming into service in 1941, it was already obsolete by World War II standards and would not have fared well had it been used heavily in the Pacific.

BATTLE. The Battle was an obsolete British single-engined light bomber. A few were still in Southeast Asia at the end of 1941, but all disappeared in 1942.

BEAUFIGHTER. The Beaufighter was a British heavy fighter that was originally designed as a long-range bomber escort and night fighter. Deliveries began in the summer of 1940, and those that reached the Pacific the next year soon became formidable tactical bombers (using torpedoes, bombs, and rockets). Also carried were four forward-firing 20mm cannon. The Japanese called the Beaufighter "Whispering Death" because of its relatively quiet engines. Nearly 6,000 were built and the last ones in the Far East were not withdrawn from service until 1960.

BEAUFORT. The Beaufort was a land-based British torpedo bomber. Although it had a 1930s design, it stayed in use well into 1944. Australia used a third of the 2,100 produced, so the Beaufort was well represented in the Pacific.

BLENHEIM. The Blenheim was the first modern British "fast bomber." When the first ones entered service in 1936, they were indeed able to outrun many fighters. But this situation did not last and the Blenheim went through several different versions until production ceased in the summer of 1943. Some 5,400 were produced. Several hundred of the Mark V version served in the Far East as light bombers until late 1943.

D3A VAL. The D3A Val was the primary Japanese carrier dive bomber for the first year of the war. While not particularly outstanding in the speed, bombload, or range department, in the hands of well-trained crews the Val did an outstanding job. The aircraft was quite maneuverable and the D3A could tangle with enemy fighters once its bombs had been dropped. Production of the D3A continued until January 1944, with 816 being delivered. The D3A ended its career as a trainer and Kamikaze.

D4Y JUDY. The D4Y Judy was a new Japanese carrier dive bomber that began replacing the older Val during the summer of 1942. By early 1943 the replacement was complete. Unfortunately, most of the well-trained prewar crews were now dead and the Judy ended up operating mainly from land bases with less skillful crews. In comparison to the older Val, the Judy was superior in nearly all aspects (speed, range, bombload).

DH 98 MOSQUITO. The British DH 98 Mosquito was one of the more remarkable aircraft of the war. Designed and built in 1940, it entered service in 1941. Most of the 7,800 built were used in Europe. Those that appeared in the Pacific served as recon, night fighter, and bomber aircraft. The DH 98 was very fast, was difficult to spot using radar (much of the fuselage was plywood), and had very long range. In effect, it was the first "Stealth bomber." Production and use continued after the war.

DH 100 VAMPIRE. Development work on the British DH 100 Vampire began in 1941, at the same time as the manufacturer was getting its famous DH 98 Mosquito bomber into production. Although the DH 100 was jet-powered, it borrowed many design concepts from the DH 98, including the extensive use of wood in the structure. This made for a light aircraft that could be easily propelled by the low-thrust jet engines available in the early 1940s. The DH 100 was to have only one engine, unlike the other early jets, which all had two. Only about forty production aircraft were ready in early 1945, too late to have much effect on the war. However, if the Pacific war had gone on longer, DH 100s would have shown up in Burma. Over 1,000 DH 100s were built, many serving into the early 1950s. With a top speed of over 500 mph, it was heavily armed (four 20mm cannon and a ton of bombs).

DH 103 HORNET. The British DH 103 Hornet was a two-engine fighter that entered service in early 1945. It also saw service on carriers such as the Sea Hornet. Over 400 were built (half for the Royal Navy, in the late 1940s), and it served into the 1950s. Had the Pacific war gone on longer, more DH 103s would have been built and sent east. The DH 103 had a top speed of 472 mph and was armed with four 20mm cannon and a ton of bombs or rockets.

E13A JAKE. The E13A Jake was the principal floatplane of the fleet. Some 1,400 were built, and they were sitting ducks for any Allied fighters (even bombers or flying boats) they came across.

E16A PAUL. The E16A Paul was the third Japanese floatplane introduced during the war. Entering service in the summer of 1944, the E16A could carry 1,000 pounds of bombs. This made it capable of effective dive-bombing. This was rarely possible, however, because most Allied ships now operated in conjunction with aircraft carriers. While faster (250 mph) than previous floatplanes, the E16A was still an easy target for Allied fighters (and most other combat aircraft).

E7K. The E7K was the original Japanese floatplane equipping cruisers and battleships. It was in the process of being replaced by the F1M2 when the war broke out. By the end of 1942, it had been withdrawn from front-line service. Like all Japanese floatplanes, it had scouting for the fleet as its primary mission.

F1M2 PETE. The F1M2 Pete was the principal Japanese float-plane for cruisers and battleships. Introduced in 1940, some 1,100 were built. It had some attack capability, with a 120-pound bomb-load. However, its slow speed (200 mph) and meager armament (one machine gun) made it an easy target for Allied fighters.

F2A BUFFALO. The F2A Buffalo was the first modern U.S. carrier fighter, reaching the fleet in 1940. The next generation (the F4F Wildcat) was much superior, and by late 1941 the Buffalo was being replaced by the F4F. But some were still on carriers at the time of Pearl Harbor, and many also served with Dutch and British forces from land bases in the East Indies. The former were quickly withdrawn, while the latter were torn up in combat. Only 500 were produced, the last one in June 1941. Most ended up serving with European nations desperate for any kind of combat aircraft.

F4F WILDCAT. The F4F Wildcat was originally designed as a biplane, and lost out to the F2A Buffalo in a flyoff competition. Redesigned as a monoplane, the F4F was clearly superior to the F2A and production began immediately. Ironically, the F4F first entered combat in British colors. An order of F4Fs for France ended up in Britain when France fell in June 1940. The Royal Navy put the aircraft into service as the "Martlet." In December of 1940, a Mart-let shot down a German bomber, scoring the F4F's first kill. The British ultimately took delivery of 1,100 F4Fs. Meanwhile, the U.S. Navy was rapidly replacing all its older carrier fighters (biplanes or F2As) with Wildcats. By the end of 1941, nearly all carrier fighters were F4Fs, and by early 1942, all of the older fighters were gone. The Wildcat was not the best fighter in the world, but it was good enough. In particular, it was rugged, being able to take more pun-ishment than its opponents. By the end of 1942, Wildcats had downed 5.9 enemy aircraft for each F4F lost.

F4U CORSAIR. The U.S. F4U Corsair, something of a dark horse in the "best fighter of World War II" competition, managed to move to the front of the pack. Originally designed as a carrier fighter, it first flew in May 1940. The Navy was dubious of its ability to operate from carriers because the pilot's view of the flight deck was quite restricted during landing, and the airplane had a relatively weak undercarriage. Admitting that the F4U was a very capable aircraft, the Navy began mass production in June 1941 anyway, deciding to have Marine pilots fly the F4U from land bases only. Entering combat in early 1943, the F4U quickly established its superiority. Through the end of the war, 2,140 enemy aircraft were shot down by the F4U, of which only 189 were lost in return. There were, as with all combat aircraft, other ways to lose F4Us. Some 1,400 F4Us were lost to other causes, including 349 to enemy antiaircraft fire, 164 in landing accidents, and the rest to other operational mishaps. While about one in 300 F4U landings resulted in damage or loss of the aircraft, this was not unusual by World War II standards. Indeed, until quite recently, getting shot down in combat was less likely than losing your aircraft through some noncombat accident. In tests, the F4U was shown capable of outflying the Zero, as well as the U.S. Army's P-47 and P-51 and all other U.S. Navy fighters. The F4U also found work as a fighter-bomber, being able to carry 3,000 pounds of bombs. It was a big airplane, weighing up to 6 tons fully loaded. By early 1944, the British (who received 2,000 F4Us) and U.S. F4U pilots convinced the Navy that the aircraft could operate safely on carriers. By the end of the war, 15 percent of F4U sorties had been flown from carriers. Some 5,000 F4U were built during the war, with even more built into the 1950s. The F4U served into the 1960s with foreign air forces.

F6F HELLCAT. The F6F Hellcat was the U.S. Navy's successor to the F4F Wildcat carrier fighter. Although the F6F didn't enter service until early 1943 (after all the crucial carrier battles of 1942 were over), it performed admirably for the rest of the war. Some 12,000 F6Fs were produced and those that got into action downed 6,477 enemy aircraft, while losing only 270 of their own in air combat. While not as capable as the F4U Corsair, the Hellcat was more than a match for any Japanese aircraft it encountered from 1943 on. Part of this was because the Japanese were unable to produce quality pilots as quickly as the Allies. No matter how much improved Japanese aircraft were, the more skillful Allied pilots more than made up for any equipment disadvantages.

F6U PIRATE. The F6U Pirate was one of several jet fighter projects the U.S. Navy began during World War II. It was not a success. Development began in 1944 and it was not ready for production until 1949. At that point, the other jet fighter projects looked more promising and the F6U was abandoned after only thirty were built. It might have turned out otherwise, although the Navy would not have had a carrier-based jet fighter until 1946 at the earliest.

F7F TIGERCAT. The F7F Tigercat was developed as a twin-engine multirole fighter-bomber for the U.S. Navy's new 45,000-ton "supercarriers." The first F7Fs arrived in the combat zone on August 15, 1945, the day Japan surrendered. Only about 100 F7Fs were produced before the war ended and most of these were the night fighter version. While the 9-ton F7F was not the best interceptor, it was capable of many other tasks. It was the first Navy fighter that could carry a torpedo. Its maximum bomb load was 2,000 pounds and its four 20mm cannon gave it substantial air-to-air firepower. Had the war continued, many more F7Fs would have been produced. As it was, the introduction of jet aircraft after World War II cut short the F7F's career. Only about 200 more were produced and all were withdrawn from service by 1952.

F8F BEARCAT. The U.S. F8F Bearcat was the replacement for the F6F Hellcat. Work began in 1943 and it was in production by early 1945. The F8F was lighter, smaller, and more capable than its predecessor. The F8F was, without doubt, the most capable propeller-driven carrier fighter ever produced. However, it never got into combat from U.S. carriers, as the first F8F unit was in transit to the Pacific when the war ended. Over 700 were eventually produced, as the F8F was to be the main Navy carrier fighter until the jets were ready in the late 1940s. Production continued until 1948 and the F8F was withdrawn from U.S. service in the early 1950s. At that point, many of the F8Fs were given to foreign governments. The French used F8Fs in their Vietnam war, the South Vietnamese government inherited some, and some were sold to Thailand.

FH-1 PHANTOM. The FH-1 Phantom was another of the U.S. Navy's jet fighter projects and probably the most successful. Work began in 1943 and the first flight took place in early 1945. In the summer of 1947, the first unit received its FH-1s. Because the war was over, only sixty-one were produced. Work went ahead on more advanced designs, although if the war in the Pacific had gone on long enough, the capable FH-1 would have been the most likely Navy jet the Japanese would have had to face.

FJ-1 FURY. The FJ-1 Fury was the third U.S. Navy project to produce a jet fighter. This one was begun in 1944, by the company that was working on what would eventually become the highly successful Air Force F-86. The FJ-1 didn't make its first flight until 1946 and it was not all that impressive. Only thirty were produced and one unit was equipped with it. More advanced designs were used for the Navy's post–World War II jet fighter.

FR-1 FIREBALL. The U.S. FR-1 Fireball was unique in the history of fighter aircraft. From a distance, the FR-1 looked like the F6F Hellcat, being about the same size and weight. But the FR-1 had a jet engine in addition to the conventional piston engine driving a prop. The jet engine would quickly give the FR-1 additional speed and power. This combination was desirable in general, and after the Kamikaze aircraft appeared, something as perky as the FR-1 was seen as a solution. With its long range, and "speed on demand" from the jet engine, the FR-1s could get out there and destroy Kamikazes before they got close to their targets. As the prospects of an invasion of Japan became more likely, the need for the FR-1 increased. Although development didn't begin until late 1942, the first FR-1 flew in June 1944 and the first deliveries of production aircraft were in March 1945. The war ended before the first FR-1 squadron could complete its training. Only sixty-six were built. The FR-1 was taken out of service in 1947, as by then it was obvious that more capable pure jet aircraft were on the way. However, if the war had continued, FR-1s would have played a major role in defending the fleet from Kamikazes.

FIREFLY. The Firefly was originally designed by the British as a two-seat carrier fighter. Entering service in late 1942, the Firefly was soon seen to be most effective as a carrier bomber. Some 600 were built and they were quite successful. The Firefly was rebuilt after the war and continued to serve into the 1950s.

FULMAR. The Fulmar was a specially built British carrier fighter. Not as effective as American and Japanese carrier aircraft, it did most of its fighting against the Italians in the Mediterranean and against German U-boats in the Atlantic. Armament was eight .30-caliber machine guns and 500 pounds of bombs. Some 600 were produced, with production ending in early 1943.

G3M NELL. The G3M Nell was the Japanese Navy's first modern land-based bomber. The G3M entered service in late 1936. These two-engine bombers were excellent, making raids over 1,000 miles from their bases. Although their bombload was only 1,700 pounds (or one torpedo), the highly trained crews made the most of it. It was G3Ms that sank the British battleship *Prince of Wales* and battlecruiser *Repulse* off Malaya on December 10, 1941. The British thought they were out of range of Japanese bombers. Early in World War II, the G3M was replaced by the G4M, which carried more fuel in the same light type of airframe, thus making it even more dangerous for the crew than the 8-ton G3M.

G4M BETTY. The G4M Betty was the Japanese Navy's principal heavy bomber. The G4M had a very long range (over 3,000 miles) for a two-engine bomber, achieved at the expense of any protection for the aircraft or crew. Carrying over 3 tons of fuel in unprotected tanks, the G4M tended to erupt in a ball of flame after taking a few hits from Allied fighters or antiaircraft guns. This made the G4M very unpopular with its crews. But deliveries began in early 1941 and the G4M was heavily used in the first year of the war. Nearly 2,500 were produced, and 250 were prominently used during the first six months of the war. The G4M had a maximum bombload of 2,200 pounds. It could also carry a single torpedo and was effective as a torpedo bomber. Typical takeoff weight was 12 tons or more. Initially, the G4M had only three 7.7mm machine guns for defense. Later versions had two 20mm cannon and two machine guns.

H6K MAVIS. The H6K Mavis was a Japanese contemporary of the American PBY flying boat. Larger than the PBY, it was roughly equal in performance. However, the limited industrial resources of Japan resulted in only about 200 of these naval reconnaissance aircraft being produced. Reliability and vulnerability problems caused the Mavis to be withdrawn from front-line service by late 1942.

H8K EMILY. The H8K Emily was a rather huge flying boat that first appeared in early 1942. Though it was an excellent recon aircraft, only 131 were produced. Since it had a one-way range of 3,800 miles, the Japanese made all sorts of interesting plans for using the H8K to bomb targets in North America. These schemes involved H8Ks being refueled by Japanese and German tanker submarines. Limited resources prevented any of these operations from being carried out.

HURRICANE. The Hurricane was Britain's first modern fighter and entered service in 1937. Production ended in 1944 after nearly 13,000 had been built. Several thousand were sent to Russia and other allies received as many. After 1941, the Hurricane was the principal British fighter in the Far East. The Hurricane had a rough time against the Zero, but Japanese Army fighters were less of a problem. However, the Hurricane, like most Allied fighters, had tremendous firepower and was well protected. This made a difference even when faced with the Zero, and Japanese bombers were easy targets for the Hurricane.

J2M JACK. The J2M Jack was a new Japanese design that flew for the first time in early 1942. Called the Raiden ("Thunderbolt") by the Japanese, this was to be a more powerful land-based interceptor. The beginning of the war threw Japanese aircraft production into turmoil and it was believed to be more efficient to turn out more of the older designs than to expend resources to switch to more modern designs. In any event, the J2M was nimble, fast (370 mph), and well armed (two machine guns and two 20mm cannon). It also had a lot of problems getting a reliable engine. Fewer than 500 were produced.

J8M SHUSUI. The J8M Shusui ("Sword Stroke") was a Japanese copy of the German Me-163 Komet, a crude, rocket-powered, short-range interceptor. The Germans were unable to do much with the Me-163 design in combat and the Japanese were able to do even less. The Germans sent plans and component samples to Japan in 1943. However, one of the two cargo submarines involved in this effort sank en route. The J8M only got as far as the prototype stage, with the engine still being perfected when the war ended. The liquid-fuel rocket engine could run for only five to six minutes, producing a top speed of 560 mph. But since the J8M could climb to 30,000 feet in less than four minutes, this gave the aircraft time to make a pass at a B-29 formation. Armed with two 30mm cannon, the J8M could do some damage. After its fuel was spent, the aircraft became a glider and landed in that mode. The concept was viable and the J8M could have turned into a formidable interceptor, or Kamikaze.

KI-100. The Ki-100 was the last fighter produced for the Japanese Army and it was by far the best. The Ki-100 was actually a redesigned and reengined Ki-61, a successful older fighter. The more powerful and reliable engine of the Ki-100 made a big difference. Fortunately for the Allies, the Ki-100 didn't enter service until March 1945. Only 396 were built (including 275 Ki-61 conversions). With a maximum speed of 360 mph, great maneuverability, and heavy armament (two 20mm cannon and two 12.7mm machine guns), the Ki-100 proved lethal to B-29s and their P-51 escorts. The U.S. Navy's F6F Hellcats (which were used on numerous raids against the Japanese home islands from carriers) took a beating from the superior Ki-100. Had the Japanese managed to improve their engine technology and quality control earlier, the Ki-100 would have been available in quantity earlier, and that would have caused far more U.S. casualties.

KI-102 RANDY. The Ki-102 Randy was a ground attack version of the Japanese Army's Ki-96 heavy (two-engine) fighter. Development work began in 1943, but production didn't begin until late 1944, and 238 were built before the war ended. The Ki-102 had better protection (armor and self-sealing fuel tanks) and armament (a 57mm gun, two 20mm cannon, and a rear-facing 12.7mm machine gun, plus half a ton of bombs or drop tanks). Fifteen high-altitude interceptor versions were also produced before the war ended. Most of these aircraft were kept in Japan; only a few were involved during the battle for Okinawa. The Ki-102 was an effective aircraft that would have been a considerable threat to Allied troops if there had been an invasion of Japan.

KI-108. The Ki-108 was a Ki-96 redesigned as a high-altitude fighter (to oppose heavy bomber raids). Work began in 1943, but the difficulty in perfecting the pressurized cabin delayed production. Testing was still going on with the four prototypes when the war ended. Had the Ki-108 gotten into service, it would have been effective. Its armament of one 37mm and two 20mm cannon would have been lethal to the B-29. Ironically, the Americans found (in early 1945) that low-altitude B-29 raids were more effective than high-altitude ones. Since these low-altitude raids tended to be at night, what the Japanese needed was a radar-equipped night fighter. Attempts to build these met with little success.

KI-109. The Ki-109 was a Japanese Army Ki-67 heavy bomber redesigned as a heavy fighter. The project began in early 1943, when the Japanese became aware of the B-29's existence and pondered how to deal with nighttime raids by this monster. The initial concept had two versions of the Ki-109. One would be a "hunter," equipped with radar and a 40cm (15.8-inch) searchlight, which would find the B-29s. The second version would be the "killer," having two 37mm cannon firing upward at an angle. This plan was soon dropped for a single version mounting a 75mm gun in its nose (and fifteen shells, to be loaded by the copilot). This would keep the Ki-109 out of range of the B-29's defensive armament and, at the time, it was thought that the B-29s would not have fighter escorts (a false hope, as it turned out). Only twenty-two of these aircraft were built before the war ended, not enough to have any noticeable effect on the B-29 raids.

KI-21 SALLY. The Ki-21 Sally was the standard Japanese Army medium bomber until 1944. First introduced in 1938, it could carry a ton of bombs and travel no faster than 262 mph. It was used mostly in China. Those that did appear in the Pacific were very vulnerable to the heavily armed Allied fighters. Like most Japanese bombers of the period, the Ki-21 was lightly constructed and lacked self-sealing fuel tanks.

KI-27 NATE. The Ki-27 Nate was the first modern Japanese Army fighter, introduced in 1937 and produced until 1940. It was used primarily in China, where it remained in service until 1943. While slow and fragile, it was possibly the most maneuverable fighter of World War II. Some 3,400 were built, and at the beginning of the war it was the most numerous Japanese fighter. Some were encountered by the Allies in the Pacific in areas where the Army was responsible for air defense.

KI-30 ANN. The Ki-30 Ann was the oldest Japanese Army light bomber to appear in the war, having first appeared in 1938. Production ceased before Pearl Harbor, as the Ki-48 and Ki-50 went into production to replace it. An unsuccessful design, used mainly in China.

KI-43 OSCAR. The Ki-43 Oscar was the Japanese Army equivalent of the Navy's A6M Zero. Entering service in 1940, it was the most heavily produced aircraft after the Zero (5,900 produced). It was not as capable as the Zero, mainly because of lower speed and inadequate armament (usually just two 7.7mm machine guns). Still, the Ki-43 was very maneuverable and a deadly dogfighter. After the Japanese saw the more heavily armed and armored Allied aircraft in action, late-model Ki-43s received self-sealing fuel tanks and some armor. Attempts were made to upgrade its armament, but these were less successful.

KI-44 TOJO. The Japanese Ki-44 Tojo was the replacement for the Ki-43. Production was delayed until 1942 so as not to interrupt the mass production of the Ki-43. The Ki-44 addressed the need for greater speed and rate of climb. Pilots new to the aircraft missed the maneuverability of the Ki-43 but came to appreciate the Ki-44's qualities when in combat against Allied aircraft. The Ki-44 saw heavy action in New Guinea during 1942 and 1943. In 1944, cannon were added, and from then through the end of the war, the Ki-44 was deadly against U.S. heavy bombers. Some 1,200 were built.

KI-45 NICK. The Ki-45 Nick was the first Japanese Army twin-engine fighter and was intended as a long-range escort for bombers. At the time, Zeros were used for this duty, but the Zeros had little fuel for fighting enemy interceptors once over the target. Although the Ki-45 entered service in 1941, it never performed in its designed role. Although speedy and maneuverable, it was no real match for most Allied fighters. It was first used as a long-range fighter and reconnaissance aircraft. It could have been used in support of the long-range bombing attacks against Guadalcanal in 1942, but the air attacks were a Navy operation and the two Japanese services rarely cooperated early in the war. By 1944, the Ki-45 found its role as a night fighter (against B-29s) and as a Kamikaze (during the daytime). Against bombers, the heavy armament of the Ki-45 was crucial. As a Kamikaze, the heavy weight of the Ki-45 was telling. Only 1,700 Ki-45s were produced.

KI-46 DINAH. All but a few (which served as interceptors) were recon aircraft, one of the best in the war.

KI-48 LILY. The Ki-48 Lily was a Japanese light bomber that entered service in 1940. A failure in combat, it was too slow and had neither exceptional range nor bombload to make up for its operational deficiencies. Nearly 2,000 were produced, most being used in China.

KI-49 HELEN. The Ki-49 Helen was the Japanese Army's most modern bomber, introduced in 1942. While faster than the earlier Japanese bomber designs, it did not have the carrying capacity or robustness of U.S. medium bombers.

KI-51 SONIA. The Ki-51 Sonia was a Japanese Army light bomber that first appeared in 1940. It was a more successful design than the Ki-49 of the same period. Nearly 2,400 were produced.

KI-61 TONY. The Ki-61 Tony was one of the better all-round Japanese fighters of the war. An Army aircraft, it was built with the help of some German technology. Entering service in 1943, it fought until the end of the war. Profiting from the experience of earlier generations of fighters, the Ki-61 was more robust, with self-sealing fuel tanks and some armor. In 1945, several hundred were fitted with a new type of engine, and the performance improvement was so dramatic that this version was called the Ki-100.

KI-67 PEGGY. The Ki-67 Peggy was a more successful Japanese Army medium bomber, appearing in early 1944. Only 700 were built and most served only to provide Allied fighters with more sturdy targets than previous Japanese bombers.

KI-84 FRANK. The Ki-84 Frank was the best fighter Japan produced. But this new Army aircraft didn't arrive until early 1944. At that point, the U.S. submarine offensive against Japanese shipping was making a noticeable dent in raw materials supplies. This meant that factories cut corners in producing the high-quality parts the Ki-

84 needed (the Japanese didn't get into high-quality manufacturing until the 1950s). As a result, the high-performance components, especially the powerful engine, were prone to frequent breakdowns. When everything was working, a Ki-84 could outfly a P-51 or P-47. But all too often, something would fail and the Ki-84 pilot would find himself at a grave disadvantage. Even when the plane was returning from a successful mission, the Ki-84's landing gear frequently failed from the stress of landing. The Ki-84 was more stoutly built (in theory) than previous Japanese fighters, and required higher-quality metals than Japanese industry was accustomed to producing. Some 3,500 were produced, but as numbers grew, their quality steadily declined. To this, many Allied pilots owed their lives.

MXY-7 BAKA. The Japanese MXY-7 Baka was the ultimate Kamikaze aircraft. It was a rocket-propelled flying bomb that was carried underneath a bomber for most of its flight. When about 50 miles from the target area, the MXY-7 was released. The pilot then guided the aircraft into a steep glide toward a target (at about 300 mph). When near the enemy ships, the pilot aimed the aircraft right at its target and ignited the rocket for the last 30 seconds of the suicide flight. The rocket provided high enough speed to get past any defending fighters and antiaircraft fire. While impressive on paper, the MXY-7 system didn't work. The lumbering bombers carrying the 1- to 1.5-ton rockets (there were two versions of the MXY-7) made easy targets for Allied interceptors. The high-flying bombers (the MXY-7 needed some altitude before dropped) were easily spotted by carrier radar. Those MXY-7s that did launch found that the new American radar-fuzed shells, and heavy flak in general, presented a wall of exploding shells they had to fly through. But the Japanese had one thing right about the MXY-7: When it did hit a ship, it had devastating results. The speedy (over 500 mph) rockets contained 1,300 or 2,600 pounds of explosive. It made quite a dent in whatever kind of ship it hit. Fortunately, only a few ships were hit by any of the 800 MXY-7s built.

METEOR. The Meteor was the world's first operational jet combat aircraft. Entering British service in the summer of 1944, eight days before the German Me-262, the Meteor promptly went to work shooting down German cruise missiles (V-1s). Armed with four

20mm cannon and able to fly higher and faster than any other fighter, the Meteor was limited only by small numbers (100 were produced during the war) and the heavy maintenance load its two jet engines put on the ground crew. No Meteors served in the Pacific, but if the war against Japan had gone beyond the summer of 1945, the Meteor would have been involved.

N1K1 GEORGE. The N1K1 George was originally developed as a Japanese floatplane fighter, but the floats were deleted and the N1K1 turned into a land-based naval fighter. The aircraft was fast, rugged, and extremely maneuverable. Entering combat in early 1944, it was quite a shock to Allied pilots. Like most other high-performance Japanese aircraft late in the war, the N1K1 suffered from repeated manufacturing defects and component failures. Only some 1,400 were produced.

P-26 PEASHOOTER. The P-26 Peashooter played only a minor role in the Pacific war, with some being used in the U.S. defense of the Philippines in late 1941. The P-26 was the U.S. Army's first all-metal monoplane fighter. It was in U.S. service between 1934 and 1938, being replaced by the P-36 (which was itself quickly replaced by the P-40). The P-26 was the last Army fighter with an open cockpit. It was a good performer, by 1930s standards. The Chinese Air Force bought some, and with these P-26s shot down many Japanese aircraft. The Philippine Army Air Force also scored some victories with its handful of P-26s during the opening weeks of the war. Fewer than 200 P-26s were produced. Several continued to serve in the Guatemalan Air Force until 1957.

P-35. The P-35 was one of the many fighters produced in America during the 1930s that eventually saw Pacific combat while serving with American allies. In this case, the P-35 flew with the newly formed Philippine Army Air Force. These P-35s had originally been ordered by Sweden, but events in Europe prevented delivery. In the summer of 1941, forty were sent to the Philippines where they were quickly lost during the Japanese invasion later that year. Lacking any armor or self-sealing fuel tanks, the P-35s didn't last long against the more maneuverable and better-armed Japanese fighters.

P-36 HAWK. The U.S. P-36 Hawk was obsolete when the war began. Even so, P-36s opposed the Japanese attack on Pearl Harbor and managed to shoot down two enemy aircraft. While it looked fairly modern, and was a contemporary of the German Me-109, the P-36 was not as well designed and its performance in combat was lower than most of the aircraft it faced in combat. While a very maneuverable and sturdy aircraft, it was relatively slow. The P-36 was built largely for export, and many nations received it (China, Thailand, France, South Africa, Argentina). Fewer than 400 were built, with production ending in early 1941.

P-38 LIGHTNING. The P-38 Lightning was one of the more successful American fighters, being the only one that was in production continuously from Pearl Harbor through V-J Day. Over 8,000 were built. But the P-38 was unusual in many respects. It had twin engines, a characteristic that does not usually produce successful fighters. The P-38 succeeded by using its high speed and superior ceiling to dive on opponents with guns blazing. If this did not work, the P-38 was usually going fast enough to escape for another try. It was heavily armed, with 37mm or 20mm cannon, plus four .50-caliber machine guns. The twin engines were often a lifesaver, as the aircraft could fly on one engine. Large and sturdy, the P-38 could absorb more punishment than most other fighters. Lastly, the P-38 had exceptional range. Twelve-hour flights were not uncommon, at a time when most fighters carried only enough fuel to stay in the air for a few hours., which made it very useful as a reconnaissance aircraft. The major disadvantage of the P-38 was its lack of maneuverability at low altitudes. Despite this, there was always enough high-altitude work available to keep the P-38 busy throughout the war.

P-39 AIRCOBRA. The P-39 Aircobra was another prewar U.S. design that came up short when the shooting started. However, in this case it was the military's fault. The original 1936 design was for a speedy, heavily armed, and robust interceptor. But the generals insisted on a ground-support aircraft and the design was changed to meet those requirements. When fighters were desperately needed in the Pacific during 1942, the P-39 was among the few aircraft available. Pilots soon found out that if they could stay away from the Japanese Zeros, the P-39 was a very effective ground-attack aircraft. The 37mm cannon also made the P-39 an excellent "bomber buster." Over 7,000 were built, with production continuing into early 1943. Many were exported to allies, and the Russians were particularly fond of the P-39's ground-attack capabilities. A number of P-39s were produced in a special export version called the P-400, and some of these saw service with U.S. Army pilots in the South Pacific.

P-40 TOMAHAWK. The U.S. P-40 Tomahawk was a follow-on to the P-36 Hawk and was a more effective aircraft. About 13,000 were built. Nevertheless, the P-40 was not quite as good as most of its opposition. The main reason that the P-40 was the most widely available fighter in 1942 was because America had waited so long to rearm. While not as capable as the contemporary Japanese Zero or German FW-190, the P-40 could hold its own if used properly. A sturdy aircraft, like its P-36 predecessor, the P-40 continued in production until late 1944. Most P-40s ended up being used as fighter-bombers, or as interceptors in secondary theaters (where first-line enemy fighters were unlikely to be encountered). Thousands were given to allies, by whom a P-40 was considered better than no fighter at all.

P-47 THUNDERBOLT. The U.S. P-47 Thunderbolt was another successful design, although it didn't enter service until late 1942 and didn't get to the Pacific until early 1944. Europe had priority on top-of-the-line Air Force aircraft and European commitments had to be filled before any could be diverted to the Pacific. Over 15,000 P-47s were produced, and more were built after the war. Some were given to allies. The P-47 was one of the heaviest single-engine fighters of the war. It was quite modern in that the aircraft was literally designed around the most powerful engine available (2,000 horsepower initially; 2,300 and then 2,800 as the war went on). Most of those in the Pacific came with the more powerful engines. The P-47's normal loaded weight of 7 to 8 tons was puny by modern standards, but it was a heavyweight in World War II. Carrying eight .50-caliber machine guns (and up to 3,000 pounds of bombs), the P-47 could inflict enormous damage on air or ground targets. Partly because of its own weight, the P-47 could take a lot of punishment and keep flying. It wasn't unusual for the P-47 to take dozens of machine gun and cannon shell hits and keep flying. Once pilots got used to the "heft" of the P-47, they loved it. At high altitudes, the aircraft was quite nimble. Its weight allowed it to dive away from trouble at high speed. With drop tanks, the P-47 was widely used as a bomber escort. The Japanese never came up with anything that could overwhelm the P-47.

P-51 MUSTANG. The U.S. P-51 Mustang was the Thoroughbred of World War II fighters. Many consider the P-51 the best of the lot. Unfortunately, few got to the Pacific. The P-51 arrived on the Pacific scene in late 1944, primarily to serve as an escort for long-range B-29 bombers. The P-51 was more agile than the P-47 and had a longer range. It weighed about half as much as the P-47 and had about half the firepower (six .50-caliber machine guns). Nevertheless, the P-51 could carry a 2,000-pound bombload. About 16,000 were delivered and production continued after the war.

P-59 AIRACOMET. The P-59 Airacomet was America's first jet fighter. Work began in 1941 using technology from the British. Although it performed satisfactorily, the design was never considered capable enough for combat use. Nearly 200 were built by late 1945 for use as trainers. The technology was transferred to Lockheed, which used it to produce the more successful postwar P-80 fighter. Had the design gone better, the P-59 could have been deployed by late 1944. Most would have probably ended up in Europe but, if the situation warranted it, P-59s could have appeared in the Pacific.

P-61 BLACK WIDOW. The U.S. P-61 Black Widow was a night fighter, a 15-ton, two-engine aircraft designed specifically to carry a large radar and heavy armament (four 20mm cannon). The pilot and radar operator would seek out and destroy enemy bombers trying to hide in the darkness. Unfortunately, development began only after Americans noted the problems the British were having with night bombers in late 1940. The first flight was just before Pearl Harbor. Thus P-61s didn't reach the front until 1943 and the Pacific Theater didn't get them until the summer of 1944. While there were few German aircraft still operating at night, the Japanese were another matter. Several Pacific P-61 pilots became aces for shooting down five or more Japanese bombers trying to attack at night. Only about 700 were built.

P-63 KINGCOBRA. The P-63 Kingcobra was a much improved version of the earlier P-39. Some 3,300 were produced between 1943 and 1945. Most of them (2,400) were sent to Russia (already an enthusiastic user of the P-39) and another 300 were given to the French. U.S. forces took the remainder, but did not use them in combat. This was another of those aircraft that could have shown up in the Pacific. As it was, the P-63 did fly for the French in Vietnam in the late 1940s.

P1Y1 FRANCES. The P1Y1 Frances was the Japanese Navy's most modern bomber, entering service during the summer of 1943. Faster and better armed than earlier models, and more robust, the P1Y1 could outrun many Allied fighters at low altitudes. The plane was hampered by shortages of fuel, spare parts, and skilled crews. About 1,100 built (including night fighter versions).

PB2Y CORONADO. The PB2Y Coronado was a four-engine U.S. floatplane developed two years after the two-engine PBY. The PB2Y was a much larger aircraft, weighing 30 tons fully loaded. It was also faster than the PBY, with a maximum speed of 224 mph and a cruising speed of 141 mph. The PB2Y was so large, in fact, that it was used primarily as a transport, getting men and supplies to front-line bases quickly. Only 210 PB2Ys were built, and one was the personal plane of Admiral Nimitz, enabling him to move across the vast Pacific comfortably, and to work with his staff while doing so.

PBM MARINER. The U.S. PBM Mariner was a follow-on to the PBY Catalina. Although the Mariner was a generally better aircraft, it wasn't superior enough to cause cessation of PBY production. The Catalina was cheaper and easier to build and it did its job well. So the PBY did most of the naval reconnaissance during the war, with PBMs being added as they were available.

PBY CATALINA. The PBY Catalina was the most common U.S. flying boat of the war, mainly because it was the first to enter service in 1936. This aircraft type served several purposes. Reconnaissance was the PBY's main job, but that could be done more effectively by B-17s and B-24s. What made the PBY unique was its ability to "land" on the water. This allowed PBYs to be stationed in places where there were no airfields, or where the local airfields were crammed with conventional bombers and fighters. Seaplane tenders (ships with fuel, repair facilities, and ground crews) would anchor in the same bays and inlets that the PBYs operated from. The ability to float also made PBYs invaluable (and quite popular) for picking up the crews of downed aircraft. Thousands of airmen owed their lives to the timely arrival of a PBY. Unfortunately, the PBY was too slow (175 mph top speed) to make an effective bomber. Submarines were a different matter, as they were less likely to shoot back and were more vulnerable to any damage. Nearly 3,300 PBYs were built during the war, about 40 percent of them being "amphibian" (with wheels allowing them to land on an airfield). Some 20 percent were given to allies. Although the PBY was slow with a cruising speed of 110 to 115 mph), it was well armed. Up to 4,000 pounds of bombs or depth charges could be carried and the average PBY was equipped with five machine guns facing in various directions. PBY range was over 2,000 miles and its maximum weight 16 tons. Normal patrols were eight to ten hours long. All in all, not too shabby for an ugly, two-engine aircraft that could float.

PV-1 VENTURA. The PV-1 Ventura was originally built by an American firm in response to a 1940 British order. After it went into action in late 1942, it was found that the PV-1 (called the Vega 36 at the time) was not a very effective bomber. The U.S. Army didn't want it and most of the 1,600 built (plus 535 improved PV-2s) were used by the U.S. Navy for ocean reconnaissance. In this role, the PV-1 was quite good.

SB2A BUCCANEER. The SB2A Buccaneer was an unsuccessful American dive bomber design. It first flew in June 1941 and 750 aircraft were produced in 1942 and 1943. None were used in combat, serving instead as trainers and target tugs.

SB2C HELLDIVER. The U.S. SB2C Helldiver was a replacement for the Dauntless dive bomber. Unfortunately, the SB2C took so long to enter production that by the time it arrived in 1943, the Avenger had already taken over many of its missions. The SB2C was a major improvement over the SBD Dauntless, but dedicated aircraft types for dive bombing and torpedo bombing were increasingly seen as unnecessary. It was obvious that carriers needed more fighters, and by 1944 many fighters were being equipped to carry bombs. The age of multipurpose aircraft was dawning and the Helldiver simply arrived at the wrong time. Although some 5,000 were produced, they were not one of the favorite carrier aircraft.

SBD DAUNTLESS. The U.S. SBD Dauntless dive bomber entered service in 1941 and was considered obsolete even then. The prewar experts were wrong, as the SBD proved one of the most effective carrier bombers of the war. Its long range (1,200 miles for bombing, 20 percent more for scouting) and reliable operation enabled the SBD to rack up a credible war record. SBDs sank 300,000 tons of enemy shipping, as well as eighteen warships of all sizes, including six carriers. It could defend itself, shooting down 138 Japanese aircraft, while losing only 80 to enemy fighters. Nearly 6,000 were delivered, including 1,000 for the U.S. Army as the A-24. Despite its excellent record, a replacement, the Helldiver, was already in the works when the war broke out. Moreover, the Avenger, the replacement for the hapless Devastator torpedo bomber, proved to be a capable dive bomber also. Torpedo bombing declined in importance as the war went on, and the Avenger was used, quite successfully, as a regular bomber most of the time. What kept the SBD in service throughout the war was its versatility and delays in getting the Helldiver into service. Even so, SBDs went from half of all carrier aircraft in mid-1942 to about 6 percent by mid-1944. Many SBDs were transferred to the Marines for land-based operations. A testimony of the SBD's worth can be seen in its use into the 1950s by many foreign air forces. The French used SBDs during the early stages of their war in Vietnam.

SC SEAHAWK. The SC Seahawk was an American floatplane used on cruisers and battleships for scouting. It was a new design, to replace the 1930s models in use through most of the war. The first SC flew in early 1944 and only 9 were built (out of 500 ordered) before the war ended. The SC had a top speed of 312 mph and a range of 625 miles. Armament consisted of two .50-caliber machine guns and up to 500 pounds of bombs or depth charges.

SO3C SEAMEW. The SO3C Seamew was a U.S. Navy floatplane used by cruisers and battleships for scouting. Although 800 SO3Cs were built between 1942 and 1944, it was an unsuccessful design that was withdrawn from service in 1944.

SOC SEAGULL. The SOC Seagull was a U.S. Navy 1930s era biplane floatplane used for scouting by cruisers and battleships. It was a very successful design. The model entered service in 1935 and over 200 were built. The SOC continued in service until the end of the war.

SEAFIRE. The Seafire was a navalized version of Britain's Spitfire fighter. Some 2,000 were built. As the Spitfire went through its many wartime versions, the Seafires were produced to the same plans with the addition of folding wings and other modifications needed for carrier operation. The Seafire was an effective carrier aircraft but had a weak undercarriage, so that the airframe tended to shake apart after too many carrier landings. Production continued after the war.

SPITFIRE. The Spitfire was the principal British fighter throughout the war. It went through continuous upgrades and modifications to keep it competitive with new enemy aircraft. This resulted in many Spitfire types, each having substantially different performance. The first (1938) Spitfire, the Mark 1, had a speed of 360 mph and four .30-caliber machine guns. The last wartime version, the Mark 18, had a top speed of 448 mph armed with two 20mm cannon and two .50-caliber machine guns. Loaded weight went from 2.6 to 4.6 tons. Ceiling, rate of climb, maneuverability, range, and bombload all improved with the many different versions. Some 20,000 were produced during the war and several hundred more into the late 1940s. By 1943, the Spitfire was a common foe for Japanese aircraft over Burma.

SWORDFISH. The Swordfish was the most successful biplane of the war. An early 1930s British design, with nearly 2,400 eventually built, the Swordfish was a torpedo bomber and had considerable success in that role in the European Theater. In the Pacific it was more commonly used as a reconnaissance aircraft (often as a floatplane). The Swordfish prototype flew in 1934 and production began shortly thereafter. The Swordfish was slow (top speed 139 mph) but had a long range (about 1,000 miles) and could carry 1,500 pounds (a torpedo or mines, rockets, and bombs). The aircraft was very steady and maneuverable, and quite rugged. Its admirable qualities were the primary reason it survived the entire war. The Swordfish would have had a harder time if it had been involved in the 1942 Pacific carrier battles. The slow speed would have been fatal in the face of carrier antiaircraft fire and Japanese fighters. Later in the war, at least the enemy fighter threat could be smothered. By then it was common to plaster Japanese ships with heavily escorted dive bombers and then bring in the torpedo bombers to finish off the stricken vessels. At this, the Swordfish would still have been effective.

TBD-1 DEVASTATOR. The TBD-1 Devastator was the standard U.S. Navy torpedo bomber at the start of World War II and was markedly ill equipped for that role. The fatal flaw of the TBD was its slow speed and the low height from which it had to drop its torpedo. This characteristic caused TBDs to take very heavy losses from Japanese flak and interceptors. At Midway, all the attacking TBDs were shot down without scoring any hits. Because the Avenger was just entering service in 1942, it wasn't until early 1944 that all the TBD-1s could be withdrawn from combat units.

TBF AVENGER. The U.S. TBF Avenger was originally designed as a new torpedo bomber, but proved so successful that it became the only bomber aircraft carriers needed. Nearly 10,000 TBFs were built from 1942 to 1945. Half a dozen participated in the battle of Midway, and by the end of 1943 the TBF was the most common bomber on carriers. The TBF was much better than the Devastator, with 50 percent more speed, nearly as much additional range, and twice the bombload (2,000 pounds), and was more heavily armed. While outclassed in most categories by the new Helldiver, the TBF still had twice the bombload. In the later stages of the war, the size of the bombload was most important. Equally important was the ease with which the TBF could be equipped with radar, making it an optimal scout aircraft. The TBF was supplied to allies, particularly Britain, with which it served well during the battle against German U-boats in the Atlantic. Avengers served with foreign air forces into the 1960s.

TEMPEST. The Tempest was Britain's second-generation fighter-bomber (after the Typhoon). Entering service in the summer of 1943, it was fast (427 mph) and heavily armed (four 20mm cannon and 2,000 pounds of bombs and rockets). It was also heavy (6.1 tons loaded) and not as nimble as fighters like the Spitfire. Nevertheless, it was a terror to Japanese ground troops in Burma. Nearly 1,000 were produced.

TYPHOON. The Typhoon was Britain's first-generation fighter-bomber. It entered service in the summer of 1941. Teething problems limited its effectiveness for about a year, but by 1943 the Typhoon was the terror of any enemy ground forces within range. Initially armed with eight .50-caliber machine guns and 1,000 pounds of bombs, it was soon changed to four 20mm cannon and 2,000 pounds of bombs and rockets. Top speed was 410 mph, and loaded weight was 6 tons. Typhoons eventually went to the Far East, where they were found to be particularly effective against Japanese shipping. Some 3,300 were produced.

VILDEBEESTE. The Vildebeeste was an early 1930s British torpedo bomber that was quickly superseded by the Swordfish. Only 200 Vildebeestes were built and only 30 New Zealand–owned aircraft were in the Pacific during the first year of the war. The aircraft had about the same speed, range, and bombload as the Swordfish.

WIRRAWAY. The Wirraway was an American design built under license in Australia. Originally intended as a two-seat trainer, the aircraft was also used as a fighter (with disastrous results) and a light bomber (a few hundred pounds of bombs, at most, were carried) in the early days of the war. Some 750 were built between 1939 and 1946.

DIFFERENT PLANES FOR DIFFERENT PURPOSES

At best, when designing airplanes one ultimately is reduced to making a series of compromises among a number of mutually desirable and mutually exclusive characteristics, such as speed, range, durability, climb rate, munitions load, and many other factors. Designing airplanes capable of operating from aircraft carriers requires even more compromises. The way an aircraft designer deals with those compromises is dictated by the characteristics deemed most desirable. What those are is determined by certain basic assumptions about the way in which the airplane is to be used.

These assumptions about "what an aircraft should do" vary between nations, and even between sister services of the same nation, each of which may have its own design philosophy. And that philosophy may be rooted not only in perceived military necessity but also in political expedience, interservice rivalry, and sheer obstinacy. The carrier aircraft that saw service in the Second World War, most spectacularly in the Pacific, reflected three very different design philosophies: British, American, and Japanese.

Britain's Royal Navy had pioneered the development of the aircraft carrier, and made the first carrier air strikes as early as 1917. However, with the formation of the Royal Air Force (RAF) in 1918, the Royal Navy began to fall behind in the evolution of naval aviation. The RAF was given control over naval aircraft. Dependent as it was upon the heavy-bomber-oriented Royal Air Force for its aircraft designs and pilots, the Royal Navy's air arm ended up decidedly inferior to the U.S. or Japanese naval air service. With the RAF largely indifferent to the unique problems of carrier aviation, British carriers, in many ways excellent vessels, went to sea with equally indifferent aircraft. For example, the performance characteristics of the Fulmar, introduced in 1940, were actually inferior to those of the Japanese Claude or the American Buffalo, which entered service in 1936 and 1938 respectively, and were both considered obsolete by 1940. Further complicating matters was the fact that the Royal Navy never permitted an aviation officer to command one of its carriers, thereby failing to develop a critical mass of aviation-oriented officers who might have been able to go to bat for the Senior Service.

Despite these handicaps, Royal Navy carriers performed yeoman service on numerous occasions, most spectacularly at Taranto Harbor on the night of November 11–12, 1940, when several Italian battleships were sunk or disabled in a nighttime air strike that forecast Pearl Harbor. British carriers that operated in the Indian Ocean during 1942–1945, often with striking success against Japanese land and naval targets, were fortunate in not having to meet any of their Japanese cousins. Had this been the case, the outcome would have been a foregone conclusion, at least in 1942. Indeed, when Britain sent a carrier task force to the Central Pacific in early 1945 it was equipped largely with American-made aircraft.

The U.S. Navy got into the aircraft carrier business in the early 1920s, at about the same time as the Imperial Navy, and nearly a decade after the Royal Navy. Several factors fostered the development of American carrier aviation. Quite early, command of aircraft carriers was reserved to aviation-qualified officers, providing fliers with a career path to high rank. This caused a flock of midlevel and even fairly senior officers to get their wings. William F. Halsey got his at age fifty-two. Moreover, despite occasional acrimony, relations between "brown shoe" officers (i.e., aviation) and "black shoe" officers (i.e., battleship) were friendlier than those prevailing in the British and Japanese navies. Although they squabbled over the details, American carrier and battleship admirals more or less agreed that carriers could have an independent role to play in a major Pacific war, albeit disagreeing on whether they might be decisive. The speed with which carriers took over as the principal arm of sea power after Pearl Harbor was one result of this attitude.

Virtually from the moment airplanes were invented, the Japanese Navy was very air-minded. Having carefully observed the development of British naval aviation during World War I, Japan promptly built the first genuine aircraft carrier, *Hosho* (completed in 1922). The evolution of carrier aviation in the Imperial Navy closely paralleled that in the U.S. Navy. There were, however, critical differences. Japanese aircraft design policy, for example, stressed speed, range, and maneuverability, while the U.S. Navy stressed pilot safety and aircraft reliability and durability.

In some ways the Japanese attitude was superior to the American, for it recognized the essentially offensive character of carrier warfare. Aircraft carriers are purely offensive weapons, much better at "giving" than at "receiving." Thus, the greater operational reach of Japanese carrier aircraft was of considerable advantage.

However, although (unlike the British) the Japanese developed a crop of senior naval officers who appreciated carrier capabilities, they produced few who were completely able to break free from traditional notions of the battleship as the ultimate arbiter of sea power. This is, perhaps, a moot point, since their basic problem was an industrial one. The critical flaw in Japanese naval aviation was Japan's limited ability to mass-produce (in increasing order of importance) carriers, aircraft, and pilots. As a result, once losses began to mount, as they did even during the victorious months from Pearl Harbor to the Coral Sea, the quality of Japan's naval air arm began to decline. Although the Japanese were able to expand aircraft carrier production by a considerable margin, through new construction and the conversion of other types of vessels, it was insufficient to meet their needs. While they greatly expanded aircraft output, they were unable to develop engines of sufficient power to compete with the higher-powered aircraft that the United States began introducing in mid-1942. By late 1942 the Japanese, who had had the best carrier aircraft at the time of Pearl Harbor, were beginning to fall behind, as newer and better American aircraft became increasingly available. And, of course, they were never able to solve their pilot production problems.

The marked differences among American and Japanese carrier aircraft design philosophies make it difficult to compare aircraft. Although the greater operational reach of Japanese carrier aircraft was theoretically a decisive advantage, it was offset by American radar and superior antiaircraft capacity. Moreover, U.S. pilots learned to cope with the speedier and more maneuverable Zeros through superior tactics.

The best example of this was the "Thatch Weave" (named after USN pilot John Thatch). The tactic required two less-maneuverable (but better-armed and -armored) U.S. F4F fighters to fly about 1,000 feet apart. When "bounced" (caught from behind) by a more nimble Japanese Zero, the two airplanes would immediately turn toward the enemy aircraft. This meant that one of the American aircraft would probably end up coming head-on at the Zero with guns blazing. Because of the superior firepower and protection of the F4F, the American plane would likely come out ahead. If that attack failed, the two U.S. aircraft would continue to turn toward the Japanese aircraft until it was shot down or ran short on fuel and had to leave the battle. This tactic was very frustrating for the Japanese, and rather boring for the Americans, but it negated Japanese fighter superiority in 1942, a time when the Japanese needed every advantage they could get.

Japanese aircraft advantages began to evaporate after 1942. With that, attrition and industrial potential became the ultimate arbiters of victory. Since the United States was not only able to expand aircraft and carrier production far more rapidly than was Japan, while simultaneously introducing more advanced aircraft, but was also able to expand pilot production enormously, the decision was inevitable.

But it wasn't just carrier-borne aircraft that ruled the seas. Land-based bombers also played a decisive role.

Although the American and British air forces favored the four-engine heavy bomber as the decisive arm of air power, most other air forces looked to the smaller two-engine medium bomber. These had the disadvantage of a relatively low bomb capacity (1 or 2 tons as against 4 or 5), but were usually faster, more maneuverable, and much cheaper to build.

Operationally, the two-engine bomber was supposed to do the same things that the heavy bombers could do—inflict decisive damage on the enemy by means of massive bombing attacks from high altitude. Like the heavy bombers, they did not prove very successful in this role. However, their greater maneuverability ultimately led them to success in a variety of other roles, especially antishipping and ground attack, which they performed at very low altitudes, often coming in "on the deck" to strike not only with bombs but also with heavy machine guns, light cannon, rockets, and even light field pieces. In this role aircraft such as the B-25 Mitchell proved enormously effective against shipping and other surface targets. The medium bomber could carry sufficient firepower to devastate a freighter or small warship in one pass. This enabled the medium bomber to achieve surprise, important because any subsequent passes would find the target ship thoroughly alerted and desperately evading and resisting.

Although in the prewar period several nations developed single-engine bombers, most of these did not prove of great value in the war, since they proved incapable of coping with even moderate fighter resistance. Medium bombers didn't carry enough firepower to defend themselves.

The two single-engine types that proved most successful were the dive bomber and the torpedo bomber, highly specialized aircraft. Although initially neither type was particularly safe in the presence of fighters, by war's end the United States had come up with a superbly versatile bomber, the Avenger; carrier-capable, it was suitable for service as a dive bomber, torpedo bomber, ground attack aircraft, antisubmarine patrol bomber, and even light transport.

DESIGNING SEAGOING AIRCRAFT

When the aircraft carrier was first developed, by the Royal Navy during World War I, there was no differentiation between carrier-capable and other types of aircraft. The primitive carriers of the day were equipped with the same aircraft that were used on land. However, the rigors of carrier operations soon caused the Royal Naval Air Service to modify existing aircraft to make them better suited to carrier operations. By the end of World War I, aircraft specially modified or designed for carrier operations were the norm on Britain's small fleet of carriers. As time went on, and more nations got into the carrier business (Japan, then the United States, and even France), the differences between carrier aircraft and land-based aircraft began to multiply. Carrier aircraft had to have sturdier frames, and particularly sturdy landing gear, to enable them to take the punishment inherent in carrier landings, described by some pilots as "controlled crashes." This made carrier planes heavier, and consequently slower and generally less maneuverable than land planes, and usually much shorter-ranged. Other differences resulted from differing national attitudes toward the importance of carrier warfare and the ways in which carriers should be operated.

The U.S. Navy designed its carrier aircraft to have folding wings in order to improve stowage, which resulted in greater weight, due to the machinery and complex bracing necessary to make folding wings work. In addition, the USN wanted to be able to stow aircraft on deck in all sorts of weather, which meant planes had to be more weatherproof than aircraft routinely stowed belowdecks. As a result, U.S. carrier aircraft were much heavier than Japanese or British ones, and in consequence rather slow and short-ranged. In compensation, they were able to take much more punishment, and U.S. carriers were able to take many more aircraft to sea with them.

The Japanese Navy dispensed with folding wings (which saved weight) and insisted on stowing all aircraft belowdecks. While this reduced the aircraft contingents of their carriers, they had lighter, and hence faster and more agile, carrier aircraft than did the U.S. Navy, at least until American industry came up with far more powerful aircraft engines.

The Royal Navy had the worst carrier aircraft in the world, due primarily to the fact that the design of carrier aircraft was in the hands of the Royal Air Force, which had little interest in the matter. As a result, British carrier aircraft were never up to the abilities of either Japanese or American ones. Since for the first two years of its war the Royal Navy was fighting Germans and Italians, the flaws of its carrier aircraft were not obvious. Moreover, the Royal Navy never clashed with the Imperial Navy in an air-sea battle, and so escaped the consequences of its inferiority in aircraft design. When the Royal Navy sent a carrier task force to fight alongside the Third/ Fifth Fleet in early 1945, it was largely equipped with American aircraft plus "navalized" versions of RAF aircraft, which, however good their tactical performance, were structurally unsuited to carrier duty at sea.

F I V E

HOW THE WAR WAS
FOUGHT IN THE AIR

A ircraft were the new element in warfare during World War II. Relatively primitive planes had been used in World War I and during the 1920s and 1930s. But World War II brought with it an explosion of innovation and technical development. Nowhere were aircraft as prominent, or as decisive, as in the Pacific. Indeed, there were more diverse forms of aerial warfare in the Pacific than in any other theater.

THE COST OF THE AIR WAR

Although the air war in the Pacific did not reach the proportions of that in Europe, it was still an extraordinary undertaking, involving literally tens of thousands of aircraft, millions of tons of supplies, and hundreds of thousands of pilots and ground support personnel.

AIRCRAFT AVAILABILITY AND EXPENDITURE: THE UNITED STATES AND JAPAN IN WORLD WAR II

	ON HAND, DEC. 7, 1941	WARTIME LOSSES	ON HAND, AUG. 15, 1945
USAAF	12,300	13,055	66,000
USNAF	5,300	8,500	41,000
Total U.S.	17,600	21,555	107,000
IJAAF	4,826	15,935	8,920
IJNAF	2,120	27,190	7,307
Total Japan	6,946	43,125	16,227

NOTES: USAAF and USNAF are the U.S. Army and Navy air forces, respectively. IJAAF and IJNAF are the Imperial Japanese Army and Navy air forces.

U.S. figures, of course, include aircraft committed to the war against Germany and Italy, as well as to that with Japan, and Japanese figures include aircraft involved in operations against China, the Netherlands, the British Commonwealth, and, right at the end, the Soviet Union, so the two sets are not totally comparable.

By the end of the war, however, over half of American aircraft were either in the Pacific or on their way there. Most Japanese aircraft losses, particularly naval aircraft losses, were inflicted by the United States, and particularly the U.S. Navy.

By the way, adding the "Wartime Losses" to the August 15, 1945, figures will not give a total for the number of aircraft available during the war, as obsolete types were withdrawn from service and scrapped, even by the Japanese.

ORGANIZING AIR COMBAT

One of the significant developments of the Pacific war was the use of mission packaging in air warfare. The term *mission packaging* refers to the process of tailoring groups of aircraft for particular operations. While the terminology is post–World War II, the notion of mixing and matching fighters, bombers, and air control aircraft to come up with a "package" best suited to the mission at hand was one that carrier air group commanders certainly understood.

The prewar theory in the U.S. Navy was that an entire air group would make a "coordinated" attack. The fighters would escort the bombers to the target. There, the dive bombers would go in first, with the fighters covering them from enemy interception. This would draw the enemy's attention (and defensive fighters) upward, permitting the torpedo bombers to go in virtually on the deck, covered by the fighters, which would descend to lower altitudes in company with the dive bombers.

In practice this didn't work out too well. The three types of aircraft had differing speeds and ranges and often arrived over the target at different times, if at all, with frequent fatal results to the bomber pilots. At Midway only one man of Torpedo Squadron Eight survived and none of their torpedoes hit anything.

Moreover, there weren't enough fighters to go around. Initially, the theory was that a strike force required about one escort for every three attacking aircraft, and in theory a carrier had just enough aircraft to do this. Unfortunately, since a typical prewar U.S. carrier air group had about fifty-four strike aircraft (TBDs and SBDs) and only eighteen fighters, this meant that a carrier commander didn't have enough resources to both provide fighters to escort his strike aircraft and maintain a CAP (Combat Air Patrol) over the carrier. Experience demonstrated that the demands for escorts and CAP pretty much reversed the prewar ratio of fighters to strike aircraft, so that by late 1944 a carrier's complement was mostly fighters and only about a third or a quarter bombers, although by then the fighters were capable of carrying out light bombing missions of their own. By then, missions were regularly composed of from one to three fighters for each bomber, depending upon the expected opposition.

Initially CAP had not been a major concern. Early war practice was to put two to eight fighters over a carrier, depending upon circumstances. This ran afoul of limited resources, there not being enough fighters on board to keep many in the air for any length of time. As fighter contingents increased, the number of fighters allocated to CAP increased. Eventually, by mid-1944, when the Third/Fifth Fleet was operating with fifteen to sixteen CVs and CVLs, not to mention supporting CVEs, the fighter contingents from a whole carrier would occasionally be earmarked for CAP. It was even suggested that some carriers be designated as CAP carriers, and assigned only fighters, with the mission of fleet defense.

Alternately, it was proposed that CVEs be mostly equipped with fighters, to provide cover for the CVs, which could then use all of their fighters to escort strike missions. These proposals were rejected. The main reason for this appears to have been that carriermen preferred to be defended by "their own guys," rather than somebody else's. Nevertheless, both suggestions seem reasonable, at least retrospectively.

One reason that the British were willing to accept the loss of aircraft capacity as a result of using armored flight decks is that they believed this would make a CAP less essential. The British also put a lot of resources into carrier defense by means of antiaircraft gunfire. British carriers did survive hits more handily than anyone else because of the armored flight decks, and managed to get by with smaller CAPs.

During the war, mission packages tended to get larger and larger. Of course, during major battles missions were flown by whole air groups (all the aircraft on one carrier). But this was not the case when air strikes were being conducted against ground targets or enemy shipping early in the war. Early on, it was not unusual for a strike to consist of literally a handful of aircraft, say a half-dozen bombers and four fighters. But as time went by strikes got larger, often comprising whole air groups, and sometimes several air groups in coordination. This was particularly the case when carriers were supporting ground operations.

GETTING THE AIRCRAFT OFF THE FLIGHTDECK

For a carrier to be useful, it had to be able to launch and recover airplanes. There was no "normal" time prescribed to arm, fuel, and launch a deckload strike by a fleet carrier. Prewar training demonstrated that this could be done in about ninety minutes, assuming all aircraft were already on deck, which was U.S. Navy policy for most of the war, even when operations were not going on. This made fueling, arming, and launching a lot easier, as bringing aircraft up from the hangar deck was a slow, tedious, and rather dangerous procedure.

Surprisingly, during the war it turned out that the ninety-minute figure was regularly bettered. Normally, a carrier always had some aircraft ready for action. These were either fighters to replace CAP, or SBDs and fighters to replace aircraft on reconnaissance and antisubmarine patrol. In addition, since the ship's skipper and the air group commander usually knew what they were doing in a particular neighborhood, they had some idea of the type of mission that they would most probably be called upon to launch. Moreover, preparing for a major mission did not require much more time than preparing for a minor one. For example, the sixteen B-25s that took part in the Doolittle Raid were armed, fueled, and away in about an hour.

As carrier "ground crews" became more skillful, the time it took to launch got shorter. In addition, in mid-1943 U.S. carriers began using jeeps to haul aircraft around their decks, which further reduced the time necessary to get off a strike, as airplanes had hitherto been manhandled from place to place. As a result, in practice, a deckload strike could get clear in thirty minutes, if some of the aircraft were armed and ready at the start, and provided there were no aircraft to recover and that the winds and seas were favorable.

Also, as radar got better, the carriers had more time to prepare to receive an attack, so they could spot and launch aircraft at relative leisure, disarming, defueling, and stowing below all those not needed to defend the ship.

In this regard it's worth recalling that at Midway Admiral Chuichi Nagumo, Japan's most experienced carrierman, thought he had enough time to rearm, and then to re-arm his aircraft in about thirty to forty-five minutes. He was wrong, but only by a little, perhaps ten minutes. His best course would have been to stick with his original decision—that is, arm his aircraft for another go at Midway Island and launch them, retaining the fighters to cover the fleet. The strike on Midway would have been a waste of ammunition, though probably not of planes, but the enhanced CAP might have saved the carriers, particularly given the fact that there would have been no fueled and ammunitioned aircraft to blow up when C. Wade McClusky showed up with his *Enterprise* dive bombers.

In the later Pacific air battles, U.S. carriers routinely launched armed torpedo and dive bombers into the blue rather than try to take a Japanese attack with them on the deck.

Assuming that there were no casualties among the aircrew or damage to the aircraft, an air strike could be recovered in about one to two minutes per plane. However, this would be an optimal situation. Damaged planes and wounded pilots made recovery much more difficult, as can be seen in some extraordinarily graphic newsreel footage. On some critical occasions the wounded guys were told to wait, so that undamaged aircraft could be recovered first, lest someone smash up the flight deck so badly operations would have to cease entirely. There were also occasions on which injured pilots bulled their way to the head of the queue. As the number of carriers multiplied, the practice of waving off the damaged aircraft fell into disuse, because there were always other carriers that could help take up the slack.

GOT NO RESPECT

Mention strategic bombing in World War II and most people will think of the B-17 Flying Fortress. The B-17 was the first heavy bomber to enter service (in 1939). But the B-17 was only second in terms of numbers built, with 12,731 produced. There were 18,325 B-24 Liberators built. The number three in this list of four-engine bombers was the British Lancaster (7,377). The B-29, the biggest four-engine bomber of the war and the only one to drop an atomic bomb, appeared in 1944 and only 3,000 were built.

More B-24s were produced because it was a more effective aircraft than the B-17. The B-24 could fly higher and faster, and carry more bombs than the B-17. B-24s had problems, however, being more difficult aircraft to fly than the B-17. The overall superiority of the B-24 over the B-17 wasn't that great, but in wartime, every little bit extra helps.

Quantity deliveries of the B-17 began in 1939, of the B-24 in 1942. Thus the B-17 had time to implant itself on the public consciousness even while larger numbers of B-24s were appearing and doing more of the work. Some missions, like hitting key targets just a little too far away for the B-17, went to the B-24.

Naval reconnaissance was also a favorite task for the B-24. The B-24 was also an escort aircraft of extraordinary capabilities. By one estimate, during the Battle of the Atlantic a B-24 saved one merchant ship for every five escort missions it flew.

Like all airplanes, the B-24 had its faults, and these were amplified in the public's mind as a means of resisting the thought that the popular "Fortress" was being replaced. To address this, the B-29 was called the "Superfortress," designating a new generation of bombers and a worthy successor to the B-17. That probably sums it up. The B-17 was the firstborn, and, like all younger siblings, the B-24 had to labor on in the shadow of its older brother.

HURTING AIRCRAFT

A study conducted by the U.S. Navy concerning causes of aircraft damage in combat between September 1944 and August 1945 proved rather interesting, although not necessarily conclusive, as the figures were based on aircraft for which it was possible to determine the cause of loss. Note the tables on page 251.

It comes as no surprise that multi-engine aircraft were more survivable than single-engine ones. After all, multi-engine aircraft have a lot of built-in redundancy. What is interesting is that for both types of aircraft, fuel system hits were less fatal than oil system hits. And it is particularly interesting that, despite their redundancy, the greatest percentage of loss for multi-engine aircraft was caused by engine hits.

PLANE FICTION

Collecting information on the Japanese military was difficult before the outbreak of the war and became almost impossible during it. As a result, a great many errors were made. Considering the surprise with which the Zero took the world, there developed a tendency to believe that Japanese aircraft engineering and industry were extremely advanced and versatile. As a result, based on fragmentary information often gathered from inept agents or unreliable sources, the Allies were led to believe that the Japanese were diligently de-

DAMAGE TO SINGLE-ENGINE AIRCRAFT

LOCALE	CASES	LOSSES	
		NUMBER	PERCENT
Control Surfaces	27	0	0
Electrical System	6	0	0
Engine	37	23	62
Fuel System	30	21	80
Hydraulics	35	21	60
Oil System	27	23	85
Pilot and Controls	97	74	76
Propeller	9	0	0
Structure	215	23	11
Other	18	5	28

DAMAGE TO MULTI-ENGINE AIRCRAFT

LOCALE	CASES	LOSSES	
		NUMBER	PERCENT
Control Surfaces	20	0	0
Electrical System	9	1	11
Engine	57	21	37
Fuel System	31	2	6
Hydraulics	17	2	12
Oil System	9	3	33
Pilot and Controls	29	6	20
Propeller	7	0	0
Structure	135	5	4
Other	40	0	0

NOTES: Single-engine aircraft were Avengers, Hellcats, Corsairs, Wildcats, and Helldivers. Multi-engine aircraft were Liberators and Privateers, both with four engines.

signing and building flocks of new and spectacularly effective airplanes. Many of these notional aircraft eventually found their way into Allied recognition books and intelligence briefings, complete with specifications, nicknames, and occasional "triviews" (pictures showing the airplane from various directions). Consider the following, none of which actually existed, yet which were taken quite seriously by Allied intelligence, even to giving them nicknames:

- Aichi Ai-104, Navy reconnaissance seaplane, "Ione"
- Mitsubishi B-97, medium bomber, "Doris"
- Mitsubishi TK-4, Army twin-engine fighter, "Frank" and later "Harry"
- Mitsubishi TK-19, Army fighter, "Joe"
- Nagoya-Sento Ki-001, carrier fighter, "Ben"
- Nakajima AT-27, twin-engine fighter, "Gus"
- Nakajima SKT-97, seaplane fighter, "Adam"
- Suzukaze 20, twin-engine fighter, "Omar"

The Japanese were also believed to be building German fighters and bombers under license. This was not the case. Although the Japanese did receive flyable examples of many German combat aircraft, these were merely for evaluation purposes. The Japanese did produce several foreign aircraft types under license during the war, but these were all (with one exception) American models, which the Japanese had legal production licenses for. Chief among these were the DC-3 transport, of which the Japanese produced over 500 aircraft. Allied pilots were often unaware of this, and when a DC-3 in Japanese colors was spotted, it gave rise to stories (largely false) of the Japanese using "captured DC-3s."

The only German aircraft produced under license was a biplane trainer. But the Japanese also produced the U.S. NA-14 advanced trainer during the war.

Two of the imaginary aircraft had particularly amusing stories behind them, the Nakajima SKT-97 "Gus" and the Suzukaze 20 "Omar." They first appeared in Allied aviation literature around the beginning of the Pacific war, in the British magazine *Flight*, and shortly turned up in the American aviation reference book *Aerosphere*, with full descriptions of their specifications. Thus, along with lots of other technicalese, we are told that the Nakajima SKT-97 was a "low-wing cantilever monoplane," with an "enclosed cockpit" in which the "pilot sits between two engines, one forward and one to the rear, with armor plate protection for both pilot and engines." The airplane was purportedly capable of 410 mph with range of 1,250 miles. The Suzukaze 20 was also a "low-wing cantilever monoplane," with an "enclosed cockpit to the rear of wing." It was supposedly capable of 478 mph.

The story of these two aircraft is an interesting lesson in how erroneous information can come to be taken as accurate, particularly in wartime. *Aerosphere* had merely copied the material from *Flight*. The British magazine, in turn, had copied its information from a German aviation publication. And the Germans had learned about the two aircraft through a mistranslation of an article that had appeared in the Japanese aviation magazine *Sora* ("*Sky*"), popular with young air enthusiasts and model builders. *Sora* had a monthly feature, "Dreams of Future Designers," in which appeared the fanciful designs of aspiring aviation engineers. The April 1941 issue of *Sora* contained two of these designs, the Nakajima SKT-97 and the Suzakaze 20. So the daydreams of a couple of Japanese teenagers ended up giving nightmares to Allied soldiers, sailors, and airmen who had to memorize all sorts of information about some aircraft that never existed.

ODD FELLOWS

One of the oddest organizations of the Pacific war was the American Volunteer Group (AVG), better known as the Flying Tigers. Quite a number of myths have grown up around this organization, most of then created by enthusiastic, and ill-informed, journalists.

The popular perception is that the Flying Tigers were volunteer American pilots fighting for the Chinese before the United States entered the war. Wrong on all counts. While the pilots were officially volunteers, they were in fact funded by the U.S. government and recruited with the assistance of the American government from the ranks of Army and Navy pilots on active duty.

The Nationalist Chinese government was using foreign pilots in an attempt to blunt the increasingly effective Japanese air power. This had not worked so well, and the American government decided to try a little unofficial military assistance. American public opinion was against any direct U.S. involvement in the China war, so the AVG was put together as if it were a private initiative with no connection to the U.S. government. It wasn't.

Recruiting of pilots and shipment of American fighters (bought with U.S. foreign aid provided to China) went on through 1941. By December of that year, the pilots and aircraft had reached Burma, where unit training would take place before the AVG moved on to China. It was here that the Flying Tigers found themselves on December 7. The AVG promptly went into combat against the Japanese invasion of Burma, inflicting heavy losses on the Japanese. Later the AVG moved on to China, where it continued flying and fighting to good effect.

By late December 1941, the American media had discovered the AVG and promptly christened it the Flying Tigers. The Walt Disney studios created a snappy logo and all the hoopla went on until July 1942 when the AVG was disbanded and their pilots and aircraft incorporated into the U.S. Army Air Force. But the AVG was as good as its reputation, destroying 296 Japanese aircraft while losing only 12 of its own in combat (another 74 were lost to accidents and other causes).

The Flying Tigers pilots were a select group of odd, but extraordinarily effective, fellows. After the war, some of them were among the founders of the Hell's Angels motorcycle club.

NO SUBSTITUTE FOR EXPERIENCE

On the eve of the Pacific war, the Japanese Navy may have had the best pilots in the world, carefully selected men, intensively trained to extraordinarily exacting standards. However, these standards could not be maintained in wartime, with deleterious and ultimately disastrous effects on the Japanese war effort.

The Imperial Navy had about 1,500 pilots in late 1941, including men who had graduated flight school but not yet completed all their training. In fact, in December 1941 there were not enough qualified pilots to man all available aircraft, which included about 550 on active carriers, plus another 100 or so on a new escort carrier and two light carriers still working up, plus some hundreds of floatplanes on battleships, cruisers, and seaplane carriers and tenders, as well as about 500 land-based aircraft, for a total of about 2,210 aircraft.

In contrast, the U.S. Navy had about 3,500 regular pilots, plus a pool of about 6,000 reservists, more than sufficient to man all available aircraft: about 600 on fleet carriers, 40 on escort carriers, about 150 to 200 floatplanes on battleships and cruisers, plus hundreds of flying boats and land-based aircraft, for a total of about 8,500 aircraft. The U.S. Navy originally had a pilot training program almost as rigorous as that of the Japanese. But in the mid-1930s it was restructured to produce more pilots, albeit less spectacularly qualified ones than their older comrades.

On the eve of the war a man needed a minimum of 700 hours of flight time to qualify as a full-fledged pilot in the Imperial Navy, while his American counterpart needed only 305 hours. About half of the active-duty pilots in the U.S. Navy in late 1941 had between 300 and 600 hours of flying experience, a quarter between 600 and 1,000 hours, and the balance more than 1,000 hours. So at the beginning of the war, nearly 75 percent of the U.S. Navy's pilots had fewer flying hours than did the least qualified of the Japanese Navy's pilots. And that was just in terms of flying hours: Many of the Imperial Navy's pilots had seen combat against the Chinese and the Russians, experiences that most U.S. Navy pilots lacked.

However, the Japanese pilot training program was so rigorous that only about 100 men a year were being qualified, in a program that required fifty to sixty-four months to complete, depending upon education on entry (high-school grads versus elementary-school grads). In January 1940, some prescient officers had proposed reorganizing the Imperial Navy's pilot training program to make it shorter, less rigorous, and more productive, in order to build up the pool of available pilots to about 15,000. This was rejected as visionary.

As a result, as soon as the war began, the Imperial Navy started losing pilots faster than they could be replaced. For example, the twenty-nine pilots lost at Pearl Harbor represented more than a quarter of the annual crop. Then came the losses at the battles of the Coral Sea and Midway, and the Guadalcanal and Solomons campaigns—literally hundreds of superb pilots. In a desperate attempt to replace the lost airmen, the Japanese began cutting corners on their pilot training program. Initially the ground component of pilot training was cut from fourteen months (for high-school grads)

FLYING HOURS TO QUALIFY FOR COMBAT		
YEAR	USN	IJN
1941	305	700
1942	305	700
1943	500	500
1944	525	275
1945	525	90

or twenty-eight months (for elementary-school grads) to three, then to one, and then virtually eliminated. Soon afterward the flight, operational, and carrier training portions of the program were cut as well, from twelve months each to four, then three, then one month each. By 1945, men were being certified fit for combat duty with less than four months' training. In contrast, the U.S. Navy was actually increasing its flight time, while keeping pilot training programs to about eighteen months.

Unlike the Japanese, the U.S. Navy applied mass-production techniques to pilot training, with the result that by mid-1944 it was qualifying about 8,000 pilots a month, at which point pilot training programs actually began to be cut. Altogether, the U.S. Navy seems to have peaked at about 60,000 pilots. Total Japanese pilot strength may actually have approached this figure, albeit with men trained to decreasingly rigorous standards.

Aside from the Imperial Navy's initially overly exacting pilot training program, there were several other factors that contributed to the decline in the quality of Japanese naval pilots:

1. LACK OF ROTATION. Japanese pilots were kept with line units until killed or wounded. This had two negative effects:

Veteran pilots were not normally available to lend a hand with training, which deprived novice pilots of their valuable advice and experience.

Experienced men soon became overexperienced, tired, and careless from excessive and continuous exposure to combat. The U.S. Navy regularly rotated men from line to training units and back again, and pulled combat-weary units out of action for regular rests. This maintained skills and morale, and helped trainees learn the ropes from the best-qualified instructors.

2. BEACHING OF CARRIER AIRCRAFT. On several occasions, notably during the Solomons campaign, entire carrier air groups were transferred to Japanese land bases to provide air support for ground operations. Carrier operations require constant training, and once committed to ongoing operations from a land base, carrier pilots quickly begin to lose the skills necessary to operate from carriers safely. The U.S. Navy occasionally committed carrier pilots to land-based operations, but with great reluctance.

3. LACK OF SEARCH AND RESCUE. As the war went on, the U.S. Navy developed an elaborate search-and-rescue system that used submarines, flying boats, and surface vessels to locate and rescue downed fliers. As a result, on average about 50 percent of U.S. airmen who crash-landed or parachuted into the sea were rescued (among them George Bush), a figure that was rising to 75 percent by the end of the war. The Japanese had no such system, which cost them the services of many valuable men.

Ill-trained pilots were not simply less effective against more experienced pilots, they were also a greater danger to themselves. Throughout the war, a quarter of the aircraft lost were due to accidents. Most of the accidents were the result of pilot error. More experienced pilots made fewer errors. When planes were operating over the open ocean, things could get particularly hairy: Navigation skills were crucial, and the weather was different. In the northern Pacific, the weather and operating conditions in general were particularly horrendous. In this region, nearly 90 percent of American aircraft losses were due to noncombat causes. The Japanese had a similar experience.

Experience was a valuable resource and the Japanese learned the hard way how easy it is to lose and how difficult it is to regain. New pilots, of any nation, are most at risk; and unless you have a few experienced pilots to help the new guys out, the survival rate will remain dismal. American pilots had a 7 percent chance of getting shot down on their first mission. This went down to under 1 percent after about ten missions.

Most pilots didn't shoot down five aircraft and become aces; only 5 percent did. But most managed to keep going and survive. American pilots knew the importance of helping the new guys along so that it evened the odds when you went into combat. The Japanese had such a low ratio of experienced to inexperienced pilots by 1944 that they were slaughtered in lopsided battles with their American counterparts. After 1943, few Japanese pilots survived long enough to become aces. From 1944 on, American pilots had more to fear from mechanical problems or bad luck than they did the skill of Japanese pilots. Meanwhile, the Japanese saw their aircraft losses from poor flying skills skyrocket. This was made worse by the increasing shortage of key raw materials for Japanese industry. Certain alloys were not available and this led to less than ideal substitutes when building aircraft engines. The Japanese aircraft engine industry was never top-of-the-line in the best of times, and by 1944 Japanese pilots had to be ever watchful of sudden engine problems. Inexperienced Japanese pilots were less able to coax a cranky engine into performing long enough to allow the aircraft to be landed, and this produced ever more noncombat losses. It saved Allied pilots some work and not a little risk.

KNIGHTS OF THE AIR

Fighters developed out of reconnaissance aircraft during World War I. Their initial function was to prevent enemy reconnaissance aircraft from doing their jobs. A logical consequence of this was that they assumed the duty of escorting friendly reconnaissance aircraft, which meant that they often had to tangle with enemy fighters intent on downing the recon planes. When bombers, also developed out of reconnaissance aircraft, came along, the fighters assumed the escort/intercept role again.

Out of the clash between escorting and intercepting fighters were born the glamorous "knights of the air," the aces.

Fighters were very difficult aircraft to design, having to combine agility, speed, endurance, and toughness in a relatively small airframe. Not until the late 1930s had technology advanced sufficiently to provide engines that could give fighters the same speed as the more advanced multi-engine bombers. This development also permitted the introduction of the monoplane fighter. It was in this period that many of the most famous fighters of World War II were designed: the Zero, the Bf-109, the Spitfire, the Wildcat, and so forth.

As with all weapons, various nations had different notions of what was most desirable in a fighter. The Japanese, for example, went in for fast, maneuverable aircraft with considerable range, such as the Zero, which were relatively lightly built, offering little protection to the pilot; in effect, the Zero was an "all offense" fighter. At least initially, the Americans also favored "long-legged" aircraft, but theirs were slower and less maneuverable, because they preferred providing the maximum possible protection for the pilot, with armor plate and self-sealing gas tanks. The war accelerated engine design, so that by midwar it became possible to build fighters that not only were fast, maneuverable, and long-legged, but also provided maximum protection for the pilot. Due to economic factors, only the Allies were really able to take full advantage of these developments.

Virtually all fighters were designed to intercept and attack bombers and tangle with enemy fighters. During the war several specialized roles developed, such as ground attack, night fighter, photoreconnaissance, and even antisubmarine fighters. Initially aircraft assigned such roles were older types, bordering on obsolescence, and those newer aircraft that proved less than effective as first-line fighters, such as the P-39 or the Me-110. The Allies, with their enormous industrial strength, soon developed specialized variants of virtually all their fighter aircraft. The Axis, with its limited ability to produce aircraft, tended to relegate older models to such specialized roles.

Fighters proved to be the most versatile aircraft of the war.

HOW FAR YOU FLY
DEPENDS ON WHAT YOU DO

The radius of air patrol shows the greatest extent to which aircraft at a land base are likely to spot ships or aircraft. No matter how many aircraft are stationed at a base, the chances of spotting something always decrease the farther away from a base you get. This is a matter of simple geometry, because the farther away from the base you get, the more area there is to cover. Reconnaissance reaches out farther than air attacks because the recon aircraft do not have to carry large weapons loads or conserve fuel for high-speed combat.

BOMBS OVER TOKYO

One thing the Japanese didn't expect was to see waves of American bombers over their cities. To the east there was the vast Pacific ocean, with no nearby islands to support airfields. To the west were Korea and China, occupied by dozens of Japanese divisions. The Japanese thought their cities were safe from air attack.

The 1942 Doolittle Raid was a shock, but was soon recognized as a special case. The Japanese did thereafter maintain hundreds of interceptors to guard against future carrier raids. But they knew these raids could do little damage because Japan's cities were vast and the bomb capacity of carrier aircraft limited.

What the Japanese didn't foresee was the B-29 bomber. They were familiar with the smaller B-17, as it had gone into service in the late 1930s. The B-17, and the subsequent B-24, didn't have the range to reach Japan from the nearest Pacific islands, the Marianas, 1,500 miles distant. The B-17 could, at most, fly nearly 1,000 miles with a minuscule bombload.

In 1940, the United States began designing the B-29, an aircraft with a 3,500-mile range, and the ability to reach a target 1,800 miles distant while carrying several tons of bombs. The B-29 first flew in 1942. The aircraft was originally conceived as a "worst case" weapon, a bomber that could reach Germany from North America (or Iceland) if the Nazis took Britain. By the time the B-29 was ready for mass production in late 1943, it was clear that the aircraft would see service in the Pacific.

The Marianas were not taken until the summer of 1944. The first B-29 units were formed in September 1943. So it was decided to send the first B-29s to India. From there they could operate against Japanese targets in Southeast Asia. The first raid was on May 27,

1944, as sixteen B-29s hit the railroad repair shops in Bangkok, Thailand (Siam). But India was just a staging area for bases in China.

The first major B-29 raids operated from Chinese bases. But because China was cut off from sea or land access, all fuel and bombs for these raids had to be flown in from India. It required 2 tons of fuel to fly in 1 ton of supplies. Some B-29 raids were made on Japan from Chinese bases, but there was no hope of flying in sufficient supplies to mount a significant air assault. The largest raids from Chinese bases were about 100 aircraft. Raids from China continued into early 1945 (when Japanese troops captured the bases), hitting targets all over the region, from Burma to Manchuria and southern Japan. Thus an effective bombing campaign against Japan would have to wait for the Marianas to be captured and bases built there (particularly on Saipan).

In October 1944, the first B-29s landed on Saipan. In November, the first B-29 raids hit Tokyo. All this while the battle for the Philippines was still raging and most of Southeast Asia and China was still under Japanese control.

After the first few months of bombing, it was noted that the European style of precision daylight bombing wasn't having the desired effect. There had long been plans to eventually switch to fire bombing of cities, but only after industrial targets (steel mills and aircraft factories) had been destroyed. But intelligence information indicated that many key weapons components were made by small shops in urban residential neighborhoods. These shops employed about one sixth of the work force. Moreover, it was known that largely wooden Japanese housing was much easier to burn than the typically brick or stone buildings found in Europe. After a few tests of fire bombing and the adoption of low-level flying tactics, the B-29s switched to this form of attack. Japan's urban areas began to burn, and with it went the nation's industrial capacity.

The damage to Japanese cities was immense. Major areas like Tokyo (equal in size to New York City) had 50 percent of their buildings destroyed. Many smaller cities suffered over 60 percent destruction. Over 2.2 million homes were destroyed and 668,000 civilians died in these raids. Although more than twice as much bomb tonnage was dropped on Germany, the losses in homes (255,000) and lives (593,000) were lower there, due to the German preference for brick and masonry construction. The bombing campaign against Germany went on for over two years, compared to less than a year for Japan. It wasn't just the two atomic bombs that made the difference, it was incendiary bombs used against exceptionally vulnerable Japanese housing. And, unlike the air war against Germany, it was bombing that brought Japan to its knees. The atomic bombs were just the final hammer blow from the air, preceded by the fire bombs and naval mines dropped by B-29s.

By the end of the war there were six B-29 wings (each with 192 B-29s and 12,000 troops). One was based in India, the others in the Marianas (Saipan, Guam, and Tinian). Most raids were small, with 25 to 50 aircraft. But every two weeks or so there were larger raids of 500 to 600 B-29s. The bombing of Japan cost about $3 million for each square mile devastated. In terms of 1995 dollars, this destruction cost about fifty cents a square foot.

It is important to note that the effectiveness of attacks from the air tended to be much overestimated by the Americans. It was one thing to go after ships with low-flying bombers, where the results of your work could be instantly seen. Attacks on land targets were another matter. One reason fire bomb raids were popular in the air assault on Japan was because the resulting damage (hundreds of acres of blackened ruins) was unambiguous.

But when attacking combat troops on the ground, it was quite another matter. This was first noted in the Aleutian Islands campaign in 1943. After the Japan bases there were captured, it was possible to assess the effectiveness of the 7,300 bombing and strafing sorties flown (and 4,300 tons of bombs dropped). One could see that most of the Japanese bomb shelters were unharmed. After the war, when Japanese records could be examined, it was discovered that only 6 percent (450 men) of the Japanese troops subjected to these attacks were killed (and about three times as many injured to one degree or another). The same result was seen on the Central Pacific islands, where U.S. Navy and Marine aircraft flew thousands of sorties against Japanese defenders. Interrogation of prisoners indicated that it was the Marines who did the most damage, followed by the big guns on the ships, and, least feared of all, the aircraft attacks.

The Japanese were well aware of the problems with air attacks. Their pilots were much more intensively trained in bombing than Americans and, as a result, were far more accurate. Fortunately, most of these pilots were dead by 1943. But the Japanese came up with some imaginative plans for getting their skilled bombardiers over North American targets. One scheme involved long-range Japanese flying boats (H8Ks) being refueled by submarine tankers until, off the coast of southern California, they would fly on to Texas, bomb vulnerable oil fields and refineries, and then fly on to be refueled by German submarine tankers. The H8Ks would then bomb up and down the east coast of America until mechanical problems, or lack of bombs, rendered the flying boats useless. Fortunately, American victories in the Pacific forced the Japanese to use their H8Ks for the more mundane task of patrolling before this scheme could be carried out. Thus while there were bombs over Tokyo, despite strenuous Japanese efforts, there were not any bombs over Brooklyn.

HOW THE WAR WAS FOUGHT ON LAND

U nlike the European portion of World War II, the Pacific saw little use of tanks and fast-moving mechanized units. In the Pacific, it was primarily an infantry war. Even on the larger islands and the mainland of Asia, most of the fighting was done by foot soldiers. Most of the battlefields were in the tropics, an area not conducive to good health even when there's not a war going on. This was, moreover, the first large-scale jungle war, as well as the first war in which amphibious landings became commonplace. The ground combat was slow and tough. Many innovations came about as both sides tried to adapt to this grueling form of warfare. While the far-ranging carrier task forces were not as dependent on bases as in the past, the war was still basically fought over the possession of bases for the ships to operate from.

DIVISIONAL ORDER OF BATTLE FOR THE PACIFIC

Although the Pacific war was one of relatively small battles, the basic ground combat unit was still the division. Often the divisions were broken up to provide garrisons or assault forces for the many small islands fought over, but everyone still kept score by counting divisions. The divisions in the Pacific varied in size from about 4,500 men (Chinese) to as many as 20,000 (U.S. Marines), depending upon their arm of service and nationality.

Regardless of size, however, a division was supposed to be a more or less self-contained combat formation of all arms (infantry, armor, artillery, support troops) capable of some degree of sustained independent operations. The principal differences among the numerous types of divisions (infantry, armor, parachute, Marine, security, fortress, and so forth) were due to the specialized missions to which they were dedicated. The vast majority of all divisions in the Paci-

ASIATIC-PACIFIC THEATER OF OPERATIONS								
	PRE	1940	1941	1942	1943	1944	1945	END
Australia	0	7	9	7	8	7	7	7
Britain	0	1	1	2	2	1	1	1
China				about 250–300				
India	3	5	6	9	11	11	14	14
Japan	36	36	39	73	84	100	145	197
New Zealand	0	1	0	1	1	0	0	0
USSR	20	20	10	10	10	10	10	80
U.S.: Army	2	2	3	3	9	13	21	21
Marines	0	0	2	3	5	6	6	6

fic were infantry divisions. The U.S. Marine division was basically an infantry division that was beefed up for amphibious assaults. There were a few parachute divisions in the Pacific and the Japanese had some armored divisions in China. But, overall, it was an infantry war.

The table on page 265 summarizes the number of divisions available to each of the belligerent powers as of the beginning of the indicated year, regardless of location. "Pre" gives strength in September of 1939, and "End" at the end of the war (September 1945).

By way of comparison with the rest of the war, the following table gives the divisions involved elsewhere ("End" means May 1945).

EUROPEAN–MIDDLE EASTERN–NORTH AFRICAN THEATER

	PRE	1940	1941	1942	1943	1944	1945	END
Australia	0	0	1	3	1	0	0	0
Britain	9	33	34	36	37	36	30	30
Bulgaria	12	14	14	16	23	29	29	20
Canada	0	1	3	5	8	6	6	6
Finland	14	17	19	20	20	20	12	12
France	86	105	0	0	5	7	14	14
Germany	78	189	235	261	327	347	319	375
Hungary	6	7	10	16	19	22	23	30
India	0	0	4	5	5	5	4	4
Italy	66	73	64	89	86	2	9	10
New Zealand	0	0	1	1	1	1	1	1
Poland	43	2	2	2	2	5	5	5
Romania	11	28	33	31	33	32	24	24
South Africa	0	0	3	3	3	4	3	1
USSR	170	180	210	240	340	390	478	411
U.S. Army	0	0	0	0	8	17	57	68

The preceding figures for the United States, some British Commonwealth nations, and the USSR (which was neutral for virtually the entire Pacific war, and for which information is very difficult to obtain) are split between the two theaters. The following table summarizes their overall strength ("End" means September 1945).

GLOBAL SUMMARY FOR THE TWO-THEATER ALLIES

	PRE	1940	1941	1942	1943	1944	1945	END
Australia	0	7	10	10	9	7	7	7
Britain	9	34	35	38	39	37	31	31
India	3	5	10	14	16	16	18	18
New Zealand	0	1	1	2	2	1	1	1
USSR	194	200	220	250	350	400	488	491
U.S.: Army	8	8	37	73	90	89	89	89
Marines	0	0	2	3	5	6	6	6

NOTES: Figures for most countries are approximate, showing divisions active at the start of the indicated year. In some cases the figures include separate brigades, lumped together on the basis of three brigades per division. All types of divisions are included except training formations, depot divisions, and inactive militia and territorial units. No attempt has been made to modify the figures on the basis of actual strength, degree of training, scales of equipment, or state of readiness. Japanese, German, and Soviet figures include "satellite" formations (for example, the German figure for 1943 includes one Serbian-manned division, two Bosnian-manned ones, eight Croatian ones, and four Slovakian ones, not to mention German divisions formed from troops of other nationalities). German figures include Air Force, Navy, and Waffen-SS ground divisions. British figures include three divisions composed primarily of African personnel. Post-1939 figures for Poland include only formations raised in exile in the West, omitting units under Soviet control: one by January 1944, twelve by January 1945, and seventeen by the war's end. French figures after 1940 include only Free French units, omitting Vichy divisions: about sixteen by mid-1941, including those in colonies that later went over to the Free French. Italian figures post-1943 omit units of Mussolini's Italian Social Republic: four by January 1944 and six by January 1945. Romanian figures from January 1945 on reflect forces fighting under Allied control. In 1939–1940, the Netherlands had nine divisions (plus about three more in the East Indies, also not shown), the Belgians twenty-two, and the Yugoslavs thirty-four, before being overrun by the Germans. Neither the Dutch nor the Belgians raised division-sized forces in exile. The Yugoslav partisans under Tito raised about twenty-four "divisions" (including one Italian-manned) from about mid-1943 onward, after Italy switched sides, opening up the Aegean to Allied shipping (and easier resupply of the Yugoslav forces). U.S. theater figures exclude units within the forty-eight states, as well as the thirteen Philippine Army divisions, activated in late 1941 and destroyed by March 1942 along with the Regular Army Philippine (12th) Division (which *is* shown above), and the half-dozen guerrilla "divisions" formed in the Philippines during the Japanese occupation. Thailand maintained four divisions through the war, although these saw little service.

THE NATIONAL ARMIES

Many nations had ground forces fighting in the Pacific. Their quality and quantity differed greatly. What follows is a brief description of each national contingent.

NETHERLANDS INDIAN ARMY

The bulk of the troops in the Dutch East Indian Army were locally raised. Organized, trained, and equipped primarily as a colonial constabulary, the Army was badly scattered in numerous small garrisons, albeit on paper two divisions and a division-sized task force existed. Total manpower was in the vicinity of 125,000, of whom about a fifth were Dutch, the rest "natives" of various sorts. When the Japanese came, the performance of the Army was very uneven. Many units simply disintegrated, while others, particularly those with high proportions of Eurasian or native Christian troops, acquitted themselves well. Ultimately the difference didn't matter; as the defense of the Dutch East Indies was a naval problem, the destruction of the ABDA fleet at the end of February 1942 sealed the fate of the Netherlands East Indian Army.

INDIAN ARMY

In origins essentially a colonial auxiliary to the British Army, by the outbreak of World War II the Indian Army was a thoroughly professional, quite modern military force. It was also quite small, with only about 160,000 men, and only three divisions. During the war expansion was rapid, peaking at something over 2 million men, all more or less volunteers, making it the largest purely volunteer army ever raised to that time. India was rife with unemployment at the start of the war, and the armed forces offered the only prospect of employment for many men. Thus the military could be selective and the quality of the troops was quite high.

Although at first virtually all of the officers in the Indian Army were British, as time went on an increasing number of Indians were given commissions. Most Indian divisions contained about 30 percent British personnel, generally technical personnel, artillerymen, and some infantry. During the war Indian units served in all theaters except northwestern Europe. The quality of the early units was quite high, but the rapid expansion of the Army in 1940–1941, caused some problems with quality among the units that served in Malaya and Burma in 1942. To some extent the difficulties lay in hasty training, poor manpower management, and equipment shortages. These problems were gradually resolved, so that when the Indian Army undertook its final offensives against the Japanese in Burma in 1944–1945, it was a highly skilled, flexible, and effective force. It was this battle-hardened, well-trained, professional force that provided the stable and effective armed forces of India and Pakistan when these two nations became independent shortly after World War II.

INDIAN NATIONAL ARMY

As part of their "Asia for the Asiatics" campaign, the Japanese supported independence movements in a number of countries, not least India, generally regarded as the basis of all British power. After overrunning Malaya and Burma, the Japanese found themselves with an enormous number of Indian prisoners of war. They also had Chandra Bose, a radical Indian nationalist.

On the run from the British, Bose had spent the early war years in Germany, unsuccessfully trying to entice Indian POWs to form Nazi collaborationist units. When Japan attacked the British Empire, Hitler thoughtfully had Bose put on a submarine and delivered to his "honorary Aryan" allies, the Japanese. Through Bose's good offices, the Japanese were able to create the "Indian National Army," a force that ultimately grew to three divisions: about 40,000 men recruited from their Indian prisoners of war and Indians resident in Malaya and Burma. The Indian National Army even included a women's regiment. Eventually committed to combat in Burma, against British and Indian troops, the Indian National Army did not do well. Many of the troops had joined only because it was better than starving or being beaten to death in a Japanese POW camp. After the war some members of the Indian National Army were subject to courts-martial, but most were given only token penalties.

THE CANADIAN ARMY

Not a whole lot of Canadian troops got into action in the Pacific Theater, but those who did fought well. The prewar Canadian Army was quite small, among the smallest in the world. Standards were high, however, and quality suffered little as a result of wartime expansion. In some ways the Canadian Army combined the best features of both the American and the British armies, being more flexible than the British but more cohesive than the American.

Canadians took part in two major operations in the Pacific. On November 16, 1941, several infantry battalions arrived in Hong Kong to strengthen the local garrison. Just three weeks later they found themselves in a desperate fight against overwhelmingly superior Japanese forces. Although the troops were neither well equipped nor fully trained, they gave a good account of themselves for three weeks, before surrendering on Christmas Day.

The second and last time Canadian ground forces were committed to action in the Pacific was at Attu, in May 1943, as part of the 1st Special Service Force, a unique commando brigade organized for special operations, consisting of several battalions each of American and Canadian troops. The 1st SSF fought for more than two weeks alongside the U.S. 7th Infantry Division, in the first significant Allied amphibious operation of the Pacific war. Once again the Canadians performed well. But Canada's primary strategic interests lay in the European Theater, rather than in the Pacific. Although Canadian troops, notably Royal Canadian Air Force units, assisted in the defense of Alaska through the balance of the war, Canadian troops did not fight again in the Pacific.

NEW ZEALAND ARMY

At the outbreak of World War II, New Zealand, which had a very small Regular Army supported by a division's worth of militia (mostly World War I veterans), promptly raised a division of volunteers and dispatched it to the Mediterranean, where it covered itself with glory in North Africa and Italy. This left only the militia and some miscellaneous units to guard New Zealand. Although an attempt was made to raise another division, it was never completed. As a result, New Zealand's contribution to the ground war in the Pacific was small, ultimately involving a number of brigade-sized actions, in which the Kiwis greatly distinguished themselves. Peak wartime strength was 157,000 troops.

PHILIPPINE ARMY

The Tydings-McDuffie Act of 1936 established an autonomous government for the Commonwealth of the Philippines, with the intention of granting full independence on July 4, 1946. Among the measures that the new Philippine government adopted upon taking office was to hire retired general Douglas MacArthur, promote him to field marshal, and put him in charge of organizing a national military force.

Recognizing the financial and industrial limitations of the infant nation, MacArthur planned for a large militia-based defensive force of some 400,000 men in forty small divisions, supported by a coast defense navy of about fifty motor torpedo boats and an air force of some 250 airplanes, mostly fighters and light bombers. This force was to be built up gradually, with an annual contingent of only 40,000 new men being drafted for about ninety days' training, with short annual refresher courses thereafter.

By mid-1941 much had been accomplished. A small Regular Army had been established, officer training programs instituted, and equipment accumulated; several thousand militiamen had actually been called up for basic training. Given six months or so, the Philippine Army would have been a rather effective force. Unfortunately, the Japanese did not cooperate.

With the threat of war rising, in late 1941 President Roosevelt federalized the entire Philippine Army, from Field Marshal MacArthur on down to the greenest private. Over 100,000 Filipino troops were hastily called up and organized into thirteen divisions during the last weeks of peace and the first weeks of war in 1941–

1942. Few of them had had any training. Despite a cadre of men trained in the Philippine Scouts (who composed several regiments of the U.S. Army), the Philippine Constabulary (a paramilitary national police force), the new military academy, or the ROTC, most of the officers had little more preparation than their men. Moreover, everything was in desperately short supply.

On paper each Philippine division was supposed to have 7,500 men in three infantry regiments, with thirty-six pieces of light artillery (twenty-four 3-inch mountain guns and twelve 75mm guns), plus small reconnaissance, engineer, and medical contingents. In practice, most divisions were woefully lacking in everything, including rifles. Aside from the 1st Division, composed mostly of the prewar regulars of the infant Philippine Army, and the 2nd, built around men of the Philippine Constabulary, the best Philippine division was the 41st, which had an unusually large proportion of men who had completed several weeks of prewar training, and most of its allotment of equipment, including all of its artillery. There were also supposed to be small contingents of army troops, including the Philippine Army Air Force, engineers, heavy artillery (105mm), and the like, to support the front-line troops, but they were pretty short of everything as well. The PAAF, for example, had only sixteen obsolete P-26 fighters, twelve equally obsolete B-10 bombers, and some other miscellaneous aircraft, with 500 men.

Nevertheless, despite their lack of equipment and training, and ultimately the debilitating effects of hunger and disease, the hardy and brave Filipino troops did extremely well during the defense of Bataan. Many of those who eluded capture by the Japanese later joined the resistance, where they proved particularly effective. The Filipinos were much encouraged in their war efforts by the prewar declaration that they would have their independence in 1946. This American decision was made not under any wartime duress, but in recognition of the desires of the Filipino people (and the desire to avoid another insurrection like the one at the turn of the century). America also had pretty good relations with Filipinos, and these emotional ties were further strengthened by the subsequent shared wartime experiences.

Had the outbreak of the war been delayed, MacArthur's timetable provided that by the late spring of 1942 each man in the Philippine Army would have had at least three months of training. And, of course, by then there would have been more equipment, albeit still not enough to outfit all the divisions properly. So had the Japanese delayed their offensive into the spring, they would have found the Philippines a far tougher nut to crack than was actually the case. As it was, the Philippines took longer to conquer than any other of Japan's Southeast Asian or Pacific targets. A better prepared Philippine Army could have made for a much more interesting first year of the war.

THAI ARMY

Siam (renamed Thailand in 1939) had maintained a precarious independence during the Age of Imperialism. By the outbreak of the war in Europe, the Thais were ruled by a military dictatorship. The fall of France led them into a brief, unsuccessful border war with the Vichyite forces in French Indochina (during which a French squadron severely punished the modest Thai Navy in the Battle of the Gulf of Siam). Despite some admiration for Japan, as an Asian nation that had modernized itself and risen to the status of a great power, the Thais decidedly wanted to remain neutral in the war. This they were not permitted to do. Japanese troops invaded Thailand within hours of Pearl Harbor. The Thai Army, four modestly equipped divisions, found itself hopelessly outclassed, and an armistice was soon arranged. Although Thailand subsequently formally allied herself with Japan, the Thai Army saw little action. Had the Thais gone into action, indications are that they would not have done well against Allied or Japanese troops. Peak wartime strength was 127,000 troops.

AUSTRALIAN ARMY

Australia was virtually bereft of military resources in the homeland on the outbreak of the Pacific war. Several fine divisions were serving with British forces in North Africa, but only one fully equipped and trained (albeit green) division remained in the South Pacific, and this was promptly lost through inept British generalship in Malaya.

There were also several partially trained divisions, and the national militia, which consisted of five divisions of World War I veterans (men in their forties and fifties). Although the Australian government successfully pressured the British to return their divisions from the Middle East, they were slow in coming home, and arrived much too late to prevent the Japanese from overrunning most of New Guinea.

Although the best Australian manpower had already been invested in the North African campaign, units raised later gave a good account of themselves during the horrors of the New Guinea campaign. It was in this hellhole that most Australian units fought until the end of the war.

The Australian Army was organized and equipped on the British model, although as the war went on it received more and more U.S. equipment. Australia produced some of its own weapons, equipment, and munitions, but was dependent on imports for most of it. Over 900,000 Australians served during the war, with over half a million being sent outside Australia. While the Australian leadership was eager to fulfill its Commonwealth obligations to Britain, many Australians became increasingly war-weary as the fighting went on year after year.

General Douglas MacArthur never cared much for the Australians, and the feeling was reciprocated. MacArthur's arrogant ways did not go down well with the more freewheeling Australians. The situation was not helped much by the caustic personality of Australia's senior military officer, General Sir Thomas Blamey. Already a veteran of campaigns in Greece and North Africa by the end of 1941, Blamey was forced to accept MacArthur as his commander. This arrangement was in recognition of the fact that, in early 1942, it was the U.S. fleet (and American supplies and reinforcements) that would keep the Japanese from descending on Australia itself. This was a real fear for the Australians, who suffered Japanese air raids along their northern coast. The Japanese did consider an invasion of Australia, but even they had to face the fact that Australia was too large and Japanese troop commitments too vast to make such an operation practicable. But in the dark days of 1942, the threat felt very real to the Australians.

Despite their mutual dislike, MacArthur and Blamey were both competent combat leaders. Australian troops did much of the jungle fighting in steamy New Guinea and the Solomons. This later led to a controversy that still lingers. In late 1944, MacArthur ordered Australian units into battle against isolated Japanese forces in the Solomons, New Britain, and Borneo. The war was obviously coming to an end, and the Australians had been at it since 1939. It seemed a waste of Australian lives to go after the still-fanatical Japanese in these out-of-the-way places. Although the subsequent fighting used tactics that minimized casualties among the nearly 100,000 Australians involved, the bad feelings about the campaign continue to this day.

BRITISH ARMY

By the outbreak of the Pacific war, the British Army had already been at war for two years, and had experienced some particularly trying times in France, North Africa, and Greece. Despite some bright moments (Dunkirk, O'Connor's Offensive in North Africa), things had not gone well for the British Army. There were a number of things wrong, not least of which was leadership, which tended to be poor at the middle levels. Doctrine was somewhat inflexible, training sometimes inadequate, equipment not always the best, and manpower, which was generally of good quality, in increasingly short supply. The generation that had been decimated in Flanders fields during World War I didn't leave enough sons to fill the ranks for the Second World War.

Some of the leadership and material problems were resolved with time, as doctrine and training were improved, better leaders came to the fore, and superior equipment was procured. Nothing could resolve the manpower crisis however, and although Britain had actually mobilized something like forty divisions by late 1942, as time went on some divisions had to be broken up in order to keep the balance at full strength.

With her resources stretched quite thin, Britain could spare few units for the Pacific war. Nearly all Pacific Theater troops served in Burma, alongside the Indian and East African divisions that had substantial British cadres. The Burma campaign, fought largely to keep the Japanese out of India, was a hard-fought infantry war that was similar to the British operations in North Africa (albeit on a smaller scale). Burma was a side show, but one in which the British Army eventually prevailed.

In order to secure the enthusiastic (or at least willing) help of the Indians, Britain promised, soon after Japan entered the war, that India would have its independence after the war was won. Although disliked as a colonial power, the British had behaved well enough in India to be taken at their word. Thus most of the fighting in Burma was undertaken willingly and competently by Indian troops (and some from colonies in Africa).

Operations in India and Burma were complicated by the fact that during the early stages of the Pacific war, British naval power in the Indian Ocean was shattered by the Japanese. Although Midway, and growing American naval power, kept the Japanese from returning to the Indian Ocean in force, the British had their hands full dealing with enemy submarines (German and Italian as well as Japanese) that operated out of Dutch East Indies bases. Eventually, the aircraft-based tactics that worked so well against submarines in the Atlantic delivered the same winning edge in the Indian Ocean. Britain was able to speed the Burma offensive along with amphibious operations along the exposed Burmese coast from 1944 on.

The biggest allies, and most formidable opponents, the British faced in Burma were not the Japanese, but the climate (tropical) and geography (mountains and soggy). The Japanese faced these same obstacles and were never able to overcome both the British and the natural obstacles. The Burmese war went on for over three years. Neither side was ever close to any kind of dramatic breakthrough, but neither side could afford to stop fighting, either. The British had to keep the Japanese out of India and the Japanese had to keep the British from getting too close to their vital oil supplies in the Dutch East Indies.

Peak wartime strength of the British Army was 4.6 million troops, of whom about 10 percent saw service in the Pacific and related areas. Additional British troops served in the Indian Army.

BURMESE NATIONAL ARMY

In furtherance of the official line that they were liberating Asia from Western domination, the Japanese created a puppet regime in

Burma and quickly recruited a small local army, mostly from dissident elements in the highly fragmented Burmese population (there is no "majority" in Burma, and ethnic and political rivalries are fierce). When finally put to the test, the Burmese National Army, which fielded several notional divisions, disintegrated.

While the Burmese people were generally enthusiastic when the Japanese first invaded, they quickly found that they had traded one colonial occupier for another. The Japanese were also considerably tougher on the people than the British, making the racial superiority of the latter seem benign by comparison.

In response, the Burmese decided to wait the situation out and do nothing that would offend either the British (who, as time went by, appeared to be winning the war) or the Japanese (who, during their occupation, quickly demonstrated a violent response to any real or perceived Burmese resistance).

CHINESE ARMIES

In a sense there was no one Chinese Army. Rather, there were several: Chiang Kai-shek's Kuomintang (KMT) Nationalist Army, various warlord armies, the Communist party's army, and even an army of Chinese serving the Japanese. Quality varied tremendously. At their best, and some Chinese units were quite good, they were able to stand up to and slug it out with Japanese units of comparable size—good examples being several of the Nationalist divisions sent into Burma under General Tai An-lan in early 1942. But this was rare, particularly outside of the Communist units. In most of the Army, equipment was always scarce, training often nonexistent, morale abysmal, rations in short supply, leadership a joke, and corruption the order of the day, which last was most responsible for the other problems.

A number of attempts were made to remedy this situation, particularly after U.S. Lieutenant General Joseph Stilwell became Chiang's Chief of Staff (one of several hats he wore) in 1942. Stilwell developed an elaborate plan to train Chinese troops in India (rather than flying in supplies from India), providing them with modern organization and equipment, and then fly them over the Himalayas to form the striking force of the KMT armies. This was done, albeit not to the extent planned. There were supposed to be several dozen such divisions, but fewer than ten were formed in this way. When tested in action, the new units proved excellent. But they were rarely used properly.

The problem was that, ultimately, neither the Nationalists nor the Communists were as much interested in fighting the Japanese (who they realized were going to lose the war in the Pacific to the Americans regardless of what was accomplished in China) as in getting ready to fight each other. While the Nationalists always had half a dozen or so excellent divisions available, these units constituted their strategic reserve. The Allies constantly demanded that these units be sent south into Burma. But the Nationalists knew that they would need these units to ward off any sudden moves by the Japanese or Communists. This was at the heart of the argument over what the Chinese Army should be doing. The Allies wanted help in Burma; the Nationalists and Communists wanted to fight each other. The Japanese were content to leave all Chinese troops alone most of the time.

Arguably, had the Chinese leadership provided for effective direction in the war against Japan, they might have been able to affect the outcome, as Japan ultimately used her enormous armies in China as a pool from which to draw units for duty elsewhere. But as a practical matter, the Chinese were virtually cut off from outside military aid for most of the war. Most of what weapons and supply they did get had to be flown over the Himalayan Mountains.

The principal weapon the Chinese had to fight the Japanese was sheer manpower. Millions of Chinese troops spent most of their time just being armed and in front of the Japanese. There were always too many Chinese troops for the Japanese to destroy, and the Japanese tied up over a million troops just keeping an eye on the numerous, albeit poorly armed and trained, Chinese units.

The Japanese supply situation was also rather poor, and when the Japanese launched several large offensives in China during 1944, they were able to keep advancing (despite heavy troop losses) until they ran out of supplies in early 1945. The resources for this offensive against the KMT armies were gathered largely by suspending operations against the Chinese Communist forces from 1943 onward. The beating the KMT units took in the last year of the war, coupled with the two-year respite the Communists had, was largely responsible for Communist military success in the civil war that followed the departure of Japanese forces in 1945.

The Chinese armies were never held in high regard during this century. Although Communist troops gave a good account of themselves in Korea, they were unable to achieve a victory. And in the late 1970s, Chinese forces were roughly handled by Vietnamese troops. There was a time, centuries ago, when Chinese armies were rightly feared. But this was definitely not the case during World War II.

Peak wartime strength was 3.8 million troops for the Nationalists and 1.2 million for the Communists.

JAPAN'S CHINESE ARMY

By 1941 Japan controlled much of the population and most of the economic resources of China. A puppet government was installed, and a considerable army recruited, eventually amounting to some twenty divisions (about a quarter-million troops). These troops proved adequate for occupation duty and combat against equally inept Chinese Nationalist (i.e., KMT) troops, but did less well against Chinese Communist troops, or those Nationalist units that had the benefit of American training and equipment. After the war most of these troops ended up in the Nationalist (KMT) or the Communist Chinese Army. These units were kept on a short leash in terms of weapons and ammunition. The Japanese did not entirely trust them, as one can imagine, and used Japanese units for all crucial combat tasks.

U.S. ARMY

Although the main event for the U.S. Army was the war against Germany, nearly a quarter of the Army's total divisional strength (twenty-one of eighty-nine divisions) ended up in the Pacific. Army units served in all parts of the Pacific Theater, some even getting into action in Burma and the Netherlands East Indies. The Army conducted seventeen division-sized assault landings, plus over fifty others on a smaller scale, so that the Army actually "hit the beach" more often than the Marine Corps.

Initially, Army units were not well prepared for the unique kind of fighting they encountered in the Pacific. The Army had been focused on affairs in Europe for a long time, and unit organization, doctrine, equipment, and training were not always well suited to the terrain most typical in the Pacific (jungle and swamp), nor to Japanese tactics. In addition, several of the first units to go into action were from the National Guard, and these sometimes experienced leadership problems. The Army's attitude toward infantry also created difficulties, as it was assumed that the infantry had the least need for quality manpower.

In time, many of these problems were ironed out (although the manpower procurement and replacement problem was never properly resolved), and Army units generally did well. Special training programs were set up in the Pacific, to get new troops in shape for the unique kind of fighting encountered in the tropics.

GROUND COMBAT DIVISIONS OF THE PACIFIC WAR, 1942

Although the Pacific is generally regarded as a maritime theater, an awful lot of ground fighting went on. Aside from China, which tied up more Japanese troops than all the other areas of the theater combined, there was considerable ground combat in Burma and many, many of the islands, from the Philippines in 1941–1942 to Okinawa in 1945.

The Chinese Army had a lot of problems. At that, it still managed to keep the Japanese occupied for most of the war. The division shown in the table on page 281 was more or less the on-paper T/O&E (table of organization and equipment) for regular divisions. Many divisions were not so well equipped as shown. There were also many variants in the divisional T/O&E, such as outfits with one or even two more brigades (six to twelve additional battalions), as well as a group of divisions organized and rather lavishly equipped on a triangular model by the United States.

Although only the British 1941 infantry division is shown here,

DIVISIONS OF THE PACIFIC WAR, 1942

	CHINESE	BRITISH	PHIL	U.S. ARMY	USMC	JAPANESE TYPE I	TYPE II
Men	10.9	17.5	7.5	15.5	19.3	15.5	12.0
Battalions							
Inf	12	10	9	9	9	9	6
Art	1	5	3	4	6	3	1
Recon	0	1	0.3	0.3	0.3	1	0
Engr	1	1	1	1	2	1	1
Sig	0	1	0.3	0.3	1	0.3	0.3
Equipment							
MG	54	867	54	280	680	412	270
Art	24	72	36	72	60	70	16
A/T	0	48	0	109	54	8	0
Mtr	24	218	24	138	162	108	72
Value	4	9	4	12	16	10	5

NOTES: All divisions are infantry. "Phil" means troops of the Philippine Commonwealth. "Men" is the number of troops in the division, in thousands. Under "Battalions," 0.3 indicates a company; "Inf" is infantry; "Art" is artillery, including antitank and antiaircraft battalions; "Recon" is reconnaissance; "Engr" is engineers; "Sig" is signals, which in some armies were subsumed in the engineers. "Equipment" excludes rifles, automatic rifles (BARs), carbines, submachine guns, and pistols. "MG" is machine guns, exclusive of those on tanks or for antiaircraft use; "Art" is artillery pieces, excluding antitank and antiaircraft pieces; "A/T" is antitank guns, very useful for "bunker busting"; "Mtr" is mortars. "Value" is a rough mathematical calculation of the relative fighting power of each division, combining manpower, equipment, experience, organizational, and doctrinal factors. Note that British and American divisions usually had some armored vehicles other than tanks, such as armored cars and self-propelled artillery pieces, which have been omitted.

this was more or less similar to those of the other imperial and Commonwealth forces throughout the war, although Australian and New Zealand divisions, which had some minor differences in organization, tended to be composed of better manpower. Note, however, that particularly during the early part of the war, in Malaya and Burma, most of the British and Indian divisions committed to action were not at full strength, about 13,500 men being common, with equipment reduced in proportion.

Usually neglected is the fact that the "U.S." troops defending the

Philippines in 1941–1942 were mostly local residents. Figures in the table on page 281 are for the optimal paper strength of the Philippine divisions. The U.S. Army division shown is on the basis of those that fought in New Guinea and Guadalcanal during 1942, as is the Marine division. In general, it's important to keep in mind that American divisions—whether Army or Marine—usually went into action with various attached combat and combat support units, such as tank battalions with seventy-two light and medium tanks, which are not shown in the table.

The Japanese Army had an extremely confusing organization. The two types of divisions shown here didn't really exist at all. They are merely given to show some idea of the broad differences between divisions. Type I divisions were "triangular" formations designed for offensive operations, while Type II divisions were "square" formations primarily for occupation duties. But in practice, there were many variations in division strength. The actual details of each type (or of any of the half-dozen or so different varieties of brigades) could vary greatly: There were Type I divisions with as many as 26,000 men, and others as small as 12,000; and while some were fully motorized, such as the 5th (15,340 men and over 1,000 motor vehicles, with no horses) or the Guards (12,650 men, over 900 motor vehicles, and no horses) when they spearheaded the conquest of Malaya, most were "leg" outfits, in which the men walked and much of the equipment was horse drawn. And there were Type II divisions as small as 8,000 men on occupation duty in China and as large as 22,000 men being used for offensive operations (such as the 18th Division in Malaya, which had just 33 motor vehicles and over 5,700 horses). In all armies, of course, there was some variation in divisional organization, but the Japanese were rather extreme in this regard.

U.S. GROUND COMBAT DIVISIONS OF THE PACIFIC WAR, 1945

During the war considerable evolution took place in divisional organization, sometimes formally, and often informally. It would be impossible to trace all the changes in divisional organization that

U.S. DIVISIONS OF THE PACIFIC WAR, 1945

	ARMY	USMC
Men	14.0	17.5
Battalions		
Tank	0	1
Inf	9	9
Art	4	6
Recon	0.3	0.3
Engr	1	2
Sig	0.3	1
Equipment		
MG	448	625
Art	99	60
A/T	57	36
Mtr	144	153
Tanks	0	46
Value	16	20

NOTES: "Men" is the number of troops in the division, in thousands; "Inf" is infantry; "Art" is artillery; "Recon" is reconnaissance; "Engr" is engineer; "Sig" is signal; "MG" is machine guns; "A/T" is antitank guns; "Mtr" is mortar; "Value" is a rough approximation of the relative combat value of the unit.

took place during the war. For example, the U.S. Army's standard infantry divisions underwent four official reorganizations between June 1941 and September 1945, with a fifth planned. The Marines went through seven reorganizations in roughly the same period. But some idea of the great changes which took place may be gained by comparing the official divisional tables of organization and equipment as they stood at the beginning of 1945.

Japanese divisions had not appreciably changed since 1942, save for an increased allocation of automatic weapons. British and Chinese divisions have been omitted from the table, because there had been little change in their organization or equipment scales since 1942, even though the British divisions were more likely to be at full T/O&E rather than at about 70 to 75 percent and had a lot more light antitank weaponry. The Philippine Army, of course, had disappeared. But great changes had occurred in the T/O&E of the American divisions.

Changes in division manpower and weapons allocations were rooted in weapons developments, the growth in firepower, the increasing role of tanks, and changes in the tactical situation, such as the greatly increased allocation of automatic weapons. In addition, there was a desperate need to conserve manpower. By eliminating a single man from each infantry platoon, the U.S. Army could realize a manpower savings of nearly 100 men per division, some 10,000 men on an Army-wide basis. Similar small economies in the manpower of other elements could yield sufficient surplus personnel to allow the Army to raise entire new divisions. Of course such changes often led to acrimonious disputes. Not every officer, for example, was sufficiently understanding as to want to lose a couple of clerks or drivers.

Note that equipment allocations were usually exceeded in the field, when units would scrounge up additional equipment, often adopting overrun enemy material. On Guadalcanal, for example, the U.S. Marines made good use of some captured Japanese 37mm guns.

THE BIG LIES OF SINGAPORE

In the years before World War II, the British built up Singapore as their principal military base in the Far East. And indeed, it was a formidable place, albeit by no means as impregnable as it was touted in the press. All the propagandizing about the fortifications was a little ploy to keep the colonials happy. Thus, when the fortress fell to the Japanese with very little fuss early in 1942, British prestige plummeted throughout Asia.

In reality, Singapore was virtually indefensible unless one commanded the seas around it, and in 1941–1942 the Royal Navy did not have the ships nor the RAF the aircraft to secure such control. Moreover, the city was on an island and its water supply came from the mainland. Should a hostile force control the mainland water (as the Japanese did when they invaded), this tropical city and its thirsty population would quickly capitulate. This was precisely what happened to the British. You can't drink fortifications.

What might have saved Singapore was the Japanese supply situation, which provided for only a week's worth of food. The average Japanese infantryman had but 100 bullets with him to last for the entire campaign. Moreover, the Japanese commander thought the British garrison comprised only 30,000 troops, not the actual 85,000 that were there. The Japanese had to storm the island of Singapore and could not wait for the British to run out of water (some was stored on the island). The British didn't know of the precarious Japanese supply situation, not that it would have done much good. But British leadership was so inept that they were unable to prevent the outnumbered and ill-supplied Japanese from getting across the water, onto the island, and into the city.

The fall of Singapore unleashed a host of rumors and tall tales. There were numerous stories of treachery (always a reliable crutch when one doesn't want to admit to ineptitude or carelessness). Incompetence in high places was also a good target. One rumor had it that the great guns of the fortress could not be swung around to fire at land-based targets. Actually this was totally untrue. In fact, the five 15-inch naval guns available were capable of firing upon targets on the landward side of the island fortress. Unfortunately, they were supplied only with armor-piercing ammunition, of dubious value against infantrymen in the jungle.

Despite their inability to hold the place, the British really had built Singapore up into an extraordinary fortress. As a result, it turned into a valuable resource for the Japanese. They very quickly began to use bits and pieces of equipment captured at Singapore to bolster their defenses elsewhere. One result of this was that U.S. Marines assaulting Tarawa found themselves being fired upon by 8-inch coast defense guns from Singapore, firing some of His Britannic Majesty's best munitions.

THE JAPANESE WAY OF WAR

Before the Pacific war began, Western nations had adopted a rather superior attitude toward the capabilities of the Japanese armed forces. While this is often blamed on racism, there were numerous historical reasons for such a perspective. For one thing, the combat experience of Japanese forces through the late 1930s had not indicated that the Japanese were capable of extraordinary battlefield performance. Western military observers had witnessed Japanese troop performance during the Russo-Japanese War of 1904–1905. During the war with Russia, the Japanese had exhibited suicidal bravery and a lack of tactical competence. Although the Japanese won that war, the consensus in the West was that it was more a case of Russian stupidity handing the bullheaded Japanese a victory.

Few Western observers bothered to look closely at exactly how the Japanese military operated. After all, every Oriental army Western troops had faced in the past century had exhibited the same ineptitude. Despite the fact that the Japanese were more diligent in following the instruction of their Western (mainly French and German) military advisers, the general attitude was that the result was just another Oriental army. There were Western military attachés in Japan during the 1930s who did note the skill possessed by Japanese troops. But their reports formed a distinctly minority opinion back home.

The Japanese had not participated in World War I, and the Western nations that had participated felt that this massive dose of combat experience simply increased the qualitative difference between Western and Japanese armed forces. When the Japanese became heavily involved fighting the Chinese during the 1930s, many Western observers explained away Japanese success by noting the very poor quality of Chinese troops.

The Japanese Navy was held in somewhat higher esteem, but it was still thought that Western ships would prove superior. The Japanese had been building all their own ships since the eve of World War I, and there had been no chance to see how these vessels would perform in combat. It was assumed that the Japanese would not soon overcome several centuries of Western experience in designing and using warships.

Combat aircraft were still relatively new, and it wasn't until World War II began that everyone got a good idea of what air power could do. The Japanese had quickly adopted military aircraft before World War I and had begun to design and build their own during the 1920s. The resulting aircraft were quite different from those built in the West. This led foreign observers to believe that the Japanese had simply made inept copies of Western designs.

The Japanese also fought a series of division-size battles with the Soviets in 1939 (before war broke out in Europe). The Japanese got the worst of it. The details of these battles were not widely known in the West, but some word did get out. To many Western officers who heard of these battles in Manchuria, it simply confirmed what they already believed.

Overall, it was not thought that the Japanese armed forces could long withstand combat with Western troops and equipment. This attitude was, of course, quite wrong, as the events of December 1941 were to demonstrate. In fact, the Japanese armed forces were quite powerful. Each of the historical examples Westerners used to downgrade the Japanese had to be hastily revisited and revised once the Japanese entered the war.

The first four months of the Pacific war were an endless string of dramatic Japanese victories. How did they do it with what everyone thought were second-rate troops and equipment? Quite simply, the Japanese adapted techniques and equipment from other nations and applied them in a typically Japanese fashion. Always a nation apart, Japan had developed a distinctive collection of traits that it still possesses. Disciplined, diligent, fearless, and convinced of their innate superiority, the Japanese spent the early part of the twentieth century building armed forces that looked Western but were uniquely Japanese. The key elements of this force, and why each was misinterpreted, were as follows.

1. HIGHLY DISCIPLINED AND WELL TRAINED

Westerners were accustomed to seeing Oriental troops whipped into shape and made to at least appear disciplined and battle ready. But it had been noted that these troops usually performed well in combat only if they had Western officers (and often Western NCOs as well). It was felt that Oriental armies were unable to provide effective training for their soldiers. This, until the Japanese were encountered, proved to be the case most of the time.

Well, the Japanese troops were well disciplined. This was a Japanese characteristic. The normal discipline of Japanese civilians was even more severe in their armed forces. And the Japanese were also well trained. The problem, for Westerners, was that you can't easily tell how effective training is until the troops go into combat. For the Western troops that had to face the Japanese in combat during the early months of the war, this was too late.

Japan managed to get a lot of combat experience out of World War I without doing a lot of fighting. Japanese officers were present at the front during World War I and they took notes. What they grasped was what the Germans (who had invented it) and everyone else called blitzkrieg. Plan carefully, move fast, attack vigorously only when you must attack, and, above all, break the enemy's will to fight. This was consistent with the traditional Japanese approach to warfare, anyway.

In effect, the Japanese practiced blitzkrieg without the tanks. This was not so much because the Japanese didn't believe in tanks, but because they often operated in areas that tanks could not operate in, against opponents for whom tanks would be overkill. Moreover, the relatively weak Japanese economy could neither build nor support many tanks. Or, put another way, the Japanese adopted the quite successful "shock troop" infantry tactics the Germans had developed in the last years of World War I. They added to it naval support and extensive use of aircraft—in effect, all the elements of blitzkrieg except the tanks.

The Japanese had also adopted the Western approach to training officers, and added a few uniquely Japanese elements. Their officer cadet schools were much harsher than anything in the West and were dedicated to turning out leaders who personified the stern traditions of the ancient samurai warrior. These officers were indoctrinated with the idea that spirit was superior to material matters. At the same time, these officers were thoroughly professional and fearless leaders. Strangely enough, their training was so Spartan that they regularly endured, and accepted, a poor diet. As a result, the officers were often smaller than their troops. Small, but tough. You could always tell who the officers were on the battlefield—they were the little guys out front waving a sword.

Training, as most Western officers knew, is not very visible. But they assumed that the Japanese troops were simply taught to look like soldiers when, in fact, the Japanese were drilled and instructed on how to be very effective in combat. Learning from past experience, they performed much of their training at night. This was a very modern attitude, but as the Japanese had long observed, the night attack was the most likely to achieve surprise. Training was also conducted under very realistic, and dangerous, conditions. This better prepared the troops for combat and, because of the Japanese attitude toward death, lethal training accidents did not cause any commotion, as they would in the West. Japanese soldiers, sailors, and airmen were all much better trained, disciplined, and mentally prepared for combat than their Western counterparts. The shock of discovering this was played out in the spectacular victories the Japanese achieved in the first six months of the war.

2. EFFECTIVE USE OF AIR POWER

The Japanese built all their own aircraft after World War I and they developed designs that reflected their own attitudes toward warfare. Key among these beliefs was the primacy of the offense. To the Japanese, attack was everything and defense was a bothersome, but sometimes necessary, detail. Thus their aircraft stressed offensive performance at the expense of protection. Japanese fighters were more nimble, carried heavier armament, and had longer range than their Western counterparts. Their bombers had heavier bombloads and longer range. But both fighters and bombers were more prone to explode into flames if they were hit. Lacking armor and self-sealing fuel tanks, Japanese aircraft were lighter, but they were quickly put out of action if hit. Western pilots soon noted this and, by the end of 1942, were able to take advantage of it.

But this was not much help during the first six months of the war. The Japanese also had a very elitist attitude toward pilot selection and training. Their pilots were probably the most capable in the world when they entered combat. Thus, when the war began, Japanese fighters were able to sweep enemy fighters from the sky while their bombers came in and hit targets with accuracy unknown in the West. As the Germans discovered with their own blitzkrieg, air superiority not only added to your combat power but also went far to demoralize the enemy troops.

While the highly capable Japanese air forces (Army and Navy) were initially a shock for their opponents, the Allies promptly learned to adapt. Moreover, the Allies (particularly the United States) had the ability to produce far more aircraft than the Japanese. By 1943, Japanese air power was no longer a decisive element in the war. At the same time, air superiority was not as decisive for the Allies as it had been for the Japanese early in the war. During 1942, Japan's foes were disorganized and not well prepared to fight. Air superiority then allowed Japan's capable forces to rapidly seize millions of square miles of land and sea. But once the Allies began attacking, they found that controlling the air did little to unnerve Japan's do-or-die troops on the ground. Air power helped, but it never caused many Japanese defenders to give up without a fight.

3. SURPRISE, SURPRISE, SURPRISE

As the Japanese had demonstrated throughout their history, they believed wars were best begun with surprise attacks. This they had done during their war with Russia beginning in 1904, as well during their initial campaigns in China. Note that their use of long-range, hard-hitting aircraft contributed considerably to the effect of surprise. Pearl Harbor was not the only swift, unexpected attack the Japanese carried out in the first weeks of the war.

While surprise was an asset for the Japanese early in the war, it became a liability later on. Their desire to achieve surprise, coupled with their belief that the "spirit" of their soldiers could overcome material shortages, led to hastily organized and unsuccessful operations later on. Moreover, Americans had a technological edge that made surprise even more difficult to achieve. One American specialty was radar, which actually spotted the Pearl Harbor air strike coming in, but no one in charge believed it. All were believers after that. By 1943, all American task forces had several radar-equipped ships, which made it nearly impossible for Japanese aircraft to achieve surprise.

The second American advantage was the breaking of Japan's radio codes. By reading messages the Japanese thought were secret, the United States destroyed Japan's ability to achieve much surprise. This second item was particularly important because the Japanese never seriously suspected that their codes were being read by the enemy. Thus surprise was a one-time advantage for Japan, and repeated attempts to achieve it later in the war only gave aid and comfort to the enemy.

Last was the American preference, and capability, to use massive amounts of firepower on the battlefield. This, coupled with the best communications systems any World War II armed forces fielded, found the Japanese running into a hail of shells and bombs soon after one of their surprise attacks was launched. December 1941 was the high point for Japanese surprise attacks. After that, it was the Japanese who were being brought up short by events they didn't expect.

4. NOT AFRAID TO DIE—OR, AS THE JAPANESE PUT IT, "TO DIE FOR THE EMPEROR IS TO LIVE FOREVER"

This attitude is something all generals wish their troops possessed. But usually, the bulk of the troops have no desire whatsoever to die. Yet a soldier who has resigned himself to death is far more clear-headed in combat. Fear of death tends to be paralyzing and, ironically, makes it more likely that one will get killed. The Japanese armed forces were unique in that most of the troops were quite accepting of the fact that they were going to die. Japanese generals tended to see that their troops did just that if those deaths would win a battle. This was part of the Japanese attitude toward war. Part of a Japanese soldier's training was constant reminders about his new relationship with death.

Until some experience was obtained in fighting Japanese troops, Western officers merely thought many Japanese soldiers were simply quite brave. It was a chilling experience when Allied soldiers realized they were facing a foe that, almost to a man, did not fear death. Throughout the war, the Japanese used this trait to good effect and the Allies had to adjust their tactics to deal with it. For one thing, there was no such thing as scaring Japanese troops into surrendering. With few exceptions, Japanese troops did not surrender. It was, quite literally, death before dishonor, as the Japanese saw defeat as the ultimate disgrace.

The Japanese had, over the centuries, developed a large repertoire of ways to kill oneself in combat. So it wasn't just a matter of accepting the fact that one could get killed in combat, but also contemplating the numerous ways one could accelerate the process in order to do the most damage to the enemy. The recognized methods ranged from looking for a way to kill as many enemy troops as possible to getting in one last shot after you have been wounded, or doing yourself in because you have been defeated and all that remains is to atone for your failure. While suicide was not considered a goal for all soldiers, it was accepted as an inevitable event in certain circumstances. Allied troops soon saw ample evidence that the Japanese view toward suicide was different from anything they had seen before.

But there was, from the Japanese point of view, a dark side to all this. Their dependence on thoroughly trained and properly indoctrinated troops meant that replacements could not be had quickly. Their pilot training, in particular, was never up to the needs of prolonged war losses. Japanese pilots, while highly skilled, were often enthusiastic to the point of ramming enemy aircraft if they found themselves out of ammunition. While this was admirable from the pilot's point of view, it took years to train a replacement and Japan soon ran out of skilled pilots. The pilot attrition situation was made worse by the lack of protection in Japanese aircraft. There were also heavy aircraft losses, but aircraft were easier to replace. By 1943 Japan had lost air superiority to better Allied pilots flying better-designed aircraft built by the more productive Western factories.

On the ground, the steady loss of infantry units seemed at first to be less of a problem because the Japanese planners always intended that their offensives would stop six months or so after the beginning of the war. Then the Japanese would dig in and inflict such losses on the counterattacking Americans that a peace could be negotiated. The negotiated peace never came, but the American infantry and the prodigious output of U.S. arms factories did. The Americans found ways to accommodate the Japanese soldiers' willingness to die. Many Japanese garrisons were simply bypassed. When Japanese troops had to be fought, firepower was used as much as possible. American losses were still heavier than if they had been fighting an opponent who would surrender when the situation was hopeless. But once the Japanese attitudes were confirmed, tactics were modified to minimize U.S. losses and accommodate the Japanese desire to die rather than surrender.

The Japanese were not relentlessly suicidal. They would withdraw their forces if that was possible and they felt that they had no chance of accomplishing anything useful. They successfully withdrew their defeated forces from Guadalcanal and the Aleutians. But when they were cornered, and withdrawal was not possible, the typical Japanese reaction was to make one last attack and sell their lives dearly. This was the fierce "banzai" attack that Allied troops came to expect when the battle seemed to be just about over.

While the Japanese were not devoted to self-destruction, they did have a cavalier attitude toward the nonspiritual aspects of soldiering. While the troops often had excellent attitudes and high morale, they just as frequently had no ammunition and were starving. This was first noted on Guadalcanal. Here, American aircraft and warships made it difficult for the Japanese to supply their troops. More troops died from starvation and lack of medical care than from enemy action. The troops died without complaint and surrender was never considered an option. In addition to being the first battle of the American counteroffensive in the Pacific, Guadalcanal was also the most lopsided battle in terms of losses. There were 1,600 American dead on the island and some 21,000 Japanese. This was largely a result of the length of the battle (six months) and the inability of the Japanese to supply their troops.

But a Western commander in Japan's place would never have let the battle go on so long like that. This was not the only battle where a Japanese commander deliberately allowed his troops to keep going to certain death. The fighting in Burma included several operations where Japanese generals sent their troops to certain death from starvation and disease on the slim chance of achieving a victory.

The Japanese attitude toward death influenced the treatment of enemy soldiers and civilians. In general, the troops treated prisoners and civilians callously. Prisoners were despised for having done what Japanese soldiers would not think of doing: surrendering. Civilians were abused simply because they were foreigners. The Japanese had a very high opinion of themselves and a correspondingly ugly demeanor regarding "barbarians" (anyone who wasn't Japanese).

These attitudes resulted in ghastly treatment of POWs and foreign civilians. Summary executions were common and rape generally went unpunished, as did looting and other forms of misbehavior. But it got worse. Japanese military physicians would practice their surgical skills on enemy civilians and POWs. The victims were usually not given any pain-killers and were killed after the procedure was completed.

Not all of these atrocities were officially condoned, but neither was there strong direction from the top against such beastly behavior. Many prisoners, especially Westerners, were treated according to the accepted (Geneva Convention) rules of war. At least the letter of the rules was often observed, but because prisoners were to be fed on the same scale as your own troops, this left the generally larger Western soldiers quite starved on the Japanese soldiers' skimpy rations. And prisoners were still brutalized and forced (despite the Geneva Convention prohibitions) to work on war-related projects. While most of the surgery practice was done on Chinese, Western POWs were sometimes used.

The attitudes toward enemy civilians led to some truly abominable practices. The most gruesome operations involved the development and use of biological weapons against the Chinese. These devices were created in Manchuria by a special unit given the innocuous name Detachment 731. In addition to developing a (bubonic) plague bomb, Detachment 731 conducted sundry forms of "medical research" on Chinese and Western prisoners.

The plague bomb never really worked. The basic idea was to spread the plague (the medieval "black death") in Chinese-held territory. The first field experiments were conducted in 1940. Few plague deaths were noted. The weapon itself was an aircraft bomb containing plague-infected fleas instead of explosives. In 1942, the fleas were released near the front to halt the advance of Chinese troops. Again, there was no particular impact on the Chinese. This may have been due to the fact that the plague was difficult to spread and that there were plenty of other diseases going around at the same time. Moreover, the fleas could not survive long without a host (usually rodents). Even attempts to spread the plague by releasing flea-infested rats had no effect.

The 3,000 members of Detachment 731 and its four subdetachments did manage to kill several thousand people with their medical experiments. These included "experimental surgery" and equally grim procedures performed in the name of medical research. Perhaps the only practical effect of Detachment 731 was letting prisoners, and captives held for interrogation, know that if they didn't cooperate they would be sent to Detachment 731 for "processing." The word got around China during the war that the detachment existed and that being sent there was worse than any of the more mundane atrocities the Japanese committed on their victims.

Like their Nazi allies, the Japanese used their fearsome reputation for brutality and atrocity, and their own disdain for death, as another weapon. It was not a decisive weapon, but it helped their cause and gave them one more reason not to clean up their act.

Oddly enough, the Japanese war criminals were not rounded up and punished to the extent that German ones were. Part of this was due to the fact many of the countries the Japanese operated in promptly erupted in civil war and rebellion after World War II ended. In the chaos this created, many Japanese war criminals were able to cover their tracks and make their escape. There were other reasons, but the fact remains that many Japanese atrocities went unpunished.

5. SPEED

The Japanese knew that if they could move faster than their opponents, they could control the action and more easily win the battle. When they were able to use their fleet and had air superiority, their nonmechanized infantry could move along quite swiftly. One thing many Western officers didn't realize was that infantry forces could move as rapidly as mechanized forces if the infantry had the opposition cleared away by bombers or warships. The Japanese were also quite adept at impromptu amphibious operations. Their infantry units could get on and off the ships quickly and sea movement was several times faster than going overland in trucks and armored vehicles. This combination was the key to their lightning conquest of the Pacific islands early in the Pacific war.

Speed, however, rarely worked for the Japanese when they did not have time to plan their operations carefully. After 1942, the Allies had the initiative and all the Japanese could do was react to the increasing number of Allied offensives. Under these conditions, the Japanese still tried to operate quickly, but now their haste merely yielded sloppiness and errors the enemy was quick to take advantage of. Speed works well when you have the initiative; otherwise it's a bad move. But the Japanese only slowly changed their style of warfare and their changes came too late.

For the first six months of the war, the skill, speed, and surprise tactics of Japanese troops carried all before them in the Pacific. The Japanese were not supermen, nor did they have any spectacular new weapons. They simply did what they did very well and, most important, did it much better than their opponents expected.

In a final irony, those Japanese who were taken prisoner (often while disabled by wounds) responded by talking freely. Japanese soldiers were not given any instruction on how to behave as prisoners because it was unthinkable that one would be taken alive. Of course, Japanese officers knew that there was a possibility that some of their troops would be taken alive while they were incapacitated by wounds, but it was felt best to ignore any possibility of surrender and not to discuss it under any circumstances. This proved to be a correct assessment of the situation, for as the war went on and the situation became more hopeless, an increasing number of Japanese overcame their conditioning and surrendered voluntarily. The number of prisoners was never that great, but in the final battles they numbered in the thousands.

Initially, only a handful of prisoners were taken. Most were seriously wounded and had to undergo extensive medical care before they could be interrogated in depth. After all possible information was obtained, the Japanese POWs were sent to camps in the United States. Some of these prisoners refused to return to Japan after the war for fear of what would become of them as soldiers who had dishonored themselves by surrendering. Many of these apprehensive POWs were allowed to remain in America, where some still live out their days, too ashamed to let their families know that they survived when so many of their comrades perished.

Hundreds of other defeated Japanese not only refused to surrender when defeated, but would not believe that the war had ended at all. In battlefields far from Japan, these troops fought on, or at least avoided any contact with the local population. From the 1950s onward, every few years, one or two of these diehards would surrender to teams of Japanese officials who made regular trips to these old battlefields. There, the officials would tramp through the jungle with loudspeakers, announcing in Japanese that the war was over and it was safe to come home now. Some old soldiers may still be out there, resourceful and unbending old men, loyal to their emperor unto the end.

THE MARINE CORPS BECOMES AN ARMY

For most of the nation's history, the Marines were a very small force. So small, in fact, that until a provisional Marine battalion landed at Guantánamo Bay in Cuba on June 10, 1898, during the Spanish-American War, most Americans had never even heard of the Marine Corps. Up until that time, U.S. Marines had served as shipboard specialists, much like marines in the world's other major navies had for the last few centuries. Of course, the Marines also occasionally provided provisional battalions for service ashore. Usually they did well in this business.

Thus, a detachment of Marines (nine of them, plus an officer and a sailor to provide medical assistance) helped storm Derna, in North Africa, on April 26, 1805 ("... to the shores of Tripoli ..."). A brigade of Marines and sailors were the only American troops who didn't run at the Battle of Bladensburg, on August 24, 1814, a disgraceful affair that resulted in the British capture of Washington. A battalion of Marines helped storm Mexico City on September 13, 1847 ("From the halls of Montezuma ..."). It wasn't all glory, however, as Marines did leave the field precipitously at Bull Run on July 21, 1861.

Normally Marines were organized as "detachments" on ships and at navy yards, only occasionally being formed into units of company size and larger, on an ad hoc basis.

In 1911, all Marines not assigned to ships were formed into companies of 103 men (identical to U.S. Army companies of that time). These companies were then organized into battalions (three companies) or regiments (ten companies) as needed. The cause of this reorganization was the fear of recurring bureaucratic and political efforts to abolish the Corps by the Army, and occasionally the Navy.

Thus the Marines began to seek a greater role for themselves than merely keeping order on warships, guarding naval bases, and occasionally landing in some remote place to "teach the natives a lesson." The Marines saw opportunities with the recent adoption of War Plan Orange, which envisioned the fleet advancing across the Pacific in the event of a war with Japan. To effect such an advance, islands would have to be occupied to serve as bases.

Although the Marines had previously never raised anything larger than a provisional regiment, quite early it was clear that seizing islands from the Japanese as the fleet advanced across the Pacific in accordance with War Plan Orange would require the services of division-sized formations. As early as 1913, the Marines began to prepare for their role in War Plan Orange, creating the Advance Base Force. This was organized and trained to make amphibious landings. Over the years it did so several times, notably at Veracruz in Mexico, in Haiti, and in the Dominican Republic.

Still, on the eve of World War I, the Marine Corps numbered only 13,700 men. During World War I, the Corps grew rapidly, reaching 75,000 by late 1918. Two Marine brigades, about 25,000 men, served with the Allied Expeditionary Force in France. The 4th Marine Brigade formed part of the 2nd Infantry Division, accumulating a distinguished record (Belleau Wood, for example). The other Marine brigade arrived later and, despite the efforts of Marine brass to create a Marine division, was used for rear-area security.

After the Great War, the Corps was cut back to about 17,000 men. But the Advance Base Force, which had been redesignated a brigade, continued to exist, effecting occasional interventions, but more importantly serving as a test bed for the development of amphibious doctrine, going through several name changes. Meanwhile, during the 1920s, a regular Marine infantry regimental organization was developed. This was a small unit, only about 1,500 men.

The Marine Corps stayed small until the 1930s, when the expansion began. On February 1, 1941, the Marines activated their first two divisions. By the end of the war they would have six.

The 1st and 2nd Marine Divisions were activated from prewar regulars. These were very good men, since the Corps could be highly selective during the Depression. When war came, these two divisions were filled out and dispatched to the South Pacific, to be "blooded" on Guadalcanal. The 1st Division went on to make a legend of itself at Guadalcanal, the first island to be reclaimed from the Japanese. After surviving that, it fought in Eastern New Guinea and New Britain, serving alongside Army units in the unglamorous jungle fighting that characterized the war in the Southwest Pacific (where it received little press coverage, it being General MacArthur's bailiwick).

In September 1944, the 1st Division finally got a chance to make the kind of amphibious landing that the Marines made famous in the Pacific. Unfortunately, it was sent against Peleliu, a heavily fortified island southeast of the Philippines. The resistance was greater than anyone expected, and the terrain totally unlike anything the troops were prepared for. The result was a hard-fought battle. To make matters worse, it was later discovered that Peleliu could have been bypassed. Later, the 1st Division ended its Pacific career by participating in the Okinawa assault in March 1945. This turned into a three-month slugging match, one of the most grueling island assaults of the Pacific war. Overall, the 1st Division had a hard time of it in the Pacific. But for a division that hadn't existed in early 1941, it acquitted itself well.

The 2nd Marine Division was also formed in February 1941. The 1st Division got priority on men and equipment and went into action first. But the 2nd Division relieved the battered 1st on Guadalcanal during late 1942 and worked with Army troops to finish running the Japanese out. With the Guadalcanal campaign over in early 1943, the 2nd Division was withdrawn for retraining. Thus prepared, the 2nd Division mounted the first modern amphibious assault at Tarawa, in November 1943. This was a tough fight. After it, the division had to be rebuilt and retrained for the Saipan invasion during June 1944. Right after that, it went on to storm Tinian during July 1944. In March 1945, the 2nd Division ended its Pacific war career with the attack on Okinawa in April 1945.

The 3rd Marine Division was formed in September 1942. This was the first case in which the 1st and 2nd Marine Divisions became "parents." About 40 percent of the men in each succeeding Marine division were drawn from the combat-seasoned veterans of the older outfits, a much higher margin of experienced troops than was the norm in most Army divisions. The 3rd Division got its first combat experience with Army troops in the Solomons (Bougainville) during 1943. Its first amphibious invasion was at Guam, in 1944. Its final assault was against Iwo Jima in February 1945.

The 4th Marine Division was formed in August 1943 by splitting up the already forming 3rd Marine Division and drawing veterans from the 1st and 2nd Divisions. It first saw action in February 1944 against Kwajalein and Roi islands. After receiving replacements and more training, it went on to invade Saipan and Tinian during the summer of 1944. Finally, the 4th Division participated in the assault on Iwo Jima in February 1945.

The 5th Marine Division was formed in January 1944 and participated in the Iwo Jima assault during February 1945.

The 6th Marine Division was formed in August 1944 and participated in the attack on Okinawa in April 1945. The 6th Marine Division had an unusual history. Its 4th Marine Regiment (named after a regiment lost on Corregidor) had been formed from the old raider and parachute battalions, which had seen action on Makin, Guadalcanal, and Bougainville in 1942–1943. The regiment served as an independent unit in the occupation of Emirau Island, and as part of the 1st Provisional Marine Brigade on Guam in 1943–1944. A second regiment, the 22nd, raised in early 1942, had occupied Eniwetok atoll in the Marshall Islands as an independent unit, and at Guam was also part of the 1st Provisional Marine Brigade. The third regiment, the 29th, was newly formed, but one battalion, the 1st, had seen action on Saipan as an independent unit. As a result, the cadre of the 6th Marine Division was unusually well seasoned.

The Marines had the distinction of having most of the commando units in the Pacific. The Army had formed six Ranger battalions, mostly for service in Europe, organized on the British model. The Army Ranger units were not as successful as was hoped, and neither were their Marine counterparts in the Pacific. As good as these troops were, and they were very good, they were not supermen. Most of the fighting in the war required good infantry, not hand-picked, highly trained commandos.

The Marines formed two raider battalions and a unit of airborne "paramarines." The 2nd Raider Battalion distinguished itself with its raid on Japanese-held Makin Island in 1942. But for the rest of the war, the Marine "commandos" served in more conventional infantry actions. This was the reason for the lack of exceptional situations that could be resolved only with elite commandos. Moreover, the Marines already considered themselves elite assault troops and saw little need for additional classes of assault specialists. Thus the absorption of the Marine commando units into the 6th Marine Division.

During the war the Marine Corps attained a peak strength of about 500,000 men, and a few women as well. It was also integrated in the course of the war, with many black riflemen in its ranks by V-J Day. The Marines also used Navaho-speaking troops to provide a form of "code" the Japanese could not break. Many Japanese-speaking Japanese-Americans also served in the ranks as translators. Both Navaho and Japanese-American Marines had to be provided with special bodyguards, lest overenthusiastic fellow Marines of the predominant racial type think they were enemy infiltrators, not to mention the necessity of preventing the capture of the Navahos by Japanese troops, since as communications personnel they knew quite a bit more than the average Marine.

In the fifty years since World War II, Marine Corps strength has never fallen below 150,000 troops. This, incidentally, was the size of the entire U.S. Army in 1940.

INVENTING THE MARINE DIVISION

As originally organized, in 1941, a Marine division was quite similar to the Army's contemporary infantry division. There were three rifle regiments of three battalions each, plus an artillery regiment (three battalions of 75mm guns and one of 105mm), plus supporting elements of reconnaissance, engineer, signal, service, and medical (supplied by the Navy) troops. In addition, there were some formations specialized in amphibious warfare, like a U.S. Navy "Beach and Shore Battalion," to help get the troops ashore, and a "Defense Battalion," intended to provide protection against attack from the sea, into a beachhead's rear.

A lot of changes in divisional organization took place even before the 1st Marine Division landed on Guadalcanal on August 7, 1942. By then the 19,300 men of a Marine division on paper had been reinforced by a tank battalion, a second engineer battalion, and a 155mm artillery battalion, while the riflemen received an increased allocation of mortars (162) and light artillery (fifty-four 37mm anti-tank guns).

Although the basic organization of the division remained more or less unchanged for the rest of the war, equipment allocations continued to evolve, particularly in terms of automatic and semiautomatic weapons. By mid-1944 the division had over 16,000 M1 carbines or M1 rifles, 625 machine guns, and 45 submachine guns, not counting machine guns on tanks and LVTs (landing vehicles, tracked). The Marines learned the hard way how useful lots of automatic weapons were.

When they first had to confront the reckless abandon of Japanese banzai attacks on Guadalcanal in 1942, they had to improvise. Some automatic weapons (machine guns and automatic rifles) were taken from all units and kept as a reserve in several trucks. When the signs of an imminent Japanese attack were detected (the Japanese were not always as stealthy as they could have been when preparing an attack), the trucks full of automatic weapons would be rushed to the threatened area and the troops promptly equipped with the needed additional firepower.

Although the number of mortars and 37mm guns fell slightly (to 153 and 36 respectively), the troops were lavishly provided with antitank rocket launchers (over 1,700) and flamethrowers, which had proven useful in "bunker busting."

As Marine Corps combat doctrine evolved, it was decided that each division should have an air wing associated with it (seventy-two aircraft of various types), to provide air defense, ground support, and reconnaissance. In practice, however, only three air wings were fully formed, and a fourth partially, so the "marriage" between ground and air elements was not as close as the Marine brass wished it to be, and Marines were often supported by Navy airmen. On their own scale of evaluation, the Marine riflemen believed air support provided by Marines was best, followed by the Navy, with the USAAF a distant third. Army troops tended to agree with the Marine assessment of who provided the best ground support.

HORSEPOWER

The image of World War II as a struggle between mechanized forces is an enduring one. It is also an erroneous one. In all theaters, including the Pacific Theater, horses and mules played a surprisingly important role.

Only two nations actually managed to more or less dispense with horses during World War II: Britain and the United States. And not even they entirely dispensed with the equine race. Although they had converted their own cavalry units to mechanized on the eve of the war, the British retained some cavalry units in the Indian Army, which were used on occupation duty in the Middle East, and in combat in Burma in 1942. The United States actually began the war with two Regular and several National Guard cavalry divisions, and actually committed some horse cavalry units to operations overseas. The 26th Cavalry Regiment (Philippine Scouts) went into action in the Philippines when the Japanese invaded in December 1941, the troopers performing yeoman service as scouts and mounted infantry, as well as mobile reserves. Later in the war, the 2nd Cavalry Division (Colored) served on occupation duty in North Africa in 1943, and the Texas National Guard's 112th Cavalry Regiment served mounted for a time on New Caledonia until converted into infantry in May 1943. Even then, some mounted units continued in service. During the Sicilian campaign, the 3rd Infantry Division created a provisional mounted reconnaissance troop, which proved so valuable the practice was adopted by other units during the Italian campaign.

Even the U.S. Navy used mounted troops, raising a regiment from local manpower in Inner Mongolia, as a security force for Navy weather stations there. The Coast Guard had mounted beach patrols along the east coast in order to prevent German submarines from landing intelligence agents and saboteurs.

Other armies made much greater use of horses than did the U.S. or the British Army. Germany and Russia used horses extensively for transport, since they were never able to mechanize their forces fully, and both countries fielded a number of cavalry divisions as well, which proved of great value on the relatively porous Eastern Front.

The Soviet Union maintained thousands of horse troopers in the Far East throughout the war, the better to keep an eye on their Japanese counterparts across the border. Mongolia was a Soviet satellite at the time, and many Mongolian cavalrymen, direct descendants of the ancient Mongol Horde, served throughout the war. Just before the war began, in 1939, there were several multidivision clashes between Japanese and Soviet forces on the Manchurian border that featured the extensive use of horse cavalry.

Japan began the war with several cavalry brigades in China, where it was also not uncommon for divisional reconnaissance regiments to be mounted. There was also a lot of horse cavalry in the Chinese collaborationist and Manchukuoan armies. Japanese cavalry brigades were eventually mechanized, but all of the rest served mounted to the end of the war. And Japanese transport tended to be horsed for much of the war, even in the South Pacific, at least for as long as the horses managed to survive. The Chinese Nationalists and Communists both made extensive use of cavalry and horse transport, as did the Soviet-dominated Mongolians.

So even in the Pacific war, the horse soldiered on.

BIG GUNS IN THE PACIFIC

Stalin called artillery "the god of war," while Louis XIV, an earlier autocrat, had called his "the king's ultimate argument." Cannon were brought down a notch or two in the Pacific because of the jungles and troops making good use of their shovels, and the abundance of trees with which to build shellproof dugouts. However, except for the opening campaign in the Philippines in 1941–1942, throughout the Pacific war that god-king was decidedly on the side of the United States.

The advantage was far more than merely that inherent in having more guns than the Japanese. There were more pieces in an American division, whether Army (72, plus about 100 antitank guns) or Marine (60, plus 54 antitank guns), than in a Japanese one (48, plus 18 small antitank guns), not to mention a more generous allocation of artillery to higher commands.

ARTILLERY OF THE PACIFIC WAR

COUNTRY	PIECE	TYPE	RANGE (IN METERS)	RPM
U.S.	37mm	A/T gun	5,000	6.0
	75mm	A/T gun	8,500	2.5
	75mm	pack hwtzr	9,800	2.5
	105mm	hwtzr	12,500	2.0
	155mm	hwtzr	16,500	1.0
Japan	37mm	A/T gun	5,000	6.0
	70mm	inf hwtzr	3,000	3.0
	75mm	inf hwtzr	8,000	2.5
	75mm	fld hwtzr	9,000	2.5
	150mm	fld hwtzr	15,000	1.0

NOTES: "A/T gun" stands for antitank gun, which was the same type of gun mounted on tanks. "hwtzr" stands for howitzer, a short-barreled weapon capable of relatively high-angled fire; most were called field howitzers, or "fld hwtzr"; a "pack" howitzer was capable of being disassembled into several more manageable pieces, for transportation on mule back; an "inf," or infantry, howitzer had a shorter range than a regular howitzer, but was much lighter. In the later stages of the war some U.S. 105mm howitzers were self-propelled. "RPM" is the number of rounds per minute that the weapon can fire on a sustained basis. The RPM can be more than doubled for a few minutes, but this leads to barrel overheating.

Moreover, while U.S. Army divisional artillery was largely composed of 105mm and 155mm guns and howitzers (Marine divisions began with 75mm and 105mm pieces, with some 155mms, but soon graduated to heavier pieces), most Japanese artillery was 75mm and 150mm. In addition, all U.S. artillery was motorized while most Japanese artillery was horse drawn, which frequently meant manhandled. U.S. artillery had an elaborate and flexible fire control system; the Japanese fire control was more rigid and unresponsive to urgent troop needs. Finally, U.S. artillery had several times more ammunition per gun than did the Japanese. In practical terms, U.S. divisions had anywhere from three to ten times as much artillery firepower at their disposal than Japanese divisions.

Not only was Japanese artillery lighter than U.S. artillery, but it was distributed differently. The United States emphasized centralized coordination of artillery, while the Japanese relied rather heavily on the 70mm and 75mm infantry howitzers. There were ten of these in each infantry regiment, in contrast to none in the comparable U.S. regiment. Japanese training and doctrine stressed the use of these for close support of their infantry, a role in which they proved very valuable. However, in very dense environments, such as the jungles of Guadalcanal or Burma, the infantry howitzers often could not be brought close enough to the front to be effective. In such situations the troops often had to attack without any artillery support, since the Japanese were unable to coordinate divisional artillery with infantry attacks.

The U.S. practice was to pool artillery assets at division level and deliver fire on call from the front-line units. Sophisticated communications and coordination techniques permitted all guns within range to fire in coordination, often with all the rounds landing on the target at the same time, a devastating experience for the troops on the receiving end. As the war progressed, it was found useful to provide some light artillery firepower to the troops right up on the front lines, in the form of bazookas (portable rocket launchers) and light antitank guns, which proved useful for busting into fortifications.

An experiment in allocating a battery of 105mm howitzers to each infantry regiment proved less than successful, however, and it was customary for these to be sent up to division artillery, where they formed an extra battalion on an ad hoc basis. As the war went on, U.S. troops also benefited from the presence of "flying artillery," aircraft equipped for ground support operations. Marine pilots were particularly good at this, since all of them had been trained as infantry officers before getting their wings.

Antiaircraft artillery played an important part in the war, as air attacks on ground troops were used by both sides until near the end of the war. Where the Japanese had lost air superiority, they usually still had aircraft and these could be sent in to attack at night. Not very accurate, but it kept the troops from getting their much needed sleep and would do some damage. The principal defense against air attacks was a variety of antiaircraft guns. Japanese and American guns were similar in caliber, but not in quality. For example, the Japanese heavy machine gun was a 13.2mm weapon with a rate of fire of 450 rounds per minute (RPM). The equivalent U.S. weapon was the .50-caliber (12.7mm) machine gun with a 540-RPM rate of fire. The Japanese weapon had a higher effective altitude (13,000 feet versus 10,000), but this was less important than rate of fire for a machine gun that typically fired at aircraft a few thousand, or a few hundred, feet away. For a weapon of that caliber, it was also important to put a lot of bullets into the aircraft to have any effect. While the Japanese used a larger-caliber (13.2mm versus 12.7mm) bullet, American aircraft were far more resistant to such damage than their Japanese counterparts.

Medium-caliber antiaircraft guns showed the same discrepancies in quality. Both sides had a 40mm gun, but the Japanese used an older British design that had a meager 250-RPM rate of fire and a ceiling of 14,000 feet. The U.S. 40mm had a 420-RPM rate and a 22,000-foot ceiling. U.S. troops were also more liberally supplied with ammunition. Nevertheless, the Japanese managed to keep some antiaircraft guns operating until the end of the war, causing steady losses among attacking American aircraft.

SHORT IS SAFER THAN LONG

The U.S. Marines undertook some of the bloodiest amphibious assaults of the war. But their overall casualty rates were not as high as those of many Army units that engaged in less intense combat over longer periods. For example, the highest casualty rate sustained by a Marine regiment in one battle was much less than 100 percent (the 29th Marine Regiment sustained 2,821 dead and wounded in eighty-two days of combat during the Okinawa campaign in 1945). By early 1945, forty-seven infantry regiments in nineteen Army divisions had suffered at least 100 percent losses, and in some cases over 200 percent casualties, all in the European Theater. All of these regiments had been in action over three months, many for eight months or more. Marines tended to be in combat for short, intense island assaults. The Army regiments endured generally less concentrated combat, but were at it for much longer periods. The record for number of days in combat for a U.S. division is held by the 2nd Infantry Division, with 305. No Marine division even came close.

TROPICAL HELL

The health of troops can be greatly affected by the climate in which they operate. In tropical areas, the heat was a not-insignificant danger. Among Allied troops operating in tropical areas between 1942 and 1943, some 15 to 20 percent were victims of heat prostration and similar afflictions. Of these, about 2 percent died. This problem even affected naval forces, particularly submarines traveling on the surface, which were very poorly ventilated, the principal reason the U.S. Navy began experimenting with air conditioning on subs during the 1930s.

At the other climatic extreme, in subarctic and arctic environments, the situation is not quite so bad, provided reasonable care is taken to provide the necessary specialized clothing and equipment. Based on its experience in operating in higher latitudes, the U.S. Army determined that men from southern states were 3 to 5 percent more likely to succumb to cold-weather-induced problems (ranging from colds to frostbite) than were men from northern states. On this basis it seems reasonable to assume that Japanese troops, who generally came from a milder environment, suffered greatly during the Aleutians campaign.

HEAVY WEAPONS IN THE PACIFIC

Most of the firepower available to the infantry is found in its "heavy weapons." Machine guns, mortars, and light artillery were the principal heavy weapons. Later in the war, rocket launchers, flame-throwers, and some even more exotic devices were added to this arsenal of gear the troops had to carry around the battlefield.

Heavy weapons are so called not only because they generate heavier firepower, but because they are literally heavy. U.S. infantrymen—whether Army or Marine—had a 33-pound .30-caliber (7.62mm) "light" machine gun, as well as the 17-pound BAR (Browning Automatic Rifle). The BAR was a successful World War I weapon. It was basically the equivalent of a fully automatic M-1 with a twenty-round magazine, and was immensely popular. The favorite infantry machine gun was the .50 caliber (12.7mm). This weapon weighed 128 pounds and was best used in defensive situations where it could be brought forward by vehicle or, as often happened, manhandled forward by the troops. The .50-caliber bullet could be lethal even at a range of 3 miles (although it couldn't be aimed that far). There was also a heavier water-cooled 7.62mm machine gun for defensive situations (where the gun would be fired a lot, so it had a cooling water jacket around the barrel). At least you could lighten this weapon by taking the water out of the water jacket.

The principal Japanese machine gun was the Model 11 light machine gun (the "Nambu light"). This was a 6.5mm weapon based on a French design. Nambu was the name of the designer, a Japanese general, who was responsible for many Japanese weapons designs. The Model 11 weighed 22 pounds, with a thirty-round magazine. The Japanese had not yet mastered quality mass production and this was the cause of frequent reliability problems with the Model 11 (and most other Japanese machine guns).

A more recent (1936) version of the Nambu light also existed (the Model 96). There was also a 7.7mm version (the Model 99). This model also weighed 22 pounds. This weapon also had reliability problems and, like the 6.5mm models, had to use slightly weaker ammo to cut down on jamming. Since machine guns are most likely to fail when they are used a lot, as in the middle of a battle, the poorly manufactured Japanese machine guns spared many American soldiers death and injury.

Because of less plentiful and capable artillery, the Japanese equipped their infantry with more mortars. One of the more common models was the 50mm "knee mortar." This was so named because at first it was thought that the concave base plate meant it was fired while resting on a soldier's thigh, an impression furthered by pictures of Japanese troops posed in this fashion. This was found to be untrue after a few Allied soldiers had their legs broken while trying it. The Japanese pictures had been made because the troops looked tough that way. Weighing 11 pounds and firing 20- to 30-ounce projectiles, the knee mortar was widely used by the infantry because of its accuracy and 120- to 600-meter range. The Japanese 52-pound 81mm medium mortar (Model 99) was more conventional and could even use the ammunition of the U.S. 81mm mortar. The mortar could be broken down to three 17-pound loads for easy battlefield mobility. The shells weighed 7 pounds each. A heavier (145-pound) 81mm mortar (Model 97) had a longer range (3,000 meters, versus 2,000 meters for the Model 99).

The Japanese had an assortment of other, generally larger, mortars that were used as artillery and not carried around by the infantry.

U.S. mortars were of 60mm and 81mm varieties. The 81mm was similar to the Japanese Model 97. The 60mm mortar weighed 42 pounds and fired 3-pound shells as far as 1,800 meters.

Both sides used "infantry guns." These were artillery guns that were customized for direct fire. That is, these guns had sights and additional armor shields so that they could be used up front with the infantry to fire at enemy positions from close range. The idea behind this was that the fire would be more accurate, and it was. It was also difficult to haul these guns through the jungle and keep them supplied with ammunition.

The Japanese had a 500-pound 70mm gun for battalion-level support and a 1,200-pound 75mm gun for regimental support. Both had a range of 3,000 meters. The United States used a modified version of its standard 105mm artillery piece. This weapon still weighed nearly 2 tons but had a range of 9,000 meters and was often used like a conventional howitzer (fired "over the hill" at targets the crew could not see). Some U.S. units also used the old 75mm pack howitzer, which had a lighter shell and shorter reach, but theoretically could be broken down into manhandleable elements.

THE SOLDIER'S BEST FRIEND

The Pacific war was an infantry war, and the infantryman's personal weapons counted for more than in Europe. Most of the Pacific fighting was done in jungles and mountains, in general under conditions where the infantryman had to depend more on his personal weapons.

Most of the troops fighting in the Pacific used a combination of older (World War I–era) and newer weapons. The Japanese used a bolt-action rifle that was literally a World War I weapon, being a 1905 design. In 1941, most Japanese troops were equipped with the original 6.5mm 1905 design rifle. Most other armies had long since

U.S. AND JAPANESE INFANTRY RIFLES				
NAME	CALIBER	WEIGHT	ACTION	CAPACITY
Model 38	6.5mm	9.4 lb	bolt action	5-round magazine
Model 99	7.7mm	8.8 lb	bolt action	5-round magazine
M1	7.62mm	9.5 lb	semiauto	8-round magazine
M1903	7.62mm	8.6 lb	bolt action	5-round magazine

upgraded to 7.5mm- to 8mm-weapons, which had longer range, greater stopping power, and superior accuracy. Gradually, throughout the war, Japanese infantry were reequipped with a newer, 7.7mm version of the 1905 Arisaka rifle.

U.S. troops were much better off. While the troops who went into combat on Wake Island, Guam, and in the Philippines in late 1941 and early 1942 were still mostly equipped with the 1903 bolt-action (7.62mm/.30-caliber) Springfield rifle, the semiautomatic M1 Garand (also 7.62mm) rapidly replaced the Springfield.

The semiautomatic M1 could deliver about thirty to thirty-six aimed shots per minute, about twice as many as a bolt-action rifle. This was because the M1 would fire as quickly as you pulled the trigger, while the bolt-action rifle required you to pull the bolt back to extract the shell casing and then move the bolt forward to load another round. In combat most fire was aimed in only a general sense. Thus the higher rate of fire of the M1 (about fifty rounds per minute compared to about twenty) gave it an edge. As a semiautomatic weapon, it could fire as fast as you could pull the trigger. In a tight spot, which was normal for infantry combat, the ability to get off eight shots in a few seconds was decisive.

For well-aimed fire, both sides had sniper versions of their rifles. The Japanese used Model 38 and 99 rifles manufactured to higher production standards and equipped with telescopic sights. The United States used special M1903 Springfield bolt-action rifles equipped with telescopes. For well-aimed fire, a bolt-action weapon had an intrinsic advantage, although a good sniper was lethal with either type.

Japanese pistols came in a wide variety of types, both revolvers and automatics, most of which were 9mm. The principal U.S. pistol was the .45 caliber (11.4mm), which was originally designed for close-in jungle combat in the Philippines at the turn of the century.

The Japanese had no submachine guns, while the United States had two. The most popular was the .30-caliber (7.62mm) M2 carbine. This was actually a small rifle (weighing 5.3 pounds) firing a pistol-type cartridge. It came with a twenty- or thirty-round magazine. The M3 (or "grease gun") was .45 caliber (11.4mm), weighed 6 pounds, and had a thirty-round magazine. Neither of these weapons was accurate beyond 100 meters. But at night, in the jungle, the action was commonly a lot closer than that. The carbine was comfortable to carry, but distrusted by combat troops for the low stopping power of its lightweight pistol cartridge. Japanese infantry attacks were carried out with so much vigor that a large bullet was often needed to stop the hard-charging Japanese troops. For that reason, the grease gun was preferred. But the M3 was heavy and awkward to carry. It was also, because of its short barrel and pistol cartridge, accurate only at very short ranges. The carbine, because of its longer barrel, had greater accuracy when aimed and fired one shot at a time at longer ranges.

THE JAPANESE
NAVY GROUND FORCES

There was a bit of culture shock when America went to war with Japan. U.S. troops knew little about Japan, and were forced to learn a lot in a short time once the shooting started. One of the "good news, bad news" surprises was the SNLF. At first, we assumed that these were Japanese marines. Well, they were, sort of. But not nearly as tough as the U.S. variety.

As with most maritime powers, Japan had occasion to send troops ashore quickly when all it had available was warships sitting off the coast. The Japanese Navy, like most navies, would simply arm sailors and have them land. If the warships involved were not going to move around or get into heavy combat themselves, a third or more of the crew could be sent ashore as infantry—for a week or so, anyway. As recently as 1914, during World War I, America had done the same thing, most obviously in Mexico where sailors landed at Veracruz as infantry and seized the city.

America also had some Marines on each ship to send along with the sailors and contribute some expert advice on infantry operations. Marines (soldiers serving on board ships) were an ancient tradition, as until the introduction of cannon, naval battles largely consisted of ships colliding and infantry fighting it out as if on land. When cannon came along, there was much less emphasis on infantry combat afloat. Some infantry troops remained on ships and these evolved during the past few centuries into soldiers who served as guards on ships, helped man the big guns, and, when needed, went ashore to take care of infantry business. Japan, because it got started late in the warship business, didn't develop marines in the traditional sense.

Yet Japan ran up against a need to land troops from warships along the China coast in the 1920s and 1930s. This worked pretty well because Japanese sailors were given infantry training as well as instruction in seamanship. By the early 1930s, the admirals were getting tired of seeing their crews stripped of sailors to take care of some emergency ashore and decided to do something about it. Thus was born the Special Naval Landing Force (SNLF). These were sailors trained and equipped to fight ashore. Their weapons were identical to those used by the Army, and their uniforms were very similar. One of the differences, however, was the use of an anchor symbol on the steel helmet instead of a star (which the Army used.)

The SNLF was organized into large battalions of 1,000 to 2,000 troops, using a wide variety of weapons. Each of the four major Japanese naval bases (Kure, Maizuru, Sasebo, and Yokosuka) was ordered to organize one or more of these units (called Rikusentai in Japanese.) A dozen SNLF battalions were organized before and during the war, as well as many other specialized Navy ground combat units. To put it in perspective, the U.S. Marines during World War II organized some 100 battalion-sized combat units, while only about three dozen (of all types) were created by the Japanese Navy's ground forces. Or, put another way, there were about five times as many American Marines as there were Japanese Navy ground troops.

After Pearl Harbor, the SNLF spearheaded the Japanese Navy's offensive into the South and Central Pacific. It was SNLF units that

seized the Pacific islands such as Wake and the Gilberts. In cooperation with Army troops, SNLF also participated in the attacks on
the Dutch East Indies (Indonesia) and Rabaul (the major naval base
just north of the Solomons and Australia).

Because of the huge size of the Pacific battlefield, the Japanese
Army and Navy had to divide the ground-fighting chores between
themselves. In the wide-open spaces of the Central Pacific, with few
islands, it was often an entirely Navy show. The Japanese Navy had,
in addition to all those warships, its own land-based aircraft and
ground forces. But the Navy was also forced to defend most of these
islands against the expected American counterattack. For this purpose, the Japanese Navy organized special "island defense units."
They were similar to SNLF except that most of their weapons were
antiaircraft guns for defending against air raids. The principal duty
of these company (100 to 200 men) and battalion (500 to 1,000
men) units was the local defense of out-of-the-way islands and their
airfields. The Japanese had dozens of these islands garrisoned in this
way. The aircraft they guarded were used to patrol the vast stretches
of the Pacific that the Japanese held sway over early in the war.

The Navy was also responsible for building these bases, or rebuilding ones they had captured. For this purpose they established
Naval Construction battalions. These were similar in function to the
U.S. Navy's famed "Seabee" battalions. The Japanese units were
much less efficient, however, as they had little in the way of earth-
moving equipment and special construction tools. Most work was
done by hand and about 80 percent of the personnel were Koreans
or Taiwanese conscripted for this purpose. Actually, there were two
types of Naval Construction battalions. One, the Setsueitai (or
Combat Engineers), was about 30 percent Japanese and did the
skilled work. These units had 800 to 1,300 troops. The other type
basically consisted of labor battalions and only 10 percent of its
strength (the supervisors) was Japanese.

When America began its drive across the Central Pacific in late
1943, the first Japanese garrisons it attacked consisted largely of
SNLF and other Japanese Navy ground forces. The closer the U.S.
Marines got to Japan, the more Japanese Army troops they encountered. General MacArthur, meanwhile, fought largely against Japanese Army units in his campaign from New Guinea to the
Philippines, as did the British in Burma and the Chinese in China.

Even in 1942, when the Marines came ashore at Guadalcanal, they encountered a Japanese Navy construction battalion (whose largely Korean troops fled into the jungle rather than fight). When the Japanese mustered forces for their counterattack on Guadalcanal, it was with Army troops.

Thus the SNLF was largely found as garrisons on small islands in the Pacific. Like the U.S. Marines, the SNLF's main purpose was seizing forward bases for the Navy, and then holding on to them. Beyond that, there were many significant differences between the SNLF and the U.S. Marines (USMC):

1. The USMC had a long tradition as highly trained and disciplined assault troops. The U.S. Marines were always distinct from the sailors they served with. The SNLF troops were sailors trained and equipped as infantry.
2. The SNLF officers were simply naval officers assigned to land combat duty. USMC officers were strictly Marine officers. Thus the USMC leadership was far more expert at commanding infantry operations than its SNLF counterpart.
3. USMC units were specially equipped for amphibious warfare. While their gear included much that was identical to what the Army used, where necessary unique weapons or equipment was developed. The SNLF had very little special equipment. In particular, the SNLF never had anything like the array of specialized amphibious equipment used by the USMC.
4. The USMC was primarily an amphibious assault force while the SNLF spent most of its time guarding bases. The USMC also had "base defense units," but these were a handful of battalions compared to nearly 100 assault units.
5. The USMC, by tradition and training, was an elite force that was expected to, and usually did, successfully undertake very difficult assignments. The SNLF, on the other hand, was not even considered as capable as its Army counterparts.

In short, there never were any Japanese marines. The SNLF troops were sailors serving ashore as infantry and that's as far as it went.

DEADLIER THAN A SPEEDING BULLET

Your chances of getting hurt by enemy action in the Pacific were much less than the risk of being laid low by disease or heat. Prior to the twentieth century, all wars had seen more troops killed by disease than enemy weapons. In this century, the weapons got more lethal, and the tools to deal with disease became more effective. But no one had fought a major war in the Pacific before, so all concerned received a rude shock when they confronted the unhealthy climate and abundance of tropical diseases there.

Early in the war, before the full extent of tropical diseases was evident, Allied troops suffered up to 100 (or more) disease and heat casualties for every combat casualty. Quickly realizing how serious the problem was, the Allies reduced this ratio to 60 to 1 in 1944 and 40 to 1 by the end of the war. While most of these injuries were not fatal, they did put the affected soldiers out of action for days, weeks, or longer. Many infected soldiers had to be discharged and left to suffer the rest of their lives from diseases that, to this day, are incurable. Many of these infections recur for the rest of the victim's life, and often shorten that life in the bargain. Many veterans of World War II still suffer from the tropical bugs they picked up during their service in the tropics.

In Europe, which was a relatively "healthy" battlefield, 51 percent of days lost were due to disease, while 49 percent were caused by combat injuries (which, while fewer, tended to tear up the victim more and require longer to recover from). In the Pacific, combat caused less than 20 percent of days lost. Don't be misled by the seemingly lower combat casualties in the Pacific. There were other enemies out there going after the troops, and the bugs and microbes were far more effective than the Japanese.

The most troublesome disease in the Pacific was malaria. This infection came in many varieties, some worse than others. None was curable. Fully half the U.S. casualties in the Pacific were caused by malaria. Although not usually fatal, it was debilitating. At any given time during the war, 3 out of every 1,000 troops in the Pacific were out of action because of malaria; many more would have the disease but be able to function, more or less. Since sailors aboard ships on the high seas were safely away from the mosquitoes that carried the disease, and most rear-area bases had exterminated the local mosquitoes, their rate of infection was much lower. But the combat units in the jungle were hit very hard. Over 10 percent of the combat troops would be out of action because of malaria in good times, and in some places, like Burma, close to half the men in a unit would be laid low.

If the troops in malarial areas took their quinine medicine daily, they could avoid infection. But the medicine was considered by many troops to be nearly as unpleasant as the disease, so many were not religious about taking it. Moreover, the quinine didn't always work. What was most effective was the use of DDT to eliminate the mosquitoes. DDT has since been outlawed (because it causes some bird species to die out) and the death and disability toll due to malaria has risen back to its normally high levels.

Early in the war, when told that measures should be taken to control mosquitoes, one Marine general—apparently Vandegrift—said, "I'm here to kill Japs, not mosquitoes." As a result, malaria casualties in his division were unnecessarily high.

To make matters worse, some islands had particularly lethal strains of malaria. In one case, an Allied air-base-building project (and the island, in the Santa Cruz group) was abandoned because the local flavor of malaria was so lethal, even with most of the mosquitoes laid low by DDT.

While malaria was the biggest health problem, there were plenty of others. One of the more obvious ones was heat. Most of the Pacific fighting was done under tropical conditions, and the summers in the tropics were brutal. In the first year or so of the war, before the troops were trained to deal with the heat, about one in six suffered from heat exhaustion and similar disabilities. About 2 percent of those so afflicted died. As usual, this fell hardest on the combat troops who, unlike their rear-area brethren, could not always "stop and cool down" or get prompt, and lifesaving, aid when the heat laid them low.

The one bright spot in all this was that the horrendous tropical living conditions hurt the Japanese even more. While the Allies had numerous highly trained doctors and medics, as well as plentiful medical supplies, the Japanese were much less well off. This was first seen clearly during the 1942 battle for Guadalcanal. American infantry battalions would lose about 25 percent of their strength to disease after three months in the jungle. The Japanese battalions lost 50 percent. While the Americans improved their techniques for dealing with tropical diseases, the Japanese did not do so to the same degree. Were it not for the Japanese custom of not surrendering and fighting to the death, they would not have been able to hold out for as long as they did in the Pacific jungles.

While U.S. practice was to get incapacitated (by wounds or disease) soldiers back to a field hospital within hours, the Japanese often had no hospital to evacuate their injured troops to. Japanese soldiers were expected to grit their teeth and endure the pain of wounds or debility of disease. Japanese soldiers would literally lie down and die without complaint. Their comrades thought nothing of it, as this was the way it was supposed to be for a Japanese soldier. Because the Japanese lacked the logistical resources of the Allies, they were unable to provide the same kind of medical support to their troops. But the Japanese did not think they would need it, and when they, and the Americans, discovered to their shock what a formidable foe the tropics were, it was too late. As much as Allied troops despised the heat and the diseases, these afflictions turned out to be remarkably effective auxiliaries in the war against Japan.

ABOVE AND BEYOND THE CALL OF DUTY

In many ways, the fighting in the Pacific was different from that in other theaters of World War II. But in one respect, it was *very* different. Infantry fighting was the most dangerous form of fighting worldwide, but in the Pacific it was particularly lethal. The vast majority of the amphibious operations in World War II took place in the Pacific and these operations featured some of the most desperate fighting ever. The U.S. Marine Corps got the bulk of the toughest amphibious landings and as a result got a higher proportion of medals for valor under fire. For example, the U.S. Army infantry (no slouches in the valor department) got one Medal of Honor for every 800 troops killed. Many troops are killed in combat without having to do much of anything. There's so much firepower and chaos in battle that just being there makes you a very bad insurance risk. But the fewer troops killed per Medal of Honor is an indicator of how desperate the fighting was and what opportunities the troops had, and took, to do something "above and beyond the call of duty."

The Army cavalry troops (who were out front doing most of the scouting) got one for every 594 killed. The U.S. Navy got one for every 550 killed, largely because damaged ships, and the resulting damage control work, provided ample opportunity for sailors to perform feats of desperate bravery trying to save other sailors as well as the ship.

But it was the Marines who had the most impressive ratio of dead to Medals of Honor: 369. Moreover, the Marines were traditionally stingy with awards for valor. The thinking was, if you were a Marine, you were normally expected to be extraordinarily brave under fire.

In some ways, however, the Marines had it easier. Unlike their Army counterparts, who stayed in action for months at a time, many of the Marine amphibious assaults were over in weeks. The Marines were then withdrawn to bases far from the fighting where they rested and trained for the next operation. The Army infantry, fighting on larger islands, were pulled out of the line and sent to another part of the same tropical hell they were fighting in to "rest." The Marine divisions often had their home base in Hawaii, a far more salubrious tropical island than New Guinea.

THE REALLY IMPORTANT STUFF:

Production and Logistics

W hile the battles of the Pacific war were won or lost according to the courage and skill of the combatants, nothing at all would have happened if one side couldn't come up with the masses of weapons and mountains of supply. Even though the Japanese displayed an uncommon courage and persistence, it was no match for the massive production and more efficient logistics of America.

"GREETINGS . . ."

Responding to the increasing threat of war, on September 16, 1940, the United States enacted its first national peacetime military-draft law. The intention was to draft up to 900,000 men annually, for one year's service, in order to create a pool of trained men in the event of a national emergency. Only men between twenty and twenty-six years of age were liable under the terms of the Selective Service Act ("selective" because the intention was to take only some of the available men). Registration began on October 16, 1940, the first names were drawn in a lottery held on October 29, and the first batch of "selectees" were inducted on November 25. Since the first draftees were to be discharged in October 1941, the men joked that they were in the Army on the "OHIO Plan" ("Over the Hill in October"). Most of them didn't get out until 1945.

In the summer of 1941, with the German invasion of Russia and the desperate desert battles in North Africa, the president requested that the Selective Service Act be amended to extend tours of duty to as much as thirty months. Despite bitter opposition from a strange mélange of both right-wing and left-wing elements (although the Communists dropped their opposition as soon as Hitler invaded Russia), the amendment passed on August 18, 1941, squeaking through the House of Representatives by just one vote. The narrowness of this vote convinced many Japanese military leaders that the United States lacked the will for war.

During the period from the enactment of the draft to the surrender of Japan, about 30 million American men were registered with the Selective Service System. Of these, only 18 million received the famous letter that began "Greetings, your friends and neighbors . . ." Of these, 6.5 million were rejected for physical, mental, or moral shortcomings, so that only 11.5 million men were taken into the service. Initially all of the draftees were assigned to the Army, so joining the Navy or the Marines was one way a young man could dodge the draft. However, wartime pressures on manpower eventually caused both the Navy and Marines to dip into the pool of draftees as well. In addition to the drafted men, about 6 million men and 350,000 women volunteered for service, so that nearly 18 million men and women saw service during the war, exclusive of Filipino personnel serving in the Philippine Army.

National guardsmen began being federalized in September of 1940, and eventually about 350,000 guardsmen were activated, an impressive proportion of whom went on to become officers.

Without Selective Service, the United States would have been even less prepared for war than was actually the case. Of course, this didn't help the poor fellows called up in 1940, who ended up being in for the duration, most not getting out until mid-1945 and a few not until early 1946.

GETTING THERE AND BACK

Counting those who got there, were killed or wounded and sent home, nearly 12 million Americans served overseas during World War II. This was 73 percent of the 16.8 million that entered service. While the average time in uniform was thirty-three months, the average time overseas was sixteen months. Most went to Europe, but over 3 million served in the Pacific. Getting them there and keeping them supplied were no easy tasks.

U.S. ARMED FORCES AND TROOPS OVERSEAS (IN THOUSANDS)

	TOTAL TROOPS	OVERSEAS	% OVERSEAS
1940	458	164	36
1941	1,801	281	16
1942	3,859	940	24
1943	9,045	2,494	28
1944	11,451	5,512	48
1945	12,123	7,447	61

Before the war, a large proportion of the active personnel of the Army, Navy, and Marines were in places like Hawaii (not yet a state), Panama, and the Philippines. In 1940, conscription was begun and manpower in uniform grew enormously.

In 1940, the distribution of troops was still along a peacetime pattern. The Army had 59 percent, the Navy 35 percent, and the Marines 6 percent of total personnel. The Army Air Corps was a bit less than 10 percent of Army strength. In December 1941, the Army was the largest service, with 75 percent of the troops. Another 5 percent, the Air Corps, belonged to the Army (and became the separate Air Force after the war). The Navy had 17 percent of manpower and the Marines only 3 percent. Since the Marines were part of the Navy, the Navy total was 20 percent. As building programs for aircraft and ships produced more equipment, the relative size of the Army Air Corps and Navy grew. By 1945, the Army had 48 percent of troops, the Army Air Corps 20 percent, the Navy 28 percent and the Marines 4 percent.

Until 1943, nearly half of the Navy was operating in the Atlantic, to battle the German submarine offensive. Many of these sailors were operating out of U.S. ports and were thus not overseas (although they were often at sea for weeks at a time). But the Battle of the Atlantic was won during the spring of 1943, and from that point on a greater proportion of ships and sailors went to the Pacific.

The Navy had little problem getting to the Pacific, as the sailors had their ships. For the ground forces, it was a different matter; they had to obtain shipping to get them to where they were needed. Because of the German submarines in the Atlantic, and the need to send supplies to Britain and Russia, there was, at first, not enough

U.S. ARMY AND MARINE DIVISIONS IN THE PACIFIC

	ARMY		MARINE		TOTAL	
	ALL	PACIFIC	ALL	PACIFIC	ALL	PACIFIC
Prewar	8	2	0	0	8	2
1940	24	2	0	0	24	2
1941	37	3	2	0	39	3
1942	73	3	3	2	76	5
1943	90	9	5	3	95	12
1944	89	13	6	4	95	17
1945	89	21	6	6	95	27

shipping to get the ground forces overseas in great numbers. Before the war, the United States already had divisions in Hawaii and the Philippines. Although it was decided early on to give priority to defeating the Germans first, most of the divisions initially sent overseas went to the Pacific. By the middle of 1943 this changed, and most divisions went to Europe. By the end of the war, all U.S. divisions were overseas. If the invasion of Japan had gone forward, there would have been over fifty American divisions in the Pacific, including the six Marine divisions.

All of the divisions sent to the Pacific were infantry units. This helped a lot, because an armored division required twice as much shipping. An Army infantry division had 14,000 men and 2,000 vehicles, which normally required 100,000 measurement tons of shipping to move. Armored divisions had a few thousand fewer troops, but did have several hundred tanks and about 10 percent more trucks.

Shipping requirements could be cut by over 40 percent if the division's equipment was broken down as much as possible and "boxed." This method, however, required a fully equipped port (with piers and cranes) at the other end to get all the stuff off the ships. Moreover, it took several extra weeks at either end to box or unbox the equipment.

Amphibious landings required four times as much shipping as the boxed method because the gear had to be stored in the order it would be needed and had to be ready to operate as soon as it left the ship. This was called combat loading. As a result of this, it was preferable to send divisions to the Pacific boxed, unload them at a port and then reload them in the combat loading manner.

As a rule of thumb, for every soldier, airman, or Marine sent overseas, you initially needed 12 tons of shipping to get each person over there with the equipment needed to do the job. Thereafter, 1 ton a month of shipping was required to keep each individual in action.

In simpler terms, to send an infantry division overseas boxed required about six Liberty ships (the most common type of ship used by the Allies). To move that same division into a combat zone for an amphibious assault took about twenty ships of various sizes. A dozen of these would be APAs (cargo ships, often Liberty types, modified to carry combat-ready troops and landing craft); the rest would be LSTs (landing ship tanks) and other specialized amphibious ships.

Marine divisions were about a third larger than Army divisions.

But then, Army divisions usually went into battle with a few additional specialized battalions (armor, artillery, and so on).

While only twenty-seven divisions fought in the Pacific (out of ninety-five), this represented twenty-seven out of seventy-one infantry divisions available to the United States. That's 38 percent of the infantry units. The Marines' support requirements were similar to those of the Army, and were provided by the Navy. Thus those twenty-seven divisions required nearly 2 million troops (including replacements for the dead, sick, and wounded) to be shipped to the Pacific and then supplied while there. That meant over 20 million tons of shipping to get them there, and then as much as 1.5 million tons of shipping a month to keep everyone supplied. Toward the end of the war, many of the ships had to make a 12,000-mile round trip to reach distant Pacific bases.

When the war ended, the movement back home was, compared to the trip out, rapid beyond comprehension. Before the war ended, plans had been made for demobilization. The public did not pay much attention to this as it was simply looking forward to an end to the fighting. The officers charged with working out the details of demobilization thus drew up plans that, while reasonable on paper, did not take into account public reaction to victory. The government was shocked by the voter response it received after Germany surrendered. The people wanted their sons, husbands, and brothers home NOW. Since America was a democracy, this opinion could not be ignored.

Moreover, President Roosevelt died shortly before Germany surrendered and President Harry Truman (the former vice president) did not have Roosevelt's stature or communications skills. In office less than a month when the Germans capitulated, Truman ordered the existing demobilization plans to be discarded and all possible efforts made to get as many troops home as soon as possible.

The only fly in this ointment was the continued resistance of Japan. While there was now peace in Europe, the war still raged in the Pacific. At the moment Germany surrendered, Allied commanders thought Japan might hold out for another year. Moreover, it looked like an invasion of Japan itself would be necessary and this would require several million troops. In other words, many veterans of the European fighting would have to be transferred to the Pacific and sent into action once more.

This did not go down well with the American public, although it was understood that it would have to be. The troops in Europe weren't too happy about their pending transfer either. This was especially true of those who had already seen a lot of combat and, in many cases, had been in uniform since late 1940.

A compromise was improvised with the establishment of a point system to determine who would go home now and who would be sent to the Pacific. The system assigned points for each month of service, each month overseas, and each month in combat, plus additional points for fathers and the like. It was thought that this would keep the most heartrending transfers to the Pacific out of the papers. It worked.

While fair in a general sense, the point system had a very negative effect on the combat capability of those units sent to the Pacific. The men with the most military, and combat, experience were sent home and discharged. Nearly a million Army men were out before Japan surrendered, leaving the Japan-bound units filled with green and untried soldiers.

All this was scary to the officers commanding units stripped of their best troops and then sent to the Pacific for, according to the stories floating about, a tougher fight than anything encountered in Europe. The Germans were tough, but at least they would surrender when they knew they were beat. The diehard spirit of the Japanese had become widely known. Since late 1944, stories of the suicidal Kamikaze pilots, and the havoc they inflicted, were received with grim foreboding by GIs in Europe. Orders to move to the Pacific were seen by many of these infantrymen as a death sentence.

Until August 1945, few people knew about the atomic bomb, and a bloody invasion of Japan seemed inevitable. On the day Germany surrendered, fighting was still raging on Okinawa and the Philippines. The euphoria of defeating Germany was tempered by the fact that Japan was fighting on. While the divisions from Europe continued to make their way to the Pacific, there was a feeling that the war would end with yet another bloodbath. In early August, however, two atomic bombs were dropped on Japan. At the same time, Russian armies invaded Manchuria. A week later, the Japanese surrendered. V-J Day was a far more joyous occasion than V-E Day, for now the war was really over.

At this point the pent-up frustration with the war became politically unbearable. The Truman administration ordered the troops released from service forthwith. By the end of 1946, only 870,000 Army troops were still overseas, many of them recent draftees hastily shipped abroad to replace combat veterans on occupation duty. Every ship and aircraft available was pressed into service for Operation Magic Carpet, this retreat from foreign battlefields. The peak month was December 1945, when the Army alone sent nearly 700,000 troops home.

There was no thought of bringing things back. Thousands of aircraft, trucks, and tanks were dumped into the ocean or just abandoned where they sat. Thousands of buildings, plus docks, airfields, and other facilities were simply turned over to the locals (if there were any, and in some isolated places, there weren't). Veterans returning decades later to visit the battlefields of their youth would find many bases as they left them. Aside from the ravages of the weather and jungle growth, nothing had changed. The retreat from wartime was that swift.

AVERAGE SPEEDS FOR THE STRATEGIC PLANNER

Since different types of ships had different speeds, coordinating movements of large forces for offensive undertakings was no easy task. Consider the difficulties a fleet commander would have if he was trying to effect an amphibious landing on a hostile shore, supported by appropriate naval forces.

The Landing Force probably could sustain 12 knots, which was very likely its maximum speed as well, because LSTs could make no more than that, although they could do so for over 3,500 miles without refueling.

The Bombardment Group, consisting of old battleships assigned to soften up the landing beaches, could sustain 15 knots, and in a pinch make 20 or so for a while.

The Escort Group, with "jeep" (CVE) carriers providing close air support to the assault force, could sustain about 15 knots for short periods, but 12 was more practical for extended voyages.

The Support Group—the cargo ships, tankers, hospital ships, repair vessels, and so forth—could sustain 15 knots, albeit not for very long periods, 12 being more practical.

The Carrier Task Force supporting the landings could cruise at 15 to 25 knots for extended periods, and could maintain as much as 30 for days on end as well.

Now, making allowances for maneuvering, replenishment, and the like, the Carrier Task Force could cover 300 to 500 miles a day, and the Bombardment and Escort groups could probably manage 300, while the Landing Force and Support Group would be lucky to make 250. In addition, it was common to have submarines support operations, as a scouting screen and to pick up downed fliers, and these could cover only 200 to 250 miles a day. Note that on land, the average speed of a mechanized unit (when not fighting) was rarely more than 100 miles a day.

So the admiral in command had to juggle his task groups. This was one factor that made life on the fast carriers a grueling experience. While the slower ships maintained steady courses, the fast carriers ended up making huge circles around the ocean, moving back and forth in irregular patterns, so as to provide cover for the slower-moving ships. And in order to confuse the enemy as to location of the landings, the carriers would probably undertake air strikes at everything within range.

"WHERE'S YOUR SHIRT?"

Anyone who has seen the film *Mister Roberts* will recall that one of the captain's hobbyhorses was that all men had to wear their shirts at all times, even when working in the ship's stifling hold. This was not a figment of the author's imagination. One of the numerous petty regulations up with which U.S. sailors had to put during the Pacific war was the mandatory wearing of shirts, with sleeves rolled down at all times.

U.S. sailors were also prohibited from wearing short pants, unlike their Commonwealth comrades. As a result, while Australian and New Zealand sailors generally sported terrific tans, being practically naked while on duty and most of the rest of the time as well, American bluejackets tended to be rather pale. This may seem to have been a manifestation of militaristic authoritarian bureaucraticism, but it was actually a very intelligent and reasonable measure.

Quite early in the war, some prescient U.S. Navy medical personnel noted that there were significant differences in the severity of burns suffered by men who had been wearing shirts and those who had not, despite the fact that they had come through the same infernos. A little experimentation soon determined that the Navy's standard blue cotton denim work shirts and jeans actually offered considerable protection from burns, especially "flash burns" from on-board explosions. If flames touched a man's bare skin it quickly began to burn, but if they licked at his shirt it burned first, and the few seconds' grace was often enough to save a man's life, not to mention a good deal of his skin. Also, the shirt offered some protection against short but intense bursts of high searing heat. So the orders went out and American sailors sweated through the rest of the war. But while they were hotter, and paler, than their Commonwealth counterparts, they also tended to get burned less often.

By the way, the flash protection works only with cotton. All bets are off with polyester, which burns hotter and faster, and in the process adheres to human flesh, causing extremely serious burns. But then, during World War II the Navy issued only cotton uniforms.

The one common exception to these dress regulations was on board destroyers. The "tin can sailors" tended to dress any way they pleased, at least when not in immediate danger of engaging the enemy (at which point the long pants and long-sleeved shirts went on). Their workaday "uniforms" consisted of regulation dungarees cut down to shorts, homemade sandals, and sundry improvised headgear. Earrings and pigtails were often quite popular, as were beards. Since senior officers rarely visited destroyers, the bohemian lifestyle was maintained until the ships returned to port, at which point a certain amount of dress discipline was restored. For a time a similar regime prevailed under Captain T. L. Gatch on the battleship *South Dakota*. Gatch was allowed to get away with this because his "wild men" proved the best shots in the fleet, even if they happened to be virtually—and sometimes totally—naked at times. But after he was promoted upstairs, a less understanding skipper came aboard and the men had to tidy up.

FERRYING AIRCRAFT

Moving aircraft from one place to another was much easier, and more efficient, if it was a one-way trip with a friendly air base at both ends. Because such aircraft could use nearly all their fuel for movement (keeping a small reserve in case bad weather was encountered), a ferry flight could cover at least three times the distance an airplane would normally fly on a combat mission. For combat missions, the aircraft had to fly out and back, plus maintain a third of their fuel load for combat itself. Even bombers would burn more fuel over the combat zone in order to dodge flak or enemy fighters. As the war went on, aircraft were equipped with extra fuel tanks. These were often drop tanks (which could be dropped like a bomb when no longer needed), and during a ferry mission the normal weapons load was usually replaced with fuel. These techniques enabled normally short-range aircraft to be ferried long distances. The biggest danger during these operations was getting lost, so a larger aircraft with a navigator on board usually accompanied groups of fighters being ferried over large expanses of open water.

MOVING THE MERCHANTMEN AROUND

Merchant shipping had to go to a great variety of destinations. The Japanese in particular had to ship supplies to a widely scattered array of destinations. While submarines were not a threat to either side's shipping in the first year of the war, the long distances were. The weather in the Pacific could be treacherous, particularly since during the war normal weather reporting was interrupted because neither side had weather stations in enemy territory. Without accurate weather reports, merchant shipping was more likely to run into bad weather, and often would never be heard from again.

Japanese shipping was particularly inefficient, as each ship could belong to one of three different organizations (Army, Navy or an industrial organization), which didn't coordinate the use of their

TYPICAL DISTANCES FROM JAPANESE PORTS

DESTINATION	DISTANCE (IN NAUTICAL MILES)	DAYS
Japanese-Held Areas		
North China, Manchuria	900	15
South China	1,600	27
Indonesia	3,200	52
Burma	4,000	65
Central Pacific (Truk)	2,600	42
South Pacific (New Guinea, Solomons)	2,900	48
Philippines	1,800	28
Potential Japanese Targets		
"Far" South Pacific (Fiji, Samoa)	4,500	73
Hawaii	3,700	60
Alaska	2,500	40
Panama	8,000	129

NOTES: "Days" indicates the number of days a typical Japanese merchant ship would take to get to that area in the second half of the war. If operated efficiently, merchant shipping could steam 200 to 300 miles a day (making allowances for time spent in port moving cargo, or waiting to load or unload). "Potential Japanese Targets" are those areas that the Japanese considered going after, and the Allies feared might be attacked. However, you can see from the distances those areas were from Japan that these targets would have been very difficult to support. Supplying Hawaii would have required nearly 50 percent more shipping than it took for the Japanese bases in the Central Pacific. Panama was so far away that it would have taken a large fraction of the Japanese tanker fleet just to support a naval attack against the canal. Alaska, on the other hand, was not that far away from Japan. Most maps do not take into account the fact that the earth is a globe and thus do not accurately portray how close Alaska is to Japan. This is one reason why Japan attacked and occupied some islands off the coast of Alaska in 1942. This also explains why the United States fought back energetically to retake these Japanese bases.

shipping. As a result, Japanese shipping moved at an average rate of 60 to 70 miles a day. This included a lot of time sitting around port waiting for a cargo, even when there was something from one of the other organizations to be carried. Often, ships simply returned empty because of this lack of coordination.

Allied shipping was far more efficient, and this enabled the Allies to bring far more men and material to bear.

Most of the resources Japan imported (raw materials and food) came from China and Korea. These areas were relatively close to Japan.

Rare (but vital) ores like tin, and oil from Indonesia, had to be moved longer distances. More important, fuel, food, other supplies, and reinforcements had to be regularly shipped to the distant Japanese military garrisons.

GETTING THE STUFF OFF THE SHIPS

Moving men, equipment, and supplies from ship to shore in the Pacific was, particularly for the Allies, little different from an amphibious invasion. They had little choice, as the Japanese had grabbed most of the good ports in the Central and South Pacific early in the war. The Allies were never able to build their own ports and instead relied heavily on amphibious vessels to bring material from freighters to land bases. But rather than use their valuable amphibious shipping, when possible they brought in thousands of lighters (flat-bottomed coastal boats) to get the supplies from the freighters anchored in the deeper water to easily built shallow-water wharves on the coast. While practical, this method doubled the time to unload a ship, as the cargo had to be unloaded twice (once to the lighter and then from the lighter to the wharf or beach).

The Japanese did not have the resources to build a lot of lighters, or the engineering equipment and trucks to quickly build the many wharves, storage areas, roads, and other cargo-handling facilities to handle numerous amphibious operations. The Japanese did use a lot of barges, not just to bring cargo ashore but also to move it between nearby islands. Overall, however, the Allies had more to unload, and greater means to unload it faster.

NAVAL LOGISTICS IN THE PACIFIC

The warships were of little value without an enormous logistical tail to move forward fuel, munitions, and other supplies. This was provided by the fleet trains, composed of numerous different types of highly specialized vessels: fleet oilers for the warships, avgas (aviation fuel) tankers for the aircraft, ammunition ships, destroyer tenders, general cargo vessels, provisions ships, seaplane tenders, heavy repair ships, hospital ships, submarine tenders, floating dry docks, and a host of others, down to net tenders, water lighters, and "honey bucket" (excrement) barges.

Prior to World War II, all navies had come up with methods for sustaining a fleet at a distance from its base. These techniques consisted of ships designed to accompany the fleet and provide it with the necessities. But nearly all navies had thought of this function as of secondary importance. It was the U.S. Navy that gave this problem the most thought, and solved it by organizing the fleet train in much the same fashion as it organized the fleet: in task forces.

Although it took time to implement, since initially there was a shortage of all types of logistical support vessels, by early 1943 the U.S. Navy had a number of "servrons" or "service squadrons." A typical one might consist of some two dozen fleet oilers and avgas tankers, four ammunition ships, three hospital ships, six provisions ships, and four general cargo vessels, all escorted by a handful of destroyers and perhaps even an escort carrier. Such a squadron could sustain a modest task force for some weeks, until, nearing depletion, it was replaced by another, and the first squadron could go "back to the barn" to replenish.

By early 1944, Pacific Fleet servrons totaled some 450 vessels. Later in the war servrons had become specialized, so that there were several that just provided fuel, and one that was in the business of sustaining the aircraft of the fleet, providing replacement aircraft, spare parts, aviation fuel, and the like.

The Japanese were never able to duplicate this effort, even in the early part of the war, when they were winning. Even the British found the task difficult. One reason for the relatively modest size of the Royal Navy task force that served with the Third/Fifth Fleet during 1945 was Britain's inability to sustain a larger force with its own fleet train.

BLITZKRIEG ACROSS THE BEACHES

Amphibious warfare, putting troops ashore on enemy territory, is as old as naval warfare itself. And in the thousands of years of amphibious operations, the techniques did not change much. Up until the early years of World War II, the same ancient methods were being used to get the troops ashore. That is, merchantmen were commandeered to carry the men and weapons, and an impromptu arrangement of barges and smaller boats was used to get the infantry and their equipment from the ships onto the enemy beaches. It was slow, it was clumsy, but for thousands of years it had worked. After Pearl Harbor, all that began to change.

During the 1920s and 1930s, American and British officers began developing new ideas on amphibious operations. The basic thrust of this work was to do for amphibious warfare what mechanization had done for ground combat in the form of the blitzkrieg. This meant getting a lot of motor vehicles, including tanks, onto the beach in the early stages of an assault. To this end, the British invented the LST, which literally ran itself up on the beach, let down a ramp in its bow, and allowed the trucks and armored vehicles to roll right onto the beach.

The American contribution came from Marine and Army officers who developed new techniques for getting the troops ashore in LST-type boats and keeping the supplies coming at a volume befitting the Americans' "pile it on" style of warfare.

Once America was in the war, the American and British ideas fused and what we now think of as amphibious warfare became a reality.

These new techniques were needed, in both Europe and the Pacific, and for quite different reasons. In Europe, one had to get ashore quickly and in force in order to avoid being shoved back into the sea by the nimble and experienced German mechanized divisions.

In the Pacific, the problems were quite different. Many of the islands to be assaulted were so small that heavy enemy fortifications were right on the beach. This was also a problem in Europe, although you could often attack somewhere that was not heavily defended on the shoreline. But in the Pacific, an old-fashioned amphibious assault would not make much progress against the strong Japanese beach defenses. Even on the larger islands where, later in the war, the Japanese did not defend the beaches, it was essential to get the maximum amount of troops and firepower ashore quickly in order to disrupt the strong Japanese defenses inland. The new amphibious warfare did not see its full potential until

1944, but even in 1943 the new equipment and techniques began to have an effect.

The Allied revolution in amphibious warfare depended, like its land counterpart, on mechanization and organization. There were three items that composed most of what is now considered modern amphibious warfare:

- Specialized amphibious warfare ships. Not just the LST, but also the many smaller amphibious ships and boats. Thousands of these had to be built and proper tactics had to be developed.
- Amphibious vehicles that could quickly go ashore and thereafter operate as land vehicles. These were the DUKWs, LVTs, and armored vehicles that could be floated ashore.
- Logistical arrangements that were capable of supporting all this new equipment once it got ashore. The U.S. Army took the lead in this area, with its amphibious engineer (actually logistical) units. The USN and the British adopted most of the techniques the U.S. Army pioneered.

By the end of World War II, Allied amphibious operations reached a peak in terms of capability that has not been equaled since.

AMPHIBIOUS WARFARE SHIPS

The most noted of these was the LST. But there were many others besides, and when used together they provided a formidable amphibious capability.

LST (LANDING SHIP TANK). Nearly 1,000 of these 300-foot ships were built from 1942 to 1945. They could carry as many as twenty tanks, and put them right onto a beach. The beaching process was not without its shortcomings. While the ship had a full load displacement of 4,000 tons, it could only be at 2,400 tons when running up on the beach. Even at that weight, there was usually damage done to the LST. The average landing operation would render 10 percent of the LSTs involved unfit for further service. Moreover, the wear and tear on those that survived the run up onto the beach was such that, during the war, only about 85 percent of the

LSTs still operational were actually fit enough for another landing. In effect, after about ten landings, an LST was a wreck and no longer usable. This was typical of all ships that ran up on beaches to disgorge their cargo. The LST was basically a modified transport and, as such, was rather slow (8 knots normally, with a maximum speed of 11 to 12 knots). Normally it carried a crew of some 100 and was usually armed with eight 40mm antiaircraft guns. LSTs were often converted to other uses, especially when they had only a few more beach landings left in their tortured hulls. Some ended up serving as repair ships, PT boat tenders, floating barracks and supply dumps, casualty evacuation ships, and even improvised air-craft carriers for light reconnaissance planes (eight of which could be operated off a portable airstrip set up on deck). It was often said that "LST" meant "large slow target," because of their slow speed and weak antiaircraft armament.

LSM (LANDING SHIP MEDIUM). This was a smaller version of the LST. Nearly 600 were built during 1944 and 1945. LSMs were, in fact, the smallest oceangoing vessels capable of making beach landings. At full load, these vessels displaced 1,000 tons, but had to be only 740 tons to run up on a beach. Some 200 feet long and with a crew of fifty to sixty, they were armed with only two 40mm antiaircraft guns and had the same speed (8 to 12 knots) as LSTs. An LSM could carry several tanks, trucks, and jeeps. Although their carrying capacity was only about the same as that of an LCT, LSMs had much superior seagoing qualities. This made them useful for small, short-range transoceanic amphibious operations, particularly in places like the Southwest Pacific. Their smaller size allowed them to get into some places LSTs couldn't reach. There were also many cases where only a few vehicles had to be delivered some-where, thus it was cheaper to risk an LSM going up on the beach rather than a larger LST. Some LSMs were converted into inshore fire support vessels, armed, for example, with a 5-inch gun, several mortars or AA guns, and several score rocket launchers. The most preferred armament was the 5-inch rocket, the LSM being capable of getting off thirty rockets a minute when equipped with an au-tomatic loader. Nearly fifty of this version were put into service, some of them being modified during construction for rocket-launching duty.

LCI (LANDING CRAFT INFANTRY). Smaller still than the LSM, being only 153 feet long and 246 tons (387 tons at full load). About 1,000 were built, plus 300 gunship versions and 49 used as flotilla flagships. LCIs could carry about 200 to 250 infantrymen with their equipment. After running aground, the craft let down two ramps, each allowing a single file of troops to walk down onto the beach. Depending on beach conditions, the troops might still have to wade through ankle- to knee-deep water. Crew size was 25 to 30 sailors. Top speed was 14 knots, making them a bit faster than LSTs and LSMs. Armament was four or five 20mm antiaircraft guns. Some were specialized for fire support missions, with crews of 78 men, armed with three 40mm antiaircraft guns and a ten-tube, 5-inch rocket launcher. LCIs were ideal for operations such as the Tinian landings or the many short-range assaults in the Southwest Pacific, since they could be loaded in friendly ports and make the short sea voyage necessary to get to their objectives. While the LCI was seagoing, its sea-keeping ability and fuel supply were too meager to get very far over open seas.

LCT (LANDING CRAFT TANK). Similar in size to the LCI, but designed to carry vehicles over short distances, up to 100 miles or so. There were two main designs; average length was 115 feet, full load weight 290 tons. They had a bow ramp for discharging three or four tanks, or several more trucks and jeeps, or about 150 tons of cargo. They were slow, with a top speed of 8 to 10 knots. The crew consisted of a dozen officers and men. About 1,000 were built, and some were converted to gunships (firing rockets).

LCVP (LANDING CRAFT, VEHICLE AND PERSONNEL). This was the amphibious assault vessel most frequently seen, especially in photos and film, landing troops and vehicles. Basically a boxy boat with a hinged front ramp, it was run up on the beach to disgorge thirty-six assaulting infantrymen directly into action, or could carry one or two jeeps or trucks, depending on size and load, or a tank. Numerous types existed, but all were very small (about 8 to 12 tons empty, and 36 feet long) and capable of being carried aboard AKAs, APAs, LSTs, and just about anything else. Somewhat larger versions were known as LCMs (landing craft medium), running about 23 tons empty, with a length of 50 feet and a capacity to lift sixty armed troops or a tank into action, or carry over 25 tons of cargo. LCVPs had a crew of three, LCMs of four. Other nations, including Japan, had adopted variations on the LCVP before World War II. But only America and Britain went on to develop a wide variety of larger "run them up on the beach and unload" craft.

In addition to those ships that literally "hit the beach," there were a number of other more conventional ship types used that did not run up on the beach.

APA (ATTACK TRANSPORT). Merchant ship of from about 6,800 to 21,000 tons at full load, modified (or built from scratch) for the transport and landing of assault troops. Most carried 1,500 troops, plus fifteen to thirty-three LCVPs and two to four LCMs. These are the ships from which the troops climbed down the cargo nets to get into the LCVPs. Nearly 150 were built or modified for APA service between 1942 and 1945. Landing a division required about a dozen APAs. Crew size was about 500 men; speed was 15 to 20 knots and armament varied, but usually included one or more 5-inch or 3-inch guns plus up to a dozen 40mm antiaircraft guns.

AKA (ATTACK CARGO SHIP). Merchant vessel of about 4,000 to 8,000 gross tonnage, specialized for the rapid unloading of military cargo in a war zone. In addition to landing craft and machinery, the cargo was loaded so that those items needed first could be unloaded first. This was called combat loading. Not all of these carried LCVPs, LCTs, and LCMs. Those that did had a dozen or so LCVPs, up to eight LCMs, and one LCT. AKAs also used the small craft from the APAs or LSDs to land supplies. Crew size (100 to 400) and armament (several 3-inch or 5-inch guns and up to eight 40mm antiaircraft guns) varied with ship size. While some were specially built as AKs, many of the early ones were merchantmen quickly taken into service. Top speed varied between 12 and 20 knots. Over 200 were put into service between 1942 and 1945.

LSD (LANDING SHIP DOCK). Twenty-two of these 454-foot, 4,500-ton ships were built between 1942 and 1945. Each literally had a dock inside its stern, so that preloaded landing craft could be carried long distances. An LSD could carry two or three loaded LCTs or LCMs or as many as fourteen loaded LCVPs or LCMs. But this was not their principal value. The internal dock allowed them to provide on-the-spot repair facilities for LCTs, LCMs, and LCVPs (and other small boats, like PTs). Given the beating these smaller craft took going up on a beach, it was quite an advantage to have an LSD handy after a landing. The amphibious craft were used heavily after the initial landing to bring supplies and reinforcements ashore. LSDs had a crew of 240, a top speed of 15 knots, and armament of one 5-inch gun and twelve 40mm antiaircraft guns. The LSD became the model for many post–World War II amphibious ships.

AGC (AMPHIBIOUS COMMAND SHIP). All but eight (two were converted prewar cargo-passenger ships, the others Coast Guard cutters) of the twenty-four AGCs were specially built from 1943 to 1945. The crew of over 600 was needed to man the elaborate communications arrangements for air control, fire support coordination, and the like. AGCs were the nerve centers of amphibious operations. The specially built ones were 435 feet long and displaced 7,430 tons. Top speed was 16 knots and they were armed with two 5-inch guns and eight 40mm antiaircraft guns. The two conversions were a bit smaller and the Coast Guard cutters were only 2,200 tons. The AGC was a small, but key, element of the amphibious armadas formed during the war. Simply having hundreds of specialized amphibious craft for an operation was not enough. All these ships had to be carefully organized and supervised during the landing and the "over the beach" support operations that followed. The Japanese never realized how crucial the one or two AGCs in each invasion fleet were. The loss of an AGC during a landing would have been catastrophic, as the resulting confusion would have made the landing force much less effective.

AMPHIBIOUS VEHICLES

Getting to the beach in force was a major accomplishment of World War II amphibious technique, but it often wasn't enough. Landings were at most risk in the first hours, and getting across the beach and inland quickly, during the first moments of the landing, was quickly seen as a crucial task. Two solutions were found and both were versions of land vehicles modified so they could get ashore on their own.

In late 1943, the U.S. Army started using the **DUKW** (called "ducks"). This was, essentially, a standard Army truck that could swim. The Army "deuce-and-a-half" truck, a six-by-six (power to all six wheels) vehicle with a 5,000-pound (21/2-ton) carrying capacity, was used. What turned a deuce-and-a-half into a DUKW was a metal box into which the truck's components were fitted. In effect, the DUKW was a cross between a truck and a flat-bottomed boat. A fully loaded DUKW weighed 8.8 tons and was 31 feet long, 8.3 feet wide, and 7.1 feet high. It could go as fast as 45 miles per hour on roads, and about 6 miles an hour in the water. One tank of fuel would carry it 220 miles on roads and 50 miles in water. There was also a smaller version of the DUKW (a "jeep" version weighing 2 tons), but few were manufactured or used. DUKWs spent most of their time ferrying supplies and troops (up to twenty-five men) from ships offshore.

A total of 21,147 DUKWs were built and they proved invaluable in getting men and matériel ashore more quickly than via larger boats that had to beach themselves. Moreover, the DUKW could go places the beaching boats couldn't. Coasts often had mud flats, sand bars, and reefs that only the DUKW could get over. The DUKW could also propel itself up to a sand spit, drive across, and then continue through the water.

Because the DUKW didn't throw itself onto a beach, it suffered less damage coming ashore than amphibious ships that did. All that sand and salt water did considerable damage to the DUKWs. Like ships and carrier aircraft, the DUKWs were constructed of sturdier materials than trucks. But even so, the tires and brake shoes had to be replaced frequently and a DUKW didn't last as long as a regular Army truck (100,000 miles or more).

By 1944, the DUKW was moved to the combat area by LSTs and then used to quickly move supplies from LSTs and cargo ships offshore to the beach and then inland to the front line. This became a remarkably efficient system, with infantry regiments able to radio the LST-based "DUKW Motor Pool Headquarters," request specific supplies, and then see them arrive within hours. Casualties could be evacuated with equal dispatch to hospital ships offshore. All of this was unprecedented in warfare at that time and was truly a revolutionary step in amphibious operations.

As useful as the DUKW was, it was basically an unarmored truck and was not capable of standing up to the enemy fire encountered during the initial landing. The U.S. Marines came up with another amphibious vehicle for that task; the "Alligator" (or LTV, for landing vehicle tracked).

The **LVT** was originally a prewar civilian vehicle developed for use in the marshlands of Florida. It was tracked like a tank and could swim. By late 1942, the Marines had it in service. Over 10,000 were produced before the war was over. Larger (several feet wider and higher, although a few feet shorter) and heavier (up to 16 tons for the armored version) than a DUKW, the LVT also cost over twice as much to build and required more effort to maintain. Moreover, it was not as fast as a DUKW. This is a common difference between wheeled and tracked vehicles. The first LVTs were very slow, being able to make only 12 mph on land and 3 to 4 mph in the water. The definitive version of the LVT, which had a top land speed of 20 mph and 5 mph in the water, came out in 1944.

The 1944 model was still slower than the DUKW, but the LVT had several key advantages. For one thing, its tracks enabled it to cross obstacles more easily than the wheeled DUKW. This was very important on the day of an assault when the beach was torn up by combat. The Marines, more than the Army, hit the most heavily defended beaches. The LVT's ability to crawl over just about anything, and relatively quickly, was often the difference between life and death in those first hours of a landing.

Like the DUKW, the original LVT was not a combat vehicle. Lacking armor and heavy weapons, it was as vulnerable as the DUKW to enemy fire. Moreover, both the DUKW and LVT were slower in getting to the beach than the existing "slide-up-on-the-beach" landing craft. What the assault troops needed was an armed and armored LVT, and that's what appeared in early 1943.

The first "assault LVTs" were simply regular LVTs with armor bolted on. This gave the troops some protection from machine-gun fire and shell fragments. By the end of 1943, some of these LVTs had a turret-mounted 37mm gun added. What the Marines really wanted was a fully armored and heavily armed LVT, and this appeared in 1944. This, the **LVT(A)**, was, for all practical purposes, an amphibious light tank. Built at the factory as such, it had a turret with a 75mm cannon plus up to four machine guns. The armor made it pretty much immune to machine-gun fire and shell fragments. Several tons heavier, the 16-ton LVT(A) was also slower on land (17 mph on land and 5 to 6 mph at sea) than the unarmored LVT. Since enemy tanks were not expected on the beach, and the LVT(A) couldn't carry a large antitank gun anyway, the 75mm cannon was intended for use against enemy troops and fortifications. The LVT(A)'s machine guns were to give the assault troops additional firepower.

Fewer than 1,000 LVT(A)s were built and they were organized into nine "amphibian tank" battalions (each with seventy-five LVT(A)s, twelve LVTs, and 700 men). Three of these were Marine units and all were used in the Pacific. Of the six Army battalions, only one was used, in the Pacific. The other five Army battalions were to be used in Europe, in support of river-crossing assaults, but the war in Europe ended before they could get into action.

Had the Army paid more attention to Marine experience with the LVT earlier than was the case, it might have had several battalions available for D Day, which would have prevented the near disaster on Omaha Beach. The LVT(A) was the future of amphibious vehicles; it became the model for the post–World War II versions of the LVT that continue in use to this day.

LOGISTIC ENGINEERING

After the troops got ashore in strength, the fighting on the beachhead often went on for weeks. All that time, supplies and reinforcements had to come across the beach, while numerous casualties had to be evacuated in the other direction. It was the U.S. Army that first recognized the potential logistic problems of modern amphibious operations and came up with the solution.

In 1942, the Army began organizing engineer amphibious brigades, one of which would support each assault division. A 7,400-man engineer amphibious brigade would have two battalions operating over 100 small amphibious craft, and another two battalions staffed with engineers trained to get the supplies off the beach and to the right destination as quickly as possible. In addition, the brigade had a small artillery detachment to protect itself (all the engineers were, as was customary, armed and trained to act as infantry when needed). There were also two ordnance companies to perform on-the-spot repair of equipment, a maintenance battalion to keep all the brigade's equipment in working order, a quartermaster battalion to run the supply dumps, an LVT or DUKW company to help move supplies around on the beach, and a medical battalion to care for the wounded troops coming back from the fighting and then evacuate them from beach.

The Navy had been less energetic in dealing with the logistics of amphibious operations, partially because the Marines took care of the assault and the Navy did all the support chores. Although the Marines were part of the Navy, they were an increasingly independent part, and this was an example of how this could cause problems. The Marines tried to take care of beachhead logistics themselves and the Navy ignored any problems unless the Marines made an issue of it. The Navy *was* most sensitive about protecting its turf. When the admirals saw that the Army had organized six of these engineer amphibious brigades, protests were made.

As in many of these interservice squabbles, a compromise was reached. The Army was allowed to keep the six brigades it had created in 1942, but promised to not create any more. Meanwhile, the Navy copied the Army's idea to beef up its own logistic support for amphibious operations. The Army made extensive use of these engineer amphibious brigades in the Pacific, particularly during the New Guinea and Philippines campaigns.

The Navy was not without its innovations in the logistics of amphibious operations. The Navy created dozens of naval construction battalions (the "Seabees"), which were crucial in rebuilding (or creating from scratch) airfields and ship support facilities on islands. The Seabees were fast, carving operational airfields out of tropical jungle in days, often while beating off Japanese attacks in the bargain. This capability shocked the Japanese, except for those who had been to America and had seen what the extensive use of bulldozers and other forms of mechanization could do to speed up construction.

The combination of improved amphibious logistics and fast construction of new facilities made the fast pace of the American Pacific offensive possible. These innovations had not been foreseen by the Japanese and they were dismayed to see heavily fortified islands assaulted, conquered, and then begin operating as air and fleet bases within weeks. This was a radically new approach to amphibious warfare. Neither the Japanese nor anyone else since has come up with an antidote for the "other" blitzkrieg of World War II, the American fast-paced island-hopping offensive across the Pacific.

NEVER ENOUGH

As successful as American amphibious capabilities were, they did have limitations. There were never enough resources for all of the attacks the generals and admirals wanted to make. Limited resources were nothing new in warfare, but amphibious tactics *were* new and no one knew exactly what benefits would accrue if the amphibious shipping was sent in this direction or that.

Amphibious operations were an essential item both in Europe and the Pacific. While the European war needed amphibious shipping from time to time, in the Pacific there was a constant need for landing on enemy islands. But the Allies had early on agreed that the European war would be settled first. Thus Europe got first call on the scarce amphibious shipping.

In late 1942, North Africa was invaded by American and British forces. This took just about all the amphibious shipping the Allies had. In the Pacific, the Marines were holding out against the Japanese on Guadalcanal while the Army fought on in New Guinea. Amphibious shipping began heading to the Pacific early in 1943, but this changed as summer approached. Europe had first call on amphibious shipping beginning in the summer of 1943, as Sicily (July) and Italy (September) were invaded, and then the largest amphibious fleet in history was assembled for the cross-Channel attack in June 1944.

Through 1944, troops in the Pacific got amphibious shipping in dribs and drabs and had to be careful using it. Until the invasion of France was carried off, Europe needed landing ships to replace those that were inevitably lost running up on beaches. After the Normandy landings in June 1944, the Pacific got the shipping, and that's the main reason so many of the major Pacific landings occurred from late 1944 through early 1945. After the summer of 1944, Europe had little need for amphibious shipping, and much of what it had used for Normandy got sent to the Pacific.

ALLIED SEAGOING AMPHIBIOUS SHIPPING IN THE PACIFIC			
TYPE	SEPT. 1943	JAN. 1944	MAY 1944
LST	67 (159)	117 (127)	125 (198)
LCT	103 (638)	130 (687)	150 (853)
LSM*	60 (143)	105 (115)	113 (188)
LCI	62 (268)	101 (196)	115 (162)
APA	22 (35)	30 (31)	40 (40)

NOTE: Allied ships of that type in other theaters are shown in parentheses.
*Estimated.

Over 4 million tons of amphibious shipping (LST, LSM, LCI, LCT) were built during the war and over a third of that was lost, mostly to wear and tear. By the end of the war, nearly all of it was in the Pacific. The APAs are listed above because, although they didn't run up on the beach, they had to get in close to load and land the troops in the LCVPs. See also the table on page 346.

AMPHIBIOUS TASK FORCES

The shipping needed for a landing depended, of course, on the size of the landing force. The table on page 347 shows two typical landing operations of the Pacific war. One was relatively small, the other quite large.

Note that each operation used a quite different combination of specialized shipping. There were several other differences between the two landings that explain this. Guam was a Navy operation deep in the Central Pacific. Leyte was an Army operation within range of several land bases. Thus the Army could use shorter-range LCIs and LCTs. Indeed, these smaller ships were preferred by the Army in the Southwest Pacific, where there were many relatively small landings within range of land-based aircraft and nearby naval bases. Another major difference between the two operations was the size of the island being assaulted. Leyte was much larger than Guam and contained a larger Japanese garrison. Thus the Leyte assault

ALLIED AMPHIBIOUS TONNAGE (IN MILLIONS OF TONS)			
	SEPT. 1943	JAN. 1944	MAY 1944
Pacific	0.4	0.66	0.71
Total	1.5	1.6	2.0
% in Pacific	26%	42%	35%

required more tanks and trucks, which is seen in the greater number of LSTs and LCTs.

The table on page 347 does not show all the shipping used, and there were a lot of cargo and tanker ships involved. Generally, you needed fifteen to twenty Liberty ships (or their equivalents) to support a division-sized landing. The Liberty ships were quite large for their time, being about 16,000 registered tons. A division also required twelve to fifteen LSTs and LSDs to carry vehicles. LCTs, LCIs, and LSMs could be used instead of LSTs if the invasion did not require a long ocean voyage. Of course, you would need several of these smaller vessels to haul the load one LST could handle.

There were many other types of support ships. These included repair and hospital ships, to care for equipment and men injured during the operation.

Each amphibious task force also included dozens of escorts (destroyers and escort carriers) as well as bombardment ships (cruisers and battleships). The larger aircraft carriers normally operated in their own task forces and, being juicy targets, tried to stay away from enemy land-based aircraft. Moreover, enemy submarines could be expected to head for an invasion site, and this was yet another reason to keep the big carriers far out to sea. The carrier task forces often did come by to launch air strikes on the invasion site, but did not stick around like the escorts assigned to the amphibious task force.

PUTTING IT ALL TOGETHER

It wasn't until 1943 that the Allies got a chance to use their new amphibious techniques fully. The special amphibious ships began to appear in 1942, but it took another year and a few false starts

	GUAM, JULY 1944	LEYTE, OCT. 1944
Divisions	1.3	4
AGC	1	5
APA	34	32
AKA	7	10
LSD	6	10
LST	30	67
LCI	0	9
LCT	0	23

before many of the kinks were worked out of the system. In its final form, the new "blitzkrieg from the sea" went through the following drill when executing their assaults:

- CAREFUL PLANNING. In addition to finding out as much as possible about the enemy troops in the target area, use of the new "beaching" ships required detailed data on local tides and underwater geography. This requirement gave rise to the use of scuba divers to sneak in to obtain this information. Later, these "beach jumpers" evolved into UDTs (underwater demolition teams) that went in to demolish any man-made or natural obstacles off the coast to be invaded. Based on all this information, plans would be made stipulating where each ship and boat would be and when, in order to get the hundreds of ships and boats onto the right part of the beach.
- FLEXIBLE EXECUTION. Plans are what you hope to do, not precisely what you will do once your forces encounter an armed enemy. The troops have to be trained to deal with the unexpected, and the support forces (gunships, aircraft, and logistics units) have to be drilled on the many changes in plans that will occur once the shooting begins. The basic assault plan included destroying enemy air power in the area and driving away or destroying enemy warships. Then began several days of air attacks on the enemy units on the beach and behind it. This was usually done by aircraft from the large (or "fast") carriers. The amphibious task force was several hundred miles away during

most of this and moved at a speed of only 200 to 300 miles a day. When the preliminary bombardment was over, the amphibious task force appeared off the enemy shore. First minesweepers, protected by small warships, went in to clear lanes for the more vulnerable (and valuable) landing ships and transports. You had to be prepared to deal with anything unusual the enemy threw at you. A good example of this was the Japanese use of Kamikaze suicide aircraft in the Philippines. U.S. commanders had to deal with this radical new tactic while still moving forward with the amphibious attack.

- THE ASSAULT. Several miles off the coast (out of machine-gun, but not artillery, range) the APAs got their infantry into the LCVPs for the actual assault. This would be launched in waves, of which there might be half a dozen or more. The LCVPs and LVTs spent half an hour or more getting to the beach. Before, and during this time, destroyers, cruisers, and battleships were shelling enemy fortifications and blasting any enemy artillery that was still functioning. The Japanese learned to hold their artillery fire until the landing craft were very close, and then blast them at point-blank range. In response, Navy destroyers would come in as close as they could (without going aground, often only a few hundred yards offshore) and shoot it out with the enemy artillery. The plans for the landings made provision for destroyers running back and forth without getting mixed up with the 100 or more LCVPs and LVTs making their way to the beach. Once the assault troops had cleared beaches of enemy troops (not an easy task), subsequent waves could bring in larger ships containing tanks and, eventually, logistics units and supplies.

- VIGOROUS FOLLOW-UP. Getting ashore was, literally, only half the battle. The assault troops would have run out of ammunition, water and food if not resupplied. Casualties had to be taken off the beach to hospital ships. Once the troops got a few miles inland, artillery and engineer troops were brought in to provide fire support and build roads and airfields. Soon, the landing force would have land-based aircraft and a lot of artillery to help finish off the enemy force. But artillery and aircraft require mountains of supply. Thus the landing beaches remained hectic places for the duration of the battle. All day long, LSTs and other ships beached themselves and unloaded vehicles and supplies. These were driven inland to supply dumps. This immense logistical support was a major innovation in amphibious operations and provided the additional firepower that saved many lives among the fighting troops.

Allied amphibious tactics and techniques changed constantly during the war. After each landing, the experience was carefully examined and lessons learned were applied to the next assault. The enemy was also learning from his mistakes, so one had to adapt quickly just to avoid running into more formidable resistance during the next operation.

SOLDIERS AS SAILORS

Over 100,000 U.S. Army troops spent most of World War II serving as sailors. In an Army tradition going back to the American Revolution, the Army supplied most of its own ships for moving troops and supplies, as well as for launching over 100 amphibious assaults. As a result, the Army ended up operating more ships and boats than the U.S. Navy during the war.

It wasn't supposed to be this way.

During the 1930s, it was agreed that the Navy would control all shipping in any future war. This was more efficient, even though it flew in the face of historical experience. In the past, the Army had been reluctant to entrust its shipping to another service. There was always a fair amount of rivalry between the Army and Navy and, until the eve of World War II, the Navy had tolerated this situation. But with a pro-Navy president in the White House and logic on its side, the Navy got its way. However, the Navy soon regretted it. As the Army began handing over its many ships in 1941, the Navy realized that it could not provide crews for these vessels as well as all the new warships it was putting into service. So the Navy agreed to let the Army keep many of its ships, for the moment.

After Pearl Harbor, the situation became even more confused. In early 1942, Army commanders operating out of Australia were told to grab shipping any which way they could. The battle with the Japanese was desperate at that point and the Navy had more important things to do than argue with the Army about who controlled

COMPARISON OF U.S. ARMY AND NAVY SHIPS OF WORLD WAR II

SHIPS	ARMY	NAVY
Over 1,000 Tons	1,665	3,436
Under 1,000 Tons (seagoing)	1,225	6,228
Under 1,000 Tons (coastal or harbor craft)	19,750	4,070
Small Amphibious Assault Boats	88,366	60,974
Total	111,006	74,708

what ship. Moreover, the situation was so chaotic in the Southwest Pacific during that period that, to this day, no one is exactly sure how many ships General MacArthur had control over.

Back in Washington, the generals and admirals went at each other throughout 1942 over who would control what ships. A compromise of sorts was reached, but in actuality it was a victory for the generals. The Army went on to control more ships than the Navy by the end of the war. While one could argue that the U.S Army had the largest fleet during World War II, this would be only technically true. While the Army had some 1,600 large ships (over 1,000 tons in displacement), the rest of its vessels were much smaller. So while the Navy put to sea with over 12 million tons of ships, the Army had only about two thirds as much.

In addition to ships counted in the table above, the Army had 16,787 pontoon "boats" that were used to build bridges across rivers and, in a pinch, as ferries to get troops across rivers or other bodies of water. Since pontoons are not very handy (or useful) in ocean waters, these boats are not counted.

Moreover, the Army did have a lot of seagoing barges (8,596) that are counted in the table because these vessels were used at sea, pulled by the 4,434 tugs the Army operated.

As you can see, the Army "fleet" was basically a logistical support outfit that did most of its work in coastal waters. The Navy fleet was a high-seas combat organization. What combat ships the Army did maintain were for coastal operations, mainly for laying mines to defend Army-controlled ports.

The other major combat mission of the Army fleet was amphibious assaults. The Army conducted more of these than the Navy, if only because there were only six Marine divisions in the Pacific and four times as many Army divisions. All of the fighting in the Pacific was on islands of one sort of another and this made amphibious capability a necessity no matter what uniform the troops wore.

The Army fleet was thus heavy on troop transports and small ships that could keep the cargo moving from ship to shore. The Army also maintained its own hospital ships and vessels needed to keep all their floating equipment in good repair.

After World War II, the Navy finally did get control of everything that floats. But not before the Army presided over "the largest fleet in history."

CUISINE DE COMBAT

Ground combat is very stressful. And the amphibious battles in the Pacific were more nerve-racking than most. To help the troops along under these chaotic and deadly conditions, a special "combat ration" was developed. This was the K ration, and it put 3,000 calories of food in a 6" × 2" × 2" container weighing a pound and a half. This ration contained "meat" (actually preserved meat in the form of pemmican, or canned Spam), crackers, candy, beverage mixes, and cigarettes.

It was found that the stress of the first few days caused most troops to throw away everything but the candy and cigarettes. In the Pacific, this was recognized and an "assault ration" was developed that contained only candy and cigarettes. Not very nutritious, but it was what the troops wanted during the first few days of an amphibious invasion.

In addition to the K ration and the assault ration, the U.S. had a wide range of different types of rations for distribution depending upon circumstances:

A rations consisted of properly cooked meals made with fresh or frozen ingredients. They were served at bases and on ships.

B rations were properly cooked meals with all perishables obtained from canned goods. Where fresh vegetables or refrigeration were not available, troops would subsist on the B ration. Sometimes they would do this for many months.

C rations were for use in combat. They came in packets that were supposed to contain a full day's meals in the form of three cans containing various combinations of "meat" (which could include Spam or poultry) and vegetables, which could be eaten cold, plus three cans containing cigarettes, sweets, and other consumables. The pound cake was quite good and troops would trade the more popular items for larger quantities of the less favored ones.

D rations consisted of the "Logan Bar," an unpalatable but nourishing confection made from chocolate, oatmeal, and sugar, which the troops disliked intensely.

The Japanese supplied their troops with a special combat (or "iron") ration, which, per meal, consisted of a half pound of biscuits and extracts that provided about 1,000 calories. However, the Japanese often had a difficult time providing their troops with any food at all.

The normal Japanese diet was quite austere, based largely on rice, barley, vegetables, and a bit of fish or meat. In garrison conditions, each soldier was provided with 20 ounces per day of rice and barley, plus a cash allowance to purchase meat, fish, and vegetables. Soldiers would pool their money for bulk purchases that would then be cooked by members of the "mess group." The standard field ration was nominally 66 ounces per man per day. About half of this was rice and barley, another third vegetables, and the remainder meat and condiments.

Overall, the Japanese rations were about two-thirds the size of Allied rations. This was sufficient for the smaller Japanese, but led to malnutrition when Allied prisoners were fed this ration (as stipulated by the Geneva Convention, which said that POWs had to be fed what your own troops got).

When supply from the home islands was available, the Japanese had a wide variety of foods available in canned form, although much of it would not have been to an American's taste (seaweed, crabmeat, rice cakes, and bean paste). Even so, Japanese troops fighting in the Solomons and New Guinea often got no food at all, or at best got "emergency rations," which were one-third or one-half the size of the standard ration. Attempts to forage in the jungle were a mixed success and thousands of Japanese troops literally starved to death.

On bypassed islands, the Japanese grew their own food as much as possible, but it is known that a number of downed Allied fliers ended up as entrées. Many thousands of Japanese died of diseases made worse by malnutrition anyway. It was noted that when Japanese troops overran an Allied position, the first "loot" they went for was the food, which was often consumed on the spot. Allied troops in similar situations preferred inedible souvenirs, such as officers' swords, flags, bits of clothing, and small weapons. Of course, the Allied troops would just as often trade these battle souvenirs to rear-area troops and ships' crews for rare (on the battlefield) delicacies such as ice cream and whiskey. It is for this reason that so many sailors and Army noncombatant types came home with battlefield souvenirs, while the combat troops returned with only the memories of those rare feasts containing ice cream, fresh meat, and strong drink.

IN SUPPORT

Although the division is the principal combat formation of an army, it represents a relatively small proportion of an army's total strength. For example, at peak strength the U.S. Army totaled some 9 million men and women in World War II, of whom about two thirds were in the Army Ground Forces or the Army Service Forces. The eighty-nine divisions—sixty-eight infantry, five airborne, and sixteen armored—in the Army averaged about 13,800 men. This totals only about 1.2 million men. Where were the balance? The balance were helping to keep the front-line troops fighting.

For each division there were:

13,800 men (on average) in the division itself
13,000 men in combat support and service units
10,000 men in communications zone troops
20,000 men in miscellaneous status

Combat support and service units contain the guys providing extra artillery fire, engineer services, tank support, medical aid, and the like to the front-line troops, sometimes being on the front lines themselves.

Communications zone troops are the men and women (nurses, clerks) behind the front, who helped pass the ammunition, run the hospitals, and guard rear-area installations, plus replacements, hospital patients, and the like.

Miscellaneous status includes troops in the United States in training and hospitals, headquarters personnel, and so forth.

Adding these troops to the division's brings the total up to about
56,800 men per division. This is referred to as a "division slice," the
total number of troops in and supporting each division, all the way
back to fellows in the recruiting stations back home. The U.S. Army
had the highest division slice in the war, partly because of its propensity for consuming enormous quantities of supplies, and partially because the Army Service Forces supported Army Air Forces operations.

The division slice varied by theater. That for troops in the Central
Pacific was higher than that for troops in the ETO. The six Army
divisions that took part in operations in the Central Pacific Theater
had a division slice of about 76,000:

17,000 with the division

28,000 in combat support and service units

11,000 in service forces

20,000 in the United States

The sixty-odd divisions in Europe had a division slice of only
about 60,000 men:

15,000 with the divisions

15,000 in combat support and service units

10,000 in communications zone forces

20,000 in the United States

Other armies got by with considerably smaller division slices. The
Japanese in particular were frugal with their division slice, preferring
to put as many troops as possible in the front line. This proved to
be a wasteful policy in the Pacific, as the troublesome geography
and climate caused unsupported troops to waste away quickly in
combat. And this happened to the Japanese time after time.

NEW KID ON THE BLOCK

Japan was a rather recent arrival on the world stage in 1941, and
the rest of the world didn't quite know what to make of it.

What got everyone's attention was Japan's growing military prowess. From a defenseless, insular nation in the 1850s, Japan had modernized itself to the point where it was making war on China with Western weapons and techniques by the end of the nineteenth century. In 1905 Japan went on to defeat a European power, Russia. Allying itself with the Western Allies during World War I, Japan entered the 1920s as a recognized and proven major military power.

But something was missing, and that vital something was an economy that could support a world-class military machine. Until the 1930s, Japan had spent more effort on its armed forces than it had on industrializing. But while the rest of the world wallowed in the Great Depression of the 1930s, Japan made great strides in expanding its manufacturing capacity. Between 1930 and 1940, truck production increased nearly a hundredfold. Aircraft production went up nearly twelve times, shipbuilding increased five times, and steel production nearly tripled.

But it wasn't enough. Japan made these great strides by concentrating on the production of military goods. Much less progress was made in the civilian sector. This can be seen by the amount of government income spent on the armed forces. In the early 1930s, 29 percent was spent on the military. By 1940, the armed forces were taking two thirds of the national budget. Moreover, the government had grabbed much of the increased production wealth for its own use. Between 1931 and 1940, government income increased sixteen times.

To put all this in perspective, consider what America and Japan spent on armaments.

Much of what Japan spent in the late 1930s went to prosecute the war in China. The territories Japan conquered in 1942 were also ruthlessly plundered through 1944. By 1945, U.S. production was decreasing at a rapid clip and Japan's had fallen even more precipitously.

Only about a third of U.S. spending went to the Pacific, while nearly half of Japanese spending went into mainland Asia operations (China, Burma, and the huge garrison in Manchuria watching the Russians). Moreover, Japan also had to face Britain in the Indian Ocean and Burma. Britain's wartime armaments spending was twice that of Japan, although less than 10 percent of it went to the Pacific.

It was America that was literally "the Arsenal of Democracy." Throughout the war, the United States alone represented 52 percent of worldwide (Allies and Axis) aircraft production, 36 percent of all artillery production, 48 percent of all vehicle production, and 66 per-

ARMAMENTS SPENDING (IN BILLIONS OF 1995 DOLLARS)		
YEAR	U.S.	JAPAN
1935–1938	13.6	18.1
1939	5.4	4.5
1940	14.5	9
1941	40.6	18.1
1942	181	27.2
1943	344	43
1944	380	55

cent of all shipbuilding. Add Britain, Canada (which produced at 30 percent of Japan's level), and Russia, and you can see what dire straits the Japanese were in. Japan's only major ally, Germany, had total armaments production that was only 50 percent of America's and had to deal with Russia (which spent about half as much as America).

The Japanese disadvantage in armaments spending manifested itself differently depending on the branch of the military. The Japanese Navy was carefully built up during the thirty years before the war. Well-designed ships and weapons plus skillful crews gave Japan an advantage at the beginning of the war. But the lack of resources did not allow for the replacement of wartime losses. Japanese admirals went into the war expecting to take up to 50 percent losses. When they suffered far less in the first few months, they got overambitious, and the result was a string of devastating defeats from Midway onward through the end of 1942. Japan didn't have the ability to replace those losses.

The Japanese air forces (both Navy and Army) were in a similar, although more complex, situation. Japan could build a lot of aircraft, but air force leaders were unwilling to lower their prewar pilot selection standards. The result was that aircraft were replaced after heavy losses in 1942, but pilots were not. U.S. air force commanders did adapt their pilot training to wartime needs and were thus able to achieve air superiority in the Pacific from 1943 on. But even if Japan had implemented more efficient pilot training, it would have done little more than cause more losses to the Americans. The United States would still have had air superiority by 1943.

The Japanese Army was least affected by Japan's armaments disadvantage. The Army was the largest of the services and its principal restriction was a lack of shipping to get the troops where they were needed in the Pacific. The Japanese style of warfare was heavy on spirit and manpower while light on equipment. Against poorly trained and equipped troops, like the Chinese, this was quite successful. Against the lavishly equipped Americans, it was disastrous.

In China, the Japanese had air superiority and the Chinese had little artillery. The situation was just the opposite against the Allies in the Pacific. Against U.S. troops, the Japanese encountered artillery fire the likes of which they had never experienced. Actually, American artillery, as used in World War II, was employed in a radical new form. In addition to prodigious use of ammunition (first seen in World War I), the Americans developed communications techniques that allowed many guns to bring their fire down on a single target more quickly than ever seen in the past. Japanese attacks, even when they had the element of surprise, were regularly blown to pieces by artillery fire. The Japanese learned to use their shovels and skill at fortification to defeat this gunfire when they were defending. But there was no way for a Japanese attack to avoid the devastating effect of the Yankee guns.

American troops were also lavishly equipped with machine guns and used them skillfully. This, combined with their artillery, demolished the Japanese offensive capability. Deprived of their ability to control battles with their fearless attacks, the Japanese were forced to defend. Even defending to the death did little for them, except to provide a means to "die honorably in battle." This does not win wars, and as a result the Japanese lost theirs.

It was possible to trade lives for a lack of guns and ammunition. Later analysis (during the Korean War) showed that a regularly supplied Chinese army could stalemate American air and artillery superiority by suffering five casualties for every American one. This was no help for the Japanese because, unlike the Chinese in Korea, the garrisons of Pacific islands were cut off from reinforcement and supply when the U.S. invasion fleet showed up. The Americans not only had material superiority, they knew how to use it.

The Japanese civilian leaders and Navy admirals were generally aware of American production superiority. Most Army generals were either ignorant of these realities or chose to ignore them. Unfortunately for Japan, the generals were running the government from the mid-1930s and it was their view of things that determined national policy.

While many civilian and Navy leaders had studied in the United States, few generals had done so. Those educated Japanese who had spent time in America came away with a clear understanding that the United States was an industrial powerhouse and not likely to back down from a fight. While the generals ruling Japan might acknowledge American industrial superiority, they dismissed the idea that Americans would not back down and ask for peace if sufficiently pummeled by Japanese military might. It was with this misunderstanding that Japan went to war, and lost everything.

RESOURCE-POOR JAPAN

Japan was critically short of every kind of raw material, including food, from the first day of the war. The Allied situation was much better, despite problems with things like rubber and tin.

Upon securing the "Southern Resources Area," the Japanese no longer had a problem with regard to access to raw materials, save in the matter of food. Existing prewar stockpiles (for example, they had 4.2 million tons of iron ore on hand at the start of the war) and output in the conquered territories were more than they required. There was enough tin stockpiled in Burma when overrun in 1942 to keep Japanese industry going for at least a year, and there was more tin in Indonesia.

Except for food, the critical problem was not the supply of materials, but sealift, since between 80 percent and 90 percent of the industry in the "Greater East Asia Co-Prosperity Sphere" was in the home islands. Since the Japanese had difficulties with shipping availability even before the submarine campaign began to bite, they were never able to import as much as they needed.

This led to one interesting staff dust-up in the CBI, when economic warfare experts tried to convince air power aficionados that bombing mining facilities that the Japanese were trying to expand was actually counterproductive, since the Japanese were actually

JAPANESE RAW MATERIALS REQUIREMENTS, 1940

ITEM	NEED	HOME (%)	IMPORT (%)	CONTROLLED (%)
Alloying Ores	0.37	37.7	62.3	0.0
Aluminum Ores	0.44	22.6	77.4	17.2
Coal	47.22	84.7	15.3	15.3
Iron Ore	6.85	16.4	83.6	24.2
Oil	40.33	7.8	92.2	0.0
Scrap Iron	2.5	1.0	99.0	7.0

NOTES: "Alloying Ores" are things like zinc, tin, nickel, and manganese, which are used to make metal alloys so essential to the manufacture of military equipment. Japan also had to import some two thirds of her lead and virtually all of her cotton, wool, and gum (not the chewing kind, but that used in various chemical processes). "Need" is the amount needed to sustain military production and the economy. Oil figures are in millions of barrels, others in millions of tons. "Home" represents the percentage available in the home islands, plus, for oil, Sakhalin and Formosa, which later also accounted for a major portion of the bauxite output. "Import" is the percentage obtained from other areas. "Controlled" indicates the proportion of the imported percentage that came from areas under Japanese control before the war began; that is, Korea, Manchuria, and China. Korea was a major source of iron ore and coal, as well as food. The United States was a major source of scrap iron, essential in the production of steel.

wasting more resources in the process than they were gaining, being unable to find enough ships to export all the ore they were digging up.

Food was actually in short supply in Japan even before Pearl Harbor. Full rationing was introduced in April 1941. Rationing of many other commodities had begun as early as 1938. Overall, about 20 percent of Japan's rice, 100 percent of its sugar, and 65 percent of its soybeans had to be imported even before the war. Korea was the big source of rice, the Japanese taking a major portion of the annual 2.5-million-ton Korean crop. However, Korean harvests were bad in 1939–1941, about 20 percent lower than normal (some 2.0 million tons), and they continued so during the war, even as Japanese agricultural output fell due to mobilization. So although the Japanese just took a larger share of the Korean crop (leaving the Koreans to eat animal-feed-quality wheat, or starve), they still didn't have enough food.

The most critical industrial resource was oil. In December 1941, the Japanese had about 61 million barrels stockpiled, enough to run the armed forces for about two years at peacetime levels of con-

ESTIMATED JAPANESE OIL AVAILABILITY AND CONSUMPTION (IN MILLIONS OF BARRELS)			
WAR YEAR	RESERVE	PRODUCTION	CONSUMPTION
1st	61.1	5.0	37.8
2nd	28.3	12.9	34.6
3rd	6.6	23.6	34.6
4th	4.4	30.0	34.6

sumption. In mid-1941 they made what they considered careful calculations as to their oil needs and resources in the coming war.

Although the Japanese had made what they thought were conservative estimates of wartime oil production and consumption, these proved wildly optimistic. For example: Peacetime yield from the Dutch East Indies was about 17.7 million barrels a year. The Japanese estimated that in the first year of the war the yield would only be about 15.4 million barrels, due to destruction of the facilities and whatnot, but that by the third year they could crank it up to about 30.0 million barrels. In fact, they were never able to even approach the prewar figure. Moreover, even their prewar figures didn't add up: Note that in the table above they should have projected *no* surplus by the end of year three, and a worsening deficit thereafter.

There were several reasons for this. The destruction of production and storage facilities was greater than expected, although it could have been worse. In addition, the Japanese do not seem to have understood the complexities of the oil industry. They were short of technical personnel, various important chemicals, and spare parts, most of which were imported from Europe or America in the prewar period. Worse yet, one of the few cargo ships sunk early in the war was the one carrying Japanese refinery technicians and their equipment from Japan. As a result of all this, they ran out of oil a lot faster than they expected. The actual figures for oil production and consumption, given in the table on page 361, are quite interesting.

So by the end of 1944, the Japanese had more or less run out of fuel. The only reason the Japanese armed forces were able to keep fighting despite the apparent deficit is that their record keeping seems to have been as faulty as their initial calculations, so that

ACTUAL JAPANESE OIL AVAILABILITY AND CONSUMPTION (IN MILLIONS OF BARRELS)				
YEAR	RESERVE	PRODUCTION	CONSUMPTION	DEFICIT
1941	61.1	—	—	
1942	52.86	12.5	51.92	
1943	14.47	20.1	41.7	−7.1
1944	0.0	9.6	29.5	−19.9

there was more fuel on hand than estimated (for example, although there supposedly was only enough fuel for a one-way trip, in 1945 the battleship *Yamato* actually did have enough fuel to make a return voyage if she survived her "suicide" mission). In addition, the table above—from Japanese sources—does not appear to include fuel derived from various improvisations, such as the use of unrefined crude and coal oil (see the table on page 362). It is, however, interesting to note that their estimates for production in war years two and three were not far off the mark. Where they failed was in estimating consumption, which was much higher than predicted. Surprisingly, there had been a minority opinion on this in the Japanese military. Although overruled before the war, this group had managed to convince the brass that an experimental coal oil production program might be useful in an emergency. Although the program was supposed to yield several million barrels a year, it never approached its goal, due largely to a lack of genuine interest and a shortage of resources.

In short, Japan began the war short of resources, and steadily fell further and further behind.

DEFINING THE TON

Although the term *ton* is used frequently with reference to both merchant ships and warships, it has a very different meaning in each case. And that meaning is not necessarily related to the familiar ton. To begin, there is the ordinary ton, by weight 2,000 English pounds, also known as the "short ton" in the United States and several other

JAPANESE COAL OIL PRODUCTION
(IN MILLIONS OF BARRELS)

YEAR	OUTPUT
1937	0.03*
1941	1.50
1942	??
1943	1.05
1944	1.20
1945	??

*The goal was 0.15 million barrels.

countries. Then there's the "long ton" or English ton or shipping ton, of 2,240 pounds. And of course there's the metric ton (or tonne), which is a 1,000 kilograms, or 2,204.6 pounds. When discussing cargo weight the U.S. armed forces sometimes used the short ton and sometimes the long, while the British always used the long ton, and the Germans, the Italians, the French, the Japanese, the Russians, and practically everyone else in the world used the metric ton. So when dealing with particularly large figures, such as thousands of tons of ammunition expended, knowing which ton is meant can be extremely important.

Merchant ships are measured in three different sorts of "ton." Gross registered tonnage (g.r.t.) is a measure of the cubic internal volume of the ship in notional "tons" of 100 cubic feet or 2.8 cubic meters, a measurement that includes all interior spaces of the ship. The g.r.t. is actually not a particularly good guide to the cargo capacity of a ship. For example, the liner *Queen Elizabeth*, the largest commercial ship in the world during the war, was about 83,000 g.r.t., but actually carried very little cargo. But by enclosing a veranda deck she once added several thousand tons to her g.r.t.

Cargo is measured in measurement tons or freight tons. These are also units of volume rather than weight, amounting to 40 cubic feet of cargo stowage capacity. Thus 1 long ton of general military cargo ran about 2.1 measurement tons. Deadweight tons measure the actual weight of everything carried in the ship, including supplies, miscellaneous equipment, fuel, and even crew, expressed in long tons: As a rule for every 1,500 deadweight tons a cargo ship could carry about 1,775 measurement tons.

Warship tonnage is measured differently, in terms of "displacement tons." Each 35 cubic feet of seawater displaced by the vessel is a displacement ton. As the volume of seawater in question actually weighs approximately 1 long ton, displacement gives a rough indication of the actual weight of the vessel.

However, as established by various international naval disarmament treaties, there are several different ways to measure the displacement of a warship, depending upon the amount of stores, ammunition, fuel, and crew carried. "Light displacement" is measured taking the bare ship, without movables such as stores, fuel, ammunition, or crew. "Standard displacement" is measured with normal stores, ammunition, fuel, and crew, necessary for peacetime operations. "Full load displacement" measures the ship when fully loaded with all possible stores, ammunition, fuel, and crew ready for a wartime mission. The differences in the three can be considerable. The German battleship *Bismarck*, for example, was approximately 39,000 tons light displacement, 44,700 tons standard, and 49,600 tons full load, while the Japanese *Yamato* ran about 59,200 tons light displacement, 64,000 tons standard, and 70,000 tons full load.

THE SHIPYARD WAR

From the mid-1930s, both the United States and Japan began building warships at a rather prodigious pace that, at least in the case of the United States, did not slacken until the war was virtually over. In the table on page 364, note particularly the sudden jump in U.S. launchings in 1942, a consequence of the "Two-Ocean Navy" bill of 1940. In the end, Japan lost the war in the shipyards as much as on the high seas.

It is interesting to note that even before the war the Japanese took much longer to build ships than the Americans, and that, although they improved considerably, it was not proportional to the reductions in time effected by U.S. yards. In fact, U.S. construction time figures for cruisers might actually have been lower, but construction of many

			MAJOR WARSHIP LAUNCHINGS, 1937–1945					
YEAR	COUNTRY	CV	CVE	BB	CA/CL	DD	DE	SS
1937–	Japan	3	0	2	4	27	0	21
1940	U.S.	2	1	3	7	47	0	28
1941	Japan	2	1	0	2	8	0	10
	U.S.	0	2	3	6	27	0	15
1942	Japan	0	1	0	3	11	0	22
	U.S.	6	14	2	10	120	25	37
1943	Japan	5	2	0	0	9	0	39
	U.S.	12	25	3	11	92	205	66
1944	Japan	6	0	0	1	5	24	31
	U.S.	8	35	1	19	64	101	78
1945	Japan	0	0	0	0	0	12	30
	U.S.	11	9	1	10	73	0	22
Total	Japan	16	4	2	10	60	36	153
	U.S.	39	86	13	63	423	331	246

NOTES: Figures for carriers (CV) include light carriers, and, as with escort carriers (CVE) include conversions. Escort carrier figures exclude aircraft transports (the Japanese Army built several of these, which looked like carriers but could not operate combat aircraft). U.S. battleship figures include three "large cruisers." Japanese submarine figures exclude numerous midgets and twenty-eight cargo boats built by the Imperial Army. Note that not all vessels launched were actually completed, particularly in the case of the United States, which canceled numerous partially completed hulls. During the war both powers also greatly reduced the time required to build ships.

vessels was deliberately delayed in order to give priority to more desperately needed carriers, destroyers, and destroyer escorts.

Liberty ships, the standard mass-produced U.S. general purpose cargo vessels of the war, were based on a prewar Maritime Commission design. Although they were larger than the average prewar merchantmen (10,000 to 14,000 g.r.t. verses about 6,000), they are useful as a basis of comparison. The Japanese, of course, did not build Liberty ships, but did produce some large *maru* (the Japanese word for "merchantman") of similar type, although smaller.

AVERAGE SHIP CONSTRUCTION TIME (IN MONTHS)				
	PREWAR		WARTIME	
TYPE	U.S.	JAPAN	U.S.	JAPAN
BB	35–42	53–61	32	—
CV	32–34	36–44	15–20	22–24
CVE	—	—	8	12
CA	32–38	40–50	24–30	—
CL	32–38	40–50	20–30	19–24
DD	13–14	24–30	5	12
SS	14–15	24–36	7	15
Liberty	12–14	20–30	1	18–24

NOTES: Each navy required about twelve months to convert a ship into a light carrier, the United States using partially complete light-cruiser hulls for this purpose and the Japanese prewar seaplane carriers and other vessels especially built to be converted in an emergency. The U.S. figure for escort carriers (CVE) is for new construction, but conversions took about the same time; the Japanese figure is for conversion.

AMERICA'S SHIPBUILDING PLAN

During the 1930s, the U.S. Navy attempted to calculate its needs in the event of a future major war. Prewar construction programs were based on these estimates, as were the emergency programs that were adopted in 1940 and 1941.

The 1940 procurement budget for the U.S. Navy was $4 billion (nearly $42 billion in 1995 terms). This nowadays seemingly trifling sum was sufficient to cover the cost of 7 battleships, 18 aircraft carriers, 27 cruisers, 115 destroyers, and 43 submarines, plus several auxiliary vessels. This seemed to fit the Navy's projected wartime needs. But the war came rather sooner than planned, and was somewhat different than anticipated. As a result, the actual Navy was quite different from that which had been planned.

The Navy certainly did not dismiss the aircraft carrier as a useful weapon; after all, it planned to have about as many flattops as battlewagons. But it certainly greatly underestimated the role that carriers would have in the war.

WARTIME STRENGTH OF THE U.S. NAVY

		PLANNED	ACTUAL	PERCENT
Battleships:	New	17	10	58.8
	Old	5	15	300.0
Carriers	Fleet	15	28	186.7
	Light	0	9	—
	Escort	5	85	1,700.0
	A/C Capacity	1,600	4,500	281.3
Cruisers:	Large	6	2	33.3
	Heavy	26	38	146.2
	Light	49	51	104.1
Destroyers:	Fleet	450	620	133.8
	Escort	0	337	—
Submarines		200	350	175.0

NOTES: The "Planned" figures indicate the number of ships that the Navy expected to have available by the outbreak of war, sometime around 1944, while "Actual" is the number of ships in commission during the Second World War (note that figures for destroyers and submarines have been rounded). "Percent" is the number of ships actually in commission as a proportion of the planned figures.

Of particular interest are the figures for escort carriers, which ultimately included about a quarter of all carrier-borne aircraft (listed under "A/C Capacity"). In fact, the escort carrier was an idea more or less foisted upon the Navy by President Roosevelt. His enthusiasm was well rewarded, for their role in antisubmarine and amphibious operations was one of the more interesting developments of the war.

Figures for cruisers are also rather interesting. The so-called large cruisers were really light battleships, often called battlecruisers, which were built on the erroneous assumption that the Japanese were building similar vessels. They turned out to be fine ships, but had even less of a role than did proper battleships. On the other hand, the predicted need for heavy cruisers was rather lower than the demand, while that for light cruisers was pretty much on target.

It is interesting to note that despite the experience of World War I, the Navy underestimated the need for destroyers to curb the sub-

U.S. SHIPS BUILDING AT THE END OF THE WAR

		TOTAL	COMPLETED	CANCELED
Battleships		2	0	2
Carriers:	Fleet	13	11	2
	Light	2	2	0
	Escort	15	11	4
	A/C Capacity	1,920	1,610	310
Cruisers:	Large	1	0	1
	Heavy	14	14	0
	Light	17	11	6
Destroyers:	Fleet	65	60	5
	Escort	0	0	0
Submarines		39	15	24

marine menace. Indeed, the underplanning in this regard was a critical factor in the creation of the destroyer escort, a sort of "second-class" destroyer designed primarily for antisubmarine operations, rather than general fleet operations. In addition, considering that the Navy's prewar plans were predicated upon a submarine campaign against Japanese shipping, the prewar estimate of the need for submarines was extremely low. Actually, the figures show only part of the difference between prewar prognostication and wartime needs, for many vessels ordered during the war were not completed in time.

THE BORING STUFF:

Policy, Politics, and Strategy

T he Pacific war was not fought in a vacuum. There was a mass of political and social events leading up to the war, and keeping it going once it started.

THE NAVAL DISARMAMENT TREATIES

The end of World War I led to an immediate reduction in armies worldwide, as victors and vanquished alike rapidly demobilized the enormous hosts that they had raised since 1914. The reductions

THE CAPITAL SHIP BALANCE, 1920–1922

	OBSOLETE	EFFECTIVE	BUILDING	TOTAL
Britain	23	19	9	51
Japan	2	8	16	26
U.S.	8	9	18	35

NOTES: Only *Dreadnought*-type "all-big-gun" battleships and battlecruisers have been included. "Obsolete" ships are those completed between 1905 and 1914. "Effective" includes vessels completed between 1914 and 1920, most of which were designed before 1914, and thus marginally out of date. "Building" includes ships under construction or already ordered but not yet laid down.

went far below the level of the "normal" peacetime establishments maintained prior to the outbreak of the war, if only because no one seriously believed there would be another major war, particularly since Germany's armed forces had been reduced to little more than a constabulary.

The end of the war also took care of two of the principal navies in the world, those of Germany and Russia, the one reduced to insignificance by the Treaty of Versailles and the other by revolution and civil war. Two others, those of France and Italy, fell decisively into the second rank of naval power, if only for lack of funds. But three navies remained strong, the American, the Japanese, and the British. Moreover, all three seemed intent on further increasing the size of their fleets.

Aside from eliminating several first class navies, the Great War vastly altered the balance of naval power in another way, for it threatened to dethrone Britain from its traditional naval supremacy. Subtracting the obsolete vessels from her inventory, Britain's margin of superiority over either of the two other major navies was so slender as to be nonexistent, and considering the number of capital ships being built, the prognosis was not good for the Royal Navy.

The strain of the war had prevented Britain from ordering very many new capital ships, while both Japan and the United States had been busy indeed. Moreover, the wily newcomers had delayed the actual start of construction so that they were able to incorporate the lessons of the war. As if that were not enough, Japan had announced that it planned to build its Navy on the basis of the "8-8-8" Plan, which stated that the first-line strength of the fleet would always be maintained at eight battleships and eight battle-cruisers no more than eight years old, plus older vessels. One did not need a degree in advanced math to realize that this meant the Japanese would add two capital ships to their fleet every year, shortly giving them the largest battle fleet in the world, a matter of concern to the United States.

America, of course, responded by planning to expand its navy as well. In the face of the Japanese and American threats to their naval primacy, the British reluctantly began planning to expand as well. A major naval arms race loomed, with all the attendant expense. The cost would be heavy for the United States, heavier still for Britain, and heaviest of all for Japan.

If the Japanese actually did try to implement the "8-8-8" Plan, they would be able to bear the expense for only six or eight years before running out of money and credit, by which time (about 1928–1930) they would have about forty serviceable battleships and battlecruisers, almost all less than fifteen years old. At that point the Japanese would either have had to abandon the "8-8-8" program, thereby admitting that Japan was not a first-class power, or go to war to secure the resources necessary to become a first-class power. In American and British naval circles, it was presumed that the latter course would be the more likely for the Japanese to take.

In an effort to halt the incipient naval arms race, in 1921 the British suggested a naval disarmament conference, in compliance with the disarmament provisions of the Treaty of Versailles. The response was surprisingly warm, and led to one of the most successful instances of international disarmament in history, the naval disarmament treaties of 1922 and 1930.

On November 12, 1921, delegates from the United States, Britain, and Japan convened in Washington (chosen to overcome isolationist fears that Uncle Sam was being hustled), with France and Italy invited out of politeness. On the very first day, the American secretary of state dropped a bombshell. Subtly observing that the United States had the economic wherewithal to outbuild both its rivals, Charles Evans Hughes announced that America would be willing to scrap a significant portion of its existing fleet and of vessels still under construction, if the other powers would do the same and agree to limitations on the size of their fleets. The offer was greeted "with almost indecent haste," as one naval historian put it.

The Washington Naval Disarmament Treaty (1921–1922) was worked out in a remarkably short time, and implemented with considerable goodwill. Including further refinements of the agreement concluded in London in 1930, 38 existing capital ships were scrapped (Britain, 29; Japan, 2; the United States, 7) and 31 of those abuilding (Britain, 8; Japan, 10; the United States, 13) were canceled or converted to aircraft carriers (2 each for the United States and Japan), although in compensation Britain was allowed to lay down and complete 2 wholly new battleships. In addition, restrictions were imposed on the replacement of existing vessels, and on the displacement (35,000 tons standard) and guns (16 inch) that future battleships could tote.

In addition, the three major powers agreed that the United States and Britain, each of which had interests in both the Atlantic and the Pacific, "needed" more capital ships than did Japan, which had interests only in the Pacific. The Japanese accepted this deal when the other powers sweetened it by barring new fortifications in the Pacific between Japan and Singapore, west of Hawaii, and by giving Japan a better ratio in some other categories of warships. A total tonnage limitation was placed on the size of the navies of all the signatories in the ratio 5:5:3:1.75:1.75 for Britain, the United States, Japan, France, and Italy. Some restrictions were placed on other classes of warships as well, which were rigidly defined as to size and armament, including the introduction of the distinction between the light cruiser and the heavy cruiser, a matter of gun caliber (6-inch or under, as opposed to anything over, up to 10-inch).

Although Britain failed to get submarines banned, these were agreements that did make a difference, as fleets actually were reduced. However, the treaty had some unintended results. Perhaps the biggest was that Japanese militarists would later use the treaty to argue that the Japanese Empire had been insulted by relegation to a state of inferiority. Efforts at further significant reductions in naval armaments, which were made well into the 1930s, came to grief due to demands for "parity" by a militarized Japan and a resurgent Germany. Thus a treaty aimed at reducing tensions and armaments eventually increased both. Disarmament doesn't always work out the way you think it will.

At the time, and afterward, particularly during World War II, many American navalists (the maritime equivalent of militarists) argued, and indeed continue to argue, that the disarmament treaties strengthened Japan, with disastrous results in 1941. This was hardly the case. In fact, had the United States adhered to the letter of the treaties, building up to allowable limits, its margin of superiority over the Japanese would have been much greater than was actually the case in 1941. However, fiscal conservatives, pacifists, and isolationists on both left and right combined to reduce the fleet to limits even lower than those prescribed by the treaties.

For example, a 1927 proposal by the Coolidge administration to build five aircraft carriers and twenty-five cruisers, as permitted by the treaty, was cut down to one carrier and fifteen cruisers, which became law in 1928, although no ships were actually laid down until 1930, and some not until 1936. As a result, on December 7, 1941, the Imperial Navy was not about 60 percent the size of the U.S. Navy, as prescribed by the disarmament treaties, but around 80 percent, and that only after President Roosevelt had been fighting for several years to strengthen the fleet.

MYTHS, CONSPIRACIES, AND COVER-UPS OF THE PACIFIC WAR

Human nature and modern media being what they are, it's not surprising that people have a tendency to come up with theories about conspiracies, treachery, cover-ups, and other nefarious Machiavellian plots, particularly in cases where unpleasant things occurred. World War II has come in for its share of such accusations. Many of these myths are the result of misinformation or, simply, information that was simply not available for a long time.

A half century later there are still a surprising number of things about the Second World War that remain secret, or are at best only partially known. Some of these unrevealed items deal with minor matters, but others are of considerable importance. For a variety of reasons, most are not likely to be revealed for many years to come, if ever. After all, some British documents dating back to the Spanish Armada (1588) apparently have never been made public.

There are many reasons for this secrecy. Bureaucratic inertia is one. At other times, such policies are designed to protect the lives, or at least the reputations, of certain people such as politicians or officers who found themselves entrapped in enemy espionage, or foreign officials, even enemy politicians and officers, who collaborated in the defeat of their own nations. And some things really ought to remain classified. Revealing where the remains of Hermann Göring and the other Nazi leaders were disposed of would undoubtedly turn the site into a Nazi shrine, grounds enough for perpetual secrecy. Of course it's true that many times it's just politically expedient to keep certain things secret, rather than open the proverbial can of worms. Here now, some questions relating to the Pacific war the answers to which are—and are likely to remain—buried in the various secret archives.

STALIN SCUTTLES JAPAN'S PEACE FEELERS

From available information it is clear that by the late spring of 1945 the Japanese government was attempting to get the Soviets to use their good offices with the United States to bring about an end to the war. Somehow the message never got to the appropriate authorities. By the time the Japanese realized what the Russians were up to (stonewalling) and attempted to reach the United States through Sweden, it was too late to avoid the final horrors of Hiroshima and Nagasaki. The extent to which Stalin deliberately impeded the peace process has never been established, although this may change now that the old Soviet archives are opening up.

CHIANG KAI-SHEK SEEKS A SEPARATE PEACE

On at least one occasion during the war, Chaing Kai-shek, the leader of Nationalist China, appears to have attempted to negotiate a separate peace with the Japanese. This seems to have been one of the sources of friction between Chiang and his principal American military adviser, General Joseph Stilwell. Moreover, Chiang's chief of intelligence (called by Stilwell "the head of Chiang's Gestapo") did maintain contact with Chinese officials working in the Japanese puppet government in China and Manchuria. What exactly was discussed via these contacts is not yet known completely. It could have been anything, or nothing. Most likely it was nothing more than the ancient Chinese custom of keeping in touch with one's enemies.

THE DOOMED PEARL HARBOR SURVIVORS

In the aftermath of the Japanese attack on Pearl Harbor, much was made of the heroic efforts to release men trapped in the hulls of the sunken ships. Nothing was said at the time, nor for some twenty-five years afterward, about the men who survived for days, and in some cases even weeks, trapped deep in the bowels of capsized battlewagons, beyond hope of rescue, who died of their injuries or slowly suffocated to death. In virtually every case, the identities of these men are known but have never been revealed, out of consideration for their families. Similarly, the Navy has never revealed the number of Pearl Harbor survivors who were eventually classified as psychological casualties, some of whom remained in institutions for the rest of their lives. Some of them still are there.

JAPANESE ASSISTANCE TO SUBVERSIVE AMERICANS

In the years before Pearl Harbor the Japanese government is known to have provided covert financial assistance to a number of organizations in the United States. While most of this money went to Japanese-American social and cultural organizations, or to groups like the Society of the Black Dragon, composed of veterans of the Russo-Japanese War, some went to radical black organizations, including one religious group that has since gained considerable prominence. The U.S. government has never revealed the extent of such aid, nor even formally acknowledged that it existed. The U.S. archives do contain information on this matter, as some of the secret Japanese radio messages that American code breakers read contained the facts.

ALLIED PRISONERS OF WAR KILLED BY "FRIENDLY FIRE"

Tens of thousands of Allied troops and civilians found themselves involuntary guests of the Japanese government during the war. A lot of these people, upward of 30 percent, did not survive the war. And some of them were killed by Allied forces. The number is not clear but is certainly in the thousands. The principal cause of such deaths among Allied prisoners was submarine attacks, the Japanese tending to ship prisoners from outlying areas to the home islands as the war dragged on. Others were killed in air attacks, including the atomic bombings. No figures on the number of such deaths have ever been revealed.

JAPANESE-AMERICANS IN THE IMPERIAL ARMED FORCES

Hundreds—perhaps thousands—of Japanese-Americans who were visiting or studying in Japan at the time of Pearl Harbor eventually found themselves drafted into the Japanese Army or Navy, many serving as junior officers. Neither the identities nor the numbers of these men have ever been published, since the men in question were not given much of a choice in the matter. A similar policy has been followed with regard to German-American and Italian-American men who found themselves serving against the United States. This has occurred in most American wars of this century, including the 1991 Gulf War with Iraq. Most of these Americans in enemy uniform were reluctant warriors. Many Japanese-Americans caught in Japan at the start of the war were, however, quite enthusiastic in their war efforts and most of these wisely stayed in Japan after the war.

THE PEARL HARBOR PLOT

The most enduring World War II conspiracy theory contends that President Roosevelt and sundry other national political and military leaders "knew" that the Japanese were about to attack Pearl Harbor and, indeed, even provoked the attack. There are numerous variations on the theme. For example, one suggests that Winston Churchill "knew," but refused to tell, so that the United States would be able to come to Britain's rescue against Germany. These theories are all based on "evidence," often "new" evidence which has "just come to light." Unfortunately, when all this evidence is examined, including the "new" evidence (which always turns out to be information of little value or relevance long available to the public, if it cared to inquire), the most charitable thing that can be said is "not proven."

Some of the "theories" about the attack rank right up there with Elvis sightings, including one contention that the attack was actually carried out by British aircraft based on one of the outlying islands of the Hawaiian group! In fact, the disaster at Pearl Harbor was the result of a lot of audacity and luck on the part of the Japanese and numerous blunders by many American political and military leaders, with no particular person being criminally responsible. As historian Gordon Prange said, "There's enough blame for everyone."

THE SAVO ISLAND COVER-UP

On the night of August 9, 1942, a Japanese squadron steamed undetected into the waters north of Guadalcanal and within a few minutes inflicted the most serious and most one-sided reverse ever suffered by the U.S. Navy in a surface action, sinking four heavy cruisers (one of them Australian) and a destroyer, killing 1,270 men and wounding 709 others, all in about thirty minutes, with no loss to themselves. These casualties amounted to about two-thirds the number of the U.S. ground troops killed during the entire Guadalcanal campaign, which lasted from August 1942 into February 1943.

The commander of the Allied squadron, British Rear Admiral V.A.C. Crutchley, was not present at the battle, having gone off to a staff conference with the overall local commander, Rear Admiral Richmond Kelly Turner, taking his flagship, the heavy cruiser *Australia*, with him. After the battle both Crutchley and Turner continued in command. As the twenty-fifth anniversary of the battle approached, a prominent conservative monthly advanced the theory that there had been a massive cover-up of Crutchley's incompetence, carried out by the Roosevelt administration (of course) in order to preserve good relations with its British masters.

In fact, aside from the general excellence of the Japanese at night naval combat, the disaster that befell the Australian and American ships off Savo Island was due more to failures of prewar doctrine and training, a continuing peacetime mind-set, a surprisingly durable contempt for the enemy, and excessive confidence in as-yet-inadequate radar, rather than command failures by Crutchley and Turner. If Crutchley had been present at the battle, the Japanese would probably have killed him and sunk his flagship as well.

DOUGLAS MACARTHUR'S REFRIGERATOR

In the closing days of the defense of Bataan, President Roosevelt ordered General Douglas MacArthur to turn command over to his principal subordinate and escape to Australia in order to coordinate Allied efforts to carry on the war in the Southwest Pacific. As a result, one night in February 1942, MacArthur, some of his close aides, and a number of high officials of the government of the Commonwealth of the Philippines boarded several torpedo boats that successfully ran the Japanese blockade. Accompanying MacArthur were his wife, his son, and his son's nurse.

Almost as soon as MacArthur had made good his escape, questions were raised as to why he had brought along his family, even though leaving them behind might have seriously impaired his abilities as a commander. Moreover, stories began to circulate that he had arranged to bring out not only members of his family but certain articles of furniture, including a refrigerator. The tale has proven extremely durable, but has no foundation in fact. None of the persons present, including the crews of the PT boats, reported carrying anything unusual during the trip.

On the other hand, although Doug didn't take his refrigerator, he also didn't take about a dozen Army nurses, who suffered the tender mercies of the Japanese for over three years, a matter about which he received little criticism.

THE HIROSHIMA PLOT

The atomic bomb attacks on Hiroshima and Nagasaki (August 6 and 9, 1945) have spawned a number of interesting conspiracy theories. The first is that senior military officers, fearful that President Harry S Truman might not let them use their new toy, falsely argued that the invasion of Japan (tentatively scheduled to begin on November 1, 1945) would result in "a million American dead," which convinced the president to use the bomb.

A variant of this has the president himself deciding to use the bomb not because it was necessary to bring Japan to a speedy surrender, but because he wanted to "send a message to the Russians." This last item has recently been revived as part of a conspiracy theory accusing Truman of having deliberately, and single-handedly, started the Cold War in order to justify a greater degree of government control over the American people and to sustain the military-industrial complex, but that's another story.

In fact, neither tale holds much water. No one in the armed forces ever suggested that the invasion of Japan would cost a million American lives. The military staff estimated there would be 250,000 to 500,000 casualties. After the war, some senior nonmilitary officials casually made this a "half-million dead" and then "a million dead." In any event, any estimate of casualties includes killed, wounded, and missing. The original estimates were a not-unreasonable figure based on recent American experience with fanatical Japanese defenders of Iwo Jima and Okinawa, and one that a postwar examination of Japanese plans for the defense of the home islands tends to bear out. There was no indication the Japanese would fight any less strenuously if their home islands were invaded. Indeed, it was a safe bet that the fighting would have been even more costly.

As for the Truman "message" theory, this rests on the assumption that no one seriously believed Japan would have to be invaded, which is patently untrue. The Russians knew of the atomic bomb (both officially and unofficially) and the Western Allies knew of Russia's plans to invade Manchuria. The main consideration was ending the war and saving American lives, not playing diplomatic games or doing warm-up exercises for the Cold War. The Japanese consistently demonstrated a marked reluctance to surrender, either on the battlefield or at the negotiating table. The American people, in light of Germany's surrender in May 1945, were eager to get the war in the Pacific over with as soon as possible. The voters were making this wish quite clear to their elected officials and the chief among these, President Truman, was listening intently. He had been told that a blockade of Japan might have to go on for a year or more before Japan finally gave in. The American people would have none of this and wanted something done. The atomic bomb was simply another incentive for the Japanese to surrender, and no one was sure it would be any more persuasive than the recent fire bomb raids (which killed more people than the atomic bombs.)

A third conspiracy theory is that the United States used the bomb on Japan because the Japanese were not white, the proof being that we did not use it on Germany. Actually, research on the atomic bomb was aimed specifically at having it available for use against Germany. In 1942, the Allies agreed that Germany must be defeated first and priority in resources was given to achieve that goal. In fact the B-36 bomber was designed specifically to deliver the bomb to Germany from bases in North America (should the Germans manage to conquer Britain). The only reason it wasn't so used was that Germany surrendered more than two months before the first bomb was even tested. Anyone who doubts that the United States would have used the bomb on Germany if it was available should consider the fire bomb raids on Hamburg and Dresden, each of which was more deadly than the combined casualties of the atomic bombings of Hiroshima and Nagasaki. Despite this intrusion of reality, the racial interpretation of the use of the bomb on Japan has proven extremely durable.

JAPAN'S IMPERIAL CONSPIRACY

This theory holds that the emperor Hirohito played an active, indeed a key role in preparing and planning for Japan's aggression in China and against the Western powers, even taking a personal interest in germ warfare experimentation. Actually, there is something to this, but not as much as has been averred. The nineteenth-century Meiji Constitution did not create a constitutional monarchy in Japan, with a figurehead sovereign. Behind a facade of parliamentary rule, Japan was essentially an authoritarian monarchy, much as Imperial Germany or Tsarist Russia had been before World War I. The emperor retained enormous power, although he usually refrained from exercising it.

This is where Hirohito's responsibility for the war lay. Not only did he fail to oppose the imposition of a militaristic regime on Japan during the early 1930s, he raised no objections to the militarists' adventurism in China. And when the armed forces asked him for a declaration of war against the Western powers, he did not hesitate to grant it. It is worth recalling in this regard that when, in mid-August of 1945—in the aftermath of Hiroshima, the Russian invasion of Manchuria, and Nagasaki—the emperor ordered Japan to surrender, the country and its armed forces did so quickly and efficiently, despite the efforts of some militaristic fanatics to prevent it from ending. So at most, Hirohito's responsibility for the war was a sin of omission, rather than one of commission. That said, it is well to remember that for most of Japan's history, the emperor was kept around as a sort of pet by the military strongmen who actually ran the country. For the emperor to go against the generals was to risk all the power he had.

THE MOUNT SURIBACHI CONSPIRACY

The ultimate image of American courage, power, and triumph in World War II is certainly Associated Press photographer Joe Rosenthal's shot of five Marines and a Navy medical corpsman raising Old Glory atop Iwo Jima's Mount Suribachi on February 23, 1945. This was actually the second flag raising that morning. A platoon of forty men from the 28th Marines had reached the summit after fierce hand-to-hand fighting and, at 10:20 A.M., three of the men raised a small American flag on a piece of pipe. Realizing that the flag was too small to be seen, and wanting to make sure that it stayed with the regiment rather than end up as a souvenir for some senior officer, the officer in command sent for a larger one even as the original flag was being raised.

Shortly afterward, the battle ensign of *LST-779* was brought up, fastened to a longer piece of pipe, and raised. The sight of the huge flag brought cheers from many of the troops hotly engaged with the enemy. It is this flag raising that was photographed by Rosenthal, who happened to be standing nearby.

Recently the claim has been made that this second flag raising was deliberately staged as a "photo opportunity" by the Marine brass, to garner more prestige for the Corps, and ultimately a bigger share of the postwar budget. Actually, the entire incident was unplanned. Both flag raisings were prompted by the men on the spot, several of whom did not survive the battle. The fact that there were two flag raisings can be found in all histories of the battle, and both flags are prominently displayed in the Marine Corps Museum, with an explanation of the circumstances and photographs of both events. Rosenthal's shot, which he almost missed taking, just happens to be the better of the two artistically. There is also a film of the second flag raising, which has not been widely seen.

Interestingly, the author who advanced this conspiratorial interpretation of the events appears to have failed to consult with any of the surviving participants in the two flag raisings. They certainly were very forthcoming when the book did appear, but their letters to various newspapers seem not to have made much of an impression, and the tale that the flag raising was staged "long after" the island was secured has received considerable circulation. It is, of course, not true that history is written by the winners; it is more often written by those with political axes to grind.

FDR CHEATED MACARTHUR

Douglas MacArthur and his numerous sycophants often claimed that his command was starved of men and resources during the war because high-ranking military and political leaders feared that if he proved too successful against the Japanese, he would almost certainly win the presidency in 1944, unseating the jealous Franklin Roosevelt.

Actually, MacArthur's command was hardly "starved." Particularly in 1942, far more men and equipment were sent to him than to Europe. Both FDR and George C. Marshall, the Army Chief of Staff, although committed to the "Germany first" strategy, recognized the desperate nature of the situation in the Southwest Pacific. An examination of available figures on troop and matériel movements bears this out. Six of the first ten divisions to ship out during the war went to the Pacific, where there were already two U.S. divisions, not counting the forces in the Philippines.

What did give MacArthur some cause for concern was that, although massive amounts of shipping, troops, and supplies were sent to the Pacific, much was diverted to the Aleutians. The Japanese occupation of several islands in the Aleutians during June 1942 caused consternation on the west coast of Canada and the United States. It became politically imperative to get the Japanese out of there as soon as possible. But this took enormous amounts of matériel and to this day it is little known that, for months at a time, over a third of the matériel sent to the Pacific went north to Alaska rather than west to New Guinea and the Solomons. By spring of 1943, the Aleutians were cleared of Japanese and all supply efforts again went west.

AMERICA'S CONCENTRATION CAMPS

America's most shameful moment in World War II was the internment of Japanese-Americans in concentration camps during World War II. This was considered a shamelessly racist attack on Japanese-Americans in the aftermath of the Pearl Harbor attack.

Or was it?

The Japanese-Americans were caught up in the ancient practice in wartime of rounding up enemy citizens and others thought to be of dubious loyalty. In one program, some 16,810 enemy aliens (noncitizens, who were not permanent residents) were rounded up, of whom 36 percent were Japanese. These "internees" were imprisoned in what we would today call medium-security prisons. But they were definitely imprisoned. This was normal in wartime; the same thing happened to Americans caught in Germany or Japan when war was declared. The only exceptions were Americans of Japanese or German ancestry caught in those nations when war was declared. In these cases, the Japanese and German governments coerced (where necessary) these Americans to "return to the fatherland" and fight against their adopted country.

The more controversial program was the relocation of Japanese-Americans (including both resident aliens and citizens) from the west coast. This began in late February 1942, on the orders of President Roosevelt, when the west coast was declared an "exclusion zone." This meant that anyone of questionable loyalty to the United States was ordered to move to another part of the country. Rather than try to separate loyal from disloyal Japanese-Americans, all persons of Japanese ancestry were removed from the zone. The program was mandatory and 110,000 Japanese-Americans (and several thousand German- and Italian-Americans as well) were sent to relocation centers. About 40 percent of these people were Japanese citizens who had not yet qualified for, or bothered to apply for, American citizenship.

Adult Japanese-Americans being relocated were questioned about their loyalty to the United States. Some 18,000 of them refused to renounce the emperor of Japan or swear allegiance to the United States and were promptly interned.

It should be kept in mind that most Japanese immigration to the United States occurred before the 1930s, a time when life was quite hard in Japan. But from the 1930s on, while the rest of the world was mired in the Great Depression, Japan prospered and Japanese at home and abroad took pride in their country's accomplishments. The improved situation in Japan, plus the usual racism immigrants suffered in their new countries, caused many Japanese to return home during the 1930s. This is why there were 20,000 Japanese with American citizenship in Japan when the war broke out.

Japanese intelligence officials were well aware of the changed attitudes of overseas Japanese and they set about creating networks of spies and informers to take advantage of it. The coded messages Japanese diplomats sent home were decrypted by American code breakers and it was this information, the shock of Pearl Harbor, the invasion of the Philippines, and the public's perception that the west coast would be attacked that led to the relocation program.

Once in the camps, those who did profess their loyalty did not have to sit out the war in the "concentration camps." If they could find jobs and housing in another part of the country, they could go there and live freely until the war was over. The west coast was still off limits because it was particularly vulnerable due to many the military bases and war factories located there. These facilities provided much of the support for the war effort in the Pacific. If Japanese agents were in place, radio messages could be sent to Japan detailing what ships were where and in what shape. A lot of information could be picked up from talkative defense workers and sailors.

Moreover, the racism worked both ways, as the Japanese were reluctant to trust a non-Japanese as an agent. The Japanese-Americans were a perfect population from which to recruit agents, and this was exactly what the Japanese did. Moreover, many Japanese-Americans made no secret of the their loyalties before the war. But it was the ones who kept quiet that had the FBI worried.

Japanese-Americans in other parts of the country were not affected by the exclusion order and went on with their lives like other Americans. By the middle of 1944, over 40,000 of the interned Japanese-Americans from the west coast had found new homes and were living freely outside the camps. Over 4,000 Japanese-Americans got away from the camps by going off to college, and about 5,000 by joining the military. While most who enlisted were sent to Europe, many of those who spoke Japanese were sent to the Pacific where they were used as intelligence specialists.

Most of those who remained in the camps were either too old, or too young, to find jobs. Many of those who remained also could not speak English. People of suspect loyalty were also kept in the camps. While most of the people in the camps were loyal American, many were not. Loyalists provided information on pro-Japanese activity among detainees, and there was quite a lot of it. The pro-Japanese internees were often quite fanatical about their beliefs and would terrorize and badger those who were patriotic Americans. After the war, some 6,000 of the detainees requested repatriation to Japan.

Some, but not many, Japanese-Americans living outside the exclusion zone moved to the camps to be close to relatives. Others who had found housing and work in other parts of the country voluntarily returned to the camps, although the government charged them a dollar a day (about five dollars in current money) for room and board if they did so. The government soon realized that it did not want to be in the camp business.

The camps were not death camps, and were not anything like the concentration camps American citizens were shut up in by the Germans or Japanese. Occupants were paid for work they did to help run the camps, and they were free to leave on a temporary or permanent basis under increasingly liberal conditions. There were still restrictions on movement, as Japanese-Americans were still forbidden to enter the west coast exclusion zone until after the war.

The camps contained a range of amenities not normally associated with concentration camps, like schools for the children (and adults), libraries, stores, banks, and medical facilities. Food was plentiful, as was medical care and education. That said, they were still detention camps, hastily built in the wilderness and closely guarded.

Of course, the most contentious issue in all this was the reasoning behind the relocation. Fear of a Japanese invasion and the presence of Japanese sympathizers was not all driven by racism against Japanese. Americans had watched in horror as the Nazis overran Europe during the last two years, often with the aid of local sympathizers. Before Pearl Harbor, there were numerous active groups of German-, Italian-, and Japanese-Americans who openly supported the aggressive ambitions of their erstwhile motherlands. What caused the panic that led to the Japanese-American roundup on the west coast, but no similar one for Germans on the east coast, was the fact that Japan was seen as the dominant naval power in the Pacific, while the Germans were, at worst, a threat to shipping with their submarines in the Atlantic. The Pearl Harbor attack was also a major factor, as it was seen as a treacherous thing to do while, at the same time, Japanese diplomats in Washington were attempting to resolve the differences between the two nations.

Fears that Japanese-Americans might represent a potential fifth column were also fanned by the Niihau incident. His airplane damaged by American antiaircraft fire over Pearl Harbor on December 7, 1941, a Japanese Navy fighter pilot managed to crash land on Niihau, the smallest of the inhabited Hawaiian Islands. The pilot convinced a local Japanese American that the arrival of the emperor's forces was imminent, the pair embarked upon a violent rampage, terrorizing the island until they were killed several days later, leaving behind a trail of dead and injured people. In addition, the collaboration of many locally resident Japanese with the Japanese army of occupation in the Philippines and other areas only strengthened the hand of those who advocated relocation of Japanese-Americans.

While an actual invasion of the west coast was beyond Japanese capabilities, public opinion in 1942 thought otherwise. "Something had to be done," and if that something meant trampling on the Bill of Rights in the process, it was done. And regretted later. Some say that the Japanese should not have been treated any differently from Germans or Italians. But the government knew something it dared not reveal at the time.

There *were* Japanese espionage networks on the west coast, and much crucial information regarding these Japanese activities remained secret for many years because this data was obtained by cryptanalysis (the MAGIC system). What MAGIC revealed was that Japanese diplomats had established an extensive network of Japanese-American agents on the west coast. Like many German-Americans and Italian-Americans, there were many Japanese-Americans who were still loyal to "the old country."

Indeed, there were some 20,000 Japanese-Americans in Japan at the beginning of the war, all of whom (with few exceptions) renounced their American citizenship and joined the Japanese war effort. Given the nature of Japanese society and the war fever then present in Japan, it is doubtful many of these Japanese-Americans had much choice in the matter. But many of them promptly joined the Japanese armed forces or enthusiastically supported the Japanese war effort. One Japanese-American, known as "Tokyo Rose," became prominent by delivering English-language radio broadcasts to American troops and was tried for treason after the war.

Many of those who remained in the camps during the war, even if they had declared their allegiance to the United States, were known to truly loyal Japanese-Americans as having pro-Japanese sympathies. The MAGIC intercepts did not detail every Japanese-American agent, because not all the messages could be deciphered, and even then, the Japanese diplomats in America did not always use names that could be traced to a specific individual in the United States. But the FBI had picked up some of this activity. What the MAGIC intercepts confirmed was that the extent of the Japanese support was larger than anyone had previously suspected and there was no way to assure that the majority of these traitors would be picked up even if the MAGIC information was used in a roundup.

So it was not all black and white. While the "invasion panic" on the west coast, along with anti-Japanese attitudes stemming from Pearl Harbor and the well-publicized Japanese atrocities in China before the war, were major causes of the exclusion zone, the main reason was the evidence of Japanese espionage activities. Germany and Italy also had thousands of pro-Fascist supporters in America, and thousands of these were also rounded up. The same could have been done among Japanese-Americans on the west coast, but the added invasion hysteria and bad feelings because of Pearl Harbor led to one of the less noble incidents in U.S. history.

The removal was not a unanimous decision. Many Americans protested, including FBI Director J. Edgar Hoover, and it was pointed out that the same kind of hysteria had been directed against German-Americans twenty-five years earlier during World War I. Of course, there had been no removal of German-Americans then, mainly because there was much less likelihood of a German invasion of America. But Americans of German extraction had been persecuted, and later apologized to, after a fashion. Here, however, was another war scare, and such events owe more to speculative futures than to unambiguous past events. It took a Supreme Court decision to affirm the removal, and thousands of Japanese-Americans endured their lot through the war.

There were also a few Japanese-Americans removed from Hawaii, where they composed a large minority of the population. The main reason why these removals were not on the same scale as on the west coast was that Hawaii was under martial law early in the war and the west coast was not. There was also the fact that it would have been a logistic nightmare early in the war to move that many people back to the mainland; there was also a labor shortage on Hawaii during the war; and, finally, the Hawaiian population was a tad less paranoid about their Japanese-American neighbors than were the folks on the mainland.

The American people, and their government, began to regret the removal even before the war was over. Japanese-Americans fought bravely in Europe and the Pacific. The accounts of their uncommon courage in the defense of their country, despite their shabby treatment, began to make headlines in 1944.

But from the beginning, there was no official policy of punishing the Japanese-Americans beyond removing them from what was then considered a war zone. The officials in charge of supervising the removal were instructed to be generous in making necessary financial arrangements. While many of the Japanese-Americans were farmers, few owned their land; most leased it. These farmers were paid for their crops in the ground and arrangements were made for leases to be taken over for the duration of the "emergency." After the war, the returning Japanese-Americans were able to make claims for losses that occurred in any event, and over a quarter-billion dollars (in current money) was paid by the government to satisfy these terms. About three dozen German- and Italian-Americans also received reparations for their losses due to internment.

Over the years, the myth has grown up that an entirely innocent Japanese-American population was thoughtlessly uprooted and tossed into concentration camps in a fit of racist hysteria. The truth was a bit more complex. Many of the Japanese-Americans so interned were disloyal. Of those military-age males who spent the war in the camps, only 6 percent volunteered for military service. And many of those interned were, by their own admission, loyal to Japan, not America. But most Japanese-Americans did not spend the war in the internment camps. Ironically, the guilt among Americans built in the decades after the war, and in the 1980s, $20,000 in further reparations was paid to each surviving Japanese-American who had spent time in the camps. This was paid to those who had been loyal as well as those who had not.

It's not enough to remember history; one must also remember the details.

THE PACIFIC COLONIES

Save for China and Siam, all of the real estate that Japan seized during the war was controlled by distant colonial powers, specifically Britain, France, the Netherlands, Portugal, and the United States. One element in Japan's strategy was its ability to manipulate the downtrodden victims of Western imperialism, by pointing out that Japan was the only Asian nation numbered among the Great Powers.

India was in ferment through the 1930s. The Indians wanted the British out but the British were in no hurry to leave. Japan's call of "Asia for the Asians" fell on receptive ears throughout India, especially during the war. At that time, Britain also controlled Burma; Holland controlled Indonesia (the "Netherlands East Indies"); France controlled Vietnam, Laos, and Cambodia; and the United

States controlled the Philippines. All of these nations were eager to get rid of their colonial rulers. When the Japanese came, many people in most of these areas at least tacitly supported them.

The exception was the Philippines, already promised it would receive independence by 1946; thus the Filipinos generally preferred to remain loyal to the United States. In between, a nervously independent Thailand was ripe for cooperation with Japan, if only to protect its fragile sovereignty. After the German conquest of France in 1940, Japan took over control of French Indochina. After Pearl Harbor, Thailand agreed to allow Japanese troops to use Thai territory to support Japanese operations in Malaya and Burma.

By early 1942, the British were being chased out of Burma by advancing Japanese troops. The Japanese carrier fleet rampaged through the Indian Ocean in March and April, bombing naval bases and sinking British warships. Although Japanese ground forces never reached densely populated Indian territory, the British diverted substantial resources to ensure that India remained British. At the end of March 1942, Britain announced that India would have its independence as soon as Germany and Japan were defeated. Burma was also liberated voluntarily, as was Malaya, albeit later. Indonesia and Vietnam had to fight for their independence when the colonial powers returned and America got drawn into the latter struggle.

The Japanese victories had a profound effect on the colonial populations. Until the Japanese came along, the Westerners were considered invincible. Although the Japanese occupation was much harsher than Western rule, the "Asia for the Asians" pitch did find receptive ears. However, no one who went through it has forgotten or forgiven the harsh treatment meted out by the Japanese, and Japan suffers from these memories to this day.

WOULD THE JAPANESE *REALLY* SURRENDER?

When the emperor announced the surrender of Japan on August 15, 1945, not all Japanese troops obeyed. The Allies had suspected that this would happen, although the scope of the refusals was not as high as they feared. At first, there were thousands of Japanese soldiers, sailors, and airmen who refused to surrender, and even a few units. Senior Japanese officers were sent out to convince leaders of combat units to lay down their arms, and this generally worked. There were a few cases of aircraft or small warships that attempted to continue the fight, but these were quickly and sharply dealt with by superior Allied force.

Individuals were another matter. Particularly in areas overseas where there were extensive forests or jungles to flee to, thousands of individual soldiers did just that. Some went in small groups, others as individuals. Many of these individuals and small groups had gotten the surrender news only secondhand (by word of mouth or rumor). They did not believe that the emperor they worshiped could ever do such a thing. It had to be an Allied trick. So they fought on, or at least maintained themselves and their weapons in the wilderness until they "received new orders." Japanese officials continued to go to countries like the Philippines and drop leaflets, or wander through the forests with megaphones, trying to convince the diehards to pack it in. By the late 1940s, most of these troops had been convinced to surrender. But hundreds fought on for decades. The vast majority of these renegades were ill-educated, but tremendously loyal (to their emperor) enlisted men. However, an elderly second lieutenant finally surrendered in the Philippines in 1974.

As late as 1990, two former soldiers (now in their seventies) surrendered in Thailand. These two, however, were an unusual case. After the war, they had joined the Communist guerrillas (as had many Axis soldiers in Europe) and fought on in Malaya and Thailand until the Thai government offered an amnesty for Communist guerrillas in the 1970s. These two knew that Japan had lost the war, but knew that they were again in trouble once the British suppressed the Malayan Communists in the 1960s. So the two old soldiers stayed where they were and went native.

There may still be old soldiers out in the bush. With rusted and useless weapons, these diehards continue the fight for the emperor by simply continuing to live out their days unrepentant and unbowing. It's all very Japanese, and those who did return over the years were considered both heroes and fools. In Japan, that is seen not as a contradiction, but simply as being very Japanese.

BIKINI

Less than a year after the surrender of Japan, a great task force once again dropped anchor in a Pacific lagoon. The lagoon was that of Bikini atoll, one of the Caroline Islands, a pleasant little place inhabited by a little more than a hundred people who were rather unceremoniously moved to another atoll.

The fleet was an odd one, ninety-five mostly obsolete vessels: a fleet carrier; a light carrier; four battleships; two heavy cruisers; seventeen destroyers; eight submarines; twenty-seven LSTs, LCIs, and LCTs; and twenty-five attack transports and cargo ships. Odder still, although most of the ships were American, there were also several former Japanese ones and even a former Germany heavy cruiser. The occasion was Operation Crossroads, a pair of tests designed to determine the probable effects of nuclear weapons on a task force at sea.

As closely as possible the ships were fitted out as if for war. The aircraft carriers had airplanes on their hangar decks, avgas in their fuel tanks, and bombs in their magazines. The battleships, cruisers, and destroyers had full magazines as well. The idea was to have everything as "normal" as possible, so that the maximum amount could be learned from the test.

The first test took place on July 1, 1946. A nuclear weapon was dropped from a B-29, to detonate in the air, just above the fleet. The results were marginal. Although there was extensive damage to the upperworks of many of the ships, few of the larger ones suffered significant damage, although the former Japanese light cruiser *Sakawa* sank the next day.

The second test, on July 25, 1946, was quite another matter. A nuclear device was suspended beneath a specially equipped LCI in the middle of the anchored vessels. The results of this underwater blast were striking. Many smaller ships and craft went down immediately; the old battleship *Arkansas* and the carrier *Saratoga*, both within a few hundred yards of ground zero, were extensively damaged, and sank within hours. Other vessels took longer to succumb. For example, the former Japanese battleship *Nagato* finally capsized on the twenty-ninth. Surprisingly, a number of the ships involved in the test

391

were salvable, particularly the old battlewagons *New York*, *Nevada*, and *Pennsylvania*, and even the carrier *Independence*. These were towed to various naval bases for study, and later expended as targets.

A lot was learned from the Bikini nuclear weapons tests, resulting in innovative developments in the design of ships built afterward. That was to the good. There was a negative side as well, however. Little was known about radiation poisoning in those days, and even less about the tolerable limits. Although some ships were deemed too "hot" to be boarded and were sunk by a few well-placed rounds, most of the others were repeatedly visited by military and scientific personnel. The resulting effects on the health of these people are still being debated, although the radiation-monitoring methods then in use did do a good job of warning sailors and technicians away from particularly hot areas.

After nearly five decades, the Bikinians (who have grown in number to nearly 2,000) are now permitted to visit their native atoll, but it will be many years before they will be able to return permanently, as certain plants and animals traditional in their diet have been found to contain higher-than-normal concentrations of several radioactive isotopes. In addition, there are all those ships lying at the bottom of their lagoon, most of them with ammunition still in their magazines. In the meantime, the Bikini islanders have been paid $100 million in compensation by the U.S. government. With this, the islanders have managed to cope somewhat better than neighboring islanders who did not have their ancestral atolls nuked.

And by the way, it isn't true, as some Japanese assert, that *Nagato* was included as a final insult to the Imperial Navy. She was included because she was available, and constructed on different principles and using different techniques than were comparable American battleships. Indeed, the presence of such former enemy vessels as *Nagato*, *Sakawa*, and the German *Prinz Eugen* could just as easily be regarded as rather insulting to the American warships present, which had fought so gallantly to oppose Japanese and German aggression.

How the Samurai Got Airborne

The development of Japan's air forces and aircraft industry in the 1920s was an extraordinary event. Japan was the only non-Western nation to develop its own aircraft industry before World War II. Moreover, Japan did not even begin industrializing until the late nineteenth century, making its leap into aircraft production even more remarkable.

Japan was, from the 1860s, eager to catch up with the West, and by the 1890s had its own arms industry. While some weapons and equipment were still bought from Western firms, Japan was increasingly self-sufficient in the construction of all modern weapons. Going into the 1920s, Japan required no outside assistance and was developing weapons and equipment that were in some cases superior to anything in the West.

Then, as now, the Japanese had a talent for taking existing technology and producing superior versions. This was the case with aircraft. In the five years following the Wright brothers' demonstration of powered flight, most of the world's major armed forces, including Japan, expressed interest. In 1910, two Japanese Army officers were sent to Europe to learn how to fly. This they did, and the next year they brought two aircraft back to Japan. In 1912, Japan built its first aircraft, an improved version of one of the aircraft brought back from Europe a year earlier. The first airplane of purely Japanese design was built in 1916. By the early 1930s, the Japanese aircraft industry was essentially free of dependence on foreign technology and assistance. Annual Japanese aircraft production went from 445 in 1930, to 952 in 1935, and 4,768 in 1940.

The Army was the first service to look into air operations. In the 1870s a balloon unit was established. Balloons were used for reconnaissance throughout the late nineteenth century and it was this experience that led to the sending of the two Army officers to Europe in 1910 to learn to fly. World War I demonstrated the value of aircraft, and a French military mission came to Japan in 1919 with pilot instructors and World War I aircraft.

By 1925, the Army had established the Army Air Corps (on a par with the other branches like infantry, artillery, and so forth). By the early 1930s, the Army was using nothing but Japanese-designed and -manufactured aircraft. Because of ongoing operations in China, Japanese Army pilots were probably the most capable in the world at that time. On the downside, the Army had decided that the Soviet Union was likely to be its most dangerous future enemy, and new aircraft designs were adjusted to deal with this threat most effectively. As a result, going into World War II, Japanese Army aircraft were optimized for relatively short-range missions in cold weather. This meant that the Japanese Army Air Force was less well equipped to deal with fighting in the Pacific than the Navy.

The Navy investigated the use of aircraft only a year behind the Army. In 1921, a British naval mission came to Japan with aircraft and instructors, and from that beginning the Japanese Naval Air Service began. Later that same year, Japan's first aircraft carrier (*Hosho*) was launched. During the 1920s, British designers working in Japan helped develop many of Japan's early domestically produced aircraft.

More carriers were built in the 1920s. As in America, these carriers were reactions to the Washington naval treaty of the early 1920s (which reduced the number of battleships the major powers could have). Rather than scrap battleships being built, Japan was allowed to convert some of them to aircraft carriers. But additional carriers, and effective aircraft to fly from them, would have to wait until the 1930s. In Japan's case, it was in the late 1930s that modern carrier aircraft were designed and built. And two of Japan's most modern carriers didn't enter service until 1941. Japanese naval aviators were able to pick up valuable experience in China during the 1930s, although these operations were minor until 1937. After that year, naval aircraft were heavily used in China, giving Japanese Navy pilots valuable experience that provided them with a decisive edge in the early battles against Western forces.

Had Western leaders paid more attention to the development of Japanese aviation, there would have been fewer unpleasant surprises in the months after Pearl Harbor. The evidence was all there, in plain sight. Western military attachés even sent back accurate reports about the advanced state of the Japanese air forces. But preconceived ideas about the Japanese led to fantasies of inept Japanese pilots barely getting into the air aboard poorly built aircraft. This is a lesson that can be applied to the future.

WHEN STRATEGIES COLLIDE

Strategy is the overall plan a nation has for winning a campaign or war. The United States and Japan had quite different strategies for winning in the Pacific.

The original, 1920s-era U.S. plan for a war with Japan (War Plan Orange) was to advance across the Central Pacific to the Philippines (whether those islands were under attack or not). Most of the Central Pacific islands were under Japanese control and many were known to be heavily fortified. The principal weapon would be the battleship, with the aircraft carriers used for scouting and support. Once the enemy battleships were found, the decisive battle would be fought, the United States would win, and it would be all over within about six months or so. Not much attention was paid to Japanese aircraft that might be on their Central Pacific islands, as aircraft had not yet demonstrated that they could demolish a large battle fleet.

By the late 1930s, prescient naval officers were beginning to realize that War Plan Orange was unworkable, but it was not really formally replaced because other officers continued to argue that the plan would work. The pessimists were right, of course. The problem now was that all those Japanese-held islands had airfields, and an increasing number of naval officers were accepting the fact that warships on the high seas would be very vulnerable to enemy bombers. The optimists were not yet convinced, although they would be during December 1941. When the war came the Philippines was lost, along with nearly everything else west of Hawaii, and the battleships that were not sunk at Pearl Harbor were now acknowledged to be quite vulnerable to aircraft.

Forced to use Australia as the main forward base in the Pacific, the primary American advance initially was from the south, through New Guinea and on to the Philippines, which was reached after nearly three years of war. All this was supported by some carrier, but mostly land-based, aircraft.

The U.S. Navy had built so many carriers and support ships by late 1943 that a second advance through the Central Pacific was proposed. This was accomplished with massive carrier air power, huge amphibious operations, and admirals determined not to let the Army run the show by itself.

This brings up another important point about Pacific war strategy: the ongoing conflict between Army and Navy commanders. This was a problem in both Japan and America. It was worse for the Japanese, where there was no one like President Roosevelt or General Marshall (the senior U.S. officer) to resolve, or at least defuse, the disputes. It's ironic that the Japanese are now known for their devotion to consensus, for they were anything but during World War II. It was the Americans who managed to work out the different approaches to strategy during the war.

In both nations, the Army and Navy had long been quite separate worlds. But there were some unique aspects to the Army-Navy situation in America.

The United States was, and is, a maritime power. Normally, it does not need much of an Army because there are no threatening armies on its land borders. But from its beginnings, America depended on overseas trade, and the protection of its shipping, in order to provide a livelihood for many of its people. In the century before Pearl Harbor:

- The Army and Navy rarely operated together. The one major exception was the Civil War. But that was seen as a unique situation and no lasting wisdom was obtained from that experience.
- The Army had always seen itself as the senior service when it came to planning and directing military operations. Of course, this began to change with the Spanish-American War, where the Navy had to go first and defeat the Spanish fleets, and then the Army followed. The Army was not happy about this new state of affairs, but it was obvious that any future war would see the Army traveling by boat, under Navy protection, to future battlefields.
- While the president was commander in chief, nothing was done to create any organization to coordinate planning and operations by the Army and Navy. Early in World War II, something was cobbled together, but it was improvisation all through the war.

The Japanese Army-Navy situation was similarly characterized by some uniquely Japanese conditions:

- The Army was heavily involved in domestic, and foreign, politics. The Navy was relatively apolitical and, as a result, kept its distance from Army commanders.
- Japan was, like America, a maritime power and even more dependent on overseas trade to sustain its people. Protecting sea lanes was, of course, a Navy responsibility. But until the war began, the most crucial routes were short (between Japan and Korea or China) and could, in theory, be secured by Army land-based air power. As a result, the Army didn't pay as much attention to working with the Navy as it should have. In effect, the Army acted like it was doing the Navy a favor by letting it help out in the China war.
- When the Pacific war began, the Army and Navy had to improvise all their cooperation. In many cases, like the Central Pacific, the Navy often did everything with its own resources, including naval infantry (SNLF) to seize islands.

Keep in mind that, whatever you might hear about American generals and admirals squabbling, their Japanese counterparts were infinitely worse. Prominent examples of the damage done by Japanese Army-Navy rivalry:

- They refused (until too late in the war) to coordinate the use of shipping. The Japanese had a shipping shortage from the beginning of the war and the situation got worse as the war went on. The Army and Navy insisted on maintaining their own separate merchant fleets and not cooperating with each other or Japanese commercial interests. In other words, if an Army cargo ship was leaving Japan for Java half full, and the Navy needed to get supplies to Java at the same time, the Army would not allow the Navy cargo in the empty space on its outgoing ship. Moreover, when these ships returned from places like Java, they would not carry commercial cargo back to Japan; they would come back empty. It was an absurd policy, but persisted for most of the war.
- The Army and Navy would not consult with each other when

they were planning operations in the same area. Part of this was the Navy's fault, because the joint planning that did occur took place in Tokyo, where the Army had the last word since it ran the government. So the Navy just went ahead and did what it thought best and hoped the Army didn't find out until it was too late.

The Army-Navy rivalry in Japan was a considerable asset to the Allied war effort. And it made similar Army-Navy conflicts in the American camp look trivial by comparison.

It's difficult to discern a coherent strategy on the part of the Japanese. In effect, their strategy was to seize as many islands as possible and fortify enough of them with so many ground troops and aircraft that the Allies would not be able to get through to Japan. This was the whole point behind Pearl Harbor, which was designed to gain as much time as possible for the Imperial Army and Navy to grab real estate that the United States would presumably eventually want to take back. If enough territory was seized, and if it was held with sufficient tenacity, the Japanese thinking went, the United States might eventually decide that the cost of recovering it wasn't acceptable, whereupon Japan would emerge with more than it had had at the start of the war. It didn't work.

The keystone of Japanese strategy, however, was not so much grabbing real estate as it was gaining economic resources. The Japanese home islands had few natural resources and nearly all the raw material for Japanese industry had to be imported. While China and Korea provided sufficient ores and food, the oil had to come from fields in Indonesia. It was to obtain access to this oil that Japan went to war with America, the British Empire, and Holland.

Japan's strategy was one of desperation, as it turned out that the Indonesian oil fields could not produce sufficient oil for Japanese needs. More to the point, Japan could not produce sufficient tankers to get the oil from Indonesia to Japan. Allied submarines kept sinking Japanese tankers, and shipping in general. Many senior Japanese military leaders recognized the futility of the war, but they carried out their orders anyway. Loyal unto death was more than just a catchphrase in the Japanese military.

JAPANESE WAR AIMS

The long-term cause of the war was Japan's rampant militarism and the consequent attitude that, as Asians, the Japanese should run Asia without interference from Western powers. The dark side of this concept was that the Japanese felt that they should be the "elder brother" to the other Asians and, in general, in charge of any part of Asia that Japanese troops could control. This point of view met with resistance from other Asians, particularly the Koreans and Chinese, who were Japan's first victims. This Japanese aggression, under way since the 1870s, came under increasing criticism from Western powers. The desire of the Western nations (particularly the United States and Britain) to rein in Japanese aggression led to an embargo on Japan when Japanese troops entered French-controlled Indochina (Vietnam and adjacent areas) in 1941 and took over. The embargo was the short-term cause of the war. Japan had few raw materials of its own. While it could get coal and mineral ores from its Chinese and Korean territories, oil was available only from Western-controlled sources such as Indonesia. Japan's Navy and air forces were useless without oil, so the embargo would eventually disarm Japan. Faced with the choice of surrender or striking back, Japan chose the action her history dictated. To many Japanese, the Pearl Harbor attack was an act of self-defense.

Japan's expansionist war aims were established half a century before Pearl Harbor. No one was able to dissuade Japan from these goals short of a full-scale war. Curiously, the Japanese still hold the view that "they couldn't help themselves" and that the war, and its consequences, made Japan a victim as much as anyone else. This is what is taught in Japanese schools today and the opinion held by many Japanese. Because of this, and Japan's current economic power, other Asian nations are still concerned about century-old Japanese war aims.

IMPERIAL JAPAN

The Japanese shared many cultural beliefs with the Chinese. One was that they, the Japanese, were a chosen people who were born to rule. Even during centuries of isolation, Japan saw itself as an empire, an empire waiting for the opportune time to assert its fore-ordained role as a world leader.

The head of the Japanese government was the emperor, in this case Hirohito, who assumed the throne in 1926 at age twenty-five. But although the constitution formally gave him considerable power, the emperor usually reigned (liked a modern European mon-arch); he did not, usually, rule, although he technically had the authority to do so.

An ancient institution in Japan, the emperors had never had as much power as they possessed in the seventy-five years prior to the surrender of Japan in 1945. Then, and now, the emperor was con-sidered a divine creature, the direct descendant of the ancient gods of Japan, but more directly from the warrior Jimmu Tenno who allegedly lived in the seventh century B.C. (but more probably about a thousand years later).

Japan was long governed by feudal tribes (or clans, as the Japanese put it) that, over the centuries, came to be dominated by one feudal clan leader who became known as the shogun. The emperor's clan was recognized as the most exalted in rank, and the keepers of im-portant religious functions. But the emperor never ruled; a succes-sion of shoguns did. From the seventeenth century to the 1860s, the undisputed shoguns of the Tokugawa clan led a peaceful, united, generally prosperous, and quite insular Japan.

But American and European warships barged into Japan in the 1850s, making the Japanese aware that their isolation had put them way behind in crucial areas of technology. A reform movement arose in Japan and, in a series of civil conflicts in the 1860s, deposed the shogunate and instituted a Western-style government using the em-peror as a head of state. In effect, the quasi-religious figure of the emperor was someone the reformers and conservatives could agree on as a unifying force in Japan.

A major samurai revolt against the reformers in the 1870s was put down by a new conscript army, and Japan began its rapid march into the industrial age. The imperial family and clan was brought along, but over 2,000 years of submitting to the will of the ruling shogun was a habit not easily discarded. While the shoguns and their hordes of samurai warriors were gone, they had, in effect, been replaced by generals and a modern army.

Non-Japanese never knew quite what to make of the emperor. The Japanese people were unrestrained in their adoration and respect for him, and this gave foreigners the impression that all the emperor had to do was issue an order and it would be done. Although Japan had a parliamentary system of government before 1945, it was a government dominated by a small number of powerful groups. The emperor had influence, but not the ability to act like an autocrat.

Japan is a nation of manners and custom. This we know today; it was even more so before 1945. Although the emperor's power was theoretically unlimited, in practice he was constrained by a mass of custom and obligation. Many things are "simply not done," or at least not done without considerable consensus building and negotiation. This approach was developed over thousands of years as the dozens of warring clans in Japan learned to resolve their differences and become a unified country.

An example of the power of consensus building and custom can be seen in the outlawing of firearms in the seventeenth century. This order actually worked, banning firearms from Japan for over two centuries. When the permanent unification of Japan occurred in the seventeenth century, and when all the fighting and talking were over, the new shogun declared that firearms made it too easy for someone to raise a peasant army and overthrow the samurai ("knights") who traditionally defended and ruled Japan. The samurai took years to train in the use of the sword and bow, and their devotion to their feudal lord, and the emperor, was considered the glue that would keep Japan together. A peasant could be trained in the use of firearms within a few weeks, and could be controlled by whoever paid him. So the shogun ordered all but a few government-owned firearms destroyed. And it was done. That's the kind of nation Japan was, and generally still is.

The modern (post-1860s) Japanese emperors have been acutely aware that their elevated status could be quickly changed back to "national historical shrine" if the imperial household stepped out of line. This did not prevent the modern emperors from grabbing all the power they could. Yet most of the emperor's power came from being in the middle of things.

A major branch of the pre-1945 government was the "Palace Institutions." The "institutions" enabled the emperor to have thousands of civil servants, family members, and retainers on the payroll serving only the emperor. Thus the emperor had experts in all areas of government at his disposal. While this still did not allow the emperor to actually issue orders to the government, it did keep him informed on what was going on and, in particular, what the many strong personalities who were running the government were up to.

The emperor could order government officials to report to him on what their departments were doing. An audience with the emperor was either a gift to bestow on a cooperative government official, or the means to punish an official whom the emperor was at odds with. All of this was done according to an immense tradition of protocol and procedure. After all, the emperor was, to the Japanese, a god that walked the earth.

Much has been written about whether or not Hirohito should have been treated as a war criminal, and punished for his role in starting (or at least for not trying to prevent) the war in the Pacific. Hirohito was not blameless. He could have refused to approve of the Army's aggressive policies in the 1920s and 1930s. But the emperor was well aware of the fact that past emperors who had overstepped their bounds had simply been ignored. A too-rambunctious emperor could be put into a form of exile, shut up in the imperial palace (which was normal anyway) and guarded by soldiers in order to "protect" him.

Thus, while Hirohito did not order the aggression that led to the war with America, he didn't make a bold move to stop it either. At least not until August 1945. At that point the emperor did stick his neck out and order the surrender. That act, no doubt, saved the imperial institution in Japan. And no doubt it was that result that crossed Hirohito's mind when he made his move.

A QUITE DIFFERENT FORM
OF GOVERNMENT

The Japanese government was organized quite differently from that of the United States, both in form and in substance. At the top of the government was the emperor, but he was the head of state, not the one who gave the orders. From the early 1930s to the end of the war the military was giving most (but not all) of the orders. This was accomplished by having a general as the prime minister and by using the government to cow the population and any other organizations that might threaten military control.

The prime minister was the one person in Japan who had the most power. The prime minister was appointed by the emperor on the advice of his principal advisers (especially senior princes) and elder statesmen. Until the armed forces forced their will on the nation in 1932, the prime minister was usually the head of the largest party in the Diet (parliament). Through the 1920s and early 1930s, the armed forces became more of a dominant force (with the aid of nationalist and expansionist civilians). Japan's overseas empire in China, Formosa, and Korea was popular with many, but not all, Japanese. The military made the overseas empire a matter of national honor and cast those in opposition as traitors. The armed forces flexed their muscles in 1932 (after assassinating two civilian prime ministers) and forced the emperor to appoint the first of a succession of generals or admirals (with a few short-term civilians) as prime minister. While the military met with resistance, they were using guns and their opponents, by and large, were not. Still, the military had, in typical Japanese fashion, accommodated their largely civilian opposition. Thus the Diet remained in session and civilians still headed many of the ministries. The prime minister presided over the following ministries:

- FOREIGN MINISTRY. The Japanese State Department.
- THE HOME MINISTRY. Controlled all the police in the nation as well as the prefectural (province) governors. There were no "states" as in America. Japan was very centralized. There was also a special national police force whose name can best be

translated as "Thought Police." This force served both as a secret police for the government and a protection against the spread of any "un-Japanese" thought or behavior.

- FINANCE MINISTRY. The Treasury Department. Controlled the national banking system and national finances.
- WAR MINISTRY. This was the department that controlled the Army's support services. This included logistics, recruiting, and so on. This ministry also controlled the semiautonomous secret police (which served mainly overseas at the behest of local commanders). The minister was always an Army officer, usually nominated by the General Staff.
- NAVY MINISTRY. Served the same function as the War Ministry, except for the Navy. The minister was always a naval officer, nominated by the Naval Staff.
- JUSTICE MINISTRY. Oversaw the court system.
- EDUCATION MINISTRY. In charge of all schools in the nation, as well as propaganda and government publications.
- COMMERCE AND INDUSTRY MINISTRY. Controlled smaller business and worked with (and sometimes for) the larger businesses.
- AGRICULTURAL AND FORESTRY MINISTRY. Controlled raw materials production within Japan.
- TRANSPORTATION MINISTRY. In charge of the national road and railroad networks as well as ports and coastal shipping.
- OVERSEAS AFFAIRS MINISTRY. Controlled the overseas colonies (China, Korea, Formosa, and later new territories conquered by Japan).
- WELFARE MINISTRY. Oversaw national health and, more important, the rationing system (which was in force long before Pearl Harbor).
- MUNITIONS MINISTRY. Coordinated (not very effectively) munitions and weapons production.
- CABINET PLANNING BOARD. Controlled the mobilization of Japan's resources for the war effort.
- MILITARY GENERAL STAFFS. There were two of these, one for the Army and one for the Navy. The Army's was the larger and more powerful. But the Navy always managed to maintain its independence. Each of the General Staffs controlled all the military units of its service. Each General Staff had a Chief of Staff

who was, in effect, the head of that service. The War and Navy ministries were subordinate (in practice) to their respective Chiefs of Staff.

THE DIET (PARLIAMENT)

Set up in the previous century, the Diet was intended to make Japan a constitutional monarchy. Until the military took over, it more or less worked. However, it was not an American-style democracy. The Diet had two chambers. The lower chamber was the House of Representatives. This comprised 466 members elected by the 14 million males who had the franchise (out of 70 million Japanese citizens; women didn't get the vote, nor did all the men, until after World War II).

There was a multiplicity of parties, and this was one thing that annoyed the military (and many conservatives and nationalists). The Diet continued to exist through the period of military rule, but all it did was approve the budget increases and discuss legislation introduced by the prime minister. The lower chamber was kept under control by secret police and various political and economic pressures.

The upper chamber was the House of Peers, whose role was to "guide" the House of Representatives. And this the House of Peers did, especially during the period of military rule. The Peers were organized in a uniquely Japanese fashion. Of the nearly 400 members, 66 were wealthy individuals elected by the 6,000 biggest taxpayers in Japan. Another 150 were nobles elected by the 1,000 or so adult male members of the nobility. The emperor selected another 125 members, based on the selectees' high achievements in the service of Japan. Finally, all the princes and marquises (senior nobles) were automatically members.

THE IMPERIAL INSTITUTIONS

The list of organizations that composed the Japanese emperor's Palace Institutions is a long one.

- IMPERIAL FAMILY COUNCIL. All adult males of the imperial family in descent from an emperor (to the fifth generation). These imperial family councillors were the princes of Japan and there were about twenty-five of them through most of Hirohito's reign. While this group was to advise the emperor on family matters (money, marriages, indiscretions in the royal family), it also served as a means for the emperor to get advice from family members concerning affairs of state. The adult princes would usually have some high government job. Even if some of these posts were largely ceremonial (it was prestigious to have a prince around), it did allow the prince to be aware of what was going on in that organization. A few princes did hold powerful posts and used these council meetings to give their relative, the emperor, frank advice.
- PRIVY COUNCIL. These were twenty-six elder statesmen (known as the privy councillors), appointed by the emperor to offer advice on any situation the emperor wanted advice on. While the prime minister "advised" the emperor on who should join this council, all of the councillors were devoted to the emperor (although some had markedly different ideas on how Japan should be governed). Not as intimate as the Imperial Family Council, the Privy Council was a better way to nudge the government to do something the emperor wanted to do but the government didn't (like surrendering at the end of the war).
- LORD PRIVY SEAL. This post was held by a loyal aristocrat. Technically, the job entailed supervising Japanese royalty. This included tasks like maintaining imperial archives, tombs, and shrines; training young nobles in protocol; and keeping track of all the documents that passed before the emperor (and especially those that had to obtain an imperial seal, the "privy seal"). In practice, the lord privy seal was the emperor's chief adviser on domestic politics. To assist in this function, the lord privy seal also supervised the Spy Service Directorate (which had access to all Japanese espionage and would prepare analyses for the emperor and his advisers). Again, in Japanese fashion, having access to all this information did little more than keep the emperor informed. He could not order the many espionage agencies to do anything. This setup did enable the emperor to dare defy the "fight to the last" government in August 1945

and broadcast his surrender announcement. In typical Japanese fashion, the emperor would not have done this unless he was pretty certain that most Japanese would accept it.

- GRAND CHAMBERLAIN. He was in charge of the emperor's personal living arrangements. This encompassed a vast bureaucracy that maintained dozens of imperial residences. The chamberlain was also in charge of the many ceremonies the emperor had to participate in. The chamberlain also looked after the living arrangements of the crown prince, the empress, and the emperor's mother (the empress dowager). In practice, the chamberlain was also the emperor's adviser on foreign affairs.

- AIDES-DE-CAMP. The emperor's personal military advisers. They were senior military officers assigned to keep the emperor informed on military affairs. There was a chief imperial aide-de-camp and dozens of assistants.

- SUPREME WAR COUNCIL. A military version of the Privy Council. It comprised senior military officers selected by the emperor (with the cooperation of the Army and Navy leaders). There was also an advisory group (the Board of Field Marshals and Fleet Admirals) that was consulted from time to time. The Supreme War Council was a means of communication between the emperor and the generals who were running the country. It was not a decision-making body, except in the sense that if a policy seemed to "displease" the emperor, it gave succor to those generals or admirals that opposed it.

- IMPERIAL HEADQUARTERS. This was formed in 1937, when it became clear that operations in China had reached wartime intensity. In effect, the establishment of this organization marked the entry of Japan (by Japanese reckoning) into a state of war. The permanent staff of the Imperial Headquarters (located in Tokyo) were staff and support personnel. Meetings with the emperor at the Imperial Headquarters were attended by the most senior military officials (the Army Chief of Staff, Navy Chief of Staff, war minister, and Navy minister). While decisions were discussed at the Supreme War Council, they were confirmed at the Imperial Headquarters.

- IMPERIAL HOUSEHOLD MINISTRY. Managed (and still manages) the emperor's wealth, which was (and still is) immense: tens of billions of dollars of assets, including millions of acres of crown lands (from which rents were collected) and two dozen palaces. In effect, this ministry (answerable to the emperor, not the prime minister) was the emperor's business manager and treasurer. The emperor held equity positions in many of Japan's largest companies, giving him a certain amount of control over the economy.

THE LARGEST ORGANIZATION IN JAPAN

The Japanese Army was the largest organization in Japan until the end of the war. At its peak, over 10 percent of the adult population was in an Army uniform, or on an Army payroll for civilian workers. There were three major organizations in the Army:

One was the General Staff, organized along the German model. It had five "bureaus," which, while comprising only a few thousand people, controlled the rest of the Army.

- The General Bureau took care of personnel affairs and organization and mobilization.
- The First Bureau was the most important, as it planned and organized military operations.
- The Second Bureau was for intelligence. Within the Second Bureau there was one section for American and European armed forces and another for Asian forces. A third section controlled secret service operations.
- The Third Bureau oversaw transport and communications.
- The Fourth Bureau was the historical bureau. It collected records of events, for later reconstruction to support future operations.

The War Ministry, another major part of the Army, was larger (in personnel) than the General Staff, but much less powerful. The War Ministry basically controlled all the civilian organizations (especially those in Japan proper) that supported the Army. There were eight bureaus in the War Ministry and the title of each accurately reflected the function of each. The Personnel Bureau looked after senior military personnel, including awards for meritorious service.

The Military Affairs Bureau kept track of the military budget and other items like ideology. The Military Administration Bureau took charge of such military details as ceremonies, duty regulations, discipline, and such. It also decided which Japanese were liable for military service and when they would be called to service. Within Japan, this bureau was responsible for the defense of installations and state secrets. The Economic Mobilization Bureau coordinated the military's control over Japanese industry and economic resources. By the end of the war, this bureau was running what was left of the Japanese economy. The Ordnance Bureau controlled the disposition of weapons and ammunition. As the war went on, this bureau spent most of its time explaining to the military why there were no more weapons and munitions. The Judicial Bureau provided legal services. The Medical Bureau organized the nation's medical resources to support the war effort. The Intendance Bureau saw to the more mundane matters of meeting payrolls and supplying food and clothing.

The field forces, the final major part of the Army, were the actual fighting forces. The field forces were organized somewhat similarly to those in the West, but there were some differences that could cause some confusion.

The smallest Army unit was the independent brigade (5,000 to 6,000 troops) commanded by a major general. Sometimes this was actually a reinforced regiment taken from a division. The most common unit in the Army (as with most armies) was the division, commanded by a lieutenant general. The normal strength of divisions was 10,000 to 15,000 troops (and much less as the war went on), even though the official full strength was 18,000 to 20,000. Transportation problems, and steady losses to enemy action or disease, kept divisions in the Pacific understrength nearly all the time.

The Japanese didn't use the "corps" as did most Western armies, but called a unit with two or more divisions an "army." These armies were commanded by a lieutenant general (as were the divisions). Just to confuse matters, the next highest level was the "area army," which contained two or more armies and an air army. These area armies were commanded by a full general or a lieutenant general. Unlike all smaller units, the area armies sometimes had a name (North China Area Army or Burma Area Army) rather than a number.

Finally, there were the army groups, which comprised two or more area armies and were commanded by a general or field marshal. Just to confuse matters, the Burma Area Army was considered an army group, but usually the name *army group* meant a larger grouping. The Southern Army Group controlled all Army forces in Southeast Asia and the Pacific (except, at times, the Burma Area Army).

The Army had its own air force (as did the Navy). The basic organization of the air force was the *sentai* (group), commanded by a colonel. A *sentai* had three or more *chutai* (companies or squadrons in U.S. parlance) of nine to twelve aircraft each, commanded by a lieutenant colonel or major. A *hikodan* (air brigade or "wing"), commanded by a major general or colonel, had four or more *sentai*, one of which was composed of reconnaissance aircraft. Larger units were *hikoshidan* (air divisions) with two or more *hikodan*, and *kokugun* (air armies) with two or more *hikoshidan*. These were considered equivalent to other Army division-size and army-size units for command purposes. There were often independent groups and squadrons, especially on out-of-the way islands in the Pacific.

Ranks were slightly different in the Japanese Army than in the American forces. America has five general ranks (brigadier general, major general, lieutenant general, general, and general of the army). The Japanese have only four ranks (major general, lieutenant general, general, field marshal).

THE IMPERIAL NAVY

The Japanese Navy's organization was similar to that of the Army in terms of the Navy General Staff and the Navy Ministry. The Navy General Staff used the term *department* rather than *bureau* (as the Army called subdivisions of the General Staff). Like the Army, the Navy adopted many organizational and command practices from European nations (particularly Germany, Britain, and France). Navy combat units were, of course, organized quite differently than those in the Army. All Navy combat units were under the command of the Combined Fleet.

Subordinate to the Combined Fleet were the area fleets, which were responsible for a geographical area. These fleets usually had a large local port as a main base (Singapore, Truk, or a base in Japan) and often many other smaller land bases. Area fleets had some major fleet units (battleships and carriers), but most of these were assigned to mobile fleets for major operations. Area fleets contained one or more fleets and air fleets. These fleets controlled the smaller units containing individual ships and aircraft.

The largest subdivision of a fleet was the group (containing two or more smaller units with individual ships). Fleets also had separate base forces, which were ports with land-based sailors (some serving as a defense garrison), small ships, and floatplanes for reconnaissance.

Individual ships were organized into divisions (two or more capital ships of one type, such as battleships or carriers) or flotillas (*sentai* of three or four cruisers or up to twelve to twenty destroyers, submarines, or smaller ships). Flotillas were also subdivided into divisions (two cruisers or two to four destroyers).

All submarines belonged to the 6th Fleet.

The mobile fleet was a temporary organization for specific operations. Subdivisions of a mobile fleet were called striking forces, and these were equivalents to U.S. task forces. Sometimes a mobile fleet would be sent to assist an operation being staged by an area fleet.

Aircraft were organized into air fleets (*koku kantai*). Two or more groups (*koku sentai*) composed an air fleet. Groups contained two or more squadrons. Squadrons (*kokutai*) contained eighteen to thirty-six aircraft of one type. Carriers had an air group attached, usually containing three squadrons (one each of fighters, dive bombers, and torpedo bombers).

THE URGE FOR EMPIRE

The cause of the war in the Pacific was not Japan itself, but that segment of the population that was fanatically devoted to expanding the Japanese "Empire." Until Japan threw off its centuries of isolationism in the late nineteenth century, Japan had had an emperor, but no empire. The reforms that transformed Japan from a feudal society into a constitutional monarchy also created a segment of the population that saw Japan's role as expansionistic and militaristic. These attitudes were the result of three influences.

- ECONOMICS. Japan was overpopulated, and the introduction of new technology from the West made the situation worse by improving living standards, increasing the birth rate, and creating a need for more resources. One solution was to seize foreign territory and send Japanese colonists overseas to the new lands. This was done, and continued until the end of World War II. Naturally, the colonists would be enthusiastic about their new opportunities, and their families became supporters of this expansion. This group included millions of Japanese from every social class.
- CULTURE. The old feudal nobility and their samurai warriors now had better weapons that they wanted to put to use. The Japanese were quite confident of their military ability, the nation never having been conquered by a foreign power. Military success against China, Korea, and Russia from 1880 to 1910 added to this sense of power. The militarists could not be denied as they piled success upon success. The military classes had lost much in the nineteenth century reforms and saw overseas expansion as a means to recover their position.
- COLONIALISM. Japan quickly became aware of how rapidly the Western nations were taking over the world. Japan realized, especially after it defeated Russia in the 1905 war, that it was the only non-Western nation that was holding its own. Its successes appealed to nearly all Japanese (who felt they were pretty special in any event). The Western nations had colonies, and now Japan also had them. During World War I, the Allies treated Japan like an equal (in order to obtain Japanese support in the Pacific) and this gave the Japanese a greater sense that Asia and the Pacific was their bailiwick and that Japan should be supreme in the region.

Although Japan's military expansion had broad appeal in the general population, it was the tacit acceptance of the extremists that caused the problems. When moderate politicians were assassinated or overseas military commanders went to war without permission, there was a tendency to indulge these acts. The perpetrators were either not punished or not punished severely. While moderate politicians held sway in Japan through the early 1930s, the hundreds of thousands of troops and colonists in Korea, Manchuria, and

China became increasingly independent. This was not an unusual situation for colonies, but it ultimately proved disastrous as the aggressive actions of the colonial armies dragged Japan into a war with the West that it could not win.

Not content to operate independently in the overseas colonies, the military pushed for control of the government at home. The politicians (and much of the population) opposed this. But the expansionists/militarists/nationalists had the guns and the fanaticism. Assassination, and the threat of assassination, cowed most politicians and the population, and by the early 1930s the generals and admirals were running the government. What made this situation worse was that most of the fanaticism was coming from junior and middle-level officers and their civilian allies. Bit by bit, like-minded generals and admirals assumed positions of power. The emperor could protest against the violence and militarization of the government, and in the case of one round of assassinations in 1936 he even responded forcefully, but the emperor knew his power was limited. It was only seventy years earlier that the emperor had been a puppet of the feudal overlords, and there was fear that this relationship would be revived.

Democracy is a fragile institution, and in prewar Japan democracy and peace lost out to authoritarianism and war.

GUERRILLA WARS

Although the Japanese actively promoted their Asian conquests as "liberations" of Asians from European colonial rule, many of the victims saw the change as just another alien occupation. The Japanese were no better, and often a great deal worse, than the European colonial powers they replaced. Japanese attitudes toward non-Japanese were callous in the extreme. Moreover, the Japanese never developed effective antiguerrilla techniques. Their response to partisan activity was brute force. Entire villages were destroyed and the inhabitants killed. This, of course, only created more hatred of the Japanese and, naturally, more guerrillas. The Japanese never learned to fight the guerrillas on the same terms. Instead they favored large-scale "search and destroy" operations that rarely found much but destroyed whatever goodwill the Japanese had obtained by expelling the colonial powers.

As a result, there were guerrilla wars in every country the Japanese occupied. The degree of resistance varied greatly from area to area. Moreover, the wartime anti-Japanese partisans usually became post–World War II freedom fighters. What Americans think of as the Vietnam War actually got its start as an anti-Japanese resistance in the early 1940s. Moreover, many of these World War II resistance efforts continue to this day, with the Japanese replaced by local "occupiers."

A country-by-country breakdown reveals as much about Asia to-day as it does World War II.

BURMA

Occupied by Britain since the nineteenth century, much to the distaste of the Burmese, this was one of those nations where the resistance was complicated by local politics. Generally, the Burmese were (and are) passive. They were unhappy with British rule, but never provided any serious military resistance. Their attitude was much the same against the Japanese. The Burmese did, however, note the postwar possibilities of making a show of resistance to the Japanese. It was clear, after 1942, that Japan would lose, so many politically active Burmese put together a "resistance movement" that existed more in word than in deed. At the same time, to placate the bloody-minded Japanese (who reacted quite harshly to any local resistance), some of these same Burmese pretended to collaborate. Contacts were made with the British and an understanding reached whereby Burma would gain its freedom after the war in return for this "resistance." The British had already reached a similar arrange-ment with the Indians. Oddly enough, there was one segment of the Burmese population that did resist actively and gave substantial armed assistance to the British. These were the Kachins and other tribal peoples in northern Burma. The "tribes" had long experienced bad relations with the mainstream Burmese, and found the Japanese to be even worse. The British, having extensive experience in dealing with tribal cultures, came off looking much better and thus were able to enlist irregular troops from among the tribes. After the war, and Burmese independence, the tribes kept fighting Burmese, and are still at it today.

CHINA

This, more than any other theater in World War II, was arguably the largest guerrilla war of the twentieth century. Because the Chinese were largely cut off from outside support after 1942, they could not afford to fight a conventional war. So several million Chinese troops played cat-and-mouse with over fifty Japanese divisions (including twenty composed of Chinese in the pay of the Japanese). The Japanese were not much better off, having limited resources to begin with, and most of that being devoted to the war with the Americans in the Pacific. There were actually three guerrilla wars going on at the same time. There was the obvious one, Chinese versus Japanese. Then there was the ongoing conflict between Chinese Nationalists and Chinese Communists. Finally, there was still a fair amount of free-lance fighting by brigands and sundry warlords. There were a number of large battles and some wide-scale offensives by the Japanese, but much of the action was between small groups of armed men (and sometimes women) sneaking around shooting at each other. While there were front lines and many organized Chinese units, the front lines were long and porous, while the Chinese had many armed supporters behind the Japanese lines. Not much about this war has been heard in the West. It was an especially ugly war, with atrocities the norm and loyalty in short supply. Americans became increasingly frustrated by the deceit they encountered from both the Communists and the Nationalists (who were more interested in fighting each other than the Japanese). It was a large war, and it didn't end on V-J Day, but continued into the early 1950s as the Communists first defeated the Nationalists and then, after establishing control over the entire country, went after sundry non-Chinese minorities. Some of these conflicts continue to the present.

INDONESIA

Even before the Japanese invasion in early 1942, there was some armed resistance to Dutch colonial rule of the Dutch East Indies. But once the Japanese were there, the Allies were eager to supply more weapons to anyone who would fight the Japanese. The Indonesians realized this would happen, but in a masterful political move, members of the resistance agreed among themselves that some Indonesians would become "collaborators" and gain aid from the Japanese also. When the Dutch returned after V-J Day, they found both "pro" and "anti" Japanese groups united and ready to fight for independence. These two groups had also equipped themselves with many of the weapons and equipment the Japanese had surrendered on the islands. After a brief but bloody struggle, the Dutch gave in.

THE ISLANDERS

The Japanese overran most of the Solomons, the Bismarcks, many of the other islands in the Southwest Pacific, and much of New Guinea rather easily, there being nothing much with which to oppose them. The local folks were Melanesians, Stone Age people with Negroid features, descended from Southeast Asians. These "stout black fellows" cooperated quite freely with their Commonwealth overlords in resisting the Japanese. This was partially out of loyalty, but mostly out of self-interest. A few weeks of Japanese domination usually convinced even the most hardened anti-British islander that the king's men were easier to get along with than the emperor's. Without the cooperation of these islanders, the task of ejecting the Japanese from the Southwest Pacific would have been far more difficult. Coastwatching operations, in which Commonwealth officers kept tabs on Japanese fleet and air movements from jungle-covered islands, would have been impossible without the assistance of the islanders. The islanders also reconnoitered Japanese positions, helped rescue downed fliers, and occasionally knocked off Japanese troops. The Allies offered a bounty for dead Japanese and live Allied pilots, a form of transaction the avid hunters among the islanders could appreciate. Many a downed Allied pilot was shocked to be confronted by a group of Stone Age warriors, one of whom would inquire in a British accent, "Are you all right, chap?" A greatly many islanders were killed, and many were subsequently decorated by the various Allied governments and awarded pensions for their wartime service.

KOREA

Unlike the other nations occupied by the Japanese, Korea had been under Japanese rule since 1905. Thus the Japanese had had over thirty years to pound the Koreans into submission. Many Koreans had fled to China and joined the Communist guerrillas there. A large Korean population existed in Manchuria, and many men from this group also fled deeper into China to join the fight. Many Koreans who stayed behind joined Japanese-controlled Army units and many more were conscripted for service as labor troops overseas. These Koreans at first confused American troops (who could not tell the difference between a Korean and a Japanese) by quickly running away or surrendering rather than fighting to the death as Japanese usually did. The Koreans were not enthusiastic about supporting the Japanese war effort, but most of their "guerrilla" activities were in the form of sabotage and lackadaisical attitudes on the job. The North Korean invasion of South Korea in 1950 was spearheaded by 100,000 Korean veterans of the war in China, while many of the South Korean officers had formerly served in the Japanese Army.

MALAYA

This area, including Singapore, was heavily garrisoned by the Japanese. A resistance movement sprang up anyway. Guerrilla operations were most enthusiastically embraced by the Chinese population of Malaya, although there were also Malay and Indian (another local minority) guerrillas. The Chinese were the core of the resistance largely because of the depredations the Japanese were committing in China. The "overseas Chinese" maintained their language and traditions, as well as links with the homeland. Another item the Malay Chinese imported from China was communism and the best-disciplined partisans were Communist led. Many native Malays, and to a lesser extent Indians, assisted the Japanese in fighting the guerrillas. This fighting continued after the war, when the Chinese Communist guerrillas continued fighting. The British, like the Japanese, used Malay assistance to eventually put down the Communist insurgency. This was something the Japanese were never able to do during the war. But the Japanese did manage to keep the guerrillas largely confined to the rural areas of Malaya.

PHILIPPINES

Of all their early campaigns, the Japanese had their hardest time in the Philippines. It took six months to defeat the American and Filipino troops, even though most of the troops were Filipino and few had more than rudimentary training. While most of the fighting was concentrated outside Manila, on the Bataan peninsula, there were thousands of American and Filipino troops elsewhere on the many islands that compose the Philippines. Not all of these troops surrendered; some simply took their weapons into the hills, there to continue the resistance. Because of the generally good relations between Americans and Filipinos (aided by the prewar promise to grant the islands their independence in 1946), the Japanese encountered a hostile population. Bolstered by popular support, the first Philippine guerrillas were able to recruit more fighters and withstand strenuous Japanese attempts to eradicate them. While there were some American officers and troops among these partisans, many of the units were led by patriotic Filipinos.

Unfortunately, the guerrillas were deep inside Japanese-controlled territory until 1944, when physical contact with the outside world was reestablished. Despite the regular radio contact with the guerrillas, Washington was rather surprised at the vigor and size of the anti-Japanese guerrilla movement. Constantly harassing the Japanese and supplying valuable information to the Allies, the guerrillas waited for the day when MacArthur would return. Meanwhile, the Japanese built up their forces in the Philippines in anticipation of a late-1944 American attack. The larger number of Japanese troops led to increased antiguerrilla activity. The clumsy and brutal Japanese tactics led to an increased number of guerrillas and a desire for revenge by the much abused Filipinos.

By the end of 1944, a steady stream of supplies arrived by submarine and long-range aircraft. Hardened by over two years of living and fighting in the jungles, the guerrillas became more numerous and effective. By the time MacArthur and his troops returned to the Philippines in late 1944, there were nearly 100,000 organized guerrillas waiting to act as scouts and fighters. The arriving American troops were surprised at the quantity, and quality, of the guerrilla troops. Although later official accounts of the Philippine fighting played down the contributions of the guerrillas, at the time American units were glad to have the guerrillas available.

Because many of the Japanese subsequently fled to the hills to fight on in early 1945, the Filipino guerrillas proved invaluable in hunting the Japanese down and limiting the damage the enemy irregulars could cause. There was a certain amount of payback involved here, as the Japanese had indulged in savage reprisals when confronted with the generally pro-American attitude of the Filipinos. Some of the Filipino guerrillas were Communist inspired and these partisans continued to fight the new Filipino government after the war and into the 1950s.

SIAM (THAILAND)

This nation was in a most bizarre situation. Siam was the only independent nation in Southeast Asia and it had maintained its independence by deft diplomacy. Even before Pearl Harbor, the Japanese made it known that they might have need to call upon Siamese "cooperation." When a Japanese army showed up on its border, demanding passage through Siam to Burma, the Siamese did what they had learned to do in order to survive. They let the Japanese march through. But the Japanese wanted more "cooperation" than that and soon had Siam under what amounted to military occupation. This did not make the Japanese popular with the Siamese people, or the government, so by late 1942 there was a typically Siamese "resistance movement." These were not your typical guerrillas, although some of them were armed and there were a few acts of sabotage during the war. What the Siamese resistance did do was get in touch with the Allies and provide a steady stream of reliable information on what the Japanese were up to in Siam. As a result, the Allies never declared Siam "hostile" and simply treated it as another victim of Japanese aggression after the war.

VIETNAM

There had already been guerrilla activity in Vietnam before World War II. In this case it was against the French, who had controlled Vietnam (and neighboring Cambodia and Laos) since late in the nineteenth century. The Japanese relationship with Vietnam proved to be a curious one. As a French colony, Vietnam had to answer to the pro-German Vichy French government established after the Germans defeated France in June 1940. This, technically, made Vietnam an "ally" of Japan (because Japan and Germany were tied by treaties). Britain and America protested when the French, under Japanese pressure, shut down Allied supply routes to China in late 1940. In July 1941, the local Vichy officials gave in to Japanese demands for access to Vietnamese ports and airfields and the right to station an unlimited number of troops in Vietnam. The local resistance then shifted operations to oppose the Japanese and, because of this, received Allied aid. The Vietnamese resistance, dominated by Communists, did not get help in keeping the French out after the war and this led to prolonged fighting that eventually dragged in the United States in the 1960s. The guerrillas were quite bitter about their treatment by the Allies. Immediately after the war, British troops moved in and rearmed Japanese soldiers to fight the Communist guerrillas for a few months.

LEGACIES OF THE PACIFIC WAR

The Pacific war left an enormous impression on the U.S. Navy, the U.S. Marine Corps, and the resuscitated Japanese armed forces. These were the military legacies of the Pacific war:

The U.S. Navy fervently embraced aircraft carriers, underway replenishment, and long-range amphibious operations. These concepts have defined the U.S. Navy and Marine Corps from 1945 to the last decade of the century. Oddly enough, these war-based concepts did not really suit postwar conditions. While the Navy was able to use its carrier aviation extensively during the Korean, Vietnam, and Gulf wars, this was not how carrier aviation was meant to operate. In those three wars, carriers were merely substitutes for additional airfields that could have been built on nearby friendly territory. But the carriers were available, even though they were more expensive to operate. Moreover, there has never been another carrier-versus-carrier naval battle since June 1944. With the collapse of the Soviet Union in 1991, there is no longer another viable carrier force to face U.S. flattops in battle.

The Marines had the same experience, having only one opportunity (at Inchon, Korea, in 1950) to practice the amphibious operations they engaged in so frequently and successfully during World War II. With the demise of the Soviet empire in 1991, the U.S. Navy and Marine Corps have had a hard time hanging on to their powerful, and expensive, World War II legacies of carriers and amphibious shipping.

The effect of the war on the Japanese armed forces is another story, however. As a result of Japan's defeat, the Japanese armed forces were discredited. They were also all but outlawed in Japan's post–World War II constitution. Once seen as a most noble career, military service is now looked down on. However, the post–World War II Japanese who do choose to serve in the "Self Defense Forces" are even more diligent and efficient than their wartime predecessors, and have gained a deserved reputation for excellence. This in spite of the fact that the best men no longer flock to the colors. In addition, although Japan's defense budget is held to 1 percent of GNP, that 1 percent grows with Japan's huge GNP. As Russia's military spending rapidly shrinks, we face the prospect that Japan will shortly have the world's second-largest defense budget.

OLD SAILORS STICK AROUND

In January 1989, Master Chief Petty Officer Clarence E. Dowden, Jr., of the Coast Guard, retired from the service. Chief Dowden was the last enlisted man in the U.S. armed forces to have served during the Second World War. Enlisting in early 1945, Dowden saw extensive service in the Pacific during the closing months of the war and remained in the service afterward.

The last World War II American officer on active duty was Rear Admiral Grace Hopper of the Navy. Admiral Hopper, who held a Ph.D. in mathematics, joined the WAVES in 1943. Discharged at the end of the war, she remained active in the Naval Reserve, while doing pioneer work in computer technology and programming (among other things, she is said to have coined the term *software bug* and was the designer of COBOL). Although she formally retired from the Naval Reserve in the 1960s, the Navy recalled her to active duty to help oversee its use of computers. One of the first women to be promoted to flag rank in the Navy, Rear Admiral Hopper remained on active duty until 1986, when she was nearly eighty years old. She told many tales about her life in the Navy, among them about how people often mistook her for a bus conductor. Opposed to the idea that women should serve in combat, Rear Admiral Hopper died in 1992. Shortly after her death the Navy announced that a new *Spruance* Class destroyer will be named in her memory, only the second American warship in this century to be named after a woman.

WHO WAS
WHO IN THE
PACIFIC WAR

O nly a handful of the key leaders in the Pacific war are known even by those who have paid attention to this conflict. But there were dozens of senior commanders who played critical roles in the progress of the campaigns and the outcomes of the battles. This chapter takes a look at many of these men, from the most famous to those whose names you may have seen only briefly in the numerous more detailed histories of World War II in the Pacific.

One of the most interesting things about Allied political and military leaders of the Second World War is the breadth of their military experience. Whereas few of the senior officers and virtually none of the political leaders of World War I had seen any serious wartime military service prior to 1914, virtually all of the senior Allied officers in World War II and many of their political leaders as well had served in the Great War, if not in other conflicts. It is generally believed that their experiences had a great influence on the character of World War II, for they were determined not to repeat the senseless slaughter they had witnessed. While most of the Japanese leaders in World War II had seen service in the Russo-Japanese War (1904–1905) or during the various "China incidents" of the 1930s, and some of their naval officers had seen action in the Mediterranean during World War I, the nature of the fighting in which they took part, the intensity of the experience, and its impact on their professional thinking was different, and apparently less, a matter that certainly affected the course of operations in the Pacific war.

Onomastic note: In Japan, China, and much of the rest of East Asia, it is the custom to put the family name before the given name, thus Yamamoto Isoroku rather than Isoroku Yamamoto. For purposes of this list, and this book in general, the Western custom of putting the given name first has been followed, excepting only some unusually well known persons.

We were also unable to find the birth and death dates of some Japanese commanders. However, we have included the important information, namely, all we could find out about that commander's abilities and, by definition, what impact that commander had on the war.

ADACHI, HATAZO. Hatazo Adachi (1884–1947) entered the Japanese Army in 1910 and saw no action thereafter until the 1930s. By Pearl Harbor he was the chief of staff of the Japanese North China Area Army. In late 1942, he commanded the Eighteenth Army, concentrated at Rabaul and northeastern New Guinea, where he continued to serve as an army commander for the remainder of the war. Although Adachi was constantly defeated, he was not relieved. This was fairly typical in the Japanese Army, where your social connections often counted for more than battlefield performance.

AKASHIBA, YAEZO. Yaezo Akashiba served as a division commander for most of the war but was given a home-islands army command in early 1945 to prepare for the final defense of Japan. Many commanders of known "spirit" (if not ability) were brought back to Japan in 1945 for "the final battle."

ALEXANDER, HAROLD. The later Field Marshal Sir Harold Alexander (1891–1969) entered the British Army in 1911 as a Guards officer, rising to lieutenant colonel during World War I, during which he commanded an infantry battalion at the front. After the war he was for a time military adviser to Latvia during its border war with Russia in 1919. By the outbreak of World War II, he was commander of the British 1st Infantry Division, among the first British units dispatched to France, in which role he greatly distinguished himself while commanding the rear guard during the Dunkirk operation. Thereafter he held a variety of commands in Britain, until March 1942, when he was sent to command in Burma, during which he made it possible for William Slim to withdraw with some semblance of order in the face of the Japanese tide. Although he failed in the impossible mission of saving Burma, Alexander had once again distinguished himself as a rearguard fighter. That August, he was sent to replace Claude Auchinleck as commander in chief in the Middle East, where Erwin Rommel's Italo-German forces had just been halted on the Alamein line. In his new command, Alexander oversaw Bernard Law Montgomery's successful defense at Alam el Halfa and his Alamein offensive, and, after the Anglo-American landings in northwestern Africa, the Tunisian campaign, the Sicilian operation, and the Italian campaign. After the war, by which time he had been promoted to field marshal, Alexander served in a variety of civil and military posts until his retirement. An extremely good officer, like many commanders Alexander tended to see his theater as the most critical one. Unwilling to see that the Italian campaign was essentially a strategic diversion, he continuously argued for more troops when the focus of Allied operations had shifted to northwestern Europe, the most decisive theater.

AMAMIYA, TATSUMI. Tatsumi Amamiya became a Japanese Army commander during the Battle for Okinawa in early 1945. Before that he had held a succession of division commands with mixed success. Often, punishment for poor performance was a posting to a truly impossible command.

ANAMI, KORECHIKA. Korechika Anami (1887–1945) served in several posts in China, Japan, and elsewhere before becoming an army commander in China in early 1941. He moved with some of these China-based units to New Guinea in late 1943, where he commanded for less than a year, and with little success. He then went on to various other posts in the Pacific and was eventually moved back to staff posts in Tokyo. By the end of the war, he was the minister of war. Anami refused to aid the abortive coup to overthrow the government when surrender was announced. He committed suicide on the day of the surrender.

ANDO, RIKICHI. Rikichi Ando joined the Japanese Army in 1914 and quickly rose through the ranks. He was one of the hotheaded generals in China who inexorably dragged Japan deeper into conflict with the West. In early 1940 he became commander of the South China Area Army. It was Ando who made an unauthorized move into French Indochina (Vietnam) after Germany had defeated France. It was this move that caused the confrontation with the West that led to the oil embargo and, soon thereafter, Pearl Harbor. If there was any one act that led inevitably to war with America, this incursion into Vietnam was it. As a result, America embargoed Japan and Japan went to war. General Ando was responsible, and he acted against orders. The Japanese government was not pleased with all the trouble Ando had caused, and recalled and retired him as punishment. However, once the decision was made (in the fall of 1941) to go to war against the West, Ando was recalled to service, promoted to full general, and given command of the Tenth Area Army in Formosa (Taiwan). This was a crucial post, as the Japanese always feared that the Allies might invade Formosa and thus cut off Japanese access to the oil and other raw materials to the south.

BLAMEY, THOMAS A. Thomas A. Blamey (1884–1951), the son of a shopkeeper, worked as a teacher for a while before being commissioned in the Australian militia in 1906. He distinguished himself during World War I (Egypt, Gallipoli, and the Western Front), rising to colonel. After the war he resigned from active service to go into business, but remained in the militia. He was appointed commander of Australia's ground forces in 1940, primarily on the basis of his considerable administrative skills, despite being tactless, often rude, and very self-aggrandizing. As a lieutenant general, in April 1941 he was briefly second-in-command to Sir Archibald Wavell in the Mediterranean–Middle Eastern Theater, during which he performed yeoman service in organizing the Allied withdrawal from Greece. Recalled from the Middle East after Pearl Harbor, Blamey was made commander of all Allied ground forces in Australia under the overall command of Douglas MacArthur. This was a difficult task, as MacArthur constantly ignored proper channels to communicate directly with units, and essentially denied Blamey any control over American troops. Blamey directed the defeat of the Japanese offensive over the Owen Stanley Mountains in New Guinea, and the Allied offensive to the Buna-Gona position, until early 1943. After the fall of Buna, Blamey was increasingly ignored by MacArthur, so that by the end of the war his effective authority was limited to Australian troops in Australia itself. Despite this, he was eventually made a field marshal, the only Australian to achieve such rank. A good officer, Blamey performed well in command, but did not "work and play well with others," which was one reason his active influence on Allied operations was limited, another being MacArthur's extraordinary hostility toward non-American troops and commanders.

BROOKE, ALAN. Alan Brooke (1883–1963), later Field Marshal Viscount Alanbrooke, the senior British military officer for most of World War II, entered the British Army as an artilleryman, in which capacity he served with great distinction for much of World War I. Between the wars he held a variety of posts, and in 1940 commanded the British II Corps with great skill during the retreat to Dunkirk. Appointed Chief of the Imperial General Staff in 1941, he is generally credited with the markedly improved British performance that characterized the rest of the war.

BROWN, WILSON, JR. Wilson Brown, Jr. (1882–1959), one of the oldest officers to serve afloat during the Pacific war, graduated from the U.S. Naval Academy in 1902. Prior to World War I his service was fairly pedestrian, but during that war he was on the staff of Admiral William S. Sims, commander of U.S. naval forces in Europe, and later commanded a destroyer. After the war he held various staff and line positions and attended several Navy schools. For a time during the 1930s he was naval aide to President Roosevelt, who got him assigned as superintendent of the Naval Academy.

On the eve of the Pacific war, he was commander of the *Lexington* task force. In this capacity he took part in the abortive Wake Island relief operation (which, but for some faintheartedness on the part of higher-ups, might have resulted in the first American victory at sea as early as mid-December 1941), in the raids on the Mandates, and in the daring Lae-Salamaua raid over New Guinea's Owen Stanley Mountains in March 1942. On April 3, 1942, Brown, already overage by Navy regulations, yielded command of his task force to Rear Admiral Aubrey Fitch and saw no further combat service in the war. Although a "black shoe" (surface warfare) officer, Brown performed well in command of a carrier task force. This was because, aside from being a capable strategist in his own right, he was aware of his lack of flying credentials, and so he listened to, and usually accepted, the advice of several of his air-qualified subordinates, such as Captain Forrest Sherman of the carrier *Lexington*. How he might have fared in a carrier battle remains an unanswerable question of the Pacific war, but he demonstrated that able admirals of the Old School could apply their talents with new technology.

BUCKNER, SIMON B., JR. The son of Confederate Lieutenant General Simon B. Buckner, Sr., Buckner (1886–1945) attended the Virginia Military Institute and West Point, being commissioned in the infantry in 1908. Before World War I, he saw service in the Philippines and on the Mexican border. When the United States entered World War I, he became a flight instructor, in which assignment he spent most of the war. He afterward held a variety of posts, while rising steadily through the ranks. In July 1940 he was named commander of all Army personnel in Alaska, where he thoroughly reorganized the defenses. Buckner remained in Alaska, while rising to lieutenant general, until March 1944 (in the meanwhile having recovered Kiska and Attu from the Japanese). Ordered to Hawaii, Buckner took command of the Tenth Army (XXIV Corps and III Marine Amphibious Corps), which he took to Okinawa the following spring. Buckner's operations on Okinawa were not brilliant, and he was severely criticized by his Marine subordinates for not making use of their amphibious capabilities. The general was killed in action by Japanese artillery on June 18, 1945, three days before the island was declared secure. He was the second-highest-ranking American Army officer killed in action during the war.

BURKE, ARLEIGH. Arleigh Burke (b. 1901) graduated from Annapolis in 1923 and held a variety of posts in the peacetime Navy. In 1940 he was assigned to the Bureau of Ordnance, where he languished until May 1943, when, promoted to captain, he was sent to the Pacific to command a destroyer squadron. Burke greatly distinguished himself during the fighting for the northern Solomons, earning the nickname "Thirty-one Knot Burke" because he seemed to press his destroyers beyond their rated capacity. In 1945 he became an acting commodore and, although a nonflier, chief of staff to Marc Mitscher, commander of Task Force 38/58. He ended the war as chief of staff to the commander, Atlantic Fleet. Burke's postwar career was equally impressive, concluding with an unprecedented six-year term as Chief of Naval Operations (1955–1961), for which post he was jumped over nearly 100 more senior officers. He retired to an active career in business.

CALLAGHAN, DANIEL. Dan Callaghan (1890–1942) graduated from the Naval Academy in 1911. He had a long and varied career, but saw little action. A naval aide to FDR in 1938, in 1941 he was given command of the heavy cruiser *San Francisco*, among the first U.S. ships to get to sea during the Pearl Harbor attack. He was named Chief of Staff to Admiral Robert L. Ghormley during the opening phase of the Guadalcanal campaign. Promoted to rear admiral, Callaghan returned to sea in time to command the U.S. squadron in the First Naval Battle of Guadalcanal (November 12–13, 1942), a major reverse for the United States, during which he was killed in action. He was a good officer; Callaghan's appointment to command the cruiser-destroyer squadron off Guadalcanal in November 1942 was an error dictated by the rigidity of naval regulations (Callaghan was senior to Norman Scott, who had already encountered the Japanese on several occasions, and bested them at Cape Esperance).

CHENNAULT, CLAIRE LEE. Claire Chennault (1890–1958) was a teacher in Texas when he joined the Army by way of a reserve officers' training camp in 1917, soon becoming a pilot and flight instructor. He passed to the Regular Army in 1920 and remained in the Air Corps, becoming an outspoken advocate of fighter aircraft and something of a critic of the bomber ring that dominated the Air Corps. He was retired in 1937, ostensibly for deafness (a common problem among open-cockpit pilots). Invited by Chiang Kai-shek to reorganize the Chinese Republican Air Force and organize an air defense system, Chennault proved surprisingly successful (he established a highly effective system of air observers to provide early warning of Japanese bomber raids). In 1940 he went to the United States to recruit the "American Volunteer Group" (AVG) and returned to China in 1941 with new pilots and aircraft for the Chinese. Most of these were still being trained in Burma in early December, and it was there that the "Flying Tigers" got their baptism of fire. Quickly moving into China, the AVG was soon made a part of the U.S. Army Air Corps, as was Chennault, who was promoted to general rank. The AVG became the Fourteenth Air Force and Chennault remained its commander for the rest of the war.

CHIANG KAI-SHEK. Chiang Kai-shek (1887–1975) came from a prosperous rural family. He entered the new Chinese Military Academy in 1906, but in 1907 was sent to study at the Japanese military academy (Japan representing the model on which progressive Chinese wished to reshape their own nation). In 1911 he resigned to join Sun Yat-sen's revolutionary army, in which he served as a senior officer. His career over the next decade was turbulent, including armed resistance to the dictatorial regime of Yuan Shih-kai, involvement in radical politics, study at a Soviet military academy, and finally, in 1923, leadership of the Kuomintang party. Chiang successfully commanded in the suppression of various warlord armies in China, and from 1927 in the crushing of the Communist party. He was never quite able to bring all China under his control, a matter that became more difficult with increasing Japanese encroachment in the 1930s. Although immensely popular in the United States, due in no small measure to the fact that the Luce family, which owned *Time* and *Life* magazines, greatly admired him, he was by no means a great commander. But it is difficult to see who would have had the ability to maintain Chinese resistance any better than he, aside from the Communists.

CHURCHILL, WINSTON. Winston Churchill (1874–1965) was the son of the distinguished British politician Lord Randolph Churchill and the American socialite Jenny Jerome. He graduated from Sandhurst (the British military academy) and had a distinguished military career. Churchill served variously as an officer or journalist on the Northwest Frontier of India, in the Sudan (where he took part in the charge of the 21st Lancers at Omdurman), in Cuba, and in South Africa, before entering politics. He began World War I as First Lord of the Admiralty, finding time to promote the invention of the tank, before commanding the 6th Battalion, Royal Scots Fusiliers, on the Western Front for several months after the disastrous Gallipoli campaign. He later became minister of munitions and secretary of state for war. For most of the years of peace he was politically on the sidelines, but was again made First Lord of the Admiralty on the eve of World War II and became prime minister upon the collapse of France in 1940.

COLLINS, J. LAWTON. J. Lawton Collins (1896–1992) graduated from West Point in 1917, but saw no service overseas in World War I. Between the wars he held a variety of posts, and attended most of the Army's higher academic institutions (Command and General Staff College, War College, Industrial College). Immediately after Pearl Harbor he was named chief of staff to the commanding general of the Hawaiian Department, and within a few months was promoted to major general and given the 25th Infantry Division, recently formed out of portions of the old Hawaiian Division. He took his division to Guadalcanal in December and later led it on New Georgia, each time distinguishing himself. In March 1944 he was sent to Europe, where he took command of VII Corps, leading it during the Normandy landings, the breakout from the beachhead, the drive across France, the Rhineland campaign, and on to the Elbe by the end of the war. After the war he held a variety of increasingly important administrative and command assignments, culminating in Chief of Staff of the Army. After his retirement he continued in public service and served on the boards of various corporations. A very good officer, "Lightning Joe" Collins, like most of the best Army commanders in the Pacific, eventually found himself fighting in Europe.

CRUTCHLEY, V.A.C. Victor Alexander Charles Crutchley (1893–1986) joined the Royal Navy shortly before World War I, in which he won a Victoria Cross. He rose steadily through the ranks thereafter, and by the outbreak of World War II was a captain. He had a distinguished combat career, the most spectacular moment being when, as skipper of the battleship *Warspite*, he led some destroyers into the narrow waters of Narvik Fjord in Norway early in 1940, to wipe out an entire German destroyer squadron. Appointed commander of the Australian cruiser squadron in mid-1942, and placed in command of part of the task force that supported the Guadalcanal landings, he was in command, though not present, at the disastrous Battle of Savo Island, for which he was found faultless, inasmuch as he was absent on orders. Crutchley continued to command the Australian squadron for most of the rest of the war, and saw considerable service in support of the Seventh Fleet. He retired as a full admiral in 1946.

CUNNINGHAM, ANDREW BROWNE. Andrew Browne Cunningham (1883–1963), the most distinguished British seadog since Nelson, was born in Scotland. He entered the Royal Navy via Dartmouth Academy in 1898, served in various ships thereafter, seeing action at the Dardanelles and in the Zeebrugge Raid during World War I, winning considerable distinction. After the war he held various posts ashore and afloat, and in 1939 was named commander of the Mediterranean Fleet. During World War II, Cunningham took part in numerous operations in the Mediterranean (Cape Spartivento, the Taranto raid, Cape Matapan, Torch, and so on), and upon the death of Sir Dudley Pound in 1943 he was made First Sea Lord, in which post he supervised all British naval operations worldwide.

DOIHARA, KENJI. Kenji Doihara (1883–1948) graduated from the Japanese Military Academy in 1904 and served on various staffs, as an intelligence officer, and as a military adviser to several pro-Japanese warlords in China for much of his career. One of the "wild men" in China, pressing for increased Japanese intervention, he was dubbed "Lawrence of Manchuria" by Western reporters for his exploits in establishing Japanese rule in northern China during the early 1930s. Doihara led the Army Secret Police in Manchuria for a time while being regularly promoted. Posted back to Japan in 1940, he commanded the Eastern Military District of Japan. Sent to command Army troops in Malaya from March 1944 to April 1945, he returned to Japan to command part of the forces to oppose the expected invasion. He commanded Japanese troops during demobilization after the surrender. Arrested, tried, and convicted, Doihara was hanged as a war criminal in 1948.

DOOLITTLE, JAMES H. James H. Doolittle (1896–1993) was a college student when he enlisted in the Army in 1917. Assigned to the Air Service, he served as a flight instructor, and remained in the service after the war, while pursuing several advanced academic degrees in science and engineering. Much of his career was spent in experimentation and in making often-spectacular test flights. Resigning from the Army in 1930, he went into business, while still racing (Harmon Trophy, 1930; Bendix, 1931; world air speed record, 1932) and serving as an adviser to government and industry on aviation. Recalled to active duty in 1940, he helped plan the expansion of the Air Corps for the coming war. In April 1942, Doolittle led the spectacular raid that bears his name, when sixteen B-25s took off from the carrier *Hornet* to bomb Tokyo and other targets in Japan. This feat, which he had suggested and planned, brought him a promotion to brigadier general and a Medal of Honor, and command of the Twelfth Air Force in England, leading it during the North African campaign. Doolittle thereafter held a variety of increasingly important posts in the air war against Germany, ending with command of the Eighth Air Force. Soon after the war in Europe ended, Doolittle began transferring his command to Okinawa in anticipation of the invasion of Japan. After the war he returned to the reserves, working in industry and as an adviser to government on numerous projects. He died in 1993, one of the last of the larger-than-life legends of the Pacific war to pass from the scene.

DOORMAN, KAREL W. The senior Dutch naval officer afloat in the Far East at the beginning of the Pacific war, Doorman (1889–1942) had had a distinguished, but peaceful, career. Nevertheless, in the interests of inter-Allied cooperation, he was appointed commander of ABDAFlot, the "American-British-Dutch-Australian" naval command in the Far East, in February 1942, as the Allies faced an overwhelmingly superior Japanese offensive. It was a hopeless command, for not only were the forces available of greatly differing capabilities, but they had never trained together, lacked a common doctrine, and could not even communicate with each other readily. Despite these handicaps, Doorman and his Allied subordinates were game, and did the only thing they could in such a situation: go down fighting in the Battle of the Java Sea.

EICHELBERGER, ROBERT L. Robert L. Eichelberger (1886–1961) was one of the most successful, and least known, U.S. commanders in World War II. Graduating from West Point in 1909, he served on the staff of the Siberian Expedition in 1918–1919, and later spent several years in the Far East. The outbreak of World War II found him as superintendent of West Point, from which post in March 1942 he went on to command various divisions and corps in training. That October, he took command of I Corps, in Australia, which he took into action in New Guinea. He was then put on the shelf for over a year, due to some favorable publicity that greatly annoyed MacArthur. However, early in 1944 he returned to operational command and thereafter held important posts in all of Douglas MacArthur's offensives, culminating in the occupation of Japan by his Eighth Army in August and September 1945. Eichelberger was one of the most competent corps and army commanders of the war and suffered relative obscurity only because his boss, Douglas MacArthur, would not tolerate subordinates' getting any attention in the press.

FITCH, AUBREY W. Aubrey Fitch graduated from Annapolis in 1906; and during World War I served aboard a battleship with the British Grand Fleet. After a variety of assignments in the peacetime Navy, he took flight training in 1929, and subsequently commanded an aircraft tender and the carriers *Langley*, *Saratoga*, and *Lexington*. On the eve of World War II, he was commander, Carrier Division 1, displaying his flag on *Saratoga*. In the opening months of the war, he commanded in the carrier raids on the Mandates and New Guinea, and was aboard *Lexington* at the Coral Sea. He thereafter commanded all Allied land-based air forces in the South Pacific, then became Deputy Chief of Naval Operations for Air, and at the end of the war superintendent of Annapolis. Retiring as an admiral, he served for a time as an adviser to industry.

FLETCHER, FRANK JACK. Frank Jack Fletcher (1885–1973) graduated from Annapolis in 1906, and had a varied and interesting career thereafter, winning a Medal of Honor at Veracruz in 1914. During World War I he commanded a destroyer on antisubmarine patrol, and afterward he served in various line, staff, and academic posts. In late 1941 he was given command of the *Yorktown* task force by Admiral Husband Kimmel, another nonflier who thought Fletcher had better qualifications to command than Aubrey Fitch, a flier. Fletcher took his command into action in the raids on the Mandates and New Guinea. He was in overall command at the Coral Sea and Midway (where he conceded command to Raymond Spruance after *Yorktown* was hit), during the Guadalcanal landings, and in the Battle of the Eastern Solomons. He later commanded all naval forces in the North Pacific, overseeing the occupation of northern Japan. Fletcher commanded in three of the five carrier battles of the war, a distinction no other officer on either side could claim. While not an outstanding commander, Fletcher was competent, and he won most of his battles.

FORRESTAL, JAMES V. James V. Forrestal (1892–1949) began life in modest circumstances, then became a journalist and later a lawyer. During World War I, he left a lucrative Wall Street law firm to serve as a naval aviator, winning the Navy Cross. After the war he returned to the law, rising to presidency of his firm. In 1940, after a brief stint as an aide to President Roosevelt, he was appointed the first undersecretary of the Navy, in which post he proved immensely effective (far more so than his immediate superior, Secretary Frank Knox). On Knox's death in 1944, Forrestal became secretary of the Navy. After the war he was influential in bringing about the creation of the Department of Defense, and was the first secretary thereof. He committed suicide shortly after resigning from this post at the president's request in 1949.

GEIGER, ROY. Roy Geiger (1885–1947) took a degree in law, but after practicing for several years enlisted in the U.S. Marines in 1907. Commissioned two years later, he served aboard ship, in Panama, in Nicaragua, and in China, before taking flight training, and, in late 1918, leading a Marine bomber squadron in France, garnering a Navy Cross in the process. After World War I he was actively involved in the development of both Marine aviation and amphibious doctrine. Shortly before Pearl Harbor he became commander of the 1st Marine Aircraft Wing, which he later led during the Guadalcanal campaign. For a time director of Marine aviation, flying a desk in Washington, in late 1943 he assumed command of III

Marine Amphibious Corps. He led this outfit in the invasions of Guam, Palau, and Okinawa, where, on the death of Lieutenant General Simon B. Buckner, Geiger assumed command of the Tenth Army, thereby becoming the only Marine ever to command a field army. He died shortly before he was scheduled to retire, and was posthumously promoted to full general.

GEORGE VI. King George VI of Great Britain (1895–1952) entered the Royal Navy on the eve of World War I, serving as a junior officer. He saw extensive service, and was under fire during the Battle of Jutland (1916). After the war, he engaged in activities normal to the second son of the king, but was thrust onto the throne by the abrupt abdication of his brother Edward VIII in 1936. Although his role in policy and strategy was constitutionally limited, he was kept constantly informed and occasionally consulted on vital matters, and is generally believed to have been a reliable source of common sense.

GHORMLEY, ROBERT LEE. Robert Lee Ghormley (1883–1958) graduated from the U.S. Naval Academy in 1906, already having taken a bachelor's degree at the University of Idaho. His career was varied, including service in Nicaragua and with the battle force of the Atlantic Fleet during World War I. Between the wars he held a variety of posts, mostly staff (he commanded only two ships in his career). From 1940 he was the Navy's special observer in Britain, from which post he was transferred in April 1942 to command in the Southwest Pacific as a vice admiral. Ghormley planned and commanded the Guadalcanal landings, an operation about which he appears to have had serious personal doubts. Although he performed adequately, in mid-October he was relieved by William F. Halsey. Thereafter he held a variety of administrative posts, culminating in May 1945 in being assigned to oversee the demobilization of the German Navy. He retired a year later. Ghormley was not a bad officer, but suffered from several handicaps, not least of which was his own pessimism and lack of command experience. In addition, he had to operate on limited resources, against an enemy who had for a long time a considerable psychological advantage, with subordinates who were often contentious, and in a type of battle that had never been fought before, a combined land-sea-air operation in three dimensions.

GOTO, ARITOMO. Rear Admiral Aritomo Goto was commander of the Japanese 6th Cruiser Squadron at the onset of the Pacific war. He was constantly in action from the initial seizure of Rabaul and the Solomons. After the U.S. invasion of Guadalcanal in August 1942, Goto and his squadron were active in resisting the American presence. Goto was killed in action during the Battle of Cape Esperance in October 1942.

HALSEY, WILLIAM F. Bill (never "Bull" except in the headlines) Halsey (1882–1959), a Navy brat, graduated from Annapolis in 1904, and shortly afterward was assigned to various battleships, sailing with the "Great White Fleet." From 1911 through 1921, he alternated command of several destroyers with a tour on the staff of the Naval Academy, winning a Navy Cross during World War I for action in the North Atlantic. In 1921 he was posted to the Office of Naval Intelligence, serving as a naval attaché in Germany and several other European countries until 1924. He returned to sea duty, commanding various destroyers and serving on battleships until 1927. He then had a round of academic posts and school assignments, emerging in 1935 as a fifty-two-year old naval aviator. Over the next few years he commanded the carrier *Saratoga*, the Pensacola Naval Air Station, Carrier Division 2, Carrier Division 1, all air units of the Pacific Battle Force, and Carrier Division 2 again (*Lexington* and *Yorktown*). Shortly before the Pearl Harbor attack his CarDiv was delivering aircraft to Wake Island; Halsey placed his division on full war alert (one of several officers who understood the meaning of "consider this a war warning"). In the war he had an active, varied, and distinguished career: the raids on the Mandates, the Doolittle Raid, the Guadalcanal campaign, the Solomons campaign, and finally as commander, Third Fleet, in the Central Pacific. He retired from the military after the war, entering business. Shortly before his death, he led an ultimately futile campaign to preserve the carrier *Enterprise* as a war memorial. Halsey was a tough, aggressive officer who made surprisingly few mistakes (the most glaring being his failure to adequately cover the "jeep carriers" off Samar during the Battle for Leyte Gulf).

HARA, CHUICHI. Rear Admiral Chuichi Hara (1889–1964) was one of the more successful, or at least luckier, of the Japanese carrier admirals. He began the war commanding the 5th Carrier Division

(*Shokaku* and *Zuikaku*), which was the busiest carrier division for the first months of the war. Because Hara's carriers fought in the Battle of the Coral Sea (May 1942), where *Shokaku* was damaged, they did not participate in the debacle at Midway a month later. His division was given a light carrier and a number of escorts and used extensively during the battles over Guadalcanal. Once Guadalcanal was abandoned, Hara and his ships retired to the main fleet base at Truk. In June 1944, Hara was made commander of the Fourth ("Mandates") Fleet (which guarded the Central Pacific islands "mandated" to Japan after World War I by the League of Nations), a post he held until the end of the war.

HART, THOMAS C. Thomas C. Hart (1877–1971) graduated from the U.S. Naval Academy in 1897 and saw service aboard the old battleship *Massachusetts* during the Battle of Santiago in the Spanish-American War. Thereafter he had a fairly routine peacetime career, while rising steadily through the ranks and becoming a submariner. During World War I he commanded a submarine squadron based in Ireland, and later served as a staff officer. After the war he held a variety of commands, attended both the Navy and Army war colleges, held several staff positions, and in mid-1939 was appointed commander of the Asiatic Fleet, based in the Philippines. One of the oldest officers still on active duty, in the months before Pearl Harbor, Hart did what he could to prepare for war. This included "stealing" a cruiser from the Pacific Fleet, conducting informal staff talks with British and Dutch naval officers, and dispersing his forces beyond the range of Japanese air power based on Formosa (a matter in which he proved far more prescient than his Army counterpart, Douglas MacArthur). When war came, Hart shifted his headquarters to the Netherlands East Indies and assumed command of all Allied naval forces under Archibald Wavell. Relieved in February, shortly before the Japanese overwhelmed the greatly outnumbered Allied surface forces, he was retired (he was already past retirement age) but immediately recalled to active duty as a member of the Navy's General Board, which advised the CNO (Chief of Naval Operations, the commander of the USN) on strategy and policy. In 1945 he returned to inactive status. Shortly thereafter, the governor of Connecticut appointed him to a U.S. Senate seat left vacant by a death. He retired from the Senate in 1946 and lived quietly thereafter. One of the oldest officers to see action in the war, Hart proved surprisingly good in a desperate situation.

HATA, SHUNROKU. Shunroku Hata joined the Japanese Army in 1901 and quickly moved up in rank. During the 1930s he commanded many of the Japanese troops fighting in China. Hata returned to Japan in 1938 and held a number of senior government posts until early 1942, when he returned to the command of the Central China Area Army, a position he held until late 1944. He was promoted to field marshal in 1943. He returned to Japan to command forces against the expected Allied invasion. Arrested, tried, convicted, and sentenced to life imprisonment as a war criminal, Hata died in 1962.

HERSHEY, LEWIS B. The man who sent "Greetings" to several generations of American youth, Lewis B. Hershey (1893–1977) was a teacher in a rural Indiana school when he joined the National Guard in 1911. Called to active duty during World War I, he served as a captain for a time in France in 1918. After the war he passed into the Regular Army as an artilleryman. He held a variety of posts in the 1920s and 1930s, becoming secretary to the Joint Army-Navy Selective Service Committee, a planning body, in 1936. In October 1940, promoted to temporary brigadier general, he became deputy head of the Selective Service System, being named director the following July. From then until his final retirement in 1970 (with a brief interval during which there was no draft, in the late 1940s), Hershey oversaw the conscription of literally tens of millions of men for the U.S. armed forces.

HIGASHIKUNI, PRINCE NARUHIKO. Prince Naruhiko Higashikuni, born in 1887, was one of the Japanese emperor's uncles. He joined the Army in 1908 and rose through the ranks until he achieved command of the Second Army in China in 1938, becoming heavily involved in combat operations there. By early 1939 he was back in Japan as adviser to the emperor and head of the Defense Command for Japan. The prince became a field marshal in 1945; agreeing with the emperor that surrender was a viable option, he became prime minister at the end of the war to speed the surrender along. He went into retailing after the war and founded a new religion (which was banned).

HIGUCHI, KIICHIRO. Kiichiro Higuchi (1888–1970) joined the Japanese Army in 1908. He served in Siberia during the Allied intervention in Russia during 1918–1922, and in a variety of posts. Promoted to lieutenant general in 1939, he commanded an army-size unit in northern Japan until the end of the war. Despite a varied career, Higuchi saw little combat, most of his duties having been as a staff officer.

HIROHITO. Emperor Hirohito (1901–1989) was the eldest son of the emperor Taisho (reigned 1912–1926) and grandson of the great emperor Meiji (1867–1912). He had only ceremonial military experience. A small child during the Russo-Japanese War, he was a carefully sheltered student during World War I. A keen anglophile, he visited Britain while still the crown prince and was impressed by what he saw. Although he came to the throne in 1926, during a period of growing democracy in Japan, his generally superior understanding of the West did not stiffen his resolve sufficiently to put him into direct conflict with the generals and admirals who shortly began to slowly take over Japan, preferring to confine himself to scientific pursuits. Although constitutionally he had enormous power, he failed to exercise it despite personal misgivings about the prospects for war.

HO CHI MINH. Born Nguyen Sinh Cung, in a traditional scholarly family, Ho (1890–1969) was a waiter at the Hotel Carleton in London at the outbreak of World War I. During the war he moved to Paris, where he joined the French Socialist party, and later helped form the French Communist party. He thereafter worked tirelessly for international communism and Vietnamese independence. During World War II he returned to Vietnam to help organize resistance against the Japanese. With the surrender of Japan, the French returned and the resistance promptly began fighting them. The result was a divided Vietnam in 1954. By the early 1960s, Communist guerrillas were active in Ho's name in South Vietnam, leading to American intervention, which ended with the achievement of Ho's goal of a unified Vietnam in 1975, six years after his death.

HOMMA, MASAHARU. Masaharu Homma (1887–1946) began his Japanese Army career in 1907, later serving with a British battalion (as an "observer") on the Western Front during World

War I. As a result of this, he had a reputation for being pro-British. A bright and capable officer, he held many staff and command positions during the 1920s. Homma commanded the Fourteenth Army, which invaded the Philippines in late 1941. While he was successful in conquering the Philippines in less than six months, this was longer than the General Staff felt was necessary. Even before the last American resistance ended on May 6, 1942, Homma was already in trouble with his superiors. As a result, the last months of fighting in the Philippines were under his control in name only. Subordinate officers were given authority by the General Staff to run operations in Homma's name, even disregarding his orders to treat prisoners humanely. Homma, being a good Japanese soldier, went along with it. One of Homma's greatest transgressions in the eyes of superiors was not making suicidal attacks with inadequate forces (a practice most other Japanese generals followed energetically). Having served in Europe during World War I, Homma knew how futile such attacks were. In Japanese eyes, he had been "tainted" by Western military thinking. As a result, he returned to Tokyo in disgrace (despite a "victory celebration" in his "honor") and spent the rest of the war on the reserve list. Because of the Bataan Death March (for which insubordinate junior officers were responsible) and other atrocities by troops under his command in 1942, he was condemned as a war criminal and sentenced to death. That he was one of the few Japanese commanders who spoke fluent (British) English, and was rather compassionate in military matters, no doubt made the Allied prosecutors uncomfortable in railroading "the Butcher of Bataan." But popular opinion demanded Homma's head, and Homma, the career soldier to the end, accepted responsibility. Unlike the other condemned war criminals, Homma was not hanged, but faced a firing squad (a "soldier's death"). Homma was cleared of his war criminal conviction by the Japanese government in 1952, it being an open secret (even to the Allied prosecutors) that Homma was not responsible for the atrocities in the Philippines. Homma was quite intelligent, a "thinker," so to speak. He was also several inches taller (at 5 feet 10 inches) than the average Japanese officer. But, as the old Japanese saying goes, "the nail that stands out must be hammered down." That Homma lasted so long in the Japanese Army, and advanced so far, is a tribute to his talents.

HONDA, MASAKI. Masaki Honda (1889–1964) joined the Japanese Army in 1910, beginning his career in the prestigious Imperial Guards Division. He held a series of command and staff positions in China during the 1930s and early 1940s, and commanded the Thirty-third Army in Burma from early 1944 until the end of the war. Honda was in charge of Japanese troops in Burma from surrender to their repatriation in 1947. He died in 1964.

HORII, TOMITARO. Tomitaro Horii (1890–1942) began his Japanese Army career in 1911 and served in staff and command positions in China during the 1930s, including the battle for Shanghai in 1932. He commanded the key South Seas Detachment, which took Guam, Rabaul, and portions of New Guinea, and commanded the Port Moresby invasion force that was turned back during the Battle of the Coral Sea. He also led the overland assault on Port Moresby and drowned crossing a river in late 1942. Horii was your typical, straight-ahead and brutal Japanese general. Had he survived the war, he would have been tried as a war criminal for his torture and execution of Australian prisoners at Rabaul.

HYAKUTAKE, SEIKICHI. Seikichi Hyakutake (1888–1947) entered the Japanese Army in 1909. Originally an infantryman, he later became a noted cryptanalyst. Passing between command and staff during the 1920s and 1930s, on the eve of the war he was in charge of signal training for the entire Japanese Army. Made a lieutenant general in 1939, in early 1942 he assumed command of the Seventeenth Army in New Guinea. After the American invasion of Guadalcanal in August 1942, he was ordered to retake it. This effort failed and he withdrew with his remaining forces to Bougainville Island (to the northwest of Guadalcanal). There he and his now-reinforced army remained until the end of the war (even though he suffered an incapacitating stroke in early 1945). He died in early 1947.

IDA, SHOJIRO. Shojiro Ida began his Japanese Army career in 1908. A fast-track officer, he served on staffs and commanded Guards units through most of the 1920s and 1930s, then commanded the Fourteenth Army during the initial invasion of Burma in December 1941. For his lack of success (as measured by his superiors), he was posted back to Japan in early 1943. Sent to Manchuria to command an army in July 1945, he was captured by the Russians the next month when the Soviet Union invaded.

IMAMURA, HITOSHI. Hitoshi Imamura (1886–1968) graduated from the Japanese Military Academy in 1907. He served in many military attaché posts (including England and India) through the 1920s and 1930s and was also active in staff and training posts. He received a series of troop commands in Japan and China during the 1930s, leading to command of the Sixteenth Army, which conquered Java and the Dutch East Indies. He used an uncharacteristically lenient policy in ruling the area, which led to his promotion to command of all troops in the Southeast Pacific in early 1943. From his headquarters in Rabaul, Imamura directed the fighting in the Solomons and New Guinea until the end of the war. He surrendered Japanese forces in the area at the end of the war.

INOUYE, SHIGEYOSHI. Shigeyoshi Inouye was one of the more original thinkers among Japanese admirals. Graduating from the Naval Academy in 1909, he studied in Switzerland and France in 1918–1921, before returning to Japan for various school and staff assignments, leading to command of a battleship in the early 1930s. Inouye (the name is also sometimes spelled Inoue) became a rear admiral in 1936 and soon began speaking out on the need for Japan to get along with the other world powers and not get into a war it could not win. Inouye opposed the Army's aggressive actions in China and was an enthusiastic supporter of carrier aviation. His opinions did not damage his career, as he became a vice admiral in 1939 and chief of naval aviation in 1940. At that point he addressed the potential war with America and correctly predicted the island-hopping strategy the United States would eventually pursue. Inouye urged that carrier aviation be given more resources than battleship building but was ignored. He finally got into trouble for stating, in early 1941, that the Japanese fleet was not capable of defeating the U.S. Navy. For this he was transferred to the command of the Fourth ("Mandates") Fleet in the Central Pacific. This fleet comprised light cruisers and destroyers, but was active in the seizure of Guam, Wake Island, and Rabaul. He was later in charge of the forces used in the abortive attempt to seize Port Moresby on the south coast of New Guinea. The resulting defeat in the Battle of the Coral Sea led to his recall to Tokyo and command of the Naval

College for the remainder of the war. Toward the end of the war he encouraged making peace. He survived the war. While not a great combat commander, he was an excellent administrator and quite intelligent. He was also an accomplished musician. Something of an intellectual in uniform, Inouye was typical of the several admirals who saw the world situation, and Japan's place in it, more clearly than the Army generals who controlled the government.

ITAGAKI, SEISHIRO. Seishiro Itagaki (1885–1946) joined the Japanese Army in 1904. He served in China during the 1930s and was in command of forces defeated by the Soviets at Nomonhan. This sidetracked his career and he spent most of the rest of the war commanding Japanese troops in Korea as a full general. In early 1945, he became commander of Japanese forces in Malaya and surrounding areas and held that post until the end of the war. He was hanged as a war criminal.

ITO, SEIICHI. Seiichi Ito (1890–1945) entered the Japanese Naval Academy in 1908 and graduated from Yale University in the 1920s. A vice admiral at the start of the war, he served on the Navy staff for most of the war. Ito became commander of the Second Fleet in late 1944. He sailed with the superbattleship *Yamato* on its death ride in April 1945 and went down with the ship.

KANDA, MASATANE. Masatane Kanda joined the Japanese Army in 1911. He served in China and the Solomons as a lieutenant general and was commander of the Seventeenth Army in Bougainville from early 1945 until the end of the war. A middling commander in the traditional Japanese style.

KAWABE, MASAKAZU. Masakazu Kawabe (1886–1965) graduated from the Japanese Military Academy in 1907. From late in World War I to 1921, he served in a diplomatic capacity in Switzerland and later traveled extensively in Europe and America. Military attaché in Berlin in the late 1920s, during the 1930s he held a variety of increasingly important posts in China. Kawabe commanded the Third Army in China at the beginning of the Pacific war and went on to command the Burma Area Army in early 1943, holding that post until September 1944. He went back to Japan to command forces to oppose the expected Allied invasion. Like a number of senior Japanese officers, he had a brother, Torashiro

(1890–1960), who was also a general. Torashiro had a distinguished career and was one of a handful of senior Army personnel who attempted to limit Japanese involvement in China.

KIMMEL, HUSBAND E. Husband E. Kimmel (1882–1968) was the son of a Confederate officer (who did not resign from the U.S. Army until after fighting against the Confederacy at Bull Run!). Kimmel graduated from the Naval Academy in 1904. Before World War I he served in various battleships, took part in the Great White Fleet's world cruise, and was wounded during the occupation of Veracruz in 1914. The following year he was assigned as an aide-de-camp to Assistant Secretary of the Navy Franklin D. Roosevelt, an assignment that would have a positive effect on his career. During World War I, Kimmel served as a gunnery officer in the American battle squadron that reinforced the Grand Fleet and as a technical adviser to the Royal Navy. He rose rapidly during the years of peace, and in early 1941 FDR jumped him over the heads of numerous other officers to command the entire U.S. fleet. Making his headquarters with the Pacific Fleet, Kimmel was at Pearl Harbor when the Japanese attacked, and was sacked ten days later. The argument as to the extent of Kimmel's responsibility for the disaster at Pearl Harbor is never ending (although Halsey thought he had been lax). Kimmel made it worse by hurling accusations in all directions, particularly at his former patron, President Roosevelt. Beached, he held no further commands until retirement. Kimmel was a good officer, and his actions after the Japanese attack were commendable. He organized a carrier sortie that might have caught two Japanese carriers unawares off Wake, he dispatched his submarines on aggressive war patrols, and he reorganized what surface and air forces remained. But all of this was after the fact. Other officers in the Pacific (Hart and Halsey) clearly understood the imminence of war on the basis of existing communications from the Navy Department. Kimmel, who lacked aviation credentials and a war college background, appears to have been lulled into complacency by the strength of his forces, the apparent impregnability of the Hawaiian Islands, and his own contempt for the Japanese.

KIMURA, HOYOTARO. Hoyotaro Kimura (1888–1948) graduated from the Military Academy in 1908. After serving in Siberia (1918–1919) he held a diplomatic post in Germany for a time.

During the 1920s he held various posts, and in 1930 went to London as a technical delegate to the disarmament conference. During the 1930s he rose through various staff appointments, and was vice minister of war in December 1941, Tojo being the minister. He became commander of the Burma Area Army in September 1944. Arrested in 1945, he was tried and was hanged as a war criminal in 1948.

KING, ERNEST J. Ernest J. King (1878–1956) graduated from Annapolis in 1901, after having served in action as a midshipman aboard the cruiser *San Francisco* during the war with Spain in 1898. Until World War I he was assigned to various ships and staffs, serving as an observer with the Japanese during the Russo-Japanese War and taking part in the occupation of Veracruz in 1914. When the United States entered World War I he was assigned to the staff of the Atlantic Fleet. After the war he specialized in submarines, but in 1928, at the age of forty-nine, he qualified as a naval aviator. King thereafter became closely identified with naval aviation. In 1933 President Roosevelt jumped him to rear admiral when he discovered that none of the candidates for chief of the Bureau of Aviation was flight-qualified. On the eve of World War II, King was serving as commander of the Atlantic Fleet, from which assignment a few days after Pearl Harbor he replaced Kimmel as commander in chief, U.S. fleet, and in March the president made him Chief of Naval Operations as well, under the terms of some special legislation. King's role in the war was indispensable. He not only oversaw the expansion of the Navy, but he was involved in plotting military strategy, directing the antisubmarine effort (he created the Tenth Fleet, a paper organization with himself as its head, to coordinate the antisubmarine war in the Atlantic), and helped coordinate American strategy and operations with those of the Allies. King retired in late 1945, shortly after having been promoted to five-star rank. For several years thereafter he served as an adviser to the secretary of the Navy and the president.

KINKAID, THOMAS C. Thomas C. Kinkaid (1888–1972) graduated from Annapolis in 1908. He served mostly in battleships until 1917, when he was assigned as a liaison officer to the British admiralty. After World War I he held various assignments, commanded several ships, held several diplomatic posts, and attended the Naval War College. Shortly after Pearl Harbor he took command of the *Enterprise* task force, which he commanded during the raids on the Mandates, at Midway, and at Santa Cruz. In early 1943 he became commander of naval forces in the North Pacific, overseeing the recovery of the Aleutians. Later that year, by then a vice admiral, he was assigned to command the Seventh Fleet ("MacArthur's Navy"), which he led during the fighting for the northern Solomons, the Bismarcks, New Guinea, and the Philippines. On the surrender of Japan he oversaw the occupation of Korea and the movement of Chinese Nationalist troops to northern China. After the war he held several administrative posts until his retirement in 1950. One of the most successful U.S. naval officers of the war, Kinkaid, who conducted more amphibious operations than any other commander in history, was little noticed by the public, overshadowed by having to work under Douglas MacArthur and by the admirals of the more glamorous fast carriers.

KITANO, KENZO. Kenzo Kitano entered the Japanese Army in 1913. He commanded the 4th Infantry Division at the start of the war and the Nineteenth Army in the Moluccas in late 1943, but returned to Japan in early 1945 for a staff job.

KOGA, MINEICHI. Mineichi Koga (1885–1944) graduated from the Naval Academy in 1906 and rose quickly through the ranks, aided by family connections with the Imperial Household. He became a rear admiral in the 1930s, when he became a major force on the Naval General Staff. Koga thought battleships could hold their own against aircraft, which put him in sync with the mainstream of Japanese naval thought. But he also believed that the Japanese Navy could not succeed against the American fleet. This caused his removal from the General Staff and a succession of fleet commands. Koga commanded the China Area Fleet early in the war. Later in 1942, he went to command the Yokosuka naval base. When Admiral Yamamoto, the commander of the Combined Fleet, was killed in early 1943, Koga took his place. Proving an able and energetic commander, Koga sought to reorganize the fleet along the obviously more efficient American lines. Koga planned to pull back Japanese naval forces and conserve them to inflict maximum damage when the American began to close in. Before Koga could complete these plans, he was killed in an airplane crash in March 1944.

KONDO, NOBUTAKE. Nobutake Kondo (1886–1953) was marked early as a potential Japanese admiral and he fulfilled that promise. Graduating from the Naval Academy in 1907, he served in staff positions. He had a lot of foreign travel, including duty in Russia in 1919–1920, and studied in Germany, becoming pro-German. Despite this, he did not believe Japan could successfully take on America. By 1939 he was a vice admiral. He commanded the naval strike force that assisted the invasion of Malaya in December 1941 and then the Dutch East Indies in early 1942. While he disagreed with the wisdom of the Midway operation, he commanded the Second Fleet there (the invasion covering force of battleships, a light carrier, and lighter units) and took over command of the surviving units of the demolished carrier forces. He commanded heavy units in battles for Guadalcanal during 1942, losing his flagship (the battleship *Kirishima*) in a night surface action off Guadalcanal in November. Kondo went on to command naval aviation (Twenty-fifth Air Fleet) in the Gilbert Islands until the American invasion in 1944. Then he moved to command the China Area Fleet until the end of the war. After the surrender, he remained in command of Japanese naval forces in Vietnam for several months to assist the British in fighting communist guerrillas (Vietminh). After the war, he became a successful businessman. Kondo was an extremely likable officer, partly because he always allowed subordinates to speak their piece. A very efficient officer and excellent bureaucrat. He became friends with many of his former enemies after the war.

KRUEGER, WALTER. Walter Krueger (1881–1967) was born in Germany, his family emigrating to the United States when he was eight. In 1898 he enlisted in the volunteers for the Spanish-American War, seeing action in Cuba. Passing to the Regulars, he served during the Philippine Insurrection, being commissioned in 1901. His career thereafter included the staff college and troop duty, and accompanying Pershing's Mexican Expedition. In 1918 he served as a staff officer with various divisions and corps in France. After the war he held various staff and line assignments, attended the Army and Navy war colleges (to the latter of which he later returned as an instructor), and by late 1941 was an acting lieutenant general in command of the Third Army. Stateside for the first eighteen months of the war, in mid-1943 Krueger took command of the

Sixth Army, organizing in Australia. He led the Sixth Army in numerous operations, including Woodlark Island, New Britain, the Admiralty Islands, New Guinea, Biak, Leyte, and ultimately Luzon, following up the war with occupation duty in Japan. Krueger was a fine commander, who managed the often difficult task of working in the shadow of Douglas MacArthur. A meticulous planner and trainer, he was also a fairly good military historian and translator, bringing over to English several military classics from his native German.

KURITA, TAKEO. Takeo Kurita (1889–1977) graduated from the Naval Academy in 1910 and specialized in torpedo warfare thereafter, while commanding successively more important vessels. By Pearl Harbor he was a rear admiral commanding the 7th Cruiser Squadron. He became a vice admiral in 1942 and commanded surface forces battling to recover Guadalcanal in that year. Kurita became commander of the Second Fleet in early 1944 and lost most of his ships in the naval battles to defend the Philippines during that year. He was relieved of command in late 1944 and returned to Japan.

KUSAKA, JUNICHI. Junichi Kusaka (1889–1972) entered the Imperial Navy shortly before World War I. He rose steadily thereafter, and in 1942 was made a vice admiral commanding the Southeast Area Fleet at Rabaul, a post that he held until the end of the war. He was the principal Japanese commander in the Bismarcks area for the entire war. His cousin was Admiral Ryunosuke Kusaka.

KUSAKA, RYUNOSUKE. Ryunosuke Kusaka (1892–1971), cousin of the above, graduated from the Naval Academy during World War I. A naval aviator between the wars, he commanded the carriers *Hosho* and *Akagi*. A rear admiral and staff officer at the start of the Pacific war, he remained a staff officer for the entire war, although he became a vice admiral. More pragmatic than most of the fleet commanders, which may be why he never got a major command, he also opposed suicide attacks.

LEE, WILLIS. Willis "Ching Chong China" Lee (1888–1945), the premier American battleship admiral of the war, graduated from Annapolis in 1908. He had an active career in surface ships, took part in the Veracruz operation in 1914, and commanded destroyers during World War I, while finding time to win a medal as part of the U.S. Olympic rifle team. Between the wars he held various command and staff assignments, and on the eve of the Pacific war was director of fleet training. In mid-1942, he was sent to command the fast battleships in the Southwest Pacific, a post he held for virtually the rest of the war. Lee developed innovative techniques for the cooperation of modern battleships with carriers in air battles (Santa Cruz Islands, for example), defeated a Japanese squadron in a wild night slug-out off Guadalcanal on November 14–15, 1942, took part in the Battles of the Philippine Sea and Leyte (where he just missed a possible battleship action off Samar by bad luck and poor guessing on Halsey's part), and right on to Okinawa (where he was denied the chance to slug it out with *Yamato* because the carrier admirals wanted to strut their stuff). Although he served most of the war subordinate to carrier admirals, he also demonstrated some ability to handle independent commands, overseeing the occupation of Baker Island (during which he had no battleships, but several carriers) and the raid on Nauru, in late 1943. On leave after Okinawa, he was temporarily assigned to Task Force 69 in the Atlantic, a special command organized to develop techniques for coping with Kamikaze attacks, an extremely critical assignment given that the Navy was then involved in planning for Operation Olympic, the invasion of Japan, scheduled for November 1, 1945. While still acting in this capacity, Lee died of natural causes in August 1945.

LEMAY, CURTIS E. Curtis E. LeMay (b. 1906) failed to get into West Point, but managed to secure a commission in the Army through ROTC. After flight training he served with various bomber units. LeMay's rise was rapid, and by the time of Pearl Harbor he was a major. Jumped to colonel the following March, LeMay was given command of the 305th Bombardment Group, which deployed to England the following month. LeMay engaged in many missions over Germany in the following months, rising to major general by early 1944. In August 1944 he was assigned to command the bomber elements of the Twentieth Air Force, operating in the CBI, rising to its command by mid-1945. In this capacity LeMay oversaw the bombing of Japan, including the use of the atomic bombs. After the war LeMay held a variety of staff posts, created the Strategic Air Command, and ultimately became Chief of Staff of the Air Force, retiring in 1965. He afterward dabbled in right-wing politics and business. An excellent pilot and officer equally capable in both combat and staff, LeMay was typical of the bomber-minded generals who tended to dominate the Air Force during the Cold War.

MACARTHUR, DOUGLAS. Douglas MacArthur (1880–1964), son of Civil War hero Arthur MacArthur (they are the only father and son to have won the Medal of Honor), graduated from West Point in 1903 with some of the highest grades ever recorded (as well as having the rather dubious distinction of being the only cadet ever whose mother lived right outside the gate for four years). An engineer, he held a variety of staff and academic posts, but no troop commands (albeit he got into action at Veracruz in 1914), until World War I, when he helped organize the 42nd "Rainbow" Division, composed of National Guard units from twenty-six states. As a staff officer, later deputy division commander, and for two days right at the end of the war acting division commander, MacArthur often went into action with the troops. After the war he reorganized West Point's academic and cadet discipline programs (he made a concerted effort to abolish hazing, which was only partially successful), served on the Billy Mitchell court-martial, commanded in the Philippines, and was Chief of Staff of the Army in the early 1930s, violently suppressing the "Bonus March," apparently against orders from the president. In 1935 he was sent to the Philippines again to help organize the commonwealth's defense forces, and in 1937 resigned from the Army in order to continue in the service of the commonwealth. When, in mid-1941, the Philippine armed forces were activated by the president and merged into the U.S. armed forces, MacArthur was recalled to duty as a full general and placed in overall command. Caught napping by the onset of the war (he lost his entire air force on the ground nine hours after Pearl Harbor), MacArthur seriously bungled the initial defense of the Philippines, but managed to salvage the situation by a belated retreat to the Bataan peninsula. Ordered to Australia by President Roosevelt in February 1942, MacArthur assumed command of Allied forces there, and shortly began an offensive that would eventually recover New Guinea and the Philippines. Army commander designate for the invasion of Japan, MacArthur instead commanded the occupation forces, and became virtual ruler of the country for several years. In

1950 MacArthur assumed command of UN forces in Korea, planning the spectacularly successful Inchon operation, but subsequently mismanaged the pursuit of the defeated North Korean Army and totally misread Chinese intentions, with disastrous results. After repeated warnings from the president about his unauthorized political statements, MacArthur was relieved of duty in April 1951. Despite the belief by many that he would undertake a political career, he spent the rest of his life in retirement. MacArthur was a commander of erratic capabilities; when he was good he was brilliant, but he was often careless and self-centered, which led to errors in planning. He also let his personal likes and dislikes, and particularly his love of publicity, interfere in his management of the war. He despised Marines and Australians, and made sure neither got any credit for operations in "his" theater. He almost fired Robert Eichelberger after a newspaper credited him (accurately) with the victory at Buna-Gona, putting him on the shelf for almost a year. Although generally regarded as a staunch conservative, MacArthur in fact had no political principles, merely saying what seemed to please whomsoever he was speaking with (among other things, he endorsed socialism and the American Civil Liberties Union). He had no friends, as he had no equals. MacArthur is buried in a pompous monument at Norfolk, Virginia.

MAO TSE-TUNG. Mao Tse-tung (1893–1976) came from a prosperous peasant family in Hunan. He received an excellent traditional education, but left school in 1911 to join Sun Yat-sen's revolutionary army. Discharged after about six months, Mao pursued a higher education, worked for a time as a librarian, and in 1921 helped found the Chinese Communist party. For a time associated with the Kuomintang party, Mao broke decisively with Chiang Kai-shek in the late 1920s; he became a notable organizer and leader of guerrilla forces, and an important theoretician of guerrilla warfare. Over the next twenty years, Mao led Communist forces in an on-again, off-again war against Chiang's Nationalists, pausing briefly to fight the Japanese as well. After World War II the civil war resumed, to be concluded with a Communist victory in 1949.

MARSHALL, GEORGE CATLETT. George C. Marshall (1880–1959) graduated from the Virginia Military Institute in 1902 and entered the infantry. He served in the Philippine Insurrection and on various staffs, attended several schools, and rose to captain by the time the United States entered World War I. Among the first American soldiers to go to France, Marshall proved an extremely able staff officer, rising rapidly to colonel and engineering the extraordinary movement of American forces from the St.-Mihiel to the Meuse-Argonne front late in 1918. After the war he rose steadily in the Army; despite the hostility of Douglas MacArthur (having John J. Pershing and Malin Craig, MacArthur's successor as Chief of Staff, as patrons probably saved his career), Marshall was named Chief of Staff in 1938 and retained the post through 1945, during which period he oversaw the expansion of the U.S. Army from 125,000 men to over 8 million. A meticulous planner and strategist of great vision, he was one of the principal architects of victory. A man of great character and dignity, he was the only person FDR never addressed by his first name, and the only professional soldier ever to win the Nobel Peace Prize, for the Marshall Plan.

MATSUYAMA, SUKEZO. Sukezo Matsuyama spent most of the war as a Japanese division commander in the Burma fighting. He became an army commander in the area during early 1945.

MIKAWA, GUNICHI. Gunichi Mikawa graduated from the Naval Academy in 1911. He had a very distinguished career, attending various schools, serving as naval attaché in Paris, on staffs, and in command of ships. Early in the Pacific war he commanded battleship divisions and cruiser squadrons (as a vice admiral). He commanded the forces that defeated the Allies at the Battle of Savo Island (the most lopsided naval defeat in American history) and surface forces throughout the battles for Guadalcanal in 1942. He was relieved in late 1943, as someone had to take the fall for Japan's steadily declining fortunes in the area after Savo. Mikawa went on to command the Southwest Area Fleet in early 1944 until U.S. naval forces seized the area in late 1944.

MITSCHER, MARC ANDREW. One of the most distinguished U.S. naval officers in history, Marc Andrew Mitscher (1887–1947) graduated from Annapolis in 1910 and spent the next five years in battleships. In 1915 he took flight training, qualifying as a pilot the following year. During World War I he commanded various naval air stations. In 1919 he took part in an attempt to fly the Atlantic.

Although his plane was forced down in the Azores by mechanical difficulties, another plane in the flight made it to Lisbon. Over the next few years he held various staff and air commands, and skippered a seaplane tender. In October 1941 he became the first captain of the carrier *Hornet*, shortly rising to rear admiral in command of the *Hornet* task force, launching the Doolittle bombers against Japan in April 1942. After taking part in the Battle of Midway, Mitscher for a time commanded a patrol wing, and in April 1943 took command of all Allied air assets in the Solomons. The following January he was put in command of the newly formed Fast Carrier Task Force, TF 38/58. This he headed for most of the rest of the war, most notably in the Battle of the Philippine Sea, the Battle of Leyte Gulf, and ultimately in raids against the Japanese home islands. After the war Mitscher was promoted to full admiral. Continuing on active service, he died while in command of the Atlantic Fleet. Although overshadowed by Halsey, and to a lesser extent Spruance, it was Mitscher who was responsible, under their overall direction, for the planning and execution of virtually all U.S. carrier operations in the Pacific from January of 1944 onward.

MIWA, SHIGEYOSHI. Shigeyoshi Miwa was a Japanese submarine officer who rose through the ranks to command the Sixth Fleet (all submarines) by the summer of 1944. He was reluctant to use his subs to carry Kamikaze mini-subs, but followed orders. These weapons did not work. He lost his command in early 1945.

MOUNTBATTEN, LOUIS. One of the youngest and most successful senior officers in the war, Louis Mountbatten (1900–1979) was not harmed by his family connections. His father had been First Lord of the Admiralty for a time, and he himself was the uncle of Prince Philip of Greece and Denmark, the prospective (and eventual) husband of Princess (later Queen) Elizabeth. A naval cadet and midshipman during World War I, by 1939 he was a destroyer skipper. Mountbatten commanded a British destroyer flotilla during the Norwegian campaign and off Crete (Noël Coward's film *In Which We Serve* is loosely based on his exploits). In 1941 he was jumped several ranks and named head of Combined Operations. In order to enhance his already considerable clout, he was simultaneously made a general and an air marshal. In this role he oversaw numerous commando operations, and helped plan the raids on

Dieppe and St.-Nazaire. From early 1943 he headed the Allied Southeast Asian Command, a post in which he rendered excellent service, being aided by a number of distinguished subordinates, most notably Bill Slim. After the war he served as the last viceroy of India, overseeing the British withdrawal and the partition. He later served in a variety of prominent military and civil posts, until killed by an IRA bomb in 1979. Mountbatten's abilities as a commander were considerable. Although his excellent political connections helped smooth the way for him, he was an excellent administrator, could get along with the most sensitive egos, had a flair for the unusual, and possessed considerable charisma.

NAGANO, OSAMI. Osami Nagano (1880–1947) was one of the senior Japanese naval admirals who got the fleet behind the idea of going to war with Britain and America. Nagano served as a military attaché in the United States just before World War I, but this did not change his attitude as a staunch Japanese nationalist. He failed to get Japan parity with Britain and America during the London Naval Conference in 1936, and pulled Japan out of the naval disarmament agreement. He served as Navy minister, and then commander of the Combined Fleet during the 1930s. In early 1941 he became Chief of the Naval General Staff. An enthusiastic supporter of the "strike south" (against Dutch oil fields) strategy, he went ahead with plans for the Pearl Harbor strike despite the Foreign Ministry's continued efforts at diplomacy. He was an advocate of taking Samoa to cut the American supply line to Australia, but the Midway operation was selected instead. Nagano was deposed by General Tojo in early 1944 when the Army seized control of the Naval General Staff. Tried as a war criminal after the war, he died of pneumonia during the trial. Nagano was smart, but not a hard worker. He preferred to get others to do the work while he concentrated on politics (at which he was pretty good). When the war began, he was already in his sixties and losing his energy. Unable to wheel and deal as he once had, he lost his support in the Naval Staff and the Imperial Household as the war went on.

NAGUMO, CHUICHI. Chuichi Nagumo (1886–1944) graduated from the Naval Academy in 1908, becoming a destroyerman and expert in torpedo warfare. During the 1920s he traveled in Europe and America, before returning to Japan to commence a series of increasingly important ship and squadron commands. Early in 1941 he was given the First Air Fleet, which he commanded in the attack on Pearl Harbor. Although Japan's premier carrier admiral, Nagumo was not an able tactician or a bold leader. At Pearl Harbor his conservative nature caused him to refuse his staff's urging that a third strike be launched to hit the American fuel supplies and other targets at the now devastated base. However, in the following six months he added to his reputation by leading strikes against Allied bases in Australia and the Indian Ocean. His shortcomings didn't catch up with him until Midway, where his indecisiveness contributed to the loss of four Japanese carriers. He survived this debacle and continued to command carrier forces during 1942 as the Japanese attempted to retake Guadalcanal. In these battles he demonstrated again a lack of drive, and by the end of 1942 he had been relegated to the command of the Sasebo naval base. In 1944, he was given command of the forces defending Saipan. On July 7, 1944, he committed suicide as invading American forces completed their conquest of Saipan.

NARA, AKIRA. Akira Nara was a "Westernized" Japanese officer. He was educated in America and graduated from the U.S. Army Infantry School. By the late 1930s he was commanding a garrison brigade on Taiwan. He was given a division to lead during the invasion of the Philippines. His unit made the final assault that captured the Bataan peninsula and caused the final American surrender. One of the few Japanese commanders to come out of the Philippines operation with his reputation intact.

NIMITZ, CHESTER W. Chester W. Nimitz (1885–1966) graduated from Annapolis in 1905 and embarked upon a career in submarines, rising to command the Atlantic Fleet submarine flotilla by 1912. The following year he toured various European nations, studying submarine development, and built the first diesel engine for the U.S. Navy. During World War I he served as chief of staff to the commander of Atlantic Fleet submarines. After the war he attended the Naval War College, served on various staffs, and rose steadily upward. At the time of Pearl Harbor he was chief of the Bureau of Navigation (i.e., personnel). From this post he was almost immediately made commander of the Pacific Fleet, to which, in early 1942, he added command of all U.S. forces in the Central and

North Pacific, as well as responsibility for coordinating operations with Douglas MacArthur in the Southwest Pacific. Nimitz oversaw all U.S. operations in the Pacific for the entire war, approving strategy, selecting personnel, ensuring the flow of men, ships, and matériel, and working with surprising smoothness with the egocentric MacArthur. After the war he was Chief of Naval Operations until his retirement in late 1947. He later served as a special assistant to the secretary of the Navy and director of the UN plebiscite in Kashmir, and wrote a reasonably sound history of the Pacific war. A capable man, Nimitz was flexible in command, willing to listen to others, even when it annoyed him. Although a nonflier, he recognized the logic behind John Towers's argument that all "black shoe" (nonaviation) officers should have a "brown shoe" (aviation) adviser, and acted on it. His relaxed, almost informal style of command masked a great deal of toughness.

NISHIMURA, SHOGI. Shogi Nishimura (1889–1944) graduated from the Naval Academy in 1911. He had a satisfactory but by no means distinguished career thereafter, rising slowly upward. At the beginning of the war he was a rear admiral. Nishimura commanded light cruiser and destroyer units through many of the 1942 battles. By 1944 he was a vice admiral and led the task force of two older battleships, one cruiser, and four destroyers that managed to avoid detection until it was in Surigao Strait, headed for the American invasion force off Leyte. Nishimura kept coming despite enormous American resistance. He went down with his flagship, the battleship *Yamashiro* (October 25, 1944).

OKAMURA, YASUJI. Yasuji Okamura joined the Japanese Army in 1904. By the outbreak of the Pacific war he was commander of North China Area Army and a full general. At the end of 1944 Okamura took command of all Japanese forces in China. At the end of the war he surrendered to Chiang Kai-shek and spent several years assisting the Nationalist Chinese in their civil war with the Communists, whom he fervently hated. His postwar service in China allowed him to return to Japan in 1949 and become involved in the creation of Japan's "Self Defense Forces."

OKOCHI, DENSHICHI. Denshichi Okoshi joined the Japanese Navy after World War I. He rose to the rank of vice admiral and commanded the Southwest Area Fleet from late 1944 until the end of the war. At this point the fleet had few ships and the command consisted largely of forces ashore. He surrendered these forces in early September 1945.

ONISHI, TAKIJIRO. Takijiro Onishi (1891–1945), one of the militaristic "wild men," and the driving force behind Japanese carrier aviation, graduated from the Naval Academy in 1912. After flight training he was thrown out of the Naval College because of his enthusiasm for gambling and chasing women, and went off to study in Britain and France for two years beginning in 1918. As one of the first Japanese naval aviators, he spent much of the 1920s and 1930s laying the foundations for the great carrier force that would forever change the nature of naval warfare, meanwhile finding time to become an ace in China. Onishi not only helped organize and train the carrier force, but was instrumental in establishing much of the industrial base necessary to build and sustain it. He became a rear admiral in 1939, after having commanded land-based naval aviation units. In 1941 he worked on the plan for attacking Pearl Harbor. His outspokenness about dumping battleships and building more aircraft and carriers prevented him from getting sea commands, and as a result he spent most of the war directing the construction of naval weapons and munitions. Onishi became a vice admiral in 1944 and was given command of Japanese naval air forces in the Philippines. He went along with Kamikaze tactics because he was pragmatic, not because he believed the quasi-religious rhetoric, and organized Kamikaze operations in the Philippines through the end of 1944, when ordered to move himself and his staff to Taiwan. There he organized more Kamikaze units, some of which operated during the battle for Okinawa. When the emperor ordered the armed forces to surrender on August 15, 1945, Onishi chose suicide instead.

OZAWA, JISABURO. Jisaburo Ozawa (1886–1966) graduated from the Naval Academy in 1909, served in destroyers, went on to various service schools, and then made his mark as a surface warfare expert in the 1920s and 1930s. He was particularly skillful in the use of torpedoes, weapons the Japanese Navy became noted for during the 1942 battles. By 1941 he was a vice admiral and commanded the surface forces that supported the invasions in Malaya and the

Dutch East Indies from late 1941 through early 1942. He became the commander of the Third Fleet at Truk in late 1942. In early 1943, he commanded a failed attempt to destroy Allied air power in the New Guinea/Solomons area. He commanded Japanese forces during the summer 1944 Battle of the Philippines Sea. The result was "the Great Marianas Turkey Shoot." Ozawa offered to resign after this, but was instead put in charge of Japanese naval forces that sortied to resist the American invasion of the Philippines in late 1944. This led to another defeat and he returned to Japan with the few surviving ships. He served on the Naval General Staff for the remainder of the war. He died in 1966, at age eighty. Ozawa was a classic "fighting admiral," but even these capabilities were not able to overcome the quantity and quality of naval forces America was able to muster. He was several inches taller than the average Japanese, but was actually rather modest in demeanor.

PATCH, ALEXANDER McCARRELL. Alexander McCarrell Patch (1889–1945) was an Army brat who graduated from West Point in 1913. Commissioned in the infantry, he saw active service on the Mexican border and in combat as commander of a machine gun battalion during World War I. He afterward held various posts, attended several Army schools, and rose slowly through the ranks. One of the officers who developed the "triangular" infantry division table of organization in 1936, Patch was in a training command at the time of Pearl Harbor, from which he was sent in January 1942 to prepare the defense of New Caledonia. Organizing the Americal (23rd Infantry) Division from odd units that he found in the South Pacific, Patch took the division to support the Marines on Guadalcanal in October 1942. Succeeding to command on Guadalcanal later that year, he oversaw the final reduction of the Japanese forces. In February 1943 Patch was ordered home to the United States, where he assumed command of a corps. In March 1944 he was given command of the Seventh Army for the invasion of southern France, which he executed flawlessly. His son, Captain Alexander McC. Patch, Jr., was killed in action under his father's command in eastern France, in late 1944. The elder Patch led his army until the end of the war, which found his troops in Bavaria. After the war assigned to head a study of how best to organize the Army for the postwar world, he died suddenly in late 1945.

PERCIVAL, A. E. A career officer with limited service in World War I, Percival (1887–1966) began World War II as chief of staff to the British I Corps, with which he saw service in France. After Dunkirk he served for a time as a division commander, and in July 1941, by then a lieutenant general, he was sent to command in Malaya and the vicinity. There were many things wrong with Percival's command. His ground troops, mostly Indians and Australians, were mostly of less than the finest quality and very unseasoned, the best units of both nations being in the Middle East. His air force was composed primarily of obsolescent aircraft. However, when the Japanese did attack, in December, although they had some material superiority, notably in the air, they were greatly outnumbered by the defenders (about 60,000 to 130,000). The Japanese didn't even realize they were outnumbered until the campaign was almost over, but were operating on a shoestring even without that knowledge. Ultimately, Percival never developed an adequate plan of campaign, so that the Japanese retained the initiative throughout, repeatedly outflanking his many attempts to form defensive lines, until he was forced onto Singapore Island, where he surrendered the remnants of his command, some 90,000 troops, to greatly inferior Japanese forces within seventy days of the beginning of the war. Percival spent the balance of the war in a Japanese prison camp, from which he was liberated in time to attend the surrender of Japan aboard USS *Missouri*. Although admittedly entrusted with a very flawed command, Percival certainly did not act with skill or determination. An inept, unlucky commander.

PHILLIPS, THOMAS. Tom Phillips (1891–1941), the son of a colonel and an admiral's daughter, entered the Royal Navy in 1904. During World War I he saw action in cruisers, notably at the Dardanelles and in the Atlantic. Between the wars he rose steadily, and at the outbreak of World War II was Vice Chief of the Naval Staff. He was still in this post in late 1941, when he was promoted two ranks and sent to command "Force Z," the Royal Navy's squadron in the Far East. Phillips was wholly unsuited to his command, having spent most of his career as a staff officer. Although it is unlikely that any British admiral could have avoided defeat at the hands of the Japanese off Malaya in December 1941, Phillips's lack of understanding of the influence of air power turned defeat into disaster.

POUND, ALFRED DUDLEY. Alfred Dudley Pound (1877–1943) entered the Royal Navy as a very young boy in the late 1880s and rose steadily, if slowly, thereafter. During World War I he served as a staff officer, being present at Jutland. After the war he held a variety of posts and commanded the Mediterranean Fleet in the late 1930s, a trying time, during which Italian submarines were illegally active against Spanish Republican shipping. In 1939 he was promoted to Admiral of the Fleet and made First Sea Lord, Chief of Staff of the Royal Navy. Pound had an enormous capacity for administrative work and was totally devoted to his duties (even having a cot placed in his office so that he could sleep there rather than return home). Unfortunately, he tended to overconcentrate control of operations in his own hands, which often led to unfortunate results. By 1942 he was aware that he had a terminal brain tumor, but remained active until the last.

PULLER, LEWIS B. Lewis "Chesty" Puller (1898–1971) enlisted in the U.S. Marines in mid-1918, after a brief stay at the Virginia Military Institute. Although he secured a commission, he was shortly discharged in the post–World War I reorganization of the Corps. He reenlisted as a private. Puller's service was typical of a Marine of his generation, including tours in Haiti, Nicaragua, and China, and aboard ship, between which he attended various schools, was recommissioned, and was repeatedly decorated. On the eve of World War II he was a battalion commander in the 7th Marines, with which he went to Guadalcanal in August 1942. Puller greatly distinguished himself on Guadalcanal, earning his third Navy Cross and sundry other decorations. He went on to command in several other operations, culminating in command of the 1st Marine Regiment on Peleliu, meanwhile earning a fourth Navy Cross. The end of the war found him in a training assignment at Camp Lejeune. In the postwar years Puller held various assignments, and then in 1950 was once more given the 1st Marines, which he led with great élan during the Inchon landings and in the battle for Seoul. Returning stateside, he rose to division command and assistant commandant before retiring for reasons of health in 1957. A short, tough, profane man, Puller, the most decorated Marine in history, was an ideal tactical commander.

ROOSEVELT, FRANKLIN D. FDR (1882–1945) came from a very prosperous family that had been prominent in New York society for generations. A Harvard man (he earned a "gentleman's C") and a graduate of Columbia Law School, Roosevelt never had any formal military training or experience. However, he was a close student of history, and during World War I he served very effectively as assistant secretary of the Navy; he wanted to resign and take a commission in the Navy, but President Wilson refused to permit him to do so. An able shiphandler himself (on several occasions he took the helm of destroyers, once even docking one), he identified so closely with the Navy that he was known to refer to it as "us" and to the Army as "them" in conversation, until George C. Marshall asked him to stop. Roosevelt's pro-Navy attitude was fortunate in many ways, for just at the moment when the nation was fighting its most important sea war, it was led by a man who had a more intimate knowledge of the Navy than any other chief executive ever.

SCOTT, NORMAN. Norman Scott (1889–1942) graduated from Annapolis in 1911 and served in destroyers, being decorated during World War I for heroic action when his ship was sunk by a U-boat in the Atlantic. Between the wars he served as a presidential aide, attended several Navy schools, and held various staff and line assignments, including the heavy cruiser *Pensacola*. By 1941 he was on the staff of the Chief of Naval Operations. From this post in June 1942 he was promoted to temporary rear admiral and given command of various task forces in the South Pacific. A tough but very well liked commander, Scott drove his men hard, training them in night tactics to meet the Japanese, hitherto masters of the art. As a result, he neatly dished up an enemy squadron in the Battle of Cape Esperance (October 11, 1942), for which Scott was named a permanent rear admiral. Scott might have gone on to greater things, but Navy regulations intervened. In early November, he was superseded in command by Dan Callaghan, whose commission as a regular rear admiral antedated his own, despite the fact that the latter had been skippering a desk for most of the war. Scott was killed in the Japanese ambush of Callaghan's squadron during the night action off Guadalcanal on November 12–13, 1942, a few minutes before Callaghan himself perished. Both men were awarded the Medal of Honor.

SHOUP, DAVID M. One of a number of controversial officers the Marines seem to produce from time to time, David M. Shoup (b. 1904) graduated from DePauw University in 1926 and was commissioned a second lieutenant in the Corps. He served afloat and in China, attended various schools, and on the outbreak of Pacific war was commanding a battalion of the 6th 'Marines in Iceland. In mid-1942 he was assigned to the staff of the 2nd Marine Division, and served in the New Georgia operation. Promoted to colonel, he commanded the Marines who assaulted Betio, the principal island within Tarawa atoll, and was awarded the Medal of Honor for refusing to be evacuated despite serious wounds. Later he was chief of staff of the 2nd Marine Division, serving during the Marianas campaign in mid-1944 and until the end of he war, when he was assigned to an administrative command in Washington. After the war Shoup held various increasingly important posts, ending his career as commandant of the Corps in 1963. Afterward an outspoken critic of intervention in Vietnam, Shoup found himself vilified and ostracized by many formerly close associates.

SLIM, WILLIAM J. Of working-class background, William Slim (1891–1970) enlisted in the Indian Army during World War I, and by its end had earned a regular commission in the Gurkhas. By the outbreak of World War II he commanded a brigade, which he led with considerable distinction in East Africa in 1940–1941, where he was wounded. During the Iraqi revolt and the Syrian campaign (spring 1941) he again proved himself. Promoted to lieutenant general in early 1942, he was sent by Sir Archibald Wavell (commander in chief, India) to try to stem the Japanese invasion of Burma, commanding the I Burma Corps. Although his troops were mostly of mediocre quality, Slim, ably supported by his superior, Harold Alexander, performed wonders. Although an attempted counteroffensive failed, Slim was able to effect a remarkably arduous retreat of some 900 miles back to India. Given command of XV Corps, Slim subjected it to an intensive regimen of physical toughening, jungle training, and irregular tactics. Appointed to command the Fourteenth Army in October 1943, Slim directed the defense of India ably, and then went over to the offensive in late 1944. By the spring of 1945 Slim had liberated most of central Burma, having inflicted over 350,000 casualties on the Japanese Army. Shortly afterward he was appointed to command all Allied ground forces in Southeast Asia. At the end of the war he was poised to liberate Malaya. After the war Slim served in several prominent military and civil posts. A simple man, Slim was a no-nonsense soldier with enormous regard for the welfare of his men. A meticulous planner, he was not averse to unconventional methods, employing irregular forces and air supply to a degree unprecedented in the war.

SMITH, HOLLAND M. Holland "Howlin' Mad" Smith (1882–1967) was a lawyer in Alabama when he received a commission in the U.S. Marines in 1905. He served in the Philippines, Panama, and the Dominican Republic before going to France in 1917 as a machine gunner and later staff officer, fighting in virtually all of the American Expeditionary Force's operations, Aisne-Marne, the Oise, St.-Mihiel, and the Meuse-Argonne. After occupation duty in Germany, he went through a series of staff and command assignments, helped develop the Corps's amphibious doctrine, and on the eve of the Pacific war was a major general in command of the newly formed 1st Marine Division. He was promoted to command what would become the V Marine Amphibious Corps, and later commander of Fleet Marine Force, Pacific. Smith directed the assaults on Tarawa, Eniwetok, Saipan, Tinian, Guam, Iwo Jima, and Okinawa, several times personally leading the assault forces. Smith retired shortly after the war, with the rank of general. A no-nonsense commander, Smith got his nickname from his occasional bursts of temper. One of his most famous acts was the so-called "War of the Smiths," in which he relieved an army division commander also named Smith during the Marianas campaign.

SMITH, OLIVER PRINCE. Oliver Prince Smith (1893–1977) graduated from Berkeley in 1916 and was commissioned in the U.S. Marines the following year. He saw no action in World War I, being in the Pacific. His interwar service was typical of a Marine of the times, serving on shipboard, in Haiti, and on various staffs, and attending several schools, including the Army's Infantry School. In May 1941 he took his 6th Marine Regiment to Iceland, where the outbreak of the Pacific war found him. In March 1942 he was transferred to Marine Corps headquarters. Not until January 1944 did he get into action, receiving command of the 5th Marines, which he led on New Britain. Shortly afterward made brigadier general, he served on Peleliu as assistant commander of the 1st Marine Division, and Okinawa as Marine deputy chief of staff to Simon B. Buckner's Tenth Army. After Okinawa he returned stateside to command the Marine schools at Quantico, in which post peace found him. After the war he was assistant commandant for a time, and in 1950 was made commander of the newly reactivated 1st Marine Division, which he led in Korea at Inchon, in the fighting for Seoul, at the Chosin Reservoir, and in the retreat to the coast, one of the most distinguished episodes in the history of American arms. Smith afterward rose to lieutenant general and retired in 1955.

SOMERVILLE, JAMES F. James F. Somerville (1882–1949) joined the Royal Navy in 1897 and, after serving in gunboats on the Nile in the Sudan, he became one of the Royal Navy's first radio specialists. During World War I he held various posts as a wireless officer, notably distinguishing himself during the Dardanelles campaign. He rose through the ranks between the wars, and actually retired from the service for reasons of health shortly before World War II broke out. Somerville remained inactive until Dunkirk, when he voluntarily offered his services to Admiral Bertram Ramsay, for whom he performed yeoman service in coordinating the movements of the numerous ships involved in the evacuation. He soon found himself back on active duty (his health problems meanwhile having been cleared up), assigned to command Force H at Gibraltar, one of the most demanding posts in the Royal Navy, from June 1940 through March 1942, during which period he commanded the attack on the French fleet at Mirs-el-Kebir and attempted with considerable success to keep the sea lanes open to Malta. In March 1942, with the Japanese overrunning much of Southeast Asia, Somerville was transferred to command the hastily assembled Far Eastern Fleet. Although his performance in this post was successful, Somerville was also quite lucky, for aside from some serious problems that spring, when the Japanese First Air Fleet (i.e., the Pearl Harbor Strike Force, of six carriers) did considerable damage (racking up a light carrier, two heavy cruisers, and much else besides), he never had to confront a Japanese offensive. In 1944 Somerville retired from this post and was sent as head of the British Naval Mission to the United States, in which capacity he ended the war, having meanwhile been promoted to Admiral of the Fleet. A good officer, Somerville was also lucky.

SPRUANCE, RAYMOND. One of the most successful American admirals of the war, Raymond Spruance (1886–1969) graduated from Annapolis in 1906, made the Great White Fleet's world cruise, commanded a destroyer, and helped complete and commission the new battleship *Pennsylvania*, all by 1916. During World War I he commanded the destroyer *Aaron Ward* in the Atlantic. After the war he held various command and staff positions, taught in several Navy schools, and attended the Naval War College. Shortly after Pearl Harbor he was given command of Cruiser Division 5, which served with Task Force 16 on the Doolittle Raid. Due to Halsey's illness, Spruance was in temporary command of TF 16 at Midway, and performed so well in this role that despite not being aviation-qualified, he continued thereafter to command carrier task forces, being provided with a staff consisting mostly of aviators. For a time chief of staff to Nimitz, Spruance was shortly put in command of what would become the Fifth Fleet (an assignment that he rotated with Halsey, under whom it was called the Third Fleet). With the Fifth Fleet, Spruance commanded in the Tarawa operation, at Eniwetok, in the Marianas (during which he won the Battle of the Philippine Sea), Iwo Jima, and Okinawa. At the end of the war, Spruance became president of the Naval War College. He retired in 1948, and served for a time as ambassador to the Philippines. Spruance proved surprisingly effective as a carrier commander. However, although he did everything right at Midway, his actions during the Philippine Sea were less perfect. Failing to realize that he had the Japanese carriers at his mercy, he defeated but did not destroy them, despite the urging of several members of his staff. This was a failure without much penalty, as the Japanese force had been basically ruined during the battle, if not completely destroyed. But in other circumstances, such a lack of follow-through on Spruance's part might have had serious aftereffects.

STILWELL, JOSEPH W. One of the most controversial American officers of the war, Joseph "Vinegar Joe" Stilwell (1883–1946) graduated from West Point in 1904 and soon afterward was in action against the Moro rebels in the Philippines. Over the next few years he rose through the ranks. The outbreak of World War I found him as an instructor at West Point, from which post he was sent to France to serve first as a liaison officer with the Allies' armies, and later as staff officer with the American Expeditionary Force. After the war he was an intelligence officer in China, attended various Army schools, commanded the 15th Infantry in China, once again served on various staffs and as an instructor, was military attaché in China, and at the time of Pearl Harbor was commanding the III Corps in California. Early in 1942 he was promoted to lieutenant general and sent to command all U.S. forces in the CBI, while simultaneously serving as chief of staff to the Chinese Nationalist Army. Although reinforced by several Chinese divisions, the Allied position in Burma collapsed, and Stilwell led a remarkably arduous retreat to the security of India. In India he reorganized U.S. forces, while training Chinese divisions that were then flown home over the Himalayas. Although he did well in these assignments, even when made deputy commander to Lord Mountbatten, Stilwell's personality was abrasive. A "tell it like it is" sort, Stilwell tended to irritate Chiang, whom he called "the Peanut," which was Chiang's name in coded messages. Although President Roosevelt attempted to get Chiang to place Stilwell in overall command of Chinese forces, in the end he had to recall the general. For a time chief of Army Ground Forces, in the spring of 1945 Stilwell was put in command of the Tenth Army on Okinawa. After the war he held an administrative command until his death. A brilliant officer, with excellent ideas that would probably have worked, but without much chance of getting them into practice due to Chinese resistance.

SUGIYAMA, HAJIME. Hajime Sugiyama joined the Japanese Army in 1901. He commanded forces in China during the 1930s and was promoted to full general in 1936. An enthusiastic supporter of Japanese expansion in China and the Pacific, he became Chief of Staff of the Army in 1940 and presided over the planning for Army operations in the Pacific during the initial expansion. Sugiyama became a field marshal in 1943 but lost the Chief of Staff post to General Tojo in 1944. He became commander of Army forces in eastern Japan until the end of the war. Sugiyama committed suicide when Japan surrendered.

SUZUKI, SOSAKU. Sosaku Suzuki joined the Japanese Army in 1912 and spent much of his early career as a staff officer and military attaché. This marked him for greater things in the future. He received troop commands in the 1930s and was chief of staff of the Twenty-fifth Army during the invasion of Malaya. Suzuki went back to a series of key staff jobs after that. In July 1944, he was given command of the Thirty-fifth Army in the Philippines and told to prepare to defend against the expected American invasion. He led his troops in resourceful resistance, successfully moving troops to other islands. Suzuki was finally killed by U.S. aircraft in June 1945, while moving by boat to another island.

TAKAGI, TAKEO. Takeo Takagi (1892–1944) graduated from the Japanese Naval Academy in 1912. He specialized in torpedo warfare and submarines, but also commanded various surface ships and served on a number of staffs over the following two decades. Late in 1941 he was given command of the Fifth Fleet as a rear admiral. He commanded the carrier strike force during the Battle of the Coral Sea and assumed command of the Sixth Fleet (submarines) in late 1943 (as vice admiral). Takagi was killed on Saipan in July 1944 during the American invasion.

TAKAHASHI, KAKUICHI. Kakuichi Takahashi joined the Japanese Navy before World War I and was on the Navy General Staff as a rear admiral in the early 1930s. He was a militant regarding the use of the Japanese fleet. Takahashi commanded the Third Fleet as a vice admiral (after being recalled from retirement) early in the war. Although active in the invasions of Dutch and British islands in the East Indies, he spent the rest of the war in Japan.

TANAKA, RAIZO. Raizo Tanaka (1892–1969) graduated from the Japanese Naval Academy in 1913, and specialized in destroyers and torpedo warfare. He rose steadily, commanding a series of ships culminating with the battleship *Kongo* in 1939. Promoted to rear admiral in 1941, Tanaka led destroyer units on escort duties during the Dutch East Indies invasion and later during the Midway operation. His main fame came when he organized and led the "Tokyo Express," which used destroyers to supply and reinforce the Japanese troops on Guadalcanal during 1942. By the end of the year he was removed from command for his outspoken criticism of how the Guadalcanal operation was being run, and spent the rest of the war commanding naval bases in Burma. Promoted to vice admiral before the end of the war, Tanaka didn't get around to surrendering until

January 1946. Tanaka was one of the most able Japanese commanders, a resourceful and wily tactician. He didn't get more important posts because he saw the situation as it was, not as many of his starry-eyed commanders wanted to see it.

TANAKA, SHINICHI. Shinichi Tanaka graduated from the Military Academy in 1913. He held a variety of posts, primarily as a staff officer, and was one of those who believed Japan should take over all of China and attack the Soviet Union. The head of the Army's Operations Division at the outbreak of the Pacific war, in 1942 he was sent as chief of staff to the Southern Area Army, which supervised operations in Indonesia and Southeast Asia. In March 1943 he received a division in Burma, leading it with great ability in tenacious rearguard actions. In September 1944, he became chief of staff, and virtual commander, of the Burma Area Army headquarters and from there constantly urged defense of Burmese positions to the last man.

TERAUCHI, HISAICHI. Count Hisaichi Terauchi (1879–1946), the son of Field Marshal Count Masakata Terauchi (who started his military career as a samurai and rose to Army command during the Russo-Japanese War, later holding important government posts as well), graduated from the Military Academy in 1899. He fought in the Russo-Japanese War, attended various schools, and spent several years as an attaché and student in Germany and Austria before World War I. Between 1914 and 1936 he rose to general and war minister, in which role he crushed the last vestiges of parliamentary authority over the military. In 1937 he commanded the forces that invaded China from Manchuria, and in 1941 was given the Southern Area Army, which controlled all Army operations in Southeast Asia and the South Pacific. Made a field marshal in June 1943, Terauchi suffered a mild stroke in April 1945, but remained in command until the end of the war because his staff did not report his ill health to Tokyo. That he did not stand trial for war crimes was due to his illness, which proved terminal. Surprisingly, he was looked after by Lord Mountbatten once the war was over. Terauchi was a soldier of the old school and did not agree with the Army involvement in politics. His noble rank and personal ability allowed him to retain his command despite these attitudes.

TOJO, HIDEKI. Hideki Tojo (1884–1948) was not a field commander during World War II. He was the most important Japanese Army general because he ran the government for most of the war and was generally considered the one man most responsible for getting Japan into a war that many senior Japanese military officers knew Japan could not win. He graduated from the Military Academy in 1905. Most of his early career was spent in staff assignments and at the War College. From 1919 through 1922 he served with the Japanese Embassy in Berlin. Considered bright, but not among the brightest, Tojo made up for this with a workaholic dedication to whatever he was doing, and an intense nationalism and ambition. Tojo was posted to the Kwantung (Manchurian) Army in the summer of 1934, as the head of the Army military police. The Kwantung Army was a hotbed of Army enthusiasm for Japanese expansion and Tojo was caught up in what was, to him, a very congenial cause. In 1937 he became chief of staff of the Kwantung Army. He actively participated in operations against Chinese troops and, in 1938, went back to Japan to become vice minister of war. He offended so many senior officials with his ultranationalist attitudes that he was removed to the more obscure post of inspector of army aviation at the end of 1938. By hard work and much politicking, he worked himself into the job of minister of war by the summer of 1940. By late 1941 he had gotten the post of prime minister and, in effect, control of the government. He retained his rank in the Army. While Japan never became a military dictatorship in the classical sense, by the end of October 1941, the Army was calling the shots (Tojo was also the minister of home affairs and minister of war). The decision to go to war was already made when Tojo took over, and he heartily supported it. Through 1942 and 1943, he became the head of even more ministries (Foreign Affairs, Education, Commerce and Industry, Munitions). By late 1943 he capped all this by becoming the Chief of Staff (commander) of both the Army and the Navy. For the first six months of 1944, Tojo was a one-man government. But he was not a complete dictator. In July 1944, the Privy Council (composed of older, semiretired senior officials) agreed that he should go and forced him to retire. The main reason for this vote of no confidence was that Japan was losing the war and Tojo refused to face reality. Although Tojo was then given a place on the Privy Council, he spent the rest of the war writing and (literally) tending his garden. Arrested as a war criminal after the war, he was tried, condemned, and hanged for atrocities. Although his body was burned and the ashes secretly buried by the Allies, Japanese crematorium workers stole some of the ashes and turned them over to the government after the occupation had ended. In 1960 an impressive tomb was constructed to contain these ashes (mixed in with those of six other war criminals). The monument is inscribed "The Tomb of the Seven Martyrs."

TOWERS, JOHN H. Among the most important molders of the U.S. Navy's carrier forces in World War II, John H. Towers was also one of the unsung heroes of the Pacific war, a man so forgotten that he is often overlooked in most standard works on naval history: He is mentioned barely a dozen times in Samuel Eliot Morison's fifteen-volume *History of U.S. Naval Operations in World War II*. A 1906 graduate of the Naval Academy, Towers earned his wings in 1911 and was thereafter closely involved with the development of naval air power. From early 1942 until the end of the war, Towers was the principal naval air officer in the Pacific, serving first as commanding officer, air forces, Pacific Fleet, and later as deputy commander in chief, Pacific. Instrumental in the development of the fast carrier task force, the evolution of air group composition, the coordination of carriers with escorts, and the assignment of flying officers as chiefs of staff to nonflying commanders (and vice versa), Towers had enormous intellectual and administrative powers that kept him from active command until virtually the end of the war, when, in August 1945, he was named commanding officer of the Second Fast Carrier Task Force, and that only on the surrender of Japan. A man who deserved better of the Republic.

TOYODA, SOEMU. Soemu Toyoda (1885–1957) graduated from the Naval Academy in 1905. A naval gunnery specialist, he had an impressive career, including numerous special assignments and duty as an admiral's aide, along with the usual run of ship and staff posts. In the late 1930s, as a vice admiral, he commanded naval forces during the heavy fighting in China. Opposed to the idea of war with America, Toyoda had little respect for the militant Army officers running the government. He spent the early part of the Pacific war commanding naval bases in Japan. In early 1944 he became commander of the Combined Fleet and was ordered to gather his forces for a "decisive battle" against the approaching American naval might. Despite his earlier attitudes toward war with America, he proposed that Japan fight on even after most of the Japanese fleet was destroyed by early 1945. Nevertheless, he accepted the emperor's surrender order. Arrested as a war criminal, he was cleared of culpability for war crimes committed by naval personnel. He had given his sword to Admiral Nimitz at the end of the war, but Nimitz returned the sword as a gesture of goodwill in 1952.

TRUMAN, HARRY S. Harry S Truman (1884–1972) came from a modest background in his native Missouri. Entering retail trade, he joined the National Guard in order to improve his business connections. Activated during World War I, Truman proved a very able artillery captain, reputedly the best mule skinner in the war and, after acquiring that skill, among the best "cussers" in the American Expeditionary Force. After the war he remained in trade and the National Guard, and entered politics. He did well in the latter two (his partner managed the business quite successfully, however), and by the outbreak of World War II was a National Guard colonel and a senator. Truman's chairmanship of one of the numerous congressional committees investigating the war brought him to the attention of President Roosevelt, with the result that he was elected vice president in 1944. Although not a member of FDR's inner circle, Truman very quickly assumed control when Roosevelt died in April 1945, proving an effective president in the final months of the war.

TURNER, RICHMOND KELLY. The unquestioned master of amphibious warfare during the Second World War, Richmond Kelly Turner (1885–1961) graduated from the U.S. Naval Academy in 1908. His early career was typical of that of a junior naval officer of his generation, including sea duty, some staff time, and some school time. During World War I he served in battleships, but did not get overseas. After the war he continued in the peacetime routine of the Navy until he took flight training in the late 1920s. Thereupon his career began to blossom. He commanded several aviation squadrons, was involved in planning the future of naval aviation, was an adviser to the U.S. delegation at the Geneva Disarmament Conference of 1932, saw some more sea time and staff duty, and in October 1940 was named director of war plans. In this post he was deeply involved not only in planning the Navy's war, but also in developing amphibious doctrine in cooperation with Marines such as Alexander A. Vandegrift. As a result, in mid-1942 he was ordered to the South Pacific to assume command of the task force that landed Vandegrift's 1st Marine Division on Guadalcanal. Despite Savo Island and other setbacks, Turner's tenacity and determination helped keep the Marines on Guadalcanal and Henderson Field in American hands. Thereafter Turner directed numerous amphibious operations with increasing skill and success. In April 1945 he was named Commander, Amphibious Forces, Pacific, comprising the III and V Marine Amphibious Corps, in anticipation of the invasion of Japan, which he would have directed. When peace came, he briefly held some minor diplomatic posts, retiring in 1947.

USHIJIMA, MITSURU. Mitsuru Ushijima (1887–1945) graduated from the Military Academy in 1908. A regimental officer during World War I, in 1918–1919 he was on the staff of the Siberian Expedition. His later career included staff, line, and school duty, and in 1939 he was given command of a division, which he led in Burma with some distinction in early 1942. There followed a tour as commandant of the Military Academy, from which post he was sent in mid-1943 to command of the Thirty-second Army on Okinawa (an island considered part of Japan proper and populated by Japanese). With nearly two years to organize the defenses, Ushijima put up a tenacious and bloody resistance against the American invasion in April 1945. About 50,000 Japanese troops were killed and 10,755, an unusually high number, were captured in this battle. Many Okinawan civilians also died, with estimates ranging from 40,000 to 110,000. The battle saw the highest American losses for any single operation, between the ferocity of the resistance and the dedication of the Kamikazes. It was these high losses that convinced American commanders and troops that resistance on the Japanese home islands would be equally fanatic and costly. After leading the stubborn defense, Ushijima committed suicide on June 21 when he saw that further resistance was futile.

VANDEGRIFT, ALEXANDER A. The first U.S. Marine to rise to four-star rank, Alexander A. Vandegrift (1887–1973) enlisted in the Marine Corps in 1908 rather than complete college. Commissioned the following year, he had an active career before World War I, serving by 1915 in Cuba, Nicaragua, Panama, Mexico, and Haiti, where, with some minor interruptions, he remained until 1923. After teaching or attending several advanced courses, he was in China for a time, and then on staff assignments at Marine headquarters. In the mid- and late 1930s he was again in China, later becoming secretary to the commandant of the Corps. When the Pacific war broke out he was assistant commander of the 1st Marine Division, assuming command in April 1942. On August 7, 1942, Vandegrift undertook the first American amphibious operation of the war, landing his division on Guadalcanal and beginning an arduous campaign that ended six months later, by which time his division had been relieved. Awarded a Medal of Honor, promoted to lieutenant general, and given command of I Marine Amphibious Corps in the spring of 1943, Vandegrift undertook the landings on Bougainville in late 1943. He was shortly afterward named commandant of the Marine Corps. Promoted to full general in March 1945, Vandegrift retired in 1949.

WAINWRIGHT, JONATHAN M. Jonathan M. Wainwright (1883–1953) came from a family with a long military tradition (even though most of them had served in the Navy). He graduated from West Point in 1906 and was commissioned in the cavalry. Aside from serving on a number of famous old posts in the West and Southwest, he saw action in the Philippines against the Moros, some staff time, and some school time. On the eve of World War I he was an instructor at the Plattsburg Officers' Training Camp, where he remained until early 1918, when he went to France. In France, Wainwright served as a divisional chief of staff during the St.-Mihiel and Meuse-Argonne offensives, and later on occupation duty in Germany, not returning to the United States until 1920. His peacetime service was a mixture of troop duty, staff time, and school time. In late 1940 he was promoted to major general and sent to command the Philippine Division, a Regular Army outfit composed primarily of Philippine troops. Upon the Japanese invasion of the Philippines, Wainwright's command formed the backbone of the defense. Given command of a corps by MacArthur, he did well on Bataan. When MacArthur was ordered to Australia in February 1942, Wainwright assumed command of U.S. forces in the Philippines. Following the surrender of Bataan he withdrew to Corregidor, which in turn surrendered on May 6, 1942. Wainwright spent the rest of the war in various Japanese prisoner-of-war camps, ending up in a Manchurian camp reserved for senior Allied officers. Convinced that he would be court-martialed upon his release, Wainwright was surprised to learn that he had been awarded a Medal of Honor and promoted to general for the tenacity with which he had held on in the Philippines. He retired in 1947.

WAVELL, ARCHIBALD. One of the few British officers to hold important commands throughout the war, Wavell (1883–1950) joined the British Army in time to see service in the South African War (1898–1902). He ended World War I as a brigade commander, and rose slowly to high command between the wars. Appointed commander in chief, Middle East, shortly before World War II broke out, he oversaw operations on as many as four fronts simultaneously: East Africa, the Western Desert, Greece, and Iraq-Syria. This disparate array of responsibilities was a critical factor in explaining the general success of Rommel's spring offensive in 1941 and the failure of British counteroffensives in the desert, for which Wavell nevertheless bore the blame. Transferred as commander in chief in India in late 1941, Wavell shortly found himself Allied supreme commander in the Far East when the Japanese launched the Pacific war. In this capacity he oversaw a succession of Allied disasters: Malaya, Singapore, the Netherlands East Indies, and Burma. By the time the situation had stabilized, Wavell's troops were confronting the Japanese along the Indo-Burmese frontier. Although he attempted an offensive on the Arakan front in late 1942, Wavell was convinced that the Allies had little hope of recovering Burma by a ground offensive, considering the manpower and logistical difficulties, not to mention the political ones (i.e., India was restive, Nationalist China unreliable, and the United States uncooperative). At American urging, Churchill jumped Wavell up to viceroy of India, in which post he exercised no control over military operations. After the war Wavell almost immediately passed into retirement. A good officer, with considerable administrative abilities, Wavell, who had only one eye as a result of an old wound, had the bad luck always to be given hopeless tasks. A man of great intellectual power, he was the author of several valuable military works, including *Generals and Generalship*, which Rommel found interesting, and an anthology of poems, *Other Men's Flowers*.

WINGATE, ORDE C. One of the most unconventional soldiers of the twentieth century, Orde Wingate (1903–1944) entered the British Army between the wars. Assigned to the Palestine garrison, during the Arab Revolt in the mid-1930s, he developed an enthusiasm for the Zionist cause, and soon went beyond his authority to train Jewish settlers for self-defense. Shortly after Italy's entry into World War II, Wingate was sent to East Africa, where he commanded Gideon Force, a guerrilla column that had enormous success in disrupting Italian defenses in 1940–1941. Sent to the Far East shortly after the Japanese overran Burma, Wingate organized and led numerous guerrilla raids into the Japanese rear, disrupting the enemy at a time when regular British Empire forces were in desperate shape. Pioneering in the use of air supply, Wingate's basic strategy was to use air supply to support raids by his specially trained troops (the "Chindits"). Sometimes he would parachute troops into an inaccessible area behind Japanese lines, where they would hack out an airstrip, air land additional troops and supplies, and then cut their way back toward British lines. His two most successful operations (February 1943 and March 1944) were very "deep penetrations," literally hundreds of miles into the enemy rear. Although enormously disruptive of Japanese logistics and communications, and although they tied down considerable Japanese forces at a critical juncture, the cost of the operations in manpower was extraordinary, and despite retaining influence with Churchill and other unorthodox thinkers, Wingate would probably have been replaced, had he not died in an aircraft accident. As the airplane was an American one, and none of the recovered bodies could be positively identified, Wingate lies in a group grave in Arlington National Cemetery. Like many other successful commanders, Wingate was an odd person, fond of quoting the Old Testament, eating raw onions, and the like, and was certainly mentally unstable (he attempted suicide after the East African campaign), but this was by no means a disqualification for military genius.

YAMADA, OTOZO. Otozo Yamada (1881–1965) graduated from the Military Academy in 1903 and entered the cavalry. Surprisingly, Yamada appears to have seen no service during the Russo-Japanese War. Over the years he passed through a variety of command, staff, and school assignments, all of which demonstrated his considerable abilities. In 1938 he was appointed to a senior command in China. At the start of the Pacific war he was a full general commanding the General Defense Command in Japan. He served on the Supreme War Council for most of the war, and was given command of the Kwantung Army in mid-1944, which was crushed by the Soviets in August 1945. Tried for war crimes by the Russians and sentenced to twenty-five years in labor camps, Yamada was released in 1956 (because of ill health; he was seventy-five years old at the time) and sent back to Japan.

YAMAGUCHI, TAMON. Tamon Yamaguchi (1892–1942), one of Japan's most talented carrier admirals, graduated from the Naval Academy in 1912. Over the years he held various posts, studied at Princeton (1921–1923), served on the Naval General Staff, was a delegate to the London disarmament conference, and served as naval attaché in Washington (1934–1937). Although a nonflier, in 1940 he was promoted to rear admiral and given the 2nd Carrier Division, *Hiryu* and *Soryu*. With his command he participated in the Pearl Harbor operation, the subsequent operations in the Dutch East Indies, and, finally, Midway. There he committed suicide by going down with his flagship, *Hiryu*. Yamaguchi was known to criticize his superiors for their narrow-minded handling of carriers. He would have been a formidable opponent had he survived Midway.

YAMAMOTO, ISOROKU. Isoroku Yamamoto (1884–1943), originally Isoroku Takano, was one of the outstanding admirals of World War II. Yamamoto graduated from the Japanese Naval Academy in 1904 and saw action during the Russo-Japanese War, losing several fingers while commanding a torpedo boat in the Battle of Tsushima in 1905. During World War I he served as a staff lieutenant commander but saw no action. He later attended Harvard as a graduate student in the 1920s, where he became well acquainted with the military and industrial potential of the United States. It was this experience that caused him constantly to counsel against war with America.

The commander of the Japanese Combined Fleet since 1939, Yamamoto was recognized by Americans and Japanese alike as the most capable commander the Japanese had, architect of the spectacular success that had attended Japanese efforts early in 1942. Yamamoto's undoing was the American success at breaking the Japanese naval codes. Yamamoto's staff suspected that their secret communications codes had been broken, but Yamamoto never believed it to be the case; at least he didn't believe it sufficiently to do much about it. As a result, American P-38 fighters ambushed Yamamoto's aircraft and its seven escorts on April 18, 1943, killing Yamamoto in the process.

Beyond being an excellent leader and combat admiral, Yamamoto spoke English, having studied for two years at Harvard shortly after World War I. For a Japanese, he was quite an independent thinker and something of an eccentric. For example, Yamamoto had a Bible with him wherever he traveled and regularly consulted it, even though he was not a Christian. What made Yamamoto dangerous to America was his pragmatism. He knew that Japan could not defeat America, but Yamamoto had the skill and rank to cause maximum casualties to American troops. The Midway operation was a workable plan, if only Yamamoto had known that his codes were compromised and been able to change the codes (thus keeping the enemy in the dark for at least a few months). The Pearl Harbor attack was his doing, and he had many other bold plans to make the American advance across the Pacific as costly as possible. The other obstacle Yamamoto faced was the Japanese Army, which saw him as a dangerous free thinker. If Yamamoto had had his way, Japan would never have gotten involved in World War II in the first place. As early as 1940 he had told senior Japanese officials that war with American would be futile, and disastrous for Japan.

But Yamamoto was still very Japanese. He allowed himself to be adopted into the Yamamoto clan when he was thirty-two years old and already a distinguished naval officer because the higher-status Yamamotos would help him overcome the stigma of his original family's lower social status (and because the Yamamotos wanted someone already famous like Isoroku Takano to be the leader of their clan). This was a typically Japanese maneuver. Yamamoto also believed in the emperor, whom he was obliged to serve as a sailor unto death. Yamamoto was typical of the many (but not nearly all) Japanese admirals who saw the Army's policy in China (and eventual takeover of the government) as not in Japan's best interest. But because the Army managed to get the emperor to agree (or at least remain silent) about its plans, there was nothing other Japanese could do but follow "the emperor's wishes."

YAMASHITA, TOMOYUKI. Tomoyuki Yamashita (1888–1946) joined the Japanese Army in 1906. In 1914 he saw action during the capture of the German colony of Kiaochow. Noted as an able officer, he spent most of the 1920s and 1930s in staff and school positions, rising rapidly in rank. By 1941 he was a lieutenant general and in command of the Twenty-fifth Army. His task was to invade Malaya and take Singapore. This he did in a stunning operation. In the summer of 1942 he moved to a command in Manchuria and the summer of 1944 was put in charge of all the forces defending the Philippines. He commanded his forces on Luzon until ordered to surrender on August 19, 1945. He still had 50,000 troops left, even though completely cut off from outside assistance. He was tried for war crimes (atrocities in Singapore and Manila), convicted, and hanged in 1946. Yamashita was considered the most able of all Japanese generals, and his final campaign in the Philippines bears this out. However, he did not get along with other Japanese leaders and was paranoid, among other things believing that Tojo was trying to have him killed. Tojo was jealous and afraid of Yamashita, but there is no evidence to support Yamashita's assassination fears.

WHAT WAS WHERE:

A Pacific War Gazetteer

C an't locate some obscure location mentioned while describing World War II operations in the Pacific? Fear not. What follows is a brief description of all those normally obscure locations. We cover all the places that might have figured in the fighting, as well as those that were actually selected as the site of a battle. Since the conflict was primarily a naval one, we cover the ports (major and minor) that featured in the action. The hinterlands of many of these ports were the locations of the principal land battles.

The Pacific Theater is a big place. In fact, the entire area comprises about a third of the planet's surface. Moreover, a lot of out-of-the-way places featured prominently in the battles. Use this listing to avoid getting lost.

To give you a better grasp of the geography of the war, consider some of the major regions and island groups that figured in the fighting. These were often referred to in one of two ways. For example, the Admiralty Islands would often be called simply the Admiralties.

REGIONS AND ISLAND GROUPS

The *Admiralty Islands* are a chain of nearly twenty mostly volcanic islands (about 800 square miles), the largest of which is Manus (about 600 square miles), in the Bismarck Archipelago, lying between New Guinea and the equator. Although rugged and extremely humid, the thinly populated jungle-clad islands were ideally suited for air bases.

The *Andaman Islands* number over 200, in the eastern Bay of Bengal, about 300 miles southwest of Rangoon, totaling about 2,500 square miles. A fairly hot, humid place, with few inhabitants, the islands are hilly and forested. The Japanese took them from the British with little effort in early 1942, and remained in control for the rest of the war.

The *Aleutian Islands* stretch about 1,100 miles westward from Alaska, between the Bering Sea and the North Pacific. A desperately bleak, rugged place, they include seventy large and numerous smaller volcanic islands in five major groupings, totaling about 6,800 square miles. They have some of the worst weather in the world. In 1942 the population was extremely thin.

Australia, the smallest continent, constitutes a member of the British Commonwealth. Relatively low, and very dry except for the eastern and northern coastal regions, Australia is about two million square miles in area. The population was relatively small, and most of it concentrated in the east.

The *Bismarck Archipelago* is an island group just northeast of New Guinea, in the Southwest Pacific, including New Britain, New Ireland, and several other large islands, as well as the Admiralty group, for a total of about 19,000 rather rugged, jungle-covered, thinly inhabited square miles.

The *Bonin Islands* are about 500 miles south of Tokyo. Although there are more than twenty-five of them, they total only about 40 square miles. Thinly populated, they were extensively fortified by the Japanese and garrisoned during World War II, but they were ignored by the United States except for occasional air raids and naval bombardments.

The *Caroline Islands* are a large archipelago in the western Pacific, totaling about 450 square miles. Thinly populated, the literally hundreds of islands, islets, and atolls had been Japanese since 1914. During World War II some of them were heavily fortified, and became the scene of desperate fighting.

Ceylon is a large (about 25,000 square miles), pearl-shaped island just southeast of India, well sited for a major base to dominate the Bay of Bengal. By 1942 the British had done little to develop the place, and it was extremely exposed to Japanese attack, as was demonstrated in the spring of that year. Now known as Sri Lanka.

The *Ellice Islands*, a group of nine islands totaling about 26 square miles, inhabited by several thousand Polynesians. Their location just south of the Gilberts made them an important Allied base during the war. When the Japanese had the chance to take them, in early 1942, they failed to do so. Funafuti was later developed into a major air base by the United States.

Fiji was a protectorate of the British Empire in 1942. Located about 1,300 miles north of New Zealand, the colony comprised more than 800 islands (of which only 105 are inhabited) totaling about 7,000 square miles, scattered over nearly a million square miles of ocean. Although few in number, the native Fijians were tough troops, serving in their own units on a number of operations. The islands were on Japan's list of objectives to be seized following the capture of Midway.

Formosa (now called Taiwan), is a large island (about 14,000 square miles) about 115 miles east of China. Held by the Japanese since 1896, the island had been turned into a major air and naval base. For a time it figured in American plans, the Navy wanting to capture the place in 1944. But it was bypassed in favor of Okinawa, probably a wise move considering the size of the island and of its garrison.

The *Gilbert Islands* straddle both the equator and the International Date Line. Although the numerous islands and islets are sprawled across over a million square miles of ocean, their total land area is only about 275 square miles. Thinly populated, they were under British control when the Japanese arrived in early 1942. Now known as Kiribati.

Hawaii is a long chain of islands in the mid-Pacific, about 2,100 miles southwest of San Francisco. The hundreds of islands and islets stretch over 1,000 miles roughly northwestward from Hawaii proper to Kure, some 60 miles northwest of Midway. Total land area is only about 11,000 square miles, virtually all of it in the eight main islands (one of which was a U.S. military target range). Oahu was the principal American military base in the Pacific for the entire war.

Korea (called Chosen by the Japanese) is a large (about 85,000 square miles) peninsula jutting southward from the Asian mainland just west of Japan. It is inhabited by an ancient and hardy people culturally and racially distinct from the Chinese, but related to the Japanese, who are descended from Korean migrants. Korea was under Japanese occupation since the Russo-Japanese War (1904–1905). After Japanese annexation in 1909, the Koreans suffered considerable oppression in a systematic attempt to obliterate their culture. The country was somewhat industrialized in the north, where there are various significant mineral deposits, and agricultural in the south, a region intensively exploited to help feed Japan. During World War II, Korea was occasionally bombed, but was largely spared the horrors of war.

The *Kuriles* are a chain of hundreds of islands, islets, and rocky outcrops stretching about 750 miles southwestward from Kamchatka in Russia to Hokkaido, the northernmost island of Japan. Only about thirty of the islands are of any size, and the total area is only about 6,000 square miles. The Kuriles, which were largely Russian before the Russo-Japanese War (1904–1905), were thinly populated, mostly by hunting and fishing tribes. Despite some of the foulest weather in the world, they were an important strategic base for the Japanese: It was from the Kuriles that the Pearl Harbor Strike Force set sail in November 1941.

The *Line Islands* comprise two chains, one on each side of the equator, totaling ten atolls, including Palmyra and Christmas, over 1,000 miles south of Hawaii. Small in area (less than 400 square miles) and thinly populated (fewer than 100 inhabitants), they were important sites for aircraft patrolling the vulnerable Allied lines of communication from North America to the South Pacific.

The *Louisiades* are a collection of numerous very small islands streaming southeastward from New Guinea, separating the Solomon Sea from the Coral Sea. They were thinly populated, by a surprisingly large number of different, if related, tribes all living close to nature. Economic resources were slight, but the islands were of some strategic value.

Manchuria (called Manchukuo by the Japanese) comprises the resource-rich and industrially advanced northeastern regions of China, partially inhabited by the Manchu, a non-Chinese people who had given China its last imperial dynasty. In 1931 the Japanese had invaded the region and set up the puppet "empire" of Manchukuo, under Pu-Yi, who had been deposed as the last emperor of China as a boy in 1911. Under Japanese rule, Manchuria was heavily exploited and settled by a surprisingly large number of Japanese. It was more or less immune from the war, save for occasional bombing raids, until the Soviet Union invaded in August 1945.

The *Mandates:* Prior to World War I, the Caroline, Marshall, and Mariana islands had been owned by Germany. In 1914 the Japanese moved in. The Treaty of Versailles in 1919 assigned the islands to Japan as a "mandate," that is, in trust for the local inhabitants, whom the Japanese were supposed to help on the road to independence. The phrase "the Mandates" became a commonplace when referring to these territories.

The *Marianas* (also known as the Ladrones, or Thieves' Islands) are a chain of fourteen islands in the western Pacific Ocean, about 1,400 miles south of Japan. The total land area is less than 400 square miles, of which Guam proper comprises 200. The other two large islands, Saipan and Tinian, account for more than half of the rest of the land area. Inhabited by Micronesians, the islands were for centuries Spanish, but Guam was taken by the United States in 1898, and the balance sold to Germany, which lost them to Japan in 1914 and they became part of the Mandates. A great many Japanese settled in the islands before World War II. Of great strategic importance, the American landings on the islands in the spring of 1944 provoked the Battle of the Philippine Sea.

The *Marquesas Islands* comprise fourteen isles (about 400 square miles) in the Pacific Ocean about 900 miles northeast of Tahiti. Part of French Polynesia, they early fell under Free French control. During the war they had some value as Allied air and naval bases.

The *Marshalls* are an archipelago in the Central Pacific, nearly 2,200 miles southwest of Hawaii in the Pacific Ocean. There are actually two chains of islands, about 125 miles apart, comprising only about 70 square miles. Japan took them from Germany in 1914, and they formed part of the Mandate territories. There was little economic development, but the Japanese began building bases in the islands in the late 1930s. The more notable of the islands are Majuro, Eniwetok, and Bikini.

The *Netherlands* or *Dutch East Indies* (now called Indonesia) comprised some 3,000 islands stretching from Sumatra to western New Guinea, and totaling about 750,000 square miles. Some areas were well developed and densely populated (Java, Amboina, Bali), while others were thinly peopled, virtually virgin tropical forests (Borneo, New Guinea). Rich in resources (oil, tin, rice, and more), the Netherlands East Indies constituted the core of the "Southern Resources Area" for which Japan was fighting.

New Caledonia was a French colony about 750 miles east of Australia and 870 north of New Zealand, totaling about 7,400 square miles, most of it in New Caledonia proper (about 6,500 square miles). Mountainous but pleasantly tropical, the islands were thinly inhabited. When the Pacific war broke out, the Free French administration placed them at the disposal of the United States, which used them as a staging area for the offensive into the Solomons during 1942.

New Guinea is the second-largest island in the world (after Greenland), and lies in the Southwest Pacific north of Australia and east of the rest of the Netherlands East Indies. The rugged, wet, tropical and jungle-clad island is about 300,000 square miles. The inhabitants were mostly Melanesians, who were divided into numerous tribes, plus a handful of Australians and Netherlanders. Politically the island was divided between Australia and the Netherlands.

The *New Hebrides* (now Vanuatu) are a group of about seventy-five islands, atolls, and islets in the Southwest Pacific, about 1,000 miles northeast of Australia. Only three of the islands are of importance (Efate, Espíritu Santo, and Tana), and they comprised most of the 5,700 square miles of the group. Thinly inhabited by

Melanesians, the islands were jointly owned by Britain and France, and made a poor living off tropical produce and fishing.

New Zealand comprises two large and numerous small islands, about 1,200 miles east-southeast of Australia, totaling about 172,000 square miles. Possessed of an advanced agricultural economy, with some industry, in 1940 New Zealand was a self-governing member of the British Commonwealth.

The *Nicobar Islands* lie south of the Andamans, east of India in the Bay of Bengal. The nineteen islands total only about 635 square miles. In 1940 they were a thinly inhabited, primitive place, and were easily captured by the Japanese, the British making no effort to defend them. Nor did the British bother attempting to eject the Japanese, so that their garrison was starving by the end of the war.

Palau is the westernmost group of the Caroline Islands, about 600 miles east of the Philippines. The hundreds of islands comprise only about 175 square miles. In Japanese hands since World War I, they were among the most developed of the Mandates. Peleliu and Angaur figured prominently in the fighting in 1944.

The *Philippines* comprises over 7,000 islands, mostly of volcanic origins and most quite small (the 11 largest constitute over 90 percent of the land area, some 115,00 square miles—about the size of Britain or Italy). Long a Spanish colony, the islands had come under U.S. control in 1898 and were slated for independence in 1946, which helps explain why the inhabitants put up the stiffest resistance of any colonial people to Japanese aggression. Although chiefly agricultural, the islands had some mining and manufacturing, and they possessed a number of excellent harbors, including Manila, which was a major world port.

The *Phoenix Islands* constituted eight uninhabited islands totaling 11 square miles, in the Pacific just south of the equator. Administered jointly by the United States and Britain (which considered them part of the Gilbert Islands), on the eve of World War II several of the islands (Canton and Enderbury) had small air bases established to help guard the supply lines from the U.S. west coast to the South Pacific.

The *Ryukyu Islands* stretch roughly southwestward for about 650 miles from Kyushu, the southernmost of the Japanese home islands, toward Taiwan. Although the 143 islands total about 700 square miles, Okinawa has more than half of the land area.

Samoa lies about halfway between Hawaii and Australia, in the South Pacific, totaling about fifteen islands (about 1,150 square miles), of which six of the smallest (about 77 square miles altogether) were under American administration and the balance British. Possessed of several useful anchorages and sites for airfields, the islands were important links in the supply route to the South Pacific.

The *Santa Cruz Islands* are a small volcanic group about 400 miles north of Espíritu Santo, in the New Hebrides. Although well sited for an advance base, the islands proved too unhealthy (the local strain of malaria was particularly nasty) to be of much use.

The *Sakishima Islands*, the southernmost group of the Ryukyu chain, contained an important Japanese naval and air station during World War II.

The *Society Islands*, which include Tahiti, form the principal part of French Polynesia. Although they were too far to the east to experience any fighting, the islands were useful for air and naval bases.

The *Solomon Islands* comprise seven large and many small islands forming two chains that stretch about 900 miles southeastward from the Bismarck Archipelago in the Southwest Pacific, totaling about 11,500 square miles. Very wet, the jungle-covered, mountainous islands were thinly inhabited, mostly by Melanesians who provided various tropical products to the world market (copra, dried coconut meat, for the soap trade, for example).

The *Volcano Islands* lie about 700 miles south of Tokyo, and total about 11 square miles, most of them barren. The principal ones, Chichi Jima and Iwo Jima, were important Japanese outposts in the final defenses of the home islands.

BASES AND BATTLEFIELDS

Now for a look at some of the actual places that figured importantly in the war in the Pacific. Not all were the scene of battles. Many were simply occupied as naval or air bases, or were potentially so if the fighting had shifted in their direction.

ADDU ATOLL, MALDIVE ISLANDS. Located just a few hundred miles southwest of India, in the northern part of the bleak Maldive Islands, Addu atoll has an ample natural harbor. Although it does not offer much protection from genuinely foul weather (the highest point on the atoll is about 20 feet above sea level), such protection is rare in the area anyway. The Royal Navy decided to develop the atoll as an advanced fleet base shortly before the Pacific war began. The Japanese apparently never learned of this, for they failed to hit it during their massive incursion into the Indian Ocean in the spring of 1942, and the Royal Navy continued to use the atoll to support operations in the eastern Indian Ocean, despite its limited facilities.

ADELAIDE, AUSTRALIA. A large port, supported by a moderately large city with a modest industrial base and considerable agricultural resources, Adelaide, on the southern coast of Australia, was not well located for a naval base.

AITAPE, NEW GUINEA. One of the few good harbors on the northern coast of New Guinea, Aitape had a safe anchorage, but virtually no port facilities. Strategically, however, a base there, whether air or naval, could enable one to project power not only along the New Guinea coast, but also well into the Philippine Sea, to the north.

AMBOINA, CERAM, NETHERLANDS EAST INDIES. Although not extensively appointed, Amboina had a good harbor, with modestly extensive port facilities, as well as a modestly good airport in 1941. Its excellent location in the eastern Netherlands East Indies made it a potentially valuable naval and air base, particularly for anyone interested in control of western New Guinea.

AMOY, CHINA. An important river port on the Chinese coast, Amoy had extensive facilities to accommodate vessels of moderate size. Its location made it valuable for control of Fukien Province.

ANCHORAGE, ALASKA. The principal city of Alaska, a small town of limited resources and poor port facilities, albeit with a decent air field. Its location, however, nearly 800 miles northeast of Dutch Harbor, made it only marginally useful as a base.

ANGAUR, PALAU. Although wholly undeveloped, and with poor possibilities as a port, Angaur had some strategic value as an air base, lying about 600 miles east of the Philippines.

APIA, SAMOA. The principal port of American Samoa, with limited facilities and only a modest anchorage, although with a fair airfield, Apia's principal value was as a base on the long route from the Americas to Australia.

AUCKLAND, NEW ZEALAND. An excellent harbor, albeit with relatively limited repair facilities and lacking in a strong industrial base to support such, Auckland was the principal port of New Zealand, and an important air transport center as well.

BAKER ISLAND. About a square mile of barren land, Baker Island lies near the equator southwest of Hawaii. The small U.S. radio facility there was evacuated in early 1942 and the island was occupied by the Japanese until 1944.

BALIKPAPAN, BORNEO, NETHERLANDS EAST INDIES. A modest harbor, on the southeastern coast of Borneo, with few facilities for docking or repairing ships, Balikpapan was important for its oil-loading facilities and its refinery.

BANGKOK, SIAM. The principal port of Siam (Thailand), Bangkok lies quite far upriver from the sea, but could accommodate vessels of considerable size, although it lacked extensive support and service facilities. There was a good airport.

BATAAN, LUZON, PHILIPPINES. Bataan is a heavily forested, mountainous peninsula on the north side of the entrance to Manila Bay. For many years, U.S. plans for the defense of the Philippines from a Japanese invasion presupposed that American and Philippine forces would immediately retire to defensive positions on the Bataan peninsula, there to hold out until relieved by the U.S. fleet. However, little was actually done to prepare the peninsula for defense. No combat positions were surveyed, no food and ammunition stockpiled, and no efforts made to improve internal communications. As a result, when the Japanese did invade in 1941, they were eventually able to batter their way into Bataan.

BATAVIA, JAVA, NETHERLANDS EAST INDIES. The capital of the Netherlands East Indies, located in western Java, Batavia had a fine harbor, with modestly extensive facilities to service ships, a small naval base, and an important airport, in terms of the standards of the region. Today called Djakarta.

BIAK, NEW GUINEA. An extensive island in the Schouten group, on Geelvink Bay, a large gulf on the northwestern coast of New Guinea, Biak was of only limited value in terms of harborage, with no port or air facilities, but great potential for dominating a large portion of the Philippine Sea and all of Western New Guinea after the building of air bases.

BOMBAY, INDIA. One of the principal ports of the world, Bombay had extensive facilities to repair and service ships, although it had limited capacity to support and maintain warships.

BOUGAINVILLE, SOLOMON ISLANDS. Largest of the Solomon Islands, Bougainville totals nearly 4,000 square miles. A rugged place, with a convoluted coastline, Bougainville was hot, humid, and jungle covered, with few inhabitants.

BREMERTON, WASHINGTON. With nearby Seattle, Bremerton was a world-class port, having important ship repair facilities and a major naval shipyard. Because of the curvature of the earth, it was the closest continental U.S. base to Japan.

BRISBANE, AUSTRALIA. One of the larger cities in Australia, Brisbane, on the central portion of the east coast, had a good harbor, with good facilities, some industrial capacity, and an excellent air base.

BRUNEI, BORNEO. On the northwestern coast of Borneo, about 700 miles northwest of Singapore, Brunei was a modest oil port with a fair harbor but few facilities. Its primary function was to pump oil into tankers and to bring in drilling equipment.

BUNA, NEW GUINEA. A worthless little trading post on the northeastern coast of New Guinea, with a very limited port. It was of value to the Japanese in order to supply their advance from nearby Gona over the Kakoda trail. The scene of heavy fighting in 1942 and 1943.

BWAGAOIA, LOUISIADES. The principal, indeed only, town in the Louisiade Archipelago, just off the northeastern tip of New Guinea, Bwagaoia had a fair harbor but little else to recommend it.

CALCUTTA, INDIA. A major port, with extensive facilities for repairing and servicing ships, Calcutta lacked the capacity to handle warships and, being a river port, was unsuited as a naval base, but did have several airports and air bases nearby.

CAMRANH BAY, INDOCHINA. Although one of the best natural harbors in the world, Camranh Bay lacked all but the most rudimentary facilities to service and repair shipping. Its fine location, however, on the central southern curve of the Indochinese coast, gave it great potential as a naval and air base for the domination of the East China Sea. It was used by the Imperial Navy during its Malayan and East Indian operations in 1941–1942.

CANTON, CHINA. A major river port, Canton had only limited facilities to repair ships, and none at all to support warships.

CANTON ISLAND, PHOENIX ISLANDS. Slightly over 3 square miles, Canton Island was an important link in the chain of air bases that the U.S. established on the route to Australia.

CEBU, PHILIPPINES. Although possessed of a decent small harbor, Cebu had only limited facilities to support shipping, and none at all to serve as a naval base, which would have been of marginal use anyway, given that the place is virtually in the heart of the Philippine archipelago.

CHANGSHA, CHINA. Although very far from the sea, Changsha was at the head of navigation for small oceangoing vessels and had surprisingly extensive port facilities, although only a limited capacity to service ships. It was an important regional center.

CHEFOO, CHINA. An important coastal city, Chefoo had some port facilities and a small airfield, and was the administrative center for the surrounding region.

CHEMULPO/INCHON, KOREA. Chemulpo (Jinsen to the Japanese) was the port of Seoul, some miles up the Han River, which was the principal city of Korea (called Chosen by the Japanese). Chemulpo was of only limited importance. Plagued by unusually severe tides, it was very unsuited for use as a naval base.

CHITTAGONG, INDIA. Although possessed of a small airfield and a good harbor, Chittagong, on the northeastern coast of the Bay of Bengal, had only limited port facilities and no industrial capacity.

CHRISTMAS ISLAND, INDIAN OCEAN. Lying south of Java and west of Australia, the small (60-square-mile), volcanic island provided some phosphates and was a useful anchorage for Allied vessels.

CHRISTMAS ISLAND, PACIFIC OCEAN. This island is almost directly south of Hawaii, in the Line Islands, near the Gilberts. The largest atoll in the world in terms of land area (about 200 square miles), Christmas was an important link in the chain of air bases that the United States established to help protect communications with the South Pacific.

CHUNGKING, CHINA. Some modest industrial facilities and the presence of the Nationalist Chinese government made Chungking of considerable importance, as did its relative inaccessibility to Japanese attack, deep in the interior of China.

COLOMBO, CEYLON. A medium-sized port on the west coast of Ceylon, with some facilities to service shipping, and a small naval base, Colombo proved too exposed to Japanese carrier raids to be of much use in the spring of 1942. Its importance grew later, once the Japanese Navy withdrew its carriers from the Indian Ocean.

CORREGIDOR, PHILIPPINES. A tadpole-shaped rocky island blocking the entrance to Manila Bay, Corregidor was heavily fortified in the decades before World War II. Properly stocked with food and ammunition, it was capable of holding out under intensive attack for long periods. However, by the early 1940s it was vulnerable to air attack.

DALNY, MANCHURIA/MANCHUKUO. A small, somewhat cramped harbor, Dalny (Dairen) had some port facilities and served as a local base for the Imperial Navy in the Yellow Sea.

DA NANG, INDOCHINA. Aside from some facilities to support coastal shipping, the fine harbor at Da Nang was of limited consequence as a port, but shared with Camranh Bay great potential value as a naval or air base.

DARWIN, AUSTRALIA. The most important city in northwestern Australia, with a roomy, sheltered harbor, fair port facilities, a small naval base, and a large airfield. However, its limited access to other parts of Australia and its relative isolation made it rather exposed for a base if nearby portions of the Netherlands East Indies were in hostile hands.

DAVAO, PHILIPPINES. Despite possessing a decent harbor, often used by the U.S. Navy, Davao had very limited facilities to support shipping, and virtually none to serve as a naval base.

DILI, TIMOR. The principal port of Portuguese East Timor, Dili was virtually bereft of facilities to service and support shipping, but was quite conveniently located with regard to Australia, less than 400 miles to the southeast.

DUTCH HARBOR, ALEUTIANS, ALASKA. Although it was the principal American naval base in Alaska, Dutch Harbor had very limited facilities to repair and service shipping, and only a tiny airfield, but was the most extensive American base in the North Pacific, and the farthest west.

ENDERBURY ISLAND, PHOENIX ISLANDS. About 4 square miles, this island lies near Canton Island. The United States established an airstrip there in the late 1930s, which served to protect the long supply lines to the South Pacific.

ENIWETOK, MARSHALL ISLANDS. A lovely atoll, with lots of room for ships but no facilities to service them, nicely located to serve as a base for the domination of the other islands in the Marshall group, many of which shared its natural assets, including strategic location.

ESPÍRITU SANTO, NEW HEBRIDES. The principal island of the New Hebrides, Espíritu Santo had a small port, with limited facilities to service ships, and a small airfield, located about 450 miles southeast of the easternmost tip of the Solomon Islands.

FOOCHOW, CHINA. An important city in southeastern China, Foochow had a river port that was adequate for small ships. The city lacked any extensive facilities to service vessels or to repair them. There was a small airfield.

FREMANTLE/PERTH, AUSTRALIA. The port of Perth, Fremantle was the principal port on the western coast of Australia, with some facilities to service shipping and a modest naval shipyard.

Perth itself, an extensive city, had some industrial facilities and was a major air base.

FRENCH FRIGATE SHOAL, HAWAIIAN ISLANDS. An uninhabitable atoll surrounding a shallow lagoon in the Pacific, about halfway between Oahu and Midway in the Hawaiian chain, French Frigate Shoal figured in Japanese war plans several times. In the spring of 1942, a submarine fueled a flying boat there, which then proceeded to make a raid over Pearl Harbor, much to the chagrin of all concerned, albeit with no material damage. Subsequent Japanese efforts to use the place were frustrated by regular U.S. Navy surface and air patrols, and the occasional stationing of a destroyer or other small warship. Several atolls in the area were made into emergency landing strips, and from the air looked like aircraft carriers.

FUNAFUTI, ELLICE ISLANDS. A pleasant atoll, with considerable room for ships, and enough land to make an air base possible, if anyone cared to build one. Strategically, Funafuti's principal value was that it is the southernmost island in the Ellice group, with Samoa about 600 miles to the east and Fiji the same distance to the south.

FUSAN/PUSAN, KOREA. The principal port of Korea (Fusan in Japanese; Pusan in Korean) had limited but satisfactory facilities to support and repair shipping, especially small coastal vessels.

GONA, NEW GUINEA. A worthless place, on the northeastern coast of New Guinea, albeit with a modest anchorage. Gona's principal value was that it lay at one end of the Kokoda trail, a barely negotiable path from the north to the south coast of New Guinea, over the Owen Stanley Mountains.

GUADALCANAL, SOLOMON ISLANDS. A large island, with an abominable climate, numerous exciting diseases, and not a single town, nor even a large village. There were no port facilities to speak of, nor even anything resembling a proper harbor, but several beaches and coves suitable for landing troops (Lunga Point, Cape Esperance, and so on) and lots of room for building air bases. Strategically, Guadalcanal is the easternmost large island in the Solomon chain, which, if held in strength, would prevent advances by an enemy up the Solomons, or farther eastward.

GUAM, MARIANA ISLANDS. The largest of the Marianas at over 200 square miles, and one of the largest islands in the Central Pacific, Guam had a small, cramped harbor with few facilities at Agana, but there were several large, deep, sheltered bays along the island's periphery. The island was valuable for supporting air bases. In addition, Guam is only about 1,000 miles from Japan.

HAIPHONG, INDOCHINA. The principal port of French Indochina, Haiphong had modest facilities to support shipping and, being several miles up the Red River, was unsuited for use as a naval base. There was a French air base nearby.

HAKODATE, HOKKAIDO, JAPAN. A small but modern port, with considerable facilities to service minor warships of all types, up to destroyers and light cruisers.

HOBART, TASMANIA, AUSTRALIA. Extensive facilities and a small naval base made Hobart of some value as a port, assuming a threat to Australia from the southeast, the least likely direction.

HOLLANDIA, NEW GUINEA. The capital and principal port of Netherlands New Guinea, Hollandia had nothing particularly noteworthy going for it as a base, aside from a roomy, well-protected harbor almost totally lacking in port facilities, and an airstrip. Strategically, its possession gives one the opportunity to develop naval and air domination over the southern half of the Philippine Sea, and air control over much of New Guinea, provided one has the resources.

HONG KONG, CHINA. One of the largest and best-equipped ports in the world. Hong Kong's value as a naval base depended totally on who controlled the surrounding portions of China, as these territories controlled access to the port and supply into the city itself.

HONOLULU, OAHU, HAWAIIAN ISLANDS. A modest harbor with some facilities to service cargo and merchant shipping, wholly overshadowed as a military base by Pearl Harbor, nearly 20 miles to the west.

HORN ISLAND, AUSTRALIA. Of only limited value as a port, with a poor anchorage and no facilities, Horn Island was well suited for use as a forward air base, being essentially the northernmost point in Australia. Although only a modest strip existed in 1941, it was an important stopover for aircraft bound for New Guinea.

ILOILO, PHILIPPINES. The major port of the southwestern Philippines, Iloilo possessed a limited harbor with very modest facilities for serving ships plus a small airstrip.

IWO JIMA, VOLCANO ISLANDS. A desolate place, with low-level volcanic activity producing noxious gases and a generally unpleasant atmosphere. The few inhabitants were of mixed American (both white and black) and Japanese descent. Shipwrecked sailors had settled down with local brides during the nineteenth century. Iwo Jima had no harbor and not even a secure anchorage. It was, however, only 600 miles south of Tokyo and capable of supporting several airfields.

JOHNSTON ISLAND. A tiny place, Johnston Island had no anchorage or port facilities, but was useful as an air base, particularly for patrol planes, since it neatly covered the southwestern approaches to Hawaii, about 700 miles to the northwest.

KAVIENG, NEW IRELAND. Although its somewhat sheltered anchorage served as a port for the shipment of copra and other tropical products, Kavieng had little else to commend itself to the curious, although there was an extensive hinterland that could be used for air bases, provided port facilities were developed to support them.

KENDARI, CELEBES, NETHERLANDS EAST INDIES. The principal port of Celebes, Kendari could accommodate and service small merchant ships and, if developed as a naval and air base, could permit one to dominate the eastern and central Netherlands East Indies.

KHOTA BARU, MALAYA. The principal British base in northern Malaya, some 400 miles north of Singapore, Khota Baru had an elaborate air base. It was also virtually impossible to defend without a large garrison and an air force, Thailand being to the north, Indochina to the northeast, and the South China Sea to the east.

KIETA, BOUGAINVILLE, SOLOMON ISLANDS. A copra (dried coconut meat) port, Kieta had no facilities beyond a modestly sheltered anchorage, not even a proper dock. Control of Kieta, however, did bring with it domination of the northern Solomons.

KING BAY, AUSTRALIA. A small town, with access to a large, fairly protected inlet on Australia's western coast, King Bay had limited facilities, but was the most important anchorage between Fremantle and Darwin.

KISKA, ALEUTIANS, ALASKA. Rarely visited, even by Aleut hunters and fishermen, Kiska did possess some ground suitable for use as an air base, should someone want to try to build one there. Even then, it had little offensive value, as there was nothing within striking distance. However, as a forward defensive position it might have some value under certain circumstances. The climate was atrocious, possibly the worst on the planet for aircraft operations.

KOBE, HONSHU, JAPAN. A major port and naval base with extensive facilities in the heart of Japan.

KUCHING, BORNEO. A small port on the northwestern coast of Borneo, mostly for coastal traders, with no significant facilities for service or repair of ships, of some value for projecting air power into the South China Sea.

KURE, HONSHU, JAPAN. The principal base of the Imperial Navy, with extensive construction and repair installations, important air bases, and excellent access to the rest of Japan by rail, securely located in the interior of the Inland Sea.

KURE ATOLL, HAWAIIAN ISLANDS. The northwesternmost islet in the Hawaiian chain, some 60 miles from Midway, Kure figured in the war several times. During the Battle of Midway, PT boats patrolled the area to ensure that the Japanese would not try using it as an advanced seaplane base. Later one islet was bulldozed into an emergency landing strip, and it still looks like an aircraft carrier from the air.

KWAJALEIN, MARSHALL ISLANDS. The largest lagoon in the world, on the most sprawling atoll of them all. Kwajalein had an extensive protected anchorage, and ample space for the establishment of naval and air base facilities. This could be used to dominate the entire region, if anyone wished to do so. The potential utility of Kwajalein in this regard had been noted by the U.S. Navy even before World War I. Surprisingly, the Japanese, who owned the place since taking it from Germany in 1914, gave little thought to developing it as a base.

LABUAN, BORNEO. A small port suitable for coastal shipping, with no facilities to repair or service vessels. As a base, nearby Brunei was more suitable.

LAE, NEW GUINEA. A fairly large town, by local standards, on the east coast of New Guinea, with a good harbor, but with limited facilities, with some potential as a base for dominating the local area.

LINGAYEN, LUZON, PHILIPPINES. Aside from a somewhat sheltered bay, the only port facilities at Lingayen, on the northwestern coast of Luzon, were a couple of simple jetties. But the local beach was broad and relatively free of obstacles, making it ideal for amphibious landings, which took place twice, once in December 1941, when the Japanese arrived, and again in January 1945, when the Americans returned.

LONG BEACH, CALIFORNIA. Including the relatively new facilities at Los Angeles and other local ports, Long Beach was one of the principal American bases on the west coast, connected to the rest of the United States by an extensive rail system, and well within range of numerous air bases.

MADRAS, INDIA. A major commercial port, with a small naval base, Madras's location on the eastern coast of India made it vulnerable to carrier air raids.

MAIZURU, HONSHU, JAPAN. Although of only modest dimensions, Maizuru, on the Sea of Japan, had been developed as a major port for destroyers and light forces.

MAJURO, MARSHALL ISLANDS. Despite a fairly extensive atoll, and some potential as an air base, Majuro was of only limited importance as a port on the eve of the war. Like most of the atolls in the area, it had considerable potential as a base.

MAKASSAR, CELEBES, NETHERLANDS EAST INDIES. A small port, accessible to tramp steamers and coastal shipping, with some potential as a base for local control via small ships and long-range aircraft.

MAKATÉA, SOCIETY ISLANDS. A useful atoll in the Society Islands, with no facilities of any sort. Strategically, its location on the northern edge of the archipelago made it of potential value if a threat were to develop from that direction.

MAKIN, GILBERT ISLANDS. A desolate island, with a British residence, a boat landing, and some shelter for ships, and room for a small airfield. Of value because it was one of the easternmost of the Gilberts.

MANDALAY, BURMA. Although Mandalay possessed some facilities as a river port, its chief importance lay in the fact that it dominated central Burma. As such it was the principal objective of the Japanese invasion of Burma in 1942 and the British counteroffensive of 1944.

MANILA BAY, LUZON, PHILIPPINES. Including not only Manila but also Cavite and several other small ports, Manila Bay was a major commercial port, with an extensive sheltered anchorage and extensive facilities to service shipping. There was also a small but well-equipped U.S. naval base at Cavite, and several important air bases in the area. The war left this area devastated.

MANUS, ADMIRALTY ISLANDS. A large island, with a modest anchorage and no port facilities. On paper, Manus was of great potential strategic value, being about 300 miles north of New Guinea and the same distance west of the Bismarcks.

MARCUS ISLAND. Although it possessed no port facilities, not even an anchorage, Marcus was valuable to the Japanese as a forward air base, since reconnaissance aircraft based there could reach far into the Central Pacific. It was located about 800 miles east of Iwo Jima and 1,200 northwest of Wake.

MEDAN, SUMATRA, NETHERLANDS EAST INDIES. An important harbor, lacking in extensive facilities, and poorly sited for use as a base.

MELBOURNE, AUSTRALIA. One of the most important ports in Australia, with a considerable capacity to service shipping, but only limited utility as a naval base, being on the country's southern coast.

MIDWAY. Midway comprises two small islands enclosed in an atoll, for a total land area of only about 2 square miles. The group, about 1,300 miles northwest of Pearl Harbor, had only a limited anchorage and no port facilities, but was of great value as an aerial reconnaissance base, and as the northernmost anchor of the Hawaiian chain. During the war, the U.S. Navy developed it into a modest base for submarines and light craft.

MILNE BAY, NEW GUINEA. A considerable anchorage, with very limited port facilities, Milne Bay was also of potential value as an air base, covering the eastern end of New Guinea.

MONO ISLAND, BOUGAINVILLE, SOLOMON ISLANDS. A small island, with a sheltered anchorage but no facilities to supply or service ships, overshadowed as a potential base by Rabaul and Kieta, both nearby.

MOROTAI, MOLUCCAS, NETHERLANDS EAST INDIES. A small port, mostly suitable for coastal shipping, with no facilities. But it had some potential and could be developed, particularly as an air base.

MUNDA, NEW GEORGIA, SOLOMON ISLANDS. A well-located peninsula, in about the middle of the Solomons, Munda had some plantation installations and a small port, of no particular importance. The plantation land was ideal for development into airfields.

MUSCAT, OMAN. A small but decent harbor with limited facilities and an important RAF base, Muscat, in South Arabia, guarded the eastern approaches to the Persian Gulf, with its important oil resources and the Allied lifeline to Russia. It would have been the principal Japanese objective if the Imperial Navy had undertaken more extensive operations in the Indian Ocean.

NAGASAKI, KYUSHU, JAPAN. A major port, with a large naval base and important air installations.

NAGOYA, HONSHU, JAPAN. One of the principal bases of the Imperial Navy, a major port with extensive facilities to construct, repair, and service ships.

NAHA, OKINAWA. The principal port of Okinawa, Naha was small and cramped, and lacked important facilities, but did provide access to the island's several actual and many potential air bases.

NAURU ISLAND. Apart from some facilities to load phosphates, Naura (8 square miles in the Central Pacific) lacked a port, although it could be said to have some value as a potential air base, lying south of the eastern Carolines and west of the Gilberts, each only a few hundred miles distant. In 1942 it was under Australian administration when the Japanese walked in.

NDENI, SANTA CRUZ ISLANDS. Poorly provided as a potential naval base, Ndeni did possess some possible value as an air base, helping to cover a wide area of the south-central Pacific, lying only about 400 miles east of Guadalcanal and the same north of Espíritu Santo. But the island was infected with a particularly virulent strain of malaria, which made it a dangerous place for foreigners. This disease problem actually stalled attempts to develop military facilities, and the island was ultimately abandoned as a potential base by the United States.

NEW BRITAIN, BISMARCK ARCHIPELAGO. New Britain is the largest of the Bismarcks, an archipelago to the northeast of New Guinea, of which it was administratively a part under an Australian mandate dating from World War I. About 14,600 square miles, the island was very undeveloped and thinly inhabited, but Rabaul, the principal town, had a fine harbor, which became an important Japanese base during the war.

NEWCASTLE, AUSTRALIA. A small but good harbor with facilities to service most merchant ships, albeit in limited numbers, and an important air base, located on the northeastern coast of Australia, giving it some value as a base for the domination of the Coral Sea.

NIIGATA, HONSHU, JAPAN. A small port, Niigata had a naval base suitable for light forces and an air base.

NOEMFOOR ISLAND. Just north of New Guinea, Noemfoor had no port, but had a good anchorage and lots of room for airfields, which made it a valuable objective during MacArthur's drive up the New Guinea coast.

NOUMÉA, NEW CALEDONIA. The capital of New Caledonia, Nouméa had a fairly good port for the region, and was located so as to give it potential as a naval and air base for control of the Coral Sea and the southern Solomons. Though it was cramped and of limited capacity, there were extensive sheltered anchorages in the area. There was a small French naval and air base. Nouméa served as a vital forward base early in the war.

OKINAWA. The largest of the Ryukyu Islands (about 450 square miles), Okinawa was the first victim of Japanese imperialism, the native dynasty being deposed in the 1870s and the islands forcibly incorporated into Japan. It was the site of important Japanese military installations by 1945; the principal reason for the American landings in the spring of that year was to seize the island as an advanced base for the pending invasion of Japan.

OLONGAPO, LUZON, PHILIPPINES. The principal American naval base in the Philippines, Olongapo, on the northwestern side of Luzon, had a fair-sized harbor, and considerable facilities to effect all but the most extensive repairs. It was also relatively isolated from Manila, the principal center of American military power in the islands, and only lightly defended.

OSAKA, HONSHU, JAPAN. One of the principal ports of Japan, with important naval and air base facilities.

PADANG, SUMATRA, NETHERLANDS EAST INDIES. A small coastal port, with a good harbor but limited resources, Padang (or Pedang) was potentially of value due to its location, on the western—mostly harborless—side of Sumatra, fronting on the Indian Ocean.

PALAWAN, PHILIPPINES. A local port, with a good anchorage but limited facilities, Palawan also had potential as an air base, given that it fronted on both the South China Sea and the Sulu Sea, as well as northern Borneo.

PALEMBANG, SUMATRA, NETHERLANDS EAST INDIES. A small upland city, with limited facilities, but the administrative center of much of Sumatra.

PALMYRA, LINE ISLANDS. Like a number of other normally useless and deserted places, Palmyra, 1,000 miles south of Hawaii, had very great potential as an air base, helping to control extensive areas of the Central Pacific.

PANAMA CITY, PANAMA CANAL ZONE. With nearby Balboa, Panama City represented a major American naval and air base, heavily defended as befit the western terminus of the Panama Canal, which provided access to the virtually unlimited facilities on the east coast of the United States. Without the Panama Canal, the war in the Pacific would certainly have dragged on into 1946.

PAPEETE, TAHITI. The principal city of Tahiti, Papeete had a large, roomy harbor, with some facilities to repair and service smaller ships, and tiny French naval and air bases.

PARAMUSHIRO, KURILES, JAPAN. A miserable place, but through perseverance and sacrifice the Japanese had developed a modest naval base and a surprisingly extensive air base, with an eye on operations toward Siberia and the Aleutians.

PEARL HARBOR, OAHU, HAWAIIAN ISLANDS. The principal American naval and naval air base in the Pacific, with extensive repair and maintenance facilities, including large dry docks, enormous workshops, great ammunition magazines, and a very large oil tank farm, not to mention vast airfields. But it had a cramped harbor (barely 3 square miles of surface area) with only a very narrow, and not easily navigated, entrance. The biggest problem, in 1941, was that its defense was based on an assumption of Army-Navy cooperation, which was not always forthcoming.

PEKING, CHINA. The capital of China, long in Japanese hands, Peking had some value as an industrial center and as a critical rail junction.

PELELIU, PALAU. A thick coat of jungle concealed the unusually rugged nature of this island. It had a small population and neither port nor air facilities, but was in an excellent strategic location, a few hundred miles east of the Philippines.

PENANG, MALAYA. On an island off the west coast of Malaya, Penang had a good harbor, with good facilities, and a small airport. It served as the principal base for Japanese, German, and Italian submarines operating in the Indian Ocean.

PONAPE, CAROLINE ISLANDS. A large island with a fairly good lagoon, Ponape had limited port facilities, although on the eve of the war the Japanese were developing it as an air base.

PORT ARTHUR, MANCHURIA/MANCHUKUO. A major port, with important docking and service facilities, and a major naval base, although one of limited strategic value.

PORT BLAIR, ANDAMAN ISLANDS. The principal port of the Andaman Islands, a small, miserable place with no particular facilities, but some potential as an air or naval base, since it could be used to project power over a wide area of the Indian Ocean and Bay of Bengal.

PORT MORESBY, NEW GUINEA. A modest-sized town, with limited use as a port, although possessing a valuable, if small, airfield. As a potential base, Port Moresby would give those holding it easy entrée into New Guinea or the Coral Sea, depending upon the direction they were going.

RABAUL, NEW BRITAIN, BISMARCK ARCHIPELAGO. A wonderful natural harbor, with very limited facilities for servicing and maintaining ships. Well suited for a naval or air base, being within easy reach of New Guinea and the Solomons, which the Japanese built it into as the war proceeded.

RANGOON, BURMA. A river port of some pretensions but only limited facilities, albeit the nerve center of British power in Burma, with an important air base and other military installations.

SABANG, SUMATRA, NETHERLANDS EAST INDIES. The westernmost important port in the Netherlands East Indies, Sabang had a good harbor but only limited resources. If properly developed, however, Sabang could be used to project power into the Indian Ocean.

SAIGON, INDOCHINA. A major city, with a good river port, but only limited facilities to service ships. There were important French military installations there in 1940.

SAIPAN, MARIANA ISLANDS. Long in Japanese hands, the island had a large Japanese population, with an extensive system of air bases under construction in 1941. There were only limited port facilities, however. Only a little more than 1,000 miles south of Tokyo.

SANDAKAN, BORNEO. A very small port, with limited capacity and no facilities, of some value as a local base for dominating the Sulu Sea and northern Borneo.

SAN DIEGO, CALIFORNIA. With nearby Coronado, the second most important American naval base in the Pacific, after Pearl Harbor, with enormous resources, extensively supported by several major air bases, and easy access by rail to the rest of the United States.

SAN FRANCISCO, CALIFORNIA. Including not only San Francisco but also the extensive port facilities surrounding San Francisco Bay, one of the premier harbors of the world, with valuable naval and air bases at Alameda and Treasure Island, considerable industrial resources, and access by rail to the rest of the United States.

SANSAPOR, NEW GUINEA. A good harbor, with no facilities, on the most northwesterly part of New Guinea, with the possibility of being used as a base to dominate portions of the Philippine Sea, the entire "Vulture's Head" region of New Guinea, and surrounding regions.

SANUIR, BALI, NETHERLANDS EAST INDIES. A small port suitable for coastal shipping, Sanuir had only limited facilities to service ships and was of little potential strategic value.

SASEBO, KYUSHU, JAPAN. A major port, with important naval and air installations.

SHANGHAI, CHINA. The largest port in China, with considerable resources to build and service all but the largest vessels,

Shanghai, which had been in Japanese hands for some years, also had considerable industrial resources and was surrounded by several air bases.

SINGAPORE, MALAYA. A major port, and the principal British naval and air base in the Far East. Although well appointed, Singapore was ill suited to its role as the bastion of British power in Southeast Asia, being an island with limited industrial resources and lacking both a fleet and an air force capable of defending it.

SKULL ISLAND. Off the southwest coast of New Guinea, of little strategic value and only occasionally visited. The island lacked even the most rudimentary anchorage, was incapable of supporting airfields, was possessed of a hostile population, and was plagued by numerous dangerous and unpleasant animals.

SOERABAJA, JAVA, NETHERLANDS EAST INDIES. The principal Dutch naval base in the East Indies, Soerabaja had good if limited facilities to service warships, even a decent dry dock, and was an important air base.

SORONG, NEW GUINEA. With no port facilities, Sorong, a few score miles southwest of Sansapor, was of value principally for its anchorage, and its potential strategic importance for control of the eastern portions of the Netherlands East Indies.

SUVA, FIJI. An important harbor, with limited resources but a fine location, about 1,200 miles north of New Zealand.

SYDNEY, AUSTRALIA. One of the roomiest harbors in the world, with considerable port facilities, extensive industrial resources, a modest naval base, and several air bases, Sydney was the most important Allied base between Pearl Harbor and Singapore.

TACLOBAN, LEYTE, PHILIPPINES. A fishing village with limited port facilities but a fine harbor.

TAINAN, FORMOSA. A major port on the southwestern edge of Formosa, with good facilities to service and repair ships, Tainan had been developed by the Japanese as their principal base against the Philippines, only a few hundred miles to the south, and it was an important air base.

TANA, NEW HEBRIDES. A small port, with limited facilities, overshadowed as a potential base by Espíritu Santo, 100 miles or so to the north.

TANKAN BAY, KURILES, JAPAN. Plagued by subarctic weather, and with only limited facilities, Tankan Bay was roomy and isolated. It served as the base from which the Pearl Harbor Strike Force sortied in late November 1941.

TARAKAN, BORNEO. An oil port, on a small island, with limited facilities to service ships, but with a refinery of some value. Strategically of some value for its location on the east coast of Borneo, about halfway between Balikpapan and Sandakan.

TARAWA, GILBERT ISLANDS. Although its atoll could protect a considerable number of ships, Tarawa had the barest port installations and no facilities to service or repair shipping. Despite its very limited land area, Tarawa was of great potential value as an air base, having the potential to dominate the Gilberts.

TAWITAWI, PHILIPPINES. A roomy but exposed anchorage in the southern Philippines (in fact, virtually the southernmost place in the Philippines), Tawitawi lacked even the most rudimentary facilities to service ships, but was convenient to the oil-producing areas of Borneo and had potential as a base for projecting naval power in a broad arc eastward (and that was how the Japanese used it).

TIENTSIN, CHINA. The port of Peking, Tientsin had limited but adequate facilities to fulfill its primary function.

TINIAN, MARIANA ISLANDS. Shortly before the war began, the Japanese had started to develop Tinian as a major base, despite the fact that it lacked a proper port. Strategically, Tinian shared with Saipan and Guam an excellent location to act either as an outlying bastion of Japan or an offensive base against her (with Tokyo only a bit more than 1,000 miles to the north).

TJILATJAP, JAVA, NETHERLANDS EAST INDIES. A small port on the south coast of Java, of some value as a base for projecting power into the eastern Indian Ocean.

TOKYO BAY, HONSHU, JAPAN. With the extensive facilities of the port of Yokohama, the naval base of Yokosuka, and the industrial and commercial resources of Tokyo itself, on the eve of World War II Tokyo Bay was one of the most important military bases on earth.

TOWNSVILLE, AUSTRALIA. Although possessed of only a modest port, Townsville had the distinction of being one of the principal air transport centers in Australia, making it an important air base.

TRINCOMALEE, CEYLON. The principal British naval and air base in the eastern Indian Ocean, Trincomalee lacked extensive facilities, making it of only limited utility.

TRUK, CAROLINE ISLANDS. A fine natural harbor in a roomy atoll, with the surrounding islands and islets suitable for several airfields, by late 1941 Truk was well on its way toward becoming one of the most important military bases in the Pacific, being roughly equidistant from New Guinea, Guadalcanal, and the Gilbert Islands. It was the principal Japanese military base in the South Pacific. Today it possesses one of the most extensive collections of sunken ships in the world.

TULAGI, SOLOMON ISLANDS. A modest island group off the much larger Florida Island, just a few miles north of Guadalcanal, Tulagi was the administrative center of the Solomon Islands. It had a fine anchorage but otherwise lacked more than very rudimentary port facilities.

UJELANG, CAROLINE ISLANDS. One of many atolls in the Carolines with a roomy anchorage, but otherwise unprovided with port facilities.

ULITHI, CAROLINE ISLANDS. A large atoll, providing an enormous protected anchorage for ships and some land for support facilities and air bases, Ulithi had been wholly neglected by the Japanese, who had owned it for over twenty-five years. It had, however, come to the notice of U.S. Navy planners as a potential advanced base for even more years than that. Ulithi became the major forward fleet base for the final U.S. advance against Japan.

VANCOUVER, BRITISH COLUMBIA, CANADA. A major port, Vancouver had extensive facilities to service and maintain ships, although it was of limited value as a naval base.

VICTORIA, AUSTRALIA. A major city, with a major port, possessed of important facilities to service and repair ships, though by no means a major naval base.

VLADIVOSTOK, SOVIET UNION. The largest and most important Russian military and naval base in the Pacific, with extensive industrial facilities, ample repair and maintenance establishments, and a number of air bases in support.

WAKDE, NEW GUINEA. Aside from a roomy harbor, and its location on the north side of New Guinea between Hollandia and Biak, Wakde had little to recommend it in 1941. Later, the Japanese turned it into a base, which was expanded considerably when taken by the Americans.

WAKE ISLAND. A small atoll (3 square miles of land on several small islands) with no anchorage and no particular value, except as a base for reconnaissance aircraft, being some 2,300 miles west by southwest from Pearl Harbor.

WELLINGTON, NEW ZEALAND. The capital of New Zealand, Wellington was an important city and port, though with only limited facilities to service vessels.

WEWAK, NEW GUINEA. A good harbor, with no facilities but a good location on the north coast of New Guinea, east of Aitape.

WONSAN, KOREA. The principal port of northeastern Korea, with a fair anchorage and good, if not extensive, port facilities.

WOTJE, MARSHALL ISLANDS. Although potentially useful as either a naval or air base, Wotje had facilities for neither in 1941.

YAP, CAROLINE ISLANDS. Although of limited potential as a naval base, Yap was well located for an air base, which the Japanese proceeded to make it. The United States considered taking the place in 1944, but dropped the project in favor of more strategically useful objectives.

ZAMBOANGA, PHILIPPINES. A small port, with limited resources and an airstrip occasionally used by the USAAF before the war.

ZANAMAI, SHAKISHIMA, JAPAN. Developed as a base for light forces, Zamanai had limited facilities.

CHRONOLOG
OF THE WAR
IN THE PACIFIC

T o give you more of a sense of the day-by-day flow of events, we have created the Chronolog. It lists significant events that occurred in the Pacific Theater on each day of the war. The Pacific war, for all its vast size and scope, tended to have long periods where not much happened. When there was action, there was a lot of it. There was always the tedium of patrolling and maintaining equipment, and for most of the troops this was how they spent most of their time.

In addition to the material on the great events, the Chronolog also covers the key dates in the career of one of the millions of troops who participated in the Pacific war. John Lindemann was a civilian on December 7, 1941. He volunteered for the Marine Corps, went on to participate in four combat landings, got promoted to corporal, and was wounded twice. He survived the war and went on to live a normal life indistinguishable from that of the other 16 million Americans who served in World War II. However, John Lindemann's career was unusual by World War II standards in that he volunteered (most troops were conscripts) and that he was engaged in heavy combat (most troops were in support jobs). He doesn't get mentioned in the history books (except this one), but it should be remembered that without the Corporal Lindemanns, there would be no history to write about. It's easy to overlook the details of history, but it is in the details that the real work is done. So consider well the experiences of John Lindemann, for you are more likely to find yourself in his situation than in that of Douglas MacArthur or Bill Halsey.

Note: The dating of events in the Pacific war is somewhat confused by the presence of the International Date Line, running roughly through the middle of the Pacific Ocean. For example, the Japanese attack on Pearl Harbor occurred on the morning of December 7, 1941, while the attacks in the Philippines and Malaya later that same day are dated December 8.

1941/NOVEMBER 26—The Japanese First Air Fleet sorties from Tankan Bay in the Kurile Islands, destination Pearl Harbor, maintaining a modest speed. If you want to pick a date for the start of the Pacific war, it's either this one, when the Japanese fleet set off for Pearl Harbor, or a few days before the attack, when the Japanese committed to the bombing raid no matter what their diplomats in Washington worked out with the Americans.

1941/NOVEMBER 27—An official communiqué from the U.S. Army Chief of Staff concludes with the line "this is to be considered a war warning." The Japanese First Air Fleet steams slowly east-southeastward.

1941/NOVEMBER 28—The U.S. Chief

of Naval Operations informs Admiral Husband Kimmel, at Pearl Harbor, "Hostile action is possible at any moment...." The carrier *Enterprise* sails from Pearl Harbor with aircraft for Wake; Rear Admiral William Halsey, the task force commander, orders the crew to full wartime alert.

1941/NOVEMBER 29—The Japanese First Air Fleet steams slowly east-southeastward.

1941/NOVEMBER 30—Japanese diplomatic efforts with the Americans seemingly go nowhere, but both sides keep trying. The Japanese in Washington are unaware of the imminent attack on Pearl Harbor.

1941/DECEMBER 1—The U.S. submarines *Argonaut* and *Trout* take station off Midway, *Triton* and *Tambor* off Wake, as a defensive measure against any approaching Japanese vessels.

1941/DECEMBER 2—President Roosevelt asks Japan to clarify its intent with regard to French Indochina, where the Japanese show signs of taking over the entire region. British "Force Z" (the battleship *Prince of Wales*, the battlecruiser *Repulse*, and four destroyers) arrives at Singapore. Reconnaissance aircraft on Hawaii are ordered to search out as far as 400 miles, in an arc from the northwest to the south. At latitude 43°N, longitude 158°30'E, about 3,200 miles northwest of Pearl Harbor, the Japanese First Air Fleet alters course due east. To thunderous cheers, the officers and crewmen of the First Air Fleet are informed that their objective is Pearl Harbor.

1941/DECEMBER 3—Reconnaissance aircraft on Hawaii are ordered to search out to 400 miles in an arc from the northwest to the south. The First Air Fleet refuels, at 45°N, 170°E, about 2,750 miles northwest of Pearl Harbor; upon completion, the tankers return to Japan and the fleet resumes its eastward course, increasing speed. The Japanese carrier fleet is now committed to the attack, no matter what.

1941/DECEMBER 4—Heavily escorted, Japanese invasion forces begin to sail for their objectives in Southeast Asia. The U.S. carrier *Enterprise* flies off reinforcements for Wake Island. Reconnaissance aircraft on Hawaii are ordered to search up to 400 miles from the northwest to the south. The Japanese First Air Fleet steams eastward.

1941/DECEMBER 5—Additional Japanese invasion forces sail from Camranh Bay and Saigon. Reconnaissance aircraft on Hawaii are ordered to search out to 400 miles in an arc from the northwest to the south. The carrier *Lexington* steams from Pearl Harbor to deliver aircraft to Midway. At 45°N, 178°W, about

1,000 miles northwest of Pearl Harbor, the Japanese First Air Fleet alters course from due east to southeast.

1941/DECEMBER 6—President Roosevelt makes a personal appeal to Emperor Hirohito, asking him to use his influence to help preserve peace in the Pacific. Reconnaissance aircraft on Hawaii are ordered to concentrate their efforts to the west and south. At 2100 hours, the Japanese First Air Fleet arrives at 31°N, 158°E, about 500 miles north of Pearl Harbor.

1941/DECEMBER 7—The First Air Fleet attacks the U.S. Pacific Fleet at its anchorage in Pearl Harbor, inflicting heavy damage at little loss to itself. Japanese destroyers shell Midway. John Lindemann, age twenty-one, is duck hunting in the swamps near Rockland Lake, 30 miles up the Hudson River from New York City, while the Pearl Harbor attack takes place. He works at a nearby pharmaceutical company. Lindemann is as angry as any American at the Japanese attack on Pearl Harbor. Unmarried, he knows he will eventually get involved more directly in the war.

1941/DECEMBER 8—Japanese aircraft destroy U.S. air power in the Philippines in a massive raid on Clark and Iba airfields on Luzon. Japanese destroyers attack Wake. Japanese troops begin landing in Malaya, attack Hong Kong, occupy the International Settlement in Shanghai, invade Siam. British Force Z sails from Singapore. An Australian independent infantry company lands on western Timor, in the Netherlands East Indies. A Dutch submarine sinks the Japanese destroyer *Isonami* off Celebes, the first Japanese warship to be sunk in the war.

1941/DECEMBER 9—Japanese troops from Kwajalein occupy Tarawa in the Gilberts. Siam agrees to a cease-fire with Japan.

1941/DECEMBER 10—Japanese aircraft sink *Prince of Wales* and *Repulse* in the South China Sea. Guam surrenders to a Japanese landing force after a two-day battle. Japanese troops begin landings in northern Luzon. Japanese naval aircraft bomb Cavite Navy Yard, Manila Bay.

1941/DECEMBER 11—Marines on Wake Island beat off a Japanese landing, sinking the destroyers *Hayate* and *Kisaragi* in the process. This was rare during World War II. Nearly all amphibious assaults succeeded, and the U.S. Marine defenders of Wake belonged to an organization that was never thrown off a beach it assaulted. U.S. submarines commence war patrols against Japanese shipping. Germany and Italy declare war on the United States.

1941/DECEMBER 12—Japanese troops land at Legaspi, in southeastern Luzon. In northern Luzon, Japanese troops advancing from Vigan and Aparri capture airstrips at Laoag and Tuguegarao. Japanese troops complete the occupation of southern Thailand, arriving at the Burmese frontier.

1941/DECEMBER 13—British and Canadian troops abandon the mainland portions of Hong Kong. The Japanese temporarily abandon the attempt to capture Wake, returning to base but continuing to subject the island to air attacks from the Mandates.

1941/DECEMBER 14—Japanese forces in Malaya occupy Kroh. Japanese air units begin repairing north Luzon airfields for their own use.

1941/DECEMBER 15—Congress votes an additional $10.1 billion (nearly $60 billion in 1995 dollars) for the war effort. Japanese forces in Malaya occupy Gurun.

1941/DECEMBER 16—Japanese troops land at Miri, in Sarawak, on Borneo. The carriers *Hiryu* and *Soryu*, with escorts, separate from the First Air Fleet to attack Wake Island. In Malaya, Japanese forces land on Penang Island.

1941/DECEMBER 17—Admiral Husband Kimmel is relieved of command of the Pacific Fleet. Vice Admiral W.S. Pye is in temporary command until Admiral Chester W. Nimitz arrives.

1941/DECEMBER 18—The Japanese 38th Division lands on the island of Hong Kong. Japanese aircraft begin operating from strips in northern Luzon. The Japanese destroyer *Shinonome* is mined and sunk off Borneo.

1941/DECEMBER 19—Japanese troops land on Mindanao, quickly occupying Davao, while completing the occupation of Penang Island off Malaya. Congress authorizes the president to draft men up to forty-four years of age.

1941/DECEMBER 20—The American Volunteer Group ("Flying Tigers") goes into action for the first time in Burma, shooting down six Japanese bombers over Kunming.

1941/DECEMBER 21—Heavily reinforced, and supported by the carriers *Hiryu* and *Soryu*, the Japanese renew their attempt to capture Wake Island. Siam (Thailand) allies itself with Japan.

1941/DECEMBER 22—Japanese troops land on Wake Island, which surrenders. Japanese troops begin a major landing on Luzon, at Lingayen Gulf in the northwest.

1941/DECEMBER 23—Japanese begin air raids on Rangoon, in British-controlled Burma. U.S. carriers speeding to support Wake Island are recalled. Heavy fighting on Luzon as U.S. and Philippine troops attempt to hold the Japanese in their beachhead.

1941/DECEMBER 24—Japanese troops land at Kuching, Sarawak. Japanese troops land at Lamon Bay, in east central Luzon, and on Jolo, in the southern Philippines. In heavy fighting the Japanese begin throwing back Philippine Army units south of Lingayen Gulf. Manila is bombed severely by Japanese aircraft. Philippine commander General Douglas MacArthur decides to retreat to Bataan. The Italian blockade runner *Orseolo* departs Kobe.

1941/DECEMBER 25—Hong Kong surrenders to the Japanese 38th Division. On Luzon the Japanese dislocate a U.S.-Philippine temporary defense line, while the South Luzon Force begins withdrawing northward. Manila is heavily bombed by Japanese aircraft.

1941/DECEMBER 26—On Luzon, the Japanese continue to press the defenders from the north and the southeast. Manila is declared an open city. Japanese columns advancing down the west coast of Malaya merge near Taiping.

1941/DECEMBER 27—On Luzon, under heavy Japanese pressure, U.S. and Philippine troops occupy a temporary line running through Gerona and San Jose.

1941/DECEMBER 28—Japanese forces in Malaya capture Ipoh, having advanced about 150 miles since landing, with 200 more to go to Singapore. On Luzon, U.S. and Philippine troops fall back to the Tarlac-Cabanatuan phase line.

1941/DECEMBER 29—On Luzon, Japanese troops eject U.S. and Philippine troops from the Tarlac-Cabanatuan line. First Japanese air raid on Corregidor.

1941/DECEMBER 30—Japanese troops occupy Kuantan, on the east coast of Malaya. On Luzon, U.S. and Philippine troops occupy the Bambang-Gapan line, but the Japanese unhinge its right flank by capturing Gapan as the Philippine 91st Division collapses.

1941/DECEMBER 31—On Luzon, by denying his right flank, Major General Jonathan Wainwright manages to preserve portions of the old Tarlac-Gapan line, hanging his right on Mount Arayat while other forces cover Paridel and Calumpit positions, vital for the withdrawal of the South Luzon Force to Bataan.

1942/JANUARY 1—United Nations Pact, representatives of twenty-six nations meeting in Washington adopt the principles of the Atlantic Charter and declare that they will make no separate peace. Philippine Army units begin holding the Borac-Guagua line, to cover the final withdrawal into Bataan, where the 15,000 U.S. and Philippine Scout troops and the 65,000 Philippine Army troops are immediately placed on half rations.

1942/JANUARY 2—On Luzon, the Japanese Army occupies Manila and Cavite, while the Borac-Guagua line holds. Japanese forces in Malaya occupy Kampar.

1942/JANUARY 3—The ABDA (American-British-Dutch-Australian) Command is formed to unite Allied efforts in Southeast Asia and the Netherlands East Indies, under the overall command of Sir Archibald Wavell. At the beginning of 1942, the Allies still possess considerable military force in the Western Pacific, but the Japanese appear more and more irresistible. The Borac-Guagua line holds on Luzon. Japanese troops continue to advance in Malaya.

1942/JANUARY 4—U.S. aircraft attack Japanese shipping in Davao Harbor, damaging the cruiser *Myoko*. The Philippine Army abandons the Borac-Guagua line and the withdrawal to Bataan is completed. Japanese troops continue to advance in Malaya.

1942/JANUARY 5—The Japanese 48th Division begins withdrawing from the Philippines for duty on Java. U.S. and Philippine troops begin consolidating the defenses of Bataan. Japanese troops continue to advance in Malaya.

1942/JANUARY 6—Philippine Army units hold the Dinalupihan-Orani line, last defensive position before Bataan. In Malaya, the British manage to hold the Japanese north of Kuala Lumpur.

1942/JANUARY 7—U.S. and Philippine forces complete occupation of the Bataan position. In Malaya, the Japanese turn the British defenses north of Kuala Lumpur.

1942/JANUARY 8—British troops in

Malaya are ordered to fall back on the "Johore line," about 50 miles north of Singapore. On Bataan, U.S. and Philippine troops continue to organize their defenses as Japanese units close with them.

1942/JANUARY 9—Japanese submarines begin operating in the Indian Ocean. First Japanese offensive against the Bataan defenses. In Malaya, the Japanese make an amphibious end run around the British left and occupy Port Swettenham on the Strait of Malacca.

1942/JANUARY 10—Japanese troops begin landing at Tarakan Bay, Borneo. Heavy fighting on Bataan. Sir Archibald Wavell arrives at Bandung, near Batavia, to take over the ABDA command.

1942/JANUARY 11—Japanese Navy airborne troops land on Celebes, in coordination with an amphibious attack. The U.S. carrier *Saratoga* is torpedoed south of Hawaii. Heavy fighting on Bataan. In Malaya, the Japanese capture Kuala Lumpur.

1942/JANUARY 12—In Malaya, the Japanese begin to advance on Malacca. A Dutch coast defense battery sinks two Japanese minesweepers off Tarakan, Borneo.

1942/JANUARY 13—The Japanese keep up heavy pressure on Philippine and American forces defending Bataan. In Malaya, the Japanese drive on Malacca.

1942/JANUARY 14—The Japanese capture Malacca in Malaya.

1942/JANUARY 15—Chinese troops halt a Japanese offensive near Changsha in Hunan Province. The Japanese Southern Army invades Burma from the Isthmus of Kra in Thailand. In Malaya, the Japanese make several small end-run amphibious landings to dislocate the British left.

1942/JANUARY 16—In Malaya, the British attempt to hold the line of the Muar River against Japanese forces advancing down the west coast.

1942/JANUARY 17—The British abandon the Muar River line in Malaya.

1942/JANUARY 18—British troops in Malaya complete withdrawal to the Johore line.

1942/JANUARY 19—The British manage to hold the Johore line in Malaya.

1942/JANUARY 20—Japanese aircraft carriers hit Rabaul. The Japanese 55th Division invades Burma from central Thailand. The British continue to hold the Japanese on the Johore line.

1942/JANUARY 21—A British task force built around the carrier *Indomitable* arrives at Addu atoll, in the Indian Ocean southwest of India. Fighting continues on Bataan, as isolated and outnumbered American and Philippine troops continue to resist, the only Allied force able to hold back the Japanese. In Malaya, the Japanese begin to dislocate the Johore line.

1942/JANUARY 22—Japanese troops begin landings on New Ireland and New Britain. Heavy fighting on the Johore line in Malaya. U.S. Army Task Force 6814 (later the Americal Division) sails from New York for the South Pacific.

1942/JANUARY 23—U.S destroyers and a Dutch submarine attack Japanese shipping off Balikpapan, Borneo. Heavy fighting on Bataan; Japanese troops land at Quinauan and Longoskayan points in the American rear but are contained. In Burma, the Japanese capture the Sittang River bridge, in the British rear, causing the collapse of the green 17th Indian Division.

1942/JANUARY 24—Australian resistance at Rabaul ends. Japanese begin landings at Balikpapan. Heavy fighting on Bataan in the Philippines and along the Johore line in Malaya.

1942/JANUARY 25—U.S. task forces built around the carriers *Enterprise* and *Yorktown* rendezvous off Samoa and proceed on a raid into the Mandates. In the Philippines, the Japanese having unhinged the first defensive line on Bataan, the American and Philippine troops fall back. In Malaya, the Johore line begins to crumble.

1942/JANUARY 26—U.S. and Philippine troops occupy the Bagac-Orion line on Bataan, Japanese troops land at Cañas Point and other headlands in their rear but are contained. In Malaya, the Japanese make major inroads into the Johore line position.

1942/JANUARY 27—HMS *Indomitable* flies off forty-eight aircraft to reinforce the defense of Java. *Enterprise* and *Yorktown* task forces raid the Marshall Islands. U.S. submarines begin supply runs to Corregidor. On Bataan, the Japanese renew their offensive. Under heavy pressure, the British forces in Malaya begin to withdraw toward Singapore.

1942/JANUARY 28—Heavy fighting on Bataan, but the Japanese are held to minimal gains. In Malaya, the British fall back toward Singapore.

1942/JANUARY 29—On Bataan, the Japanese are held to minimal gains. Philippine troops eliminate the Japanese at Longoskayan Point. In Malaya, the British fall back on Singapore.

1942/JANUARY 30—Japanese undertake a surprise attack on Moulmein, Burma.

1942/JANUARY 31—British abandon Moulmein, Burma, and retire across the Salween River. Japanese begin landings on Amboina. British troops in Malaya are withdrawn to Singapore.

1942/FEBRUARY 1—On Bataan, the Japanese land reinforcements at Cañas Point. The U.S. carriers *Enterprise* and *Hornet* raid Japanese bases in the Gilbert and Marshall islands.

1942/FEBRUARY 2—The British carrier *Indomitable* arrives at Trincomalee, on Ceylon. The Japanese complete occupation of Amboina. In the Philippines, U.S. and Philippine troops counterattack in Bataan.

1942/FEBRUARY 3—U.S. and Philippine troops on Bataan effectively restore the Bagac-Orion line, but the Japanese continue to attack. The Japanese advance in Burma.

1942/FEBRUARY 4—Japanese aircraft catch the ABDA cruiser-destroyer squadron in Madoera Strait, north of Bali, inflicting heavy damage on the U.S cruisers *Marblehead* and *Houston*.

1942/FEBRUARY 5—Japanese artillery begins bombarding Singapore from across the Johore Strait.

1942/FEBRUARY 6—The Japanese advance in Burma. Japanese aircraft make intensive attacks on refugee ships fleeing Singapore.

1942/FEBRUARY 7—Japanese aircraft make intensive attacks on refugee ships fleeing Singapore.

1942/FEBRUARY 8—Japanese troops begin crossing the Johore Strait, to land on Singapore island. Japanese land at Makassar, Celebes. Philippine troops eliminate Japanese troops holding Quinauan Point. The Japanese call off their offensive on Bataan, frustrated by the dogged resistance of American and Philippine troops.

1942/FEBRUARY 9—Japanese troops effect a second beachhead on Singapore island, which is subject to a heavy-bombardment air raid. Japanese troops on Bataan suspend offensive operations and begin a long period of rest and reorganization; for the first time since the Pacific war began in early December, the Japanese have been stopped cold.

1942/FEBRUARY 10—On Bataan, U.S. and Philippine troops consolidate their position and prepare to eliminate the last Japanese position in their rear, at Cañas Point.

1942/FEBRUARY 11—The Japanese move a paratrooper force south for use in the Netherlands East Indies.

1942/FEBRUARY 12—The British see their situation in Singapore as grave and consider surrender without further resistance.

1942/FEBRUARY 13—Philippine troops eliminate Japanese forces at Cañas Point on Bataan. Japanese light surface forces sink the British gunboat *Scorpion* in Banka Strait, prompting the ABDA cruiser-destroyer force to sortie from Batavia.

1942/FEBRUARY 14—Japanese paratroopers land near Palembang. Attempting to intercept a convoy proceeding through Banka Strait, Allied cruisers and destroyers are attacked by Japanese aircraft and break off the effort.

1942/FEBRUARY 15—Singapore surrenders to the Japanese, depriving the Allies of one of the major British naval bases in Asia. Japanese amphibious troops land at Palembang, where there is heavy fighting. The Dutch destroyer *Van Ghent* runs aground in Banka Strait and must be abandoned. The Japanese First Air Fleet departs Palau for the Netherlands East Indies.

1942/FEBRUARY 16—Japanese secure Palembang. Minor actions in the Philippines, as both sides rest and reorganize. An Australian and American convoy attempting to reach Timor is turned back by Japanese air attack.

1942/FEBRUARY 17—The Japanese expand their footholds in the Netherlands East Indies. The Japanese advance in Burma. The Dutch destroyer *Van Ness* is sunk by Japanese aircraft in Banka Strait.

1942/FEBRUARY 18—The Japanese expand their footholds in the Netherlands East Indies. The Japanese advance in Burma. The Japanese First Air Fleet arrives in the Banda Sea, north-northwest of Australia. The Dutch coast defense ship *Soerabaja* and a submarine are destroyed by air attack on Soerabaja Naval Base.

1942/FEBRUARY 19—The Japanese First Air Fleet raids Port Darwin, in northwestern Australia, inflicting heavy damage (seven merchant ships totaling over 43,000 tons are sunk, plus a destroyer and four small craft, with six other merchant ships and two warships damaged). Japanese troops begin landing on Bali. Later that night, the ABDA cruiser-destroyer force engages Japanese shipping, losing the Dutch destroyer *Piet Hein* and suffering a cruiser and two destroyers damaged, while damaging two Japanese destroyers (Battle of Lombok Strait).

1942/FEBRUARY 20—USS *Lexington* beats off a Japanese air attack some 300 miles east-northeast of Rabaul, but is forced to abandon a planned raid on that place. In a combined amphibious and airborne attack, Japanese troops land at Kupang and Dili, on Timor. Allied surface ships skirmish inconclusively with Japanese ships in Bandung Strait.

1942/FEBRUARY 21—On Timor, Dutch and Australian troops begin a guerrilla resistance.

1942/FEBRUARY 22—The Japanese 48th Division arrives at Balikpapan from the Philippines.

1942/FEBRUARY 23—The Japanese submarine *I-17* shells Elwood, California. President Roosevelt orders General Douglas MacArthur from the Philippines to Australia to assume command of all Allied forces there.

1942/FEBRUARY 24—The *Enterprise* task force raids Wake Island. The Japanese complete occupation of Timor, aside from the mountainous interior. Japanese convoys put to sea for the invasion of Java. The Italian blockade runner *Orseolo* arrives at Bordeaux from Kobe.

1942/FEBRUARY 25—The Japanese Java invasion force converges on its objectives. The Japanese continue their advance in Burma.

1942/FEBRUARY 26—Allied warship movements in the Netherlands East Indies convince the Japanese to delay the Java operation. The Japanese continue their advance in Burma. The Japanese First Air Fleet enters the Indian Ocean.

1942/FEBRUARY 27—Battle of the Java Sea: Under Vice Admiral Karel Doorman, the ABDA cruiser-destroyer force attempts to intercept the Japanese invasion force, only to be intercepted by a superior Japanese squadron, losing two light cruisers and three destroyers, with heavy damage to his other ships. The U.S. aircraft transport *Langley* (the first U.S. aircraft carrier) is sunk by Japanese aircraft south of Java.

1942/FEBRUARY 28—Battle of Sunda Strait: As Japanese troops begin landing on Java, USS *Houston* and HMAS *Perth* attempt to escape from the Java Sea by way of Sunda Strait, only to be sunk by overwhelming Japanese forces.

1942/MARCH 1—Japanese troops begin landing on Java. Battle off Soerabaja: HMS *Exeter* and an American and a British destroyer are intercepted and sunk by Japanese naval and air forces while trying to escape eastward from Java. The Japanese battleship *Hiei*, supported by cruisers and destroyers, sinks two U.S. destroyers south of Java.

1942/MARCH 2—Japanese troops occupy Zamboanga, on Mindanao in the Philippines. Japanese encounter heavy fighting on Java.

1942/MARCH 3—Having refueled from a submarine at French Frigate Shoal, two Japanese flying boats raid Pearl Harbor. Heavy fighting on Java, while Japanese cruisers and destroyers sink the destroyer HMS *Stronghold*, several smaller warships, and a merchant ship south of Java.

1942/MARCH 4—The *Enterprise* task force raids Marcus Island. In the Netherlands East Indies, heavy fighting continues on Java, while three damaged Allied destroyers in Soerabaja Navy Yard are scuttled.

1942/MARCH 5—The First Air Fleet raids Tjilatjap, sinking several vessels. Japanese troops land at Salamaua, in

northeastern New Guinea. General Harold Alexander is appointed British commander in Burma.

1942/MARCH 6—Dutch resistance on Java becomes fragmented; the Dutch Navy begins scuttling its last vessels in Javan ports.

1942/MARCH 7—Japanese surface units shell Christmas Island (the one off Australia), sinking one ship. British troops evacuate Rangoon. Having just recently arrived, the U.S. Americal Division sails from Melbourne, Australia, for Nouméa.

1942/MARCH 8—Japanese troops land at Lae, in northeastern New Guinea. Japanese naval units reconnoiter Buka, north of Bougainville. Japanese troops depart Singapore for northern Sumatra.

1942/MARCH 9—Allied forces on Java (about 20,000) surrender.

1942/MARCH 10—The carriers *Lexington* and *Yorktown* make a daring raid over the Owen Stanley Mountains in New Guinea, to hit Japanese shipping at Lae and Salamaua, sinking an auxiliary cruiser and two merchant ships, and damaging four warships and several merchantmen. The U.S. 27th Infantry Division sails from San Francisco for Hawaii.

1942/MARCH 11—Over two weeks after receiving orders to proceed to Australia, Douglas MacArthur finally leaves Corregidor, on a PT boat, which takes him to Mindanao, where a B-17 will fly him to Australia. Major General Jonathan Wainwright assumes command in the Philippines.

1942/MARCH 12—The U.S. Americal Division lands at Nouméa. Japanese troops land at Sabang, in northern Sumatra. U.S. General Joseph Stilwell arrives in Burma to assist Sir Harold Alexander, as combined U.S. and Chinese commander.

1942/MARCH 13—Japanese troops land at Buka, north of Bougainville, and begin building an airfield. British (actually mostly Indian and Burmese) and Chinese troops establish the Prome-Toungoo line in Burma.

1942/MARCH 14—Japanese forces in Burma halt in order to rest and reorganize, as the British and Chinese hold on the Prome-Toungoo line.

1942/MARCH 15—In Burma, the British and Chinese consolidate the Prome-Toungoo line. The U.S. 27th Infantry Division arrives in Hawaii.

1942/MARCH 16—A battalion of the U.S. Americal Division sails from Nouméa bound for Efate, in the New Hebrides. In Burma, British and Chinese troops hold on the Prome-Toungoo line.

1942/MARCH 17—General Douglas MacArthur arrives in Australia by B-17 from Mindanao. In Burma, British and Chinese troops hold on the Prome-Toungoo line.

1942/MARCH 18—A battalion of the U.S. Americal Division occupies Efate, in the New Hebrides. In Burma, British and Chinese troops hold on the Prome-Toungoo line.

1942/MARCH 19—British General William Slim takes command of the British Burma Corps, while the Prome-Toungoo line holds. The Japanese 56th Division sails from Singapore for Rangoon. The U.S. 41st Infantry Division sails from San Francisco for Australia.

1942/MARCH 20—Elements of the Japanese 18th Division sail from Penang, Malaya, for the Andaman Islands. In Burma, British and Chinese troops hold on the Prome-Toungoo line.

1942/MARCH 21—In Burma, a massive Japanese air raid on Magwe virtually eliminates Allied air power in the theater, as the Japanese prepare a new offensive to break the Prome-Toungoo line.

1942/MARCH 22—The British 5th Division departs from Britain bound for Madagascar. In Burma, Japanese preparations for a new offensive proceed, while British and Chinese troops continue to hold on the Prome-Toungoo line.

1942/MARCH 23—Troops of the Japanese 18th Division occupy Port Blair, in the Andaman Islands. In Burma, British and Chinese troops hold on the Prome-Toungoo line, as Japanese preparations for a new offensive are completed.

1942/MARCH 24—Japanese forces conduct mopping-up operations throughout the Netherlands East Indies, landing troops at numerous small ports bypassed during the invasion. In Burma, the Japanese open an offensive up the Sittang, Irrawaddy, and Chindwin rivers.

1942/MARCH 25—Task Force 39 (the carrier *Wasp*, a fast battleship, two heavy cruisers, and eight destroyers) steams from the east coast bound for Scapa Flow, northern Scotland, where it will relieve British forces earmarked for operations in the Indian Ocean.

1942/MARCH 26—The Japanese First Air Fleet departs Celebes bound for the Indian Ocean.

1942/MARCH 27—British Admiral Sir James Somerville assumes command of the Far Eastern Fleet (three carriers; five battleships; seven cruisers, including one Dutch; and fourteen British, Dutch, and Australian destroyers; divided into a "fast" division, able to make 24 knots, and a "slow" one able to make 18), based on Ceylon. A Japanese submarine flotilla (six boats) departs Penang for the Indian Ocean.

1942/MARCH 28—The Japanese First Air Fleet enters the Indian Ocean.

1942/MARCH 29—Japanese troops capture Lashio, in northern Burma, from Chinese troops. After reconnaissance reports the presence of the Japanese First Air Fleet in the Indian Ocean, Admiral Somerville concludes it will attack his bases in Ceylon and orders his ships to deploy so as to ambush them.

1942/MARCH 30—British and Japanese fleets concentrate on Ceylon in the Indian Ocean.

1942/MARCH 31—The British Far Eastern Fleet reaches its patrol area south of Ceylon. Japanese troops in Burma drive Chinese troops out of Toungoo, thus unhinging the Prome-Toungoo line.

1942/APRIL 1—U.S. and Philippine troops on Bataan go on quarter rations because of the inability to get supplies through the Japanese naval blockade. The British Far Eastern Fleet continues to search for the Japanese First Air Fleet south and east of Ceylon. The First Air Fleet refuels south of Java. A Japanese destroyer carrying reinforcements for the Andaman Islands departs Penang. A Japanese cruiser-destroyer force departs Megui for operations in the Bay of Bengal.

1942/APRIL 2—The carrier *Hornet*, carrying sixteen USAAF B-25 medium bombers, sails from San Francisco with her escort, intending to stage an air raid on Tokyo. Low on fuel, the British Far Eastern Fleet is ordered to retire to Addu atoll in the Maldive Islands, as the whereabouts of Japanese First Air Fleet are still unknown, making Ceylon too dangerous. The Japanese 18th Division sails from Singapore for Rangoon.

1942/APRIL 3—Heavily reinforced with fresh troops, heavy artillery, and lots of ammunition, the Japanese launch a major offensive on Bataan in the Philippines.

1942/APRIL 4—The Japanese offensive on Bataan begins cracking the main line of resistance. The British Far Eastern Fleet reaches Addu atoll. A Japanese destroyer lands reinforcements in the Andaman Islands. The Japanese First Air Fleet is detected south of Ceylon, where all operational ships are ordered to put to sea.

1942/APRIL 5—The British Far Eastern Fleet hastily sorties from Addu atoll in an attempt to intercept the Japanese First Air Fleet. Japanese aircraft from the First Air Fleet strike Colombo, Ceylon, sinking a destroyer, an auxiliary

cruiser, and another minor warship, while, out at sea, the British heavy cruisers *Cornwall* and *Dorsetshire*, as well as many auxiliaries and merchant ships, are sunk. The British and Japanese fleets in the Indian Ocean fail to spot each other, although coming within 200 miles of each other. On Bataan, Japanese troops capture Mount Samat, unhinging the defenses. When a counterattack by U.S. and Philippine troops fails to throw them back, a U.S. withdrawal is ordered.

1942/APRIL 6—Japanese drive forward on Bataan. Elements of the Japanese First Air Fleet begin a raid into the Bay of Bengal. In the Indian Ocean, the British Far Eastern Fleet and Japanese First Air Fleet continue to fail to locate each other.

1942/APRIL 7—Japanese troops land on Bougainville. The Japanese 18th Division lands at Rangoon. In the Indian Ocean, the British Far Eastern Fleet is ordered to return to Addu atoll.

1942/APRIL 8—The carrier *Enterprise* and her escorts, under Rear Admiral William F. Halsey, sail from Pearl Harbor. The British Far Eastern Fleet reaches Addu atoll.

1942/APRIL 9—Aircraft from the Japanese First Air Fleet sink nine merchant ships off the coast of Orissa, India, while cruisers raid commerce in the Bay of Bengal, accounting for three more ships, for a total of about 92,000 tons. Japanese carrier aircraft raid Tricomalee, inflicting little damage save to defending aircraft, but sink the carrier *Hermes*, two smaller warships, and two tankers in nearby waters. U.S. and Philippine forces on Bataan surrender to the Japanese, ending the desperate resistance of the "Battling Bastards of Bataan." But U.S. troops still hold the island of Corregidor, which lies astride the entrance to Manila Bay.

1942/APRIL 10—The British Far Eastern Fleet (mostly older battleships and cruisers, plus the carriers *Indomitable* and *Formidable*) retires to Bombay and East Africa. Japanese troops land on Cebu, in the central Philippines. The Japanese renew their offensive in Burma. In the Philippines, the Japanese begin a systematic bombardment of Corregidor and the smaller island forts in Manila Bay.

1942/APRIL 11—Corregidor is subjected to intensive bombardment. The Japanese continue to advance in Burma.

1942/APRIL 12—The Japanese continue bombardment of Corregidor. They continue to advance in Burma.

1942/APRIL 13—Task Force 16 is formed when *Enterprise* and her escorts rendezvous with *Hornet* and hers, west of Pearl Harbor.

1942/APRIL 14—Japanese troops overcome final U.S. resistance on Cebu. In Burma, the Japanese continue to press the British.

1942/APRIL 15—The Japanese continue to attack in Burma. Heavy bombardment of Corregidor.

1942/APRIL 16—Japanese troops land on Panay, in the southern Philippines. Japanese troops occupy Magwe, in central Burma.

1942/APRIL 17—In the Philippines, the Japanese begin to spread out on Panay, and continue heavy bombardment of Corregidor.

1942/APRIL 18—The Doolittle Raid (or Tokyo Raid). From a position little more than 650 miles east of Honshu, the carrier *Hornet* launches sixteen B-25 medium bombers against Tokyo and other targets. This comes as quite a shock to the Japanese, even though the damage is slight. The Japanese attack the Chinese Sixth Army in northern Burma, while the British are hard pressed before the Yenangyaung oil fields.

1942/APRIL 19—The British are forced to abandon the Yenangyaung oil fields

in Burma, after heavy fighting since April 10.

1942/APRIL 20—British troops fall back in Burma.

1942/APRIL 21—The Japanese continue their bombardment of Corregidor.

1942/APRIL 22—The U.S. 32nd Infantry Division sails from San Francisco for Australia.

1942/APRIL 23—Uncovered by the British withdrawal to their west, Chinese troops in central Burma begin to pull out northward to avoid being outflanked by the Japanese.

1942/APRIL 24—Japanese troops advance on all fronts in Burma.

1942/APRIL 25—Task Force 16 returns to Pearl Harbor; its mission (the Doolittle Raid) remains a closely guarded secret for months afterward.

1942/APRIL 26—Japanese reaction to the Doolittle Raid is to recall some fighter groups from the front, while Admiral Isoroku Yamamoto is inspired to propose a plan to expand Japan's defensive perimeter to the Aleutians and Midway.

1942/APRIL 27—In Burma, the Japanese advance threatens Mandalay.

1942/APRIL 28—The British situation in Burma becomes critical, with a Japanese invasion of India becoming more likely as Japanese troops advance on all fronts.

1942/APRIL 29—Japanese troops occupy Cotabato, Mindanao.

1942/APRIL 30—British troops evacuate Mandalay in Burma.

1942/MAY 1—Task Force 17 (the carrier *Yorktown* and escorts, under Fletcher) rendezvouses with TF 11 (the *Lexington*, under Fitch) on the eastern edge of the Coral Sea. In Burma, Japanese troops occupy Mandalay and press on.

1942/MAY 2—The Japanese bombard Corregidor from Bataan, preparatory to a landing. The U.S. submarine *Drum* torpedoes the Japanese seaplane carrier *Mizuho* off Honshu.

1942/MAY 3—Japanese troops land on Tulagi, near Guadalcanal, in the eastern Solomon Islands. Japanese troops land at Cagayan, Mindanao, last important town in the Philippines still in U.S. hands. Japanese troops capture Lashio, in northern Burma, from Chinese troops, severing the "Burma Road" to China (which is useless anyway, since all Allied troops in Burma are cut off from external supply, the Japanese having occupied all the ports).

1942/MAY 4—The carrier *Yorktown* attacks the Japanese at Tulagi, seriously damaging a destroyer, which has to be beached and abandoned. Corregidor is subjected to an intense artillery and aerial bombardment.

1942/MAY 5—The Japanese carriers *Zuikaku* and *Shokaku* enter the Solomon Sea from the north, intent upon supporting operations against the eastern Solomons and Port Moresby. Japanese troops land on Corregidor. British troops land at Diégo-Suarez, a Vichy-held naval base in northern Madagascar. Japanese Imperial General Headquarters orders the Combined Fleet to prepare for an attack on Midway and the Aleutians.

1942/MAY 6—U.S. and Japanese carriers search for each other in the Coral Sea/Solomon Sea area. Corregidor surrenders, after several gunboats are scuttled by the U.S. Navy.

1942/MAY 7—The Battle of the Coral Sea begins. U.S. carrier aircraft sink the carrier *Shoho*, while Japanese carrier aircraft sink a U.S. oiler and destroyer. Japanese submarine-borne aircraft reconnoiter Aden. The British capture Diégo-Suarez, Madagascar, from the Vichy French.

1942/MAY 8—The Battle of the Coral Sea continues. U.S. and Japanese carrier task forces trade blows, the U.S. losing the carrier *Lexington* while the Japanese suffer heavy damage to *Shokaku* and se-

vere aircraft loss. The Japanese abandon the Port Moresby operation and withdraw northward. This is the first setback for the Japanese Navy since the war began. Japanese submarines begin reconnaissance operations off East Africa. In Burma, Japanese troops close on Myitkyina, in the far north, held by the Chinese. Douglas MacArthur urges the Joint Chiefs of Staff to authorize an offensive in the Solomons, under his command, to stop the Japanese from advancing any farther.

1942/MAY 9—The Port Moresby invasion force returns to Rabaul.

1942/MAY 10—U.S. troops on Mindanao surrender to the Japanese, ending formal resistance, but some flee to the interior to conduct guerrilla operations.

1942/MAY 11—The British fight a desperate rearguard battle at Kalewa in Burma, and manage to retreat westward. The U.S. submarine *S-42* sinks the Japanese merchant cruiser *Okinoshima* in St. George's Channel, New Britain.

1942/MAY 12—In revenge for the Doolittle Raid on Tokyo, and Chinese assistance in getting the American airmen safely away, the Japanese launch a punitive expedition in China, eventually killing thousands of Chinese.

1942/MAY 13—British troops in Burma retreat westward while preparations are made to keep the Japanese out of India.

1942/MAY 14—U.S. troops in the mountains of North Luzon surrender to the Japanese, but some resort to guerrilla warfare. In Burma, the Japanese reach the foothills of the Arakan Mountains near Shwegyin, leaving the British in control of only small areas of the country along the Indian frontier, the Burma Army having been completely shattered, although small groups (including Stilwell and his staff) would exfiltrate from Japanese-held territory over following months. The U.S. 32nd Infantry Division arrives in Australia.

1942/MAY 15—The U.S. 41st Infantry Division completes its movement to Australia. British headquarters for the Burma front is established at Imphal, in the mountainous eastern portion of Assam, in the extreme northeast of India.

1942/MAY 16—In Burma, the Japanese press the Chinese defenders of Myitkyina (a key station on the Burma Road).

1942/MAY 17—In Burma, Japanese troops threaten to overwhelm the Chinese at Myitkyina.

1942/MAY 18—U.S. and Philippine troops on Panay surrender to the Japanese, ending formal resistance in the Philippines. The American and Philippine troops, despite being cut off from aid because of the Japanese naval blockade, fought on until food and ammunition were gone. On Panay, as elsewhere in the islands, many refused to surrender and, in effect, deserted to form guerrilla bands that would fight on until MacArthur returned in thirty months. No Allied force gave the Japanese as much trouble as these stalwart fighters, which indicated what could be expected as the war went on.

1942/MAY 19—The Japanese engage in mopping-up operations in Burma.

1942/MAY 20—Japanese submarine-borne aircraft reconnoiter Durban, in South Africa. The last organized British and Chinese forces retire from Burma.

1942/MAY 21—Japanese troops occupy Samar and Leyte, in the eastern Philippines.

1942/MAY 22—The Japanese carriers *Ryujo* and *Junyo* concentrate at Ominato, northern Honshu, while the balance of the First Air Fleet concentrates in the Inland Sea.

1942/MAY 23—The Japanese are completing preparations for the Midway Operation.

1942/MAY 24—Japanese submarine-borne reconnaissance aircraft scout Kodiak Island, south of Alaska.

1942/MAY 25—Japanese submarine-borne reconnaissance aircraft scout Kiska, in the Aleutians. Japanese carriers sortie from Ominato, northern Honshu, for the Aleutians.

1942/MAY 26—Japanese submarine-borne reconnaissance aircraft scout Kiska, in the Aleutians. Task Force 16 (*Enterprise* and *Hornet*) arrives at Pearl Harbor. The Japanese First Air Fleet sorties from the Inland Sea, bound for Midway. The U.S. 37th Infantry Division sails from San Francisco for the Fiji Islands. In North Africa, Rommel attacks the Gazala line.

1942/MAY 27—*Yorktown* arrives at Pearl Harbor and immediately goes into dry dock for emergency repairs. A Japanese troop convoy and escorts leave Ominato bound for the Aleutians. A Japanese troop convoy and escorts leave Saipan and Guam bound for Midway.

1942/MAY 28—The Main Body of the Japanese Combined Fleet sorties from the Inland Sea for Midway. Task Force 16 puts to sea from Pearl Harbor, followed later in the day by TF 17, with *Yorktown* under way but still under repair. U.S. army and naval personnel from Efate begin to establish a base on Espíritu Santo.

1942/MAY 29—A Japanese submarine-borne reconnaissance plane scouts Diégo-Suarez, in northern Madagascar. Japanese and U.S. naval forces begin converging on Midway.

1942/MAY 30—A Japanese midget submarine torpedoes the British battleship *Ramilles* and a tanker at Diégo-Suarez, off Madagascar. Japanese and U.S. fleets converge on Midway.

1942/MAY 31—Japanese midget submarines penetrate Sydney Harbor, sinking one old vessel and causing considerable panic. U.S. battleships sortie from San Francisco to support the carriers in the Central Pacific. Japanese and U.S. fleets converge on Midway.

1942/JUNE 1—The carrier *Saratoga*

and escorts sortie from San Diego to support carriers in the Central Pacific. Japanese and U.S. fleets continue converging on Midway. Japanese submarines begin taking station off Midway and the Hawaiian Islands.

1942/JUNE 2—U.S. Task Forces 16 and 17 join forces northeast of Midway. The Japanese fleet nears Midway from the west and south.

1942/JUNE 3—The Japanese carriers *Ryujo* and *Junyo* raid Dutch Harbor in the Aleutians. The Japanese invasion force is attacked southeast of Midway by B-17s and Catalinas, the latter torpedoing a tanker. Combined Task Forces 16 and 17 keep station northeast of Midway as the Japanese fleet approaches.

1942/JUNE 4—The Battle of Midway begins. Japanese aircraft raid Midway, sparking daylong action that leaves four Japanese carriers sunk and one U.S. carrier, *Yorktown*, so badly damaged that it has to be abandoned. Japanese carrier aircraft bomb Dutch Harbor in the Aleutians.

1942/JUNE 5—The Battle of Midway continues. Attacks by B-17s on damaged Japanese cruisers retiring from Midway have no effect. Although damaged, the carrier *Yorktown* remains afloat and is taken in tow. Admiral Isoroku Yamamoto orders the Combined Fleet to retire. Japanese submarines operating in Mozambique Channel.

1942/JUNE 6—The Battle of Midway continues. U.S. carrier aircraft attack damaged Japanese cruisers retiring from Midway, sinking *Mikuma* and severely damaging *Mogami*. Japanese troops land on Kiska in the Aleutians. The Japanese submarine *I-168* torpedoes *Yorktown*, further damaging her, and sinks an escorting destroyer.

1942/JUNE 7—The Battle of Midway ends. The carrier *Yorktown* sinks. U.S. carriers begin to retire from the vicinity of Midway. The Japanese fleet is retiring

from Midway. Japanese troops land on Attu in the Aleutians.

1942/JUNE 8—MacArthur again urges the Joint Chiefs of Staff to undertake an offensive in the Solomon Islands.

1942/JUNE 9—Consternation in Tokyo as the news of the Midway disaster sinks in. It is kept a secret initially, but details are soon circulating throughout the Japanese Navy's officer corps; the Army is not informed of the disaster until much later.

1942/JUNE 10—As damaged U.S. ships from Midway begin reaching Pearl Harbor, major reinforcements to the U.S. fleet enter the Pacific via the Panama Canal (the carrier *Wasp*, a fast battleship, a heavy cruiser, and eight destroyers). Lead elements of the U.S. 37th Infantry Division reach Fiji.

1942/JUNE 11—Japanese ships from the Midway operation begin returning to bases in the Marianas. U.S. survivors of the battle are undergoing repair.

1942/JUNE 12—Japanese submarines withdraw from Mozambique Channel.

1942/JUNE 13—The Combined Fleet begins to return to bases in Japan.

1942/JUNE 14—Japanese troops are consolidating their positions in the Aleutians. The German merchant cruiser *Thor* begins operating in the Indian Ocean. Headquarters and the first echelon of the 1st Marine Division debark in New Zealand.

1942/JUNE 15—U.S. and Australian Pacific fleets are reorganized into TF 1 (battleline of battleships) at San Francisco; TF 8 (cruisers and destroyers) in the Aleutians; TF 11 (*Saratoga* and escorts), TF 16 (*Enterprise* group), and TF 17 (*Hornet* group) at Pearl Harbor; and TF 18 (*Wasp* group) temporarily at San Diego, plus TF 44 (cruisers and destroyers) in Australian waters. John Lindemann enlists in the Marine Corps, along with several friends. He will be given orders to report for boot camp (basic training) in August. This is a typical procedure at this point of the war, with more volunteers available than facilities to train them.

1942/JUNE 16—A Japanese submarine-borne aircraft reconnoiters Mauritius in the Indian Ocean.

1942/JUNE 17—Japanese deploy a flotilla of six submarines in the Aleutians.

1942/JUNE 18—Marines on New Zealand begin an intensive training program.

1942/JUNE 19—The U.S. submarine S-27 is lost when she goes aground in the Aleutians.

1942/JUNE 20—The Japanese submarine I-26 shells Port Estevan, near Vancouver.

1942/JUNE 21—Japanese land-based air strength in the Solomons, Bismarcks, and northeastern New Guinea is estimated at 126 combat and reconnaissance aircraft by Allied intelligence; a further 33 two-engined bombers based at Timor are believed capable of intervening in operations around the Solomon Sea.

1942/JUNE 22—The Japanese are estimated by Allied intelligence as having about two brigades at Rabaul, two companies on New Ireland, a battalion in the Admiralties, a regiment at Tulagi, and a few companies on Bougainville, plus air base and service personnel. An estimated 1,000 SNLF troops ("Marines") are believed to be at Lae and Salamaua.

1942/JUNE 23—U.S. staff discussions continue as to the merits of an offensive in the Solomons-Bismarcks-Rabaul area (MacArthur wants a single offensive under his command; the Navy would prefer not to have him controlling its carriers and Marines).

1942/JUNE 24—The Japanese submarine I-25 shells Port Stevens, Oregon.

1942/JUNE 25—The U.S. submarine Nautilus sinks the Japanese destroyer Yamakaze about 50 miles southeast of Tokyo Bay. Chief of Naval Operations

(CNO) Ernest J. King suggests to Army Chief of Staff George C. Marshall that an amphibious offensive be undertaken in the Solomon Islands on August 1, to be under Navy control.

1942/JUNE 26—The Germans begin unrestricted submarine warfare off the east coast of the United States (limited attacks had begun earlier). The carnage wrought put a further strain on U.S. naval resources and made it more difficult to divert ships to the Pacific.

1942/JUNE 27—Japanese shellings (by submarine) of U.S. and Canadian coastal installations in the past week bring a call for more naval resources to guard the west coast of North America.

1942/JUNE 28—U.S. staff discussions continue as to the best options for undertaking an offensive in the New Guinea–Bismarcks–Solomons area.

1942/JUNE 29—U.S. staff discussions continue as to the best options for undertaking an offensive in the New Guinea–Bismarcks–Solomons area.

1942/JUNE 30—Congress votes $42 billion (about $400 billion in 1995 dollars) for defense for the next fiscal year.

1942/JULY 1—Task Force 18 sorties from San Diego, bound for the South Pacific, escorting the 2nd Marine Regiment, to complete the 1st Marine Division already in the South Pacific, at New Zealand.

1942/JULY 2—The Joint Chiefs of Staff finally adopt a compromise plan to begin pushing back the Japanese in the South Pacific: The Navy is to drive up the Solomon Islands while MacArthur recovers northeastern New Guinea and then drives on Rabaul, authorizing Operation Watchtower, the seizure of Guadalcanal.

1942/JULY 3—Japanese troops land on Guadalcanal from Tulagi and begin constructing an airfield (to be completed by August 15).

1942/JULY 4—Australian coastwatchers report Japanese airfield construction on Guadalcanal. The Japanese destroyer *Nehoni* is sunk in the Aleutians by the U.S. submarine *Triton*.

1942/JULY 5—Aerial reconnaissance confirms Japanese airfield construction on Guadalcanal. The U.S. submarine *Growler* sinks the Japanese destroyer *Arare* in the Aleutians, near Kiska.

1942/JULY 6—Based on reconnaissance information, Chief of Naval Operations Ernest J. King orders Operation Watchtower (the capture of Guadalcanal) implemented immediately.

1942/JULY 7—Task Forces 11 (*Saratoga*) and 16 (*Enterprise*) sortie from Pearl Harbor to support the Guadalcanal operation.

1942/JULY 8—Vice Admiral Robert L. Ghormley and General Douglas MacArthur confer in Melbourne over details of Operation Watchtower.

1942/JULY 9—The general plans for Operation Watchtower take shape, as the 1st Marine Division practices amphibious landings in New Zealand, between which it helps load and unload ships due to local labor union problems.

1942/JULY 10—The USAAF agrees to increase the allocation of aircraft to the Pacific Theater, thereby slowing its planned buildup in Britain.

1942/JULY 11—Japanese Imperial General Headquarters acknowledges the results of the Battle of Midway (the destruction of Japanese carrier superiority) and cancels its orders of May 5 to capture Midway and other outlying islands. The second echelon of the 1st Marine Division debarks in New Zealand.

1942/JULY 12—The U.S. Joint Chiefs of Staff propose that following the completion of an offensive up the Solomons to Rabaul, the logical course of action would be to proceed northward along the axis Truk-Guam-Saipan "and/or" through the Netherlands East Indies to the Philippines.

1942/JULY 13—Allied ground combat forces potentially available for offensive operations in the Pacific are: the U.S. 37th Infantry Division, in the Fiji Islands; the U.S. Americal Division, on New Caledonia; the Australian 7th Division, in Australia; the U.S. 1st Marine Division (understrength), in New Zealand; the New Zealand 4th Brigade, in Fiji; the U.S. 7th Marine Regiment (of the 1st Marine Division), in Samoa; the U.S. 147th Infantry Regiment, in Tongatabu. Several additional U.S. and Australian divisions are available, in Australia, but are either committed to the defense of the western and northern portions of the country or not yet trained.

1942/JULY 14—Admiral Yamamoto reorganizes the Combined Fleet as a consequence of Midway, among other things creating the Eighth Fleet, at Rabaul under Vice Admiral Gunichi Mikawa, to oversee operations in the Solomons and New Guinea.

1942/JULY 15—The U.S. submarine *Grunion* sinks three Japanese submarine chasers and a large merchant ship (about 8,600 tons) in the Aleutians. The interdiction (with subs, surface ships, and aircraft) of Japanese supply efforts eventually leads to Japanese abandonment of Aleutian bases.

1942/JULY 16—The Allies make intensive preparations for the Guadalcanal operation, but the target date must be postponed from August 1 to August 7, as the convoy transporting the 7th Marine Regiment is delayed. The Japanese push preparations for operations in New Guinea.

1942/JULY 17—Massive amounts of manpower are committed to building up military strength in Alaska, and the west coast of North America in general. This is a considerable drain on resources for the Pacific Theater, and slows down offensive operation farther west.

1942/JULY 18—U.S. planners see reconquest of Japanese bases in the Aleutian Islands (off Alaska) in 1943. It is politically impractical (due to public fears) to simply cut off the Japanese in the Aleutians and leave them there. This is similar to the effects of the Doolittle Raid on Tokyo earlier in the year. As a result of that raid, the Japanese greatly strengthened their air and land forces in northern Japan, to the detriment of efforts elsewhere in the Pacific. Thus the United States and Canada have to devote enormous resources to conquer the essentially useless Japanese Aleutian bases.

1942/JULY 19—U.S. naval forces available to support Operation Watchtower total three aircraft carriers, one fast battleship, nine heavy cruisers, two antiaircraft cruisers, thirty-one destroyers, six submarines, and numerous smaller vessels. Australian naval forces total two heavy cruisers and a light cruiser.

1942/JULY 20—Task Forces 11, 16, and 18 unite near Fiji, for the Guadalcanal operation. All but one of six Japanese submarines that have been operating there withdraw from the Aleutians, having sunk only one ship in thirty-four days of patrolling. Escorted by a cruiser-destroyer force, Japanese troops depart Rabaul for Buna and Gona, in New Guinea. The German merchant cruiser *Thor* sinks a British freighter in the Indian Ocean.

1942/JULY 21—Japanese troops land at Gona, northeastern New Guinea.

1942/JULY 22—Japanese troops land at Buna, northeastern New Guinea. Japanese troops at Gona begin to advance up the Kokoda trail, toward Port Moresby on the southern coast. Allied aircraft attack Japanese shipping off Buna and Gona, inflicting some damage. The 1st Marine Division sails from Auckland, New Zealand, for the Fiji Islands.

1942/JULY 23—Japanese ships at Buna and Gona depart for Rabaul.

1942/JULY 24—U.S. submarines begin operating in the Kurile Islands. Japanese warships and merchantmen from the Buna-Gona landings return to Rabaul.

1942/JULY 25—U.S. carrier aircraft available to support Operation Watchtower total 240 (99 fighters, 102 dive bombers, and 39 torpedo bombers) aboard the carriers *Saratoga, Enterprise,* and *Wasp.* This is the bulk of U.S. carrier assets in the Pacific.

1942/JULY 26—Japanese reinforcements land at Buna. The 1st Marine Division arrives at Fiji for amphibious landing rehearsal; virtually all Navy and Marine elements involved in Operation Watchtower are now concentrated.

1942/JULY 27—Allied land-based or amphibian combat and reconnaissance aircraft concentrated for Operation Watchtower total 321 (196 U.S. Navy or Marine, 95 U.S. Army, and 30 Royal New Zealand Air Force) organized into Task Force 63 and deployed mostly in the New Hebrides and on New Caledonia. In addition, about 175 aircraft (about 120 USAAF, 30 RAF, and 20 RAAF) based in Australia and New Guinea are capable of supporting operations at Guadalcanal by air attacks on Rabaul and surrounding Japanese-held areas. The 1st Marine Division conducts amphibious landing rehearsals at Fiji, in cooperation with carrier aircraft and cruiser and destroyer gunfire support.

1942/JULY 28—Rear Admiral Fletcher, overall commander of the landing forces and covering forces in Operation Watchtower, issues his operational orders, detailing the courses and duties of all forces for the invasion of Guadalcanal. U.S. forces continue amphibious assault rehearsals at Fiji.

1942/JULY 29—Japanese reinforcements land at Buna, northeastern New Guinea, despite the loss of one transport to Allied air attack.

1942/JULY 30—The U.S. submarine *Grunion* is declared "overdue" while on patrol in the Aleutians, probably lost to hazards of the sea. Vice Admiral Gunichi Mikawa arrives at Rabaul to assume command of the Eighth Fleet.

1942/JULY 31—Task Force 62 (the 1st Marine Division) sails from Fiji toward Guadalcanal, escorted by Task Force 61 (TFs 16, 17, and 18). The fast division of the British Far Eastern Fleet returns to Colombo from East Africa. The U.S. aircraft carrier *Essex* is launched at Newport News, Virginia, the first of an order of twenty-six to the same design. A Japanese convoy bound for Buna (New Guinea) with reinforcements is forced to return to Rabaul by intensive Allied air attack, although no vessels are lost.

1942/AUGUST 1—Allied movements designed to mask the Guadalcanal operation: the U.S. Pacific Fleet battleline (seven old battleships, ten destroyers) is transferred from San Francisco Bay to Pearl Harbor, while the British "Force A" (two carriers, one battleship, several cruisers and destroyers) sorties from Colombo toward the Andaman Island operation.

1942/AUGUST 2—The battleship *South Dakota* (of a powerful new design) begins operating in the Pacific.

1942/AUGUST 3—In Manchuria, the Japanese Army begins the formation of three tank divisions.

1942/AUGUST 4—The U.S. destroyer *Tucker* is mined at Espíritu Santo.

1942/AUGUST 5—The Japanese submarine *I-30* arrives at Lorient, France, after running the Allied blockade. The Japanese superbattleship *Musashi* is commissioned. A Japanese convoy leaves Rabaul with reinforcements for Buna (New Guinea).

1942/AUGUST 6—Task Force 62 arrives southwest of Gaudalcanal.

1942/AUGUST 7—Operation Watchtower. The 1st Marine Division is landed on Guadalcanal and nearby Tulagi and some smaller islands by Task Force 62, finding spotty resistance. A Japanese convoy bound for Buna (New Guinea) with reinforcements from Rabaul is recalled.

1942/AUGUST 8—Marines on Guadalcanal advance westward from their landing beaches and capture the unfinished Japanese airstrip. The first Japanese air raid on Guadalcanal occurs.

1942/AUGUST 9—The Marines on Guadalcanal consolidate their hold on Henderson Field, and occupy several small islands in the vicinity of Tulagi. The Battle of Savo Island: Around midnight seven Japanese cruisers and one destroyer smash an Allied squadron in the waters north of Guadalcanal, sinking four heavy cruisers (one Australian) and one destroyer with no loss to themselves. Chinese forces defeat a Japanese offensive in Kiangsi Province.

1942/AUGUST 10—Task Force 62 pulls out of Guadalcanal waters. A U.S. submarine sinks the Japanese heavy cruiser *Kako*, one of the ships retiring from the Battle of Savo Island. Marines on Guadalcanal are put on two-thirds rations because many of the supply ships withdrew before they could be unloaded. The British Far Eastern Fleet returns to Colombo from its diversionary mission near the Andaman Islands.

1942/AUGUST 11—The Combined Fleet begins to move from the Inland Sea to Truk, in order to support operations at Guadalcanal. Marines consolidate their position on Guadalcanal.

1942/AUGUST 12—Japanese convoys land reinforcements at Buna, in northwestern New Guinea. U.S. destroyer-transports land supplies on Guadalcanal. Japanese troops reach Kokoda, the principal pass across the Owen Stanley Mountains on New Guinea.

1942/AUGUST 13—Japanese take control of the vital main pass in the Owen Stanley Mountains, on the Buna-Kokoda trail in New Guinea.

1942/AUGUST 14—Japanese complete landing 3,000 construction troops near Gona, in New Guinea.

1942/AUGUST 15—U.S. transports land supplies at Guadalcanal. The last Japanese submarine in the Aleutians, *I-6*, is withdrawn.

1942/AUGUST 16—Heavily escorted, the Ichiki Detachment (about 1,000 infantry) sails from Truk for Guadalcanal. Japanese convoys land reinforcements at Buna, in northwestern New Guinea.

1942/AUGUST 17—The U.S. 2nd Marine Raider Battalion, landed from submarines, raids Makin Island, in the Gilberts. The raid is a success, even though the small Japanese garrison fights to the death. An unfortunate aftereffect of this raid is that the Japanese decide to heavily fortify the many small islands they occupy in the Central Pacific, which comes back to haunt the Marines when they storm Tarawa in the following year.

1942/AUGUST 18—The Ichiki Detachment lands on Guadalcanal, east of the U.S. 1st Marine Division positions.

1942/AUGUST 19—Japanese convoys land reinforcements at Buna, in northwestern New Guinea. Marines on Guadalcanal skirmish with elements of the Japanese Ichiki Detachment.

1942/AUGUST 20—Henderson Field completed, 31 Marine Corps fighters are landed from the U.S. escort carrier *Long Island*.

1942/AUGUST 21—Before dawn the Ichiki Detachment attacks the eastern face of the Gaudalcanal beachhead and is crushed by the defenders, who envelop their rear (Battle of the Tenaru River). U.S. destroyers and fast transports deliver supplies to Guadalcanal, at the cost of one escorting destroyer.

1942/AUGUST 22—Marines continue to consolidate their hold on Guadalcanal and Tulagi. U.S. Army fighters begin landing at Henderson Field (five P-400s) from New Caledonia. Off Savo Island, the Japanese destroyer *Kawakaze* torpedoes the U.S. destroyer *Blue*, which is towed to Tulagi.

1942/AUGUST 23—Japanese cruisers and destroyers shell Nauru Island. U.S. reconnaissance aircraft spot a Japanese force intent on reinforcing Guadalcanal. That night Japanese destroyers shell the Marines on Guadalcanal. The U.S. destroyer *Blue*, damaged on the twenty-second, is scuttled at Tulagi. The U.S. 40th Infantry Division begins leaving San Francisco for Hawaii.

1942/AUGUST 24—Battle of the Eastern Solomons: Aircraft from the carrier *Saratoga* sink the Japanese carrier *Ryujo*, while Japanese carrier aircraft damage *Enterprise*. Before she retires for repairs, *Enterprise* lands eleven dive bombers at Henderson Field. That night Japanese destroyers shell Henderson Field, while Japanese SNLF (naval infantry) troops land on the Goodenough Islands, off northeastern New Guinea. John Lindemann reports to Parris Island for ten weeks of Marine Corps boot camp. It is tough, hot, but survivable.

1942/AUGUST 25—Marine and Navy aircraft attack a Japanese reinforcing squadron near Guadalcanal. Japanese SNLF troops land at Milne Bay, in southeastern New Guinea, but are contained by Australian defenders. North of the Solomons, USAAF B-17s sink the Japanese destroyer *Mutsuki* with high-altitude bombing, the first, and only, time this tactic works against an underway warship.

1942/AUGUST 26—Japanese troops occupy Nauru Island against no resistance. Australian troops at Milne Bay stoutly resist the Japanese landing force.

1942/AUGUST 27—Japanese reinforcements are landed at Milne Bay, where Australian and U.S. troops put up heavy resistance. Nine U.S. Army P-400 fighters land at Henderson Field.

1942/AUGUST 28—Some Japanese destroyer transports are intercepted by U.S. aircraft and sunk or damaged, but others manage to land reinforcements on Guadalcanal later that night. That night aircraft from the Japanese submarine *I-15* drop incendiary bombs on Oregon forests. The battleship *Washington* and several destroyers enter the Pacific via the Panama Canal.

1942/AUGUST 29—Initial elements of the Japanese Kawaguchi Detachment are landed on Guadalcanal from destroyers and high-speed transports. A Japanese cruiser squadron attempts to support SNLF troops at Milne Bay, New Guinea, with little success. The battleship *Yamato* arrives at Truk as flagship of Admiral Isoroku Yamamoto. Save for one day, when she changes her anchorage, she will swing at her anchor for the next seven months.

1942/AUGUST 30—Japanese aircraft sink a U.S. destroyer transport attempting to reinforce Guadalcanal. U.S. troops land on unoccupied Adak Island, in the Aleutians.

1942/AUGUST 31—The carrier *Saratoga* is torpedoed by the Japanese submarine *I-26*. U.S. destroyers and fast transports land reinforcements on Guadalcanal. The Japanese decide to abandon their landing at Milne Bay.

1942/SEPTEMBER 1—Japanese "Tokyo Express" destroyers en route to resupply Guadalcanal are slightly damaged by U.S. B-17s. The U.S. 40th Infantry Division begins landing at Hawaii. U.S. fast transports run supplies into Guadalcanal.

1942/SEPTEMBER 2—Marines on Guadalcanal consolidate beach-front defenses (the USMC 3rd Defense Battalion in position).

1942/SEPTEMBER 3—Japanese "Tokyo Express" destroyers continue to encounter resistance from U.S. aircraft as increased efforts are made to strengthen Japanese ground forces on the island. U.S. Marines are also forced to continue reliance on fast transports (older destroyers converted to carry cargo) for supply from Allied bases to the south.

1942/SEPTEMBER 4—The "Tokyo Express" lands the last elements of the Kawaguchi Detachment on Guadalcanal. Off Lunga Point, Japanese destroyers sink two U.S. destroyer transports. Japanese aircraft also threaten U.S. daytime supply efforts.

1942/SEPTEMBER 5—Japanese troops withdraw by sea from Milne Bay, in eastern New Guinea.

1942/SEPTEMBER 6—On New Guinea, Japanese troops occupy Efogi on the Kokoda trail, about 50 miles north of Port Moresby.

1942/SEPTEMBER 7—U.S. transports land supplies on Guadalcanal.

1942/SEPTEMBER 8—On Guadalcanal some 700 U.S. Marines effect a landing at Tasimboko, in the rear of the Kawaguchi Detachment, disrupting Japanese preparations for an offensive, and then withdraw. Japanese air raids on Guadalcanal. That night a Japanese destroyer squadron shells Tulagi.

1942/SEPTEMBER 9—Major elements of the Combined Fleet (Second and Third Fleets) sortie from Truk to cover reinforcements to Guadalcanal from Rabaul and support an offensive planned for September 12.

1942/SEPTEMBER 10—British troops effect a landing on the west coast of Vichy-French-controlled Madagascar. On Guadalcanal, the Kawaguchi Detachment prepares for an offensive.

1942/SEPTEMBER 11—Having failed to secure a lodgment at Milne Bay, the Japanese also withdraw from the nearby Trobriand Islands.

1942/SEPTEMBER 12—An Australian ship steams from Darwin to reinforce Allied troops still holding out on Timor, in the East Indies. Battle of Bloody Ridge: The Japanese Kawaguchi Detachment attacks the southeastern face of the Guadalcanal beachhead with heavy losses.

1942/SEPTEMBER 13—Battle of Bloody Ridge on Guadalcanal: After the last efforts of the Kawaguchi Detachment attack are beaten off, Marine Raiders and paratroopers attempt to probe the Japanese positions but are driven back.

1942/SEPTEMBER 14—On Guadalcanal the Japanese retire from Bloody Ridge in great disorder. The *Wasp* and *Hornet* task forces join south of the Solomons in order to support a convoy reinforcing Guadalcanal.

1942/SEPTEMBER 15—The Carrier *Wasp*, battleship *North Carolina*, and destroyer *O'Brien* are torpedoed south of the Solomons ("Torpedo Alley"), the carrier sinking. U.S. reinforcements reach Guadalcanal.

1942/SEPTEMBER 16—The 3rd Marine Division is activated at San Diego. A convoy with the 7th Marine Regiment arrives south of Guadalcanal.

1942/SEPTEMBER 17—An Australian ship lands reinforcements on Timor. On New Guinea, Japanese troops are halted at Ioribaiwa, 32 miles north of Port Moresby, by the Australian 7th Division.

1942/SEPTEMBER 18—The U.S. 7th Marine Regiment is landed on Guadalcanal, with extensive supplies. British troops land at Tamatave, on the east coast of Madagascar.

1942/SEPTEMBER 19—Before dawn, Japanese destroyers patrol the waters between Guadalcanal and Tulagi. Marines on Guadalcanal have full rations restored because of their improved supply situation.

1942/SEPTEMBER 20—The Combined Fleet is ordered back to Truk. Japanese intelligence estimates that there are only 7,500 U.S. troops on Guadalcanal, when the actual figure is over 19,000.

1942/SEPTEMBER 21—Marines on Guadalcanal prepare an offensive, to disrupt Japanese concentrations west of the beachhead.

1942/SEPTEMBER 22—Confronted by advancing British and Free French forces, Vichy French troops on Mada-

gascar abandon the capital, Tananarive, and withdraw southward.

1942/SEPTEMBER 23—The Combined Fleet arrives at Truk. British troops occupy Tananarive, Madagascar. On Guadalcanal a battalion of the 7th Marines (commanded by Lieutenant Colonel Lewis "Chesty" Puller) infiltrates through the Japanese lines and advances on Mount Austen, deep in the interior.

1942/SEPTEMBER 24—On Guadalcanal, having passed through the Japanese lines stealthily, a battalion of the 7th Marines engages and scatters Japanese troops concentrated at the foot of Mount Austen.

1942/SEPTEMBER 25—On Guadalcanal a battalion of the 5th Marines reinforces that of the 7th Marines at Mount Austen. Attempting to run supplies to Dutch and Australian guerrillas, the Australian destroyer *Voyager* goes aground off Timor; attacked by Japanese aircraft before she can be towed off, she is scuttled.

1942/SEPTEMBER 26—On Guadalcanal, Marines of the 5th and 7th regiments advance from Mount Austen to the mouth of the Mataniko River, where they are reinforced by a Marine raider battalion. Stealthily entering Singapore Harbor in three canoes, British raiders manage to sink or damage about 40,000 tons of shipping.

1942/SEPTEMBER 27—The U.S. 32nd Infantry Division begins moving to Port Moresby from Australia, some elements going by air. On Guadalcanal, frustrated in an attempt to attack across the Mataniko River, one attacking Marine battalion is sealifted to Point Cruz, where it is hoped it will enable the other two battalions to break across the Mataniko, but the Japanese counterattack in a double envelopment, pocketing the battalion, which nevertheless manages to cut its way back to the coast. Japanese aircraft bomb Guadalcanal.

1942/SEPTEMBER 28—The Marines

abandon their positions on the Mataniko River, on Guadalcanal.

1942/SEPTEMBER 29—South African troops land at Tuléar, in southwestern Madagascar.

1942/SEPTEMBER 30—Marines on Guadalcanal expand their defensive perimeter.

1942/OCTOBER 1—The U.S. 43rd Infantry Division begins sailing from San Francisco for New Zealand and Espíritu Santo. The Italian blockade runner *Orseolo* departs Bordeaux for Kobe.

1942/OCTOBER 2—U.S. air raid on Rabaul damages the cruiser *Yubari* and other shipping. U.S. troops occupy Funafuti in the Ellice Islands, southeast of the Japanese-held Gilberts.

1942/OCTOBER 3—In the Aleutian Islands off Alaska, U.S. troops occupy the Andreanof Islands.

1942/OCTOBER 4—Marines on Guadalcanal continue to expand their defensive positions.

1942/OCTOBER 5—U.S. Navy and Marine aircraft raid Japanese shipping in the Shortland Islands.

1942/OCTOBER 6—On Guadalcanal, Marines prepare a renewed attack on the Mataniko River line.

1942/OCTOBER 7—On Guadalcanal, the 5th Marines advance westward along the coast from the beachhead to the Mataniko River against some resistance from the Japanese 4th Infantry Regiment, while the 2nd and 7th Marines advance across country farther inland, meeting no resistance.

1942/OCTOBER 8—On Guadalcanal, heavy rains prevent any offensive operations, but while the 5th Marines feint preparations for a major assault and mop up some Japanese holdouts east of the Mataniko River, the 2nd and 7th Marines quietly bivouack in the interior, further scouting for Japanese positions.

1942/OCTOBER 9—Japanese destroyers land elements of the 2nd Division on Guadalcanal. As the 5th Marines

hold Japanese attention on the Mataniko River, the 2nd and 7th Marines advance westward, and then northward, trapping the Japanese 4th Infantry and inflicting heavy casualties before falling back eastward across the Mataniko in the afternoon.

1942/OCTOBER 10—On Guadalcanal, the Marines who conducted the Mataniko operation rest and reequip, as intelligence concludes a Japanese offensive is in preparation.

1942/OCTOBER 11—Battle of Cape Esperance: U.S. cruisers and destroyers ambush the "Tokyo Express" off Guadalcanal, sinking a heavy cruiser and destroyer, while losing one destroyer. This is the first surface action in which U.S. ships defeat their Japanese counterparts.

1942/OCTOBER 12—U.S. aircraft sink two Japanese destroyers, one near Savo Island and the other nearly 90 miles northwest of it. A Japanese submarine begins operations in the Gulf of Oman, threatening Allied oil being shipped from the Persian Gulf.

1942/OCTOBER 13—U.S. destroyers shell Japanese positions on Guadalcanal. Japanese battleships and escorts shell Marine positions on Guadalcanal. The U.S. 164th Infantry Regiment (Americal Division) lands on Guadalcanal, raising the garrison to over 23,000.

1942/OCTOBER 14—Japanese cruisers shell Marine positions on Guadalcanal, while covering the landing of reinforcements.

1942/OCTOBER 15—Before dawn, four Japanese transports have to be beached on Guadalcanal under U.S. air attack. That night Japanese cruisers again shell Henderson Field. The U.S. destroyer *Meredith* is sunk by *Zuikaku* aircraft off San Cristóbal.

1942/OCTOBER 16—The USAAF sinks a Japanese destroyer near Kiska, off Alaska. *Enterprise* and escorts sortie from Pearl Harbor for the South Pacific. The U.S. destroyer *O'Brien*, damaged by a torpedo on September 15, founders off Samoa, en route to Pearl Harbor. Japanese submarines, ignoring plentiful Allied supply ships, concentrate on attacking warships (as is their custom) to increasing effect. The area south of Guadalcanal is christened "Torpedo Alley" because of all the Japanese subs lurking there.

1942/OCTOBER 17—Vice Admiral Robert L. Ghormley and other commanders in the South Pacific appear to have lost confidence in the probability of success on Guadalcanal. This is more a result of Ghormley's pessimism than a realistic appraisal of the situation. The Japanese forces in the area are in bad shape, although this is not readily obvious to the Americans just yet.

1942/OCTOBER 18—William F. Halsey replaces Ghormley as Allied commander in the South Pacific. A U.S. submarine damages a Japanese "Tokyo Express" light cruiser off Guadalcanal.

1942/OCTOBER 19—U.S. aircraft damage a Japanese destroyer off Guadalcanal.

1942/OCTOBER 20—British East African troops overcome resistance from Vichy French troops and continue their conquest of Madagascar in the Indian Ocean.

1942/OCTOBER 21—U.S. destroyers land supplies on Guadalcanal.

1942/OCTOBER 22—Australian troops land on Goodenough Island to find the Japanese have evacuated.

1942/OCTOBER 23—The Battle of Edson's Ridge begins. A fierce Japanese assault against the southern face of the Guadalcanal beachhead is stopped. A Japanese ground attack on the Marines' Mataniko line is defeated. The U.S. 43rd Infantry Division begins arriving in New Zealand.

1942/OCTOBER 24—Battle of the Santa Cruz Islands preparations: *Enter-* *prise* and *Hornet* rendezvous northeast of Espíritu Santo to block a move by Japanese carrier force known to be in the area. The Battle of Edson's Ridge ends. A fierce Japanese assault against the southern face of the Guadalcanal beachhead is thrown back for good.

1942/OCTOBER 25—Battle of Lunga Point at Guadalcanal: Japanese cruisers and destroyers engaged in daylight bombardment of Henderson Field chase two U.S. destroyers and sink two small U.S. harbor craft, before being attacked by Marine and USAAF aircraft, suffering one destroyer lost and damage to other vessels. Battle of the Santa Cruz Islands: U.S. and Japanese carriers are searching for each other northeast of the Solomons. A Japanese attempt to flank the Marine Mataniko line is defeated.

1942/OCTOBER 26—Battle of the Santa Cruz Islands. *Hornet* is put out of action, eventually to be sunk by Japanese destroyers, while Japanese carriers are heavily damaged. Thus the Japanese attempt to use carrier aviation to support efforts on Guadalcanal fails. Elements of the U.S. 43rd Infantry Division arrive at Espíritu Santo. On Guadalcanal, the Marines begin preparing for a new offensive westward toward Kokumbona.

1942/OCTOBER 27—On Guadalcanal, Marine engineers begin fabricating bridging materials for the proposed offensive to Kokumbona.

1942/OCTOBER 28—The Japanese "Tokyo Express" uses its destroyer transports to land troops on Guadalcanal from Kokumbona to Cape Esperance.

1942/OCTOBER 29—The ALCAN (Alaska-Canadian Military) Highway is opened, the only motor road to Alaska. Now most supply for Alaska can go by road, thus freeing shipping for service in the western Pacific.

1942/OCTOBER 30—As the Marines complete preparations for an offensive toward Kokumbona, assault units begin moving up to the Mataniko River. Meanwhile, heavy losses have caused the Japanese to withdraw.

1942/OCTOBER 31—America announces that 800,000 U.S. troops are now serving overseas.

1942/NOVEMBER 1—On Guadalcanal, supported by heavy naval, air, and artillery bombardments, the Marines attack across the Mataniko River. Now out of Marine boot camp, John Lindemann is given some leave and then sent to Camp Lejeune and assigned to the 3rd Marine Division (23rd Marine Regiment) to continue his training.

1942/NOVEMBER 2—On Guadalcanal, the Marine Kokumbona offensive gains ground, isolating Japanese troops on Point Cruz and pressing on westward. During the night, the "Tokyo Express" lands reinforcements at Tetere, about 15 miles east of the main beachhead.

1942/NOVEMBER 3—On Guadalcanal, the Marines secure Point Cruz, west of Henderson Field, as other Marines and Army infantrymen press westward. Japanese troops newly landed at Tetere attempt to advance westward, but collide with a Marine battalion (sent there the previous day) near Koli Point, which falls back slowly before their advance, supported by cruiser and destroyer gunfire.

1942/NOVEMBER 4—On Guadalcanal, reinforcements reach the battalion holding Koli Point, while the Kokumbona offensive is suspended. The USAAF bombs Kiska in the Aleutians.

1942/NOVEMBER 5—Marines and Army troops attack the Japanese concentration east of Koli Point on Guadalcanal, flanking them from the south. The Japanese land reinforcements on Guadalcanal. Vichy French troops on Madagascar surrender to the British at Fort-Dauphin in southeastern Madagascar.

1942/NOVEMBER 6—On Guadalcanal, having driven the Japanese back from Koli Point, Marines and Army troops press them eastward.

1942/NOVEMBER 7—While the Japanese land reinforcements on Guadalcanal, Marines and Army troops press them back from Koli Point.

1942/NOVEMBER 8—The Japanese land reinforcements on Guadalcanal, but east of Koli Point the Marines and Army troops make an amphibious end run around them, pocketing them at the mouth of the Gavaga Creek. A large U.S. reinforcement convoy sails from Nouméa for Guadalcanal, supported by a heavy escort (*Enterprise,* two battleships, eight cruisers, twenty-three destroyers). Operation Torch begins when U.S. and British forces begin landing in northwestern Africa. Because of this operation, the Pacific has been somewhat starved of amphibious shipping and, to a lesser extent, warships.

1942/NOVEMBER 9—Despite desperate resistance, Marines and Army troops begin to eliminate the Japanese concentration at the Gavaga Creek on Guadalcanal, in a combined land and sea attack. The Japanese Second Fleet sorties from Truk to support a planned major naval offensive at Guadalcanal on November 12 and 13.

1942/NOVEMBER 10—On Guadalcanal, Marine and Army troops whittle down the Gavaga pocket as the Japanese try desperately to break out. The Japanese land reinforcements on Guadalcanal.

1942/NOVEMBER 11—As the U.S. lands reinforcements on Guadalcanal, Marines and Army troops eliminate the Gavaga pocket, while other Marines and Army infantrymen resume the Kokumbona offensive, pressing the Japanese slowly westward. Japanese aircraft raid Henderson Field. West of Australia, the Royal Indian Navy minesweeper *Bengal,* escorting a tanker, beats off an attack by two Japanese auxiliary cruisers, sinking one.

1942/NOVEMBER 12—As U.S. reinforcements land on Guadalcanal, Major General Vandegrift calls off the Kokumbona offensive, having gotten word that a major Japanese naval force is due off Guadalcanal that night. Japanese aircraft raid Henderson field. The Naval Battle of Guadalcanal begins. Shortly before midnight, Japanese cruisers and destroyers inflict a severe defeat on the U.S. Navy, which loses one cruiser and four destroyers sunk, three cruisers and two destroyers damaged, at a cost to the Japanese of one destroyer sunk, plus severe damage to the battleship *Hiei* and several destroyers.

1942/NOVEMBER 13—The Naval Battle of Guadalcanal continues. U.S. aircraft further damage the Japanese battleship *Hiei*, which has to be scuttled, while a U.S. cruiser sinks a disabled Japanese destroyer. A Japanese submarine sinks the antiaircraft cruiser *Juneau*; the five Sullivan brothers perish.

1942/NOVEMBER 14—The Naval Battle of Guadalcanal continues. In "The Slot," *Enterprise* and Marine aircraft from Henderson Field batter Japanese ships, sinking a cruiser and two transports, and damaging several others. Japanese transports beach on Guadalcanal in order to land reinforcements. During the night, large Japanese forces (one battleship, two heavy cruisers, two light cruisers, and eight destroyers) try to bombard Henderson Field, to be ambushed around midnight by the U.S. battleships *Washington* and *South Dakota* with four destroyers. *South Dakota* is badly damaged, but the Japanese lose a destroyer and the battleship *Kirishima* is reduced to a burning wreck. The first time U.S. battleships are in a surface action with enemy warships since the Spanish-American War (1898).

1942/NOVEMBER 15—Unable to provide air cover for a tow, the Japanese scuttle *Kirishima* off Guadalcanal.

1942/NOVEMBER 16—Marines and Army troops on Guadalcanal begin to reorganize for a new offensive.

1942/NOVEMBER 17—Marines and Army troops on Guadalcanal prepare for a new offensive, reconnaissance patrols penetrating west of their position.

1942/NOVEMBER 18—U.S. and Australian troops reach the heavily fortified Japanese positions at Buna and Gona, in northeastern New Guinea. On Guadalcanal, an Army infantry battalion advances west of the Mataniko River; although resistance is slight, the troops make slow progress, being green and unacclimated.

1942/NOVEMBER 19—Soviets launch a major counteroffensive at Stalingrad, heralding a major turning point of the war in Russia. This is a blow to Japanese morale, as they expected eventual assistance from the Germans once the Nazis had conquered southern Russia and driven on into the Persian Gulf area. In the wake of the Stalingrad battle, the Germans would not be advancing anywhere anymore. On Guadalcanal, the drive westward is strengthened with seasoned troops, but resistance remains slight. During the night Japanese troops move up.

1942/NOVEMBER 20—On Guadalcanal, the Japanese launch a surprise attack at the two battalions west of the Mataniko River, but U.S. troops hold with air and artillery support, as reinforcement begin moving toward them.

1942/NOVEMBER 21—On Guadalcanal, troops resume the offensive westward with difficulty against well-prepared Japanese positions.

1942/NOVEMBER 22—On Guadalcanal, a renewed attack westward achieves small gains, and the 8th Marines are ordered up.

1942/NOVEMBER 23—On Guadalcanal, after a thirty-minute preliminary bombardment the 8th Marines attack but, after a day of heavy fighting, make slight gains. Concluding that further attacks would be equally profitless, General Vandegrift cancels the offensive.

1942/NOVEMBER 24—U.S. aircraft sink a Japanese destroyer attempting to reinforce Guadalcanal. On Guadalcanal, Marines and Army troops west of the Mataniko dig in to consolidate their positions.

1942/NOVEMBER 25—The fighting on New Guinea develops into a stalemate, with neither side able to keep an offensive going in the pestilential jungles.

1942/NOVEMBER 26—In the Indian Ocean, the cruisers HNMS *Jacob van Heemskerk* and HMAS *Adelaide* intercept a German blockade runner bound for France from the Netherlands East Indies.

1942/NOVEMBER 27—On Guadalcanal, both sides regroup and reorganize.

1942/NOVEMBER 28—The Teheran Conference begins, as President Roosevelt, Prime Minister Churchill, and Secretary Stalin and their staffs discuss policy and strategy for three days. The Allies have much to celebrate. Their forces are on the offensive in Russia (Stalingrad), North Africa (El Alamein and Algeria), and in the Pacific (Guadalcanal). After years of victories, the Axis is reeling.

1942/NOVEMBER 29—Japanese troop strength on Guadalcanal peaks in November, at 30,000 troops (about equal to U.S. strength), then rapidly declines in the next two months due to lack of food and medicine. U.S. strength rises to 40,000 well-supplied troops in December, while Japanese strength plummets toward 20,000.

1942/NOVEMBER 30—Battle of Tassafaronga: In a night action, eight Japanese destroyers attempting to reinforce Guadalcanal get the better of five U.S. cruisers and six destroyers trying to stop them, sinking one heavy cruiser and

damaging three others while losing one destroyer, but are forced to break off their mission. The German merchant cruiser *Thor* is destroyed in a fire while docked at Yokohama. At Teheran, the "Big Three" reach tentative agreements on strategy.

1942/DECEMBER 1—Lieutenant General Robert L. Eichelberger is put in command of the Buna-Gona operation in New Guinea. Eichelberger is to become one of the most successful ground force commanders in the Pacific and his first success will be in turning around the stalemated situation in New Guinea. On Guadalcanal, staff officers from the U.S. American Division assume control of supply functions from Marine Corps personnel.

1942/DECEMBER 2—On Guadalcanal, the 1st Marine Division prepares to be relieved, as the American Division begins to take over defensive positions. The Italian blockade runner *Orseolo* arrives at Kobe from Bordeaux.

1942/DECEMBER 3—Japanese destroyers land reinforcements on Guadalcanal, where the 1st Marine Division is preparing to be withdrawn. U.S. aerial reconnaissance discovers that the Japanese are building an airstrip on Munda, in the central Solomons.

1942/DECEMBER 4—On Guadalcanal, personnel of the American Division take increasing responsibility from those of the 1st Marine Division. The Marines are very debilitated from four months of combat operations in the disease-ridden jungles of Guadalcanal and need rehabilitation before their next operation.

1942/DECEMBER 5—On Guadalcanal, the Japanese consolidate new defensive positions in the interior, at Mount Austen.

1942/DECEMBER 6—The Japanese continue to build new defensive positions in the interior of Guadalcanal, at Mount Austen. U.S. aircraft bomb

Munda to slow Japanese work on a new air base.

1942/DECEMBER 7—Japanese destroyers attempting to land reinforcements on Guadalcanal are beaten off by a combination of aircraft and PT boats (including *PT-109*, skippered by future U.S. president John F. Kennedy).

1942/DECEMBER 8—On Guadalcanal, troops of the Americal Division land and officers of the Americal Division assume full control of all staff duties. U.S. aircraft turn back a Japanese attempt to land more troops on New Guinea.

1942/DECEMBER 9—Australian troops capture Gona, in northeastern New Guinea. On Guadalcanal, Major General Alexander A. Vandegrift and the 1st Marine Division are officially relieved and Army Major General Alexander Patch assumes command. The 5th Marines board transports and sail away that afternoon. Guadalcanal was the first major Marine operation of the Pacific war and one of the longest, lasting four months. The British prepare an offensive from India into Arakan, the westernmost coastal province of Burma.

1942/DECEMBER 10—Australian troops land at Oro Bay, New Guinea, near Buna. U.S. aircraft bomb Munda. The British offensive in Arakan gets under way, moving between the sea and the mountains.

1942/DECEMBER 11—Japanese destroyers land reinforcements on Guadalcanal, but lose one of their number to PT boat attacks. U.S. aircraft bomb Munda. The British (actually the 14th Indian Division) advance slowly in the Arakan region of Burma.

1942/DECEMBER 12—The Japanese destroyer *Teruzuki* is sunk by U.S. *PT-45* northeast of Kolombangara. On Guadalcanal, Japanese infiltrators destroy a P-39 and a fuel truck.

1942/DECEMBER 13—Australian troops prepare to make an "end run" around Buna, in New Guinea. U.S. aircraft bomb Munda. The British advance cautiously in the Arakan region of Burma.

1942/DECEMBER 14—Australian reinforcements land at Oro Bay, near Buna. Japanese destroyers reinforce Buna. On Guadalcanal, the U.S. Americal Division prepares an offensive, reconnoitering Mount Austen. The British advance cautiously in Arakan; rather than resist, weaker Japanese forces begin to retire.

1942/DECEMBER 15—On Guadalcanal, U.S. reconnaissance patrols scout Mount Austen. U.S. aircraft bomb Munda. The British advance cautiously in the Arakan region of Burma, even though the Japanese are beginning to fall back.

1942/DECEMBER 16—The British offensive on the Arakan coast takes Maungdaw, only to discover that it has been abandoned by the Japanese.

1942/DECEMBER 17—The U.S. Americal Division attacks toward Mount Austen on Guadalcanal. Elements of the U.S. 25th Division land on Guadalcanal. U.S. aircraft bomb Munda.

1942/DECEMBER 18—The Japanese cruiser *Tenryu* is sunk by the U.S. submarine *Albacore* near the Bismarck Archipelago. On Guadalcanal, the U.S. Americal Division presses its advance on Mount Austen; resistance is slight.

1942/DECEMBER 19—The malaria rate among U.S. troops on Guadalcanal reaches a statistical rate of 972 cases in every 1,000 men per year. As bad as this is for U.S. troops, it is even worse for the Japanese, who are losing most of their troop strength on the island to disease and malnutrition. The British advance in Arakan; the outnumbered Japanese begin to develop a major defensive position in front of Akyab, more than 100 miles to their rear, giving themselves time to bring up reinforcements.

1942/DECEMBER 20—The new U.S. policy of using submarines to mine the waters off major Japanese ports finds its first victim. An 8,000-ton Japanese transport goes down off Tokyo.

1942/DECEMBER 21—On Guadalcanal, the Americal Division's Mount Austen offensive falters. U.S. aircraft bomb Munda.

1942/DECEMBER 22—Australian and American troops overcome the last Japanese resistance at Buna, in northeastern New Guinea. On Guadalcanal, the Americal Division's Mount Austen offensive continues to run into problems.

1942/DECEMBER 23—The U.S. 41st Infantry Division ships out from Australia for New Guinea. On Guadalcanal, the Americal Division finally makes significant gains against Mount Austen.

1942/DECEMBER 24—On Guadalcanal, the Americal Division encounters the main Japanese defenses, the "Gifu," in the Mount Austen area.

1942/DECEMBER 25—U.S. aircraft continue their incessant bombing of Munda, slowing Japanese efforts to build a base there. On Guadalcanal, the Americal Division undertakes an unsuccessful assault on the Gifu.

1942/DECEMBER 26—Japanese 20th Division movement from Korea to New Guinea is under way. The British advance cautiously in Arakan; Japanese preparations at Akyab continue.

1942/DECEMBER 27—Lead elements of the U.S. 27th Infantry Division land at Port Moresby, New Guinea. On Guadalcanal, the Americal Division suspends its offensive against Mount Austen and reconnoiters.

1942/DECEMBER 28—Despite constant U.S. bombing, the Japanese begin using their new airstrip on Munda, in the central Solomons. On Guadalcanal, the Americal Division probes the Japanese fortifications in the Mount Austen area.

1942/DECEMBER 29—The U.S. destroyer-minesweeper *Wasmuth* sinks off the Aleutians, after a gale causes two of her depth charges to detonate, causing extensive damage.

1942/DECEMBER 30—On Guadalcanal, the Americal Division rotates fresh units into the line and prepares for a renewed attack on Mount Austen.

1942/DECEMBER 31—Prime Minister Tojo decides to abandon Guadalcanal. On Guadalcanal, the Americal Division rotates fresh units into the line and prepares for a renewed attack on Mount Austen. Japanese troops are driven from defensive positions at Tassafaronga Point, Guadalcanal. The U.S. aircraft carrier *Essex* is commissioned.

1943/JANUARY 1—Japanese destroyers run supplies into Guadalcanal, despite attempts by U.S. aircraft and PT boats to interfere. Additional elements of the U.S. 25th Infantry Division land on Guadalcanal, where the Americal Division resumes its assault on Mount Austen.

1943/JANUARY 2—The U.S. I Corps secures the Buna area, on the northwestern coast of New Guinea. U.S. forces on Guadalcanal (one Marine, two Army divisions) reorganized as XIV Corps. The British continue their advance in the Arakan region of Burma; Japanese resistance stiffens.

1943/JANUARY 3—U.S. Americal Division pockets Japanese forces defending Mount Austen on Guadalcanal.

1943/JANUARY 4—Imperial General Headquarters issues orders for the evacuation of Guadalcanal. Elements of the 2nd Marine Division and last echelon of the U.S. 25th Infantry Division land on Guadalcanal. A U.S.-Australian cruiser-destroyer force shells Munda, suffering slight damage in a Japanese air attack. In this action, proximity-fuzed antiaircraft ammunition is used for the first time in the Pacific, by USS *Helena*.

1943/JANUARY 5—On Guadalcanal, Army engineers complete a motor bridge across the Mataniko River, greatly easing supply problems; meanwhile Japanese troops in the Gifu continue to resist. In Arakan a stalemate begins to develop, as the Japanese hold the British before Akyab.

1943/JANUARY 6—On Guadalcanal, General Patch lays plans for a major offensive that will drive the Japanese from the island. In the Arakan region of Burma, the British become bogged down before Akyab.

1943/JANUARY 7—U.S. strength on Guadalcanal reaches 50,000 men, Marine, Army, and Navy; Japanese strength is less than 25,000. On Guadalcanal, small detachments of soldiers and Marines begin to be sealifted to strategic locations along the coast in the rear of the Japanese, to establish "block" positions should the enemy attempt to retreat. A stalemate develops in Arakan; the British will take heavy losses in several major attacks over the next weeks.

1943/JANUARY 8—British occupation forces turn control of Madagascar over to the Free French. On Guadalcanal, the U.S. 25th Infantry Division is ordered to make a major attack on the tenth. Stalemate in the Arakan region of Burma.

1943/JANUARY 9—An Australian brigade is airlifted to a jungle airstrip at Wau, near Salamaua in northeastern New Guinea, where it begins to build a major base.

1943/JANUARY 10—Japanese destroyers bringing supplies to Guadalcanal are ambushed by U.S. PT boats, which sink two of the Japanese ships with slight damage to themselves. U.S. forces on Guadalcanal begin a general offensive to eliminate Japanese forces. Henderson Field is now usable in all weather conditions because of an improved runway. The U.S. 25th Infantry Division attacks to clear the area southwest of the Mataniko River and envelop the Kokumbona position.

1943/JANUARY 11—On Guadalcanal, fierce resistance, the jungle, and a short-

age of drinkable water combine to limit the gains of the U.S. 25th Infantry Division's attack, but the 35th Infantry Regiment captures the "Sea Horse" area and begins to encircle the Gifu area in the island's interior.

1943/JANUARY 12—Losing a destroyer to the hazards of the sea, U.S. troops land on unoccupied Amchitka in the Aleutians and commence building an airstrip. On Guadalcanal, the U.S. 25th Division makes limited gains against the Japanese.

1943/JANUARY 13—The U.S. submarine Guardfish torpedoes a Japanese patrol vessel off New Ireland. On Guadalcanal, the U.S. 25th Division, in a daring attack, breaks Japanese resistance and occupies the "Galloping Horse" area of the island, clearing the entire western flank of the American beachhead, while the 2nd Marine Division attacks westward along the coast.

1943/JANUARY 14—Japanese destroyers bringing reinforcements (about 600 men) and supplies to Guadalcanal are attacked by U.S. aircraft and PT boats with little effect. On Guadalcanal, the 2nd Marine Division makes gains west of the beachhead. The Casablanca Conference is held. President Roosevelt and Prime Minister Churchill begin ten days of meetings; enunciate the "unconditional surrender" policy, and outline future Allied global strategy.

1943/JANUARY 15—The Japanese superbattleship Musashi arrives at Truk. On Guadalcanal, despite the employment of tanks and flamethrowers, the 2nd Marine Division is held to limited gains by Japanese defenders west of the Mataniko.

1943/JANUARY 16—On Guadalcanal, the 2nd Marine Division cautiously clears Japanese defenders out of "the Ravine," a tangled gully blocking their advance.

1943/JANUARY 17—On Guadalcanal, the 2nd Marine Division secures the Ravine, but farther east Japanese troops in the Gifu continue to resist the 25th Infantry Division.

1943/JANUARY 18—A U.S. cruiser-destroyer force bombards Japanese-held Attu, in the Aleutians. On Guadalcanal, having gained only 1,500 yards in five days of fighting, the 2nd Marine Division halts its offensive against the last Japanese stronghold in the interior. In New Guinea, Sanananda, on the northeast coast, falls to Allied troops.

1943/JANUARY 19—U.S. destroyers shell Japanese positions on Guadalcanal. On Guadalcanal, as front-line elements are rotated with reserve troops, General Patch prepares for a new assault on the Japanese, as the 25th Infantry Division pockets the Gifu.

1943/JANUARY 20—On Guadalcanal, the U.S. 25th Infantry Division tightens its hold on the Gifu. Stalemate in the Arakan region of Burma as the British offensive grinds to a halt.

1943/JANUARY 21—On Guadalcanal, the U.S. 25th Infantry Division tightens its hold on the Gifu, as Japanese troops try to escape from the position during the night.

1943/JANUARY 22—On Guadalcanal, the U.S. 25th Infantry Division tightens its hold on the Gifu, despite a Japanese "banzai" attack after nightfall, while other elements of XIV Corps undertake a major offensive westward along the coast, making surprising gains. The Papuan campaign ends in New Guinea. Some 7,000 of 16,000 Japanese troops sent in were killed. Total U.S. and Australian casualties were 8,500, with less than 2,000 dead from all causes.

1943/JANUARY 23—U.S. cruisers and destroyers, supported by aircraft from *Saratoga*, bombard Japanese positions on Guadalcanal, in support of the XIV Corps offensive, which overruns Kokumbona. U.S. troops eliminate the Gifu pocket, on Mount Austen on Guadalcanal. The Casablanca Conference of Allied leaders agrees on a strong offensive in Burma and "unconditional surrender" for the Axis.

1943/JANUARY 24—On Guadalcanal, the U.S. XIV Corps advances from the Kokumbona position.

1943/JANUARY 25—On Guadalcanal, the U.S. XIV Corps reaches the Poha River. The Italian blockade runner *Orseolo* departs Kobe for Bordeaux.

1943/JANUARY 26—On Guadalcanal, Marines and soldiers of the U.S. XIV Corps consolidate their positions along the Poha River.

1943/JANUARY 27—On Guadalcanal, a combined Army-Marine provisional division attacks westward along the coast.

1943/JANUARY 28—On Guadalcanal, the U.S. combined Army-Marine division reaches the Nueha River, having advanced about 2 miles.

1943/JANUARY 29—The Japanese submarine *I-1* is sunk off Cape Esperance by two New Zealand corvettes, which salvage important cryptographic equipment. American experts have been cracking Japanese codes since before the war began, but the capture of code machines with current settings, as well as code books, speeds up the process.

1943/JANUARY 30—The U.S. lands reinforcements and supplies on Guadalcanal. In the Air Battle of the Rennell Islands, Japanese aircraft sink the heavy cruiser *Chicago*.

1943/JANUARY 31—On Guadalcanal, the combined Army-Marine division crosses the Bonegi River, upstream from Cape Tassafaronga, to flank the Japanese positions there. The bulk of the Japanese 20th Division is concentrated at Wewak, New Guinea.

1943/FEBRUARY 1—A U.S. Marine regiment lands on the west coast of Guadalcanal, in an attempt to outflank the defending Japanese. Twenty Japanese destroyers sortie from Rabaul to evacuate remaining troops on Guadalcanal, and are virtually uninjured in a running fight with U.S. aircraft and PT boats, but lose one of their number to a mine, while sinking three PT boats.

1943/FEBRUARY 2—Nineteen Japanese destroyers evacuate thousands of Japanese troops from Guadalcanal, where the U.S. combined Army-Marine division captures Cape Tassafaronga. In the Netherlands East Indies, the last Australian guerrillas on Timor (operating there since December 8, 1941) are withdrawn by sea.

1943/FEBRUARY 3—The battleship *Massachusetts* begins operating in the Pacific. On Guadalcanal, the U.S. combined Army-Marine division secures the Tassafaronga area. Heavy skirmishing between Allied and Japanese troops along the Indo-Burmese frontier.

1943/FEBRUARY 4—The U.S. lands reinforcements and supplies on Guadalcanal. The Japanese light cruiser *Isuzu* and twenty-two destroyers sortie from Rabaul to evacuate troops from Guadalcanal, suffering serious damage from U.S. aircraft. Heavily escorted, the battle-hardened Australian 9th Division sails home from Suez.

1943/FEBRUARY 5—*Isuzu* and escorts evacuate thousands of Japanese troops from Guadalcanal, where the U.S. combined Army-Marine division continues to advance along the northern coast.

1943/FEBRUARY 6—On Guadalcanal, the U.S. combined Army-Marine division reaches the Umasani River, having advanced about 5 miles in eleven days.

1943/FEBRUARY 7—Eighteen Japanese destroyers sortie from Rabaul to evacuate troops from Guadalcanal, suffering some damage from U.S. air attacks. On Guadalcanal, U.S. troops advance on both the northern and the northwestern coasts. Admiral Halsey authorizes Operation Cleanslate, the occupation of the Russell Islands.

1943/FEBRUARY 8—Eighteen Japanese destroyers evacuate the last of nearly 12,000 Japanese troops from Guadalcanal. On Guadalcanal, U.S. troops advance on both the northern and the northwestern coasts.

1943/FEBRUARY 9—No organized Japanese forces remain on Guadalcanal, as U.S. troops advancing along the northwestern and northern coasts make contact at Cape Esperance. U.S. Chief of Naval Operations Ernest J. King "invites" CINCPAC Chester W. Nimitz to consider the possibility of capturing the Gilbert Islands.

1943/FEBRUARY 10—The major ground fighting on Guadalcanal is now over, and has cost the U.S. 1,600 Army and Marine troops killed and 4,245 wounded, plus thousands of casualties from disease. Japanese Army losses were at least 14,800 killed, 9,000 dead of disease, and about 1,000 prisoners. Casualties in the naval battles off Guadalcanal and in the general area were far more numerous. But it was the land battle that decided the issue. Guadalcanal was a sobering experience for the Japanese, who had never been so soundly defeated on land before. Some Japanese leaders realized that Guadalcanal would be the pattern in the future.

1943/FEBRUARY 11—At Nouméa preparations for Operation Cleanslate, the occupation of the Russell Islands, proceed. On Guadalcanal, Marine and Army troops mop up Japanese stragglers. Heavy skirmishing between Allied and Japanese troops along the Indo-Burmese frontier.

1943/FEBRUARY 12—At Nouméa, a small naval task force is organized to support Operation Cleanslate: four destroyers, four destroyer-transports, five minesweepers, and twelve LSTs, plus some smaller vessels.

1943/FEBRUARY 13—The Japanese 41st Division arrives at Wewak, New Guinea, from China.

1943/FEBRUARY 14—At Nouméa, elements of the U.S. 43rd Infantry Division are embarked for Guadalcanal.

1943/FEBRUARY 15—Convoys for Operation Cleanslate approach Guadalcanal.

1943/FEBRUARY 16—Elements of the U.S. 43rd Infantry Division land at Koli Point, Guadalcanal, to prepare for the occupation of the Russell Islands.

1943/FEBRUARY 17—The second echelon of the U.S. 43rd Infantry Division arrives off Koli Point, Guadalcanal, but is delayed in landing by a Japanese air raid, which causes no damage. The New Zealand corvette *Moa* lands a reconnaissance team on Banika, the easternmost large island in the Russell group.

1943/FEBRUARY 18—U.S. cruisers and destroyers shell Japanese positions on Attu in the Aleutians. In Burma, the first "Chindit" raid gets under way, as Orde Wingate's British 77th Brigade enters Japanese-controlled territory from Assam. Over the next few weeks its several columns will spread out over central Burma inflicting great destruction on bridges, roads, isolated Japanese installations, and the like, before the survivors return to India. The second echelon of the U.S. 43rd Infantry Division lands at Koli Point, Guadalcanal. The New Zealand corvette *Moa* lands a reconnaissance team on Pavuvu, the largest of the Russell Islands, and concludes that the Japanese have evacuated the group. U.S. cruisers and destroyers shell Japanese positions on Attu.

1943/FEBRUARY 19—On Guadalcanal, the U.S. 43rd Infantry Division prepares to land on the Russell Islands, the operation having been turned into a large-scale drill. U.S. cruisers and destroyers shell Japanese positions on Attu.

1943/FEBRUARY 20—The U.S. submarine *Albacore* sinks the Japanese destroyer *Oshio* near the Admiralty Islands. The first RCT of the U.S. 43rd Infantry Division sails from Guadalcanal for the Russell Islands. Continued

stalemate in the Arakan region of Burma.

1943/FEBRUARY 21—The first RCT of the U.S. 43rd Infantry Division lands in the Russell Islands. The second RCT of the U.S. 43rd Infantry Division sails from Guadalcanal for the Russell Islands.

1943/FEBRUARY 22—The second RCT of the U.S. 43rd Infantry Division lands in the Russell Islands.

1943/FEBRUARY 23—U.S. troops in the Russell Islands consolidate their positions. On Guadalcanal, the Army and Marines are still coping with Japanese stragglers, most of whom refuse to surrender and fight on as snipers.

1943/FEBRUARY 24—U.S. troops in the Russell Islands begin construction of an airfield. Heavy skirmishing between Allied and Japanese troops along the Indo-Burmese frontier; the Japanese decide to withdraw to the Burmese side of the mountains because of their tenuous logistical situation.

1943/FEBRUARY 25—The U.S. Navy establishes a motor torpedo boat base in the Russell Islands.

1943/FEBRUARY 26—Stalemate in the Arakan region of Burma. U.S. construction projects in the Russell Islands include an airfield, three landing craft bases and repair facilities, and training grounds for combat divisions.

1943/FEBRUARY 27—The Australian 9th Division arrives at Sydney from the Middle East, after twenty-three days at sea.

1943/FEBRUARY 28—Escorted by cruisers and destroyers, eight Japanese transports (about 7,000 troops) sail from Rabaul bound for Lae, in eastern New Guinea. U.S. troops in the Russell Islands reach 9,000.

1943/MARCH 1—Aided by unusually hazy weather, a Japanese troop convoy bound from Rabaul to Lae is undetected by U.S. reconnaissance.

1943/MARCH 2—Battle of the Bismarck Sea: A Japanese convoy bound for Lae is attacked by USAAF aircraft, losing one transport.

1943/MARCH 3—Two Japanese destroyers are sunk northeast of New Guinea by U.S. and Australian aircraft. The Battle of the Bismarck Sea continues: Just off the coast of New Guinea, the Japanese convoy is attacked by over 350 U.S. and Australian aircraft, plus surface forces, with the loss of all transports and four destroyers, at a cost of 21 Allied aircraft.

1943/MARCH 4—In an official report to Army units throughout the South and Southwest Pacific, a senior Japanese staff officer criticizes American combat methods on Guadalcanal, concluding that the Americans have many admirable qualities ("they are quite brave"), but many faults as well ("infantry forces do not engage in night attacks"), and that leadership is poor ("officers of middle rank and below possess little tactical ability").

1943/MARCH 5—The Japanese 54th Division arrives at Java from Japan.

1943/MARCH 6—Much action in the Solomon Islands. U.S. destroyers shell Japanese positions on Munda. U.S. cruisers and destroyers ambush and sink two Japanese destroyers attempting to reinforce Vila in the same area. Japanese aircraft raid the Russell Islands. Stalemate in the Arakan region of Burma, but the Japanese begin preparing for an offensive.

1943/MARCH 7—U.S. and Japanese forces conduct regular naval and air patrols throughout the Solomons. The Japanese refuse a German request to join the war against Russia.

1943/MARCH 8—U.S. commanders assess the lessons of Guadalcanal; the Marines call for more firepower and special training. The Japanese advance across the Yangtze River in China.

1943/MARCH 9—British Chindit com-

mandos in Burma advance to the Irrawaddy River.

1943/MARCH 10—The Chinese resist the Japanese spring offensive in China.

1943/MARCH 11—The American Volunteer Group ("Flying Tigers") in China is redesignated the Fourteenth Air Force, under General Claire Chennault. Admiral Isoroku Yamamoto transfers his flag to the battleship *Musashi*, at Truk.

1943/MARCH 12—Stalemate in the Arakan region of Burma, as the Japanese offensive preparations are completed.

1943/MARCH 13—In the Arakan region of Burma, the Japanese 55th Division undertakes an attack against the British 14th Indian Division.

1943/MARCH 14—Heavy fighting in the Arakan region of Burma; Japanese forces begin an arduous crossing of "impassable" mountains, which will bring them into the British rear.

1943/MARCH 15—The U.S. Seventh Fleet is formed to conduct operations in the Solomons and Southwest Pacific, the Fifth to conduct operations in the Central Pacific.

1943/MARCH 16—More action in the Solomon Islands. U.S. destroyers shell Vila. U.S. troops in the Russell Islands reach 16,000.

1943/MARCH 17—In Arakan, flanked by Japanese troops who have crossed "impassable" mountains, British troops begin a retreat.

1943/MARCH 18—In Burma, the Chindits, having already cut several rail lines, raid across the Irrawaddy River. In Arakan, the Japanese press the retreating British.

1943/MARCH 19—The Chindits begin to withdraw from Burma, back to their bases in India.

1943/MARCH 20—The U.S. submarine *Pollack* sinks the Japanese merchant cruiser *Bangkok Maru* in the Marshall Islands. In Arakan, the retreat of the

14th Indian Division becomes disorderly.

1943/MARCH 21—The British begin rushing reinforcements to bolster their position in the Arakan region of Burma.

1943/MARCH 22—The Japanese are alarmed at their deteriorating position in the Aleutian Islands and decide to be more aggressive with their naval patrols off the Alaskan coast, and to clear the way for sending supplies to their garrison there.

1943/MARCH 23—The British retreat from the Arakan region of Burma shows signs of turning into a rout, with the Japanese turning or infiltrating every position the British attempt to hold and unhinging it.

1943/MARCH 24—A Japanese cruiser-destroyer force sorties from Paramushiro for the Aleutians.

1943/MARCH 25—The Japanese cruiser-destroyer squadron from Paramushiro nears the Komandorski Islands on a mission to Kiska.

1943/MARCH 26—Battle of the Komandorski Islands, the last daylight naval shoot-out in history without interference from aircraft or submarines. U.S. cruisers and destroyers barely beat off a stronger Japanese squadron (two cruisers and four destroyers versus four cruisers and four destroyers, with a transport) attempting to reinforce Japanese garrisons in the Aleutians.

1943/MARCH 27—Orde Wingate's Chindit commandos have been ordered back to their Indian base after nearly two months of rampaging about the Japanese rear area in Burma. Their most notable (and useful) achievement was to make over seventy cuts in Japanese rail lines.

1943/MARCH 28—The Japanese squadron defeated at the Komandorski Islands returns to Paramushiro, where its commander is sacked.

1943/MARCH 29—Japanese gather hundreds of aircraft in bases throughout the northern Solomons and Rabaul. Their plan is to launch decisive attacks on the growing Allied base on Guadalcanal.

1943/MARCH 30—The British situation in the Arakan region of Burma continues to deteriorate, as Japanese troops keep advancing (despite an increasingly dire logistical situation).

1943/MARCH 31—The Italian blockade runner *Himalaya* awaits in Bordeaux to make an attempt to run the Allied blockade and get to the Far East.

1943/APRIL 1—The Italian blockade runner *Orseolo* arrives at Bordeaux from Kobe.

1943/APRIL 2—Plans go forward to create the 4th Marine Division using officers, NCOs, and troops from the existing 3rd Marine Division as a cadre. This would slow down the training of the 3rd Division. But since large-scale Marine operations would not be taking place until 1944, it was thought prudent to take advantage of the time, and the thousands of men who had volunteered for the Marines, to create the new division. By the end of summer, the 3rd and 4th Divisions are hard at work getting ready for future battles.

1943/APRIL 3—Public unease over the "Europe First" policy grows in Australia. The Japanese still have plenty of fight in them and the Australians have seen their troops hammered in North Africa, Singapore, and New Guinea without much benefit to the folks down under.

1943/APRIL 4—While Australians fret over the lack of Allied resources devoted to their homeland's defense, much of the matériel and shipping available in the Pacific is being massed for an attack on small Japanese bases on the Aleutian Islands off Alaska. This huge commitment in resources is partially in response to unease among the citizens of western Canada and the United States.

1943/APRIL 5—A British brigade headquarters is overrun by advancing Japanese in the Arakan region of Burma.

1943/APRIL 6—Although scant help to sagging Australian morale, another nation (Bolivia) decides to declare war on the Axis.

1943/APRIL 7—Nearly 190 Japanese aircraft from Rabaul (reinforced by aircraft landed from four carriers) attack Allied shipping at Guadalcanal and Tulagi, sinking a destroyer, a tanker, and the New Zealand corvette *Moa*, and damaging other vessels, while losing only 21 of their number.

1943/APRIL 8—The Japanese press on with their offensive in the Arakan region of Burma. This, coupled with their recent success in the air over the Solomons and their continued hold on bases in the Aleutians, gives some Japanese cause to believe that the war is going their way.

1943/APRIL 9—The Japanese destroyer *Isonami* is sunk southeast of Celebes by the U.S. submarine *Tautog*.

1943/APRIL 10—U.S. construction troops rush to complete an airfield on the Russell Islands, which will allow more efficient use of aircraft in the Solomon Islands area.

1943/APRIL 11—Japanese aircraft from Rabaul raid Oro Bay, near Buna in northeastern New Guinea, burning two merchant ships.

1943/APRIL 12—Japanese aircraft from Rabaul make a major raid on Port Moresby, in southern New Guinea, but cause little damage.

1943/APRIL 13—Japanese troops in China continue to improve their positions by seizing more territory from the Nationalist Chinese.

1943/APRIL 14—Japanese aircraft from Rabaul make a major raid on Milne Bay, sinking two transports. The Japanese submarine *Ro-102* is sunk by *PT-150* and *PT-152*, off Lae, in eastern New Guinea.

1943/APRIL 15—The U.S. completes a major airfield on Banika, the Russell Islands.

1943/APRIL 16—American code breakers have discovered that Japanese Navy commander in chief Isoroku Yamamoto will be flying to visit bases in the Solomons. A risky decision is made to attempt to shoot down Yamamoto's aircraft and deprive Japan of one of her most capable admirals. There is a chance that the Japanese will realize that their codes are being broken and expend the enormous effort needed to change their code system. If that happens, it will take the Allies months (at least) to regain their ability to read secret Japanese transmissions.

1943/APRIL 17—The British situation in the Arakan region of Burma is becoming hopeless, as nothing seems able to stop the Japanese infantry.

1943/APRIL 18—Acting on deciphered Japanese codes, U.S. P-38 fighters intercept two airplanes carrying Japanese Admiral Isoroku Yamamoto and his staff, shooting down both planes and killing the admiral, at Buin, Bougainville.

1943/APRIL 19—The U.S. submarine *Scorpion* lays mines in Japanese waters.

1943/APRIL 20—The U.S. submarine *Runner* lays mines off Hong Kong.

1943/APRIL 21—The U.S. submarine *Stingray* lays mines in Chinese waters.

1943/APRIL 22—Australians complain to their allies about the "Europe First" policy and the strain it is putting on depleted Australian resources.

1943/APRIL 23—The U.S. submarine *Seawolf* sinks a Japanese patrol vessel in the Yellow Sea.

1943/APRIL 24—The U.S. 7th Infantry Division sails from San Francisco for Alaska for the final assault on Japanese bases in the Aleutians.

1943/APRIL 25—A U.S. Navy amphibious task force steams north from San Francisco toward Japanese bases in the Aleutian Islands off Alaska.

1943/APRIL 26—U.S. cruisers and destroyers shell Japanese positions on Attu in the Aleutians. Off Mauritius, the German submarine *U-180* transfers Indian radical nationalist leader Subhas Chandra Bose to the Japanese submarine *I-29*.

1943/APRIL 27—Chinese resistance to the Japanese advance in Hupeh Province begins to stiffen. The Japanese are attacking with scant resources and depend on marginal Chinese performance to keep the offensive going.

1943/APRIL 28—The U.S. submarine *Scamp* sinks the Japanese seaplane carrier *Kamikawa Maru* off New Ireland.

1943/APRIL 29—The British consider abandoning their operations in the Arakan due to implacable Japanese resistance.

1943/APRIL 30—The U.S. 7th Infantry Division begins debarking in Alaska. The U.S. submarine *Snook* lays mines in Chinese waters.

1943/MAY 1—John Lindemann finds himself shifted from the 3rd Marine Division to the newly formed 4th Marine Division. Here he is assigned to the 25th Marine Regiment (2nd Battalion, E Company), the outfit he will serve in through four battles. This splitting of units to form new ones was a common practice early in the war. When new divisions had to be formed, troops would be taken from an existing unit for the nucleus of the new one.

1943/MAY 2—Darwin, Australia, is bombed by Japanese aircraft based in New Guinea.

1943/MAY 3—The British-held town of Maungdaw in the Arakan is threatened by advancing Japanese troops.

1943/MAY 4—The U.S. 7th Division and the U.S.-Canadian First Special Service Force set sail from Cold Bay, Alaska, bound for Attu.

1943/MAY 5—Thousands of Japanese troops continue to fight on in the Solomons, even though Allied air and naval forces increasingly dominate the sea and skies in the area. Allied forces increase patrols and mining to restrict Japanese resupply efforts. This is largely successful, although supplies continue to get through and Japanese forces fight on in the area until the end of the war.

1943/MAY 6—Japanese hopes of a German advance into the Middle East (to meet Japanese troops moving through India) are dashed as the Allies launch their final offensive in North Africa. Within a week, all Axis troops in North Africa will surrender. This will be followed by an invasion of Sicily and, before the end of the year, the surrender of Italy (one of the charter members of the Axis).

1943/MAY 7—U.S. destroyers mine the Blackett Strait, under cover of a cruiser-destroyer raid into Vella Gulf.

1943/MAY 8—Three Japanese destroyers are lost to a U.S. mine barrage in the Blackett Strait, near New Georgia. The battleship *Yamato* puts to sea from Truk, her first activity in the war since August 29, 1942. The U.S. 7th Infantry Division arrives off Attu, but cannot land due to poor weather.

1943/MAY 9—In May of 1943, the Battle of the Atlantic is, for want of a better date, won. From this point on, German U-boats markedly decline as a threat to Allied shipping. As a result, more naval resources are available for the Pacific. The large concentration of Allied anti-submarine forces in the North Atlantic causes the Germans to redeploy their U-boats. This includes stationing several dozen in the Indian Ocean, operating from bases in the Netherlands East Indies.

1943/MAY 10—Off Attu, the U.S. 7th Infantry Division and her escorts ride out poor weather awaiting an opportunity to launch their landing.

1943/MAY 11—Elements of the U.S. 7th Division and the U.S.-Canadian First Special Service Force commence landings on Attu in the Aleutians. The

Japanese battleship *Yamato* arrives at Kure for a refit. The Italian submarine *Capellini* departs La Pallice, France, on a blockade-running mission to Japan.

1943/MAY 12—U.S. cruisers and destroyers shell Vila and Munda and mine Kula Gulf. Additional elements of the U.S. 7th Infantry Division land on Attu. In Arakan, having driven the British back roughly to the line of the front in mid-December, the Japanese halt their advance.

1943/MAY 13—Axis troops in Tunisia, North Africa, surrender.

1943/MAY 14—Japanese minesweepers clear Kula Gulf.

1943/MAY 15—Heavy fighting on Attu in the Aleutians, as Japanese defenders fight to the death.

1943/MAY 16—The Italian submarine *Tazzoli* departs La Pallice, France, on a blockade-running mission to Japan and is never heard from again (probably sunk by British aircraft in the Bay of Biscay that same day).

1943/MAY 17—The Japanese complete preparations for yet another offensive in China.

1943/MAY 18—The Japanese open a new offensive across the Yangtze River in China.

1943/MAY 19—Heavy fighting on Attu.

1943/MAY 20—The U.S. Joint Chiefs of Staff approve a plan for the defeat of Japan, to include simultaneous offensives through the Gilbert and Marshall islands, the Bismarck Archipelago, and Burma, preparatory to further advances, and ultimately to the air and sea blockade of Japan and possible invasion.

1943/MAY 21—The battleship *Musashi* and escorts arrive at Tokyo Bay, for a possible sortie to the Aleutians, but the mission is abandoned.

1943/MAY 22—Heavy fighting on Attu, with outnumbered Japanese troops fighting to the death.

1943/MAY 23—The Italian submarine *Giuliani* departs La Pallice, France, on a blockade-running mission to Japan.

1943/MAY 24—Churchill and Roosevelt meet and agree to increase aid to China and adopt an "island-hopping" strategy in the Pacific.

1943/MAY 25—Elements of the Japanese Fifth Fleet (northern Pacific) are at sea for a possible rescue of the Attu garrison.

1943/MAY 26—The Japanese commence covert evacuation of troops on Kiska, in the Aleutians, by submarine. Heavy fighting on Attu. Elements of the Japanese Fifth Fleet (northern Pacific) are at sea for a possible rescue of the Attu garrison.

1943/MAY 27—The Chinese put up stiff resistance to the latest Japanese offensive in China.

1943/MAY 28—Aircraft drop surrender leaflets on remaining Japanese troops of the Attu atoll garrison. This has no perceptible effect on the Japanese. By the end of 1943, American commanders realize that Japanese troops, with a few individual exceptions, do not surrender.

1943/MAY 29—The Japanese abandon plans to evacuate the Attu garrison, which undertakes a major "banzai" attack in recognition of its desperate position.

1943/MAY 30—Organized Japanese resistance on Attu ends.

1943/MAY 31—Chinese troops in Hopeh Province halt a Japanese drive on Chungking.

1943/JUNE 1—The Japanese Army decides to reorganize the Imperial Guard, forming a second division at Tokyo, which is designated the 1st, while the original Imperial Guards Division, in Sumatra since early 1942, is redesignated the 2nd.

1943/JUNE 2—Pope Pius XII denounces air bombardment. This does not in any way delay U.S. plans to deploy the B-29 bomber in the Pacific in 1944.

1943/JUNE 3—The Japanese offensive in China succeeds after hard campaigning, as the Japanese take control of all shipping on the upper Yangtze River.

1943/JUNE 4—The German auxiliary cruiser *Michel* sails from Batavia, Java, bound for the Indian Ocean.

1943/JUNE 5—Air Battle of the Russell Islands: Over 80 Japanese aircraft from Rabaul tangle with over 100 U.S. aircraft from Henderson (Guadalcanal) and other fields, losing 24 aircraft to 7 American ones.

1943/JUNE 6—The Japanese assess their situation on Kiska, in Alaska's Aleutian Islands, and decide that it is hopeless. Evacuation is the only option.

1943/JUNE 7—The Japanese resume air attacks on Guadalcanal.

1943/JUNE 8—The Japanese battleship *Mutsu* is destroyed by an internal explosion while lying in Hiroshima Harbor.

1943/JUNE 9—On convoy duty off Fremantle, an Australian minesweeper is sunk in a collision with a merchant ship.

1943/JUNE 10—The U.S. submarine *Trigger* torpedoes the Japanese carrier *Hiyo* off Japan, but it does not sink. The Japanese submarine *I-24* is sunk off Kiska by a U.S. patrol boat.

1943/JUNE 11—The Japanese submarine *I-9* is sunk off Kiska by the U.S. destroyer *Frazier.*

1943/JUNE 12—Prime Minister General Tojo grapples with the problem of how to present Japan's declining fortunes to the rest of the Japanese leadership. It is decided to simply make an announcement to the Diet (parliament). So far in 1943, Japan has had to abandon Guadalcanal, the Aleutians and an offensive in China. Only Burma has been a success, and there it was simply throwing back a British offensive.

1943/JUNE 13—The blockade-running Italian submarine *Capellini* arrives off Cape Town, bound for the Japanese-held Netherlands East Indies.

1943/JUNE 14—Tojo meets with Indian nationalist leader Subhas Chandra Bose (who had fled trial in India in 1941, making his way to Germany and then, via submarine, to Tokyo) and agrees to allow Bose to set up a government to control Indian territory when Japanese forces in Burma move into eastern India, and an army to assist in the "liberation" of India.

1943/JUNE 15—West of Australia the German merchant cruiser *Michel* sinks a 7,700-ton merchant ship. The Italian submarine *Barbarigo* departs La Pallice, France, with critical matériel and electronic equipment for Japan, and is never heard from again.

1943/JUNE 16—A Japanese air attack from Rabaul and New Georgia against ships in the vicinity of Guadalcanal meets with total failure, only 1 of 94 aircraft returning to base, after inflicting minor damage on two vessels.

1943/JUNE 17—The Italian submarine *Giuliani* reaches the East Indies, bringing critical matériel and documents for the Japanese. West of Australia, the German merchant cruiser *Michel* sinks a 9,900-ton tanker.

1943/JUNE 18—The Italian submarine *Torelli* departs La Pallice, France, on a blockade-running mission to Japan.

1943/JUNE 19—Allied preparations for Operation Cartwheel concluding, convoys begin sailing. This campaign will take islands surrounding the major Japanese base at Rabaul and isolate it.

1943/JUNE 20—Operation Cartwheel fleet units begin to deploy. The blockade-running Italian submarine *Capellini* enters the Indian Ocean, bound for the Japanese-held Netherlands East Indies. John Lindemann is promoted to Pfc. (private first class).

1943/JUNE 21—Operation Cartwheel: Fast transports covertly land U.S. Marine 4th Raider Battalion on New Georgia.

1943/JUNE 22—Operation Cartwheel: Fast transports covertly land reconnaissance elements of the U.S. 43rd Division on New Georgia. The Japanese submarine 1-7 is damaged off Kiska by the U.S. destroyer *Monaghan*, and puts in to Kiska Harbor.

1943/JUNE 23—Operation Cartwheel: The U.S. 112th Cavalry Regiment (dismounted) lands on Woodlark Island, off New Guinea. The Japanese submarine *Ro-103* sinks two transports involved in Operation Cartwheel off Guadalcanal.

1943/JUNE 24—In a radio broadcast from Tokyo, Indian nationalist Chandra Bose calls for the Indian people to rise up in armed revolt against British rule. The appeal goes largely unheeded.

1943/JUNE 25—U.S. submariners finally get the Navy to admit their torpedoes are faulty and take measures to fix them. Meanwhile, the Navy agrees to temporary fixes to provide decent armament and, schooled in effective tactics, U.S. subs begin to make big inroads against the Japanese transport fleet.

1943/JUNE 26—The U.S. 1st Cavalry Division (dismounted) sails from San Francisco for Australia.

1943/JUNE 27—Operation Cartwheel: The first troop convoys arrive off their objectives.

1943/JUNE 28—Operation Cartwheel: A U.S. 158th Infantry RCT lands on Kirwina Island, east of New Guinea.

1943/JUNE 29—Operation Cartwheel: U.S. cruisers and destroyers shell Japanese installations at Shortland, near Bougainville. The Japanese submarine *Ro-103* encounters troop convoys, but her report is dismissed by higher headquarters.

1943/JUNE 30—In New Guinea, Allied troops feint an offensive against Salamaua, with a U.S. amphibious landing at nearby Nassau Bay while Australian troops advance from Wau, to cover Allied occupation of the Trobriand and Woodlark islands, east of New Guinea.

Operation Cartwheel: Heavily supported by naval and air forces, elements of the U.S. 43rd Infantry Division land at Rendova against slight resistance, while small detachments begin landing on New Georgia.

1943/JULY 1—Operation Cartwheel: The U.S. lands reinforcements at Rendova; the Marine 4th Raider Battalion captures Viru Harbor on New Georgia. The Japanese destroyer *Hokaze* is damaged by the U.S. submarine *Thresher* in the Southwest Pacific. Pfc. John Lindemann and the 4th Marine Division are shipped, via the Panama Canal, from Camp Lejeune to San Diego.

1943/JULY 2—Operation Cartwheel: Japanese cruisers and destroyers shell U.S. positions at Rendova; the U.S. 37th and 43rd Divisions and Marines, supported by artillery fire from Rendova and large naval and air forces, land on both sides of Munda on New Georgia.

1943/JULY 3—Operation Cartwheel: Japanese destroyers on a resupply mission depart Rabaul; heavy fighting on New Georgia.

1943/JULY 4—Operation Cartwheel: Elements of the U.S. 37th Infantry Division land at Bairoko, on Kula Gulf; Japanese destroyers, landing reinforcements at Vila, on Kula Gulf, sink a U.S. destroyer; heavy fighting on New Georgia.

1943/JULY 5—Japan cedes five provinces of Malaya to Siam. Operation Cartwheel: A major "Tokyo Express" supply mission departs Rabaul; heavy fighting on New Georgia. At Kiska, the damaged Japanese submarine *I-7* is scuttled.

1943/JULY 6—U.S. cruisers and destroyers shell Japanese positions on Kiska in the Aleutians, a mission that is repeated several times over the next two weeks. Operation Cartwheel: In the Battle of Kula Gulf, Japanese destroyers attempting to land troops at Vila, on Kula Gulf are ambushed by a U.S. cruiser-destroyer force, but sink the cruiser *Helena*, while losing the destroyer *Nagatsuki*, grounded and then attacked by Allied aircraft; heavy fighting on New Georgia.

1943/JULY 7—A Japanese destroyer force sets out from Paramushiro in the Kuriles to evacuate the remaining garrison on Kiska. The U.S. 33rd Infantry Division sails from San Francisco for Hawaii. Heavy fighting on New Georgia.

1943/JULY 8—Heavy fighting on New Georgia. U.S. destroyers shell Kiska. The Japanese 15th Division begins movement to Burma from Nanking, China.

1943/JULY 9—Operation Cartwheel: U.S. destroyers shelling Japanese positions at Munda beat off attacks by about 100 enemy aircraft; heavy fighting on New Georgia. The Italian submarine *Capellini* reaches Sabang, Sumatra, bringing mercury, electronic equipment, and other items for the Japanese.

1943/JULY 10—Heavy fighting on New Georgia. U.S. destroyers shell Kiska.

1943/JULY 11—Operation Cartwheel: U.S. cruisers and destroyers shell Munda. The U.S. 1st Cavalry Division debarks in Australia.

1943/JULY 12—The U.S. 33rd Infantry Division debarks in Hawaii.

1943/JULY 13—Operation Cartwheel: In the Battle of Kolombangara, eight Japanese destroyers and a light cruiser attempting to land reinforcements on New Georgia are ambushed by three cruisers (one a New Zealander) and ten destroyers, losing the light cruiser *Jintsu*, while sinking a destroyer and heavily damaging all three Allied cruisers.

1943/JULY 14—The Japanese submarine *I-179* is lost to an accident in Japanese home waters.

1943/JULY 15—Heavy fighting on New Georgia.

1943/JULY 16—Unable to reach Kiska due to adverse weather, Japanese destroyers that sailed on July 7 return to Paramushiro. Two Australian cruisers and four U.S. destroyers are ordered from Espíritu Santo to join Seventh Fleet forces engaged off New Guinea.

1943/JULY 17—U.S. aircraft from Henderson Field and other bases in the Solomons attack Japanese shipping off Buin, Bougainville, sinking a destroyer and damaging several other vessels. U.S. destroyers shell Kiska.

1943/JULY 18—U.S. destroyers shell Kiska.

1943/JULY 19—Heavily escorted, three Japanese destroyers land supplies at Vila on Kula Gulf.

1943/JULY 20—Retiring from Kula Gulf, a Japanese cruiser-destroyer force is attacked by U.S. aircraft, with two destroyers lost and a cruiser damaged. A Japanese submarine torpedoes, but does not sink, the Australian light cruiser *Hobart* in the Solomons. The Joint Chiefs of Staff issue orders for Operation Galvanic, the seizure of the Gilbert Islands.

1943/JULY 21—The U.S. 6th Infantry Division sails from San Francisco for Hawaii. The U.S. Navy cancels an order for five new battleships. U.S. Army Chief of Staff George C. Marshall proposes bypassing Rabaul, leaving the large garrison isolated and ineffective because of a lack of supplies of fuel and ammunition.

1943/JULY 22—U.S. battleships, cruisers, and destroyers shell Kiska and nearby islets in the Aleutians. Japanese cruisers, destroyers, and support ships sail from Paramushiro in the Kuriles to complete the evacuation of Kiska. The Japanese seaplane carrier *Nisshin* is sunk by U.S. aircraft off Bougainville.

1943/JULY 23—Heavy fighting continues on New Georgia as a Japanese attempt to land troops using motorized barges is frustrated by U.S. motor torpedo boats.

1943/JULY 24—U.S. destroyers land supplies at Bairoko on Kula Gulf. Admiral Chester W. Nimitz orders U.S. submariners to deactivate magnetic exploders on their torpedoes, as these are finally admitted to be defective.

1943/JULY 25—Retiring from Kula Gulf, U.S. destroyers shell Munda and Lailand. The U.S. 25th Infantry Division reinforces New Georgia, where heavy fighting continues. Mussolini is deposed as dictator of Italy, effectively taking Italy out of the Axis.

1943/JULY 26—Two ships of the Japanese Kiska evacuation squadron are forced to turn back to Paramushiro due to damage caused by collisions in heavy seas. U.S. destroyers shell Munda. Heavy fighting on New Georgia as a renewed Japanese attempt to land troops using motorized barges is frustrated by U.S. motor torpedo boats.

1943/JULY 27—"The Battle of the Pips": U.S. battleships, cruisers, and destroyers expend hundreds of rounds against a false radar blip (or "pip") west of Kiska. Heavy fighting on New Georgia. The Japanese destroyers Ariake and Mikazuki are sunk off New Britain by U.S. Army aircraft. In Chinese waters, the U.S. submarine Sawfish sinks the Japanese minelayer Hiroshima and a merchant ship.

1943/JULY 28—After nightfall the Japanese Kiska evacuation squadron evacuates over 5,000 troops in less than an hour and departs for Paramushiro.

1943/JULY 29—The U.S. 6th Infantry Division debarks in Hawaii.

1943/JULY 30—U.S. destroyers shell suspected Japanese positions on Kiska.

1943/JULY 31—The Japanese 17th Division begins moving to Rabaul from central China. Experienced troops are being steadily withdrawn from China for service in the Pacific and Burma, to be replaced (if at all) by green troops from Japan.

1943/AUGUST 1—The Japanese Kiska evacuation squadron returns to Paramushiro in the Kuriles, having suffered

no losses due to enemy action. In the Blackett Strait, off New Georgia, five Japanese destroyers intent upon resupplying Kolombangara tangle with fifteen U.S. PT boats, sinking one, PT-109.

1943/AUGUST 2—U.S. battleships, cruisers, and destroyers shell suspected Japanese positions on Kiska. Pfc. John Lindemann arrives in San Diego with the 4th Marine Division.

1943/AUGUST 3—The Japanese 17th Division begins moving to Rabaul from central China.

1943/AUGUST 4—U.S. troops close in on the Japanese airfield on Munda (New Georgia).

1943/AUGUST 5—U.S. troops on New Georgia capture the Japanese airfield at Munda. The battleship Musashi and her escorts return to Truk. Pfc. John Lindemann and the 4th Marine Division are moved up the coast from San Diego to Las Pogas, where a primitive tent camp is built. The division begins training for operations in the Pacific.

1943/AUGUST 6—Battle of Vella Gulf. Four Japanese destroyers attempting to land troops on Kolombangara are ambushed by six U.S. destroyers, with only the lucky Shigure getting away. U.S. troops on New Georgia pursue Japanese forces into the interior, as engineers begin to repair the airstrip.

1943/AUGUST 7—U.S. troops on New Georgia break Japanese resistance.

1943/AUGUST 8—Air combat over New Georgia has resulted in the loss of 93 U.S. and 350 Japanese aircraft. Fighting continues on Munda in the Solomons.

1943/AUGUST 9—U.S. troops on New Georgia pursue Japanese forces into the interior.

1943/AUGUST 10—Japanese troops on New Georgia effectively become guerrillas, fighting on in the wild interior of the island.

1943/AUGUST 11—Admiral Chester W. Nimitz proposes to Vice Admiral

William Halsey that Kolombangara be isolated and bypassed, a plan that is adopted.

1943/AUGUST 12—While the USAAF drops tons of bombs, U.S. battleships, cruisers, and destroyers shell suspected Japanese positions on Kiska.

1943/AUGUST 13—Heavily escorted, nearly 35,000 U.S. and Canadian troops sail from Adak in the Aleutians, bound for Kiska. Flying from Australia, U.S. B-24s bomb the oil fields at Balikpapan in Borneo.

1943/AUGUST 14—Quadrant Conference: President Roosevelt and Prime Minister Churchill meet at Quebec for ten days of conferences concerning Allied policy and strategy, definitively setting Operation Overlord (the landings in France) for the spring of 1944. It is agreed that the Pacific offensive will be on two fronts, one an island-hopping drive through the Central Pacific, the other the ongoing advance up the Solomons toward the Philippines.

1943/AUGUST 15—U.S. and Canadian troops begin landings on Kiska heavily supported by naval and air bombardments. Five days pass before it is established that the Japanese have definitely evacuated the island. Allied casualties are a score of deaths from "friendly fire" and a number of men killed on a destroyer damaged by a mine. Elements of the U.S. 25th Infantry Division begin landing on Vella Lavella in the central Solomons, getting ashore against no opposition except by Japanese aircraft.

1943/AUGUST 16—The 4th Marine Division is activated at Camp Pendleton. Having completed a refit, the battleship *Yamato* arrives at Truk. On Vella Lavella, the 25th Infantry Division encounters moderate resistance.

1943/AUGUST 17—Japanese light forces land reinforcements on Vella Lavella, while their covering force of four destroyers beats off an attempt by four U.S. destroyers to intervene, with little effect on either side. A major U.S./Australian air raid on Japanese installations at Wewak, northern New Guinea, destroys over 100 aircraft.

1943/AUGUST 18—The Nationalist Chinese complain of being left out of decision making by the Allies. China has been acknowledged as one of the "Big Four" (U.S., Britain, Russia, China) Allies, but only for propaganda purposes. China wants real power among the Big Four, but lacks the military or political clout to obtain it.

1943/AUGUST 19—Off Espíritu Santo, the Japanese submarine *I-17* is sunk by U.S. aircraft and a New Zealand corvette. Heavy Allied air raids on Wewak, New Guinea.

1943/AUGUST 20—On New Georgia, surviving Japanese troops are hunted down.

1943/AUGUST 21—Heavy Allied air raids on Wewak, New Guinea.

1943/AUGUST 22—U.S. destroyers shell Finschhafen, in eastern New Guinea. U.S. Marines occupy Nukufetau in the Ellice Islands, which is undefended.

1943/AUGUST 23—The Japanese submarine *I-25* reconnoiters Espíritu Santo with a small scout plane.

1943/AUGUST 24—The British decide to appoint Lord Louis Montbatten supreme Allied commander for Southeast Asia.

1943/AUGUST 25—Organized Japanese resistance on New Georgia ends. The Inter-Allied Quebec Conference ends, with a recommendation that MacArthur and Halsey leapfrog Rabaul, occupying outlying portions of New Britain and New Ireland to isolate the enormous (over 100,000 troops) base at Rabaul.

1943/AUGUST 26—Operating from bases in China, U.S. bombers attack Japanese installations in Hong Kong. The Italian submarine *Torelli* reaches Sabang, Sumatra, bringing critical materials, documents, and a Japanese intelligence officer.

1943/AUGUST 27—The bulk of the Japanese 17th Division is concentrated at Rabaul.

1943/AUGUST 28—U.S. Marines occupy Nanomea in the Solomons while elements of the 43rd Division occupy Arundel Island, both of which are undefended by the Japanese.

1943/AUGUST 29—On Vella Lavella, the 25th Infantry Division advances slowly against moderate resistance.

1943/AUGUST 30—The U.S. Navy Fast Carrier Task Force approaches Marcus Island to stage a raid. This type of operation is an opportunity to train pilots and ship crews under combat conditions without a great deal of risk.

1943/AUGUST 31—Escorted by elements of the Seventh Fleet, the Australian 9th Division sails from Milne Bay for a landing near Lae, in northeastern New Guinea. A small task force lands U.S. Army personnel on Baker Island in the Central Pacific, which is not held by the Japanese.

1943/SEPTEMBER 1—The U.S. Fast Carrier Task Force hits Marcus Island, in the western Central Pacific, with both air and gunnery attacks. The Japanese submarine I-182 is sunk by the U.S. destroyer Wadsworth off Espíritu Santo.

1943/SEPTEMBER 2—USAAF aircraft bomb Lae, in northeastern New Guinea, sinking a patrol vessel, while another patrol vessel is torpedoed near Truk by the U.S. submarine Snapper.

1943/SEPTEMBER 3—The Japanese submarine I-25 is sunk near Espíritu Santo by the U.S. destroyer Ellet; I-20 is sunk in the New Hebrides by the U.S. destroyer Patterson.

1943/SEPTEMBER 4—Elements of the Australian 9th Division land near Lae, in New Guinea. On Vella Lavella, the 25th Infantry Division makes gains against Japanese resistance.

1943/SEPTEMBER 5—Elements of the Australian 9th Division complete landings near Lae, despite Japanese air attacks that sink one landing craft and damage several ships.

1943/SEPTEMBER 6—The U.S. 503rd Parachute Regiment airdrops 1,700 men at Nadzab, northwest of Lae, securing the airstrip, into which is flown the Australian 7th Division. The U.S. submarine Halibut torpedoes, but does not sink, the Japanese heavy cruiser Nachi off Japan.

1943/SEPTEMBER 7—Heavy fighting around Lae and on Vella Lavella. The Japanese 54th Division moves from Java to Burma.

1943/SEPTEMBER 8—U.S. destroyers bombard Lae in support of operations of the Australian 9th Division.

1943/SEPTEMBER 9—Formal announcement is made of the surrender of Italy. The Italian sloop Eritrea, in Japanese-controlled Sabang, escapes to sea, eludes pursuit, and eventually reaches Ceylon, but the Italian submarines Capellini, Giuliani, and Torelli are captured by the Japanese, who turn them over to the Germans, who commission them as UIt-24, UIt-23, and UIt-25.

1943/SEPTEMBER 10—The German merchant cruiser Michel sinks a tanker (about 10,000 tons) in the eastern Pacific.

1943/SEPTEMBER 11—The Japanese minesweeper W-16, attempting to clear mines off Makassar, Celebes, is sunk by one. Japanese submarine I-26 reconnoiters the Fiji Islands.

1943/SEPTEMBER 12—Australian and U.S. troops capture Salamaua, in northeastern New Guinea.

1943/SEPTEMBER 13—Nationalist Chinese leader Chiang Kai-shek consolidates his power by becoming president of China. While not an important post, it adds to Chiang's stature.

1943/SEPTEMBER 14—The U.S. 25th

Division prepares to turn operations on Vella Lavella over to the New Zealand 3rd Division. Heavy fighting around Lae.

1943/SEPTEMBER 15—The U.S. 25th Division prepares to turn operations on Vella Lavella over to the New Zealand 3rd Division. The Japanese submarine Ro-101 is sunk by the U.S. destroyer Saufley aided by two aircraft, in the South Pacific.

1943/SEPTEMBER 16—Allied troops capture Lae, in northeastern New Guinea. The U.S. 25th Division prepares to turn operations on Vella Lavella over to the New Zealand 3rd Division.

1943/SEPTEMBER 17—U.S. B-24s bomb Tarawa, in the Gilbert Islands, from air bases on Canton and Funafuti. The New Zealand 3rd Division begins to relieve the U.S. 25th Division on Vella Lavella.

1943/SEPTEMBER 18—B-24s bomb Tarawa, in the Gilbert Islands. On Vella Lavella the U.S. 25th Infantry Division is officially relieved by the New Zealand 3rd Division.

1943/SEPTEMBER 19—Aircraft of the U.S. Fast Carrier Task Force and U.S. B-24s raid Tarawa.

1943/SEPTEMBER 20—In the aftermath of the previous day's attack by U.S. carrier aircraft on their base at Tarawa, the Japanese redouble their efforts to fortify the island against amphibious attacks.

1943/SEPTEMBER 21—Australian raiders in six canoes enter Singapore Harbor, to sink two ships with limpet mines.

1943/SEPTEMBER 22—On Vella Lavella the New Zealanders undertake a two-pronged offensive, driving along both coasts.

1943/SEPTEMBER 23—The New Zealander offensive on Vella Lavella presses the Japanese back. Heavy fighting near Finschhafen, New Guinea, as the Australians attack the Japanese garrison.

1943/SEPTEMBER 24—The U.S. sub-

marine Cabrilla damages the Japanese escort carrier Taiyo near Japan.

1943/SEPTEMBER 25—The Japanese begin concentrating light craft on the north coast of Kolombangara in order to evacuate the garrison.

1943/SEPTEMBER 26—The Japanese oceangoing torpedo boat Kasasagi is sunk off Flores in the Netherlands East Indies.

1943/SEPTEMBER 27—Heavy fighting near Finschhafen, as the Australians defend against fierce Japanese attacks.

1943/SEPTEMBER 28—The Japanese minelayer Hoko is sunk east of Buka by U.S. Army aircraft.

1943/SEPTEMBER 29—Heavy fighting near Finschhafen, as the Australians attack the Japanese garrison.

1943/SEPTEMBER 30—On Vella Lavella the New Zealanders confine the Japanese (about 600) to a small pocket on the northwestern tip of the island. The U.S. submarine Barb departs Pearl Harbor carrying the new Mark-18 torpedo.

1943/OCTOBER 1—On Vella Lavella the New Zealanders suspend offensive operations, containing the Japanese pocket on the northwest of the island.

1943/OCTOBER 2—The Australian 20th Brigade secures Finschhafen, in eastern New Guinea. The U.S. destroyer Henley is sunk off Finschhafen by the Japanese submarine Ro-103.

1943/OCTOBER 3—The Japanese begin another offensive in central China, this one to grab as much of the local rice harvest as possible.

1943/OCTOBER 4—In the Indian Ocean, the Japanese submarine I-37 scouts the Chagos Islands with a small reconnaissance plane.

1943/OCTOBER 5—U.S. carrier aircraft raid Wake Island, in the Central Pacific, while cruisers shell Japanese installations there; in retaliation, the Japanese execute U.S. civilians interned on the island.

1943/OCTOBER 6—Japanese destroyers attempt to evacuate troops on Vella Lavella and are intercepted by U.S. destroyers, one on each side being lost before the Japanese turn away, leaving the U.S. with three damaged destroyers. Meanwhile, Japanese small craft succeed in getting most of the surviving Japanese troops off Vella Lavella.

1943/OCTOBER 7—U.S. carriers and cruisers raid Wake Island.

1943/OCTOBER 8—Japanese leader General Tojo assumes more power by taking over as minister of commerce and industry.

1943/OCTOBER 9—U.S. carriers retire from Wake.

1943/OCTOBER 10—The Japanese naval command concludes that the U.S. plans a landing at Wake Island. In the Indian Ocean, the Japanese submarine I-37 scouts Diégo-Suarez with a small reconnaissance plane.

1943/OCTOBER 11—The Combined Fleet is ordered to prepare for action if the U.S. attacks Wake Island. The U.S. submarine Wahoo is sunk by Japanese aircraft in La Pérouse Strait.

1943/OCTOBER 12—The USAAF begins heavy bombardment raids on Rabaul.

1943/OCTOBER 13—Several Japanese submarines converge on Hawaii on reconnaissance missions, but are unable to ascertain the presence of the bulk of the U.S. fleet.

1943/OCTOBER 14—The USAAF subjects Rabaul to a major air raid.

1943/OCTOBER 15—Admiral Sir Andrew Cunningham is appointed First Sea Lord of the British Admiralty (Chief of Naval Operations).

1943/OCTOBER 16—The Japanese declare the Philippines an independent republic under "temporary Japanese supervision." Filipinos continue their guerrilla war against the Japanese.

1943/OCTOBER 17—In the Indian Ocean, the Japanese submarine I-37 scouts Kilindini, East Africa, with a small reconnaissance plane. The Japanese submarine I-36 scouts Pearl Harbor with a reconnaissance plane, determining that the fleet is at sea. Based on this evidence, and the heavy pounding to which Wake has been subjected in recent weeks, Japanese naval headquarters feels certain the U.S. Navy is about to conduct a landing at Wake, and orders the Combined Fleet to sea. The U.S. submarine Tarpon sinks the German merchant cruiser Michel in the Bonin Islands.

1943/OCTOBER 18—The Japanese Combined Fleet steams northward from Truk, bound for Wake. The Japanese submarine I-19 is reported overdue.

1943/OCTOBER 19—British, American, and Russian foreign ministers meet in Moscow and agree that Russia will enter the war against Japan once Germany has been defeated. The Japanese are not informed.

1943/OCTOBER 20—Aircraft from six Japanese carriers based at Truk are transferred to bases at Rabaul; the carriers then steam for Japan, to pick up new air groups. Thus there are no operational Japanese carriers available in the Pacific. The Japanese Combined Fleet steams northward from Truk, bound for Wake.

1943/OCTOBER 21—The Japanese Combined Fleet steams northward from Truk, bound for Wake. Operation Galvanic (invasion of the Gilberts) gets under way. Transports and escorts begin movements toward troop concentration areas.

1943/OCTOBER 22—Sir Archibald Wavell is made viceroy of India, with the urgent mission of keeping India loyal and in the war.

1943/OCTOBER 23—The Japanese conclude that there is no American threat to Wake Island, and recall the Combined Fleet to Truk.

1943/OCTOBER 24—The Combined

Fleet steams for Truk after its abortive sortie toward Wake. The Japanese destroyer *Mochizuki* is sunk by Marine aircraft southwest of Rabaul.

1943/OCTOBER 25—USAAF bombers based in China raid Japanese airfields in Formosa for the first time. Battle of Cape St. George: Six U.S. destroyers intercept six Japanese destroyers carrying reinforcements for Bougainville, sinking three.

1943/OCTOBER 26—Chandra Bose proclaims a provisional Indian government in Singapore and declares war on Britain.

1943/OCTOBER 27—The New Zealand 8th Brigade (about 8,000 men) occupies Mono and Stirling in the Treasury Islands and the USMC 2nd Parachute Battalion lands amphibiously on Choiseul, against no resistance, as a deceptive measure designed to mask operations against Bougainville. The Japanese Combined Fleet returns to Truk after its abortive sortie toward Wake Island.

1943/OCTOBER 28—The Japanese evacuation of Kolombangara ends, only about 1,000 out of nearly 11,000 men of the garrison failing to get away safely.

1943/OCTOBER 29—The USAAF subjects Rabaul to a major air raid. The newly activated Japanese 31st Division reaches Burma.

1943/OCTOBER 30—U.S. subs mine the waters off Indochina. Before long, Hainan Strait and the water off Saigon are heavily mined.

1943/OCTOBER 31—The Japanese 2nd Division, withdrawn from Guadalcanal in February 1942 for rest, reinforcement, and reorganization in the Philippines, is deployed to Malaya.

1943/NOVEMBER 1—The 3rd Marine Division lands at Cape Torokina, at Empress Augusta Bay, Bougainville, easily overcoming initial resistance on the ground (the local Japanese garrison was only 270 men and one 75mm gun) and in the air. U.S. destroyers shell the Japanese air base at Buka. Japanese surface forces sortie from Rabaul. U.S. carrier aircraft raid Japanese installations at Buin and Buka.

1943/NOVEMBER 2—Battle of Empress Augusta Bay: In a nighttime attempt to interfere in the landings at Cape Torokina, four Japanese cruisers and six destroyers are intercepted by four U.S. cruisers and nine destroyers, the Japanese being beaten off after losing a light cruiser and a destroyer and incurring heavy damage to two cruisers and two destroyers, the U.S. suffering two damaged destroyers. The Marine 2nd Parachute Battalion withdraws from Choiseul. U.S. ships off Empress Augusta Bay are subject to a Japanese air attack, with little damage. U.S. carrier aircraft raid Japanese installations at Buin and Buka. In China, the Japanese undertake a "rice offensive" (to steal the recent harvest for their own troops) in Hunan Province.

1943/NOVEMBER 3—Major elements of the Japanese Combined Fleet (ten cruisers and about a dozen destroyers) set sail from Truk to reinforce ships at Rabaul. Marines on Bougainville meet little resistance, as the Japanese are as yet on the wrong (i.e., northern and southern) parts of the island.

1943/NOVEMBER 4—U.S. aerial reconnaissance spots the Japanese cruiser-destroyer force bound for Rabaul from Truk.

1943/NOVEMBER 5—The U.S. submarine *Halibut* sinks the Japanese carrier *Junyo*, en route to Japan from Truk. Massive U.S. Navy and Army air strikes at Rabaul severely damage six cruisers and several destroyers; most damaged ships promptly depart for Truk.

1943/NOVEMBER 6—The New Zealand 8th Brigade is withdrawn from the Treasury Islands. Light action on Bougainville, where a Japanese cruiser-destroyer force from Rabaul lands over 1,000 troops.

1943/NOVEMBER 7—Japanese cruisers and destroyers damaged at Rabaul on November 5 reach Truk. Japanese troops make a weak attack on Marine positions at Cape Torokina, Bougainville.

1943/NOVEMBER 8—Despite Japanese Rabaul-based air strikes on transports, the U.S. 37th Infantry Division reinforces the Marines at Cape Torokina, but fighting continues to be light.

1943/NOVEMBER 9—The Japanese 36th Division reaches Halemhera, New Guinea.

1943/NOVEMBER 10—Task Force 52 sails from Pearl Harbor bound for the Gilbert Islands.

1943/NOVEMBER 11—Major U.S. carrier air strikes on Japanese air bases at Rabaul sink one destroyer and damage a cruiser and a destroyer; forty-one Japanese aircraft attack U.S. carriers with no success, only eight returning to base. Desultory action on Bougainville.

1943/NOVEMBER 12—Japanese carrier air groups landed at Rabaul on October 20 are withdrawn for reorganization after loss of 121 of their 173 aircraft. Light combat on Bougainville, while the U.S. lands additional Marine and Army troops at Cape Torokina, despite Japanese air strikes on the covering force, which cause some damage.

1943/NOVEMBER 13—Operation Galvanic (invasion of Tarawa) under way; Task Force 53 sails from the New Hebrides bound for the Gilbert Islands. U.S. Army and Navy B-24s from Funafuti and Canton bomb Tarawa and Makin, in the Gilberts.

1943/NOVEMBER 14—Moderate fighting on Bougainville continues; U.S. forces at Empress Augusta Bay total nearly 34,000, while Japanese forces on Bougainville and surrounding islands may total 40,000, but are unable to concentrate effectively.

1943/NOVEMBER 15—Task Force 74 (two Australian cruisers and two destroyers, plus two U.S. destroyers) arrives at the New Hebrides from Milne Bay. U.S. bombers based in China attack harbor installations in Hong Kong. Operation Galvanic: Task Force 52 refuels near Baker and Howland islands, in the Central Pacific, while Task Force 53 refuels near Funafuti, before resuming course for the Gilbert Islands. U.S. Army and Navy B-24s from Funafuti again bomb Tarawa and Makin.

1943/NOVEMBER 16—The Japanese minelayer *Ukishima* is lost to an unknown cause near Hatsushima (possibly sunk by a U.S. submarine later lost). The U.S. submarine *Corvina* is sunk by the Japanese submarine *I-179* near Truk.

1943/NOVEMBER 17—A U.S. destroyer transport is sunk off Empress Augusta Bay by Japanese aircraft. Operation Galvanic: Task Forces 52 and 53 unite about 500 miles east of the Gilbert Islands, and begin softening-up air strikes on Makin and Tarawa, supported by battleship and cruiser gunfire.

1943/NOVEMBER 18—The Japanese destroyer escort *Sanae* is sunk by the U.S. submarine *Bluefish* in the Philippines. Operation Galvanic: Makin and Tarawa are subjected to intense air and sea bombardment.

1943/NOVEMBER 19—Fighting continues on Bougainville. Operation Galvanic: The Fast Carrier Task Force raids Japanese-held islands in the Gilberts and Nauru. U.S. Army and Navy B-24s from Funafuti bomb Tarawa and Makin atolls, in the Gilberts. The Japanese light cruisers *Isuzu* and *Nagara* sail from Truk for Mili in the Marshalls, while *Naka* departs for Kwajalein.

1943/NOVEMBER 20—Operation Galvanic goes into high gear. The 2nd Marine Division lands on Betio Island, Tarawa, while the 27th Infantry Division lands on Makin Island, in the Gilberts. Heavy fighting on Tarawa. Japanese air attacks on the fleet cause damage to the carrier *Independence*.

1943/NOVEMBER 21—Operation Galvanic: Heavy fighting on Tarawa; troops advance on Makin; seventy-eight Marines land on Abemama atoll, about 75 miles southeast of Tarawa.

1943/NOVEMBER 22—Operation Galvanic: Heavy fighting on Tarawa, where the Japanese make a "banzai" charge after dark; on Makin, Army personnel advance slowly; Seabees begin construction of an air base at Abemama.

1943/NOVEMBER 23—Operation Galvanic continues: Makin Island is secured by the U.S. 27th Infantry Division; Marines secure Betio. In India, the Chinese 38th Division essays an offensive into Burma across the Assamese mountains. Chinese troops in Hunan begin stout resistance to a Japanese "rice offensive" at Changteh. The Japanese light cruisers *Isuzu* and *Nagara* arrive at Mili in the Marshalls; the former then proceeds to Kwajalein, while the latter returns to Truk. The Japanese light cruiser *Naka* arrives at Kwajalein from Truk. In the Indian Ocean, the Japanese submarine I-37 scouts the Seychelles with a small reconnaissance plane.

1943/NOVEMBER 24—The U.S. escort carrier *Lipscombe Bay* is torpedoed by the Japanese submarine I-175 in the Gilbert Islands, sinking with heavy loss of life (including Pearl Harbor hero Dory Miller). A Japanese cruiser-destroyer force (three heavy cruisers plus a destroyer squadron) departs Truk for Kwajalein. The Chinese 38th Division advances across the mountains on the Burma-India frontier.

1943/NOVEMBER 25—First major Japanese operation on Bougainville, as a Japanese infantry regiment attacks the U.S. defense perimeter, to be beaten off with heavy losses. Battle of Cape St. George: Five U.S. destroyers intercept five Japanese destroyers near New Geor-

gia, sinking three. Operation Galvanic reaction: Japanese aircraft from Kwajalein make two unsuccessful attempts to raid the U.S. fleet off Tarawa and Makin (one a "spectacular" night attack), as Marines eliminate final Japanese pockets on outlying islets of Tarawa atoll. The Chinese 38th Division attacks into Burma from India.

1943/NOVEMBER 26—Marines mop up Japanese pockets on outlying islets of Tarawa atoll. The Japanese submarine I-39 is sunk near Makin by the U.S. destroyer *Boyd*. A Japanese cruiser-destroyer force (three heavy cruisers plus a destroyer squadron) arrives at Kwajalein from Truk. In Burma the Chinese 38th Division advances into the Hukawng Valley.

1943/NOVEMBER 27—Marines eliminate final Japanese pockets on outlying islets of Tarawa atoll. The Japanese light cruiser *Isuzu* arrives at Kwajalein from Mili. A Japanese cruiser-destroyer force (three heavy cruisers plus a destroyer squadron) departs Kwajalein for Eniwetok.

1943/NOVEMBER 28—The Japanese light cruiser *Nagara* departs Truk for Maloelap. A Japanese cruiser-destroyer force (three heavy cruisers plus a destroyer squadron) arrives at Eniwetok from Kwajalein.

1943/NOVEMBER 29—U.S. and Australian destroyers bombard Japanese positions on New Britain. The U.S. destroyer *Perkins* is sunk off Cape Vogelkop in New Guinea in a collision with an Australian troop transport. The U.S. submarine *Sculpin* is sunk by a Japanese destroyer near Truk. Aircraft from the U.S. escort carrier *Chenango* sink the Japanese submarine I-21 in the Gilberts. A Japanese cruiser-destroyer force (three heavy cruisers plus a destroyer squadron) departs Eniwetok for Kwajalein.

1943/NOVEMBER 30—U.S. destroyers bombard Japanese positions near Cape

Torokina on Bougainville, where heavy fighting continues. A Japanese cruiser-destroyer force arrives at Kwajalein from Eniwetok. In Burma, the Japanese begin to counterattack the Chinese 38th Division.

1943/DECEMBER 1—The 5th Marine Division begins organizing at Camp Pendleton, California.

1943/DECEMBER 2—The Japanese light cruiser *Nagara* arrives at Maloelap from Truk.

1943/DECEMBER 3—The Japanese light cruiser *Nagara* departs Maloelap for Kwajalein. In Burma, the Japanese attempt to wipe out isolated elements (three battalions) of the Chinese 38th Division.

1943/DECEMBER 4—The U.S. Fast Carrier Task Force raids Kwajalein and Wotje, sinking six transports while damaging three more plus two light cruisers, and destroying fifty-five aircraft at a cost of five U.S. planes lost and an aerial torpedo hit on the carrier *Lexington*. The Japanese escort carrier *Chuyo* is sunk and the carrier *Ryuho* damaged about 250 miles southeast of Tokyo Bay by the U.S. submarine *Sailfish*. The Japanese light cruiser *Nagara* arrives at Kwajalein from Maloelap, joining a light cruiser, three heavy cruisers, and a destroyer squadron that have been there for several days.

1943/DECEMBER 5—Major Japanese air raid on port facilities at Calcutta, India. A Japanese cruiser-destroyer force (three heavy cruisers, two light cruisers, and a destroyer squadron) sails from Kwajalein for Truk.

1943/DECEMBER 6—During November–December 1943, the Japanese Army activates ten "independent mixed brigades" (four or five infantry battalions, an artillery battalion, an engineer battalion, and some services) by reorganizing occupation forces in the Netherlands East Indies (four), the Philippines (four), Thailand (one), and Indochina (one), to release troops for combat elsewhere while still maintaining local control.

1943/DECEMBER 7—A Japanese cruiser-destroyer force arrives at Truk from Kwajalein.

1943/DECEMBER 8—A U.S. fast battleship task force bombards Japanese positions on Nauru. Australian troops capture Wareo in New Guinea.

1943/DECEMBER 9—The Japanese break off their attempt to take Changteh, in Hunan, China.

1943/DECEMBER 10—U.S. Navy Seabees complete an airstrip at Empress Augusta Bay, Bougainville, where Army and Marine personnel are pushing their defensive perimeter outward. The resistance is so dogged that Japanese troops will still be fighting on Bougainville at the end of the war.

1943/DECEMBER 11—A U.S. Army amphibious task force forms up for landing on the Arawe Peninsula of New Britain (nearly 300 miles west of Rabaul).

1943/DECEMBER 12—The U.S. and Nationalist Chinese governments cannot agree on the extent to which Chinese troops should get involved in Burmese fighting. The U.S. wants more action; the Chinese want more aid.

1943/DECEMBER 13—Heavily escorted by U.S. and Australian warships of the Seventh Fleet, the U.S. 112th Cavalry Regimental Combat Team (converted to infantry) sails from Goodenough Island for New Britain.

1943/DECEMBER 14—The Japanese destroyer *Numakaze* is sunk by the U.S. submarine *Grayback* about 50 miles east of Okinawa.

1943/DECEMBER 15—After a major aerial bombardment, the U.S. 112th Cavalry RCT lands at Arawe, New Britain.

1943/DECEMBER 16—The Japanese submarine *I-29* departs Penang for France.

1943/DECEMBER 17—The Allies battle the last Japanese defenders on the Arawe Peninsula of New Britain.

1943/DECEMBER 18—The Japanese stage air raids in southern China (Kunming) to cripple Chinese forces advancing into Burma.

1943/DECEMBER 19—The U.S. 1st Marine Division makes final preparations for Operation Dexterity, the invasion of Cape Gloucester, New Britain.

1943/DECEMBER 20—The Japanese destroyer *Fuyo* is sunk about 60 miles west of Manila by the U.S. submarine *Puffer*.

1943/DECEMBER 21—In southern China, Japanese air raids have little effect on Chinese preparations to send more troops south into Burma.

1943/DECEMBER 22—Japanese bombers again hit Kunming in China.

1943/DECEMBER 23—USAAF aircraft operating from bases in China sink a Japanese gunboat about 35 miles south of Formosa. The U.S. 1st Marine Division completes preparations for the invasion of Cape Gloucester.

1943/DECEMBER 24—In northern Burma, General Joseph Stilwell undertakes an offensive to rescue remnants of the Chinese 38th Division, which has been bottled up by the Japanese. The U.S. 1st Marine Division is aboard ship and ready for the invasion of Cape Gloucester.

1943/DECEMBER 25—Japanese reinforcements for Rabaul and New Ireland depart from Truk. U.S. carrier aircraft raid Kavieng, New Ireland, sinking or damaging several ships. The battleship *Yamato* is damaged by a torpedo from the U.S. submarine *Skate* about 180 miles north of Truk. The Japanese submarine *I-29*, bound for France, replenishes from the German supply ship *Bogota* in the Indian Ocean. The U.S. 1st Marine Division sails for Cape Gloucester, New Britain.

1943/DECEMBER 26—The 1st Marine

Division lands at Cape Gloucester, New Britain. The U.S. destroyer *Brownson* is sunk by Japanese Army aircraft off Cape Gloucester, New Britain. The Japanese submarine *I-29*, bound for France, replenishes from the German supply ship *Bogota* in the Indian Ocean.

1943/DECEMBER 27—Heavy fighting on Cape Gloucester, New Britain, as follow-up elements of the 1st Marine Division land.

1943/DECEMBER 28—The U.S. Americal Division relieves the 3rd Marine Division on Bougainville.

1943/DECEMBER 29—On Cape Gloucester, the 1st Marine Division captures the Japanese airfield.

1943/DECEMBER 30—The Royal Navy dispatches two carriers, two battleships, a battle cruiser, and seven destroyers from Britain for the Far Eastern Fleet.

1943/DECEMBER 31—In northern Burma, Chinese forces under Stilwell break the Japanese encirclement of their 38th Division and clear portions of the Tarung River valley of the enemy. The U.S. 38th Infantry Division sails from New Orleans for Hawaii.

1944/JANUARY 1—Fighting in Cape Gloucester on New Britain ceases as all Japanese resistance is overcome. The Allies now control western New Britain, further isolating Rabaul, at the eastern end of the island.

1944/JANUARY 2—Allied troops land on Saidor, New Guinea. This isolates 12,000 Japanese troops at Sio.

1944/JANUARY 3—The Chinese 38th Division battles to secure its positions along the Tarung River in Burma.

1944/JANUARY 4—Australian forces struggle to reach Kelanoa in New Guinea, bringing them within 60 miles of linking up with U.S. forces.

1944/JANUARY 5—On New Guinea, American and Australian offensives struggle on to combine at Kelanoa. This juncture will greatly improve the Allied position in New Guinea, and render the Japanese position strategically hopeless.

1944/JANUARY 6—The Nationalist Chinese government faces crisis because President Roosevelt demands greater Chinese operations against Japan. Pfc. John Lindemann and the 4th Marine Division ship out from California to the Marshall Islands in the Central Pacific.

1944/JANUARY 7—Japanese resistance in Arawe (New Guinea) weakens.

1944/JANUARY 8—U.S. Navy ships bombard the Japanese base on Shortland Island in the Solomon Islands.

1944/JANUARY 9—In the Arakan area of Burma, British troops recapture Maungdaw.

1944/JANUARY 10—British bombers begin dropping naval mines at the mouth of the Salween River in Burma.

1944/JANUARY 11—The Japanese make a desperate attempt to hold their Tarung River positions in northern Burma in the face of a Chinese advance.

1944/JANUARY 12—Chinese forces gain the upper hand over Japanese defenders along the Tarung River.

1944/JANUARY 13—Chinese forces complete their operation to secure the Tarung River line.

1944/JANUARY 14—President Roosevelt threatens the Chinese with loss of Lend-Lease aid if more Chinese forces are not committed to fight against Japan.

1944/JANUARY 15—Australian troops reach the north coast of the Huon Peninsula in New Guinea near Sio.

1944/JANUARY 16—The Chinese reply to the U.S. threat of Lend-Lease loss by threatening to halt all Chinese aid for U.S. forces unless America comes across with a billion dollars in new aid.

1944/JANUARY 17—After desperate last-ditch resistance, Allied troops subdue the last Japanese defenders at Arawe on the southern coast of New Britain.

1944/JANUARY 18—The Japanese make preparations for a major counteroffensive against British forces in the Arakan area of Burma.

1944/JANUARY 19—Chinese and Japanese troops struggle for control of Taro Plain in northern Burma.

1944/JANUARY 20—The Allies prepare to unleash thousands of commandos in northern Burma against Japanese rear-area installations. This, combined with the advance of U.S., British, and Chinese troops, is to reopen the Burma Road to allow supply of China overland from India.

1944/JANUARY 21—Fighting on the Burmese coast near Maungdaw between British (Indian) and Japanese troops continues.

1944/JANUARY 22—Allied air units in the Solomons prepare to stage a major air strike on the large Japanese base at Rabaul.

1944/JANUARY 23—The Chinese government is caught in a quandary. The Americans insist that the Chinese commit their strategic reserve of capable divisions to fighting in Burma, but this leaves them without any reserve if the Japanese in eastern China attack again.

1944/JANUARY 24—U.S. naval aircraft prepare for a major series of attacks against Japanese bases in the Marshall Islands.

1944/JANUARY 25—A major Allied air raid on the main Japanese base at Rabaul results in destruction of eighty-three enemy aircraft.

1944/JANUARY 26—A minor diplomatic coup for the Allies: Liberia declares war on, while Argentina severs diplomatic relations with, Germany and Japan.

1944/JANUARY 27—The U.S. issues a report on Japanese atrocities against U.S. and Filipino troops after the surrender of Bataan in early 1942 ("The Bataan Death March").

1944/JANUARY 28—U.S. Navy Task Force 58 (nine carriers, several battleships, many cruisers and destroyers) steams within striking distance of the Marshall Islands.

1944/JANUARY 29—Major U.S. Navy air offensive against Japanese bases in the Marshall Islands begins.

1944/JANUARY 30—Chinese forces oust Japanese from Taro Plain in northern Burma.

1944/JANUARY 31—U.S. troops land on Japanese-held Kwajalein Island (and other nearby islands in the Marshalls). These are the first of Japan's prewar territories to fall. Pfc. John Lindemann lands on Roi Island as part of the U.S. offensive in the Marshalls. His unit, the 25th Marines, takes the island with little loss and remains there until March 25. Other Marine units have a harder time on nearby Kwajalein Island.

1944/FEBRUARY 1—The Japanese leadership learns that Australia has formed a commission to investigate Japanese war crimes.

1944/FEBRUARY 2—American troops advance rapidly against light resistance on Kwajalein and other islands in the Marshalls.

1944/FEBRUARY 3—In a daring raid, U.S. warships based in Alaska bombard the northern Japanese island of Paramushiro in the northern Kuriles. This was the first time any of the Japanese "home" islands was shelled by Allied ships.

1944/FEBRUARY 4—Japanese troops launch their major offensive against British forces in the Arakan region of Burma.

1944/FEBRUARY 5—Except for a few isolated holdouts, Kwajalein is conquered. The Japanese have lost 5,100 troops (all dead, save for 200 POWs). U.S. losses are 142 dead.

1944/FEBRUARY 6—Chinese troops advance from the north in Burma, while British Chindit irregulars to the south try to distract and delay Japanese reinforcements.

1944/FEBRUARY 7—Japanese offensive in the Arakan area of Burma has some success, as British units pull back.

1944/FEBRUARY 8—Some British troops encircled in the Arakan region of Burma prepare to fight their way past Japanese forces.

1944/FEBRUARY 9—The Americans ask Nationalist Chinese permission to send a military mission to the Chinese Communists (to try to get the Communists to help against the Japanese, or frighten the Nationalists into doing so).

1944/FEBRUARY 10—Australian troops complete their takeover of the Huon Peninsula in New Guinea.

1944/FEBRUARY 11—Japan stops using Truk (in the Carolines) as a major naval base. It has become too difficult to get merchant shipping to Truk to keep the fleet supplied.

1944/FEBRUARY 12—U.S. Marines occupy Umboi Island (off the western end of New Britain).

1944/FEBRUARY 13—U.S. Marines take possession of Arno in the Marshall Islands.

1944/FEBRUARY 14—Pfc. John Lindemann's unit, the 4th Marine Division, is shipped from the Marshall Islands back to Maui in the Hawaiian Islands.

1944/FEBRUARY 15—New Zealand troops land on Green Island in the northern Solomons.

1944/FEBRUARY 16—U.S. Army and Marine units coordinate their attacks to secure the entire western half of New Britain.

1944/FEBRUARY 17—The Allies complete a massive two-day attack (six battleships and nine carriers) on the main Japanese base on Truk. Although most Japanese warships have earlier been withdrawn, Allied ships and aircraft still sink two cruisers, three destroyers, and over 200,000 tons of merchant shipping (including several tankers). The island's airstrips are destroyed. Truk is now neutralized, and will be bypassed, leaving many of its garrison to starve before the war ends.

1944/FEBRUARY 18—Allied destroyers shell Japanese bases at Rabaul and Kavieng.

1944/FEBRUARY 19—Fighting continues on the Marshall Islands at Engebi and Eniwetok. Resistance ends on February 21 and these islands become major bases for further American advances.

1944/FEBRUARY 20—New Zealand troops complete their conquest of Green Island. This cuts off all remaining Japanese troops in the Solomon Islands. The Allies now have an air base only 117 miles from the main Japanese base at Rabaul. This short distance permits steady aerial bombing of Rabaul, escorted by fighters. Japanese air power at Rabaul will soon be neutralized as a result.

1944/FEBRUARY 21—General Tojo takes over direct control of the Japanese Army by assuming the position of Army Chief of Staff.

1944/FEBRUARY 22—U.S. Navy Task Force 58, while approaching the Mariana Islands, is attacked by Japanese aircraft. The attack is defeated with heavy losses to the Japanese.

1944/FEBRUARY 23—For the first time in the Burma war, British forces defeat the Japanese in a pitched battle; Japanese forces at Sinzweya withdraw after their attacks on the 7th Indian Division fail. The Japanese style of warfare has been difficult for the British to deal with. The dramatic Japanese victories over the British early in the war (particularly the fall of Singapore) played a part, as did the British use of a variety of different troops (Indian and British). But there was also the Japanese fatalistic perseverance and refusal to surrender when beaten. Eventually, the British learned to cope.

1944/FEBRUARY 24—U.S. carrier aircraft complete a series of attacks against Japanese positions in the Marianas (Saipan, Tinian, Rota, and Guam), the first such attacks of the war.

1944/FEBRUARY 25—British, U.S., and Chinese forces all advance in Burma.

1944/FEBRUARY 26—The U.S. fleet carrier *Bennington* and escort carrier *Steamer Bay* are launched. Since Pearl Harbor, the U.S. Navy has commissioned eight fleet carriers (728 total aircraft capacity), nine light carriers (370 aircraft), and forty-three escort carriers (729 aircraft) for its fleet, while the Imperial Navy has commissioned only three fleet carriers (about 160 aircraft), four light carriers (121 aircraft), and five escort carriers (138 aircraft).

1944/FEBRUARY 27—A U.S. amphibious task force approaches the Admiralty Islands.

1944/FEBRUARY 28—U.S. air and naval forces begin softening up the Admiralty Islands preparatory to an amphibious landing on Los Negros. Pfc. John Lindemann and the 4th Marine Division arrive at Maui (Hawaii) and begin a training program in preparation for their next amphibious assault.

1944/FEBRUARY 29—U.S. Army troops invade Los Negros in the Admiralty Islands, to complete the encirclement of Rabaul.

1944/MARCH 1—American troops on Los Negros Island defeat Japanese attacks on their beachhead.

1944/MARCH 2—The Japanese airfield at Momote on Los Negros Island is seized by U.S. troops.

1944/MARCH 3—The Japanese make a final effort to force U.S. troops off Los Negros Island. The attack fails, and with it goes most of the remaining Japanese combat capability.

1944/MARCH 4—In northern Burma, American commandos (Merrill's Marauders) and the Chinese First Army begin an offensive against the Japanese to reopen the Burma Road into China.

1944/MARCH 5—U.S. Navy ships bombard Manus in the Admiralty Islands.

1944/MARCH 6—U.S. Marines make a landing on New Britain and establish a beachhead over a mile deep near Talasea.

1944/MARCH 7—Three brigades of British Chindit commandos begin attacking Japanese rear-area installations in northern Burma. The Chindits were dropped behind the Japanese lines two days earlier.

1944/MARCH 8—While part of the Japanese force desperately struggles against Chinese Regulars and British and American commandos in north Burma, another Japanese force launches an offensive against British forces near Imphal in eastern India.

1944/MARCH 9—U.S. Marines seize the Talasea airstrip in New Britain; there is no resistance.

1944/MARCH 10—Chinese troops and Merrill's Marauders seize full control of the Walawbum Valley in northern Burma.

1944/MARCH 11—British troops continue to advance on the Arakan front in Burma, closing in on the town of Razabil.

1944/MARCH 12—Ireland refuses to oust Axis (Japanese and German) diplomats (who act, in effect, as spies). Britain enacts sanctions.

1944/MARCH 13—The British launch an outflanking amphibious operation in the Arakan area of Burma.

1944/MARCH 14—A Japanese surprise attack at Imphal (eastern India) threatens to surround retreating British units.

1944/MARCH 15—U.S. Army troops invade Manus Island in the Admiralties.

1944/MARCH 16—The Japanese destroyer *Shirakumo* is torpedoed east of Hokkaido by the U.S. submarine *Tautog*. Since Pearl Harbor, Japan has lost 62 of her 129 destroyers.

1944/MARCH 17—U.S. amphibious task forces move toward Emirau in the Bismarck Archipelago.

1944/MARCH 18—U.S. Task Group 50.1 bombards Mili atoll in the Marshall Islands.

1944/MARCH 19—General Tojo and his aides debate whether to announce to the Japanese people that the outlook for the war is dire. Several days later, the announcement is made.

1944/MARCH 20—U.S. Marines occupy Emirau Island in the Bismarck Archipelago. The island will be used to further isolate Rabaul and neutralize it.

1944/MARCH 21—The final phase of fighting on Los Negros Island begins.

1944/MARCH 22—Japan's offensive in Burma gains momentum as its troops approach the Indian border.

1944/MARCH 23—Japanese troops launch attacks on Bougainville in the Solomons. The attacks are halted by U.S. artillery. This was the last major battle in the Solomons.

1944/MARCH 24—British Major General Orde Wingate is killed in a plane crash in Burma. He developed the commando tactics and organization used with much success against the Japanese in Burma.

1944/MARCH 25—Last organized Japanese resistance on Manus Island is put down.

1944/MARCH 26—USS *Tullibee* sinks itself when one of its torpedoes circles and hits the sub. One survivor lives to tell the tale.

1944/MARCH 27—Chinese forces in northern Burma keep up the pressure on the Japanese to aid British troops farther south who are being forced back into India.

1944/MARCH 28—The U.S. Navy prepares Task Force 58 for a major raid into the western Caroline Islands.

1944/MARCH 29—Advancing Japanese

troops in eastern India cut the road between Imphal and Kohima, threatening the entire British position in the area.

1944/MARCH 30—U.S. Task Force 58 begins several days of raids into the western Carolines (Palau, Yap, and Ulithi). At a cost of 20 aircraft, the U.S. forces destroy 150 enemy aircraft, 6 warships, and over 100,000 tons of shipping.

1944/MARCH 31—Admiral Mineichi Koga, commander of the Japanese Combined Fleet, dies in an airplane crash in the Philippines. Admiral Soemu Toyoda succeeds him.

1944/APRIL 1—U.S. Navy Task Force 58's raid into the western Carolines continues, with the Japanese unable to offer any effective resistance.

1944/APRIL 2—The USAAF stages a campaign to destroy Japanese air power around Hollandia, New Guinea.

1944/APRIL 3—The USAAF launches a large raid on the major Japanese base at Hollandia, New Guinea. Over 300 Japanese aircraft are destroyed, most of them caught on the ground before they can take off.

1944/APRIL 4—In eastern India, the Japanese move on Kohima, having cut the road from Kohima to Imphal.

1944/APRIL 5—British forces are unable to halt the Japanese forces advancing on Kohima.

1944/APRIL 6—Several days of U.S. air raids leave the Japanese with only twenty-five flyable aircraft in Hollandia, New Guinea.

1944/APRIL 7—British forces at Kohima are brought under more pressure as advancing Japanese cut off the town's water supply.

1944/APRIL 8—In a skillful, and lucky, bit of bombing, B-24s bring down the Sittang Bridge in Burma. This cripples Japanese railroad traffic to crucial battle areas for two months.

1944/APRIL 9—The Japanese offer to mediate a peace agreement between Germany and Russia. The Germans are perplexed and the Russians turn the offer down.

1944/APRIL 10—British forces on the Imphal-Kohima front in eastern India are ordered to take the offensive. The Japanese have gambled everything on their offensive and soon run out of resources. The Japanese troops are left largely without food, ammunition, or other supplies.

1944/APRIL 11—The Japanese destroyer *Akigumo* is sunk off Zamboanga, the Philippines, by the U.S. submarine *Redfin*.

1944/APRIL 12—Australian light forces depart Finschhafen, New Guinea, to escort convoys carrying reinforcements to the Admiralty Islands and to shell bypassed Japanese positions.

1944/APRIL 13—Japan masses forces on its front line in China, in preparation for an offensive into the interior areas of China.

1944/APRIL 14—In one of those all-too-common wartime accidents, the ammunition ship *Fort Stikene*, carrying 1,300 tons of TNT, explodes in Bombay Harbor. Another ammunition ship nearby explodes, and in the ensuing blast a total of twenty-one ships are destroyed. Nearly 1,000 people are killed.

1944/APRIL 15—Task Force 58 is en route from its base at Majuro to the Admiralty Islands for the Hollandia invasion.

1944/APRIL 16—Senior American military planners address the question of what must be done to defeat Japan and whether an invasion of Japan itself will be necessary, leading to preliminary studies for Operation Olympic, the invasion of Japan.

1944/APRIL 17—Japan begins its last major offensive in China as one division crosses the Yellow River. The objective is the U.S. airfields in China that are supporting raids by long-range bombers as far as Japan itself.

1944/APRIL 18—Fighting in New Britain begins to die down and, by the end of the month, is over save for some sporadic Japanese holdout activity.

1944/APRIL 19—Japan sends two more divisions south from Peking toward U.S. air bases in China.

1944/APRIL 20—A British division lifts the Japanese siege of Kohima in eastern India. The Japanese still hold the key road to Imphal.

1944/APRIL 21—U.S. Task Force 58 raids Hollandia, Wakde, and other points in northern New Guinea with aircraft and gunfire in preparation for the Hollandia landings.

1944/APRIL 22—U.S. Army troops make an amphibious landing near Hollandia in New Guinea.

1944/APRIL 23—Staff officers at the U.S. War Department conclude that Japan can be defeated only with an invasion of Japan itself. This becomes an objective for the rest of the war, until the unexpected success of the atomic bomb test in July 1945 provides an alternative.

1944/APRIL 24—Australian troops occupy Madang in New Guinea. This provides another airfield for Allied use, and Australian aircraft promptly begin using it.

1944/APRIL 25—The Japanese offensive in China intensifies, with Honan Province being the center of most of the fighting.

1944/APRIL 26—More Allied gains in New Guinea. Australians take Alexishafen; U.S. troops take the airfield at Hollandia.

1944/APRIL 27—Heavy fighting continues at Imphal (eastern India) as the Japanese attempt to defeat the British before the start of the rainy season.

1944/APRIL 28—The Japanese advance in China continues. USAAF planes attack Yellow River bridges in an attempt

to slow down the Japanese by cutting off their supply.

1944/APRIL 29—U.S. Navy carriers again raid Truk and destroy over 100 aircraft.

1944/APRIL 30—U.S. Navy carrier aircraft continue a second day of raids on the Truk naval base, destroying most of the remaining fuel supplies. This effectively neutralizes Truk's ability to support naval or air operations against Allied forces.

1944/MAY 1—Ponape Island in the Carolines is worked over by U.S. battleships and carrier aircraft.

1944/MAY 2—U.S. and Chinese forces continue advancing through the Mogaung Valley of northern Burma.

1944/MAY 3—Allied aircraft begin mining waters off Rangoon and Bangkok, making it nearly impossible for the Japanese to bring merchant shipping into those ports.

1944/MAY 4—Chinese troops battle to the vicinity of Kamaing in northern Burma.

1944/MAY 5—The British, feeling their military position in Burma and political position in India is now stable, release nationalist leader Mahatma Gandhi (who has been imprisoned since August 1942).

1944/MAY 6—Fighting in the Aitape area of New Guinea goes poorly for the Japanese, who, in several weeks of fighting, have lost over 500 dead to only 19 Americans killed. Allied reinforcements and supplies continue to land amphibiously.

1944/MAY 7—Allied air raids against the sea routes off Rangoon and Bangkok virtually drive Japanese shipping from the Bay of Bengal.

1944/MAY 8—Chinese forces mass for a major advance in northern Burma.

1944/MAY 9—The Japanese offensive in China succeeds in capturing Lushan, thus securing complete control of the Peking-Hankow railroad.

1944/MAY 10—The Chinese launch a major offensive in north Burma, crossing the Salween River and advancing on a 100-mile front.

1944/MAY 11—Japanese forces in China continue to battle for control of the Peking-Hankow rail line.

1944/MAY 12—The Japanese beat off Chinese attempts to again sever the Peking-Hankow rail line.

1944/MAY 13—One of several Japanese submarines operating outside the Pacific is sunk in the mid-Atlantic by a U.S. destroyer escort.

1944/MAY 14—U.S. commandos (Merrill's Marauders) in Burma plan a surprise attack on the Japanese airport at Myitkyina. The attack succeeds on the seventeenth.

1944/MAY 15—British troops finally break down the Japanese defenses of Kohima in eastern India.

1944/MAY 16—The siege of Kohima in eastern India is finally ended, with the last Japanese resistance crushed.

1944/MAY 17—U.S. and British aircraft attack Soerabaja in Java and sink ten enemy ships.

1944/MAY 18—Japanese and Chinese forces engage in street fighting in the Chinese city of Loyang.

1944/MAY 19—U.S. Army troops make an amphibious assault on Wakde Island (off the north coast of New Guinea).

1944/MAY 20—U.S. Navy aircraft attack Japanese-held Marcus Island.

1944/MAY 21—Japanese resistance on Wakde Island is crushed. The island will support an air base that will provide air cover for the coming Allied invasion of Mindanao in the Philippines. Meanwhile, another disaster unfolds at Pearl Harbor. Often, just getting ready for combat was lethal. While ships are being loaded for the coming invasion of Saipan, one LST filled with extra fuel and ammunition (because of a shortage of specially built ammunition ships) explodes while docked next to several other LSTs. This happens in the West Loch area of Pearl Harbor, near the ammunition depot. The LSTs are swarming with sailors and Marines, all working on a Sunday to get the ships ready for the upcoming operation. Pfc. John Lindemann is one of the Marines working on the loading. Fortunately, his LST is the last in a line of ten ships from the one that blows up. He and some others cut the lines securing their LST to the pier and their ship drifts out of danger before the chain reaction of exploding ships reaches them. Six LSTs are lost, as are 207 Marines (and many sailors.) Nearly 400 Marines are also injured. This disaster delays the 4th Division's sailing by twenty-four hours, the lost time being made up on the voyage to Saipan.

1944/MAY 22—The campaign in the Admiralty Islands ends. The Japanese have lost over 3,000 dead; the U.S., 326.

1944/MAY 23—The Japanese offensive in China is hit by a Chinese counteroffensive.

1944/MAY 24—U.S. Navy carrier aircraft attack Wake Island.

1944/MAY 25—Japanese lose ground in fighting around Myitkyina in Burma, but reinforce their troops for a counteroffensive.

1944/MAY 26—U.S. commandos in Burma lose some of their gains in the battle for Myitkyina.

1944/MAY 27—The U.S. Army 41st Division meets only token resistance when it lands on Biak Island. This brings Allied troops to within 900 miles of the Philippines.

1944/MAY 28—The Chinese commit all their available forces to their advance across the Salween River in north Burma.

1944/MAY 29—The first tank battle of the Pacific war takes place as Japanese and American armor clash on Biak. The Japanese lose. Pfc. John Lindemann and the 4th Marine Division ship out from

Maui to Saipan, in the Marianas Islands.

1944/MAY 30—Despite increased Chinese resistance, two Japanese divisions force their way across the Hsiang River in their attempt to shut down Allied air bases in China.

1944/MAY 31—Allied air attacks and air-dropped mines keep nearly all Japanese ships out of the Bay of Bengal.

1944/JUNE 1—Monsoon rains begin in Burma. Most military operations begin to slow down because of the reduced mobility.

1944/JUNE 2—Japanese forces in Honan Province of China halt their operations, having achieved all of their objectives.

1944/JUNE 3—The Battle of Kohima in eastern India ends in a British victory.

1944/JUNE 4—The fighting at Myitkyina, Burma, stalls as casualties force the U.S. and Chinese troops to regroup.

1944/JUNE 5—Several more Chinese divisions cross the Salween River in Burma.

1944/JUNE 6—Pentagon planners set October 1, 1945, as the date for the first landings on the Japanese home islands. The vast logistical preparations for such an operation move forward using that date as a target.

1944/JUNE 7—A U.S. Navy task force steams toward the Marianas Islands, to soften up the objective for later invasion.

1944/JUNE 8—A desperate Japanese attempt to resupply Biak Island with five heavily laden destroyers ends with one ship being sunk and the other four turned back.

1944/JUNE 9—The U.S. amphibious task force steams toward Saipan in the Marianas.

1944/JUNE 10—The U.S. and Chinese assault on Myitkyina, Burma, resumes.

1944/JUNE 11—U.S. Navy ships and aircraft attack the Marianas (Guam, Saipan, and Tinian), losing a dozen aircraft but destroying 200 Japanese planes and damaging installations.

1944/JUNE 12—The Chinese Communists, fearful of the recent Japanese offensive, pledge support of the Chinese Nationalists in the fight against the Japanese.

1944/JUNE 13—Fighting at Myitkyina, Burma, turns against the Allies as the Japanese gain ground.

1944/JUNE 14—The Japanese offensive in China rolls on, as the city of Liuyang falls.

1944/JUNE 15—Saipan, in the Marianas, is stormed by two U.S. Marine divisions. The 27,000 Japanese defenders are hit by the firepower of seven battleships and eleven cruisers. Saipan and other islands in the Marianas will be bases for B-29 attacks on Japan. Pfc. John Lindemann is among those landing on Saipan, and runs into a lot more opposition than he did in the Marshall Islands.

1944/JUNE 16—Returning to their China bases, U.S. B-29s have made their first air attacks on Japan since the Doolittle Raid in early 1942.

1944/JUNE 17—U.S. Navy carrier aircraft attack Iwo Jima and the Bonin Islands. Pfc. John Lindemann, in the midst of the fierce fighting on Saipan, is promoted to corporal and given command of a rifle squad. Casualties have been heavy. Corporal Lindemann discovers that the most effective weapon at night is the hand grenade. Many a night, Corporal Lindemann and his Marines spend a lot of time tossing grenades at Japanese infantry creeping toward their positions. The enemy also realizes the value of grenades (which don't give your position away as the flash of a rifle does). So Marines and Japanese toss grenades, and scurry out of the way of what may be hurled toward them.

1944/JUNE 18—In China, the Japanese offensive takes the city of Changsha, an area the Japanese had twice earlier in the war reached and failed to take. Corporal John Lindemann is on patrol during the continuing Saipan fighting. While he is moving through a cane field, a Japanese mortar opens up. One of the shells lands near Corporal Lindemann, sending metal tearing through his knee. It is not a serious wound, but it is messy and has to be treated quickly before infection sets in. Lindemann is evacuated to an offshore hospital ship in a few hours.

1944/JUNE 19—The three-day Battle of the Philippine Sea begins. It ends in a defeat for the Japanese (they lose three carriers and 426 of the 473 aircraft committed). This was a major Japanese attempt to slow the American advance across the Pacific. After their failure in this battle, Japanese senior leaders know that the war is lost.

1944/JUNE 20—Allied troops in New Guinea advance on the last Japanese airfield on the island.

1944/JUNE 21—After ten weeks of fighting over Imphal in eastern India, the Japanese find they have suffered nearly 44,000 casualties, compared to 14,000 British, including 2,700 dead.

1944/JUNE 22—The battle of Imphal comes to an end as British troops open the road from Kohima to Imphal. The Japanese troops begin to retreat.

1944/JUNE 23—Savage fighting continues on Saipan, as the Japanese defenders fight to the last man.

1944/JUNE 24—Corporal John Lindemann, after six days on a hospital ship off Saipan, finds that his knee wound is sufficiently healed to allow him to return to his unit (E Company, 2nd Battalion, 25th Marines). It is common for lightly wounded soldiers to be sent back into action before their wounds are completely healed. The experienced troops are needed, and often the wounded man himself is eager to rejoin his buddies while they are still under fire.

1944/JUNE 25—The Japanese emperor, Hirohito, calls a conference of senior generals and admirals to discuss Japan's worsening situation. The military admits that the "outer" defenses like Saipan cannot be held and that emphasis must be placed on bases closer to Japan.

1944/JUNE 26—The U.S. air base at Hengyang, China, is overrun by Japanese troops.

1944/JUNE 27—Fighting on Saipan continues at an intense level, as the dug-in Japanese have to be rooted out by advancing Marines.

1944/JUNE 28—Around Hengyang, Chinese forces put up stiff resistance to advancing Japanese.

1944/JUNE 29—There is heavy U.S. submarine activity, as *Archerfish* sinks Japanese *Patrol Boat Number 24* off Iwo Jima, while *Darter* sinks minelayer *Tsugaru* off Morotai. During June 1944, U.S. submarines in the Pacific sink about 260,000 tons of Japanese merchant shipping, exclusive of vessels under 500 tons, not to mention two aircraft carriers, six destroyers, and these two smaller warships.

1944/JUNE 30—U.S. Navy warships steam toward Iwo Jima and the Bonin Islands.

1944/JULY 1—Japanese resistance on Saipan crumbles. Admiral Chuichi Nagumo commits suicide. He led Japanese fleets to victory early in the war, until defeated at Midway. He was then demoted to command of the naval forces in the Saipan area, which is how he comes to end his life in a bunker surrounded by U.S. Marines.

1944/JULY 2—Surviving Japanese forces fall back to the north end of Saipan to make a last stand.

1944/JULY 3—U.S. Navy ships bombard Iwo Jima and the Bonin Islands. Several Japanese transports are sunk.

1944/JULY 4—U.S. Marines on Saipan force the remaining Japanese defenders to a small corner of the island.

1944/JULY 5—Japanese commanders at Imphal in eastern India discuss calling off the operation. After several days' debate, the decision is made to withdraw. The Japanese find that they have lost 53,000 out of the 85,000 troops committed. Many of the losses were due to disease and starvation because of inadequate logistical arrangements.

1944/JULY 6—Surviving Japanese troops on Saipan resolve to make one last attack to reverse their desperate situation. The attack is made the following day, with most of the 3,000 attacking troops being killed, but not before inflicting heavy casualties on the defending Marines.

1944/JULY 7—U.S. B-29s from Chinese bases again attack targets in Japan. On Saipan, the remaining Japanese forces are cornered and desperate. Corporal John Lindemann's Marine rifle company is hit by a Japanese "banzai" charge. Marine artillery is called in to help halt this attack. Unfortunately, the shells fall short of their intended target. E Company is hit pretty bad, with over half the Marines being killed or wounded by the friendly fire. The Japanese assault is halted, but E Company ends up with only 40 Marines fit for action (down from 240 at the beginning of the battle).

1944/JULY 8—Guam is bombarded by U.S. Navy ships, beginning a series of daily attacks in preparation for landings later in the month. On Saipan, after the friendly fire incident on the seventh, E Company is considered too weak to stay in the line and is detailed to provide security for battalion headquarters. This is hardly a withdrawal from combat, as Japanese and American troops are intermixed on the island, with Japanese soldiers preferring to get behind American lines and cause maximum mayhem. E Company also receives replacements while out of the line, and gradually builds its strength

back up for the invasion of Tinian later in the month.

1944/JULY 9—Saipan finally falls to American forces. Nearly the entire Japanese garrison of 27,000 men is dead. U.S. casualties are 3,700 soldiers and 10,500 Marines. There are 3,200 American dead. In addition, thousands of Japanese civilians commit suicide.

1944/JULY 10—Cut off from supply and air support, desperate Japanese troops launch a counterattack at Aitape, New Guinea.

1944/JULY 11—U.S. Vice President Henry Wallace, having been sent to China to investigate the situation, reports that Nationalist leader Chiang Kai-shek is more interested in fighting the Communists than the Japanese. Wallace suggests that the U.S. try to mediate the disputes between the Nationalists and Communists.

1944/JULY 12—Another Allied attempt to capture Myitkyina, north Burma, fails. The attack is compromised when Allied aircraft mistakenly bomb their own troops.

1944/JULY 13—The fighting in the Myitkyina region has so far caused the Japanese nearly 2,000 casualties (including 790 dead).

1944/JULY 14—Senior members of the Japanese government increasingly suggest that, in the wake of the loss of Saipan, it might be a good idea if General Tojo resigned as prime minister.

1944/JULY 15—The Japanese commander at Myitkyina considers withdrawing in the face of constant Allied attacks and lack of much support from his own side.

1944/JULY 16—Australian cruisers and destroyers shell Japanese positions near Aitape, New Guinea.

1944/JULY 17—The Japanese minister of the navy, Admiral Shigetaro Shimada, resigns.

1944/JULY 18—Pressure from senior members of the government, and the "elders" (retired politicians and senior officers), forces General Tojo to resign his government posts (prime minister, minister of the Army and Army Chief of Staff, minister of the interior, minister of munitions, etc., etc.). A new government is formed, with much the same policies as the old one.

1944/JULY 19—In the aftermath of the battle for Saipan, U.S. commanders note that more Japanese have surrendered than in any previous battle. Still, the POWs number only a few hundred out of the 27,000-man garrison.

1944/JULY 20—An American invasion force approaches Guam and begins shelling and bombing the island intensively.

1944/JULY 21—Two divisions (one Marine, one Army) storm ashore on Japanese-held Guam in the Marianas.

1944/JULY 22—After allowing American troops to advance a mile or so inland on Guam, the Japanese launch a fierce counterattack, which is defeated.

1944/JULY 23—From Saipan, an American invasion force of U.S. Marines puts to sea for nearby Tinian in the Marianas.

1944/JULY 24—After two weeks to recuperate from the Saipan fighting, two Marine divisions land on Tinian. Corporal John Lindemann of the 4th Marine Division leads his squad into action once more, this time coming away without a scratch. Well, there are plenty of scratches and bruises, but nothing requiring a trip to the hospital ship. Only one Japanese regiment is defending. On Saipan, each U.S. division suffered 1,000 dead and over 4,000 wounded. On Tinian, each division averages less than 200 dead and 900 wounded. Tough fighting, but not nearly as severe as Saipan. In large part, the lower losses are the result of a successful deception. Going ashore on Saipan, there were heavy losses from Japanese machine guns and mortars just approaching and crossing the beach. There is one large beach in the southern part of Tinian, but only two smaller ones (65 and 130 yards wide) in the north. The Japanese on Tinian are fooled, as each of these small beaches is hit by a Marine regiment, which quickly pushes past the few Japanese stationed there.

1944/JULY 25—U.S. Army and Marine units are still 4 miles away from linking up their separate beachheads on Guam. Japanese resistance is stiffening.

1944/JULY 26—U.S. President Roosevelt holds a conference in Hawaii with MacArthur and Nimitz. The Navy wants to take Formosa in order to cut Japan off from its oil and resource supplies in the Netherlands East Indies (and to make it easier to supply the Chinese). MacArthur proposes the Philippines, and wins the argument (even though he offers a larger and more difficult operation).

1944/JULY 27—U.S. Marines clear most of northern Tinian and begin rebuilding the airfield they found there.

1944/JULY 28—The Japanese commander at Myitkyina, Burma, orders his troops to withdraw, but decides to commit hara-kiri to atone for the shame of withdrawing in the face of the enemy.

1944/JULY 29—U.S. Marines capture the Orote airstrip on Guam, despite fierce Japanese resistance.

1944/JULY 30—The U.S. 6th Infantry Division lands on the Vogelkop Peninsula on the northwest coast of New Guinea, as well as the nearby islands of Amsterdam and Middleburg.

1944/JULY 31—British assist in forming an anti-Japanese Burmese government in exile in India.

1944/AUGUST 1—U.S. Marines crush Japanese resistance on Tinian.

1944/AUGUST 2—Chinese and American forces detect Japanese withdrawal in the Myitkyina area of northern Burma, and cautiously close in.

1944/AUGUST 3—The key Burmese town of Myitkyina falls to U.S. and Chinese troops. This permits the reopening of the Burma Road, providing a land route into China for military aid. The fierce fighting deep in the jungle costs the Allies over 5,400 casualties (including 972 Chinese and 272 Americans killed).

1944/AUGUST 4—U.S. Army and Marine divisions link up on Guam, cutting the Japanese defenders into two groups.

1944/AUGUST 5—Elements of Task Force 58 attack Iwo Jima and Chichi Jima with air strikes and shellings, sinking one destroyer and two transports, and destroying or damaging many aircraft.

1944/AUGUST 6—Japanese troops in China advance toward Hengyang, in the face of heavy Chinese resistance.

1944/AUGUST 7—The Japanese light cruiser *Nagara* is sunk in Japanese waters by the U.S. submarine *Croaker*. Since Pearl Harbor, Japan has lost sixteen of her forty-four cruisers.

1944/AUGUST 8—The Japanese offensive in China rolls on, taking the city of Hengyang, despite stiff Chinese resistance.

1944/AUGUST 9—The fall of Hengyang causes some of the warlords in the Nationalist coalition to seek to replace Chiang Kai-shek as leader of the Nationalist cause.

1944/AUGUST 10—Organized Japanese resistance on Guam is stamped out. Some 10,000 Japanese defenders have died. American casualties are 5,000, including 1,400 killed. The U.S. now has an island large enough, and close enough, to support hundreds of B-29 bombers with which to bomb Japan.

1944/AUGUST 11—U.S. B-29s flying out of bases in India complete the first of over 150 missions to drop marine mines in rivers and ports in China, Indochina, Malaya, and Sumatra.

1944/AUGUST 12—Mopping up proceeds on Guam, continuing until the end of the war.

1944/AUGUST 13—The 5th Marine Division begins moving from San Diego to Hawaii.

1944/AUGUST 14—With the fighting over on Tinian for nearly two weeks, Corporal John Lindemann and the 4th Marine Division ship back to their home base in Maui, Hawaii.

1944/AUGUST 15—During August 1944, U.S. submarines operating in the Pacific have sunk 245,000 tons of Japanese merchant shipping, not counting vessels of under 500 tons, plus an escort carrier, two light cruisers, two destroyers, and six smaller warships. A further 50,000 tons of shipping have been sunk by aircraft and surface ships.

1944/AUGUST 16—The U.S. 81st Infantry Division completes its movement from San Francisco to Hawaii.

1944/AUGUST 17—The last Japanese troops to have entered Indian territory during the Imphal-Kohima offensive are killed or driven over the border into Burma.

1944/AUGUST 18—The U.S. submarine *Rasher* sinks the Japanese escort carrier *Taiyo* off Luzon. Since Pearl Harbor, the Imperial Navy has lost twelve aircraft carriers (with a total capacity of 525 aircraft) of all types, out of a total of twenty-three.

1944/AUGUST 19—The White House announces that President Roosevelt has appointed a special envoy to China in order to effect a military alliance between Nationalist and Communist forces.

1944/AUGUST 20—After three months of fighting in the jungle, Biak Island, northwest of New Guinea, is finally cleared of Japanese forces. The U.S. Army has suffered 2,400 casualties (including 400 dead). The Japanese have lost nearly 5,000 dead, although 220 were taken prisoner.

1944/AUGUST 21—U.S. B-29s operating out of bases in Ceylon begin a series of raids on Japanese installations on Sumatra.

1944/AUGUST 22—Japanese abandon Ulithi in the western Carolines, not realizing that the Americans want the atoll as a forward base.

1944/AUGUST 23—Formation of the new 6th Marine Division begins on Guadalcanal.

1944/AUGUST 24—The British Far Eastern Fleet makes a carrier raid on Padang, in southwestern Sumatra.

1944/AUGUST 25—U.S. Army troops finally overcome all Japanese resistance in the Aitape region of New Guinea. The Japanese have suffered 8,800 dead, while 98 Japanese surrendered. American dead number 440.

1944/AUGUST 26—Preparations for the first landings in the Philippines proceed. Philippine guerrilla organizations begin to receive orders concerning their role in the coming battle.

1944/AUGUST 27—The Royal Navy doubles its submarine strength in the Far East with the arrival of the 2nd Submarine Flotilla at Ceylon.

1944/AUGUST 28—Task Force 38 departs Eniwetok atoll for raids in the western and central Carolines.

1944/AUGUST 29—The Japanese offensive in China continues. Eleven divisions advance from Hengyang toward the major U.S. air bases at Kweilin and Liuchow.

1944/AUGUST 30—The U.S. 96th Infantry Division completes its movement from San Francisco to Hawaii. Allied ground forces in the Pacific (Pacific Ocean areas and Southwest Pacific) total thirty-four divisions (seven Australian, twenty-one U.S. Army, and six U.S. Marine divisions, plus a large New Zealand brigade, and numerous inde-

pendent brigades, regiments, and battalions). In these same areas Japanese ground forces total thirty divisions and about as many independent brigades, plus numerous separate regiments and battalions, plus large numbers of troops in the home islands.

1944/AUGUST 31—Chinese forces in northern Burma and South China approach a linkup and reestablishment of access between the two nations severed by the Japanese in 1942.

1944/SEPTEMBER 1—The 4th Marine Division and Corporal John Lindemann arrive at Maui, after having invaded and conquered Saipan and Tinian. The division has a 28 percent casualty rate (5,981 killed or wounded), most of them in the twenty-seven 240-man rifle companies. The 6,480 Marine infantry have suffered over 50 percent casualties. It will take several months to train the replacements up to the level of the experienced survivors of Saipan and Tinian. Corporal Lindemann has lost several men in his squad and works hard to get his new troops into shape for their next Pacific battle.

1944/SEPTEMBER 2—Task Group 38.4 raids the Bonin Islands.

1944/SEPTEMBER 3—U.S. Navy ships attack the Japanese base on Wake Island.

1944/SEPTEMBER 4—Task Force 38 begins concentrating in the Philippine Sea for operations against the Palau Islands and the Philippines.

1944/SEPTEMBER 5—Chinese forces moving from Burma reach the Kaolikung Pass, to link up with Chinese forces from Yunan Province in China. This reestablishes the land link that was served by the Japanese in 1942.

1944/SEPTEMBER 6—The U.S. Navy uses sixteen carriers to launch air strikes against Japanese-held islands in the western Carolines (Yap, Ulithi, and Palau).

1944/SEPTEMBER 7—Chinese forces in the Salween area of Burma finally clear out all resistance, killing most of the 2,000 Japanese defenders. The Chinese suffer 7,700 dead in the process. This is another vital area that has to be cleared in order to reopen the Burma Road.

1944/SEPTEMBER 8—Two and a half Japanese divisions stationed in South China join the attack on the U.S. airfields at Kweilin and Liuchow.

1944/SEPTEMBER 9—A dozen carriers of Task Force 38 begin two days of raids against Japanese bases on Mindanao.

1944/SEPTEMBER 10—The Japanese prepare a counteroffensive in the Salween area of Burma, in order to prevent reopening of the Burma Road.

1944/SEPTEMBER 11—Three U.S. submarines sink two Japanese transports on their way from Singapore to Formosa. The transports carry 1,274 Allied POWs. Over 300 of the POWs die, with 159 rescued by the subs and the rest by the Japanese.

1944/SEPTEMBER 12—Allied leaders hold a conference in Canada where Churchill and Roosevelt agree that emphasis should be shifted to the Pacific now that the Germans appear to be at the end of their rope. It is also reaffirmed that the first invasion of the Japanese home islands will take place in October 1945.

1944/SEPTEMBER 13—U.S. Navy ships and aircraft pound Peleliu Island (in Palau) preparatory to an invasion.

1944/SEPTEMBER 14—The Japanese abandon their efforts at a counteroffensive in the Salween area of Burma. This eliminates a major threat to the reopening of the Burma Road.

1944/SEPTEMBER 15—In a U.S. one-two punch, Marines land on the Japanese-held island of Peleliu, 450 miles east of the Philippines (Mindanao), while the Army's 31st Division lands on Morotai in the Admiralty Islands, about 350 miles southeast of

Mindanao, in preparation for the scheduled liberation of the Philippines.

1944/SEPTEMBER 16—Aided by the terrain, Japanese troops on Peleliu offer fierce resistance, although greatly outnumbered by U.S. Marines.

1944/SEPTEMBER 17—The USAAF abandons a major air base at Kweilin, China, as the Japanese close in.

1944/SEPTEMBER 18—Task Force 38 is replenishing in the western Pacific.

1944/SEPTEMBER 19—Fierce fighting continues on Peleliu between Marines and Japanese troops.

1944/SEPTEMBER 20—U.S. troops land on Angaur Island in Palau, readily overcoming resistance.

1944/SEPTEMBER 21—U.S. Navy Task Force 38 launches air strikes from a dozen aircraft carriers against Japanese targets in the Luzon, Philippines, area.

1944/SEPTEMBER 22—A U.S. Army regiment lands unopposed on Ulithi atoll in the western Carolines.

1944/SEPTEMBER 23—The airfield on Peleliu is repaired and U.S. Marine aircraft begin operating from it.

1944/SEPTEMBER 24—Part of a U.S. Army division is sent to reinforce the Marines on Peleliu; the Japanese promptly counterattack.

1944/SEPTEMBER 25—Admiral Halsey proposes, and Nimitz and MacArthur accept, changing the operational agenda, canceling the landings on Mindanao scheduled for October 10 in favor of a landing on Leyte at that date.

1944/SEPTEMBER 26—Task Force 38 continues strikes against the Philippines.

1944/SEPTEMBER 27—Japanese troops in the Philippines increase preparations to resist a possible U.S. invasion.

1944/SEPTEMBER 28—Task Force 38 prepares to return to Ulithi.

1944/SEPTEMBER 29—Heeding a message from Filipino guerrillas, a U.S. sub comes to Mindanao to pick up eighty-one Allied POWs who survived the sinking of a Japanese transport (sunk by another U.S. sub). The POWs had made contact with the guerrillas, who used their radio to arrange the rescue.

1944/SEPTEMBER 30—U.S. and Filipino guerrillas complete preparations to support expected American landings, having mobilized their entire strength and deployed to do maximum damage to the Japanese once the invasion gets under way.

1944/OCTOBER 1—Allied (mainly U.S.) submarines in the Pacific have their best month of the war in October, sending 328,000 tons of Japanese shipping to the bottom. Allied aircraft and ships sink another 186,000 tons. From this point on, the sinking of Japanese merchant shipping will decline, simply because there aren't many Japanese ships left to sink.

1944/OCTOBER 2—U.S. Navy Task Group 38.4 operates between Palau and the Philippines.

1944/OCTOBER 3—Although cut off from any meaningful supply, thousands of Japanese troops in the Solomons and New Guinea continue to fight on. Many will do so until the war ends, and a few for several decades after that.

1944/OCTOBER 4—Task Force 38 completes replenishment and rest at Ulithi, which has been turned into an enormous Navy logistical base.

1944/OCTOBER 5—Japanese troops continue to resist on Peleliu, a battle that is turning out to be more difficult than the Marines had first thought.

1944/OCTOBER 6—U.S. Navy Task Force sorties from Ulithi atoll for raids against the Philippines, Formosa, and the Ryukyu Islands (Okinawa group).

1944/OCTOBER 7—U.S. Navy Task Group 38.4 joins Task Force 38 in the Philippine Sea.

1944/OCTOBER 8—U.S. Task Force 38 refuels in the Philippine Sea and prepares for massive raids against Japanese

air installations in the Ryukyus, Formosa, and the Philippines.

1944/OCTOBER 9—U.S. Navy ships bombard Japanese-held Marcus Island.

1944/OCTOBER 10—Moving ever closer to Japan itself, the U.S. Navy launches air strikes from seventeen carriers, to hit targets in the Ryukyus (especially Okinawa).

1944/OCTOBER 11—Japanese military leadership develop a series of plans for Operation Victory ("Sho-Go"). These plans spell out the desperate measures Japan will take when the home islands are threatened. Basically they come down to "fight to the last man, woman, child, weapon, and piece of equipment."

1944/OCTOBER 12—The U.S. Navy carrier task force launches air strikes against Formosa, in order to destroy Japanese air power in the area. The Japanese commanders are shocked at the ineffectiveness of their air forces against the better-trained and -equipped Americans.

1944/OCTOBER 13—The U.S. Navy carrier task force launches its second day of air strikes against major Japanese air strength in Formosa.

1944/OCTOBER 14—The U.S. Navy carrier task force completes three days of air strikes against Formosa, breaking the back of Japanese air power in the area (destroying 280 aircraft).

1944/OCTOBER 15—Peleliu is finally secured after a month of heavy fighting. Small-scale action continues into November against Japanese holdouts. The Japanese lose nearly 12,000 troops, the Marines over 1,200.

1944/OCTOBER 16—Chinese forces in Burma launch another offensive to clear remaining Japanese forces that might block the land route (the Burma Road) between India and China.

1944/OCTOBER 17—Admiral Nimitz announces that during the second week of October, Allied forces destroyed nearly 700 Japanese aircraft and over seventy Japanese ships.

1944/OCTOBER 18—In preparation for the coming invasion of the Philippines, U.S. Army Rangers are landed on islands off Leyte Gulf.

1944/OCTOBER 19—General Stilwell is relieved of his posts in China. This is as a result of the Chinese leader Chiang Kai-shek seeing Stilwell as the cause of all the problems Chiang is having with the Nationalist, American, and Communist leaderships.

1944/OCTOBER 20—General MacArthur returns to the Philippines, as he promised he would two and a half years earlier. In the first twenty-four hours of the invasion, nearly 200,000 troops are landed on the east coast of Leyte.

1944/OCTOBER 21—Japanese forces on Leyte counterattack, although their long-term strategy is to defend, not attack. The fighting in the Philippines will go on until the end of the war.

1944/OCTOBER 22—Japanese naval forces close in on Leyte in order to oppose the American invasion.

1944/OCTOBER 23—The Japanese meet the American invasion of the Philippines with a naval attack. The resulting Battle of Leyte Gulf is the largest naval battle in history and goes on for three days. The Japanese fleet is smashed, losing three battleships, four carriers, ten cruisers, and seventeen other warships. The U.S. loses three small carriers and three destroyers.

1944/OCTOBER 24—The Japanese split their remaining warships between the Inland Sea (between Honshu, Shikoku, and Kyushu) and the waters off Singapore.

1944/OCTOBER 25—The advance of U.S. forces in the Philippines is held up by dug-in and determined Japanese defenders.

1944/OCTOBER 26—The Japanese offensive in China, stalled because of logistical problems and increased Chinese resistance, starts rolling again toward the U.S. air bases at Kweilin and Liuchow.

1944/OCTOBER 27—The Japanese begin launching Kamikaze suicide plane attacks at U.S. ships off the Philippines.

1944/OCTOBER 28—The Kamikazes draw first blood, with a U.S. cruiser being damaged by suicide aircraft crashing into it.

1944/OCTOBER 29—Chinese forces in northern Burma continue to clear out Japanese forces capable of blocking the Burma Road.

1944/OCTOBER 30—Covering the troops on Leyte, U.S. Task Group 38.4 is attacked by Kamikaze aircraft, which severely damage two carriers.

1944/OCTOBER 31—Chinese troops continue to battle Japanese in the border area of China and Burma. By the end of the year, the area will be clear.

1944/NOVEMBER 1—Despite the enormous U.S. naval and air forces in the area, the Japanese are able to land reinforcements on Leyte.

1944/NOVEMBER 2—The U.S. Army clears Japanese troops from the central valley on Leyte.

1944/NOVEMBER 3—The Japanese Army's "Special Balloon Regiment" begins releasing the first of over 9,000 hydrogen-filled balloons. These are expected to float with the prevailing westerly winds all the way from Japan to the west coast of North America. Each carries a 40-pound bomb that will explode on landing, injuring anyone in the vicinity or starting a fire. Nearly 300 of the balloons actually will reach North America, but only three will cause any known damage (six dead and two brush fires).

1944/NOVEMBER 4—The Japanese launch air attacks against Saipan and Tinian in the Marianas to disrupt preparations for further attacks against Japan.

1944/NOVEMBER 5—B-29s fly from Chinese bases to bomb Singapore.

1944/NOVEMBER 6—The Soviet Union accuses Japan of aggression, a prelude to eventually declaring war on Japan.

1944/NOVEMBER 7—The Chinese take the town of Shwebo in northern Burma.

1944/NOVEMBER 8—Japanese transports get through the U.S. naval and air blockade to land another division as reinforcements for their troops on Leyte.

1944/NOVEMBER 9—Another reinforcement landing by Japanese troops on Leyte is only partially successful. The troops get ashore, but U.S. Navy aircraft sink the transports before the ammunition and supplies can be unloaded.

1944/NOVEMBER 10—The Japanese offensive in China finally captures the two major U.S. air bases at Kweilin and Liuchow.

1944/NOVEMBER 11—In response to the vast number of U.S. aircraft carriers, Japan sends its newest carrier, *Shinano*, off to war. While this carrier has only seventy aircraft, it has 12 inches of armor on its flight deck and is considered unsinkable. However, seventeen days later a U.S. sub sends *Shinano* to the bottom with a spread of torpedoes. This is the shortest combat life of any major ship in World War II.

1944/NOVEMBER 12—Task Force 38 refuels and resupplies in the Philippine Sea.

1944/NOVEMBER 13—U.S. Task Force 38 makes new air strikes on Luzon, concentrating on Japanese shipping in Manila Bay.

1944/NOVEMBER 14—U.S. Task Force 38 pounds Japanese shipping in Manila Bay; in two days of raids the Japanese lose a light cruiser, four destroyers, and ten transports sunk, plus a destroyer and five transports damaged.

1944/NOVEMBER 15—Escorted by U.S. and British warships, an American infantry regiment storms Pegun Island, near Morotai.

1944/NOVEMBER 16—U.S. Task Force 38 refuels and resupplies in the Philippine Sea. At this point in the war, U.S. ships are staying at sea for many months at a time, being replenished by fleets of cargo ships and oilers. Hospital ships and special repair ships tend to injured sailors and equipment.

1944/NOVEMBER 17—The Japanese offensive in China continues, with the next objectives being Kweiyang, then the key cities of Kunming and Chungking.

1944/NOVEMBER 18—A British carrier task force raids oil facilities, air bases, and port installations in Sumatra.

1944/NOVEMBER 19—U.S. troops make an amphibious landing on Asia Island (off the northwest coast of New Guinea).

1944/NOVEMBER 20—British troops cross the Chindwin River to begin a monsoon season offensive to drive the Japanese from central Burma.

1944/NOVEMBER 21—Chinese forces move in on Bhamo in northern Burma.

1944/NOVEMBER 22—The "British Far Eastern Fleet," in the Indian Ocean, is reorganized, as the "British Pacific Fleet" is formed (four new carriers, two new battleships, plus cruisers and destroyers) for operations with the U.S. Third/Fifth Fleet.

1944/NOVEMBER 23—Japanese troops from Indochina move north to link up with Japanese troops approaching the Chinese city of Nanning.

1944/NOVEMBER 24—The first B-29 raid from bases in the Marianas (Saipan) is launched. Tokyo is hit by 111 B-29s.

1944/NOVEMBER 25—Japanese Kamikazes launch more attacks at U.S. Navy carriers off the Philippines. Four carriers are damaged.

1944/NOVEMBER 26—Japanese troops in central Burma begin to withdraw.

1944/NOVEMBER 27—B-29s from the

Marianas hit Tokyo; B-29s from India hit Bangkok.

1944/NOVEMBER 28—Japanese resistance on Peleliu and other Palau islands finally ends. Most of the Japanese garrison of 14,000 has been killed, 400 captured. U.S. ground forces have suffered nearly 10,000 casualties (including 1,800 dead, more than at Guadalcanal).

1944/NOVEMBER 29—Chinese Nationalist leader Chiang Kai-shek refuses to allow U.S. ammunition to be shipped through his territory to Communist forces.

1944/NOVEMBER 30—With the Japanese closing in, Nationalist Chinese divisions in Burma are ordered north to aid in the defense of Kunming.

1944/DECEMBER 1—Japanese troops on Leyte exhaust their food supplies. The U.S. blockade prevents everything except supply submarines from getting through.

1944/DECEMBER 2—British troops continue their advance into central Burma, as the Japanese continue to withdraw.

1944/DECEMBER 3—The Japanese Eleventh Army, which advanced into South China against orders from Tokyo, runs out of supplies and slows down.

1944/DECEMBER 4—The new U.S. military representative in China, General Albert Wedemeyer (who replaced Stilwell), requests that remaining B-29s in China be withdrawn. The Burma Road is not yet functional and all supplies for the B-29s in China have to be flown in over the Himalayan Mountains (a very inefficient and meager source of supply).

1944/DECEMBER 5—The U.S. Sixth Army on Leyte is ordered to destroy the stubborn Japanese resistance around Ormoc.

1944/DECEMBER 6—Despite a lack of supply, Japanese forces on Leyte continue to resist and even launch counterattacks.

1944/DECEMBER 7—The Japanese attempt to resupply their forces on Leyte. The effort fails and thirteen transports are sunk by U.S. aircraft.

1944/DECEMBER 8—U.S. land-based bombers and carrier aircraft begin a seventy-two-day pounding of Iwo Jima in preparation for an amphibious assault.

1944/DECEMBER 9—British troops continue advancing into central Burma as they realize that the Japanese are pulling out without (much of) a fight.

1944/DECEMBER 10—U.S. Army troops finally break stubborn Japanese resistance at Ormoc, Leyte, in the Philippines.

1944/DECEMBER 11—U.S. forces capture Ormoc, and discover why the Japanese fought so stubbornly to hold it. Ormoc contains the main supply dumps for the Japanese troops on Leyte. With Ormoc gone, the remaining 35,000 Japanese troops on Leyte are short on ammo and food.

1944/DECEMBER 12—U.S. Task Force 38 (thirteen carriers plus escorts) sorties from Ulithi atoll for a new series of air strikes against Japanese bases on Luzon.

1944/DECEMBER 13—Chinese forces in northern Burma enter outskirts of the town of Bhamo.

1944/DECEMBER 14—U.S. Navy amphibious task force approaches Philippine island of Mindoro.

1944/DECEMBER 15—Mindoro is invaded by U.S. troops. There is no opposition on the beaches, but Kamikazes attack landing ships, damaging several and sinking two LSTs.

1944/DECEMBER 16—Chinese forces in northern Burma capture the town of Bhamo.

1944/DECEMBER 17—Five hundred miles east of the Philippines, the U.S. Third Fleet is caught in a mighty typhoon for two days.

1944/DECEMBER 18—The losses suffered by the Third Fleet in the typhoon that first hit it on December 17–18 prove greater than those in many naval battles. Three destroyers are sunk, over 140 aircraft destroyed, and severe damage inflicted on eight carriers, a cruiser, seven destroyers, and many support ships. Nearly 800 sailors lose their lives and many more are injured.

1944/DECEMBER 19—B-29s in China begin hitting Japanese targets in China rather than in Japan. The success of the Japanese offensive in China requires that all available resources be used to stop it.

1944/DECEMBER 20—Japanese troops on Leyte are told by Tokyo that they can expect no further reinforcements or supplies.

1944/DECEMBER 21—British troops in Burma capture Kawlin.

1944/DECEMBER 22—The Vietnamese Liberation Army is formed in Vietnam by Vo Nguyen Giap. This is the core of the Communist army that will eventually overcome Japanese, French, and American forces.

1944/DECEMBER 23—Task Force 38 proceeds to Ulithi atoll, after eleven days of operations in support of the fighting on Leyte.

1944/DECEMBER 24—U.S. cruisers and destroyers bombard Iwo Jima.

1944/DECEMBER 25—British troops move into the Akyab district of Burma, as the Japanese withdraw.

1944/DECEMBER 26—Japanese ships attack U.S. beachhead on Mindoro in the Philippines.

1944/DECEMBER 27—B-29s flying out of the Marianas (Saipan) make their fifth major raid on Tokyo.

1944/DECEMBER 28—The Japanese assess the aftereffects of five B-29 raids and find that the damage being done is not crippling. Soon the Americans realize the same thing and this leads to the switch to fire bomb raids and a much less favorable outcome for the Japanese.

1944/DECEMBER 29—Stepping up

their attack against Japanese forces on Leyte (now low on food and ammo), in less than two weeks U.S. Army forces kill nearly 6,000 Japanese while losing only 11 of their own troops.

1944/DECEMBER 30—U.S. Army aircraft attack Japanese shipping in the Manila Bay area.

1944/DECEMBER 31—Task Force 38 (thirteen carriers) sorties from Ulithi for renewed air strikes against the Japanese in the Ryukyus, Formosa, and the Philippines.

1945/JANUARY 1—The U.S. Eighth Army on the Philippine island of Leyte begins a campaign to clear still-active Japanese troops. This fighting will continue until the end of the war.

1945/JANUARY 2—As U.S. Navy ships leave Leyte for the invasion of Luzon, they are attacked by more Kamikazes.

1945/JANUARY 3—The U.S. Third Fleet stages raids on Okinawa, Formosa, and the Pescadores. American losses are 18 aircraft, but the Japanese lose a dozen ships and over 100 aircraft.

1945/JANUARY 4—A U.S. amphibious invasion force approaching the main Philippine island of Luzon suffers heavy Japanese air attack.

1945/JANUARY 5—Fighting continues on the Chinese-Burma border, with key towns continuing to change hands.

1945/JANUARY 6—The Japanese air force on Luzon is reduced to only 35 aircraft, down from 150 at the end of 1944.

1945/JANUARY 7—British troops occupy Akyab, in the Arakan area of Burma, as the Japanese situation continues to deteriorate in the region.

1945/JANUARY 8—Task Force 38 refuels in the Philippine Sea preparatory to renewing air strikes on Formosa and the Ryukyus and in support of the Luzon landings.

1945/JANUARY 9—The main Philippine island of Luzon is invaded by the

U.S. Sixth Army. Nearly 100,000 troops are landed at Lingayen Gulf, 100 miles north of Manila, in the first twenty-four hours.

1945/JANUARY 10—U.S. Army troops on Luzon move inland meeting little opposition.

1945/JANUARY 11—The Japanese leadership examines the situation and decides to put all its remaining resources into Kamikaze-type weapons. By the end of the month, all industrial and military organizations have channeled their energies to building suicide weapons, and providing crews to man them.

1945/JANUARY 12—U.S. Navy Task Force 38 sweeps the Indochinese coast, its carrier aircraft sinking over three dozen Japanese ships.

1945/JANUARY 13—Japanese forces in the Philippines launch their few remaining aircraft against recently landed U.S. troops on the coast of Luzon.

1945/JANUARY 14—British troops crossing the Irrawaddy River in Burma are hit by a Japanese counterattack, which results in a month-long battle.

1945/JANUARY 15—The Japanese offensive in China continues, with Japanese forces advancing on the U.S. air base at Sui-ch'uan.

1945/JANUARY 16—U.S. carrier aircraft attack Japanese-held Hong Kong. The Japanese defenses are found to be meager, having been stripped for other fronts.

1945/JANUARY 17—The U.S. Sixth Army on Luzon steps up its drive on Manila.

1945/JANUARY 18—Although Peleliu is "secured," fighting continues, with Japanese stragglers forming raiding parties to attack the U.S. ammo dumps and air base.

1945/JANUARY 19—In China, Japanese troops seize control of the Canton-Hankow rail line.

1945/JANUARY 20—The first convoy navigates the Burma Road. The route needs repair and rebuilding before full-scale use is possible. Corporal John Lindemann and the 4th Marine Division ship out from Maui, Hawaii. Destination: Iwo Jima, and their toughest battle yet.

1945/JANUARY 21—U.S. carrier aircraft attack Japanese air bases on Okinawa and Formosa, destroying some 100 enemy aircraft in the process.

1945/JANUARY 22—Corregidor, the island fortress guarding Japanese-held Manila Bay, is attacked by U.S. aircraft.

1945/JANUARY 23—The Burma Road is declared open, but small, scattered Japanese units in the area make travel on the route dangerous.

1945/JANUARY 24—In China, advancing Japanese troops cause the U.S. air base at Sui-ch'uan to be evacuated.

1945/JANUARY 25—U.S. B-29s undertake a major mining effort in the waters off the ports of Singapore, Saigon, Camranh Bay, and Penang. This is the largest mining operation of the war, with 366 mines dropped off Singapore alone.

1945/JANUARY 26—The Japanese government orders its troops in China to call off their offensive and concentrate on defending the China coast and key Japanese installations in North China. As is customary, the commanders in China do not instantly or consistently comply.

1945/JANUARY 27—A U.S. amphibious assault force leaves Hawaii, destination Iwo Jima.

1945/JANUARY 28—The Philippine island of Mindoro is declared free of organized Japanese resistance and under U.S. control.

1945/JANUARY 29—Additional U.S. troops land northwest of Subic Bay, on the Philippine island of Luzon. They promptly move southward toward Bataan.

1945/JANUARY 30—Task Force 63, the British Pacific Fleet (four carriers, a fast battleship, four cruisers, and eleven destroyers), refuels at sea in the Indian Ocean and then proceeds eastward to join the U.S. Pacific Fleet.

1945/JANUARY 31—The U.S. 11th Airborne Division is landed—by amphibious craft—at the south entrance to Manila Bay.

1945/FEBRUARY 1—The Japanese offensive in China captures Kukong, the last Chinese stronghold on the Hankow rail line. This cuts off Chinese forces to the east from the rest of China.

1945/FEBRUARY 2—Combat operations come to a halt on Leyte in the Philippines, although small pockets of Japanese resistance remain.

1945/FEBRUARY 3—On the Philippine main island of Luzon, the U.S. Sixth Army is poised to fight its way into the Philippine capital of Manila.

1945/FEBRUARY 4—The first large supply convoy makes it from Ledo in India to Kunming in China along the full length of the Burma Road. It's been nearly three years since the last convoy arrived.

1945/FEBRUARY 5—Australian troops land on the island of New Britain.

1945/FEBRUARY 6—The battle for the Philippine capital, Manila (on Luzon), begins in earnest. Over 4,000 American POWs are freed from prison camps in the area, after nearly three years' imprisonment.

1945/FEBRUARY 7—The Japanese offensive in China captures another U.S. air base, this one at Kanchow.

1945/FEBRUARY 8—Japanese resistance in Manila stiffens.

1945/FEBRUARY 9—Elements of Task Force 58 (sixteen carriers and escorting warships) begin departing Ulithi atoll for raids on the Tokyo area and to support the Iwo Jima landings.

1945/FEBRUARY 10—The Japanese begin to wonder if the gods are on their side, as Tokyo is hit with a severe earth-

quake shortly before a raid by nearly 100 B-29 bombers.

1945/FEBRUARY 11—British forces close in on Mandalay, in Burma.

1945/FEBRUARY 12—Off the Philippine coast, the U.S. sub *Batfish* sinks its third Japanese submarine in four days.

1945/FEBRUARY 13—Japanese forces in Mandalay are being surrounded as additional British forces move around the city.

1945/FEBRUARY 14—U.S. troops reach the Bataan peninsula outside Manila on Luzon in the Philippines as U.S. PT boats enter Manila Bay.

1945/FEBRUARY 15—U.S. troops make a landing on the southern tip of the Bataan peninsula. Japanese troops in nearby Manila are surrounded.

1945/FEBRUARY 16—American troops make a surprise attack on Corregidor (guarding the entrance to Manila Bay), using paratroopers and troops coming ashore from nearby Bataan. Over 4,000 Japanese defenders on Corregidor are killed, with the loss of only 136 American dead.

1945/FEBRUARY 17—Attempts to clear beach defenses on Japanese-held Iwo Jima encounter unexpected problems and nearly 200 U.S. Navy frogmen are killed.

1945/FEBRUARY 18—British troops land on the Burmese coast in the Arakan region and cut off the retreat of Japanese forces.

1945/FEBRUARY 19—Nearly 800 miles south of the Japanese home islands, 30,000 U.S. Marines land on Iwo Jima. The Japanese planned to use Iwo Jima as a launching platform for suicide aircraft attacks against Allied forces attempting to invade the Japanese home islands, as well as a forward fighter base to oppose B-29 raids from the Marianas Islands. Three U.S. Marine divisions are involved in the assault on this 8-square-mile island defended by 22,000 fanatical Japanese. Corporal John Lindemann, of the 4th Marine Division, comes ashore in the second wave of the landings. This is scant comfort, as most of the Japanese are still sitting in fortified positions away from the beaches. Even so, the resistance on the beach is fierce.

1945/FEBRUARY 20—U.S. Army troops land on Samar and Capul islands, giving them control of the vital San Bernardino Strait in the Philippines. On Iwo Jima, Corporal John Lindemann's squad has lost four of its twelve men by the second day. At that point, the Marines can only measure their progress in tens of yards.

1945/FEBRUARY 21—Japanese resistance on Iwo Jima is fierce, with the invading Marines already losing half their tanks. The fighting increases in intensity. Corporal John Lindemann's squad has now lost half its strength. That's not too shabby by Iwo Jima standards, where many Marine squads are a lot worse off and some have been wiped out. John Lindemann himself becomes a casualty, suffering a concussion from a nearby explosion. He is not evacuated, however, and quickly returns to action with an awful headache.

1945/FEBRUARY 22—Very heavy fighting on Iwo Jima.

1945/FEBRUARY 23—On Iwo Jima, elements of the 28th Marines raise the U.S. flag on Mount Suribachi.

1945/FEBRUARY 24—Most of the Manila area on Luzon, in the Philippines, is under U.S. control.

1945/FEBRUARY 25—In a major change in tactics against Japanese cities, U.S. B-29 bombers switch from high-altitude daylight raids with high-explosive bombs, to low-level night raids with incendiary bombs. The first raid against Tokyo, with 334 B-29s, burns out nearly 10,000 acres of the city.

1945/FEBRUARY 26—The British offensive against remaining Japanese forces in Burma continues with moves against Mandalay and Pagan.

1945/FEBRUARY 27—As the U.S. Navy has shut down, captured, or isolated most Japanese naval bases in the Pacific, the Japanese submarine threat has diminished to the point where it is no longer a danger to Allied ships in the Pacific. The only major Japanese submarine base still intact outside of the home islands is Penang, Malaya. It is from Penang that German submarines have been operating for several years, and they continue to operate from this base (along with Japanese subs) after Germany surrenders in May.

1945/FEBRUARY 28—U.S. forces land on Palawan Island in the Philippines. Occupation of this island effectively cuts Japan off from its resource areas in the East Indies.

1945/MARCH 1—U.S. Navy ships and aircraft attack the Japanese-held Ryukyu Islands.

1945/MARCH 2—Japanese resistance on Corregidor Island at the entrance of Manila Bay ends, less than three years after the Japanese first took the island fortress from American defenders.

1945/MARCH 3—Japanese resistance in the Philippine capital of Manila ends.

1945/MARCH 4—Advancing British troops cut off Japanese forces in central Burma.

1945/MARCH 5—U.S. Marines have cleared most of Iwo Jima, and U.S. fighters begin operating from a captured airstrip.

1945/MARCH 6—British units continue to close in on Mandalay, in Burma.

1945/MARCH 7—Trapped Japanese troops in central Burma counterattack to break out, bringing the British advance to a halt.

1945/MARCH 8—British troops fight

their way into Japanese-held Mandalay, Burma.

1945/MARCH 9—Japanese troops attack French garrisons in Indochina, thus eliminating the last remnant of pro-German Vichy French rule. The Japanese feared that Free French troops would be landed (via the Allied-controlled waters around Indochina) and the Vichy troops would join the Free French.

1945/MARCH 10—Dawn over Tokyo reveals a man-made hell. The previous night, 279 low-flying B-29 bombers dropped 1,665 tons of incendiary bombs, which created a firestorm that killed 84,000 Japanese. This is a greater death toll than either of the later A-bomb raids produced.

1945/MARCH 11—Emperor Bao Dai of Vietnam, a puppet of the French and later the Japanese, declares Vietnam's independence from France. The Japanese ignore this and remain in control.

1945/MARCH 12—Japanese forces in Mandalay, Burma, are surrounded.

1945/MARCH 13—Only a few pockets of Japanese resistance remain on Iwo Jima.

1945/MARCH 14—U.S. B-29s raid the Japanese city of Osaka, inflicting 13,000 casualties.

1945/MARCH 15—In central Burma, British and Japanese forces are intermingled as fighting continues.

1945/MARCH 16—Iwo Jima is declared free of organized Japanese resistance.

1945/MARCH 17—U.S. B-29s raid the Japanese city of Kobe, inflicting 15,000 casualties.

1945/MARCH 18—U.S. troops land on the island of Panay, in the Philippines, and push inland.

1945/MARCH 19—U.S. Navy aircraft attack the Kure naval base area on the Japanese home islands. With Iwo Jima secured, the 4th Marine Division and Corporal John Lindemann ship out for Maui.

1945/MARCH 20—The last ship of a twenty-one-vessel Japanese convoy is hunted down and destroyed. The convoy attempted, for ten weeks, to carry supplies from Japan to its beleaguered forces in Southeast Asia. None of the ships made it as far as Singapore, being constantly harried by U.S. aircraft and submarines.

1945/MARCH 21—British forces take control of Mandalay, with surviving Japanese troops in the area retreating toward Thailand (Siam).

1945/MARCH 22—The Japanese offensive in China continues, with an attack toward the U.S. air base at Laohokow.

1945/MARCH 23—A British carrier task force joins the U.S. fleet for operations against the Japanese home islands.

1945/MARCH 24—The last pocket of 200 Japanese troops on Iwo Jima is cornered in an area about 50 yards square. The Japanese eventually launch an attack from this position and nearly all are killed.

1945/MARCH 25—The U.S. air base at Laohokow in China is destroyed as the Japanese close in. This is the last U.S. air base in China that the Japanese will capture.

1945/MARCH 26—A U.S. Army division lands on the Philippine island of Cebu.

1945/MARCH 27—B-29s begin mining operation in the waters around Japan. In the space of a few weeks, the mining brings Japanese shipping to a standstill and makes the blockade of Japan nearly complete.

1945/MARCH 28—A U.S. Army division lands on the Kerama Islands in the Ryukyus, providing a forward base to support an assault on Okinawa.

1945/MARCH 29—U.S. troops clearing the Kerama Islands in the Ryukyus discover 350 suicide boats, held there for use against any force that attempted to land on Okinawa.

1945/MARCH 30—A U.S. amphibious task force approaches Okinawa.

1945/MARCH 31—Japanese naval commanders, sensing the approaching battle for Okinawa, prepare plans for remaining Japanese Navy ships to make suicide attacks on the U.S. fleet. Attacking Japanese ships will be provided with only enough fuel for a one-way trip.

1945/APRIL 1—Okinawa is assaulted by 60,000 U.S. Army and Marine troops (two divisions of each). The island is only 360 miles south of the Japanese home islands and the battle of Okinawa is the last major assault of the war, and the bloodiest.

1945/APRIL 2—On Okinawa, the Japanese pull back, rather than oppose the invading American troops on the beach, to await them in fortifications farther inland.

1945/APRIL 3—The Soviet Union decides to renounce the five-year Soviet-Japan neutrality pact signed in April 1941.

1945/APRIL 4—U.S. troops on Okinawa finally encounter the dug-in Japanese garrison, and bloody battle for the island ensues. The 4th Marine Division and Corporal John Lindemann arrive back at Maui after the Iwo Jima operation. The Marines are ordered to start training for the invasion of Japan, the first operation to take place in October 1945. The Marines are to lead the way. But first the damage from Iwo Jima has to be repaired. The division has suffered over 8,000 casualties. Over half of these were wounded who gradually return from hospitals. The rest of the losses have to be made up by fresh replacements. While the war in Europe looks close to ending, the Marines on Maui know they are likely to be in action again before the year is out.

1945/APRIL 5—In the wake of the Soviets' abrogation of the April 1941 five-year neutrality pact with Japan, the Japanese cabinet resigns.

1945/APRIL 6—The Japanese launch a mass Kamikaze attack on U.S. ships off Okinawa. The 355 aircraft fly from one of the home islands (Kyushu) and only 24 of them hit anything. Six small ships (destroyers and support vessels) are sunk, but many more are damaged by friendly fire, as all U.S. ships in the area open up to stop the Kamikazes.

1945/APRIL 7—The Japanese Second ("Suicide") Fleet is intercepted by U.S. carrier aircraft before they can reach Okinawa. Some 900 U.S. aircraft are involved in this battle, of which 10 are lost. The Japanese lose the superbattleship *Yamato*, a cruiser, four destroyers, and 54 aircraft.

1945/APRIL 8—British forces in Burma isolate more Japanese troops as the British offensive moves on toward Rangoon.

1945/APRIL 9—U.S. forces land on the island of Jolo in the Sulu Sea (off the Philippines).

1945/APRIL 10—British carrier aircraft attack Japanese air bases on Formosa to stop Japanese air raids on U.S. ships off Okinawa.

1945/APRIL 11—British forces in Burma hustle toward Rangoon (300 miles) in order to take the city before the monsoon rains begin.

1945/APRIL 12—Over 150 Japanese Kamikazes are shot down off Okinawa, although a Baka flying bomb hits and sinks a U.S. destroyer.

1945/APRIL 13—Chinese and Japanese forces both begin offensives in different parts of China. President Roosevelt collapses and dies of a cerebral hemorrhage (April 12 in North America). Radio Tokyo broadcasts a dignified notice.

1945/APRIL 14—Japanese forces in China are again ordered to withdraw troops for the defense of the Chinese coast and this time they comply, abandoning several captured U.S. air bases in the process. A B-29 air raid on Tokyo damages the Imperial Palace.

1945/APRIL 15—In Burma, the first use of helicopters in a rescue takes place. The crew of a transport has to bail out high in the mountain jungles. A search plane crashes during the search. When a patrol reaches the injured search plane survivor on foot, it radios back that he is too ill to move. The nearest U.S. air base has an experimental Sikorsky YR-4 helicopter on hand for testing, and the helicopter pilot decides to attempt the risky mission in an area where no aircraft can land. He succeeds, and thus effects the first use of a helicopter as a rescue aircraft.

1945/APRIL 16—Ie Shima, a smaller island off Okinawa, is invaded by a U.S. Army division.

1945/APRIL 17—The last invasion of the Philippines campaign, as U.S. forces land on Mindanao Island.

1945/APRIL 18—Popular American war correspondent Ernie Pyle is killed by a Japanese sniper on Ie Shima, near Okinawa.

1945/APRIL 19—Assisted by an enormous amount of naval gunfire and aircraft support, U.S. Army forces launch a major offensive to break Japanese resistance on Okinawa.

1945/APRIL 20—Japanese troops in Burma continue to be hunted down or trapped by advancing British forces. The British are closing in on the Yenangyaung oil fields, the largest in Burma.

1945/APRIL 21—Advancing British forces move to within 200 miles of Rangoon in Burma. The Japanese decide to abandon Rangoon and pull back farther to reorganize their forces.

1945/APRIL 22—The island of Palawan in the Philippines is declared secure.

1945/APRIL 23—The battle for the central Philippines ends as Japanese resistance is crushed on the island of Cebu.

1945/APRIL 24—Around Japan, Allied air power, submarines, and especially naval mines, begin to shut down Japanese ports. By the end of April, the port

of Nagoya becomes the first of many to cease operations.

1945/APRIL 25—The Japanese army in China still has fight left in it. At Wukang, a Chinese division is routed by Japanese forces.

1945/APRIL 26—Japanese resistance on Okinawa intensifies, stalling U.S. efforts to secure the island.

1945/APRIL 27—U.S. and Australian warships begin four days of bombarding the Japanese-held oil facilities on Tarakan Island (off the northeast coast of Borneo).

1945/APRIL 28—Japanese Kamikaze attacks on U.S. ships off Okinawa continue. During the month of April, over 1,000 Japanese aircraft are destroyed. But 20 Allied ships are sunk and 157 damaged, mostly by Kamikazes.

1945/APRIL 29—Fighting is so intense on Okinawa that one U.S. Army division has to be pulled out of the line because of heavy losses.

1945/APRIL 30—British forces reach the town of Pegu in Burma.

1945/MAY 1—Australian forces land on Tarakan, off Borneo. The island had been held by the Japanese since early 1942.

1945/MAY 2—Advancing British troops discover that Rangoon, Burma, has been abandoned by the Japanese.

1945/MAY 3—The Japanese attempt to reverse their declining position on Okinawa by making a pair of amphibious landings behind American lines. Nearly 1,000 Japanese troops are involved and most are quickly killed or captured.

1945/MAY 4—British warships bombard Japanese installations in the Sakishima Islands in the southern Ryukyus.

1945/MAY 5—Japanese Kamikazes score a major success off Okinawa, sinking seventeen ships at the loss of only 131 aircraft.

1945/MAY 6—British declare the

Burma campaign over, although isolated Japanese units will fight on for several more weeks.

1945/MAY 7—British forces in southern Burma advance to link up with Allied units in the interior.

1945/MAY 8—The war in Europe ends with the surrender of Germany. Japan now stands alone against the massed military might of the Allied powers. With the defeat of Germany comes the announcement of a "leave plan" to determine who will get some relief now that only Japan is left and not as many troops are needed at the front. What this means to the Marines of the 4th Division at Maui, Hawaii, is that those who have seen the most action are eligible for transfer back to the mainland for six months of easier duty. Corporal John Lindemann, with four invasions, two wounds, and two decorations to his credit, qualifies for such a transfer. It is understood that if the invasion of Japan goes forward, these troops will end up back in the Pacific as replacements for those lost in the initial invasion.

1945/MAY 9—The Marines continue to advance on Okinawa, but Japanese resistance shows no sign of slackening.

1945/MAY 10—U.S. Army troops on Okinawa advance to positions overlooking the island's capital, Naha. Japanese Kamikaze attacks continue.

1945/MAY 11—Australian troops land in the Wewak area of New Guinea.

1945/MAY 12—Heavy Japanese Kamikaze attacks on the U.S. and British ships off Okinawa. The battleship New Mexico is badly hit.

1945/MAY 13—U.S. Army troops move into the Cagayan Valley on Luzon, in the Philippines. Japanese resistance continues.

1945/MAY 14—U.S. Army troops on the Philippine islands of Mindanao and Negros continue to battle feisty Japanese.

1945/MAY 15—British warships and aircraft attack Japanese installations on the Andaman Islands.

1945/MAY 16—The most intensive use of napalm in the war occurs near the Philippine capital, Manila, where Japanese troops threaten the city's water supply. Over 300 tons of napalm are dropped over several days. U.S. troops are then able to go in and mop up remaining Japanese resistance.

1945/MAY 17—The last surface battle of the war takes place, as the Japanese cruiser Haguro is sunk by five British destroyers in the Strait of Malacca.

1945/MAY 18—Chinese troops take the port of Foochow on the China coast.

1945/MAY 19—On Okinawa, another U.S. Army division has to be pulled out of combat because of high casualty rates. Even the Marines are suffering an exceptionally high rate of combat fatigue losses.

1945/MAY 20—The Japanese begin withdrawing divisions from China to shore up the defenses of the home islands.

1945/MAY 21—Japanese resistance on Okinawa shows signs of weakening.

1945/MAY 22—Okinawa is hit with heavy rains, which stall offensive operations for nearly two weeks.

1945/MAY 23—Japan's largest port, Yokohama, ceases operations because of Allied air and naval operations, as well as mines offshore.

1945/MAY 24—In addition to Kamikaze attacks, Japanese suicide paratroopers land on a U.S. airfield on Okinawa. Several U.S. aircraft are destroyed before the paratroopers are all killed.

1945/MAY 25—U.S. military planners set November 1 as the date of the first invasion of the Japanese home islands.

1945/MAY 26—Chinese troops reoccupy the city of Nanning, cutting off 200,000 Japanese troops in Indochina (who no longer have access to sea movement).

1945/MAY 27—The port of Tokyo is closed because of damage to port installations and Allied military activity in the surrounding waters.

1945/MAY 28—The Japanese make a last attempt to reverse their situation on Okinawa with Kamikaze attacks. Over 100 Japanese aircraft are destroyed, but only one U.S. destroyer is sunk.

1945/MAY 29—Organized Japanese resistance on the Philippine island of Negros collapses.

1945/MAY 30—The Okinawan capital of Naha is almost completely under U.S. control. On a memorable Memorial Day, Corporal John Lindemann, late of the 4th Marine Division, arrives at Treasure Island naval base. Corporal Lindemann has been away from North America for seventeen months. It is good to be back.

1945/MAY 31—Japanese forces on Okinawa begin pulling back to make their last stand.

1945/JUNE 1—Japanese resistance on Luzon in the Philippines is reduced to small-unit actions. Without supplies of food or ammunition, the surviving Japanese troops begin acting like guerrillas.

1945/JUNE 2—Nationalist Chinese leader Chiang Kai-shek gives up his title of premier of the Nationalist government, but remains the president and strongman.

1945/JUNE 3—Japanese troops on Okinawa, increasingly cornered, fight desperately against U.S. troops. Heavy rains make it difficult for the attackers to support their offensive efforts.

1945/JUNE 4—Corporal John Lindemann reports to San Diego to draw new equipment. His threadbare uniforms, having survived four Pacific battles, are replaced with new outfits. He is now fit for stateside duty, and a little peace and quiet.

1945/JUNE 5—A typhoon hits Okinawa, damaging four battleships, eight carriers, seven cruisers, eleven destroyers, and dozens of support ships.

1945/JUNE 6—U.S. Marines on Okinawa clear the Naha airfield of Japanese resistance. Corporal John Lindemann boards a troop train in San Diego for his trip to the east coast (Jersey City, New Jersey) and his new assignment. Because he is going all the way to the east coast, Lindemann gets a sleeping-car assignment. Troops going shorter distances simply get a seat and have to sleep in it if their trip lasts overnight.

1945/JUNE 7—In China, the Japanese have been forced back to the starting point of their spring offensive.

1945/JUNE 8—On Luzon in the Philippines, U.S. Army patrols reach deep into the back country, finding only scattered Japanese resistance.

1945/JUNE 9—Desperate Japanese forces on Okinawa's Oroku Peninsula are trapped when advancing U.S. Marine units close off any escape.

1945/JUNE 10—Australian troops land on Borneo.

1945/JUNE 11—British warships steam into the Caroline Islands to attack the Japanese base at Truk.

1945/JUNE 12—Trapped Japanese troops on the Oroku Peninsula of Okinawa begin committing suicide or surrendering.

1945/JUNE 13—Japanese resistance on the Visayan Islands ends. Nearly 10,000 Japanese died, compared to 3,200 U.S. casualties (including 835 dead).

1945/JUNE 14—The Pentagon orders commanders in the Pacific to prepare plans to deal with a sudden surrender by the Japanese.

1945/JUNE 15—In China, Chinese forces advance on a broad front into territory formerly held by Japanese troops (most of whom have been pulled back to Manchuria or Japan itself).

1945/JUNE 16—British warships bombard Truk, in the Carolines.

1945/JUNE 17—On Okinawa, U.S. Army troops breach the final defensive line of the Japanese forces. The Japanese commander commits suicide.

1945/JUNE 18—Having burned out Japan's major cities, U.S. B-29s begin attacking the smaller ones.

1945/JUNE 19—British forces move out of Burma into Thailand.

1945/JUNE 20—In an unprecedented event in the war, over 1,000 Japanese soldiers surrender on Okinawa. Civilians, who so far have actively assisted the soldiers, also begin to surrender in great numbers.

1945/JUNE 21—All of the islands in the southern Philippines are declared clear of organized Japanese resistance.

1945/JUNE 22—The U.S. declares the battle for Okinawa over. In eighty-one days of fighting, the 118,000-man Japanese garrison has been killed, except for 7,400 who were captured (usually while wounded or otherwise incapacitated) or surrendered. U.S. casualties are 49,000, of which 12,520 were killed. Japan has lost 7,800 aircraft in Kamikaze attacks, as well as ships. Allied forces have lost 800 aircraft, nearly 5,000 sailors dead, and thirty-six ships sunk (none larger than a destroyer). Deaths among the Okinawan civilian population may have reached 150,000 (we will never know for sure). It is the ferocity of this battle, more than anything else, that makes the use of atomic bombs against Japan preferable to attempting a landing on the home islands.

1945/JUNE 23—On Luzon, the U.S. uses paratroopers, glider troops, Philippine guerrillas, and U.S. Army troops to close the net around surviving Japanese troops.

1945/JUNE 24—Australian forces capture Sarawak.

1945/JUNE 25—Japanese forces continue to pull back in China, closely followed by advancing Chinese troops.

1945/JUNE 26—B-29s begin night raids on Japanese oil-refining facilities (to deny aviation fuel for remaining Japanese aircraft).

1945/JUNE 27—The campaign against the Japanese on Luzon in the Philippines is declared over, although individual Japanese soldiers and small units still resist.

1945/JUNE 28—Australian troops capture Kuala Belait in the East Indies.

1945/JUNE 29—Chinese forces begin advancing into Indochina.

1945/JUNE 30—On Luzon, 23,000 remaining Japanese soldiers continue to resist, but throughout the Philippines the war is largely over. The Japanese have lost 317,000 troops in the Philippines, plus 7,236 captured. Total U.S. casualties are 60,000. Philippine losses (including civilians) are far higher.

1945/JULY 1—Australian troops invade Balikpapan, Borneo, the largest oil field in Asia. Japanese troops resist.

1945/JULY 2—Japan announces that over 5 million of its citizens have been killed or injured in the U.S. air raids so far; the actual figure is about 672,000 killed, with several million more injured, depending on how you count "war-related injuries."

1945/JULY 3—Australian troops take over oil fields at Balikpapan, Borneo.

1945/JULY 4—U.S. troops, working with Philippine guerrilla units, track down and kill surviving, but still resisting, Japanese troops. Few Japanese will surrender.

1945/JULY 5—Australian troops continue their conquest of Borneo.

1945/JULY 6—Chinese forces continue moving north toward Manchuria. Japanese troops offer less resistance.

1945/JULY 7—Dutch troops enter the fighting in Borneo.

1945/JULY 8—Task Force 38 refuels and resupplies at sea in preparation for operations against the Japanese home islands.

1945/JULY 9—Task Force 38 arrives off Japan; except for the rotation of individual ships to rear areas for rest, refit, or repair, the fleet (sixteen U.S. carriers with escorting vessels, later joined by four British carriers and escorts) will remain in Japanese waters until the war is over.

1945/JULY 10—In the largest air assault to date, over 1,000 U.S. and British carrier aircraft bomb airfields and industrial installations in the Tokyo area. Corporal John Lindemann, late of the 4th Marine Division, reports for duty with Marine security detachment at the Quonset Point Naval Air Station in Rhode Island. This is pretty cushy duty compared to storming ashore on defended beaches. Nevertheless, this security duty is not permanent. Lindemann knows that if the invasion of Japan goes forward, Marines like him will be shipped back to the Pacific to replace the many casualties.

1945/JULY 11—Allied bombers turn their attention to the Japanese home islands of Shikoku and Honshu.

1945/JULY 12—Japan asks the Soviets to assist in negotiating a cease-fire with the Allies; somehow the message doesn't get through.

1945/JULY 13—Italy declares war on Japan.

1945/JULY 14—U.S. battleships shell the Japanese home islands (the port of Kamamishi), a first in the war.

1945/JULY 15—Australian troops continue to overrun Japanese positions in Borneo.

1945/JULY 16—The first atomic bomb is tested in New Mexico. It works.

1945/JULY 17—The U.S. Third Fleet (with the British carrier task force) shell and bomb the Tokyo area.

1945/JULY 18—Australian troops take the Sambodja oil field in Borneo.

1945/JULY 19—Surrounded Japanese units in Burma make a coordinated attack to break out of their encirclement.

1945/JULY 20—Japanese units in China continue to withdraw in the face of advancing Chinese troops.

1945/JULY 21—U.S. radio broadcasts demand that Japan surrender or be destroyed.

1945/JULY 22—British troops in Burma generally defeat Japanese attempts to break out.

1945/JULY 23—U.S. Navy warships sweep past the Japanese home islands of Shikoku and Kyushu, sinking over 100 Japanese transports as they go.

1945/JULY 24—Over 1,500 Allied aircraft attack the Japanese naval base at Kure (on the Inland Sea), sinking three of Japan's four remaining battleships.

1945/JULY 25—In response to a call from the Allies to surrender, Japan says it will surrender, but not unconditionally.

1945/JULY 26—British warships and aircraft attack Japanese installations on the west coast of Malaya.

1945/JULY 27—Japan's cities are "bombed" with leaflets telling them that Japan must surrender or be destroyed.

1945/JULY 28—Around midnight, Kamikazes sink their last ship, the U.S. destroyer *Callaghan*, off Okinawa.

1945/JULY 29—U.S. warships shell naval and air bases on Honshu.

1945/JULY 30—Two British midget submarines sneak into Singapore Harbor and sink a Japanese cruiser by attaching mines to it.

1945/JULY 31—Malnutrition grows rampant in Japan, with the average citizen getting only 1,680 calories a day (22 percent less than the minimum to survive).

1945/AUGUST 1—U.S. air-dropped mines on the Japanese-controlled Yangtze River sink thirty-six Japanese transports and damage another eleven.

1945/AUGUST 2—B-29s drop 6,600 tons of bombs on five Japanese cities.

1945/AUGUST 3—The blockade of Japan is complete. Nothing gets in, nothing gets out.

1945/AUGUST 4—The last organized Japanese troops in Burma are killed or captured, with only 1,700 of the remaining 10,000 Japanese troops escaping to fight on individually or in small groups.

1945/AUGUST 5—In China, Chinese troops continue to advance with little opposition from the retreating Japanese.

1945/AUGUST 6—A 4.5-ton atomic bomb is dropped on the Japanese city of Hiroshima. Over 80,000 Japanese die, with many more injured.

1945/AUGUST 7—Russian troops mass on the Manchurian and Korean borders, ready to invade those Japanese-held territories.

1945/AUGUST 8—The Soviet Union declares war on Japan, and the Red Army begins its invasion the next day.

1945/AUGUST 9—A second atomic bomb is dropped on Nagasaki, killing over 30,000 Japanese.

1945/AUGUST 10—Discovering that the Japanese were keeping their Kamikaze aircraft in northern airfields on Honshu, Allied carrier aircraft make a massive attack, destroying 400 Japanese aircraft and damaging over 300. The Allies lose 34 of their own planes.

1945/AUGUST 11—U.S. and British battleships shell Japanese steel mills near the coast.

1945/AUGUST 12—Leaflets are dropped on Japanese cities, calling on the people to surrender or face "utter devastation."

1945/AUGUST 13—Japan's leaders offer to surrender unconditionally if the emperor's status is left unchanged. This is refused, and the debate rages on in the Japanese government about what to do.

1945/AUGUST 14—Japan agrees to surrender unconditionally.

1945/AUGUST 15—Despite a last-minute coup attempt by Army officers, the emperor's surrender message is broadcast. The Japanese people accept the emperor's order.

1945/SEPTEMBER 15—Japan formally signs an instrument of surrender aboard the battleship USS *Missiouri* in Tokyo Harbor. World War II is over. However, it will be six months before the last of the far-flung Japanese garrisons actually lay down their arms. Indeed, Japanese troops are used as local police in many areas through late 1945, until the Allies can get their own troops in place. The repatriation of former Japanese soldiers to Japan continues through 1946.

1945/OCTOBER 29—Corporal John Lindemann is given his honorable discharge for thirty-eight months of service, four battles, a Bronze Star, and a banged-up knee (and the Purple Heart medal that goes with it). And then there are the memories. John Lindemann would not talk much about his wartime experiences for some twenty years. His outfit, the 4th Marine Division, went to war with about 19,000 men. In thirteen months of action, the division suffered 14,736 casualties. Members of the division were awarded 8 Medals of Honor, 111 Navy Crosses, 646 Silver Stars, and 2,517 Bronze Stars. John Lindemann marries in 1949, raises a family and, for want of a better term, lives happily ever after. But he will never go duck hunting again.

S O M E

R E C O M M E N D E D

R E A D I N G

T his does not purport to be an exhaustive, or even extensive, bibliography of materials on the Pacific war. There are literally thousands of books on the subject, and even a volume about the size of the present one would not be enough to cover works in English alone. However, some works are more important, or at least more unusual, than others, and make for particularly rewarding reading.

Brown, Robert. *Warship Losses of World War Two.* New York: Sterling/ Arms and Armour, 1990. A valuable compendium of all warship losses during the war, including those of neutrals. In addition to the basic chronological presentation of ship losses, with location, circumstances, and often extensive explanatory notes, there are statistical tables and several analyses of the causes of ship loss. Very handy for the serious student of World War II at sea.

Dorrance, William H. *Fort Kamehameha*. Shippensburg, Pa.: White Mane, 1993. Takes a look at the fixed fortifications of Pearl Harbor, with considerable detail on the theory and practice of coast defense, a matter in which all of the Pacific powers had invested enormous sums in the years before the war.

Dunnigan, James F. *How to Make War*. Third edition. New York: William Morrow, 1993. Focuses on the theory and practice of warfare in the late twentieth century, but contains much that is useful in helping to understand the conduct of the Second World War as well.

Dunnigan, James F., and Nofi, Albert A. *Dirty Little Secrets of World War II*. New York: William Morrow, 1994. A general look at the entire war, putting the Pacific war more firmly into perspective within the global struggle.

Dunnigan, James F., and Nofi, Albert A. *Shooting Blanks*. New York: William Morrow, 1991. Looks at the problem of understanding military power, with numerous examples drawn from World War II.

DuPuy, Trevor N. *Numbers, Predictions, and War*. Indianapolis: Bobbs-Merrill, 1979. Discusses the Quantified Judgment Model, an attempt to develop a mathematical model capable of comparing the military capabilities of various military forces, based on the experience of several dozen battles during the Second World War.

Greenberg, Eli, and Associates. *The Ineffective Soldier: Lessons for Management and the Nation*. Three volumes. New York: Columbia University, 1959. Analyzes where and how the U.S. armed forces mismanaged their manpower; one volume is titled *The Lost Divisions*.

Harris, Merion and Susie. *Soldiers of the Sun: The Rise and Fall of the Japanese Imperial Army*. New York: Random House, 1991. Although not entirely successful as a history of the Imperial Army, this comes into its own in a series of chapters that analyze the doctrine, character, equipment, and philosophy of the Japanese Army in the period of World War II.

Miller, Edward S. *War Plan Orange: The U.S. Strategy to Defeat Japan, 1897–1945*. Annapolis: U.S.N.I., 1991. Presents a superbly detailed analysis of U.S. planning for a war with Japan, with an examination of the personalities involved and the ways in which changing world events influenced such planning, plus a look at the ways in which the various prewar plans influenced the actual development of U.S. strategy in the Pacific war.

Millett, Allan Reid, and Murray, Williamson, editors. *Military Effectiveness*. Three volumes. Boston: Allen & Unwin, 1988. A collection of essays by noted specialists on the military capabilities and limitations of the armed forces of each of the Great Powers during World War I (Vol. I), the interwar period (Vol. II), and World War II (Vol. III), with many valuable insights and much food for thought. The same editors' *Calculations: Net Assessment and the Coming of World War II* (New York: The Free Press, 1992) contains a series of essays on how each of the great powers dealt with the problem of evaluating the military capabilities and limitations of their opponents.

Morison, Samuel Eliot. *History of United States Naval Operations in World War II*. Fifteen volumes. Boston: Little, Brown, 1947–1962. A remarkably literate, very complete treatment of the subject in sometimes extraordinary detail, which has stood the test of time rather well. For those short of the leisure to read it all, the same author's *The Two Ocean War* (Boston: Little, Brown, 1963) presents a shorter treatment of the subject.

Overy, R. J. *The Air War, 1939–1945*. New York: Stein & Day, 1981. A critical analytic look at the nature of the war in the air, with many valuable perspectives, such as the importance not merely of aircraft production, but also of the production of spare parts.

Parillo, Mark P. *The Japanese Merchant Marine in World War II*. Annapolis: U.S.N.I., 1993. Deals with the subject in considerable detail, with numerous tables, maps, and diagrams to help the reader develop a better understanding of the Japanese failure at sea.

Perret, Geoffrey. *There's a War to Be Won: The United States Army in World War II*. New York: Random House, 1991. Presents a pretty good look at the U.S. Army in World War II, weaving together the diverse trends in doctrine, organization, equipment, and planning that ultimately led to the Army with which the United States fought the Second World War, while looking into everything from the personalities of the Army's leaders to problems and surprises in weapons development, racial policies, the medical corps, the famous maneuvers of 1940–1941, and, of course, the experience of battle.

Prange, Gordon R., with Goldstein, Donald M., and Dillon, Katherine V. *At Dawn We Slept*. New York: McGraw-Hill, 1981. Along with the same authors' *Pearl Harbor: The Verdict of History* (New York: McGraw-Hill, 1986), provides the most detailed and exhaustive inquiry into the American disaster at Pearl Harbor. Going to considerable lengths to examine the numerous conspiracy theories (some of which—such as the claim that the attack was actually carried out by British pilots operating from a secret base on one of the other Hawaiian Islands as a result of a deal between Roosevelt and Churchill—are remarkable indeed), the authors conclude that "there is enough blame for everyone," and not a little credit for the Japanese. Their *Miracle at Midway* (New York: McGraw-Hill, 1982) carries the story forward to the series of Japanese blunders and American successes that led to the Japanese disaster just seven months later.

Ready, J. Lee. *Forgotten Allies* Two volumes. New York: McFarland, 1985. Takes an in-depth look at the role in the war of the minor powers, and the numerous resistance movements, with one volume for the war against Germany and another for that against Japan. A valuable and very neglected book.

Reynolds, Clark G. *The Fast Carriers.* New York: McGraw-Hill, 1968. Although relatively old, and rather focused on the American point of view, this is still the best overall treatment of the carrier war in the Pacific.

Stouffer, Samuel A., et al. *The American Soldier: Studies in Social Psychology in World War II.* Two volumes. Princeton: Princeton University Press, 1949. Written because, by an extraordinary bit of military mismanagement, upon being drafted into the Army, Stouffer and several other sociologists were assigned to study the troops. The result was a series of opinion polls and surveys that are unmatched for the insight they give into the mind and attitudes of the common soldier on everything from Army chow to race relations to the nature of the enemy. The volumes are *Adjustment During Army Life* and *Combat and Its Aftermath.*

The United States Army in World War II. Washington, D.C.: OCMH, 1947–to date. The nearly eighty-volume official account of the U.S. Army in the war, probably the best official history ever written. While the operational volumes are literate, well reasoned, critical, and worth reading, the really good stuff is in the technical volumes, on matters from the procurement of aircraft to racial policies to logistical support. No other major-power official history even comes close to the objectivity, scholarship, and readability of this series.

The United States Strategic Bombing Survey. Washington, D.C.: USSBS, 1945–1949. A 200-volume look at the war, focusing on the influence of strategic bombing, with many valuable insights.

Warship International. A quarterly published for many years, now by the International Naval Research Organization (5905 Reinwood Dr., Toledo, Ohio 43613), this is an extraordinary source of detailed historical, technical, and operational information about fighting ships, with frequent articles, letters, and reviews related to the naval war in the Pacific, marred only by the lack of an index.

Wood, Pamela, editor. *Fourth Marine Division.* One of the thousands of unit histories to come out of World War II. This one was used to fill out the details of Corporal John Lindemann. These books add a dimension to the war that is missing from most other historical works. Most can be found only in large research libraries, as they are normally sold only through unit veterans' organizations.

INDEX

INDEX